6. Can a local account be used in a trust relationship? Explain.

7. In a complete trust domain model that uses 4 different domains, what is the total number of trust relationships required to use a complete trust domain model?

Exam Questions

The following questions are similar to those you will face on the Microsoft exam. Answers to these questions can be found in section Answers and Explanations, later in the chapter. At the end of each of those answers, you will be informed of where (that is, in what section of the chapter) to find more information..

1. ABC Corporation has locations in Toronto, New York, and San Francisco. It wants to install Windows NT Server 4 to encompass all its locations in a single WAN environment. The head office is located in New York. What is the best domain model for ABC's directory services implementation?

   A. Single-domain model

   B. Single-master domain model

   C. Multiple-master domain model

   D. Complete-trust domain model

2. JPS Printing has a single location with 1,000 users spread across the LAN. It has special printers and applications installed on the servers in its environment. It needs to be able to centrally manage the user accounts and the resources. Which domain model would best fit its needs?

   A. Single-domain model

   B. Single-master domain model

   C. Multiple-master domain model

   D. Complete-trust domain model

5. What must be created to allow a user account from one domain to access resources in a different domain?

   A. Complete Trust Domain Model

   B. One Way Trust Relationship

   C. Two Way Trust Relationship

   D. Master-Domain Model

Answers to Review Questions

1. Single domain, master domain, multiple-master domain, complete-trust domain. See section, Windows NT Server 4 Domain Models, in this chapter for more information. (This question deals with objective Planning 1.)

2. One user, one account, centralized administration, universal resource access, synchronization. See section, Windows NT Server 4 Directory Services, in this chapter for more information. (This question deals with objective Planning 1.)

6. Local accounts cannot be given permissions across trusts. See section, Accounts in Trust Relationships, in this chapter for more information. (This question deals with Planning 1.)

Answers and Explanations: For each of the Review and Exam questions, you will find thorough explanations located at the end of the section.

Exam Questions: These questions reflect the kinds of multiple-choice questions that appear on the Microsoft exams. Use them to become familiar with the exam question formats and to help you determine what you know and what you need to review or study more.

Suggested Readings and Resources

The following are some recommended readings on the subject of installing and configuring NT Workstation:

1. Microsoft Official Curriculum course 770: *Installing and Configuring Microsoft Windows NT Workstation 4.0*

   • Module 1: Overview of Windows NT Workstation 4.0

   • Module 2: Installing Windows NT Workstation 4.0

2. Microsoft Official Curriculum course 922: *Supporting Microsoft Windows NT 4.0 Core Technologies*

   • Module 2: Installing Windows NT

   • Module 3: Configuring the Windows NT Environment

3. *Microsoft Windows NT Workstation Resource Kit Version 4.0* (Microsoft Press)

   • Chapter 2: Customizing Setup

   • Chapter 4: Planning for a Mixed Environment

4. Microsoft TechNet CD-ROM

   • *MS Windows NT Workstation Technical Notes*

     • MS Windows NT Workstation Deployment Guide – Automating Windows NT Setup

     • An Unattended Windows NT Workstation Deployment

5. Web Sites

   • www.microsoft.com/train_cert

Suggested Readings and Resources: The very last element in each chapter is a list of additional resources you can use if you wish to go above and beyond certification-level material or if you need to spend more time on a particular subject that you are having trouble understanding.

Use of the Microsoft Approved Study Guide logo on this product signifies that it has been independently reviewed and approved in complying with the following standards:

● Acceptable coverage of all content related to Microsoft exam number 70-029 titled Designing and Implementing Databases with Microsoft SQL Server 7.0

● Sufficient performance-based exercises that relate closely to all required content

● Technically accurate content, based on sampling of text

Exam 70–029 – Designing and Implementing Databases with Microsoft SQL Server 7.0

OBJECTIVE	CONTENT	EXERCISES	ASSESSMENT QUESTIONS
DEVELOPING A LOGICAL DATA MODEL			
Group data into entities by applying normalization rules.	Chapter 1 Normalizing Your Database Design p. 39	1.4 (p. 50)	22, 25 (p. 55–56)
Identify primary keys.	Chapter 1 Choosing and Defining the Primary Key p. 24	1.1 (p. 48) 1.2 (p. 48) 1.3 (p. 49) 1.4 (p. 50) 1.5 (p. 51)	23 (p. 55)
Choose the foreign key that will enforce a relationship between entities and that will ensure referential integrity.	Chapter 1 Primary Keys and Foreign Keys p. 30 Referential Integrity, p. 31	1.2 (p. 48) 1.3 (p. 49) 1.4 (p. 50)	6, 15–22 (p. 53–55)
Identify the business rules that relate to data integrity.	Chapter 1 Column Constraints p. 26	1.1 (p. 48)	8, 11–13 (p. 53–54)
Incorporate business rules and constraints into the data model.	Chapter 1 Column Constraints p. 26	1.1 (p. 48)	8, 11–13 (p.53–54)
In a given situation, decide whether denormalization is appropriate.	Chapter 1 Impact of Normalization p. 44	1.5 (p. 51)	25 (p. 56)
DERIVING THE PHYSICAL DESIGN			
Assess the potential impact of the logical design on performance, maintainability, extensibility, scalability, availability, and security.	Chapter 1 Impact of Normalization p. 44	1.5 (p. 51)	25 (p. 56)
CREATING DATA SERVICES			
Access data by using the dynamic SQL model.	Chapter 10 Dynamic Model versus Stored Procedure Model p. 387	10.1 p. 402–403	1, 3, 4, 10 p. 404–406
Access data by using the stored procedure model.	Chapter 10 Dynamic Model versus Stored Procedure Model p. 387	10.2 p. 403–404	1, 3, 4 p. 404–405
Manipulate data by using Transact–SQL cursors.	Chapter 8 Implementing Cursors p. 323	8.4, 8.5 p. 336–337	5, 7 p. 340
Choose the appropriate type of cursor.	Chapter 8 Implementing Cursors p. 323	8.4, 8.5 p. 336–337	5, 7 p. 340
Define the appropriate level of sensitivity to change.	Chapter 8 Implementing Cursors p. 323	8.4, 8.5 p. 336–337	5, 7 p. 340
Choose the appropriate navigation.	Chapter 8 Implementing Cursors p. 323	8.4, 8.5 p. 336–337	5, 7 p. 340
Choose the scope of the cursor, specifically global or local.	Chapter 8 Implementing Cursors p. 323	8.4, 8.5 p. 336–337	5, 7 p. 340

OBJECTIVE	CONTENT	EXERCISES	ASSESSMENT QUESTIONS
CREATING A PHYSICAL DATABASE			
Implement constraints.	Chapter 3 Using Constraints p. 105	3.1 p. 126 3.4 p. 127	1, 5, 8, 10–15 p. 128–130
Create and maintain indexes.	Chapter 4 Managing Indexes with Transact–SQL p. 147 Managing Indexes with Enterprise Manager p. 154	4.1, 4.2 p. 171	1–13 p. 173–175
Choose an indexing strategy that will optimize performance.	Chapter 4 Types of Indexes p. 140 Guidelines for Indexing p. 145	4.1, 4.2 p. 171	1–13 p. 173–175
Given a situation, choose the appropriate type of index to create.	Chapter 4 Choosing an Index Type Choosing an Index Type p. 146	4.1, 4.2 p. 171	1–13 p. 173–175
Choose the column or columns to index.	Chapter 4 Choosing Which Columns to Index p. 146	4.1, 4.2 p. 171	1–13 p. 173–175
Choose the appropriate index characteristics, specifically ILLFACTOR, FDROP_EXISTING, and PAD_INDEX.	Chapter 4 Creating Indexes p. 148	4.1, 4.2 p. 171	1–13 p. 173–175
Populate the database with data from an external data source. Methods include the bulk copy program and Data Transformation Services (DTS).	Chapter 5 Objective covered in entire chapter.	5.1, 5.3 p. 216–218	1–10 p. 218–220
Implement full–text search.	Chapter 4 Implementing Full–Text Search p. 157	4.3, 4.4 p. 171–173	14, 15 p. 175
MAINTAINING A DATABASE			
Evaluate and optimize the performance of an execution plan by using DBCC SHOWCONTIG, SHOWPLAN_TEXT, SHOWPLAN_ALL, and UPDATE STATISTICS.	Chapter 11 Creating, Examining, and Optimizing Execution Plans p. 413	11.1, 11.2 p. 433	1–4 p. 436–437
Evaluate and optimize the performance of query execution plans.	Chapter 11 Creating, Examining, and Optimizing Execution Plans p. 413	11.1, 11.2 p. 433	1–4 p. 436–437
Diagnose and resolve locking problems.	Chapter 11 Diagnosing and Resolving Locking Problems p. 425	11.3 p. 434	5, 10 p. 437–438
Identify SQL Server events and performance problems by using SQL Server Profiler.	Chapter 11 Using SQL Server Profiler p. 426	11.4 p. 434–436	6–9 p. 437

OBJECTIVE	CONTENT	EXERCISES	ASSESSMENT QUESTIONS
CREATING DATA SERVICES			
Implement error handling by using return codes and the RAISERROR statement.	Chapter 9 Returning Information from a Stored Procedure p. 352	9.5 p. 375–376	13, 14 p. 379
Choose appropriate recompile options.	Chapter 9 Creating Stored Procedures p. 350	9.5 p. 375–376	13, 14 p. 379
Create triggers that implement rules, that enforce data integrity, and that perform cascading updates and cascading deletes.	Chapter 9 Triggers p. 362	9.3, 9.4 p. 374–375	5–12 p. 378–379
Implement transactional error handling.	Chapter 9 Implementing Transactional Error Handling in Triggers p. 364	9.3, 9.4 p. 374–375	5–12 p. 378–379
Create result sets that provide summary data. Query types include TOP *n* PERCENT and GROUP BY, specifically HAVING, CUBE, and ROLLUP.	Chapter 6 Generating Summary Data p. 244	6.4–6.6 p. 365	14 p. 269
Configure session–level settings.	Chapter 10 Configuring Session Level Options p. 391	10.1, 10.2 p. 402–404	5–9 p. 405–406
Access data from static or dynamic sources by using remote stored procedures, linked servers, and OPENROWSET.	Chapter 9 Distributed Queries p. 367	9.6 p. 376–377	15, 16 p. 379–380
Evaluate where processing occurs when using OPENQUERY.	Chapter 9 Accessing Data Using the OpenQuery Function p. 369	9.6 p. 376–377	15, 16 p. 379–380
CREATING A PHYSICAL DATABASE			
Create and manage files, filegroups, and transaction logs that define a database.	Chapter 2 Entire chapter covers objective.	2.1 p. 83 2.2 p. 84	1–6, 9, 10 p. 85–86
Create tables that enforce data integrity and referential integrity.	Chapter 3 Managing Tables p. 97 Declarative Referential Integrity (DRI) Constraints p. 112 Data Validation Constraints p. 120	3.1 p. 126 3.4 p. 127	1, 5, 8, 10–15 p. 128–130
Choose the appropriate data types.	Chapter 3 Understanding Data Types p. 91	3.1 p. 126 3.4 p. 127	1, 5, 8, 10–15 p. 128–130
Create user–defined data types.	Chapter 3 User–Defined Data Types p. 95	3.1 p. 126 3.4 p. 127	1, 5, 8, 10–15 p. 128–130
Define columns as NULL or NOT NULL.	Chapter 3 Managing Tables p. 97	3.1 p. 126 3.4 p. 127	1, 5, 8, 10–15 p. 128–130
Define columns to generate values by using the IDENTITY property, the uniqueidentifier data type, and the NEWID function.	Chapter 3 System Data Types p. 92 Using an IDENTITY Column p. 110	3.1 p. 126 3.4 p. 127	1, 5, 8, 10–15 p. 128–130

OBJECTIVE	CONTENT	EXERCISES	ASSESSMENT QUESTIONS
CREATING DATA SERVICES			
Create and manage explicit, implicit, and distributed transactions to ensure data consistency and recoverability.	Chapter 8 Using Transactions p. 316	8.6 p. 338	8–10 p. 340–341
Define the transaction isolation level.	Chapter 8 Define the Transaction Isolation Level p. 307	8.6 p. 338	8–10 p. 340–341
Design transactions of appropriate length.	Chapter 8 Design Transactions of Appropriate Length p. 318	8.6 p. 338	8–10 p. 340–341
Avoid or handle deadlocks.	Chapter 8 Avoid or Handle Deadlocks p. 319	8.6 p. 338	8–10 p. 340–341
Use optimistic locking appropriately.	Chapter 8 Use Optimistic Locking Appropriately p. 320	8.6 p. 338	8–10 p. 340–341
Implement error handling by using @@TRANCOUNT.	Chapter 8 Implement Transactional Error Handling p. 321	8.6 p. 338	8–10 p. 340–341
Write INSERT, DELETE, UPDATE, and SELECT statements that retrieve and modify data.	Chapter 6 Writing SELECT Statements: An Overview p. 226 Choosing Columns p. 228 Using DISTINCT and ALL Keywords p. 232 Choosing Rows p. 233 Sorting Result Rows p. 244 Using Sub–Queries p. 258	6.1–6.3 p. 264	1–6 p. 267–268
	Chapter 7 Objective covered in entire chapter.	7–1–7.3 p. 293–294	1–13 p. 294–296
Write Transact–SQL statements that use joins or subqueries to combine data from multiple tables.	Chapter 6 Using Joins p. 253 Using Sub–Queries p. 258	6.7, 6.8 p. 266	11–13, 15 p. 269–270
Create scripts by using Transact–SQL. Programming elements including control–of–flow techniques, local and global variables, functions, and error handling techniques.	Chapter 8 Control–of–Flow Statements p. 302 Managing Errors p. 310	8.1–8.3 p. 334–336	1–4, 6 p. 267–268
Design, create, use, and alter views.	Chapter 9 Views p. 355	9.1, 9.2 p. 374	1–4 p. 377–378
Modify data through a view.	Chapter 9 Recognizing the Limitations of Views p. 358	9.1, 9.2 p. 374	1–4 p. 377–378
Query data through a view.	Chapter 9 Recognizing the Benefits of Using Views p. 355	9.1, 9.2 p. 374	1–4 p. 377–378
Create and execute stored procedures to enforce business rules, to modify data in multiple tables, to perform calculations, and to use input and output parameters.	Chapter 9 Stored Procedures p. 348	9.5 p. 375–376	13, 14 p. 379

MCSE

SQL Server 7 Database Design

Exam: 70-029

David Besch
Contributing Authors
Sean Baird
Chris Miller
Denis Darveau
Wayne Smith
Deanna Townsend

New Riders

MCSE Training Guide: SQL Server 7 Database Design

Copyright® 1999 by New Riders Publishing

International Standard Book Number: 0-7357-0004-4

Library of Congress Catalog Card Number: 98-83034

Printed in the United States of America

First Printing: May, 1999

03   02   01   00   99   7   6   5   4   3   2   1

Trademarks

All terms mentioned in this book that are known to be trademarks or service marks have been appropriately capitalized. New Riders cannot attest to the accuracy of this information. Use of a term in this book should not be regarded as affecting the validity of any trademark or service mark.

Microsoft is a registered trademark of Microsoft Corporation in the United States and other countries. New Riders is an independent entity from Microsoft Corporation and is not affiliated with Microsoft Corporation in any manner. This publication may be used in assisting students to prepare for a Microsoft Certified Professional exam. Neither Microsoft Corporation, its designated review company, nor New Riders warrants that use of this publication will ensure passing the relevant exam.

Warning and Disclaimer

Every effort has been made to make this book as complete and as accurate as possible, but no warranty or fitness is implied. The information provided is on an "as is" basis. The authors and the publisher shall have neither liability nor responsibility to any person or entity with respect to any loss or damages arising from the information contained in this book or from the use of the CD or programs accompanying it.

EXECUTIVE EDITOR
Mary Foote

ACQUISITIONS EDITOR
Sean Angus

DEVELOPMENT EDITOR
Stacia Mellinger

MANAGING EDITOR
Sarah Kearns

PROJECT EDITOR
Clint McCarty

COPY EDITOR
Daryl Kessler

INDEXER
Lisa Stumpf

TECHNICAL REVIEWERS
Sean Baird
Gordon Baker

SOFTWARE DEVELOPMENT SPECIALIST
Michael Hunter

PROOFREADER
Elise Walter

PRODUCTION
Cheryl Lynch
Jeanette McKay

Contents at a Glance

Table of Contents

Part II: Final Review

Part III: Appendixes

About the Author

David Besch lives in Olathe, Kansas, where he is a database administrator in the managed health care service industry. He is an MCSD and has been in the computer science field for four years. David is the co-author of *MCSE Training Guide: SQL Server 6.5 Design and Implementation* and served as the technical editor for *Teach Yourself MCSE SQL Server 6.5 Administration in 14 Days*. David, married to a beautiful, highly intelligent, and supportive wife, Cheryl, is expecting the arrival of their first child in the spring of 1999. He spends his spare time reading the latest Robert Jordan, *The Wheel of Time* series, or playing Ultima on the computer. (So if you have any theories on whether Moraine is still alive or any other topic in *The Wheel of Time* series, email him at DavidB@geoaccess.com.) You can also send any comments or questions on this book to the same email address.

ABOUT THE REVIEWERS

Sean Baird is the senior architect for the Software Solutions group at Empower Trainers & Consultants, Inc. He has worked on a wide variety of business solutions for Empower's clients and has technical experience with much of the Microsoft Product line, especially SQL Server. Sean has also co-authored two books on SQL Server and presented at MCP Magazine's TechMentor conference. He obtained a bachelor's degree in Computer Science from the University of Missouri-Rolla and holds the MCSE, MCSD, and MCT certifications. Sean lives in Kansas City, where he enjoys piloting the Empower hot-air balloon in his spare time.

Gordon Barker is currently working for Microsoft Canada Co. as a consultant specializing in SMS, SQL Server, networking, and the core NT technologies. He received his B.S. in Geology in 1976 from the University of Western Ontario but immediately went to work for the University Computing Centre as a Technical Writer. Gordon had worked as Technical Support on Control Data, Digital, and Unisys mainframes before working in Unix support to move a large Canadian manufacturer from mainframes to Unix support for all business functions. Gordon has also worked as a developer in Cobol Fortran, Pascal, C, C++, Java, and SQL Forms application, as well as having played the role of D.A. and D.B.A. in large Oracle and SQL Server database shops. He is certified as an MCSE, with product certifications in SQL Server. Gordon lives in Alberta with his wife Christina and their Gold Wing, Columbus.

Dedication

This book is dedicated to my family. Cheryl: Thanks for the lonely days and quiet nights that you spent while giving me time to work. All, of course, helped to take the edge off the everlasting deadlines. My parents: For all the help and advice given to get me to this most wonderful and charmed life that Cheryl and I share with you.

Acknowledgments

I need to acknowledge all the people who made this project possible. Chris Miller and Sean Baird: For getting me into writing this book and the expert advice. Sean Angus and Stacia Mellinger: Your attention to detail and scheduling made the whole book possible.

And I'd like to acknowledge all the people we neglected during the long hours and weekends we dedicated to the writing of this book, without whose prayers and encouragement we would have not have fared so well.

Tell Us What You Think!

As the reader of this book, you are our most important critic and commentator. We value your opinion and want to know what we're doing right, what we could do better, what areas you'd like to see us publish in, and any other words of wisdom you're willing to pass our way.

As the Executive Editor for the Certification team at New Riders Publishing, I welcome your comments. You can fax, email, or write me directly to let me know what you did or didn't like about this book—as well as what we can do to make our books stronger.

Please note that I cannot help you with technical problems related to the topic of this book, and that due to the high volume of mail I receive, I might not be able to reply to every message.

When you write, please be sure to include this book's title and author, as well as your name and phone or fax number. I will carefully review your comments and share them with the author and editors who worked on the book.

Fax: 317-581-4663

Email: certification@mcp.com

Mail: Mary Foote
        Executive Editor
        Certification
        New Riders Publishing
        201 West 103rd Street
        Indianapolis, IN 46290 USA

How to Use This Book

New Riders Publishing has made an effort in the second editions of its Training Guide series to make the information as accessible as possible for the purposes of learning the certification material. Here, you have an opportunity to view the many instructional features that have been incorporated into the books to achieve that goal.

CHAPTER OPENER

Each chapter begins with a set of features designed to allow you to maximize study time for that material.

List of Objectives: Each chapter begins with a list of the objectives as stated by Microsoft.

Objective Explanations: Immediately following each objective is an explanation of it, providing context that defines it more meaningfully in relation to the exam. Because Microsoft can sometimes be vague in its objectives list, the objective explanations are designed to clarify any vagueness by relying on the authors' test-taking experience.

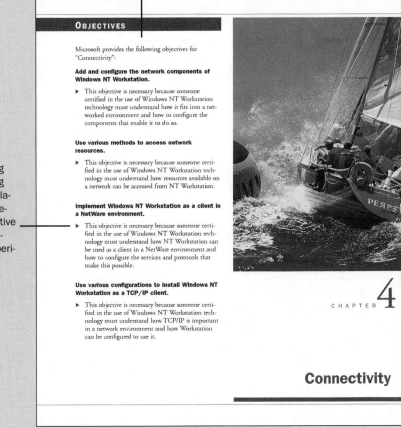

OBJECTIVES

Microsoft provides the following objectives for "Connectivity":

Add and configure the network components of Windows NT Workstation.

▶ This objective is necessary because someone certified in the use of Windows NT Workstation technology must understand how it fits into a networked environment and how to configure the components that enable it to do so.

Use various methods to access network resources.

▶ This objective is necessary because someone certified in the use of Windows NT Workstation technology must understand how resources available on a network can be accessed from NT Workstation.

Implement Windows NT Workstation as a client in a NetWare environment.

▶ This objective is necessary because someone certified in the use of Windows NT Workstation technology must understand how NT Workstation can be used as a client in a NetWare environment and how to configure the services and protocols that make this possible.

Use various configurations to install Windows NT Workstation as a TCP/IP client.

▶ This objective is necessary because someone certified in the use of Windows NT Workstation technology must understand how TCP/IP is important in a network environment and how Workstation can be configured to use it.

C H A P T E R 4

Connectivity

OUTLINE

Chapter Outline: Learning always gets a boost when you can see both the forest and the trees. To give you a visual image of how the topics in a chapter fit together, you will find a chapter outline at the beginning of each chapter. You will also be able to use this for easy reference when looking for a particular topic.

STUDY STRATEGIES

▶ Disk configurations are a part of both the planning and the configuration of NT Server computers. To study for Planning Objective 1, you will need to look at both the following section and the material in Chapter 2, "Installation Part 1." As with many concepts, you should have a good handle on the terminology and know the best applications for different disk configurations. For the objectives of the NT Server exam, you will need to know only general disk configuration concepts—at a high level, not the nitty-gritty. Make sure you memorize the concepts relating to partitioning and know the difference between the system and the boot partitions in an NT system (and the fact that the definitions of these are counter-intuitive). You should know that NT supports both FAT and NTFS partitions, as well as some of the advantages and disadvantages of each. You will also need to know about the fault-tolerance methods available in NT—stripe sets with parity and disk mirroring—including their definitions, hardware requirements, and advantages and disadvantages.

Of course, nothing substitutes for working with the concepts explained in this objective. If possible, get an NT system with some free disk space and play around with the Disk Administrator just to see how partitions are created and what they look like.

You might also want to look at some of the supplementary readings and scan TechNet for white papers on disk configuration.

▶ The best way to study for Planning Objective 2 is to read, memorize, and understand the use of each protocol. You should know what the protocols are, what they are used for, and what systems they are compatible with.

As with disk configuration, installing protocols on your NT Server is something that you plan for, not something you do just because it feels good to you at the time. Although it is much easier to add or remove a protocol than it is to reconfigure your hard drives, choosing a protocol is still an essential part of the planning process because specific protocols, like spoken languages, are designed to be used in certain circumstances. There is no point in learning to speak Mandarin Chinese if you are never around anyone who can understand you. Similarly, the NWLink protocol is used to interact with NetWare systems; therefore, if you do not have Novell servers on your network, you might want to rethink your plan to install it on your servers. We will discuss the uses of the major protocols in Chapter 7, "Connectivity." However, it is important that you have a good understanding of their uses here in the planning stage.

Study Strategies: Each topic presents its own learning challenge. To support you through this, New Riders has included strategies for how to best approach studying in order to retain the material in the chapter, particularly as it is addressed on the exam.

INSTRUCTIONAL FEATURES WITHIN THE CHAPTER

These books include a large amount and different kinds of information. The many different elements are designed to help you identify information by its purpose and importance to the exam and also to provide you with varied ways to learn the material. You will be able to determine how much attention to devote to certain elements, depending on what your goals are. By becoming familiar with the different presentations of information, you will know what information will be important to you as a test-taker and which information will be important to you as a practitioner.

EXAM TIP

Only One NTVDM Supports Multiple 16-bit Applications Expect at least one question about running Win16 applications in separate memory spaces. The key concept is that you can load multiple Win16 applications into the same memory space only if it is the initial Win16 NTVDM. It is not possible, for example, to run Word for Windows 6.0 and Excel for Windows 5.0 in one shared memory space and also run PowerPoint 4.0 and Access 2.0 in another shared memory space.

Exam Tip: Exam Tips appear in the margins to provide specific exam-related advice. Such tips may address what material is covered (or not covered) on the exam, how it is covered, mnemonic devices, or particular quirks of that exam.

Note: Notes appear in the margins and contain various kinds of useful information, such as tips on the technology or administrative practices, historical background on terms and technologies, or side commentary on industry issues.

---

8   Chapter 1   PLANNING

INTRODUCTION

Microsoft grew up around the personal computer industry and established itself as the preeminent maker of software products for personal computers. Microsoft has a vast portfolio of software products, but it is best known for its operating systems.

Microsoft's current operating system products, listed here, are undoubtedly well-known to anyone studying for the MCSE exams:

◆ Windows 95

◆ Windows NT Workstation

◆ Windows NT Server

NOTE

Strange But True Although it sounds backward, it is true: Windows NT boots from the system partition and then loads the system from the boot partition.

Some older operating system products—namely MS-DOS, Windows 3.1, and Windows for Workgroups—are still important to the operability of Windows NT Server, so don't be surprised if you hear them mentioned from time to time in this book.

Windows NT is the most powerful, the most secure, and perhaps the most elegant operating system Microsoft has yet produced. It languished for a while after it first appeared (in part because no one was sure why they needed it or what to do with it), but Microsoft has persisted with improving interoperability and performance. With the release of Windows NT 4 which offers a new Windows 95-like user interface, Windows NT has assumed a prominent place in today's world of network-based computing.

WINDOWS NT SERVER AMONG MICROSOFT OPERATING SYSTEMS

▶ As we already mentioned, Microsoft has three operating system products now competing in the marketplace: Windows 95, Windows NT Workstation, and Windows NT Server. Each of these operating systems has its advantages and disadvantages.

WARNING

Don't Overextend Your Partitions and Wraps It is not necessary to create an extended partition on a disk; primary partitions might be all that you need. However, if you do create one, remember that you can never have more than one extended partition on a physical disk.

Looking at the presentation of the desktop, the three look very much alike—so much so that you might have to click the Start button and read the banner on the left side of the menu to determine which operating system you are looking at. Each offers the familiar Windows 95 user interface featuring the Start button, the Recycling

---

Objective Coverage Text: In the text before an exam objective is specifically addressed, you will notice the objective is listed to help call your attention to that particular material.

Warning: In using sophisticated information technology, there is always potential for mistakes or even catastrophes that can occur through improper application of the technology. Warnings appear in the margins to alert you to such potential problems.

STEP BY STEP

5.1 Configuring an Extension to Trigger an Application to Always Run in a Separate Memory Space

1. Start the Windows NT Explorer.

2. From the View menu, choose Options.

3. Click the File Types tab.

4. In the Registered File Types list box, select the desired file type.

5. Click the Edit button to display the Edit File Type dialog box. Then select Open from the Actions list and click the Edit button below it.

6. In the Editing Action for Type dialog box, adjust the application name by typing **cmd.exe /c start /separate** in front of the existing contents of the field (see Figure 5.15).

FIGURE 5.15
Configuring a shortcut to run a Win16 application in a separate memory space.

Step by Step: Step by Steps are hands-on tutorial instructions that walk you through a particular task or function relevant to the exam objectives.

Figure: To improve readability, most figures have been placed in the margins so they do not interrupt the main flow of text.

14   Chapter 1   PLANNING

You must use NTFS if you want to preserve existing permissions when you migrate files and directories from a NetWare server to a Windows NT Server system.

Windows 95 is Microsoft's everyday workhorse operating system. It provides a 32-bit platform and is designed to operate with a variety of peripherals. See Table 1.1 for the minimum hardware requirements for the installation and operation of Windows 95. Also, if you want to allow Macintosh computers to access files on the partition through Windows NT's Services for Macintosh, you must format the partition for NTFS.

MAKING REGISTRY CHANGES

To make Registry changes, run the REGEDT32.EXE program. The Registry in Windows NT is a complex database of configuration settings for your computer. If you want to configure the Workstation service, open the HKEY_LOCAL_MACHINE hive, as shown in Figure 3.22.

The exact location for configuring your Workstation service is

    HKEY_LOCAL_MACHINE\System\CurrentControlSet\Services\
    LanmanWorkstation\Parameters

To find additional information regarding this Registry item and others, refer to the Windows NT Server resource kit.

This summary table offers an overview of the differences between the FAT and NTFS file systems.

In-Depth Sidebar: These more extensive discussions cover material that perhaps is not as directly relevant to the exam, but which is useful as reference material or in everyday practice. In-Depths may also provide useful background or contextual information necessary for understanding the larger topic under consideration.

REVIEW BREAK

Choosing a File System

But if the system is designed to store data, mirroring might produce disk bottlenecks. You might only know whether these changes are significant by setting up two identical computers, implementing mirroring on one but not on the other, and then running Performance Monitor on both under a simulated load to see the performance differences.

This summary table offers an overview of the differences between the FAT and NTFS file systems.

Review Break: Crucial information is summarized at various points in the book in lists or tables. At the end of a particularly long section, you might come across a Review Break that is there just to wrap up one long objective and reinforce the key points before you shift your focus to the next section.

CASE STUDIES

Case Studies are presented throughout the book to provide you with another, more conceptual opportunity to apply the knowledge you are developing. They also reflect the "real-world" experiences of the authors in ways that prepare you not only for the exam but for actual network administration as well. In each Case Study, you will find similar elements: a description of a Scenario, the Essence of the Case, and an extended Analysis section.

CASE STUDY: REALLY GOOD GUITARS

ESSENCE OF THE CASE

Here are the essential elements in this case:

- need for centralized administration
- the need for WAN connectivity nation-wide
- a requirement for Internet access and e-mail
- the need for Security on network shares and local files
- an implementation of Fault-tolerant systems

SCENARIO

Really Good Guitars is a national company specializing in the design and manufacturer of custom acoustic guitars. Having grown up out of an informal network of artisans across Canada, the company has many locations but very few employees (300 at this time) and a Head Office in Churchill, Manitoba. Although they follow the best traditions of hand-making guitars, they are not without technological savvy and all the 25 locations have computers on-site which are used to do accounting, run MS Office applications, and run their custom made guitar design software. The leadership team has recently begun to realize that a networked solution is essential to maintain consistency and to provide security on what are becoming some very innovative designs and to provide their employees with e-mail and Internet access.

RGG desires a centralized administration of its

continues

Essence of the Case: A bulleted list of the key problems or issues that need to be addressed in the Scenario.

Scenario: A few paragraphs describing a situation that professional practitioners in the field might face. A Scenario will deal with an issue relating to the objectives covered in the chapter, and it includes the kinds of details that make a difference.

Analysis: This is a lengthy description of the best way to handle the problems listed in the Essence of the Case. In this section, you might find a table summarizing the solutions, a worded example, or both.

CASE STUDY: PRINT IT DRAFTING INC.

continued

too, which is unacceptable. You are to find a solution to this problem if one exists.

ANALYSIS

The fixes for both of these problems are relatively straightforward. In the first case, it is likely that all the programs on the draftspeople's workstations are being started at normal priority. This means that they have a priority of 8. But the default says that anything running in the foreground is getting a 2-point boost from the base priority, bringing it to 10. As a result, when sent to the background, AutoCAD is not getting as much attention from the processor as it did when it was the foreground application. Because multiple applications need to be run at once without significant degradation of the performance of AutoCAD, you implement the following solution:

1. On the Performance tab of the System Properties dialog box for each workstation, set the Application Performance slider to None to prevent a boost for foreground applications.

2. Recommend that users keep the additional programs running alongside AutoCAD at a minimum (because all programs will now get equal processor time).

The fix to the second problem is to run each 16-bit application in its own NTVDM. This ensures that the crashing of one application will not adversely affect the others, but it still enables interoperability between the applications because they use OLE (and not shared memory) to transfer data. To make the fix as transparent as possible to the users, you suggested that two things be done:

1. Make sure that for each shortcut a user has created to the office applications, the Run in Separate Memory Space option is selected on the Shortcut tab.

2. Change the properties for the extensions associated with the applications (for example, .XLS and .DOC) so that they start using the /separate switch. Then any file that is double-clicked invokes the associated program to run in its own NTVDM.

EXTENSIVE REVIEW AND SELF-TEST OPTIONS

At the end of each chapter, along with some summary elements, you will find a section called "Apply Your Knowledge" that gives you several different methods with which to test your understanding of the material and review what you have learned.

CHAPTER SUMMARY

KEY TERMS

Before you take the exam, make sure you are comfortable with the definitions and concepts for each of the following key terms:

- FAT
- NTFS
- workgroup
- domain

This chapter discussed the main planning topics you will encounter on the Windows NT Server exam. Distilled down, these topics revolve around two main goals: understanding the planning of disk configuration and understanding the planning of network protocols.

◆ Windows NT Server supports an unlimited number of inbound sessions; Windows NT Workstation supports no more than 10 active sessions at the same time.

◆ Windows NT Server accommodates an unlimited number of remote access connections (although Microsoft only supports up to 256); Windows NT Workstation supports only a single remote access connection.

Key Terms: A list of key terms appears at the end of each chapter. These are terms that you should be sure you know and are comfortable defining and understanding when you go in to take the exam.

Chapter Summary: Before the Apply Your Learning section, you will find a chapter summary that wraps up the chapter and reviews what you should have learned.

Chapter 1 PLANNING   23

APPLY YOUR KNOWLEDGE

This section allows you to assess how well you understood the material in the chapter. Review and Exam questions test your knowledge of the tasks and concepts specified in the objectives. The Exercises provide you with opportunities to engage in the sorts of tasks that comprise the skill sets the objectives reflect.

Exercises

1.1 Synchronizing the Domain Controllerys

The following steps show you how to manually synchronize a backup domain controller within your domain. (This objective deals with Objective Planning 1.)

Estimated Time: Less than 10 minutes.

1. Click Start, Programs, Administrative Tools, and select the Server Manager icon.

2. Highlight the BDC (Backup Domain Controller) in your computer list.

3. Select the Computer menu, then select Synchronize with Primary Domain Controller.

12.2 Establishing a Trust Relationship between Domains

The following steps show you how to establish a trust relationship between multiple domains. To complete this exercise, you must have two Windows NT Server computers, each installed in their own domain. (This objective deals with objective Planning 1.)

Estimated Time: 10 minutes

1. From the trusted domain select Start, Programs, Administrative Tools, and click User Manager for Domains. The User Manager.

FIGURE 1.2
The login process on a local machine.

2. Select the Policies menu and click Trust Relationships. The Trust Relationships dialog box appears.

4. When the trusting domain information has been entered, click OK and close the Trust Relationships dialog box.

Review Questions

1. List the four domain models that can be used for directory services in Windows NT Server 4.

2. List the goals of a directory services architecture.

3. What is the maximum size of the SAM database in Windows NT Server 4.0?

4. What are the two different types of domains in a trust relationship?

5. In a trust relationship which domain would contain the user accounts?

Exercises: These activities provide an opportunity for you to master specific hands-on tasks. Our goal is to increase your proficiency with the product or technology. You must be able to conduct these tasks in order to pass the exam.

Review Questions: These open-ended, short-answer questions allow you to quickly assess your comprehension of what you just read in the chapter. Instead of asking you to choose from a list of options, these questions require you to state the correct answers in your own words. Although you will not experience these kinds of questions on the exam, these questions will indeed test your level of comprehension of key concepts.

6. Can a local account be used in a trust relationship? Explain.

7. In a complete trust domain model that uses 4 different domains, what is the total number of trust relationships required to use a complete trust domain model?

Exam Questions

The following questions are similar to those you will face on the Microsoft exam. Answers to these questions can be found in section Answers and Explanations, later in the chapter. At the end of each of those answers, you will be informed of where (that is, in what section of the chapter) to find more information..

1. ABC Corporation has locations in Toronto, New York, and San Francisco. It wants to install Windows NT Server 4 to encompass all its locations in a single WAN environment. The head office is located in New York. What is the best domain model for ABCís directory services implementation?

    A. Single-domain model

    B. Single-master domain model

    C. Multiple-master domain model

    D. Complete-trust domain model

2. JPS Printing has a single location with 1,000 users spread across the LAN. It has special printers and applications installed on the servers in its environment. It needs to be able to centrally manage the user accounts and the resources. Which domain model would best fit its needs?

    A. Single-domain model

    B. Single-master domain model

    C. Multiple-master domain model

    D. Complete-trust domain model

5. What must be created to allow a user account from one domain to access resources in a different domain?

    A. Complete Trust Domain Model

    B. One Way Trust Relationship

    C. Two Way Trust Relationship

    D. Master-Domain Model

Answers to Review Questions

1. Single domain, master domain, multiple-master domain, complete-trust domain. See section, Windows NT Server 4 Domain Models, in this chapter for more information. (This question deals with objective Planning 1.)

2. One user, one account, centralized administration, universal resource access, synchronization. See section, Windows NT Server 4 Directory Services, in this chapter for more information. (This question deals with objective Planning 1.)

6. Local accounts cannot be given permissions across trusts. See section, Accounts in Trust Relationships, in this chapter for more information. (This question deals with Planning 1.)

Exam Questions: These questions reflect the kinds of multiple-choice questions that appear on the Microsoft exams. Use them to become familiar with the exam question formats and to help you determine what you know and what you need to review or study more.

Answers and Explanations: For each of the Review and Exam questions, you will find thorough explanations located at the end of the section.

Suggested Readings and Resources

The following are some recommended readings on the subject of installing and configuring NT Workstation:

1. Microsoft Official Curriculum course 770: *Installing and Configuring Microsoft Windows NT Workstation 4.0*

    • Module 1: Overview of Windows NT Workstation 4.0

    • Module 2: Installing Windows NT Workstation 4.0

2. Microsoft Official Curriculum course 922: *Supporting Microsoft Windows NT 4.0 Core Technologies*

    • Module 2: Installing Windows NT

    • Module 3: Configuring the Windows NT Environment

3. *Microsoft Windows NT Workstation Resource Kit Version 4.0* (Microsoft Press)

    • Chapter 2: Customizing Setup

    • Chapter 4: Planning for a Mixed Environment

4. Microsoft TechNet CD-ROM

    • *MS Windows NT Workstation Technical Notes*

        • MS Windows NT Workstation Deployment Guide – Automating Windows NT Setup

        • An Unattended Windows NT Workstation Deployment

5. Web Sites

    • www.microsoft.com/train_cert

    • www.prometric.com/testingcandidates/ assessment/chosetest.html (take online

Suggested Readings and Resources: The very last element in every chapter is a list of additional resources you can use if you want to go above and beyond certification-level material or if you need to spend more time on a particular subject that you are having trouble understanding.

Introduction

MCSE Training Guide: SQL Server 7 Database Design is designed for advanced endusers, service technicians, and network administrators with the goal of certification as a Microsoft Certified Systems Engineer (MCSE). The Designing and Implementing Databases with Microsoft SQL Server 7 exam (70-029) measures your ability to implement, administer, and troubleshoot information systems that incorporate SQL Server 7.

This book is your one-stop shop. Everything you need to know to prepare for the exam is in here, and Microsoft has approved it as study material. You do not have to take a class in addition to buying this book to pass the exam. However, depending on your personal study habits or learning style, you may benefit from buying this book *and* taking a class.

This book also can help advanced users and administrators who are not studying for the exam but are looking for a single-volume reference on SQL Server 7 Database Design and Implementation.

HOW THIS BOOK HELPS YOU

This book conducts a tour of all the areas covered by the 70-029 exam and teaches you the specific skills you need to achieve your MCSE certification. You'll also find helpful hints, tips, real-world examples, exercises, and references to additional study materials. Specifically, this book is set up to help you in the following ways:

◆ **Organization.** This book is organized by major exam topics and individual exam objectives. Every objective you need to know for the 70-029

exam is covered in this book. The objectives are not covered in exactly the same order as they are listed by Microsoft, but we have attempted to organize the topics in the most logical and accessible fashion to make it as easy as possible for you to learn the information. We have also attempted to make the information accessible in the following ways:

- The full list of exam topics and objectives is included in this introduction.

- Each chapter begins with a list of the objectives to be covered in that chapter.

- Each chapter also includes an outline that provides an overview of the material and the page numbers on which particular topics can be found.

- The objectives are repeated (in color) in the text directly preceding the material most directly relevant to it (unless the whole chapter addresses a single objective).

- Information about where the objectives are covered is also conveniently condensed in the tear card at the front of this book.

◆ **Instructional Features**. This book has been designed to provide you with multiple ways to learn and reinforce the exam material. Following are some of the helpful methods:

- *Objective explanations.* As mentioned previously, each chapter begins with a list of the objectives covered in the chapter. In addition, immediately following each objective is an explanation of it in a context that defines it more meaningfully.

- *Study strategies.* Early in each chapter, you will also find strategies for how to study and retain the material in the chapter, particularly as it is addressed on the exam.

- *Exam tips.* Exam tips appear in the margin to provide specific exam-related advice. Such tips might address what material is covered (or not covered) on the exam, how it is covered, mnemonic devices, or particular quirks of that exam.

- *Review breaks and summaries.* Crucial information is summarized at various points in the book in lists or tables. A chapter summary appears before each chapter's exercises and review and exam questions.

- *Key terms.* A list of key terms appears as part of the chapter summary for each chapter.

- *Notes.* These appear in the margin and contain various kinds of useful information, such as tips on technology or administrative practices, historical background of terms and technologies, or side commentary on industry issues.

- *Warnings.* When using sophisticated information technology, there is always the potential for mistakes or even catastrophes to occur because of improper application of the technology. Warnings appear in the margin to alert you to such potential problems.

- *In-depth notes.* These more extensive discussions cover material that may not be directly relevant to the exam, but which is useful as reference material or in everyday practice. These notes might also provide useful background or contextual information necessary for understanding the larger topic under consideration.

- *Step-by-step tutorials.* These are hands-on, tutorial instructions that lead you through a particular task or function relevant to the exam objectives.

- *Exercises.* Found near the end of each chapter in the "Apply Your Knowledge" section, exercises might include additional tutorial material as well as other types of problems and questions.

- *Case studies.* Presented throughout the book, case studies provide you with a more conceptual opportunity to apply and reinforce the knowledge you are developing. They include a description of a scenario, the essence of the case, and an extended analysis section. They also reflect the real-world experiences of the authors in ways that prepare you not only for the exam but for actual network administration as well.

◆ **Extensive practice test options.** The book provides numerous opportunities for you to assess your knowledge and practice for the exam. The practice options include the following:

- *Review questions.* These open-ended questions appear in the "Apply Your Knowledge" section that appears at the end of each chapter. These questions allow you to quickly assess your comprehension of what you just read in the chapter. Answers to the questions are provided later in the section.

- *Exam questions.* These questions also appear in the "Apply your Knowledge" section of each chapter. They reflect the kinds of multiple-choice questions that appear on the Microsoft exams. Use them to practice for the exam and to help you determine what you know and what you need to review or study further. Answers and explanations for them are provided.

- *Practice exam.* A practice exam is included in the "Final Review" section of the book. The "Final Review" section and the practice exam are discussed later in this Introduction.

- *Top Score software.* The Top Score Test Simulation Software Suite on the included CD-ROM provides further self-evaluation opportunities in the form of practice exams, study cards, flash cards, and product simulations.

> **NOTE** For a complete description of the New Riders Top Score test engine, please see Appendix D, "Top Score User's Manual."

◆ **Final Review.** This part of the book provides you with three valuable tools for preparing for the exam.

  - *Fast Facts.* This condensed version of the information contained in the book will prove extremely useful for last-minute review.

  - *Study and Exam Prep Tips.* Read this section early on to help you develop study strategies. This section also provides you with valuable exam-day tips and information on new exam and question formats, such as adaptive tests and simulation-based questions.

  - *Practice Exam.* A full practice exam is included. Questions are presented in the styles used on the actual exam. Use it to assess your readiness for the real thing.

For more information about the exam or the certification process, contact Microsoft:

Microsoft Education: (800) 636-7544

Internet:
ftp://ftp.microsoft.com/Services/MSEdCert

World Wide Web:
http://www.microsoft.com/train_cert

CompuServe Forum: **GO MSEDCERT**

> **NOTE** The book also includes other features, such as sections titled "Suggested Readings and Resources," which direct you toward further information that could aid you in your exam preparation or your actual work. There are several valuable appendixes as well, including a glossary (Appendix A), an overview of the Microsoft certification program (Appendix B), and a description of what is on the CD-ROM (Appendix C). (You will recall that the "Top Score User's Manual" appears in Appendix D.) These and all the other book features mentioned previously will provide you with thorough preparation for the exam.

WHAT THE 70-029 EXAM COVERS

The 70-029 exam covers the five main topic areas represented by the conceptual groupings of the test objectives: developing a logical database, deriving the physical design, creating data services, creating a physical database, and maintaining a database. The exam objectives are listed by topic area in the following sections.

Developing a Logical Database

◆ Group data into entities by applying normalization rules.

◆ Identify primary keys.

◆ Choose the foreign key that will enforce a relationship between entities and that will ensure referential integrity.

◆ Identify the business rules that relate to data integrity.

◆ Incorporate business rules and constraints into the data model.

◆ In a given situation, decide whether denormalization is appropriate.

Deriving the Physical Design

◆ Assess the potential impact of the logical design on performance, maintainability, extensibility, scalability, availability, and security.

Creating Data Services

◆ Access data by using the dynamic SQL model.

◆ Access data by using the Stored Procedure model.

◆ Manipulate data by using Transact-SQL cursors.

  • Choose the appropriate type of cursor.

  • Define the appropriate level of sensitivity to change.

  • Choose the appropriate navigation.

  • Choose the scope of the cursor, specifically global or local.

◆ Create and manage explicit, implicit, and distributed transactions to ensure data consistency and recoverability.

  • Define the transaction isolation level.

  • Design transactions of appropriate length.

  • Avoid or handle deadlocks.

  • Use optimistic locking appropriately.

  • Implement error handling by using @@TRANCOUNT.

◆ Write INSERT, DELETE, UPDATE, and SELECT statements that retrieve and modify data.

◆ Write Transact-SQL statements that use joins or sub-queries to combine data from multiple tables.

◆ Create scripts using Transact-SQL. Programming elements include control-of-flow methods, local and global variables, functions, and error handling methods.

◆ Design, create, use, and alter views.

  • Modify data through a view.

  • Query data through a view.

◆ Create and execute stored procedures to enforce business rules, to modify data in multiple tables, to perform calculations, and to use input and output parameters.

  • Implement error handling by using return codes and the RAISERROR statement.

  • Choose appropriate recompile options.

◆ Create triggers that implement rules, that enforce data integrity, and that perform cascading updates and deletes.

  • Implement transactional error handling.

◆ Create result sets that provide summary data. Query types include TOP n PERCENT and GROUP BY, specifically HAVING, CUBE, and ROLLUP.

◆ Configure session-level options.

◆ Access data from static or dynamic sources by using remote stored procedures, linked servers and openrowset.

  • Evaluate where processing occurs when using OPENQUERY.

Creating a Physical Database

◆ Create and manage files, file groups, and transaction logs that define a database.

◆ Create tables that enforce data integrity and referential integrity.

  • Choose the appropriate data types.

  • Create user-defined data types.

  • Define columns as NULL or NOT NULL.

  • Define columns to generate values by using the IDENTITY property, the uniqueidentifier data type, and the NEWID function.

  • Implement constraints.

◆ Create and maintain indexes.

  • Choose an indexing strategy that will optimize performance.

  • Given a situation, choose the appropriate type of index to create.

  • Choose the column or columns to index.

  • Choose the appropriate index characteristics, specifically FILLFACTOR, DROP_EXISTING, and PAD INDEX.

◆ Populate the database with data from an external data source. Methods include bulk copy program (BCP) and Data Transformation Services (DTS).

◆ Implement full-text search.

Maintaining a Database

◆ Evaluate and optimize the performance of an execution plan by using DBCC SHOWCONTIG, SHOWPLAN_TEXT, SHOWPLAN_ALL, and UPDATE STATISTICS.

◆ Evaluate and optimize the performance of query execution plans.

◆ Diagnose and resolve locking problems.

◆ Identify SQL Server events and performance problems by using SQL Server Profiler.

HARDWARE AND SOFTWARE YOU'LL NEED

A self-paced study guide, this book was designed with the expectation that you will use Windows NT 4.0 as you follow along through the exercises while you learn. However, the theory covered in *MCSE Training Guide: SQL Server 7 Database Design* is applicable to a wide range of network systems in a wide range of actual situations, and the exercises in this book encompass that range.

Your computer should meet the following criteria:

◆ On the Microsoft Hardware Compatibility List

◆ 486DX2 66-Mhz (or better) processor for Windows NT Server

◆ 340MB (or larger) hard disk for Windows NT Server

◆ VGA (or Super VGA) video adapter

◆ VGA (or Super VGA) monitor

◆ Mouse or equivalent pointing device

◆ Double-speed (or faster) CD-ROM drive (optional)

◆ Network Interface Card (NIC) (optional for most work if SQL Server is installed locally)

◆ Presence on an existing network (optional for most work if SQL Server is installed locally)

◆ Microsoft Windows NT Server version 4.0

◆ Microsoft SQL Server version 7.0 client utilities, including the following:

  • SQL Server version 7.0 Enterprise Manager

  • SQL Server version 7.0 Query Analyzer

  • SQL Server version 7.0 Profiler

◆ Microsoft SQL Server version 7.0 (can be installed on your local machine or present on the network to which you are connected)

It might be easier to obtain access to the necessary computer hardware and software in a corporate business environment. It can be difficult, however, to allocate enough time within the busy workday to complete a self-study program. Most of your study time will occur after normal working hours, away from the everyday interruptions and pressures of your regular job.

ADVICE ON TAKING THE EXAM

More extensive tips are found in the "Study and Exam Preparation Tips" element of the "Final Review" section, but keep the following advice in mind as you study:

◆ **Read all the material.** Microsoft has been known to include material not expressly specified in the objectives. This book has included additional information not reflected in the objectives in an effort to give you the best possible preparation for the examination—and for the real-world network experiences to come.

◆ **Do the step by step tutorials and complete the exercises in each chapter.** They will help you gain experience using the Microsoft product. All Microsoft exams are task and experience based and require you to have experience using the Microsoft product in a real networking environment.

◆ **Use the questions to assess your knowledge.** Don't just read the chapter content; use the questions to find out what you know and what you don't. Study some more, review, and then assess your knowledge again.

◆ **Review the exam objectives.** Develop your own questions and examples for each topic listed. If you can create and answer several questions for each topic, you should not find it difficult to pass the exam.

> **NOTE**
> **Exam-Taking Advice** Although this book is designed to prepare you to take and pass the Designing and Implementing Databases with Microsoft SQL Server 7.0 exam, there are no guarantees. Read this book, work through the questions and exercises, and when you feel confident, take the practice exam and additional exams using the TestPrep test engine. Your results should reflect whether you are ready for the real thing.
>
> When taking the actual certification exam, make sure you answer all the questions before your time limit expires. Do not spend too much time on any one question. If you are unsure about a question, answer it as best you can; then mark it and review it when you have finished the rest of the questions.

Remember, the primary object is not to pass the exam—it is to understand the material. After you understand the material, passing the exam should be simple. Knowledge is a pyramid: To build upward, you need a solid foundation. This book and the Microsoft Certified Professional programs are designed to ensure that you have that solid foundation.

Good luck!

Exam Preparation

9   Miscellaneous Programming Techniques

10   Client Accessibility

11   Maintaining a Database

This chapter helps you prepare for the Microsoft exam by covering the following objectives:

Group data into entities by applying normalization rules.

▶ You'll need to understand the first three normal forms and how to apply them to derive a well-tuned data model.

Identify primary keys.

▶ By applying the normalization rules, you'll have a data model that will present obvious candidates for primary keys. The most important question to answer is "Are these values *guaranteed* to be unique?".

Choose the foreign key that will enforce a relationship between entities and ensure referential integrity.

▶ The important point here is to identify the fact that a relationship exists between two entities. Then, of course, that relationship should be enforced in the final data model.

Identify the business rules that relate to data integrity.

▶ These are the simple rules that ensure that only the proper kinds of data are allowed for an attribute. They include datatypes, nullability, uniqueness, and whether changes should be allowed.

CHAPTER 1

Database Design

Incorporate business rules and constraints into the data model.

▶ This point is a matter of applying the rules identified by the previous objective. The previous objective required familiarity with the types of business rules that were appropriate for data modeling; this one requires you to apply those rules to specific entities and attributes.

In a given situation, decide whether denormalization is appropriate.

▶ Just as it is important to know the normalization rules that will enforce a well-behaved data model, it is important to know when your model has features that just don't fit the rules. Most importantly, knowing when it is advisable to break the rules will force you to recognize the vast majority of the situations when it is *not* advisable to denormalize.

Assess the potential impact of the logical design on performance, maintainability, extensibility, scalability, availability, and security.

▶ This point is really a recap of all the previous rules. The purpose is to put an emphasis on applying the logical design to a physical SQL Server database.

▶ Be familiar with the terms entity, attribute, and relationship and how they relate to data modeling.

▶ Learn the first three normal forms. You should be able to read a case study and derive a data model from it.

▶ Be sure you know the basic data integrity constraints and in what situations you would apply them.

INTRODUCTION

Creating a simple database in SQL Server is relatively easy; however, one of the most important tasks you will perform as a database developer has little to do with the SQL Server product itself. Before creating a database, you should spend some time thinking about how it will be designed. You also must decide how you will represent the real-world information of your application in a relational database. Understanding the concepts presented in this chapter on design, or database modeling, is vital to a successful database implementation.

This chapter covers the fundamentals of designing a database by using relational database design methods. In addition, you learn how these modeling concepts are implemented in SQL Server. Because the process of data modeling deals with several abstract concepts, a case study is presented at the beginning of the chapter and is used to make the concepts and principles more accessible. This case study will be referred to throughout the chapter to illustrate key concepts in clear, practical terms.

Keep in mind that an in-depth discussion of relational database design is outside the scope of this book. Numerous reference materials are available on this topic, such as the following:

◆ Graeme Simsion, *Data Modeling Essentials* (Van Nostrand Reinhold, 1994).

◆ David C. Hay, *Data Model Patterns, Conventions of Thought* (Dorset House Publishing, 1996).

◆ E. F. Codd, *The Relational Model for Database Management* (Addison-Wesley Publishing Company, 1990).

The following topics are covered in this chapter:

◆ Case study: A college enrollment database

◆ Introducing data modeling concepts: entities, attributes, and relationships

◆ Implementing entities and attributes

◆ Implementing relationships

◆ Incorporating business rules into the database

◆ Normalizing your database design

Case Study: A College Enrollment Database

A small Midwestern engineering college has contracted you to design and develop a database to automate its student enrollments and class scheduling. You begin by interviewing the Registrar to determine what types of information will be stored in the database. The Registrar offers you the following information:

"We have ten departments on campus that offer about 400 different courses—everything from Astronomy 101 to Zoology 410. Of course, we don't have enough professors to teach every course every semester, but we do manage to offer about 150 different courses each semester.

"One of the problems we'd like this database to solve is the difficulty we have scheduling all of the courses we do offer in a semester. Typically, a course is offered at several different times during the week. For instance, Physics 150 may be offered on Monday, Wednesday, and Friday from 1:30 to 2:30 p.m., and it may also be offered on Tuesdays and Thursdays from 7:30 to 9:00 a.m.. Right now, we have to worry about the different time slots and rooms assigned to each class. We stick bits of paper up on the wall to show what's been used and what hasn't. It's difficult and time-consuming to do it this way, especially if someone leaves a window open and the papers get scattered! Just to keep everything straight, we refer to these different scheduled courses as "classes." Because professors are in short supply, only one professor teaches a particular class.

"Sometimes we don't even have a tenured professor available to teach a class and we need to have a teaching assistant do the job. There isn't any difference as far as the class is concerned—we just assign the T/A as the teacher—but we do keep fairly different types of information on the two different categories of teachers. For instance, our T/As are paid by the hour, whereas the professors are salaried.

"Oh! Another interesting point about our teachers—we're very proud of the new mentoring program we've just put in place. Our more experienced professors have the option to mentor some of our newer professors. This program ensures that our newer professors have someone to talk to in case they need advice. We're not forcing this on anyone, so not everyone will have a mentor, but we would like to document in the database who has a mentor and who doesn't.

"Now, we have about 4,000 students who can enroll themselves in any of these classes. Right now we use paper enrollment forms—you can imagine the paperwork we have to go through in order to process everyone's enrollments! Eventually, we'd like the students to be able to enroll over the Internet, but before we can have someone write that application, we need this database to keep track of everything. Not only that, but several professors want to start tracking attendance more closely so they can correlate attendance with students' grades. They want to be able to do this each time the class meets."

The Registrar concludes by telling you that her descriptions of the campus's operations are not at all complete, and that you should interview the department heads for more information. However, you decide to begin modeling the database on what you've learned so far.

As you are introduced to new concepts of data modeling throughout the chapter, an example from this case study may be used to solidify an abstract concept in real terms. You can also use points from this study yourself to help place an idea in a context that makes sense to you.

INTRODUCING DATA MODELING CONCEPTS: ENTITIES, ATTRIBUTES, AND RELATIONSHIPS

The relational design process provides a structured approach to modeling an information system's data and the business rules for that data. After you learn the fundamentals of this process, you should be able to take the information learned from the requirements gathered for the system (such as the information presented in the case study) and easily design a database.

The three key components used in relational database design (*entities*, *attributes*, and *relationships*) are outlined in Table 1.1.

TABLE 1.1

THE THREE KEY COMPONENTS USED IN RELATIONAL
DATABASE DESIGN

Design Component	Implemented in SQL Server	Examples
Entities	Tables	Student, Course
Attributes	Columns in a Table	Student's Name, Course number
Relationships	Primary/Foreign Key Columns or Tables	Teacher to Class

The upcoming subsections describe each component in more detail.
The chapter then discusses in general terms how these components
are implemented in SQL Server. Don't worry about the details for
now; implementing tables, columns, and relationships is covered in
more detail in Chapter 6, "Retrieving Data."

Entities

Entities are the basic building blocks of relational database design.
An *entity* defines any person, place, thing, or concept for which data
will be collected. Some examples of entities include the following:

◆ Person: student, teacher

◆ Place: classroom, building

◆ Thing: computer, lab equipment

◆ Concept: course, student's attendance

When you attempt to discover possible entities in your data model,
it is often helpful to look (or listen) for nouns/noun phrases during
the requirements analysis. Because nouns describe people, places,
things, or concepts, this trick usually leads you to an entity. The
challenge is to distinguish between the relevant and the irrelevant
concepts. Consider the following excerpt from the case study:

"We have ten *departments* on campus that offer about 400 different
courses—everything from Astronomy 101 to Zoology 410. Of
course, we don't have enough *professors* to teach every course every

semester, but we do manage to offer about 150 different courses each semester."

The highlighted words or phrases are likely candidates for modeling as an entity. The *professor*, or *teacher*, concept is an obvious choice, as are the ideas of a *course* and a *department*. The database will have to keep track of many different teachers and courses. In addition, the database will be used over many semesters, so if detailed information needs to be kept about each semester, the concept of a *semester* should be modeled as an entity. Notice that the idea of a campus, while important to a college, is not a candidate for an entity in this example. This is because a small college with only one campus will probably build any campus-specific information directly into its data model. If the college were planning to expand to multiple campuses in the future, creating a campus entity then would be important because it would allow you to collect information about each distinct campus.

A good practice is to list all the entities in your database with a one-sentence description of what that entity represents. For example, a teacher may be defined as "a person employed by the college who is responsible for instructing students in a class." Usually, a good entity can be described in one sentence, unless it is a very abstract concept.

Review the case study to see if you can identify some entities that will be used in the data model. Then, review the following list of entities:

◆ Teacher: A person employed by the college who is responsible for instructing a class of students.

◆ Student: A person who is enrolled in classes at the college and attends class sessions.

◆ Course: The subject material taught in a class.

◆ Class: A scheduled instance of a course that is taught by one teacher and that meets in a particular room during specific times of the week.

◆ Class Session: An instance of a class that occurs at a particular date and time.

When speaking of an entity in the data model, one usually is referring to an *instance* of that entity. An *instance* is a particular occurrence of an entity that is distinguishable from all other occurrences

> **NOTE**
>
> **Tedious Practice Can Yield Large Rewards** Defining each entity in your database in this way may seem unnecessary, but it is especially helpful when you're dealing with concepts that are more abstract than a teacher. Also, creating these definitions can draw attention to any relationships between entities.

of that entity. For example, the college has multiple professors, such as Professor Noel, Professor Press, and Professor Smith. Each is an instance of a teacher. The concept of an instance is important to understanding relationships.

In a data model diagram (often referred to as an *Entity-Relationship (ER) diagram*, or the database *schema*), entities are most often drawn as boxes, occasionally with their definition inside. See Figure 1.1 for an example of the case study's data model up to this point.

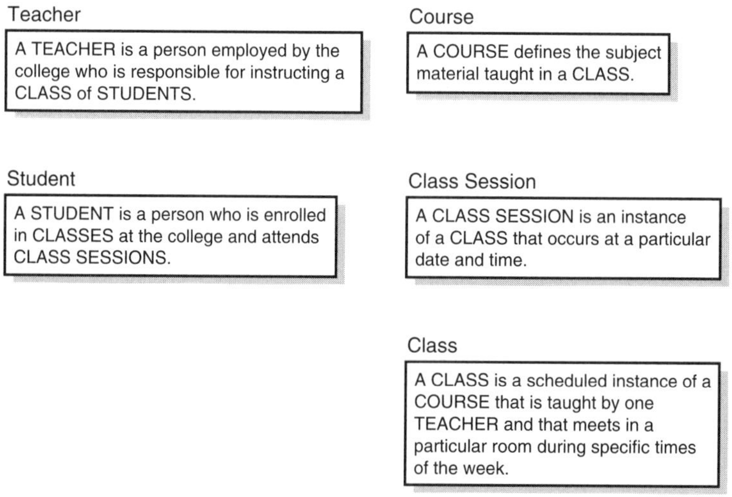

Teacher

> A TEACHER is a person employed by the college who is responsible for instructing a CLASS of STUDENTS.

Course

> A COURSE defines the subject material taught in a CLASS.

Student

> A STUDENT is a person who is enrolled in CLASSES at the college and attends CLASS SESSIONS.

Class Session

> A CLASS SESSION is an instance of a CLASS that occurs at a particular date and time.

Class

> A CLASS is a scheduled instance of a COURSE that is taught by one TEACHER and that meets in a particular room during specific times of the week.

FIGURE 1.1

Example ER diagram (entities and definitions) for the college enrollment database.

Now that you are familiar with the concept of an entity, you are ready to describe your entities in greater detail.

Attributes

The second major data-modeling concept that you must understand is that of attributes. *Attributes* are additional characteristics or information defined for an entity.

An entity's attributes don't define an entity, but they provide additional information about an entity that may be useful elsewhere. The concept of a *teacher* can be defined (definition) without knowing the teacher's name, salary, or educational level (attributes). However, knowing nothing about its teachers does the college little good. And that's where the attributes come in handy.

> **NOTE**
>
> **Use a Data Modeling Tool**   Several good data modeling tools are available on the market. These tools help you create professional ER diagrams and fully define all aspects of your data model. In addition, many of these tools automatically create the final database in SQL Server.

Review the case study and the entities described in the previous section. Try to list some attributes for each entity, then review the following list of possible attributes for each entity:

- Teacher: Name, gender, social security number, address, salary, years tenured
- Student: Name, gender, social security number, billing address, college address, class level, grade point average

  Course: Course number, course name, prerequisites
- Class: Course number, scheduled meeting times, scheduled room, assigned teacher, maximum enrollment, students enrolled
- Class Session: Course number, date and time of session, students attending

There is no set method or trick for discovering attributes of a particular entity. Usually, brainstorming on the different characteristics of an entity is sufficient. If you find that you are having difficulty, you may want to check your definition of the entity to see if it is specific enough.

In an ER diagram, attributes are listed by name inside their entity's box, as shown in Figure 1.2.

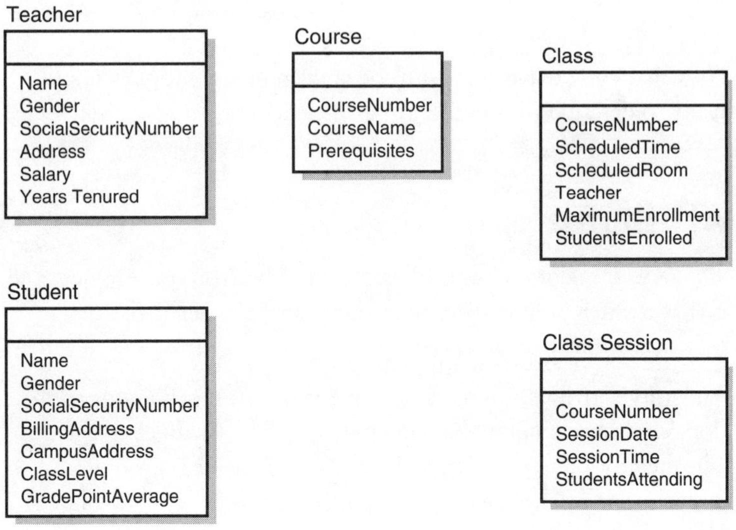

FIGURE 1.2
Example ER diagram (entities and attributes) for the college enrollment database.

Relationships

Entities and attributes enable you to explicitly define what information, or data, is being stored in the database. Relationships are the other powerful feature of relational modeling and give the modeling technique its name. A *relationship* is a logical linkage between two entities that describes how those entities are associated with each other. Think of relationships as the logical links in a database that turn simple data into useful information.

For instance, our definition of a teacher reads: "A person employed by the college who is responsible for instructing students in a class." Clearly, the teacher entity and the class entity are somehow associated with each other. Creating a relationship explicitly defines an association between entities in the data model.

You will now see how to identify not only the need for a relationship, but also the type of relationship.

Identifying Relationships in a Data Model

If entities can be thought of as the nouns in data modeling, then relationships are best described as the verbs. In fact, relationships often have a verb phrase associated with them in the data model, much like entities have an associated definition. One trick to discovering relationships between entities is to look closely at the entity definitions. Consider the following entity definitions from earlier in the chapter:

◆ Teacher: A person employed by the college who is responsible for *instructing* a CLASS of STUDENTS.

◆ Student: A person who is *enrolled* in CLASSES at the college and *attends* CLASS SESSIONS.

◆ Course: *Defines* the subject material taught in a CLASS.

◆ Class: A scheduled instance of a COURSE that is *taught* by one TEACHER and that meets in particular room during specific times of the week.

◆ Class Session: An instance of a CLASS that *occurs* at a particular date and time.

Notice that the definitions now are written to show other entities in all caps, and significant verbs or verb phrases appear in italics.

Formatting your entity definitions in this way makes it easy to identify possible relationships between entities. These definitions can be distilled into several simple statements that highlight the relationships between the entities in this case study:

A TEACHER instructs CLASSES.

A COURSE defines subject material for CLASSES.

STUDENTS are enrolled in CLASSES.

STUDENTS attend CLASS SESSIONS.

A CLASS occurs as CLASS SESSIONS.

In an ER diagram, relationships are represented as lines drawn between entities. Often, the verb phrase appears near the line to describe the relationship further. See Figure 1.3 for the case study's data model with relationships.

FIGURE 1.3
Example ER diagram (entities and relationships) for the college enrollment database.

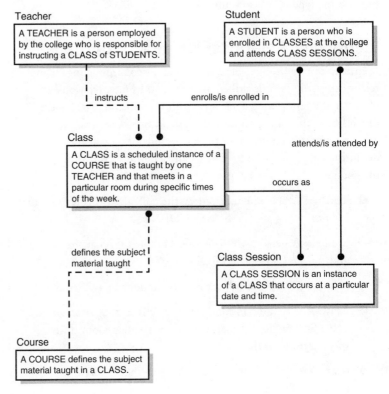

Types of Relationships

You may notice that some of the relationship lines in Figure 1.3 have dots on one or both of their ends. This is because there are several different ways to classify a relationship.

The identifying property of a relationship is called its cardinality. The *cardinality* of a relationship allows the database modeler to specify how instances of each entity relate to each other. There are three major types of cardinality:

◆ **One-to-One**. A single instance of one entity is associated with a single instance of another entity. This type of relationship is relatively uncommon; it is typically used when an entity can be classified into several subtypes. See Exercise 1.4 for an example of when a One-to-One relationship might be used.

A single line drawn between the entities involved indicates a relationship. If that relationship is more complicated than a simple One-to-One cardinality, the line is usually denoted in some way (such as with a dot) to indicate the cardinality.

◆ **One-to-Many**. An instance of an entity (called the *parent*) is associated with zero or several instances of another entity (called the *child*). An example of this type of relationship can be found by examining the teacher and class entities. A teacher may instruct zero or more classes during the course of a semester.

A One-to-Many relationship is drawn as a line between the entities involved. The child end of the relationship typically has a dot.

◆ **Many-to-Many**. Many instances of an entity are associated with many instances of another entity. Consider the enroll-ment relationship between a student and a class. A single stu-dent may be enrolled in many classes, and a single class may enroll many students. SQL Server's implementation of the relational model does not directly support a Many-to-Many relationship; however, it is possible to model this type of car-dinality using two One-to-Many relationships to a third entity (table). This implementation is described fully in the section "Many-to-Many Relationships" later in this chapter.

A Many-to-Many relationship is drawn as a line between the entities involved. Both ends of the line have a dot.

Later in the chapter you learn how each of these types of relationships is implemented in SQL Server.

NOTE

Different Degrees of Relationships
The One-to-Many relationship actually has a sub-classification. Typically, the One-to-Many cardinality means "one to zero, one, or more." It is possible to specify that at least one instance of the child entity must exist; in other words, "one to one or more." In most notation systems, this is denoted by an uppercase P near the child end of the relationship line.

The One-to-One relationship is actually a special case of a "one to exactly *n*" type of relationship, in which exactly *n* instances of the child entity must exist. Most notation systems denote this type of relationship by putting the number of instances required near the child end of the relationship line.

Finally, another special type of cardi-nality is the "one to zero or one." This specifies that either zero or one instances of the child entity exist for each instance of the parent. Most notation systems denote this condi-tion with an uppercase Z near the child end of the relationship.

Data Modeling Concepts

You have just learned about entities, attributes, and relationships in an abstract sense. The most important things to take away from this section are the following definitions:

▶ An *entity* defines any person, place, thing, or concept for which data will be collected.

▶ *Attributes* are additional characteristics or information defined for an entity.

▶ A *relationship* is a logical linkage between two entities that describes how the entities are associated with each other.

You should now know what each of these terms means in the context of data modeling, and so are ready to see how these ideas are used in SQL Server. The following sections introduce more concrete terminology that will rigidly define entities, attributes, and relationships in the terms that SQL Server understands.

IMPLEMENTING ENTITIES AND ATTRIBUTES

Now that you've become familiar with the three main concepts used in relational modeling, it's time to see how these concepts are used in SQL Server. Entities and attributes are implemented in SQL Server as tables and columns, respectively. The following subsections describe table and column characteristics in SQL Server's terminology. You'll see how to choose a primary key and apply appropriate column constraints. The following main section deals with how relationships are defined between tables in a database in SQL Server.

Chapter 3, "Implementing a Physical Design," covers the actual commands used to define tables and relationships in a database.

Characteristics of Tables

Recall that the earlier discussion of entities introduced the concept of an *instance* of an entity. In SQL Server, tables are used to store information about each instance of an entity. A sample table for the teacher entity is presented in Figure 1.4.

First Name	Last Name	Gender	Social Security Number	Salary	Years Tenured
Warren	Press	M	001-03-1869	$45,000	12
Marie	Noel	F	079-91-2060	$52,500	15
Michael	Barry	M	114-78-1342	$59,000	16
Christopher	Smith	M	001-23-1903	$60,100	18

FIGURE 1.4
The teacher entity as a table.

Note that a table stores each instance of an entity as a row in the table, with each attribute stored in a column. So, in Figure 1.4, the table has four teachers, and each column describes information about one of the four teachers. Rows and columns are sometimes referred to as *records* and *fields*, respectively. The order of the rows and columns in a table is not important, although columns that store related information should be grouped together. Note that in the example table, the FirstName and LastName columns are grouped in this way.

The following list summarizes the terminology just mentioned:

◆ *Entities* are modeled as *tables*.

◆ In a *table*, each instance of an entity is called a *row*.

◆ *Attributes* are modeled as *columns* in a table.

◆ Programmers often refer to *rows* and *columns* as *records* and *fields*, respectively.

Although you can choose any names you want for tables and columns, following a few guidelines can make your data model consistent and easier to read. These guidelines include:

◆ Table and column names are usually singular; this is a relational modeling convention.

◆ Tables are almost always named after the entity they represent.

◆ Mixed case is preferable to using underscores to separate words.

◆ Ensure that columns that store the same type of information in different tables have the same name. For instance, if the teacher table and the student table both store address information, make sure that the column storing the ZIP code has the same name in both tables.

◆ Ensure that similarly named columns all have the same data types.

These guidelines may seem basic, but developers writing applications that use your database will appreciate the consistency.

SQL Server does place some restrictions on table and column names. The restrictions include the following:

◆ Table and column names cannot be longer than 128 characters.

◆ Table names must be unique within the database.

◆ Column names must be unique within a table.

> **NOTE**
>
> **Most Object Names Follow the Same Rules**   Most object names within SQL Server are limited to 128 characters.

SQL Server enforces the uniqueness of table and column names for you, but for a relational model to work properly, each row must also be unique. This concept is known as *entity integrity* or *row integrity*. In other words, each instance of an entity must be distinguishable from all other instances. Otherwise, it would be very difficult to change a particular instance of an entity. Imagine trying to change some information about one teacher without knowing how to distinguish that teacher from the others! Because SQL Server does not automatically enforce it, the person designing the database must build this row uniqueness into the data model. Row uniqueness is enforced by using a special column in the table called the *primary key*.

Choosing and Defining the Primary Key

▶ Identify primary keys.

As mentioned in the preceding section, the *primary key* is a special column or group of columns in the table that can be used to identify any one row. The important thing to remember is that the value in the primary key column (or combination of values in the group of columns) *must be unique in the table in which it resides.* Fortunately,

SQL Server provides several ways to enforce the uniqueness of the primary key:

◆ Using a primary key constraint when the table is defined. See Chapter 3 for more information about constraints.

◆ Using the sp_primarykey stored procedure to define the primary key for an existing table.

◆ Creating a unique index on the primary key column(s). See Chapter 4, "Indexing," for more information about indexes.

A primary key can be chosen out of the existing columns in a table, or a new column can be created expressly for this purpose.

The easiest way to create a primary key is to create a special column called an *identity* column, also known as an *auto-number* or a *sequence* column. An identity column contains numbers assigned automatically by SQL Server. SQL Server just adds one to the prior value in the column to get a new, unique number to use as a key value. In data modeling terms, this type of primary key is known as a *surrogate key*, because the key values themselves have no inherent meaning.

To choose a primary key, look at the existing attributes of an entity to see whether there's an attribute or group of attributes that could serve to identify instances of that entity. The important question to ask yourself when you're considering these possible keys is, "Are the values of this column or group of columns guaranteed to be unique?" If the answer is yes, then you have found a *candidate key*. You will ultimately define a primary key by choosing one of these candidate keys. This type of primary key is known as an *intelligent key*, because the key value has some business meaning associated with it as well.

Consider the teacher table shown in Figure 1.4. We could choose to identify a teacher by name, using a combination of the FirstName and LastName columns. Of course, we know that many people have the same name, so this is a poor choice for a primary key. Now, consider the teacher's social security number. Social security numbers are supposed to be unique, which would make this column a good choice for a primary key. Unfortunately, social security numbers can be duplicated by accident, which not only causes a lot of confusion for the people involved, but causes our choice of a primary key to fail. So, for the teacher table, we will just assign a surrogate key called TeacherID, as shown in Figure 1.5.

NOTE

Choosing the Primary Key Type
There are advantages and disadvantages to using surrogate and intelligent keys. Consult one of the data modeling texts listed near the beginning of the chapter for more information.

FIGURE 1.5
The teacher table with a primary key defined.

Teacher ID (PK)	First Name	Last Name	Gender	Social Security Number	Salary	Years Tenured
1	Warren	Press	M	001-03-1869	$45,000	12
2	Marie	Noel	F	079-91-2060	$52,500	15
3	Michael	Barry	M	114-78-1342	$59,000	16
4	Christopher	Smith	M	001-23-1903	$60,100	18

> **NOTE**
>
> **Identifying Alternate Keys** SQL Server allows only one primary key to be defined per table, even though there may be several valid candidate keys. In situations like this, the data modeler usually defines the other candidate keys as *alternate keys* by creating a uniqueness constraint on the candidate key column(s). SQL Server then enforces uniqueness on the alternate key(s) as well as the primary key.
>
> Alternate keys are usually denoted in a data model by the letters *AK*.

Surrogate primary key names usually end with *Code, Number,* or *ID.* Primary keys are denoted in the data model with the letters *PK,* or separated from the other attributes by a line in the ER diagram. Typically, the primary key column(s) are the first in the table.

In addition to defining a column as a primary key, the database designer can define additional constraints on columns. These constraints are discussed in the next section.

Column Constraints

▶ Identify the business rules that relate to data integrity.

▶ Incorporate business rules and constraints into the data model.

You may specify additional constraints on columns when designing your database. These constraints enable you to build basic business requirements into your data model. There are three fundamental types of column constraints used in a database design:

◆ Not null (NN)

◆ No duplicates (ND)

◆ No changes (NC)

These constraints can be combined, as in the case of a primary key, which is usually marked as NN and ND.

The *not null* concept allows the database designer to require the entry of a value in a particular column. For example, if a teacher's name, gender, and social security number are *required* for tax purposes, these columns can be marked as not null. The not null concept is also used for columns involved in a primary key. SQL Server implements the not null concept by keeping information about the *null option* of each column. This option must be set when a table is created, and is set by using the NULL or NOT NULL keyword. See Chapter 3 for more information about creating tables.

The *no duplicates* concept specifies that the values in a column must be unique. This concept is used in primary keys and alternate keys. For example, disallowing duplicates on the TeacherID column in the teacher table allows that column to be used to uniquely identify any row in that table. SQL Server implements this concept in a number of ways, including a primary key constraint, a unique constraint, or a unique index. Chapters 3 and 4 describe in detail how to implement these ideas.

The *no changes* concept allows the database designer to prohibit changes to the values in a column. This concept is used mainly for columns participating in a primary key. Preventing changes to a primary key is recommended because primary key values are used to create relationships between tables, and changes to a primary key could result in a referential integrity violation. (For more information on the role of primary keys in relationships, see the following section on implementing relationships.) SQL Server implements this concept using check constraints or triggers. Constraints of all types are covered in detail in Chapter 3, and triggers are explained in Chapter 9, "Miscellaneous Programming Techniques."

SQL Server also enables you to build custom constraints on columns to enforce more complex rules, such as "the number of years tenured for a teacher cannot be less than zero." Custom constraints are discussed in Chapter 3.

Figure 1.6 shows the sample teacher table with constraints defined. Note that the primary key column, TeacherID, has several constraints defined.

> **NOTE**
>
> **Properties of Null Values** *Null* is a special value used in relational databases that means "no value has been entered" or "the value is unknown." It is not the same as an empty string ("") or a zero value.
>
> Null has two special properties of which you should be aware. First, it propagates through any arithmetic expression, so "2 + null" results in null. Next, comparing null to any value, including itself, results in a null.

> **NOTE**
>
> **Protect Data by Assigning Column Permissions** You also can assign security permissions to columns so that only certain users of the database may make changes to values in those columns. For instance, you might want only the department chairs at the college to have the ability to change teachers' salaries.

Teacher ID (NN,NC,ND)	First Name (NN)	Last Name (NN)	Gender (NN)	Social Security Number (NN)	Salary	Years Tenured
1	Warren	Press	M	001-03-1869	$45,000	12
2	Marie	Noel	F	079-91-2060	$52,500	15
3	Michael	Barry	M	114-78-1342	$59,000	16
4	Christopher	Smith	M	001-23-1903	$60,100	18

FIGURE 1.6
The teacher table with column constraints.

Non-Decomposable Columns

One important consideration when implementing attributes in a table involves *decomposing* an attribute into several columns. Typically, attributes should be broken down into columns that contain information that cannot be decomposed any further. Consider the Teacher entity shown in Figure 1.2. Two attributes in this entity—name and address—should be broken into multiple columns. The name attribute should be decomposed into columns for FirstName, LastName, and MiddleInitial. The address attribute should be decomposed into columns for Address1, Address2, City, State, and ZipCode (and possibly Country). Storing values in columns that cannot be decomposed further has several advantages:

◆ Columns are easier to update. For instance, decomposing the address attribute into multiple columns allows a developer to easily change any part of the address without having to worry about the other parts.

◆ Columns are easier to query. For instance, finding all teachers that live in a certain city can be accomplished by querying the city portion of the address. If this attribute were not decomposed, finding where the city was in the address would be difficult.

◆ Data integrity is more specific. Each column can have its own data type, null option, or other constraints as needed. For instance, not every person has a middle initial, so this column could allow nulls, whereas the FirstName and LastName columns would require a value.

There are no specific rules about when to decompose a column or how far to decompose a column. Phone numbers are a good example of columns that could be decomposed further. It would be possible to decompose a phone number into its area code and number, or area code, prefix, and number. Another example is a ZIP code field, which could be decomposed into a ZIP code and a ZIP+4 code. Both of the aforementioned examples are rarely decomposed into separate columns. As a database designer, you need to evaluate the need to decompose these types of columns, based on how the information is updated or queried, or based on special data integrity rules.

Entity and Attribute Implementation

The consideration of all the implementation issues presented in this section leads to the data model presented in Figure 1.7. This diagram shows a typical implementation of the entities and attributes for the enrollment database.

R E V I E W   B R E A K

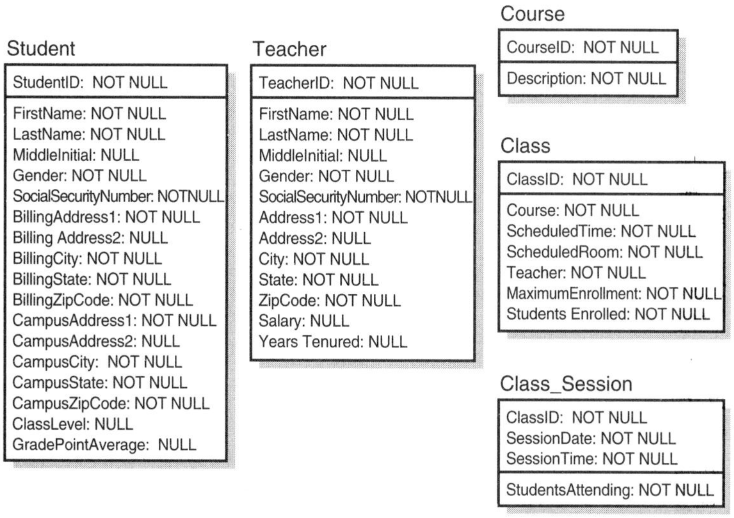

FIGURE 1.7
The enrollment database ER diagram (Completed Entities and Attributes) with primary keys and column characteristics shown.

Student

StudentID: NOT NULL
FirstName: NOT NULL LastName: NOT NULL MiddleInitial: NULL Gender: NOT NULL SocialSecurityNumber: NOTNULL BillingAddress1: NOT NULL Billing Address2: NULL BillingCity: NOT NULL BillingState: NOT NULL BillingZipCode: NOT NULL CampusAddress1: NOT NULL CampusAddress2: NULL CampusCity: NOT NULL CampusState: NOT NULL CampusZipCode: NOT NULL ClassLevel: NULL GradePointAverage: NULL

Teacher

TeacherID: NOT NULL
FirstName: NOT NULL LastName: NOT NULL MiddleInitial: NULL Gender: NOT NULL SocialSecurityNumber: NOTNULL Address1: NOT NULL Address2: NULL City: NOT NULL State: NOT NULL ZipCode: NOT NULL Salary: NULL Years Tenured: NULL

Course

CourseID: NOT NULL
Description: NOT NULL

Class

ClassID: NOT NULL
Course: NOT NULL ScheduledTime: NOT NULL ScheduledRoom: NOT NULL Teacher: NOT NULL MaximumEnrollment: NOT NULL Students Enrolled: NOT NULL

Class_Session

ClassID: NOT NULL SessionDate: NOT NULL SessionTime: NOT NULL
StudentsAttending: NOT NULL

IMPLEMENTING RELATIONSHIPS

Entities and attributes are physically represented in a SQL Server database by tables and columns. Relationships between tables differ in that they are not represented by any particular object in the database. Instead, relationships are created by logically linking the primary key column(s) of the parent table with a *foreign key* column (or columns) in the child table.

In the following subsections, you will see how to choose primary keys and foreign keys in your model, determine the correct cardinality of the relationships, and finally learn how SQL Server enforces these relationships.

Primary Keys and Foreign Keys

▶ Choose the foreign key that will enforce a relationship between entities and that will ensure referential integrity.

Understanding how primary keys and foreign keys relate to each other is vital to understanding relationships in SQL Server. When a relationship is created between two tables (say, teacher and class), the parent table in the relationship contributes its primary key to the child table, where it is known as a foreign key, as shown in Figure 1.8.

FIGURE 1.8

Implementation of the relationships between the teacher, class, and course tables.

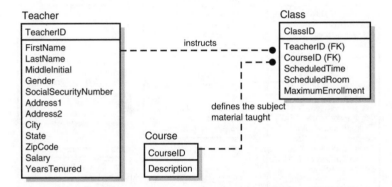

Note how a new TeacherID column is present in the class table and that it carries the *FK* (foreign key) designation. Note also how the CourseID column (the primary key of the course table) is contributed to the class table as a foreign key. The foreign key columns in the class table are said to have a *reference* to the associated primary key columns in the parent tables.

The link between entities in the tables is created by storing the value of the primary key for the parent row in the foreign key column of the child row. See Figure 1.9, which shows some sample data for these three tables to illustrate this concept.

By looking at the class table, you can determine the teacher and the course by looking at the value in the appropriate foreign key column, then finding the value in the related primary key column. For instance, the class with ID 3 is taught by Professor Press, because the TeacherID in the class table matches with that professor's primary key value. Also, we know that the subject of this class is Computer Science 284 because of the value stored in the CourseID column. SQL Server uses primary key and foreign key values to *join* tables when querying information from more than one table. For more information, see Chapter 6.

Teacher ID (PK)	First Name	Last Name	Gender	Social Security Number
1	Warren	Press	M	001-03-1869
2	Marie	Noel	F	079-91-2060
3	Michael	Barry	M	114-78-1342
4	Christopher	Smith	M	001-23-1903

Course ID (PK)	Description
1	Physics 109
2	Electrical Engineering 213
3	Computer Science 284

Class ID (PK)	Teacher ID (FK)	Course ID (FK)	Scheduled Time		Scheduled Room	Maximum Enrollment
1	2	1	MWF	7:30 AM	Phys 104	30
2	4	1	TR	11:30 AM	Phys 114	35
3	1	3	M	6:00 PM	CSC 215	40
4	3	2	TR	2:30 PM	EE 119	20
5	1	3	MWF	4:30 PM	CSC 210	25

FIGURE 1.9

The teacher, course, and class tables, showing the related data in the primary key and foreign key columns.

Now that you have seen how primary keys and foreign keys are used in relationships, let's look at some specifics of implementing relationships of different cardinalities.

One-to-One and One-to-Many Relationships

One-to-One and One-to-Many relationships are implemented as described in the previous section. The primary key of the parent table is contributed to the child table as a foreign key. In the case of a One-to-One relationship, one row with a particular primary key value in the parent table corresponds to one row in the child table with the same value as a foreign key. In the case of a One-to-Many relationship, one row with a particular primary key value in the parent table corresponds to multiple rows in the child table with the same value as a foreign key.

If the primary key column is contributed to the child table's primary key (in other words, the foreign key is one of the columns in the child table's primary key), then this relationship is known as an *identifying* relationship. In this case, the child entity is known as a *dependent* entity because its identification depends on the parent entity. Foreign keys in identifying relationships cannot contain null values.

The relationships in Figure 1.8 could be implemented as identifying relationships, because a class can be identified uniquely by the combination of its teacher, course, scheduled time, and scheduled room attributes.

The other type of relationship (in which the foreign key is not part of the child's primary key) is known as a *non-identifying* relationship, because the child entity can be identified without knowing about the parent. In this case, the child entity is said to be *independent* of its parent. Foreign keys in non-identifying relationships can be marked as not null (NN), in which case they are known as a *mandatory non-identifying* relationship.

Figure 1.8 shows two non-identifying relationships between the Class table and the Teacher and Course tables. A class is identified by its class ID, and the relationships provide additional information about the class. The relationships are mandatory because that information about a class must be known.

Many-to-Many Relationships

A Many-to-Many relationship is implemented a bit differently than a One-to-One or One-to-Many relationship. A simple primary key to foreign key link does not suffice. Consider the relationship between the student entity and the class entity. This relationship defines which classes students are enrolled in, or which students are enrolled in which classes. Simply taking the primary key from one table and using it as a foreign key in another will not work, because only half of the relationship is defined; furthermore, this would result in the duplication of data in one or the other tables.

One possible way to implement this type of relationship would be to use a column in each table that lists all the classes for each student, or all the students in each class. This type of implementation is shown in Figure 1.10.

Student ID	Name	Class Enrollment
1	C. Brunswick	1,3,4
2	D. Hughes	2,4
3	B. Smith	1,4,5
4	K. Davies	2,5

Class ID	Teacher ID	Course ID	Scheduled Time	Students Enrolled
1	2	1	MWF 7:30 AM	1,3
2	4	1	TR 11:30 AM	2,4
3	1	3	M 6:00 PM	1
4	3	2	TR 2:30 PM	1,2,3
5	1	3	MWF 4:30 PM	3,4

FIGURE 1.10
A Many-to-Many relationship between the student table and the class table, using multiple primary key values in a column.

Unfortunately, although a person can look at the two tables and determine which students are enrolled in which class, SQL Server has no way to efficiently use this information. SQL Server has no built-in way to match key values stored in this manner. In addition, implementing the relationship in this way violates the idea of using non-decomposable columns (as discussed earlier in the chapter).

Because the enrollment columns shown in Figure 1.10 can be decomposed, take a look at how effective that implementation option is. Consider Figure 1.11. In this case, the enrollment column in the student and class tables has been decomposed into a list of columns.

Student ID	Name	Enrollment 1	Enrollment 2	Enrollment 3	Enrollment 4	Enrollment 5
1	C. Brunswick	1	3	4	Null	Null
2	D. Hughes	2	4	Null	Null	Null
3	B. Smith	1	4	5	Null	Null
4	K. Davies	2	5	Null	Null	Null

FIGURE 1.11
Many-to-Many relationship between the student table and the class table, using multiple primary key values in multiple columns.

Class ID	Teacher ID	Course ID	Scheduled Time	Enrollment 1	Enrollment 2	Enrollment 3	Enrollment 4	Enrollment 5
1	2	1	MWF 7:30 AM	1	3	Null	Null	Null
2	4	1	TR 11:30 AM	2	4	Null	Null	Null
3	1	3	M 6:00 PM	1	Null	Null	Null	Null
4	3	2	TR 2:30 PM	1	2	3	Null	Null
5	1	3	MWF 4:30 PM	3	4	Null	Null	Null

This may seem like a viable solution at first, because now SQL Server has distinct columns that it can use to join the tables. However, this implementation has two problems. First, SQL Server cannot join multiple columns in this manner any easier than it can join columns with lists of values. Secondly, this implementation restricts students to enrolling in only five classes, and restricts classes to a maximum of five students. True, it would be possible to increase the number of enrollment columns in each table to handle all possible situations, but this would waste storage space if a student was enrolled in only a few classes, or a class only had a few students enrolled.

So how is a Many-to-Many relationship implemented? The trick is to use another table. In data modeling lingo, the entity used in building a Many-to-Many relationship is called an *associative entity*, but many database designers simply refer to it as a *join table*. To implement a Many-to-Many relationship, define the associative entity in the data model and create a one-to-many relationship from each of the original entities to the associative entity, as shown in Figure 1.12. Note that the primary keys of the original tables migrate as foreign keys to the primary key of the join table. In most Many-to-Many implementations, the join table is a dependent entity.

> **NOTE**
>
> **Normal Form Violation** The second implementation option presented is also a violation of first normal form. For more information on normal forms, see the later section "Normalizing Your Database Design."

FIGURE 1.12

An ER diagram of a Many-to-Many relationship between the student table and the class table, using an associative entity.

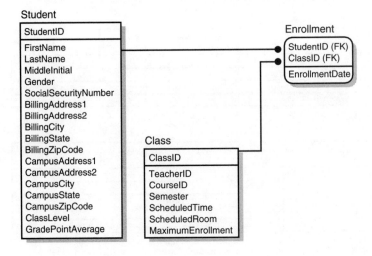

You also can define additional columns for the primary key to ensure that it will be unique—refer again to Figure 1.12. In this case, no additional fields are required because the combination of a student ID and class ID is guaranteed to be unique. If a student has the misfortune to fail a course and has to repeat it in a later semester, he or she will be enrolled in a new instance of a class because a course has new classes defined for each semester. See Exercise 1.3 for an example of when additional primary key attributes are required.

Creating a new entity for a Many-to-Many relationship also opens an opportunity for defining new attributes for this entity. Doing this enables you to store additional information about the relationship. Figure 1.12 illustrates this by adding an enrollment date column to the enrollment table. Now you know not only that a student *is* enrolled in a class, we know *when* that student enrolled.

Implementing a Many-to-Many relationship in this way eliminates the problems discussed at the beginning of this section. All columns are nondecomposable, and first normal form isn't violated. See Figure 1.13 for an example of a correct Many-to-Many implementation.

Student ID (PK)	Name
1	C. Brunswick
2	D. Hughes
3	B. Smith
4	K. Davies

FIGURE 1.13

Example of a Many-to-Many relationship between the student table and the class table, using the enrollment table as a join table.

Student ID (PK)	Class ID (PK)	Enrollment Date
1	1	5/20/1997
1	3	5/20/1997
1	4	5/20/1997
2	2	5/22/1997
2	4	5/22/1997
3	1	5/22/1997
3	4	5/23/1997
3	5	5/22/1997
4	2	5/19/1997
4	5	5/20/1997

Class ID (PK)	Teacher ID	Course ID	Scheduled Time	
1	2	1	MWF	7:30 AM
2	4	1	TR	11:30 AM
3	1	3	M	6:00 PM
4	3	2	TR	2:30 PM
5	1	3	MWF	4:30 PM

Recursive Relationships

Recursive relationships aren't covered on the exam, yet they are used in some special cases. Consider the following excerpt from the case study:

"Oh! Another interesting point about our teachers—we're very proud of the new mentoring program we've just put in place. Our more experienced professors have the option to mentor some of our newer professors. This program ensures that our newer professors have someone to talk to in case they need advice. We're not forcing this on anyone, so not everyone will have a mentor, but we would like to document in the database who has a mentor and who doesn't."

In this case, the teacher entity needs to have a relationship to itself, because a more experienced teacher acts as a mentor to a less experienced teacher. A recursive relationship is implemented just like a normal One-to-One or One-to-Many relationship, except that the same table acts as both the parent and the child in the relationship. Figure 1.14 shows how the relationship described in the case study would be modeled.

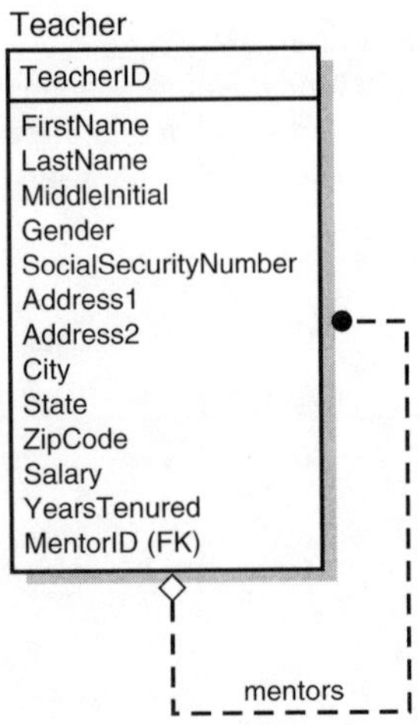

Note how the primary key of the teacher table is contributed back to the teacher table as a foreign key. Also, note that the foreign key is renamed from `TeacherID` to `MentorID`—this is known as *rolenaming*, and clarifies the foreign key's role in describing the entity.

A recursive relationship is always non-identifying, and may be either mandatory or non-mandatory. In the example presented in Figure 1.14, the relationship is non-mandatory, because not every teacher has a mentor. If every teacher were required to have a mentor, then the relationship would be made mandatory by indicating that the MentorID column could not contain nulls. Figure 1.15 shows a sample teacher table.

In the example, professors Press, Noel, and Smith do not have mentors, and this is represented by a null in the MentorID column. All other professors do have mentors, and the value in the MentorID column refers back to the primary key of that professor's mentor. For instance, Professor Noel mentors Professor Joshua Smith.

FIGURE 1.14

ER diagram of a recursive relationship on the teacher entity.

Teacher ID (PK)	First Name	Last Name	Mentor ID (FK)
1	Warren	Press	Null
2	J.C.	Brunswick	8
3	Marie	Noel	Null
4	Joshua	Smith	3
5	Elizabeth	Green	6
6	Michael	Barry	3
7	Janice	Saint	1
8	Christopher	Smith	Null

FIGURE 1.15
Example teacher table, showing the relationship between the TeacherID column and the MentorID column.

Referential Integrity

▶ Choose the foreign key that will enforce a relationship between entities and that will ensure referential integrity.

One final concept important to implementing relationships deals with referential integrity. *Referential integrity* is a way of ensuring that the primary key and foreign key values used to create a relationship never get out of sync. Otherwise, it would be possible to have child entities that had no corresponding parent entity. If this happens, the child entity is said to be *orphaned*. Figure 1.16 and the next few paragraphs describe how this can happen.

NOTE **Use Rolenaming to Avoid Conflicts**
Rolenaming can be used in any type of relationship, but is required for a recursive relationship. Otherwise, the foreign key would have the same name as the primary key!

Course ID (PK)	Description
1	Physics 109
2	Electrical Engineering 213
3	Computer Science 284

FIGURE 1.16
Course and Class tables, with relational data.

Class ID (PK)	Teacher ID (FK)	Course ID (FK)	Scheduled Time		Scheduled Room	Maximum Enrollment
1	2	1	MWF	7:30 AM	Phys 104	30
2	4	1	TR	11:30 AM	Phys 114	35
3	1	3	M	6:00 PM	CSC 215	40
4	3	2	TR	2:30 PM	EE 119	20
5	1	3	MWF	4:30 PM	CSC 210	25

Referential integrity violations are a concern any time data is inserted into a table, removed from a table, or updated in the table:

◆ **The insert problem**. If a row is inserted into a child table that has a foreign key value that does not match any primary key in the parent table, then the child row will be an orphan. For instance, inserting a class that has a CourseID of 4 results in a class that has no corresponding course (refer to Figure 1.16).

The two options for preserving referential integrity are to restrict the insert—to not allow it to happen—or to set the CourseID column to null. Typically, the insert is restricted.

◆ **The delete problem.** If a row is deleted from the parent table, then any rows in the child table that refer to the parent row are orphaned. For example, deleting the Physics 109 course in Figure 1.16 leaves the associated classes without a valid CourseID. When a parent row is deleted, there are three options. The delete may cascade to the child rows, in which case they are also deleted. For example, deleting the Physics 109 course in Figure 1.16 would also delete the classes with IDs of 1 and 2. To prevent cascading, the delete can be restricted, or the child rows' foreign key values can be set to null. Typically, the delete is restricted.

Recall the information gained in the interview: "We have ten departments on campus that offer about 400 different courses—everything from Astronomy 101 to Zoology 410. Of course, we don't have enough professors to teach every course every semester, but we do manage to offer about 150 different courses each semester." In this database, you would probably restrict deletes because not having any classes some semester is no reason to forget that you have a course to teach!

◆ **The update problem.** If the primary key value of the parent table is changed, then any rows in the child table that refer to the parent row are orphaned. Also, if the foreign key value in a child row is updated to refer to a nonexistent parent row, then the child row is orphaned. For updates to the parent table, the update can be cascaded to the child table, the update restricted, or the child's foreign key set to null. For updates to the child table, the update can be restricted or the foreign key set to null. It is standard practice to disallow updates to a primary key column, and to restrict updates to foreign key columns so that only valid values can be entered.

Referential integrity is maintained by using triggers or declarative referential integrity (DRI) constraints. *DRI constraints* can only restrict inserts, deletes, or updates to preserve referential integrity. *Triggers* are more flexible and can implement a restriction, a cascade, or a set null operation to preserve referential integrity. Triggers are discussed more thoroughly in Chapter 9, and constraints are covered in Chapter 3.

WARNING

Use Caution with Cascading Deletes   Use cascading deletes with caution: If a lot of child tables reference a single parent table and cascading deletes are in place, it is possible to destroy a large amount of data very quickly!

Relationship Implementation

As its name implies, relationships are the very basis of a relational model. You should now have a solid understanding of how to implement relationships in your data model. Remember also that you saw how to identify a primary key in each table of your data model.

Now that you can implement relationships in your data model, you can use that knowledge to normalize your database design. Through the process of normalization you learn to apply three simple rules to find potential weaknesses in your design. By following the principles of normalized design you can be certain to have a solid data model to implement.

NORMALIZING YOUR DATABASE DESIGN

▶ Group data into entities by applying normalization rules.

In 1970, E.F. Codd formalized three rules for relational database design known as *normal forms.* In later years, additional normal forms have been defined (there are now six), but the first three are the most widely used. Normalizing your database ensures the following three things:

◆ Dependencies between data are identified.

◆ Redundant data (and all of the problems associated with it) is minimized.

◆ The data model is flexible and easier to maintain.

Codd's normal forms were derived from set-based calculus, but you don't need to be a mathematician to use them. The next three sections discuss the three normal forms and how to identify and correct violations of each. Before normalizing an entity, it is helpful to first identify or create a primary key. In addition, columns should be decomposed before normalization.

Normalization, if carried too far, can adversely affect performance by increasing the number of tables joined in a query. In some cases, *denormalizing* the data model is appropriate. However, it is usually best to take the data model to third normal form before considering what data to denormalize.

The following sections discuss the first (1NF), second (2NF), and third (3NF) normal forms, respectively.

First Normal Form

The purpose of first normal form (1NF) is to eliminate repeating groups of attributes in an entity. In general, 1NF violations cause the data model to be less flexible and less efficient in storing data. For example, suppose the college wants to track students' degrees—whether a degree has already been earned (as in the case of a graduate student that already has a BS degree), or if the degree is still in progress (such as a freshman who has just started working towards his BS). The initial ER diagram for the student entity could look something like the one presented in Figure 1.17.

To discover a violation of first normal form, look at each attribute for an entity and ask yourself whether the attribute occurs repeatedly for any particular instance of this entity. If the occurrence is repeated, as in the case of the DegreeID, DegreeName, DegreeWhenEarned, and DegreeInProgress attributes in Figure 1.17, then you must correct the 1NF violation.

To correct a violation of first normal form, create and name a new entity that describes the repeating groups. For this example, create a new entity called *Student Degree*. Eliminate the repeating groups of attributes and move them to the new entity. Finally, decide on a primary key for the new entity (in this example, use the DegreeID) and create an identifying One-to-Many relationship between the original entity and the new entity. The results will be similar to those shown in Figure 1.18.

Student

StudentID
FirstName
LastName
MiddleInitial
BillingAddress1
BillingAddress2
BillingCity
BillingState
BillingZipCode
CampusAddress1
CampusAddress2
CampusCity
CampusState
CampusZipCode
DegreeID1
DegreeName1
DegreeWhenEarned1
DegreeInProgress1
DegreeID2
DegreeName2
DegreeWhenEarned2
DegreeInProgress2

FIGURE 1.17
First normal form violation in the student entity.

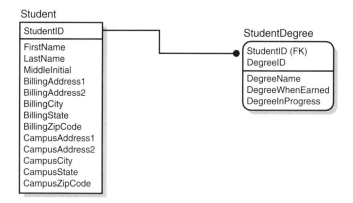

Student

Student
StudentID
FirstName
LastName
MiddleInitial
BillingAddress1
BillingAddress2
BillingCity
BillingState
BillingZipCode
CampusAddress1
CampusAddress2
CampusCity
CampusState
CampusZipCode

StudentDegree

StudentDegree
StudentID (FK)
DegreeID
DegreeName
DegreeWhenEarned
DegreeInProgress

FIGURE 1.18
Resolved first normal form violation in the student entity.

Resolving the preceding violation has made the data model more flexible because the limitation of storing two degrees per student has been removed. In addition, we save storage space when a student has only one degree.

Second Normal Form

The purpose of second normal form (2NF) is to eliminate partial key dependencies. In other words, each attribute in an entity must depend on the whole key, not just a part of it.

Consider Figure 1.19. This ER diagram shows the data model from the last section, with an additional attribute (DegreeCreditsRequired) stored about each degree in the StudentDegree entity.

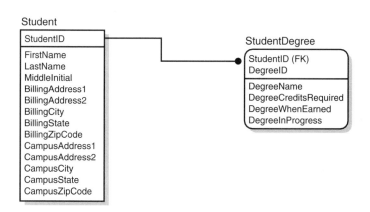

Student

Student
StudentID
FirstName
LastName
MiddleInitial
BillingAddress1
BillingAddress2
BillingCity
BillingState
BillingZipCode
CampusAddress1
CampusAddress2
CampusCity
CampusState
CampusZipCode

StudentDegree

StudentDegree
StudentID (FK)
DegreeID
DegreeName
DegreeCreditsRequired
DegreeWhenEarned
DegreeInProgress

NOTE **Exceptions to the Rule**   The address fields in the student table also are a violation of 1NF. In this case, however, you should leave these fields in the student table because the college only requires these two addresses to be kept for a student. On the other hand, you would normalize the degree fields because a student can potentially hold any number of degrees, and normalizing makes the data model more flexible.

If the college were interested in storing a variety of different addresses for each student, or past addresses for each student, however, those attributes would be a good candidate for normalization.

FIGURE 1.19
Second normal form violation in the StudentDegree entity.

How to Spot Second Normal Form Violations   Second normal form violations can occur only in entities that have primary keys composed of more than one attribute.

To identify a 2NF violation, look at each attribute not involved in the primary key and ask yourself whether this attribute depends on only part of the primary key. In Figure 1.19, the dependence is indeed only partial for the DegreeName and DegreeCreditsRequired attributes, which depend only on the DegreeID. In other words, you don't need to know about a student to know a degree's name or the credit hours required to obtain it. You do, however, need to know about the particular student for the DegreeWhenEarned and DegreeInProgress attributes.

To correct a violation of second normal form, create a new entity for the attributes that depends on only part of the primary key. In this example, create a new *Degree* entity that describes each degree program and the credit hours required to obtain it. Then, move the partially dependent attributes to the new entity and create an identifying relationship between the new entity and the entity that had the violation, as shown in Figure 1.20.

FIGURE 1.20
Resolved second normal form violation in the StudentDegree entity.

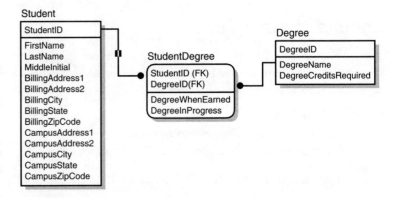

2NF violations typically cause data to be duplicated. In this example, the degree name and credit hours required were duplicated for each student that had a particular type of degree (BA, BS, MS, and so on). Moving the attributes for a degree to the new entity eliminates this redundancy.

Third Normal Form

Third normal form (3NF) also helps eliminate redundant information by eliminating interdependencies between non-key attributes. To identify a violation of this kind, look at each attribute not participating in the primary key and ask yourself whether the attribute depends on some other non-key attribute. See Figure 1.21 for an example of a violation of third normal form in the Class entity.

In this diagram, there are actually two violations of the third normal form. The first occurs because of the dependency between the CourseNumber and CourseName attributes, and the second occurs because of the dependency between the TeacherID, TeacherFirstName, and TeacherLastName attributes.

To resolve a 3NF violation, create a new entity that contains all of the non-key attributes that depend on each other. In this example, create two new entities—one for the interdependent course attributes, and one for the interdependent teacher attributes. For the new entity, choose or create a primary key, then create a non-identifying relationship back to the original entity. The resolution of the normal form violations shown in Figure 1.21 is shown in Figure 1.22.

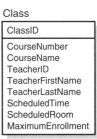

FIGURE 1.21
Third normal form violation in the Class entity.

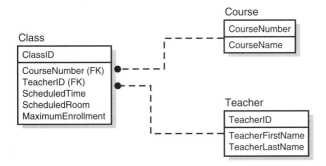

FIGURE 1.22
Resolution of the third normal form violations in the Class entity.

The third normal form is very similar to the second normal form, except that it deals entirely with dependencies that don't involve the key. In both cases, however, redundant data is eliminated, which makes the database more reliable and easier to update.

Impact of Normalization

▶   In a given situation, decide whether denormalization is appropriate.

▶   Assess the potential impact of the logical design on performance, maintainability, extensibility, scalability, availability, security.

Know the Terminology for the Test
One of the objectives for the test is to "assess the potential impact of the logical design on performance, maintainability, extensibility, scalability, availability, and security." Because some of these terms aren't very precise, all of the terms have been replaced in this section with the three terms performance, flexibility, and consistency, which are carefully defined in the preceding paragraph. *Performance* is the same in both lists so there is no problem there. Maintainability, extensibility, and scalability all relate to a model's ability to accommodate change and growth, so they are combined under the term *flexibility*. In addition, a data model that accommodates change without requiring a complete overhaul will be more available as well. Security and a measure of maintainability are addressed by the *consistency* of the data. Inconsistent data is difficult to maintain because of its chaotic nature, and for the same reason it is more difficult to track changes. If a particular attribute is duplicated in many entities, it is also more difficult to assign appropriate permissions to all those areas.

Database design is vitally important to the performance and scalability of any application that uses the database. Database applications are often designed around the database. A good database design allows superior performance from a good application. After the database is designed, it can be very difficult to modify that design. After applications have been written against a database design, radical changes to the database design usually require changes to the applications. These dependent changes can quickly lead to small changes requiring huge expense. A good database design has a great deal of flexibility built into it, however, and can accommodate more changes easily.

There are three primary factors that a good database design will enhance:

◆   Performance

◆   Flexibility

◆   Consistency

Performance relates to the speed at which data can be found and returned to the user. Flexibility is a measure of changes that can be allowed without affecting the number of entities, attributes, or relationships in the data model. Consistency is a measure of redundancy in the data. When redundancy is reduced, you are assured that the data returned is always correct and concise.

Recall the example used to describe first normal form. Before applying first normalization rules, a student record could store only a set number of degrees. This was an unnecessary limitation that could have been very difficult to change after applications had been written that relied on the original structure. In this way, following the rules for first normal form enhances the data model's flexibility.

Even after applying the first normal form to the data model, how-ever, there was a problem of duplicate data. Both the second and third normal forms worked together in different ways to reduce redundant data. Storing duplicate data is obviously wasteful of storage space, which can hurt performance by requiring a larger volume of data to be searched and transferred to the client applica-tion. A more subtle problem is that of consistency. When storing both DegreeID and DegreeName in the StudentDegree table as shown by Figure 1.19, there is a chance that the name associated with a DegreeID could be different in different records. By fol-lowing the rules of the second and third normal forms, redundancy is reduced and consistency increased.

Even in the example of first normal forms, the student table was left denormalized in that it contained two different addresses. In this case, it was determined that the university would never need to track more than the two addresses. Therefore, it was decided that better performance could be achieved by incorporating both addresses directly into the student table because there would be no need to join to additional tables to obtain address information. Denormalization can therefore improve the performance of a data model, but this performance always comes at the price of decreased flexibility.

CASE STUDY: LEWIS, OSWALD, AND CARREY

ESSENCE OF THE CASE

Here are the essential elements of the case:

- ▶ Performance is currently lacking.
- ▶ Data integrity is a problem.
- ▶ The current model is not flexible.
- ▶ The application and data model will both be redesigned.

SCENARIO

Lewis, Oswald, and Carrey is a small but aggres-sively growing accounting firm. It used in-house talent to develop a simple client database years ago, but as the firm grows, its members are becoming increasingly disappointed in the perfor-mance of the database. In preparation for a planned IPO, the members are reviewing their internal processes and have decided to contract with you to update and expand this database pro-gram professionally. You interview the original author of the program, Jeff, who readily admits that although he is a computer enthusiast, he is not a skilled developer. Rather, he cobbled

continues

CASE STUDY: LEWIS, OSWALD, AND CARREY

continued

together a simple database application using Microsoft Access to help track his contacts with various clients for billing purposes. Other members of the firm thought the application was pretty neat and asked to use it as well. The whole thing has just grown in complexity from there.

You hear from most users that the system loses data from time to time. Jeff says that the users are really just careless when entering the data and sometimes misspell a client name when entering their time. Then when a user looks for all the time entered against that client, the misspelled record isn't returned. Lately, Jeff estimates that he's spending almost a full day every month just fixing these kinds of mistakes, in addition to his regular duties. He also says that two months ago he had to rework the main table to allow users to bill against more than six clients—now everyone can enter time against fifteen clients at once. However, only a few people need this many clients, and now the database is almost three times its original size.

ANALYSIS

You have the opportunity to completely redesign this application and the database that it references. Because data can be misplaced due to a simple misspelling, and employees can only bill against a set number of clients, you are sure that an improved database design would improve the application. These are classic cases of an improperly normalized data model.

You know that the users currently must enter the entire name of a client that they want to enter their time against. This could be better implemented by having a Client entity that could provide a list of all possible clients to choose from. Choosing the client from a list would eliminate the problem of misspellings. It is also clear that because the data model had to change to allow people to bill to more than a set number of clients, there is a violation of second or third normal form as well. This could be fixed by implementing an associative entity that would allow a Many-to-Many relationship between the employees entering their time and the Client entity.

All the changes predicted here could be as easily implemented in the Access environment they are currently using as they could in SQL Server. Because the firm is expecting rapid growth and performance is already limited, it would probably be best to dedicate a small server to running SQL Server. SQL Server would definitely scale better than Access would to accommodate the future growth.

CHAPTER SUMMARY

This chapter covered the fundamentals of designing a database using relational database design methods. You learned the data modeling concepts that must be understood before the database can be implemented. You also learned how these modeling concepts are executed in SQL Server. Although it is important to learn the SQL Server commands and code, you must first understand the basic concepts of entities, attributes, and relationships before you can successfully design a database.

KEY TERMS

- entity
- attribute
- relationship
- normalization
- primary key
- foreign key
- referential integrity
- denormalization
- One-to-One relationship
- One-to-Many relationship
- Many-to-Many relationship
- surrogate key
- candidate key
- normal forms

Exercises

1.1   Modeling a New Entity

Recall that the case study at the beginning of the chapter made mention of the fact that several academic departments existed at the college. This exercise walks you through the steps required to create the department entity, define its attributes, and identify a primary key.

Estimated Time: 5 minutes

1. Identify the person, place, thing, or concept that will be represented in the data model by the new entity. This exercise uses the concept of an academic department at the college.

2. Develop a sentence that defines the entity. For example, for the academic department, you might use the following: "A department is a unit of administration that offers at least one type of degree and employs one or more teachers."

3. Identify any attributes of the entity. For this example, you want to store information about the department's name and chairperson, as well as the office location and phone number for the department.

4. Place restrictions on any attributes as required. For the department entity, because the department name and chairperson are required information, place a no nulls restriction on those attributes.

5. Identify or create a primary key attribute. For the department entity, you could use the department name as the primary key because two departments on campus are unlikely to have the same name. However, remember that a primary key usually has a no changes restriction, which in this

case would make it difficult to change a department's name if required. Therefore, create a surrogate key called DepartmentID.

6. The new entity should look similar to the one presented in Figure 1.23. You may now implement the new entity in SQL Server. For more information on how to do this, see Chapter 3.

Department

DepartmentID: NOT NULL
DepartmentName: NOT NULL
DepartmentChairperson: NOT NULL
OfficeLocation: NULL
MainOfficePhoneNumber: NULL

FIGURE 1.23
The Department entity.

1.2   Creating a One-to-Many Relationship

Exercise 1.1 walked you through the process of creating the department entity. You may have noticed that the definition of a department includes the phrase "employs one or more teachers." This phrase indicates that a relationship exists between the department entity and the teacher entity. This exercise walks you through the steps required to create this relationship (a One-to-Many relationship).

Estimated Time: 5 minutes

1. If you have not already done so, define each entity that participates in the relationship and define the primary key for each. The department and teacher entities participate in the relationship in this example.

2. Create the foreign key attribute in the child table for the relationship and denote it with the *FK* indicator. If the parent entity helps define the child entity, then include the foreign key in the child entity's primary key. Otherwise, just include the foreign key with the other attributes of the child entity.

APPLY YOUR KNOWLEDGE

In the department-teacher example, a department does not help define a teacher, so the foreign key from the department entity is not included in the primary key of the teacher entity.

3. Draw a line between the two entities and indicate the cardinality of the relationship. In this case, the relationship requires that a department employ at least one teacher. The *P* designation indicates that the cardinality is "One-to-One or more."

4. If desired, write the verb phrase that describes the relationship on or near the relationship line. The resulting data model should look similar to the one presented in Figure 1.24.

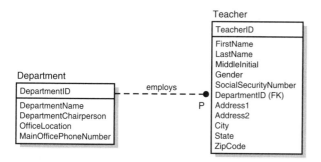

FIGURE 1.24
The One-to-Many relationship between the department entity and the teacher entity.

1.3 Creating a Many-to-Many Relationship

Recall that a Many-to-Many relationship exists between the student entity and the class session entity. This relationship defines which students attended a particular class session. This exercise walks you through the steps required to create the Many-to-Many relationship.

Estimated Time: 5 minutes

1. If you have not already done so, define each entity that participates in the relationship and define the primary key for each. The student and class session entities participate in the relationship in this example.

2. Define and name the associative entity used in the Many-to-Many relationship. In this example, name the entity `ClassSessionAttendance.`

3. Create an identifying One-to-Many relationship from each of the original entities to the associative entity. In other words, create foreign keys in the associative entity's primary key. These foreign keys reference the primary keys of the original entities in the relationship.

   The class session attendance example entity will have a primary key composed of the StudentID and SessionID foreign key attributes.

4. Verify that the primary key of the new table will be unique, and add any attributes to the primary key if required. For this example, the combination of the student and session information is sufficient.

5. Add any non-key attributes to the associative entity if needed. In this example, the associative entity is simply used to record whether a student attended the session or not. One example of a non-key attribute that could have been added to this entity is a flag to indicate if the student was tardy.

   The final data model should look something like the one presented in Figure 1.25.

APPLY YOUR KNOWLEDGE

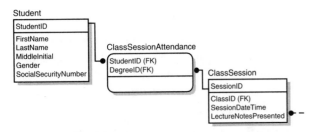

FIGURE 1.25
The Many-to-Many relationship between the class session entity and the student entity.

1.4   Creating a One-to-One Relationship

Exercise 1.4 explains one scenario in which a One-to-One relationship is useful and shows you how to create a One-to-One relationship in a data model. Consider the following excerpt from the case study:

"Sometimes we don't even have a tenured professor available to teach a class and we need to have a teaching assistant do the job. There isn't any difference as far as the class is concerned—we just assign the T/A as the teacher—but we do keep fairly different types of information on the two different categories of teachers. For instance, our T/As are paid by the hour, whereas the professors are salaried."

The previous paragraph explains that there are two different categories of teachers about which data is maintained. It would be possible to store all of this information in a single teacher table, but if the two categories of teacher don't share much common information, many columns in the teacher table would contain null values. A better solution is to categorize the entity, as outlined in this exercise.

Estimated Time: 5 minutes

1. Determine which attributes are common to all categories of the entity. For this example, every teacher has a name and address. These attributes stay in the main entity.

2. Determine how many categories exist for the entity, and create that number of new entities. In this example, the teacher entity can be categorized into a T/A type or a tenured professor type, so two new entities should be created.

3. Move the attributes specific for each category to the new entities. In this example, the TeacherTADetail receives the hourly rate attribute and a foreign key that links a T/A's information to a student's information. The TeacherTenuredDetail receives the attributes specific only to tenured professors, such as salary and benefits information.

4. Create the primary keys for the new entities by creating a foreign key that references the original entity. In this example, both the TeacherTADetail and TeacherTenuredDetail entities have a TeacherID foreign key as their primary keys.

Because the primary key of each child entity is composed of only the foreign key from the parent table, there can be at most one row in the child table for each row in the parent table. The resulting data model should look something like the one presented in Figure 1.26.

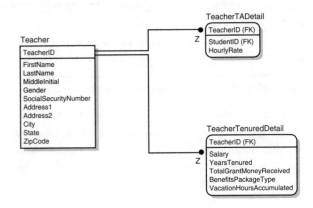

FIGURE 1.26
Teacher entity after being categorized into T/A detail and tenured professor detail. Note the One-to-One cardinality in the relationships.

APPLY YOUR KNOWLEDGE

1.5   Assessing the Logical Model for Performance

Exercise 1.5 explains one scenario in which a normalized logical model might have poor performance for a specific report. In this scenario a case is made for violating second normal form in order to significantly reduce the number of entities that will need to be examined in a common report.

A common report that is needed by both students and faculty for a variety of reasons is one to list a student or students, and the names of all the courses they are enrolled in. In further interviews with department heads you are told that although this is a simple query, it is run very frequently and must be highly optimized.

Figure 1.27 depicts the relationship between a student and a course.

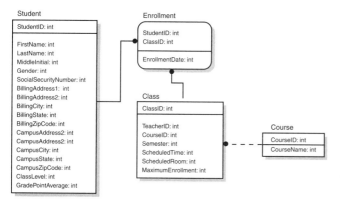

FIGURE 1.27
Normalized relational chain from the Student entity and the Course entity.

Estimated Time: 5 minutes

1. Examine Figure 1.27. Think about the rules of normalization and determine whether this model meets the conditions of third normal form. You should notice that the address fields in the student table violate first normal form as was described in the section "First Normal Form."

2. The query that needs to be optimized is one that will return student names and the names of all the courses in which the student is enrolled. Pay attention to the fact that in order to accomplish this objective, four different tables need to be consulted.

3. Examine the degree of each relationship in this model. Notice that one student is enrolled in many classes, and that each class represents one course. To optimize the report, you will want to copy the CourseName attribute from the Course entity to an entity as close to the Student entity as is possible without changing the degree of any relationship.

   By storing the CourseName attribute in two different locations, you will already be increasing the amount of data stored in your model. (If you were to choose to store CourseName in the Student entity, then the degree of the relationship between Student and Enrollment would be One-to-One because all student information would be repeated for every course in which the student was enrolled. This would be too great of a sacrifice in normalization to justify the performance of this particular report.)

4. Alter the Enrollment entity to store the CourseName attribute. Note that this is a violation of second normal form because the CourseName is entirely dependent on the ClassID. The benefit is that in order to report student names along with course names only the Student and Enrollment entities must be examined.

Keep in mind that this exercise was intended to show the thought processes behind identifying a performance problem, and solving it through careful denormalization. Although the process is correct, it is unlikely that a small midwestern collage would be dealing with the

APPLY YOUR KNOWLEDGE

sheer volume of data that would make the original four-table scan prohibitive. On all but the most underpowered servers, the hundreds or thousands of rows in these tables could be handled without difficulty. Nonetheless Figure 1.28 shows the modified data model.

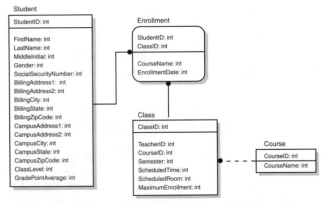

FIGURE 1.28
Denormalized relational chain from the Student entity and the Course entity.

Review Questions

1. What is an entity?

2. What is an attribute?

3. What is a relationship?

4. What is the defining characteristic of a primary key?

5. What are the three main types of relationships used in a database model?

6. How are primary keys and foreign keys used to create a relationship?

7. How is a no nulls constraint implemented for an attribute?

8. How is a no changes constraint implemented for an attribute?

9. How is a no duplicates constraint implemented for an attribute?

10. Briefly describe each of the three normal forms.

11. Why would you normalize a database?

12. Why would you violate a normal form?

Exam Questions

1. Before it is implemented in SQL Server, a data model is most often represented in what kind of diagram?

    A. Object-Relational diagram

    B. Codd diagram

    C. Entity-Relationship diagram

    D. Table structure diagram

2. Which of the following is an instance of a particular entity implemented in SQL Server?

    A. View

    B. Table

    C. Column

    D. Row

3. In a database model, each entity may have multiple what?

    A. Attributes

    B. Primary keys

    C. Names

    D. Relationships to other entities

APPLY YOUR KNOWLEDGE

4. In a data model, any person, place, thing, or concept about which data is collected is called what?

    A. A relationship

    B. An attribute

    C. An object

    D. An entity

5. In a data model, an attribute is used to do what?

    A. Store specific information about an entity.

    B. Define an entity.

    C. Create an instance of an entity.

    D. Enforce entity integrity.

6. Which of the following statements are true about relationships? Select all that apply.

    A. Relationships are stored in the database as relationship objects.

    B. Relationships explicitly define an association between two entities.

    C. Relationships are most easily identified during requirements analysis by looking or listening for noun phrases.

    D. Relationships are a logical link between tables implemented with primary keys and foreign keys.

    E. Relationships are most often characterized by their cardinality.

7. By which of the following terms is an attribute also known?

    A. Column

    B. Field

    C. Row

    D. Table

8. What are the three general types of constraints used for attributes in a data model?

    A. no updates

    B. no duplicates

    C. no nulls

    D. no deletes

    E. no changes

9. Using what type of columns makes them easier to update and query?

    A. Decomposable

    B. Unique

    C. Not null

    D. Nondecomposable

10. Which of the following are true about table and column names? Select all that apply.

    A. Table and column names are limited to 40 characters.

    B. Table names must be unique within the database.

    C. Column names must be unique within the database.

    D. Table and column names must be in all uppercase.

    E. Column names must be unique within a table.

APPLY YOUR KNOWLEDGE

11. How is a no nulls restriction implemented for a column in SQL Server?

    A. By using a not null constraint when the table is created

    B. By using an index that does not allow nulls

    C. By specifying the null option on the column when the table is created

    D. By using a reference constraint

12. How is a no changes restriction implemented for a column in SQL Server?

    A. By using a check constraint

    B. By using a primary key constraint

    C. By using a trigger

    D. By using column permissions

13. How is a no duplicates restriction implemented for a column in SQL Server?

    A. By using a reference constraint

    B. By using a unique index on the column

    C. By using a unique constraint

    D. By using column permissions

    E. By using a trigger

    F. By using a primary key constraint

14. What does the primary key of a table enforces?

    A. Referential integrity

    B. Entity or row integrity

    C. Column integrity

    D. Identity constraints

15. What is the relationship between a primary key and a foreign key?

    A. A foreign key value is contributed to a primary key value in a column to create a link between two instances of an entity or two instances of two different entities.

    B. A primary key value is contributed to a foreign key value in a column to create a link between two instances of an entity or two instances of two different entities.

    C. There is no relationship; primary keys and foreign keys are two different ways to ensure entity integrity.

16. In a One-to-Many relationship,

    A. The foreign key value of a single instance of the parent entity is contributed to a primary key value in multiple instances of the child entity.

    B. The primary key value of a single instance of the parent entity is contributed to a foreign key value in multiple instances of the child entity.

    C. A parent entity may be identified by its child entity.

    D. A child entity may be identified by its parent entity.

17. Which of the following best describes a One-to-One relationship?

    A. Is typically the result of normalizing an entity

    B. Is characterized by one primary key value corresponding to zero or one foreign key values

    C. Is characterized by one primary key value corresponding to zero or more foreign key values

    D. Is typically the result of an entity being categorized into two or more different types

APPLY YOUR KNOWLEDGE

18. Which of the following best describes a One-to-Many relationship?

    A. Is typically the result of normalizing an entity

    B. Is characterized by one primary key value corresponding to zero or one foreign key values

    C. Is characterized by one primary key value corresponding to zero or more foreign key values

    D. Is typically the result of an entity being categorized into two or more different types

19. What is the most commonly used cardinality in a relationship?

    A. One-to-Many

    B. One-to-One

    C. Many-to-One

    D. Many-to-Many

20. A Many-to-Many relationship is implemented with which of the following?

    A. Two One-to-Many relationships

    B. Multiple columns in each participating entity that contain the primary key values of the referenced entity

    C. A column in each participating entity that lists the primary keys referenced in the other entity

    D. An associative entity

21. Which of the following is true of a recursive relationship?

    A. The parent instance of one entity is associated with one or more child instances of another entity.

    B. The parent instance of one entity is associated with one or more child instances of the same entity.

    C. An instance of an entity always has an association with itself.

    D. Multiple parent instances of one entity are associated with one child instance of another entity.

22. Referential integrity refers to what?

    A. The enforced uniqueness of a row in a table

    B. The enforced uniqueness of a column in a table

    C. Ensuring that a foreign key attribute cannot be null

    D. The enforced synchronization of primary key and foreign key values

23. An identity column is used to do which of the following?

    A. Identify an attribute.

    B. Provide unique, sequenced primary key values.

    C. Enforce the no changes restriction on a column.

    D. Define a foreign key.

24. What are the benefits of a normalized data model?

    A. Redundant data is minimized.

    B. Storage space is used more efficiently.

    C. The data model is more flexible.

    D. Performance is improved.

APPLY YOUR KNOWLEDGE

25. In which circumstance is denormalizing a data model best done?

    A. Only after fully normalizing the database

    B. When the entities are being designed

    C. If performance is slow due to many tables being joined together

    D. To reduce redundant data

Answers to Review Questions

1. An entity defines any person, place, thing, or concept for which data will be collected. (Refer to the section "Entities" for more information.)

2. An attribute is any additional characteristic or information defined for an entity. (Refer to the section "Attributes" for more information.)

3. A relationship is a logical linkage between two entities that describes how the entities are associated with each other. (Refer to the section "Relationships" for more information.)

4. A primary key must first and foremost be unique. (Refer to the section "Choosing and Defining the Primary Key" for more information.)

5. The three main types of relationships used in a database model are One-to-One, One-to-Many, and Many-to-Many. (Refer to the section "Types of Relationships" for more information.)

6. The primary key value for an instance of an entity is used in the foreign key attribute of the instance(s) of the associated entity. (Refer to the section "Primary Keys and Foreign Keys" for more information.)

7. Use the SQL Server null option for a column when creating a table to define whether or not the column may contain nulls. (Refer to the section "Column Constraints" for more information.)

8. Use an identity property on the column (when creating a table), or use a trigger to prevent changes to a column. Security permissions also may be assigned to a particular column to prevent certain users from modifying its contents. (Refer to the section "Column Constraints" for more information.)

9. Use a primary key or unique constraint on a column to ensure its uniqueness. The stored procedure sp_primarykey also may be used to define a primary key, and a unique index on a column prevents duplicate values. (Refer to the section "Column Constraints" for more information.)

10. First: No groups of attributes should be repeated in an entity. Second: All attributes should depend on the entire primary key. No attribute should depend on only part of a candidate key. Third: No attribute should be wholly dependent on other non-key attributes. (Refer to the section "Normalizing Your Database Design" for more information.)

11. The three main reasons are that dependencies between data are identified, redundant data (and all of the problems associated with it) is minimized, and the data model is flexible and easier to maintain. (Refer to the section "Normalizing Your Database Design" for more information.)

12. It is common to allow small violations to the normal forms in an attempt to achieve a specific performance gain. Denormalization always comes at the price of decreased flexibility. (Refer to the section "Impact of Normalization" for more information.)

APPLY YOUR KNOWLEDGE

Answers to Exam Questions

1. **C.** A logical data model is often depicted in an Entity-Relationship diagram, or ER diagram. Although this modeling technique is based on Dr. Codd's work, it does not bear his name. (Refer to the section "Introducing Data Modeling Concepts: Entities, Attributes, and Relationships" for more information.)

2. **D.** This was a deliberately tricky question. Entities are represented as tables in ER diagrams, but an *instance* of an entity would be a particular data row in the table. Attributes of entities are columns in a table. Views are not covered in this chapter. (Refer to the section "Entities" for more information.)

3. **A, D.** An entity is represented as a table in a data model. A table can have only one primary key (though it can be made of multiple columns, which are attributes of the entity), and it can have only one name. An entity can have many attributes, and can have many different relationships to other entities. (Refer to the section "Introducing Data Modeling Concepts: Entities, Attributes, and Relationships" for more information.)

4. **D.** Data modeling terminology primarily deals with entities, attributes, and relationships; they don't normally address objects. Entities model people, places, things, and concepts. (Refer to the section "Entities" for more information.)

5. **A.** Attributes are specific characteristics of an entity. Although the attributes that make up the primary key can be used to uniquely define an entity, this is not an inherent property of all attributes. Attributes can not be said to perform the action of creating an entity, and constraints enforce data integrity, not attributes. (Refer to the section "Attributes" for more information.)

6. **B, D, E.** Foreign key constraints enforce relationships; there is no such thing as a relationship object. Relationships are most easily identified during requirements analysis by looking or listening for *verbs* rather than nouns. (Refer to the section "Implementing Relationships" for more information.)

7. **A, B.** Columns and fields are interchangeable terms for the physical implementation of attributes. A row is a collection of all attributes in a particular instance of an entity, so it would not describe a single attribute. A table is the physical implementation of an entity, not an attribute. (Refer to the section "Characteristics of Tables" for more information.)

8. **B, C, E.** Both no updates and no deletes are rough variations on the actual constraint no changes. (Refer to the section "Column Constraints" for more information.)

9. **D.** The uniqueness or nullability of a column has no real effect on the ease of queries or updates. A decomposable column is made up of multiple distinct attributes, and therefore is not as specific as a collection of non-decomposable columns, making it more difficult to work with. (Refer to the section "Non-Decomposable Columns" for more information.)

10. **B, E.** Table and column names are limited to 128 characters, not 40. Different tables can have columns with the same name—there can be two tables both having a FirstName column for example. Table and column names can be of mixed case. (Refer to the section "Characteristics of Tables" for more information.)

APPLY YOUR KNOWLEDGE

11. **C.** SQL Server implements an option of NULL or NOT NULL on every column rather than implementing a true null constraint. Although unique constraints are implemented through indexes, this is not true of no null restrictions. A reference constraint would not work for enforcing nullability. (Refer to the section "Column Constraints" for more information.)

12. **A, C, D.** SQL Server does not specifically implement a no changes constraint; however, there are several ways to gain this functionality. Either a trigger or a check constraint can apply robust logic to entered values that can prevent changes. You could optionally apply permissions to columns to prevent users from changing values. (Refer to the section "Column Constraints for more information.)

13. **B, C, E, F.** Applying a unique index to a column will guarantee that duplicates cannot be added. Applying either a unique constraint or a primary key constraint will implicitly create a unique index. Technically, a trigger allows enough programmability to enforce a no duplicates restriction, but this would be overly complicated and not recommended. (Refer to the section "Column Constraints" for more information.)

14. **B.** A primary key guarantees the uniqueness of every row. A row in a table is a specific instance of an entity; therefore a primary key enforces the integrity of entities. (Refer to the section "Characteristics of Tables" for more information.)

15. **B.** Relationships are made by storing a primary key value in a foreign key column. Setting up a relationship constrains the foreign key column to store only values that can be found in the primary key, therefore the direction is important. (Refer to the section "Implementing Relationships" for more information.)

16. **B, D.** Primary keys can not be duplicated; therefore a single foreign key cannot be contributed to many primary key values, as is suggested in choice A. Choices C and D differ as a matter of direction. Remember that the child entity is said to be dependent on the parent; therefore the child can be identified by the parent, but not the other way around. (Refer to the section "Types of Relationships" for more information.)

17. **B, D.** A One-to-One relationship is certainly not characterized by a single primary key corresponding to many foreign key values—this would be a One-to-Many relationship instead. When an entity is categorized into one of two or more types then you would typically have a single record pointing to a single record that contains some code indicating which type. (Refer to the section "Types of Relationships" for more information.)

18. **A, C.** When an entity is normalized, attributes are often removed to form a new entity and a relationship is established between the two entities. This relationship is most commonly One-to-Many from the one original entity pointing to zero, one, or more new entities. (Refer to the section "One-to-One and One-to-Many Relationships" for more information.)

19. **A.** One-to-One relationships are rare because they indicate situations where the two related tables could be combined without violating third normal form. Therefore most One-to-One relationships are combined to reduce the number of joins needed to collect all the information needed about an entity. A Many-to-Many relationship is implemented through two One-to Many relationships, so the One-to-Many relationships will always be more numerous of the two by definition. Many-to-One relationships are the same as

APPLY YOUR KNOWLEDGE

One-to-Many just seen from the other direction. (See section "Implementing Relationships" for more information.)

20. **A, D.** A Many-to-Many relationship needs to have an associative entity between the two primary entities in the relationship. Two One-to-Many relationships are needed to join the three tables together. (Refer to the section "Many-to-Many Relationships" for more information.)

21. **B.** A recursive relationship is a relation between two instances of the same entity. (Refer to the section "Recursive Relationships" for more information.)

22. **D.** Answers A and C refer to entity integrity, and answer B would be attribute integrity. (Refer to the section "Referential Integrity" for more information.)

23. **B.** An identity column is often called a surrogate key because it is provides a candidate key to the entity, but has no inherent meaning. (Refer to

the section "Choosing and Defining the Primary Key" for more information.)

24. **A, B, C.** Normalizing your data model will provide many benefits and will often improve the overall performance of a database, but any performance gains are secondary to the gains in consistency and flexibility. Data models are often denormalized for specific performance gains. (Refer to the section "Normalizing Your Database Design" for more information.)

25. **A, C.** Denormalization will reduce the flexibility and consistency of your database; however, it also will reduce the number of joins required to access your data, which can improve performance. By first fully normalizing your data model, you will be sure to denormalize only the specific attributes you want, and you will be fully aware of the extent of the tradeoffs between flexibility and performance. (Refer to the section "Impact of Normalization" for more information.)

Suggested Readings and Resources

We recommend the following resources for further study in the area of planning:

1. Graeme Simsion, *Data Modeling Essentials* (Van Nostrand Reinhold, 1994).

2. David C. Hay, *Data Model Patterns, Conventions of Thought* (Dorset House Publishing, 1996).

3. E. F. Codd, *The Relational Model for Database Management* (Addison-Wesley Publishing Company, 1990).

This chapter helps you to prepare for the Microsoft exam by covering the following objective:

Create and manage files, file groups, and transaction logs that define a database.

▶ The key to this chapter (and this objective) is the CREATE DATABASE statement. You'll need to be able to use both the CREATE DATABASE statement and the Enterprise Manager graphical interface to create databases. Know how to create a database with a single primary file, or using secondary files and multiple file groups. Make sure you know the use of the Model database to initialize your own user databases.

CHAPTER 2

Creating
Physical Storage

▶ Make sure you have a firm grip on files and file groups. You should know the kinds of performance benefits that multiple file groups can give you.

▶ Know the standard file extensions of primary data files (.mdf), secondary data files (.ndf), and log files (.ldf). Because the standard isn't enforced by SQL Server, Microsoft will want to be sure that Certified Professionals know what they are supposed to use. This should make for a couple of easy points to pick up on the test.

▶ Be certain of the Transact-SQL (TSQL) syntax for CREATE DATABASE. The user interface of Enterprise Manager is pretty intuitive to use, so the test will likely focus more on the TSQL statements.

INTRODUCTION

Chapter 1, "Database Design," discusses the process of creating a model, or schema, for a database. Before such a schema can be implemented, some physical storage, such as files on a hard drive, must be created for the database schema to reside in. This chapter covers the information you need to know in order to create the database to allocate this physical storage.

To this end, this chapter first enters a brief discussion of the units of storage that SQL Server uses to allocate space on the physical media (hard disks). You also learn about the files that are created on the physical media that hold a database's information. A database can use two or more files to hold its information, and these files can be allocated to specific sizes and locations to affect performance and reliability. With all this information, you will finally see exactly how to create a database with the proper configuration and size to suit your needs.

UNITS OF STORAGE IN SQL SERVER

There are two basic units of storage in SQL Server:

- ◆ Page
- ◆ Extent

A *page* is the fundamental unit of storage that SQL Server uses. A page either belongs to a specific object or is used for one of several kinds of internal record keeping data structures. Pages are 8KB in size, which is a change from previous versions of SQL Server, which used 2KB pages. This change causes the SQL Server page size to match the Windows NT I/O block size of 8KB. The larger page size is therefore more efficient and causes less overhead.

An *extent* is the fundamental unit of allocation in SQL Server. When more space within a data file is needed for an object, at least one full extent is allocated. Although a page belonging to a certain object belongs only to that object, an extent can contain pages belonging to many different objects. An extent contains eight pages, which results in 64KB. Although small objects are initially assigned to mixed extents that contain pages belonging to as many as eight objects, SQL Server attempts to keep larger objects assigned to uniform extents in which all the pages belong to a single object.

DATABASE FILES AND FILE GROUPS

Create and manage files, file groups, and transaction logs that define a database.

Databases store their information in dedicated files on the server. Every database has at least two files:

◆ Primary data file

◆ Log file

In addition, a database can have multiple secondary data files. The secondary data files can optionally be combined into file groups, which provides for some specific performance enhancements in certain situations.

All of these files are created through the CREATE DATABASE statement along with the database that will use them. Note that this is different from previous versions of SQL Server, which first allocated storage space and then created the database to use that space. The current use of multiple data files and file groups is considered one of the most significant improvements in SQL Server 7.0.

A *file group* is a collection of one or more data files. All data files belong to some file group. Just as every database has a single primary file, there is also a single primary file group, which always includes the primary file. This primary file group is also the default file group unless a user file group is specifically named the default. Objects created in the database can be created in a specific file group; otherwise these objects are created in the default file group. All information written to a file group is spread out among all files in the group, proportional to the amount of free space in the files. In this way, all files in a file group tend to fill at the same time, and information is distributed as evenly as possible.

By defining multiple data files on separate physical disks on a server and then combining those files into a file group, all data in that file group is spread across the multiple disks, which can shorten each

NOTE

Backward Compatibility for Existing Scripts   SQL Server 7.0 actually still supports the use of the DISK INIT statement that was required in earlier versions. This statement would create the disk files for databases, and then the CREATE DATABASE statement would reference the existing files. This arrangement is still allowed in SQL Server 7.0 for backward compatibility, but it is not recommended for normal use and is not covered on the test. This feature is therefore outside the scope of this book. You can find more information by looking in SQL Server Books Online in "Getting Started: Backwards Compatibility."

single disk's access time. Alternatively, multiple data files can be created on separate physical disks, and each file made into a group of its own. Different highly utilized objects in the database can then be put on different file groups that are on different physical disks. In this approach, user requests for one of the objects do not contend with requests for objects in a different file group. This is a much more targeted solution, requiring more planning to be effective. These two solutions can be combined, by putting different objects in distinct file groups where each file group spans multiple disks. Note that in these scenarios, a RAID array is considered a single disk.

The following three subsections cover in greater detail primary data files, secondary data files, and transaction log files, respectively.

Primary Data File

As was stated earlier, all databases have a *primary data file*. This file contains all of the system tables and other system objects. The primary data file will also contain the links to all secondary data files and log files. Microsoft recommends that most databases will work very well with only a single primary data file and log file. The only reason to use multiple secondary files and file groups is to obtain specific performance gains on servers with multiple physical disks. Primary data files should be given an .mdf extension to identify them as such. More information on filenames can be found in the later section "Creating a Database."

Secondary Data Files

Secondary data files can be used to spread data over multiple disks. When using multiple data files, Microsoft recommends that the primary data file be left empty of user data and that all user data be placed in the secondary data files. This strategy keeps all of the system information needed for internal administration of the database in a separate, safe location so that damage to a secondary data file is more likely to be isolated. Secondary data files should be given a standard extension of .ndf for consistency with Microsoft's declared standards. More information on filenames can be found in the later section "Creating a Database."

N O T E **RAID Systems are Groups of Disks Acting as One** The word *RAID* is an acronym for *Redundant Array of Inexpensive Disks*. RAID systems are a method of combining multiple physical disk drives into a single unit in which all data is spread among all the drives in the array. There are many different implementations of RAID. Two common RAID systems are RAID 1 (disk mirroring) and RAID 5 (disk striping with parity). With *disk mirroring*, the identical data is written on all disks in the array (the array nearly always consists of multiple of two disks). RAID 1 improves read performance by accessing both disks and provides a backup if either disk fails. With *disk striping with parity*, data is broken into multiple pieces and parity information is calculated. Each parity information piece is written to a different disk than the data piece it is calculated from. In this way, if any single disk fails, the data lost on that disk can be recovered using the remaining data and the parity.

WARNING

Write-Caching Disk Controllers Can Interfere with Logging For this recovery process to work, SQL Server must accurately know when log changes have been written to disk. Disk controllers that perform write caching can destroy the usefulness of the transaction log by making SQL Server believe that log changes have been written to disk when they have not. In this situation, SQL Server's copy of the log and the copy of the log on disk are out of sync, and automatic recovery may fail.

Because write caching almost always improves disk performance, many high-performance servers have write-caching controllers. Most of the better controllers have a battery backup that maintains the cache in event of a power failure. Using write-caching controllers with a battery backup is acceptable because cached information can be written to disk on startup, and the SQL Server log will remain intact. If your server has a write-caching controller, make sure it also has a battery backup.

Write-caching software cannot guarantee that cached information will be written to disk in event of a system failure. Therefore, you should never use write-caching software with SQL Server.

Transaction Log Files

Transaction log files hold all the data of the transaction log. Every database must have one log file but may have many. The transaction log is the heart of SQL Server's ability to recover a database in the event of a system crash. SQL Server uses a *write-ahead* log, which means that database changes are logged before they are applied. If the server fails because of a power outage or other problem, SQL Server automatically recovers the database by applying committed transactions and rolling back incomplete transactions.

The following list of steps offers an overview of how SQL Server uses the transaction log:

1. Some sort of change to the database is made. Except for a few cases, every modification to a database is logged. Some examples of logged modifications follow:

    *   Direct changes to the data caused by the execution of an INSERT, UPDATE, or DELETE statement

    *   Creation of a database object

    *   Page and extent allocations caused when information is added to a table or index

2. The pages to be modified are loaded into memory.

3. As each modification is made, the change is written to the transaction log before the change is applied to the data. Transaction log changes must be flushed before any data page holding a modification logged in the log page. The log page can be retained in memory so long as none of the associated data pages are flushed. SQL Server ensures that log pages are flushed before any associated dirty data pages but does not necessarily flush a log page immediately. Changes to the data pages are just modified in memory.

4. About once a minute, the SQL Server CHECKPOINT process looks at the database and flushes any modified pages in memory to the disk. The checkpoint marks the transaction log to indicate which transaction was last written to disk.

In the event of a system failure, SQL Server performs automatic recovery on startup. SQL Server looks at the transactions in the transaction log after the last CHECKPOINT because these are database changes that have not been written to disk. Completed transactions are applied to the database (rolled forward), and incomplete transactions are backed out (rolled back).

Although a log file can have any legal operating system name, Microsoft recommends that the .ldf extension be used for consistency with primary data files and secondary data files.

> **NOTE**
>
> **Non-Logged Operations Trade Safety for Speed**   Non-logged operations operate significantly faster than logged operations because SQL Server does not have the additional overhead of writing log records. Bulk-copy and SELECT INTO operations can be non-logged, and are usually used for handling large amounts of data.
>
> Non-logged operations make the transaction log useless for database recovery, so the database should be fully backed up after performing a non-logged operation.

Database Files and File Groups

REVIEW BREAK

Database files are the objects of physical storage for your database. You can create multiple database files to spread disk access over multiple disks to improve performance. Regardless of the number of files you create, you will always have only one *primary data file*. You will also have at least one transaction log file, but you could, in fact, have many. Additional data files are called *secondary data files*, as opposed to the single primary data file.

Whereas database files are the physical files that allow you to target specific physical disks for data access, *file groups* are logical groups of the database files. Any object in your database can be created on a specific file group. By creating that file group on a specific database file you can control which objects are written to specific physical disks. By grouping multiple database files into a single file group, SQL Server automatically spreads data written to the file group evenly across all database files. This enables you to spread the load of data access across multiple physical disks which can increase performance.

Now that you are familiar with database files and file groups, you are ready to learn how to actually create databases that put these concepts into action. In the following section, you use both Enterprise Manager and Transact-SQL statements to create and alter databases using multiple database files and file groups.

CREATING A DATABASE

▶ Create and manage files, file groups, and transaction logs that define a database.

Before implementing a data model in SQL Server, you must create a database to store the various tables and other objects required to store the information. By default, only the system administrator can create databases, though this permission may be transferred to other users. When you create a database, you give it a name, define the database files it will reside on, and specify the size for these data and log files. When you are creating a database, keep the following in mind:

◆ The database name can be up to 128 characters in length, and must be unique on the server.

◆ The default size of a database's primary file if no size information is specified is the size of the Model database (.75MB). The default size of any secondary or log file is 1MB. The minimum value the size parameter can have is 512KB, which is the smallest size a log file can be set to.

◆ Generally, the log size should be about 10–25% of the expected size of the data.

◆ Data and log files are allocated in 64KB increments.

With the preceding caveats in mind, you are ready to put the information into action. In the next two subsections you will create a database, first with Enterprise Manager, and then with the CREATE DATABASE Transact-SQL statement.

Enterprise Manager

To create a database from Enterprise Manager, perform the tasks outlined in Step by Step 2.1.

STEP BY STEP

2.1 Using Enterprise Manager to Create a Database

1. Select the server you want to work with, and expand the tree view by clicking the plus sign (+) to the left of the server icon. Select the Databases folder, right-click so that the context menu appears, and select the New Database option. The Database Properties dialog box appears, as shown in Figure 2.1.

(You also can get to a New Database dialog box by selecting Action, New, Database from the Enterprise Manager menu after choosing a server.)

2. Enter the name of the database in the Name box.

3. In the Database Files grid you can enter the primary and multiple secondary data files. You'll see that after entering the database name the first line auto-populated for the primary data file. Review this data and make changes to fit your naming conventions.

4. Check the size column in particular to size the primary data file correctly.

5. Notice that you cannot change the File group of the primary data file. Every database has a primary data file that always belongs to the primary file group.

6. Below the grid are options for the automatic growth of the file selected in the grid. You can set the growth rate as a percentage, or by megabytes, and you can select the maximum size as either unlimited, or as a set size in megabytes.

7. Use the blank row in the grid to enter secondary data files. As you complete a row, new blank rows will appear for more files. For secondary data files you can enter new file groups.

8. For each of your secondary data files, review the growth options below the grid.

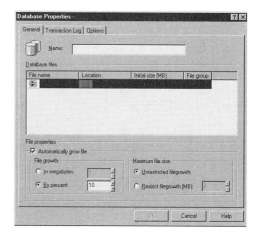

FIGURE 2.1
The Database Properties dialog box for a new database.

continues

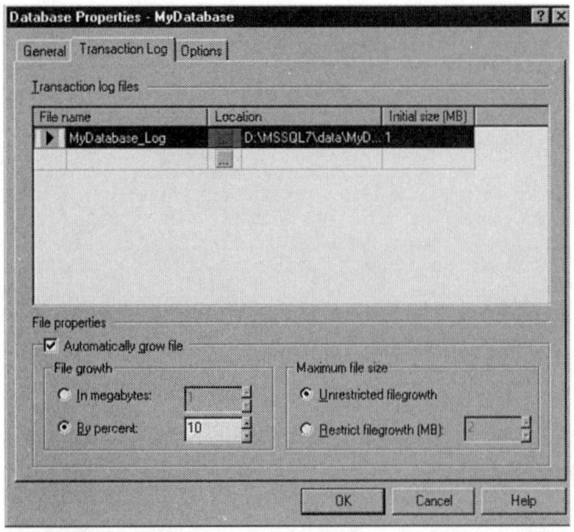

FIGURE 2.2
The Transaction Log tab of the Database Properties dialog box.

continued

9. Click the Transaction Log tab of the dialog box to set the name, location, and size of the transaction log file. This tab will look very similar to the General tab you just left. Figure 2.2 shows a sample of this tab of the dialog box.

10. Review the default log file information in the grid, and make changes to fit your naming standards and to set the size correctly. Except for the lack of file groups (log files never belong to file groups), the Transaction Log tab works identically to the General tab. You can enter additional log files, and set the growth parameters of each.

11. The Options tab is described later in this chapter (see section "Database Options"). Go ahead and take a peek if you're curious, but you won't need to worry about these options for now.

12. Click the OK button when you have all the data and log files set the way you want them. SQL Server starts allocating file space and closes the dialog box when it's finished, and your database is complete.

> **NOTE**
>
> **Use Stored Procedure to Create a Removable Media Database** SQL Server enables you to create databases on removable media, such as a floppy disk, CD-ROM, or ZIP drive. This feature is most useful for distributing read-only databases on CD-ROM. To create a database of this type, use the sp_create_removable system stored procedure.
>
> For more information about creating and using databases on removable media, see SQL Server Books Online.

An existing database can be modified using the same interface you just used. Simply right-click the database in Enterprise Manager and choose Properties. The same Database Properties dialog box is shown, allowing you to rename, resize, and reorganize files and file groups.

TSQL

To create a database using the Transact-SQL CREATE DATABASE command, perform the tasks outlined in Step by Step 2.2.

STEP BY STEP

2.2 Using Transact-SQL Command CREATE DATABASE to Create a Database

1. Start the SQL Server Query Analyzer, and log on to the server on which you want to create the new database. You should see an empty query window similar to the one shown in Figure 2.3.

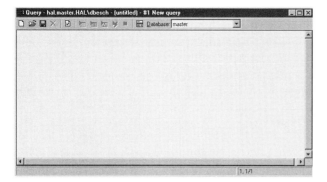

FIGURE 2.3
The SQL Query Analyzer connected to the Master database.

2. You must be in the Master database to create a database. Use the Database combo box to select the Master database.

3. The syntax for the CREATE DATABASE command is as follows:

```
CREATE DATABASE database_name
[ ON [PRIMARY]
        [ <filespec> [,...n] ]
        [, <filegroup> [,...n] ]
]
[ LOG ON { <filespec> } ]
[ FOR LOAD ¦ FOR ATTACH ]

<filespec> ::=
  ( [ NAME = logical_file_name, ]
    FILENAME = 'os_file_name'
    [, SIZE = size]
    [, MAXSIZE = { max_size ¦ UNLIMITED } ]
    [, FILEGROWTH = growth_increment] ) [,...n]

<filegroup> ::=
FILEGROUP filegroup_name <filespec> [,...n]
```

The following list explores each of the main syntax parts:

- The ON keyword is used to specify the number, name, and size of data files to use. If this keyword is omitted, a minimum sized database is created with a primary data file having the same name as the database name supplied in the data directory of the SQL Server installation directory.

- The optional PRIMARY keyword indicates that the list of files that follows belongs to the primary file group. Even if the PRIMARY keyword is omitted, a file group definition may not appear in the syntax

continues

continued

until at least one data file is defined. The first data file defined is the primary data file. Any other data files following the first will be secondary data files in the primary file group, until a user file group is explicitly defined.

- The LOG ON keyword is used to specify the number, name, and size of log files to use. If this is omitted, a single log file is created with a system-defined name and the size of 25% of the total data size.

- The FOR LOAD keyword is provided only for backward compatibility. It creates the database with the DBO Use Only option turned on, and an internal status set to Loading. The database is unusable until an existing backup is restored into it. This option is unnecessary because the RESTORE statement in SQL Server 7.0 can create the database automatically if needed, eliminating the need for this step.

- Use the FOR ATTACH keyword to indicate that you are attaching a previously created database to this server. Only a single <filespec> is needed following the ON keyword to indicate the primary data file. The primary data file contains all information needed to attach the remaining data and log files.

- The <filespec> marker in the syntax indicates that a data or log file definition is allowed. A <filespec> defines a single data or log file by specifying a name, filename, size, and growth parameters. These parameters are defined independently in the following bullet points.

- The NAME keyword of the <filespec> definition should be followed by a logical name for the file that SQL Server will use internally. The logical name must conform to the usual rules for identifiers, the most important of which is the 128-character limit. Note that the NAME keyword is only optional if the FOR ATTACH option is used.

- The FILENAME keyword is required, and is followed by the full pathname of the file to use, or create, on the server. This pathname must be valid for the operating system on which SQL Server is running.

- The SIZE keyword is followed by a beginning size for the file. The minimum size is 512KB. The size may be followed by a KB or MB qualifier, indicating whether the number appears in kilobyte units or megabyte units, respectively. If no qualifier is used, the size is assumed to be given in megabytes (MB). If SIZE is omitted, 1MB is assumed. All sizes are rounded to the nearest 64KB increment.

- The MAXSIZE keyword is used to indicate the maximum allowable size for the file. This is used when the file is filled and SQL Server attempts to autogrow the file. The maximum size can be qualified just like the preceding SIZE parameter. MAXSIZE can also be followed by the UNLIMITED keyword, which indicates that the file will grow until the disk is full. If MAXSIZE is not specified, the maximum file size will be unlimited.

- The FILEGROWTH keyword is used to indicate how much the file should grow each time it fills. The number following FILEGROWTH can be a number qualified with KB or MB, or it can be a percentage qualified with %. The default qualifier is megabytes (MB). If no FILEGROWTH is specified, 10% is used. The number entered cannot exceed the MAXSIZE parameter. Any FILEGROWTH increment is rounded to the nearest 64KB increment.

- The <filegroup> marker in the syntax indicates that a new file group can be begun at this location. A file group is denoted by the keyword FILEGROUP followed by an identifier for this group. All data files that follow this point are members of this file group, until a new file group is defined.

continues

continued

Following are some examples of the CREATE DATABASE statement:

- The following statement creates a database named Sample in the data directory of the SQL Server installation directory with a default data size .75MB, an default log size of .5MB:

```
CREATE DATABASE Sample
```

- The following statement creates Sample with two data files, both of which are in the primary file group:

```
CREATE DATABASE Sample
ON
(NAME = DataFile1,
 FILENAME = 'c:\mssql7\data\DataFile1.mdf'),
(NAME = DataFile2,
 FILENAME = 'c:\mssql7\data\DataFile2.ndf')
LOG ON
(NAME = LogDevice1,
 FILENAME = 'c:\mssql7\data\LogFile1.ldf')
```

- The following statement creates a database named Sample with multiple data files according to Microsoft's standards. The secondary data file is placed its own file group to separate it from the primary data file. It is assumed that the server in this example has two physical disks—C: and D:—both of which have an \mssql7\data directory off the root. The log file is place on a separate physical drive from the data file to improve performance:

```
CREATE DATABASE Sample
ON PRIMARY
(NAME = SampleData1,
 FILENAME = 'c:\mssql7\data\SampleData1.mdf',
 SIZE = 5MB,
 MAXSIZE = UNLIMITED,
 FILEGROWTH = 10%),
FILEGROUP Secondary
(NAME = SampleData2,
 FILENAME = 'c:\mssql7\data\SampleData2.ndf',
 SIZE = 100MB,
 MAXSIZE = UNLIMITED,
 FILEGROWTH = 10%)
LOG ON
(NAME = SampleLog,
 FILENAME = 'd:\mssql7\data\SampleLog.ldf',
 SIZE = 20MB
 MAXSIZE = UNLIMITED,
 FILEGROWTH = 10%)
```

4. Execute the query by typing **Alt + X** or by clicking on the Execute Query button. The database is created. SQL Server reports the actual size of the database files it created.

After the database is created, there may still come a time when you want to make changes to way the files are arranged. Just as changes can be made through Enterprise Manager, as was described previously, all the same changes can be made with the ALTER DATABASE statement in SQL Server. Most of the options in the ALTER DATABASE statement are self explanatory, so they are not detailed here. Following is the syntax for the ALTER DATABASE statement:

```
ALTER DATABASE database
{    ADD FILE <filespec> [,...n] [TO FILEGROUP
filegroup_name]
     ¦ ADD LOG FILE <filespec> [,...n]
     ¦ REMOVE FILE logical_file_name
     ¦ ADD FILEGROUP filegroup_name
     ¦ REMOVE FILEGROUP filegroup_name
     ¦ MODIFY FILE <filespec>
     ¦ MODIFY FILEGROUP filegroup_name filegroup_property
}
```

The <filespec> found in the ALTER DATABASE statement conforms to the same syntax as the <filespec> previously described in the CREATE DATABASE statement. When modifying a file using the MODIFY FILE option, you should only change one property of the <filespec> at a time. The MODIFY FILEGROUP option has three options for the filegroup_property parameter:

◆ **READONLY.** This option prevents data modifications against objects in the file group. You must have exclusive access to the database to set this option.

◆ **READWRITE.** Use this option to undo the results of the READONLY option.

◆ **DEFAULT.** This option sets the file group as the default file group where all new objects are created if not specified elsewhere.

The important option here is the MODIFY FILEGROUP option, which allows you to change the default file group. When creating a database the primary file group is the default. If you want to keep your user objects in a separate file group from the system objects, as

Microsoft recommends, you should change the default file group so that all objects you create will go to the correct file group. This is accomplished with the following command:

```
ALTER DATABASE database_name MODIFY FILEGROUP filegroup_name
➥DEFAULT
```

DATABASE OPTIONS

▶ Create and manage files, file groups, and transaction logs that define a database.

If you created a database using SQL Enterprise Manager, you saw an Options tab in the Database Properties dialog box. On this tab are a number of configuration options specific to that database. The options made available from Enterprise Manager are only a subset of the most commonly changed options. Other options can be set only with the sp_dboption stored procedure, which is described later in this section. By default, only the system administrator or DBO can set database options. The complete list of database options follows:

◆ **Autoclose.** This option specifies that the database remains active only while users are connected to it. When the last connection to the database is closed, all resources held by the database are freed and the database shuts down. When a user tries to use the database again, it reopens automatically.

◆ **Autoshrink.** When this option is set to True, the files of the database are checked periodically to determine if space is available to be reclaimed. This periodic checking adds a small amount of overhead to the system, so it is False by default. This option can only be set by sp_dboption.

◆ **ANSI Null Default.** This option specifies whether columns are *NULLable* by default. If this option is turned on, then columns that do not have their NULL options explicitly defined during a CREATE TABLE or ALTER TABLE statement default to allowing NULLs.

◆ **ANSI Nulls**. If this option is set to True, then all comparisons to NULL evaluate to NULL (unknown). The default value in SQL Server is False, which allows comparison of two values to evaluate to True if both values are NULL. This option can be set only by sp_dboption.

◆ **ANSI Warnings.** The ANSI standard requires that warnings be returned to the user when many non-fatal error conditions, such as division by zero, occur. This option can be set only by `sp_dboption`.

◆ **Concat Null Yields Null.** This option determines whether concatenating a NULL value to a string returns a NULL or if the string is unaffected. By default, in SQL Server, using a NULL in a concat will not affect the original string. This option can be set only by `sp_dboption`.

◆ **Cursor Close on Commit.** This option determines whether open cursors are closed when a transaction is committed or rolled back. By default, cursors remain open across transactions. This option can be set only by `sp_dboption`.

◆ **DBO Use Only.** If this option is turned on, then only the database owner (DBO) or users aliased to the DBO can access the database.

◆ **Default to Local Cursor.** This option determines whether cursors default to a local or global scope. By default, cursors have a global scope. This option can be set only by `sp_dboption`.

◆ **Merge Publish.** When this option is set to True, the database is allowed to be published for a merge replication. By default, Merge Publish is not allowed. This option can be set only by `sp_dboption`.

◆ **Offline.** This option is primarily used for databases stored on removable media. When a database is offline, no users can access the database. SQL Server does not open the database's files, and the database is not automatically recovered upon server startup. This option can be set only by using `sp_dboption`.

◆ **Published.** This option determines if a database is allowed to provide publications for replication. By default, this option is turned off and is usually set only when replication is set up on a server. This option can be set only by `sp_dboption`.

◆ **Quoted Identifier.** When this option is True, any strings enclosed in double quotes are treated as identifiers. These quoted identifiers do not have to follow the standard rules for identifiers, meaning they can be reserved words and can contain spaces. All string literals must be enclosed in single quotes while this option is True. When this option is False (the default), all strings enclosed in either single or double quotes are treated as literals, and identifiers cannot be enclosed in quotes. This option can be set only by sp_dboption.

◆ **Read Only.** If this option is turned on, users (including the system administrator and DBO) cannot modify any data in the database.

◆ **Recursive Triggers.** This option determines whether triggers can be fired recursively—that is, whether the same trigger can be executing twice; the second being due to a data modification made by the execution of the first instance. When this option is True, care should be taken that triggers do not cause themselves to execute indefinitely. By default, this option is set to False.

◆ **Select Into/Bulkcopy.** If this option is turned on, then non-logged operations are permitted in the database.

◆ **Single User.** Turning this option on restricts the number of connections into the database. Only one user at a time can access the database. This option can be set only by sp_dboption.

◆ **Subscribed.** Determines whether a database is allowed to subscribe to publications from other databases involved in replication. This option can be set only by using sp_dboption, and is usually set only when replication is set up on a server.

◆ **Torn Page Detection.** Setting this option causes SQL Server to perform additional checks to recognize I/O errors in updating the database on disk. If a power failure or disk failure occurs between the start and completion of a page write, the database appears to be updated; however, the data may not be consistent. When such an error is discovered, the database must be restored from a good backup to fix the error. This option is less important if your server has a write-caching disk controller with a battery backup because such a controller is protected from power failure events that require backup, though they are still vulnerable to disk failures. By default, this option is off.

◆ **Trunc. Log On Chkpt.** If this option is set, committed transactions are removed from the transaction log every time the CHECKPOINT process occurs. Very useful in databases in which transaction log dumps are not needed, such as a database under development, this option reduces the likelihood of the transaction log filling up. This option also causes a CHECKPOINT to occur if the log ever reaches 70% of capacity, and then again at 100% of capacity. Note that because a CHECKPOINT cannot free space in the log associated with an active transaction, a single transaction can still overwhelm a log of limited size.

Database options can be set by using the sp_dboption system stored procedure or through Enterprise Manager. A few of the options can only be set using sp_dboption. To use sp_dboption to set a database option, perform the tasks outlined in Step by Step 2.3.

> **NOTE**
> **Use Model Database to Control Default Options** Setting a database option in the Model database causes that option to be set in all newly created databases. This can be especially useful for the options that control ANSI default behavior.

STEP BY STEP

2.3 Using sp_dboption to Set a Database Option

1. Load the SQL Query Analyzer, and log on to the server on which the database resides. The Query window appears (refer to Figure 2.3).

2. The syntax of the sp_dboption stored procedure is as follows:

```
sp_dboption [dbname] [, 'optname' [ , {TRUE ¦ FALSE
➥} ]]
```

sp_dboption behaves differently when different options are specified. Consider the following examples:

- Calling sp_dboption without any parameters causes all database options to be listed:

```
sp_dboption
```

- Calling sp_dboption with only a database name returns a list of all enabled options in that database:

```
sp_dboption pubs
```

- Calling sp_dboption with a database name and option name returns the current setting for that option:

```
sp_dboption pubs,'read only'
```

continues

continued

- Calling sp_dboption with a database name, option name, and setting value turns the option on or off:

  sp_dboption pubs, 'read only', true

3. Type in the sp_dboption command in a format similar to that shown previously.

4. Execute the query by typing **Alt + X** or by clicking the Execute button on the toolbar of the query window. The database option is changed.

To set database options from Enterprise Manager, perform the tasks outlined in Step by Step 2.4.

STEP BY STEP

2.4 Setting Database Options from Enterprise Manager

1. Load Enterprise Manager and select the server on which the database resides. Expand the tree view by clicking the plus sign (+) to the left of the server icon.

2. Select the Databases folder, and expand the tree view to show all the databases on this server.

3. Select the database for which you want to change an option, and right-click it so the context menu appears. Click the Properties option. The Database Properties dialog box appears. Select the Options tab, as shown in Figure 2.4.

4. Turn an option on or off by checking or unchecking its check box. Click the OK button to save your changes.

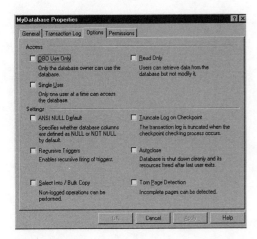

FIGURE 2.4
The Options tab on the Database Properties dialog box in Enterprise Manager.

CASE STUDY: BUILDING AN OPTIMAL SERVER

ESSENCE OF THE CASE

Here are the essential elements of the case:

- ▶ The current SQL Server database is using one primary data file and a log file on the same physical drive.

- ▶ There are four distinct groups of tables in the data model.

- ▶ The current applications tend to access only one of these groups at a time, but new applications are being developed that will take the entire data model into account.

- ▶ There is a single table of enormous size that is commonly referenced by users.

SCENARIO

Your company has recently undergone a major development effort to migrate several loosely related Access databases into a single unified database on SQL Server. During the migration, a lightly used file server—really nothing more than a desktop machine with a big hard drive—was used to host SQL Server. Now that the migration has been declared a success, more people than ever are starting to use the database. Different departments are now able to see the "big picture" because data from all aspects of the companies business is all in one place, increasing the reliability and consistency of the information. New applications are under development that will use this wealth of information more effectively for more users. Meanwhile, that poor fileserver is starting to smoke. You have been asked to recommend a server configuration that will give SQL Server the best performance for the money.

You find that there are four distinct groups of tables in the data model, loosely representing four original Access databases from different departments. In addition, there is one key table that represents more than a quarter of the entire data space. The total space required for the data files are currently just under 1GB.

ANALYSIS

You have a golden opportunity to set this database up right. You have a clean slate from which to work to avoid hardware bottlenecks in the future. You also don't know what kind of budget constraints you are under. Nonetheless, there are some important decisions you can make. Of course, more and faster processors will improve

continues

CASE STUDY: ADD TITLE HERE

continued

performance, more memory is better than less, and mirrored or RAID 5 disk arrays will offer better reliability and speed than a single large drive. However, these specifics can all be balanced against each other later when you have solid quotes on hardware prices to compare to your budget. The most important thing you can do from a SQL Server standpoint is to determine what kinds of file groups your database would benefit from.

First, you know that if you put the transaction log on its own physical drive you will improve update performance. The transaction log has little effect on reads, but when data is being modified, all modifications must go to both the transaction log and the data files. Separating these two components is always a good idea.

You also may want to set each of the four table groups of the data model onto its own physical drive, but remember that the whole database is only around 1GB in size. You also know that soon, users will be accessing all of these tables equally. A single RAID 5 array will spread the I/O against several disks, and should be able to handle the data requests against this size of data. More beneficial would be to separate that one large table into its own file group on a separate drive or possibly its own drive array. Your recommendation therefore would be to ensure that the server can provide three fault-tolerant disk systems for SQL Server to achieve maximum benefits.

CHAPTER SUMMARY

KEY TERMS

Before you take the exam, make sure you are comfortable with the definitions and concepts for each of the following key terms:

• CREATE DATABASE

• ALTER DATABASE

• primary data file

• secondary data file

• log file

• file group

This chapter discussed how databases are implemented and managed in SQL Server. This information allows you to create a database and manage the data and log files efficiently. On a server with multiple physical disks, you can optimize your database to minimize disk contention.

APPLY YOUR KNOWLEDGE

Exercises

2.1 Creating a Database Using Enterprise Manager

This exercise walks you through the steps of creating a database using the Enterprise Manager application. The database you create here is used in the next exercise. In this exercise you create a simple database, and the following one alters it to a size that is useful for exercises in the next chapter.

Estimated Time: 10 minutes

1. Start the SQL Enterprise Manager application.

2. Choose a server from the tree in the left pane of the window. If necessary, expand the server groups to reveal the server you want to work with. Expand the server of your choice.

3. Select the Database folder, right-click so the context menu appears, and select the New Database option. The Database Properties dialog box appears.

4. Enter the name of the database in the Name box. This may be up to 128 characters in length. To create the example database that will be used in the following exercises, use the name MyDatabase.

5. There is a grid in the middle of the screen labeled Database Files. The first line in this grid is already filled in. This first line represents the primary data file. Overwrite the default values with the following information:

   • **File name:** MyDatabasePrime

   • **Location:** c:\mssql7\data\ MyDatabasePrime.pdf

Leave the Initial Size and File Group columns at the defaults. Note that you cannot change the value of the File Group for the primary data file even if you try.

6. You will create other data files later to hold the user data, so the primary data file shouldn't need more space that it has now. Ensure that the primary data file is highlighted in the grid, and uncheck the Automatically Grow File check box in the bottom area of the screen. The screen should look similar to that shown in Figure 2.5.

FIGURE 2.5
The Database Properties dialog box for MyDatabase.

7. Click the Transaction Log tab. Change the defaults for the log data file to match the following:

   • **File name:** MyDatabaseLog

   • **Location:** c:\mssql7\data\MyDatabaseLog.ldf

   • **Initial Size:** 2MB

APPLY YOUR KNOWLEDGE

Again, you have the option of restricting the growth of the log data file. To avoid complications, however, leave the defaults alone to allow unlimited growth, at 10% at a time.

8. Click the Options tab to set the default options for this database. Choose the Truncate Log On Checkpoint option. Because this is a test database, the Truncate Log On Checkpoint option obviates the need for backups to prevent the log from filling up. If you encounter any problems with the database, it will be just as easy to re-create the database as it would be to restore it from a backup.

9. Click the OK button to create the database. Use File Manager or Explorer to find the database files that were created.

2.2 Altering a Database Using Transact-SQL

Exercise 2.2 shows you how to alter a database using Transact-SQL. It walks you through the process of using the ALTER DATABASE Transact-SQL command to expand the size of a database.

Estimated Time: 5 minutes

1. Start the SQL Query Analyzer application.

2. Log on to your server, and the Query Analyzer window appears.

3. If it is not already selected, select the Master database in the Database combo box on the query window's toolbar.

4. Type the following commands, making modifications as necessary for your system:

```
ALTER DATABASE MyDatabase
ADD FILEGROUP UserData
go
```

```
ALTER DATABASE MyDatabase
ADD FILE
(NAME = MyDatabaseUserData,
 FILENAME =
'c:\mssql7\data\MyDatabaseUser.ndf',
 SIZE = 10MB
) TO FILEGROUP UserData
go
ALTER DATABASE MyDatabase
MODIFY FILEGROUP UserData DEFAULT
```

Notice that you are executing three different ALTER DATABASE commands. Because the ALTER DATABASE command can only perform one action on the database at a time, multiple commands are needed. The go statement that separates the ALTER DATABASE commands instructs SQL Server to run each statement independently. These statements create a separate file group—UserData—and create a secondary data file in that group. Finally, the UserData file group becomes the default file group.

5. Execute the query by typing **Alt + X** or by clicking the Execute Query button. A 10MB datafile named MyDatabaseUserData is created on the disk. Use File Manager or Explorer to verify that the device was created.

Review Questions

1. What is the purpose of the transaction log?

2. What is a data file?

3. What is a log file?

4. What TSQL command is used to create a new database?

5. How large is a page?

6. Why are data files expanded in 64KB increments?

7. What is the advantage to placing the transaction log on multiple file groups?

8. What command creates the data and log files for the database to use?

9. How many file groups can a data file belong to?

10. What does the Truncate Log On Checkpoint database option do?

11. What is special about the default file group?

12. Describe how data is allocated in a file group.

Exam Questions

1. What is the standard extension for primary data file names?

   A. .pdf

   B. .ldf

   C. .dat

   D. .mdf

2. What is the minimum size of a data or log file?

   A. 1MB

   B. 2MB

   C. 64KB

   D. 512KB

3. Data and Log files expand by what increments?

   A. 8KB

   B. 64KB

   C. 512KB

   D. 1MB

4. When creating a database with the CREATE DATABASE command, in what units can the file sizes be expressed? Select all that apply.

   A. MB

   B. Number of pages

   C. Number of extents

   D. KB

5. When creating a database with the CREATE DATABASE command, in what units are the file sizes expressed, by default?

   A. MB

   B. Number of pages

   C. Number of extents

   D. KB

6. When creating a database through Enterprise Manager, in what units are the file sizes expressed?

   A. MB

   B. Number of pages

   C. Number of extents

   D. KB

7. What is the size of a page?

   A. 2KB

   B. 8KB

   C. 64KB

   D. 128KB

APPLY YOUR KNOWLEDGE

8. What is the size of an extent?

 A. 2KB

 B. 8KB

 C. 64KB

 D. 128KB

9. A company is building a new SQL Server database, to be used primarily to support a web page. The database will be marked as read-only during normal operations and will receive only small data updates through a batch process once a month. The server being used has two physical disk devices: One is a mirrored drive in which the operating system files are stored, and the other is a larger RAID 5 array. The problem is to configure the database files to offer maximum performance. It has been decided to put the primary data file on the RAID 5 array, the transaction log on the mirrored system physical drive, and to use no secondary files.

 Rate the solution as one of the following:

 A. This is an outstanding solution to the problem. The solution will offer maximum performance to the database.

 B. This is a fair solution to the problem. The solution will work, but it offers no special performance gains.

 C. This is a poor solution to the problem. Although the solution will work, it ignores simple methods that would increase performance.

 D. This is a bad solution to the problem. A database cannot be created in this manner.

10. Phil has created a new database that takes advantage of multiple physical disks on his server. He has created his primary data file on one disk and placed a secondary data file on another physical disk. The transaction log resides on the same disk as the primary data file. Phil's plan is to keep his user objects on the secondary data file and leave the system tables on the primary data file. He quickly discovers, however, that after creating his user-defined objects, they all were created on the primary file group. What might he have done wrong?

 A. All objects are created on the primary data file until there is no more room. Only after the primary data file is full will objects be created on the secondary data file.

 B. He probably forgot to define the secondary data file as part of a separate file group. Objects are created on file groups rather than on specific data files.

 C. He probably forgot to define the secondary data file as the default data file. Objects are created on the default data file unless a different data file is specified.

 D. Nothing is actually wrong. SQL Server automatically assigns the secondary data file as the primary file group so that user objects will be created separately from the system objects on the primary data file.

Answers to Review Questions

1. The transaction log holds information about what changes have been made to the database. The transaction log can be used to rebuild the

state of the database since the last backup. (Refer to the section "Transaction Log Files" for more information.)

2. A data file in a database holds information about objects in the database. A database can have a single primary data file and multiple secondary data files. (Refer to the section "Database Files and File Groups" for more information.)

3. A log file in a database holds the information from the transaction log. The transaction log never shares space in a data file. (Refer to the section "Database Files and File Groups" for more information.)

4. The CREATE DATABASE command is used to create a database in Transact-SQL. (Refer to the section "Creating a Database" for more information.)

5. A SQL Server page is 8KB in size. (Refer to the section "Units of Storage in SQL Server" for more information.)

6. An extent is the basic unit that SQL Server uses for allocating space. An extent is 64KB in size. Therefore, data pages are allocated in 64KB increments. (Refer to the section "Units of Storage in SQL Server" for more information.)

7. A transaction log cannot be allocated to a file group. A transaction log can be made up from multiple log files, but none of these files belong to a file group. (Refer to the section "Database Files and File Groups" for more information.)

8. Data and log files are created at the same time as the database that uses them, through the CREATE DATABASE command. In previous versions of SQL Server, physical files were created independently of the database that would use them, with the DISK INIT command. DISK INIT still exists for

backward compatibility, but this command has only very limited functionality and should not be used. (Refer to the section "Database Files and File Groups" for more information.)

9. A data file can belong to only one file group. In fact, a data file *must* belong to a file group as well. (Refer to the section "Database Files and File Groups" for more information.)

10. When the Truncate Log On Checkpoint option is set to True, all committed transactions in the log are truncated whenever a checkpoint occurs. A checkpoint is forced whenever the log reaches 70%, and then again at 100% of capacity. (Refer to the section "Database Options" for more information.)

11. When objects are created, it is possible to specify which file group they should be created in. If no file group is specified, then objects are created in the default file group. If no default file group is explicitly set through the ALTER DATABASE command, the primary file group is the default file group. (Refer to the section "Database Files and File Groups" for more information.)

12. When new space is allocated to objects in a file group, the space is allocated proportional to the amount of space that is left in each data file, so that all data files will tend to fill at the same rate. (Refer to the section "Database Files and File Groups" for more information.)

Answers to Exam Questions

1. **D.** Although SQL Server does not enforce a naming standard for data and log files, Microsoft recommends .mdf for primary data files, .ndf for

APPLY YOUR KNOWLEDGE

secondary data files, and .ldf for log files. (Refer to the section "Database Files and File Groups" for more information.)

2. **D.** The minimum sizes for a data or log file is 512KB, although the primary data file must be large enough to accommodate the model database, which is usually 768KB. (Refer to the section "Creating a Database" for more information.)

3. **B.** Data and log files expand by 64KB, which corresponds to the size of an extent, SQL Server's basic unit of allocation. (Refer to the sections "Creating a Database" and "Units of Storage in SQL Server" for more information.)

4. **A, D.** When using the CREATE DATABASE statement, sizes can be expressed with either an MB qualifier or a KB, indicating megabytes or kilobytes, respectively. (Refer to the section "Creating a Database" for more information.)

5. **A.** Although either megabytes (MB) or kilobytes (KB) can be specified, sizes in the CREATE DATABASE default to megabytes. (Refer to the section "Creating a Database" for more information.)

6. **A.** When creating a database through Enterprise Manager, the file sizes must be specified in megabytes. (Refer to the section "Creating a Database" for more information.)

7. **B.** A page, the fundamental unit of storage, is 8KB in size. (Refer to the section "Units of Storage in SQL Server" for more information.)

8. **C.** An extent, the fundamental unit of allocation, is 64KB in size. (Refer to the section "Units of Storage in SQL Server" for more information.)

9. **C.** Because this will be a read-only database, there is nothing to be gained by placing the transaction log on a separate physical device. In fact, this solution overlooks the ability to spread data across the two physical devices in order to increase performance. (Refer to the section "Database Files and File Groups" for more information.)

10. **B.** All data files will be part of the primary file group unless other file groups are specifically created. The primary data file is always part of the primary file group. File groups can group one or more data files together, and objects are then created on specified file groups. (Refer to the section "Database Files and File Groups" for more information.)

Suggested Readings and Resources

We recommend the following resources for further study in the area of planning:

1. SQL Server Books Online
   - Pages and Extents
   - Files and Filegroups
   - Setting Database Options

2. Transact-SQL Help File
   - CREATE DATABASE
   - ALTER DATABASE
   - sp_dboption

This chapter helps you prepare for the Microsoft exam by covering the following objectives:

Create tables that enforce data integrity and referential integrity:

- **Choose the appropriate data types.**

- **Create user-defined data types.**

- **Define columns as** NULL **or** NOT NULL.

- **Define columns to generate values by using the** IDENTITY **property, the** uniqueidentifier **data type, and the** NEWID **function.**

- **Implement constraints.**

▶ This objective is very straightforward. You should be able to create tables, and use all possible table options effectively. You need to be familiar with all data types, and be able to create your own user-defined data types. In particular, pay attention to the uniqueidentifier data type. You also should know the different kinds of constraints that can be used on tables and columns.

CHAPTER 3

Implementing a Physical Design

STUDY STRATEGIES

▶ There is a lot of information to learn for just one test objective. By the end of this chapter you'll need to know just about everything there is to know about creating tables. This includes data types and other column options, and both table constraints and column constraints. Study the CREATE TABLE syntax in depth. Most everything else in this chapter ties directly back to the CREATE TABLE syntax, so it's very important. You should find the data types to be just what you'd expect to find in any database. Just remember that every character data type has an equivalent Unicode character type. Finally, learn all the constraints. Remember that column and table constraints differ only in the way they are created and named. A primary key constraint, for example, works exactly the same whether it was defined at the column level or the table level.

INTRODUCTION

This chapter discusses implementing the physical design of a logical data model. The logical data model was described in Chapter 1, "Database Design." There you learned that entities are implemented as tables, and that attributes equate to columns in those tables. In this chapter, you learn how to create the actual tables in SQL Server and implement all of the logical properties of attributes through column data types, properties, and constraints.

Finally, in this chapter you learn how to implement the relationships found in your data model. By explicitly declaring these relationships, you enable SQL Server to automatically enforce the rules on the data that you insert into the tables. In this way, you ensure that the entities you store in your database will correctly support and describe each other.

By correctly implementing the logical design, you will have created a strong foundation for your database. All other objects that are created in your database relate to various methods of manipulating the data you store. All the data, however, are stored in tables, so a proper implementation of the tables and their relationships structures the data in a way to ease the tasks of storing, retrieving, and manipulating the data.

In order to prepare you for these areas of the exam, this chapter covers the following topics:

◆ Understanding data types

◆ Managing tables

◆ Using constraints

UNDERSTANDING DATA TYPES

▶ Create tables that enforce data integrity and referential integrity:

Choose the appropriate data types.

Create user-defined data types.

Define columns as NULL or NOT NULL.

Define columns to generate values by using the IDENTITY property, the uniqueidentifier data type, and the NEWID function.

Implement constraints.

Before creating tables in a database, it is helpful to understand what kinds of data can be stored in SQL Server. SQL Server uses 24 different *data types* to identify the type of information (be it numeric, character based, or some other type) stored in a column. In addition, database users can define their own data types based on the system supplied data types.

Data types also are used to define the type of data passed as a parameter to a stored procedure or the type of data used in a local variable.

System Data Types

The 24 system data types can be grouped into eight broad categories (for more information about each specific data type, see the SQL Server Books Online):

◆ **Binary.** The binary, varbinary, and image types are used to store streams of binary information. The binary type is fixed length, whereas the varbinary and image types are variable in length. Use the image type to store extremely large values greater than 8,000 bytes.

◆ **Character.** The char, varchar, and text types store alphanumeric characters. The char type is fixed length, whereas the varchar and text types are variable in length. Use the char data type when you expect each value to be roughly the same size; use the varchar type if a character field can contain NULLs or will have data of widely varying lengths; use the text type to store extremely large strings longer than 8,000 characters.

◆ **Unicode Character.** The nchar, nvarchar, and ntext types store unicode characters. Because unicode characters are twice the size of standard characters, each of these types stores only half as much data as their standard character counterparts. Use the ntext data type to store strings larger than 4,000 unicode characters.

◆ **Date & Time.** The datetime and smalldatetime types both store date and time values. The difference between the two is the range of dates each can store and the accuracy of the time. smalldatetime is accurate to one second, whereas datetime is accurate to 3.33 milliseconds.

◆ **Exact Numeric.** The decimal, numeric, money, and smallmoney types can all store decimal numbers exactly. The numeric datatype is actually just a synonym for the decimal type.

◆ **Floating Point (approximate numeric).** The float and real types both provide for the approximate storage of decimal numbers; the main difference between the two is the range of values each can store.

◆ **Integer.** The bit, int, smallint, and tinyint types all store integer data in varying ranges.

◆ **Special Numeric.** These are numerically based data types that have special properties beyond simply storing user-supplied data:

  • *cursor*. The cursor data type can be assigned the instance of a cursor that was defined with the DECLARE CURSOR syntax. The cursor type variable then maintains a reference to the cursor, and can be used to manipulate the cursor.

  • *uniqueidentifier*. The uniqueidentifier is a 16-byte number formatted as a globally unique identifier (guid) as defined by Microsoft. The NEWID function provided by SQL Server generates numbers of this type that are guaranteed to be unique throughout the world.

  • *timestamp*. The timestamp data type provides a value unique to the database every time a column is inserted or updated. Note that this value is guaranteed to be unique to the database, but could conceivably be duplicated on other databases. Unlike uniqueidentifier values, which must be set using some function, timestamp columns are updated by the system automatically when an insert or update occurs to the row.

Knowing what data types SQL Server supports allows you to best choose which data type to use for any situation. The most basic decision to make is whether your data binary, character, or numeric.

Binary data is generally any data that is not human readable. More specifically, it is data that you want to store untranslated and untouched by SQL Server. Common examples of binary data include graphics and application data files, such as word processing documents and spreadsheets. The binary and varbinary data types allow you to store up to 8,000 bytes of data, and the image data type can store 2GB of data.

Character data is data that contains alphanumeric characters. As a rule, you should store only data that cannot be stored as a number in character data fields, but there several notable exceptions. Social security numbers, phone numbers, and ZIP codes are all technically numeric values, but experience has shown that these are almost always best off stored as character data. Because all of these numbers have inherent formatting in them, it is often easier to store the formatted string, rather than reformatting the data every time it is displayed.

Character data comes in two broad types: standard characters and Unicode characters. A *standard* character set contains 255 different characters, and requires one byte to store each character. The *Unicode* character set requires 2 bytes of storage, and it contains enough characters to support most of the world's languages. The standard character data type requires less space to store, and offers a greater compatibility with other systems. You should use Unicode data types whenever you may need to store international text.

You can choose to store character data in either a fixed-width or variable-length format. In a *fixed-width* format, an exact amount of space is allocated for the field in the table. In a *variable-length* field, a maximum size is set, but less data will take up less space. Variable-length fields require slightly more overhead to process than fixed width fields, due to their unpredictable nature. As a rule, fields that require fewer than 20 characters should be fixed length, whereas longer fields tend to save enough space when defined as variable length to justify the greater overhead. In any case, if the data to be stored requires more than 8,000 standard or 4,000 Unicode characters, you must use the text or ntext data type. These data types require noticeably greater overhead for SQL Server to process, but they can store 2GB of data.

Numeric data fields are used to store numbers. Numeric data types are much more efficient at storing numbers than are character data types. Therefore, wherever you can represent a column's data as numbers, you should probably use a numeric rather than a character type. (Recall, however, that social security numbers, telephone numbers, and ZIP codes are often better candidates for character fields than numeric, for the reasons stated previously. In most other cases however, numeric fields should be preferred.)

Beware of using short character codes for key fields. These types of identifying codes are common in mainframe environments where it was easier for operators to make read a mnemonic character code than it was to use an integer. In today's client-server environment, however, data is more often presented to a user through a graphical interface that can translate simple integer fields to human-readable text. Therefore, it is better to use a more efficient integer code that relates to a translation table containing a description field, than it is to use character codes for key fields.

User-Defined Data Types

SQL Server allows custom data types to be defined. *User-defined data types (UDTs)* help ensure that similar columns have the same data type, NULL option, default, and rule, and help document the database. A user-defined data type has the following characteristics:

◆ **Base type.** This defines the main SQL Server data type for the user-defined type (UDT).

◆ **NULL option.** Specifies the default NULL option for columns that use this user-defined type. The UDT NULL option can be overridden when a table is created or changed.

◆ **Rule.** A UDT may have a rule bound to it that defines a range of values acceptable for the column. For more information about rules, see Chapter 9, "Miscellaneous Programming Techniques."

◆ **Default.** A UDT can have a default bound to it that defines an initial value for the column. Default values are most often used with columns that do not allow NULLs. For more information about defaults, see Chapter 9.

Note that through the base type, user-defined data types always represent a type that could be represented as a real SQL Server data type, without the use of a UDT. User-defined data types simply allow a shorthand data type notation for a commonly used field.

UDTs may be added and deleted through Enterprise Manager, or by using the sp_addtype and sp_droptype system stored procedures. The stored procedures have a simple syntax defined as follows:

```
sp_addtype [@typename =] type,
       [@phystype =] system_data_type
       [, [@nulltype =] 'null_type']

sp_droptype [@typename =] 'type'
```

In both stored procedures, the @typename parameter represents the name of the UDT. The additional parameters allowed by the sp_addtype stored procedure define the system data type and the nullability of the UDT.

To create a user-defined data type through Enterprise Manager, follow Step by Step 3.1.

STEP BY STEP

3.1 Creating a User-Defined Data Type with Enterprise Manager

1. Start the SQL Enterprise Manager application.

2. In the left pane of Enterprise Manager, select the server that contains the database you want to work with. You might need to expand a server group first to find the server you want. Expand the tree view by clicking on the plus (+) sign to the left of the server name.

3. Expand the Databases folder by clicking the plus sign to the left of the folder icon. A list of all of the server's databases appears.

4. Select the database to which you wish to add the table. Click the plus sign to the left of the database icon to expand the tree view that contains the User-Defined Data Type node.

5. Click the User-Defined Data Type icon to display the UDTs already defined in your database. Any existing UDT can be selected by clicking it. You can drop the selected UDT by pressing the Delete key.

6. To add a new user-defined data type, right-click anywhere in the right pane to display the context menu. Choose the New User-Defined Data Type option, and the User-Defined Data Type Properties window is displayed, as shown in Figure 3.1.

7. In the Name field, type the name of the UDT you want to create.

8. Choose the base data type from the Data Type drop-down list box, and, if appropriate for the chosen data type, enter the length.

9. Use the Null check box to select whether you want the UDT to be nullable.

10. If you wish to associate an existing rule or default to the UDT, you can select it from the remaining drop-down list boxes.

11. Click OK to create the user-defined data type.

FIGURE 3.1
The User-Defined Data Type Properties window.

Managing Tables

▶ Create tables that enforce data integrity and referential integrity:

Choose the appropriate data types.

Create user-defined data types.

Define columns as NULL or NOT NULL.

Define columns to generate values by using the IDENTITY property, the uniqueidentifier data type, and the NEWID function.

Implement constraints.

After you are finished with defining the physical storage for a database (refer to Chapter 2, "Creating Physical Storage"), you can add tables and other objects to your database to implement the data model. Tables are used to store all of the data in a database and are the most structurally complex of all the database objects. The remainder of this chapter covers how tables are implemented in SQL Server, and how data integrity is maintained.

When working with tables, it is helpful to remember the following facts:

◆ Table names can be up to 128 characters in length, and must be unique in a database.

◆ A table can contain up to 1,024 columns, and the combined row length (sum of all of the bytes of storage for all columns) can be no more than 8,092 bytes.

◆ Column names must be unique within a table.

◆ A SQL Server database can contain up to two billion tables (although a database with this many tables would be difficult to administer).

Each column in a table has four important characteristics. The first is the column *name*; this identifies the column in the table. Next, the column *data type* specifies the type of information stored in the column. The column's NULL option defines whether the column can contain NULLs. Remember that the NULL value can be used in any data type to indicate an unknown value. Refer to the Chapter 1 section "Column Constraints" for more information. Finally, the column can have one or more *constraints* associated with it. Constraints are discussed later in the chapter. But first, take a closer look at managing tables in a more general sense: creating a table, modifying a table, and dropping a table.

Creating a Table

When you create a table, you are really defining the table's structure in terms of its columns. This can be done by using the Transact-SQL CREATE TABLE statement, or by using Enterprise Manager.

The CREATE TABLE statement can be rather complex. Because constraints, for example, haven't been discussed yet, a simplified version of the syntax is described here:

```
CREATE TABLE [database.[owner].]table_name (
 {col_name datatype [null_option]
 ¦ col_name AS computed_column_expression
 } [, ...]
)
[ON {filegroup ¦ DEFAULT} ]
[TEXTIMAGE_ON {filegroup ¦ DEFAULT} ]
```

The following list addresses this syntax:

◆ The col_name must follow the standard rules for identifiers.

◆ The datatype option specifies one of the standard SQL Server data types or a user-defined data type.

◆ The null_option in the syntax is either the keyword NULL or NOT NULL.

◆ The computed_column_expression represents a mathematical expression that can make use of other column names in the table and literals. This column is a virtual column for which no data is stored; rather the data is calculated according to the function supplied. The computed column can be used just like any other column except that it cannot be used in a constraint, and it cannot be the target of an INSERT or UPDATE statement.

◆ The optional ON parameters after the column definitions allow you to force the creation of the table or text and image data type columns in a specific file group. Because of the exceptional size of text and image data type columns, it is sometimes desirable to place the data for these columns in a separate file group. File groups are explained in Chapter 2.

To create a table using Transact-SQL, perform the tasks outlined in Step by Step 3.2.

> **NOTE**
>
> **Know the Setting of ANSI NULL Default** Enabling the ANSI NULL default database option causes table columns to allow NULLs if no NULL option is specified for the column.

STEP BY STEP

3.2 Creating a Table Using TSQL

1. Open the SQL Query Analyzer and log on to the server.

2. Select the database that contains the new table from the Database combo box.

3. Type the CREATE TABLE statement. In this example, a table named MyTable is created in the MyDatabase database with five columns. Note that the second column has no NULL option set, so it defaults to NOT NULL. The ON DEFAULT option is specified here to demonstrate the

continues

continued

syntax, but unless a file group other than the default is
specified there is really no reason to include this option:

```
CREATE TABLE MyDatabase..MyTable (
    ID int NOT NULL,
    LastName varchar(30) NOT NULL,
    MiddleInitial varchar(1) NOT NULL,
    FirstName varchar(30) NULL,
    TaxID int NOT NULL
)
ON DEFAULT
```

4. Execute the query by typing **Alt + X** or by clicking the
   Execute button on the toolbar. The table is added to the
   database.

To create a table in Enterprise Manager, perform the tasks outlined
in Step by Step 3.3.

STEP BY STEP

3.3 Creating a Table Using Enterprise Manager

1. In the left pane of Enterprise Manager, select the server
   that contains the database to which you want to add the
   table. You might need to expand a server group first to
   find the server you want. Expand the tree view by clicking
   the plus sign (+) to the left of the server name.

2. Expand the Databases folder by clicking the plus sign to
   the left of the folder icon. A list of all of the server's databases appears.

3. Select the database to which you want to add the table.
   Click the plus sign to the left of the database icon to
   expand the tree view. The resulting display looks similar
   to the one shown in Figure 3.2.

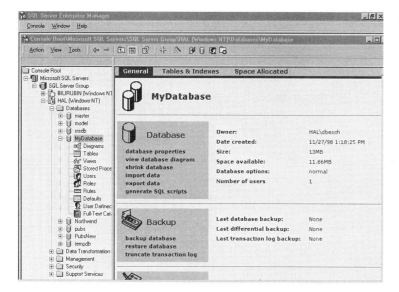

FIGURE 3.2
Navigating to the Tables folder for a database in Enterprise Manager.

4. Right-click the Tables folder so that the context menu appears. Select the New Table option. You are presented with the New Table window similar to the one presented in Figure 3.3.

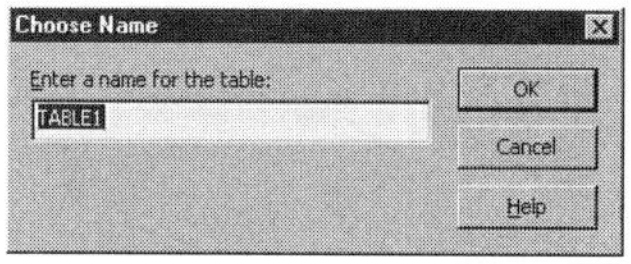

5. Enter a name for the new table in the Choose Name dialog box that appears. For this example, use the name MyTable, although any other name would work just as well.

6. Define each column for the table by typing a column name in the grid, selecting a data type, entering a data type length, precision, and scale (for some data types), and entering a NULL option. Note that you could also add a default value, and choose the Identity or IsRowGuid option. These extra options are discussed in later sections of this chapter. For this example, enter five columns as shown in Figure 3.4.

continues

FIGURE 3.3
The New Table window in Enterprise Manager.

continued

FIGURE 3.4
Columns defined in the New Table window.

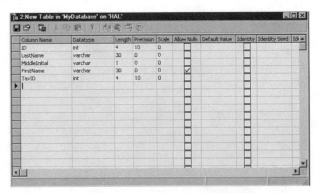

7. When you are done entering the columns for the table, click the Save button on the window's toolbar. The table is added to the database.

Modifying a Table

After you create a table, you can modify its structure by adding columns, and adding, changing, or removing constraints (constraints are covered in more detail later in the chapter). Be aware of one primary restriction when altering the columns in a table: You can add a new Identity column to the table if one does not exist, but you cannot change an existing column to an Identity column. (Identity columns are covered in more detail later in this chapter.)

A table can be modified by using the Transact-SQL ALTER TABLE statement or by using Enterprise Manager. Step by Step 3.4. shows you how to modify an existing table with the Transact-SQL ALTER TABLE statement.

> **EXAM TIP**
>
> **New Feature of SQL Server 7**
> The ability to drop a column or to change its data type is new to SQL Server 7.0. Because this was a highly requested and much-anticipated new feature, Microsoft wants to be sure you are familiar with it by including it on the test.

STEP BY STEP

3.4 Altering a Table Using TSQL

1. Open the SQL Query Analyzer and log on to the server.

2. Select the database that contains the new table from the Database combo box.

3. Type the ALTER TABLE command. The simplified syntax is as follows:

```
ALTER TABLE [database.[owner].]table_name {
 ALTER COLUMN col_name new_datatype [null_option]
¦ADD {col_name datatype [null_option]} [,...]
¦DROP {COLUMN col_name} [,...]
}
```

Constraints also can be defined in the ALTER TABLE statement—the syntax is covered later in this chapter. Every column must be named and have a data type defined.

4. For this example, first modify the MyTable table to add a column.

```
ALTER TABLE MyDatabase..MyTable
ADD SocialSecurityNumber varchar(11) NULL
```

Execute the query by typing **Alt + X** or by clicking the Execute Query button on the toolbar. The table is modified.

5. Now alter the existing MiddleInitial column to use the char data type, and to allow NULLs.

```
ALTER TABLE MyDatabase..MyTable
ALTER COLUMN MiddleInitial char(1) NULL
```

Execute the query by typing **Alt + X** or by clicking the Execute Query button on the toolbar. The table is modified.

6. Finally, drop the existing column TaxID.

```
ALTER TABLE MyDatabase..MyTable
DROP COLUMN TaxID
```

Execute the query by typing **Alt + X** or by clicking the Execute button on the toolbar. The table is modified.

Tables can also be modified from the Design Table window in Enterprise Manager (see Figure 3.5). Select the Tables folder for the database in the right pane of Enterprise Manager to see a list of tables in the left pane. Right-click the table you want to modify and choose Design Table.

FIGURE 3.5

The Design Table window of MyTable used to
change table structure.

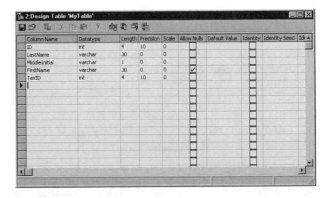

Dropping a Table

A table can be *dropped* (deleted) from a database by its owner, the
system administrator, or the DBO. When a table is dropped, all
data, indexes, triggers, and constraints associated with the table also
are deleted.

A table can be dropped by using Transact-SQL or by using
Enterprise Manager. To drop a table using Transact-SQL, perform
the tasks outlined in Step by Step 3.5.

STEP BY STEP

3.5 Dropping a Table Using TSQL

1. Open the SQL Query Analyzer and log on to the Server.

2. Select the database that contains the new table from the
Database combo box.

3. Type the DROP TABLE command. The syntax is as follows:

```
DROP TABLE <tablename>
```

For example, to drop a table named MyTable, type the
following:

```
DROP TABLE MyTable
```

4. Execute the query by typing **Alt** + **X** or by clicking the
Execute button on the toolbar. The table is dropped from
the database.

To drop a table by using Enterprise Manager, perform the tasks outlined in Step by Step 3.6.

STEP BY STEP

3.6 Dropping a Table Using Enterprise Manager

1. Navigate to the Tables folder for the database containing the table to drop, as explained in previous examples, including Step by Step 3.3.

2. Expand the Tables folder by clicking the plus sign to the left of the folder icon.

3. Select the table you want to drop, and right-click so the context menu appears. Select the Drop option, and the Drop Objects dialog box appears, as shown in Figure 3.6.

4. Click the Drop All button. The table is dropped from the database.

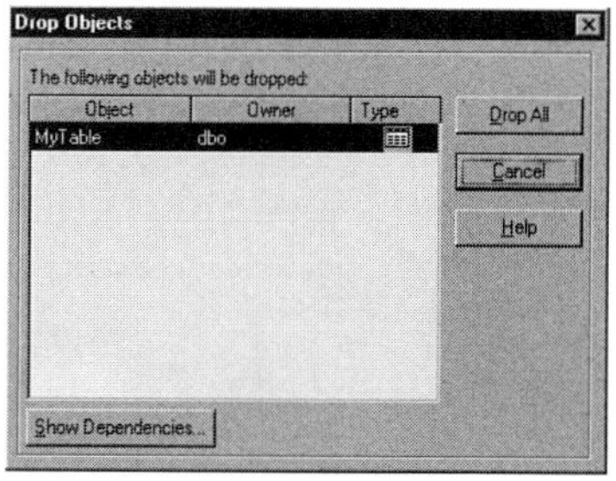

FIGURE 3.6
The Drop Objects dialog box in Enterprise Manager.

USING CONSTRAINTS

▶ Create tables that enforce data integrity and referential integrity:

> Choose the appropriate data types.
>
> Create user-defined data types.
>
> Define columns as NULL or NOT NULL.
>
> Define columns to generate values by using the IDENTITY property, the uniqueidentifier data type, and the NEWID function.
>
> Implement constraints.

Data integrity is an important concept to keep in mind when designing a database. *Data integrity* is a broad term that simply refers to the correctness of data in a database. One of the benefits of using SQL Server is that all of the data integrity rules can be defined in a central location—namely, the database. There are three main types of data integrity:

◆ **Entity integrity.** Recall from Chapter 1 that one of the requirements in a relational database design is the ability to distinguish different instances of an entity. This concept is known as *entity integrity*, and it is accomplished by creating a primary key in a table.

◆ **Domain integrity.** *Domain integrity* is concerned with ensuring that column values fall within an acceptable range of values (the *domain*). Domain integrity also refers to the data type and nullability of a column.

◆ **Referential integrity.** *Referential integrity* refers to the requirement that primary and foreign keys remain synchronized between parent and child tables.

SQL Server supports two different implementations of data integrity. *Procedural* data integrity, which is available in all versions of SQL Server, relies on views, triggers, stored procedures, defaults, and rules to enforce domain and referential integrity. Procedural data integrity is the most flexible, but incurs the most execution overhead and can be error-prone.

SQL Server 6.0 introduced constraints as a way to maintain *declarative* data integrity. Constraints provide a concise, consistent way to manage all three types of data integrity by extending the SQL syntax used to create and modify tables. In other words, the data integrity is declared when a table is created. Constraints are less error-prone and incur less execution overhead than procedural methods; however, constraints are somewhat less flexible.

There are no clearly defined rules for when one type of data integrity should be used rather than another. Usually, a mix of methods is used. The remainder of the chapter covers the different types of constraints and how they enforce each type of data integrity.

Managing Table Constraints

As mentioned previously, constraints can be created on a table when the table is initially defined. Another benefit of constraints is that they may be added or removed from the table without the need to drop or modify the table itself. Using the Transact-SQL CREATE TABLE and ALTER TABLE statements gives you the most flexibility in defining constraints, though you may find that using Enterprise Manager's Design Table window is easier.

When using constraints in a database implementation, be aware that constraint names must be unique in the database. If you do not explicitly assign a name to a constraint, SQL Server provides one.

N O T E   **System-Stored Procedures Can Show Table Constraints**   Use the system-stored procedure sp_help or sp_helpconstraint to see each constraint placed on a table.

Adding and Dropping Constraints with Transact-SQL

The previous discussions of the CREATE TABLE and ALTER TABLE statements excluded the syntax used to manage table constraints. This section shows you the full syntax diagram for each statement and gives examples of adding and dropping constraints on a table. More detailed Transact-SQL syntax is shown for each constraint type later in the chapter.

When using Transact-SQL statements to manage constraints, you declare constraints at either the column level or the table level. Where you declare the constraint has no bearing on how it functions; the syntax is merely different. Constraints that involve more than one column, however, must be declared at the table level.

Constraints are usually first declared when a table is created with the CREATE TABLE statement. Here is the full syntax for CREATE TABLE:

```
CREATE TABLE [database.[owner].]table_name (
  { column_name data_type [null_option] [col_constraint
  ➥[, ...]]
   ¦table_constraint
  } [,...]
)
[ON {filegroup ¦ DEFAULT} ]
[TEXTIMAGE_ON {filegroup ¦ DEFAULT} ]
```

Note that constraints may be declared in-line with the column definition, such as the following:

```
EmployeeSalary money not null CHECK (EmployeeSalary > 0)
DEFAULT 50000
```

This example defines both an unnamed (left to the system to supply) CHECK constraint and a DEFAULT constraint on the EmployeeSalary column. Both constraints are said to be defined at the column level.

NOTE

Column-Level Constraints Are Favored over Table Level Constraints
Typically, column-level constraints are used when possible because they make the CREATE TABLE statement easier to read.

Constraints declared at the table level can be interspersed with the column definitions, or can be included at the end of the column definitions in the statement. This example shows a PRIMARY KEY constraint and a UNIQUE constraint both declared at the table level:

```
CREATE TABLE Employee (
EmployeeID        int  IDENTITY,
PRIMARY KEY (EmployeeID),
FirstName         char(30),
LastName          char(30),
SocialSecNumber   char(11),
CONSTRAINT UQ_EmployeeSSN
UNIQUE (SocialSecNumber)
)
```

Typically, all table-level constraints are included at the end of the column list to improve readability. Note that in the preceding example, a name was explicitly assigned (UQ_EmployeeSSN) to the UNIQUE constraint on the social security number column.

You can use the ALTER TABLE statement to add or drop constraints after a table has been created. The full syntax of ALTER TABLE is as follows:

```
ALTER TABLE [database.[owner].]table_name [WITH CHECK ¦
➥WITH NOCHECK]{
 ALTER COLUMN col_name new_datatype [null_option]
➥[RowGUID_option]
¦ADD {[col_name datatype
[null_option][Identity_option][RowGUID_option][column_
➥constraints]]
       ¦[table_constraint]
     } [, ...]
¦DROP {COLUMN col_name ¦ [CONSTRAINT] constraint_name}
➥[,...]
¦ {CHECK ¦ NOCHECK} CONSTRAINT {ALL ¦ constraint[,...n]}
¦ {ENABLE ¦ DISABLE} TRIGGER {ALL ¦ trigger[,...n]}
```

You have already seen how to add columns by using the ALTER TABLE statement. When you add new columns with constraints, or add new table-level constraints, the syntax used to describe columns and constraints is exactly the same as the CREATE TABLE syntax.

Because there are many types of constraints, upcoming sections describe how to create each type independently. Dropping a constraint, however, is straightforward. All that is needed to drop a constraint is the name. Executing the following statement drops the UNIQUE constraint defined earlier on the Employee table:

```
ALTER TABLE Employee
DROP CONSTRAINT UQ_EmployeeSSN
```

Enabling and Disabling Constraints

When using the ALTER TABLE syntax, the tables you alter will likely already have data in them. It is possible that some of this data could be invalid for the constraints you add. For this reason, SQL Server automatically checks the existing data for correctness when adding FOREIGN KEY and CHECK constraints. In a table with a large set of data, these checks can take quite some time to perform, so SQL Server allows you to specify options that will disable these checks.

The WITH NOCHECK option in the ALTER TABLE statement disables constraint checking for new FOREIGN KEY and CHECK constraints being added. This enables these constraints to be added even if the existing data violates these constraints. Conversely, applying the WITH CHECK option, which is the default, explicitly applies the integrity constraints.

To disable an existing FOREIGN KEY or CHECK constraint for troubleshooting or bulk data modifications, use the NOCHECK CONSTRAINT option in the ALTER TABLE syntax. All that is needed is the name of the FOREIGN KEY or CHECK constraint to disable. The constraint will remain disabled until the CHECK CONSTRAINT option of the ALTER TABLE syntax is used. When a disabled CHECK or FOREIGN KEY constraint is re-enabled, SQL Server assumes a "WITH NOCHECK" by default and does not recheck existing data against the constraint.

The NOCHECK option has no effect on PRIMARY KEY, UNIQUE, or DEFAULT constraints.

Triggers can also be enabled or disabled by using the ENABLE TRIGGER or DISABLE TRIGGER options of the ALTER TABLE syntax. Triggers are discussed fully in Chapter 9.

Adding and Dropping Constraints with Enterprise Manager

Constraints can be added and removed from the Design Tables window in Enterprise Manager as well. When this window is first opened, it simply shows the columns in the table and their various properties. Clicking the Table and Index Properties button on the window's toolbar opens the Table and Index Properties dialog box, shown in Figure 3.7.

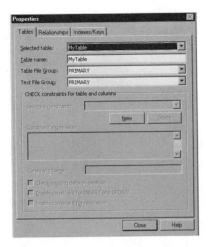

FIGURE 3.7
The Table and Index Properties dialog box in the Design Tables window.

The Table and Index Properties dialog box is used to manage every constraint type, except for defaults, which are managed from the grid containing the table columns and their properties, and Foreign Key constraints. Note that when you use Enterprise Manager to modify a table's constraints, you cannot name PRIMARY KEY or DEFAULT constraints, and you do not need to make a distinction between constraints declared at the column level or the table level.

Using an IDENTITY Column

Technically, the IDENTITY property for a column is not a constraint. Nevertheless, IDENTITY columns are often used to provide entity integrity, so they are included in this section.

An IDENTITY column is a special column in a table that provides a sequential, auto-incrementing number generated every time a record is inserted into the table. The number for a new row is determined by taking the last value in the column and adding an *increment* value supplied during the column's definition. In this fashion a unique value is guaranteed for each new entity inserted. Ensuring the uniqueness of entities is what entity integrity is all about. Keep the following in mind when using IDENTITY columns:

◆ A table can only have one IDENTITY column.

◆ The column must use an integer data type (*int*, smallint, or tinyint) or an exact numeric data type (*numeric* or *decimal*) with no fractional component. In other words, the column must contain only whole numbers.

◆ The column is automatically restricted from containing NULLs.

◆ The column cannot be updated.

Do not confuse an IDENTITY column with a column containing a timestamp. A new timestamp value is supplied when a column is inserted or updated. The IDENTITY column only supplies values when a row is inserted.

Creating an IDENTITY Column

An IDENTITY column is created when a table is created with the
CREATE TABLE statement, or when a table is modified via an ALTER
TABLE statement. Recall that the syntax for creating a column in
either one of these statements takes on the following form:

```
column_name data_type [null_option]
```

Adding the IDENTITY option into the syntax diagram gives you the
following:

```
column_name data_type [null_option] [IDENTITY
➥[(seed,increment)]]
```

The seed and increment values are optional. If one is specified, however, both must be specified. The *seed* value indicates what the value
of the IDENTITY column will be when the first row is inserted
into the table. The *increment* value specifies the step used to increment to the next value in the column. If these values are omitted,
then seed and increment both default to 1.

Following are some examples of CREATE TABLE statements using
IDENTITY columns:

1. This example creates a table with several columns. The first
   column, ID, is an IDENTITY column with seed and
   increment of 1:

   ```
   CREATE TABLE IdentityEx1 (
       ID          int          IDENTITY,
       FirstName   varchar(30)  NOT NULL,
       LastName    varchar(30)  NOT NULL
   )
   ```

2. This example shows how the seed and increment values are
   explicitly defined:

   ```
   CREATE TABLE IdentityEx2 (
       ID          int          IDENTITY(100,5),
       FirstName   varchar(30)  NOT NULL,
       LastName    varchar(30)  NOT NULL
   )
   ```

3. This example shows that the increment value can be a
   negative number:

   ```
   CREATE TABLE IdentityEx3 (
       ID          int          IDENTITY(0,-1),
       FirstName   varchar(30)  NOT NULL,
       LastName    varchar(30)  NOT NULL
   )
   ```

An IDENTITY column also can be added to a table in the Design Tables window in SQL Enterprise Manager.

Special Considerations for IDENTITY Columns

Tables with IDENTITY columns require some special considerations when inserting data. When inserting information into the table by way of the INSERT statement, the identity column should be omitted from the list of columns to insert. For example, to insert data into any of the three preceding sample tables, the syntax would be as follows:

```
INSERT IdentityEx1 (FirstName,LastName) VALUES
➥('John','Smith')
```

Note how the ID column is omitted from the INSERT statement. SQL Server automatically provides the value for this column when the row is inserted. See Chapter 7, "Modifying Data," for more information about the INSERT statement.

It is possible to query a table to determine the last identity value inserted into that table. This information is obtained by querying the value of the @@IDENTITY system function, as in the following example:

```
SELECT @@IDENTITY from IdentityEx1
```

This query returns the last identity value used in the IdentityEx1 table.

NOTE

The IDENTITY_INSERT Option It is possible to explicitly provide a value for an identity column when using the INSERT statement. Turning on the IDENTITY_INSERT option for the table enables you to explicitly enter values in an identity column. For more information about the IDENTITY_INSERT option, see the SQL Server Books Online.

Declarative Referential Integrity (DRI) Constraints

The *Declarative Referential Integrity (DRI)* constraints are used by SQL Server to enforce both entity and referential integrity. All referential integrity enforced with DRI constraints is restrictive. In other words, updates to key values are not permitted, parent records cannot be deleted if child records exist, and a child record cannot be inserted if its foreign key value does not match a parent's primary key value.

Note that it is possible to implement your data design without utilizing the DRI constraints available to you. As long as you can absolutely guarantee that *all* data put into your database is thoroughly checked for correctness, you can save a small amount of SQL Server's overhead during data modifications by eliminating DRI checks. However, your application developers may find it convenient to allow SQL Server to provide their integrity checks for them. In fact, in most cases, SQL Server can run these checks more efficiently than a remote application can. Microsoft has taken great pains to integrate DRI integrity checks directly into the query processor where they are done with maximum efficiency. For these reasons, DRI should be used in your data design in all but the most specialized cases.

In the following sections you will learn about Primary Key, and Unique constraints to provide entity integrity, and you will see how Foreign Key constraints use these to provide referential integrity.

PRIMARY KEY Constraint

The PRIMARY KEY constraint is used to enforce entity integrity because the primary key can be used to uniquely identify any row in a table. A PRIMARY KEY constraint may be created as a column level constraint (for single column keys) or as a table level constraint (for multiple column keys). Keep the following facts in mind when using a PRIMARY KEY constraint:

◆ Only one PRIMARY KEY constraint can be created per table.

◆ The column(s) participating in a primary key cannot enable NULLs. The key can be composed of up to 16 columns.

◆ A PRIMARY KEY constraint is enforced by creating a unique index on the key column(s). The type of index (clustered or non-clustered) can be specified when the constraint is defined; the default is a clustered index. The index cannot be dropped without dropping the constraint.

◆ A PRIMARY KEY constraint is required if the table will be referenced by a FOREIGN KEY constraint or if the table will be replicated.

The simplified syntax of the PRIMARY KEY constraint, when used with the CREATE TABLE or ALTER TABLE statement, is as follows:

```
[CONSTRAINT pk_name]
PRIMARY KEY [CLUSTERED ¦ NONCLUSTERED]
(column1 [,column2 [,...column16]])
```

Following are some examples of the syntax used to create this constraint:

1. This example creates a table with a column-level PRIMARY KEY constraint on the ID column. SQL Server provides a system name for the constraint, and the resulting index is clustered:

```
CREATE TABLE Employee
(
    EmployeeID int          IDENTITY PRIMARY KEY,
    FirstName  varchar(30)  NOT NULL,
    LastName   varchar(30)  NOT NULL,
    HireDate   datetime     NULL
)
```

2. This example creates a table with a table-level PK constraint on two columns. The name of the constraint is PK_EmployeeReview. The resulting index is clustered:

```
CREATE TABLE EmployeeReview
(
    EmployeeID      int        NOT NULL,
    ReviewDate      datetime   NOT NULL,
    PerformanceRank tinyint    NOT NULL,
    Comments        text       NULL,
    CONSTRAINT PK_EmployeeReview
        PRIMARY KEY (EmployeeID, ReviewDate)
)
```

3. This example is similar to example 2, except the resulting index is non-clustered:

```
CREATE TABLE EmployeeReview
(
    EmployeeID      int        NOT NULL,
    ReviewDate      datetime   NOT NULL,
    PerformanceRank tinyint    NOT NULL,
    Comments        text       NULL,
    CONSTRAINT PK_EmployeeReview
        PRIMARY KEY NONCLUSTERED (EmployeeID, ReviewDate)
)
```

A PRIMARY KEY constraint also can be added from the Design Tables window in SQL Enterprise Manager. Right-clicking on the row selector will show a context menu that allows you to set the primary key, as shown in Figure 3.8.

FIGURE 3.8
Setting a primary key through Enterprise Manager.

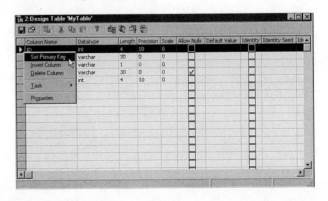

FOREIGN KEY Constraint

The FOREIGN KEY constraint is used to enforce referential integrity between tables. A FOREIGN KEY constraint can be created as a column-level constraint (for single-column foreign keys) or as a table-level constraint (for multiple column foreign keys). Keep these facts in mind when using an FOREIGN KEY constraint:

◆ A FOREIGN KEY must reference a PRIMARY KEY or UNIQUE constraint in the referenced table. The FOREIGN KEY may reference the same table (a recursive relationship) or another table in the same database. For cross-database referential integrity, use a trigger.

◆ The number of columns in the FOREIGN KEY must match the number of columns in the referenced PRIMARY KEY or UNIQUE constraints. In addition, the data types of each column must match.

◆ No index is automatically created on the column(s) participating in a foreign key. You should build an index on the FOREIGN KEY column(s) to improve the performance of queries using the FOREIGN KEY in a join.

Here is the simplified syntax of the FOREIGN KEY constraint as it is used with the CREATE TABLE or ALTER TABLE statement:

```
[CONSTRAINT fk_name]
[FOREIGN KEY (column1 [,column2 [,...column16]])]
REFERENCES referenced_table (ref_column1 [,ref_column2
➥[,...ref_column16]])
```

Following are examples of the syntax used to create this constraint:

1. This example creates the EmployeeReview table shown previously and adds the foreign key reference back to the Employee table. The FOREIGN KEY constraint has a system-supplied name:

```
CREATE TABLE EmployeeReview
(
    EmployeeID      int        NOT NULL REFERENCES
Employee (EmployeeID),
    ReviewDate      datetime   NOT NULL,
    PerformanceRank tinyint    NOT NULL,
    Comments        text       NULL,
    CONSTRAINT PK_EmployeeReview
      PRIMARY KEY (EmployeeID, ReviewDate)
)
```

(This example assumes that the Employee table has a PK or UNIQUE constraint on the EmployeeID column.)

2. This example shows how to define the same FK constraint shown in #1 as a table-level constraint:

```
CREATE TABLE EmployeeReview
(
    EmployeeID       int         NOT NULL,
    ReviewDate       datetime    NOT NULL,
    PerformanceRank  tinyint     NOT NULL,
    Comments         text        NULL,
    CONSTRAINT PK_EmployeeReview
        PRIMARY KEY (EmployeeID, ReviewDate),

    FOREIGN KEY (EmployeeID)
        REFERENCES Employee (EmployeeID)
)
```

3. This example shows how a recursive relationship is implemented. The Employee table self-references itself to model the employee-manager relationship. The constraint is given a name (FK_ManagerID) in this example:

```
CREATE TABLE Employee
(
    EmployeeID int          IDENTITY PRIMARY KEY,
    FirstName  varchar(30)  NOT NULL,
    LastName   varchar(30)  NOT NULL,
    HireDate   datetime     NULL,
    ManagerID  int          NULL,

    CONSTRAINT FK_ManagerID
    FOREIGN KEY (ManagerID)
        REFERENCES Employee (EmployeeID)
)
```

A FOREIGN KEY constraint also can be added from the Manage Tables window in SQL Enterprise Manager. The second of the Advanced Features tabs enables you to define a table's foreign key(s).

A FOREIGN KEY constraint cannot be created from the Design Tables window in SQL Enterprise Manager. Instead, FOREIGN KEY constraints are created using the Database Diagrams folder in the database. Step by Step 3.7 demonstrates how to implement, through Enterprise Manager, the recursive relationship on a table, Employee, described earlier.

STEP BY STEP

3.7 Creating a FOREIGN KEY Constraint in Enterprise Manager

1. Before a foreign key can be defined, you must create a table to work with. Create the following table either by executing the following command in a TSQL query tool, or by copying the relevant information to create an equivalent table in SQL Enterprise Manager:

```
CREATE TABLE Employee
(
    EmployeeID int         IDENTITY PRIMARY KEY,
    FirstName  varchar(30) NOT NULL,
    LastName   varchar(30) NOT NULL,
    HireDate   datetime    NULL,
    ManagerID  int         NULL,
)
```

2. Now use SQL Enterprise Manager to view the contents of the database you created the table in by expanding the database.

3. Right-click the Database Diagrams folder to show the context menu. Choose the New Database Diagram option as shown in Figure 3.9.

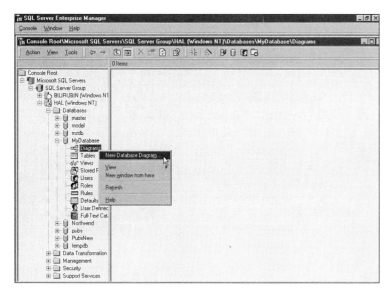

FIGURE 3.9
Choose the New Database Diagram option from the Database Diagrams context menu.

continues

continued

FIGURE 3.10
The Select Tables to be Added screen of the Create Diagram Wizard.

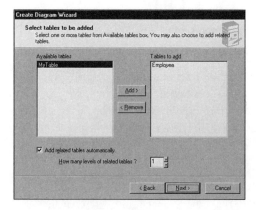

4. The Create Diagram Wizard appears. Click Next on the introductory screen to get to the Select Tables to be Added screen. Add the Employee table as shown in Figure 3.10 and then choose Next.

5. Choose Finish on the last screen of the wizard, and then confirm that the tables have been added and arranged on the diagram by clicking OK on the pop-up dialog box that follows.

6. You should see a diagram similar to the one shown in Figure 3.11. Click and hold on the row selection box for ManagerID that is on the left edge of the Employee table and drag the mouse off the left edge of the table. Drag the relationship onto the title bar of the Employee table.

7. By dragging the relationship from ManagerID to the Employee title bar you have indicated that you want to establish a relationship between the ManagerID field and the primary key of the Employee table. SQL Server then presents you with the Create Relationship dialog box as shown in Figure 3.12.

FIGURE 3.11
Database diagram of the Employee table.

8. SQL Server has supplied default values for all the parameters needed to create the relationship. You can change the name of the relationship or you can even completely redesign the relationship by changing the primary key table columns or the foreign key table columns.

9. There are three options available at the bottom of the Create Relationship dialog box. The first option (Check Existing Data on Creation) is analogous to the WITH CHECK or WITH NOCHECK options for the CREATE TABLE or ALTER TABLE statement, and can be unchecked to avoid the initial data integrity checks.

The second option, Enable Relationship for INSERT and UPDATE, allows you to disable the relationship just as though you had used the NOCHECK CONSTRAINT option of the ALTER TABLE syntax. Although the constraint will exist, it will not be enforced until it is re-enabled.

The third option, Enable Relationship for Replication, can be disabled to prevent the relationship from being enforced for data entered into the table by the replication process.

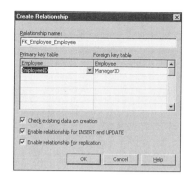

FIGURE 3.12
The Create Relationship dialog box.

UNIQUE Constraints

UNIQUE constraints are very similar to PRIMARY KEY constraints in that both are used to enforce entity integrity. There are a number of subtle differences between the two types of constraints, however:

◆ Only one PRIMARY KEY constraint can exist on a table, but multiple UNIQUE constraints can exist. UNIQUE constraints are usually used to define alternate keys on a table.

◆ UNIQUE constraints create an index just like PRIMARY KEY constraints, but the UNIQUE constraint's index defaults to being non-clustered.

◆ Columns participating in a UNIQUE constraint can contain NULLs.

The syntax to create a UNIQUE constraint is very similar to that of a PRIMARY KEY constraint:

```
[CONSTRAINT unique_constraint_name]
UNIQUE [CLUSTERED ¦ NONCLUSTERED]
(column1 [,column2 [,...column16]])
```

The above syntax is used in the same manner as when creating a PRIMARY KEY constraint. UNIQUE constraints also can be added from the Manage Tables window in SQL Enterprise Manager. The third of the Advanced Features tabs enables you to define UNIQUE constraints for the selected table.

Data Validation Constraints

Data validation constraints are used to enforce domain integrity in SQL Server by ensuring that columns have valid values. This is accomplished in one of two ways: by checking the column's value against a predefined rule (on insert and update), and by providing a default value for a column if a value is not specified (on insert).

CHECK Constraint

A CHECK constraint provides a way for SQL Server to validate the value in a column (or columns) when a row is inserted or updated. For instance, a CHECK constraint can be used to enforce the entry of a phone number field as (###) ###-####. Keep the following in mind when using CHECK constraints:

◆ The CHECK constraint's data validation rule must evaluate to a Boolean expression.

◆ CHECK constraints can only reference a single table, and they cannot use sub-queries.

◆ Unlike rules, CHECK constraints can reference other columns in the table.

◆ CHECK constraints can be created at the column or table level.

CHECK constraints can be created from the Table and Index Properties button on the Design Table window in Enterprise Manager. CHECK constraints also can be defined with Transact-SQL; the following is the simplified syntax of the CHECK constraint as it is used with the CREATE TABLE or ALTER TABLE statement:

```
[CONSTRAINT check_constraint_name]
CHECK (check_expression)
```

For example, this CREATE TABLE statement shows a data validation rule that forces the user to enter a formatted phone number. The CHECK constraint is declared at the table level and named CK_ValidPhone:

```
CREATE TABLE Employee
  (
EmployeeID int          IDENTITY,
FirstName  varchar(30)  NOT NULL,
LastName   varchar(30)  NOT NULL,
HireDate   datetime     NULL,
HomePhone  char(14)     NOT NULL,

CONSTRAINT CK_ValidPhone
CHECK (HomePhone LIKE '([0-9][0-9][0-9]) [0-9][0-9][0-9]-
➡[0-9][0-9][0-9][0-9]')
  )
```

DEFAULT Constraint

A DEFAULT constraint is used when rows are inserted into a table. If a column has a default constraint, and the user does not explicitly specify a value for the column, then the constraint's value is used instead. DEFAULT constraints are useful for providing values for columns that do not enable NULLs. Keep the following in mind when using DEFAULT constraints:

◆ Only one DEFAULT constraint can be defined per column.

◆ This constraint cannot be placed on an IDENTITY column, or a column that has a timestamp data type.

◆ DEFAULT constraints can be created at the column or table level.

DEFAULT constraints can be created in the Transact-SQL CREATE TABLE or ALTER TABLE statement. The basic Transact-SQL syntax for a DEFAULT constraint is as follows:

```
[CONSTRAINT default_constraint_name]
DEFAULT {constant_value ¦ niladic-function ¦ NULL}
[FOR column_name]
```

The constraint name is optional, and the FOR keyword need only be used when the constraint is declared at the table level. A default can consist of a constant value (such as the number 42 or the string abc), a NULL, or the result of a niladic function. A *niladic* function returns a value without accepting any parameters; examples include user_name() and getdate(), which return the database user's name and the current date, respectively.

You also can use the Design Table window in Enterprise Manager to add DEFAULT constraints to columns. The grid containing the table columns and their properties has a place to enter a default value for each column. Simply enter the default value in the space provided.

It is important to note that DEFAULT constraints are particularly important to columns with the UniqueIdentitfier data type. As was described earlier in the chapter, the UniqueIdentifier data type holds a 16-byte hexadecimal value. The values in this field are always supposed to be system supplied by using an algorithm that is guaranteed to generate values that are unique in the whole world. You can insert previously generated values from another source into a UniqueIdentifier field, but if you are using this field as a primary key, it should be set with the NewID() function. The NewID() function generates values according to the unique algorithm referred to earlier. By using the NewID() function in a DEFAULT constraint for a UniqueIdentifier column, you can automatically assign globally unique values to the column.

CASE STUDY: DERIVING A PHYSICAL DESIGN FROM A LOGICAL DATA MODEL

ESSENCE OF THE CASE

Here are the essential elements of the case:

- ▶ You must implement a logical database design.
- ▶ You must determine specific SQL Server data types.
- ▶ You must determine specific SQL Server constraints.

SCENARIO

You have developed a logical data model for a training company that will help track classes and student enrollment. This model has identified all of the entities, attributes, and relationships for the database, but the details about each attribute are not yet defined. Specifically, you still need to choose the data types and implement the constraints for the columns in the database.

ANALYSIS

This is a fairly broad task to tackle. Fortunately, it's also relatively straightforward. All the hard work of creating the data model is done, and the challenge of determining all relationships has been met. You should have an idea of what kind of data is expected in each field already; you just need to choose between the different integers, and the different character types, and so on.

The first thing you should do is identify any user-defined data type candidates. Common choices are phone numbers, Social Security numbers, and ZIP codes. Anywhere that you have the same kind of field appearing in multiple tables you have a candidate for a user-defined data type. Scan through your data model one table at a time to find such candidates and jot down the entity and attribute name as well as the base data type. Don't be too specific on the data type—you'll be coming back to that later. Simply noting integer, decimal, or character is good enough for now. When you are done, you should have several lists of similar attributes. Set this list aside until you've made all your data type choices in the rest of the data model.

continues

CASE STUDY: DERIVING A PHYSICAL DESIGN FROM A LOGICAL DATA MODEL

continued

Next, you'll need to start specifying the actual data types for your tables. To begin, pick the most central table you can find. In most data models there tend to be tables that sit in the center of a "web" with relations leading off to many tables. The choices you make in setting the data types and nullability of these central tables will tend to spill over and make the determinations in many other instances. Make your data type and nullability choices for each attribute in this table. Then check all the relationships and be certain that the data types match on both sides. While you are going through this process, attribute by attribute, you should explicitly define defaults, check constraints, and identity columns as well.

Keep the following in mind as you make your specific data type choices: When determining numeric values you want to choose the smallest type possible, while still erring on the side of caution. Remember that using a data type which is too small is the basis of the Y2K bug! For character data, a good rule of thumb is to use fixed length for expected lengths of less than 30 characters, and variable length for those over 30 characters. Remember that you have the choice of using Unicode character strings now as well.

When determining constraints, think about what would be an illegal value for an attribute. Those that have strict rules about what is and isn't allowed are good candidates for check constraints. Think also about attributes that are informational, or otherwise seldom used or known. Examples might be marital status, or a flag indicating whether a student is using a coupon to reduce his tuition. These attributes make good candidates for defaults. Primary keys, foreign keys and alternate keys should all be determined by the data model—these constraints are obvious. Watch for surrogate keys as well; these keys, which are just made-up numbers to uniquely identify rows in a table, are obvious candidates for Identity fields.

Repeat the process of determining the data types of the other "central" tables you identified and their immediate relationships. Eventually work your way down to smaller tables until you've completed the data model.

After you've made the data type and constraint choices for all attributes in the data model, you can apply a test for consistency by going back to your list of user-defined data type candidates. Make sure that all the like members on your list truly have the same data type and nullability. If any don't match, be sure you can isolate a good reason why. Go ahead and implement the remaining user-defined data types.

CHAPTER SUMMARY

In this chapter you have learned how to implement a database design in SQL Server. The concepts presented here have completed the ideas presented in Chapter 1. You should now be able to create tables to reflect the entities in your data model, and implement the attribute constraints and entity relationships. You were introduced to the data types SQL Server provides, and saw how these data types helped to accurately constrain the data for the table's columns.

KEY TERMS

Before you take the exam, make sure you are comfortable with the definitions and concepts for each of the following key terms:

- data type
- user-defined data type
- CREATE DATABASE
- ALTER DATABASE
- Constraint
- IDENTITY
- Entity Integrity
- Domain Integrity
- Relational Integrity

APPLY YOUR KNOWLEDGE

Exercises

The exercises in this chapter build on each other, and so are best done in sequential order.

3.1 Creating a Table

In Exercise 3.1, you create a table to store a company's employee information.

Estimated Time: 5 minutes

1. If it is not already loaded, open the SQL Query Analyzer and log on to your server.

2. Use the Database combo box to select your test database.

3. Type the following query in the query window:

```
CREATE TABLE Employee
(
    FirstName            varchar(30) NOT
➡NULL,
    LastName             varchar(30) NOT
➡NULL,
    MiddleInitial        char(1)  NULL,
    SocialSecurityNumber char(11) NOT NULL,
    HireDate             datetime NULL
)
```

4. Execute the query by typing **Alt + X** or by clicking the Execute Query button on the query window's toolbar. The Employee table is created.

5. In the query window, execute this query:

```
exec sp_help Employee
```

6. Check to see that the columns were created with the proper data types and NULL options.

3.2 Adding an IDENTITY Column to a Table

Exercise 3.2 walks you through the steps required to add an IDENTITY column (EmployeeID) to the Employee table you created in Exercise 3.1.

Estimated Time: 5 minutes

1. If it is not already loaded, open the SQL Query Analyzer and log on to your server.

2. Use the Database combo box to select your test database.

3. Type the following query in the query window:

```
ALTER TABLE Employee
ADD   EmployeeID   int   IDENTITY
```

4. Execute the query by typing **Alt + X** or by clicking the Execute Query button on the query window's toolbar. A new column called EmployeeID is added to the Employee table. The column is an IDENTITY column with a seed and increment of 1.

5. In the query window, execute this query:

```
exec sp_help Employee
```

6. Check to see that the IDENTITY column has been added.

3.3 Adding Constraints to a Table

In this exercise, you add three constraints to the Employee table you created in Exercise 3.1. EmployeeID will have a PRIMARY KEY constraint, and SocialSecurityNumber will have a DEFAULT constraint and a UNIQUE constraint.

Estimated Time: 5 Minutes

1. If it is not already loaded, open the SQL Query Analyzer and log on to your server.

2. Use the Database combo box to select your test database.

APPLY YOUR KNOWLEDGE

3. Type the following query in the query window:

```
ALTER TABLE Employee
ADD
    CONSTRAINT PK_Employee
        PRIMARY KEY (EmployeeID),
    CONSTRAINT UQ_SSN
        UNIQUE (SocialSecurityNumber),
DEFAULT '000-00-0000' FOR
SocialSecurityNumber
```

4. Execute the query by typing **Alt + X** or by clicking the Execute Query button on the query window's toolbar. The constraints are added to the table.

5. In the query window, execute this query:

```
exec sp_help Employee
```

Notice that the three constraints show up in the results. The PRIMARY KEY and UNIQUE constraints show the names specified in step 3, and the DEFAULT constraint has a system-supplied name. Note also that the table has two new indexes to enforce the PRIMARY KEY and UNIQUE constraints.

3.4 Implementing a Relationship Using a FOREIGN KEY Constraint

Exercise 3.4 walks you through the process of building a new table, EmployeeCertification, which will store information about an employee's professional certifications. The table is a child of the Employee table and has a relationship enforced by a FOREIGN KEY constraint.

Estimated Time: 5 minutes

1. If it is not already loaded, open the SQL Query Analyzer and log on to your server.

2. Use the Database combo box to select your test database.

3. Type the following query in the query window:

```
CREATE TABLE
        EmployeeCertification
(
    EmployeeID          int       NOT NULL
REFERENCES Employee(EmployeeID),
    CertificationTestNumber  char(5)   NOT NULL,
    DateTestPassed           datetime  NOT NULL,
    PRIMARY KEY (EmployeeID,
CertificationTestNumber)
)
```

4. Execute the query by typing **Alt + X** or by clicking the Execute Query button on the query window's toolbar. The new table is created. The first two columns are the primary key, and the EmployeeID column references the EmployeeID column in the Employee table.

5. In the query window, execute this query:

```
exec sp_help EmployeeCertification
```

Notice the two constraints on the table. Because the preceding query did not specify constraint names, system-supplied names will be used. Notice also that the index created on the primary key is clustered.

Review Questions

1. What data type should you use to store a comment field in a table in which the user is allowed to enter comments of arbitrary length?

2. What are the uses of user-defined data types?

3. What are the advantages and disadvantages of unicode data types?

4. Explain how an identity column works.

5. Describe the meaning of the seed and increment values of the Identity property.

APPLY YOUR KNOWLEDGE

6. Contrast the UNIQUE constraint and the PRIMARY KEY constraint.

7. How is a UNIQUE constraint enforced?

8. Name the two main categories of constraints.

9. What are the advantages of using constraints rather than triggers, defaults, or rules?

Exam Questions

1. What are the Transact-SQL commands used to create and delete user-defined data types?

    A. CREATE UDDT and DROP UDDT

    B. sp_bindtype and sp_droptype

    C. sp_addtype and sp_droptype

    D. sp_addtype and sp_unbindtype

2. What are some benefits of user-defined types? Select all that apply.

    A. UDTs give SQL Server the flexibility to store future data types.

    B. UDTs help document a database.

    C. UDTs provide consistent column properties for similar columns.

    D. UDTs help enforce column naming conventions.

3. Data types are used to define which of the following? Select all that apply.

    A. The type of information stored in a table's column

    B. The type of information used in a local variable

    C. The type of information passed between triggers and tables

    D. The type of information used in a stored procedure's parameters

4. SQL Server maintains what types of information about a column in the table definition?

    A. Name, NULL option, and constraints

    B. Name, data type, and NULL option

    C. Name, data type, NULL option, and bytes of overhead

    D. Name, data type, NULL option, and constraints

5. Which statement is *not* true about tables and columns?

    A. A table can contain up to 1024 columns.

    B. Column names must be unique within the database.

    C. Table and column names can be up to 128 characters in length.

    D. A table definition is really just a collection of column definitions.

6. When altering the structure of a table, which of the following rules apply? Select two answers.

    A. New columns can be added with either NULL option.

    B. New columns can be added only if they allow NULLs.

    C. An existing column can be converted to an IDENTITY column.

D. Columns of the `timestamp` data type cannot be added.

E. A new IDENTITY column can be added if one does not already exist.

7. What is the purpose of the `WITH NOCHECK` option in the `ALTER TABLE` statement?

A. All constraint checking is disabled to improve performance.

B. Constraint checking is turned off for the table until turned back on with the `WITH CHECK` keywords.

C. `PRIMARY KEY` and `UNIQUE` constraints are not checked for the duration of the table modification.

D. `CHECK` and `FOREIGN KEY` constraints are not checked for the duration of the table modification.

8. What are the three main types of data integrity implemented by SQL Server constraints?

A. Domain integrity

B. Attribute integrity

C. Entity integrity

D. Referential integrity

E. Data type integrity

9. How is a NOT NULL column added to an existing table?

A. By using the `ALTER TABLE` statement

B. By dropping and recreating the table

C. By using `ALTER TABLE` to add a nullable column, then using `sp_changenull` to change the column's `NULL` option

10. What are the benefits of procedural data integrity implemented using views, triggers, rules, and defaults? Select all that apply.

A. Fewer error-prone than constraints

B. Lower execution overhead than constraints

C. Cross-database referential integrity

D. Maximum flexibility in handling data integrity violations

11. Which of the following statements about `PRIMARY KEY` constraints are true? Select all that apply.

A. They are implemented via a unique index.

B. The key column(s) allow `NULL`s.

C. They enforce entity integrity.

D. The constraint's index is clustered by default.

12. A `FOREIGN KEY` constraint requires what types of constraints in the referenced table? Select all that apply.

A. `PRIMARY KEY`

B. `CHECK`

C. `FOREIGN KEY`

D. `UNIQUE`

13. Which of the following statements applies when a constraint is declared at the column level?

A. It has a lower execution overhead than a constraint declared at the table level.

B. It only applies to that column.

C. The `WITH NOCHECK` option must be used.

D. No other constraints can be defined for that column.

APPLY YOUR KNOWLEDGE

14. How does an administrator replace a missing row in a table with an IDENTITY column?

    A. By turning on the IDENTITY_INSERT option for the table and inserting a record with an explicit IDENTITY value

    B. By executing sp_insert_identity on the table

    C. By using sp_dboption to configure the database so that identity columns may be updated

    D. By dropping and re-creating the table, then inserting the old records in the correct order

15. Steve works at an auto parts distributor. He maintains a database that tracks, among other things, products and suppliers. Currently, the database maintains a supplier ID for every product that Steve's business sells. Steve needs to modify the database to list all possible suppliers to every product. To do this, he knows he will have to drop the supplier ID from the Products table, and then add a new table, ProductSupplier, that will allow a Many-to-Many join between product and supplier. He writes the following script to make the changes:

```
ALTER TABLE Products
DROP        Constraint FK_Products_Suppliers,
Column SupplierID
GO

CREATE TABLE ProductSupplier (
    ProductID int NOT NULL References
Products(ProductID),
    SupplierID int NOT NULL References
Suppliers(SupplierID),
    Primary Key (ProductID, SupplierID)
)
GO
```

Rate the solution as one of the following:

    A. This is an optimal solution. It not only performs the necessary changes, but it also fully implements referential integrity.

    B. This is a good solution. All necessary changes are completed.

    C. This is a poor solution. The script stops short of implementing all necessary changes.

    D. This is not a solution. This script contains bogus commands and does not form valid TSQL statements.

Answers to Review Questions

1. Any time character data of arbitrary length is used, you should consider using a text data type. Keep in mind, however, that even an ordinary char data type can hold up to 8,000 characters, which should be adequate for most cases. For data with a truly arbitrarily large size, however, the text data type will accommodate 2GB of data. (For more information, refer to the section "Understanding Data Types.")

2. User-defined data types help document a database by providing consistent data types and properties to similar fields. (For more information, refer to the section "User-Defined Data Types.")

3. Unicode data types allow a broad range of characters to be used in a string, most notably characters from international languages. The drawback of Unicode data is that each character requires twice the storage space of regular character data, and that older applications and utilities cannot read the new Unicode data of SQL Server 7.0. (For more information, refer to the section "Understanding Data Types.")

4. An identity column is automatically populated during an insert to the table. The numbers used are monotonically increasing integers, although

APPLY YOUR KNOWLEDGE

you are not guaranteed that no numbers will be skipped. When an INSERT statement in a transaction is rolled back, the Identity value assigned is lost and will not be reused. (For more information, refer to the section "Using an IDENTITY Column.")

5. The seed value specifies the starting number for the auto-increment, and the increment value specifies the step used to increment to the next value. (For more information, refer to the section "Using an IDENTITY Column.")

6. Unique columns allow NULL values, whereas primary key columns do not. (For more information, refer to the section "Declarative Referential Integrity (DRI) Constraints.")

7. Both UNIQUE and PRIMARY KEY constraints are enforced through the use of unique indexes. (For more information, refer to the section "Declarative Referential Integrity (DRI) Constraints.")

8. The two main categories of constraints are as follows: Declarative Referential Integrity (DRI) constraints, which are used to enforce entity integrity and referential integrity, and Data Validation constraints, which are used to enforce domain integrity. (For more information, refer to the sections "Declarative Referential Integrity (DRI) Constraints" and "Data Validation Constraints.")

9. Constraints have lower execution overhead than triggers, defaults, or rules, and tend to be less error-prone. (For more information, refer to the section "Using Constraints.")

Answers to Exam Questions

1. **C.** SQL Server provides the system-stored procedures sp_addtype and sp_droptype to add and drop user-defined data types. User-defined data types are not "bound" in any way, nor is there a CREATE and DROP TSQL syntax for them. (For more information, refer to the section "User-Defined Data Types.")

2. **B, C.** User-defined data types do not provide for future data types; rather, they are built only from existing data types. User-defined data types also do not have any effect on column names. They can, however, help document a database by providing consistent data types and properties to similar fields. (For more information, refer to the section "User-Defined Data Types.")

3. **A, B, D.** Columns, variables, and the parameters of stored procedures are all assigned data types. Triggers are not passed information from tables; they operate directly on the information they collect from any part of the database. (For more information, refer to the section "Understanding Data Types.")

4. **D.** SQL Server needs to know a column's name, data type, NULL option, and what constraints are applied against the column. (For more information, refer to the section "Managing Table Constraints.")

5. **B.** Column names must be unique within a table, but not within an entire database. The maximum columns per table are 1024, and the length of an identifier is 128 characters. All information about a table can be applied to one or more of that table's columns; in this sense a table represents the grouping of individual columns. (For more information, refer to the section "Creating a Table.")

APPLY YOUR KNOWLEDGE

6. **A, E.** Unlike earlier versions of SQL Server, NOT NULL columns can be added to a table as well as NULL columns. Whereas an existing column cannot be turned into an Identity column, a new Identity column can be added to the table if one does not already exist. (For more information, refer to the section "Modifying a Table.")

7. **D.** When the WITH NOCHECK option is invoked in the ALTER TABLE statement, FOREIGN KEY and CHECK constraints that are created will not be checked for initial accuracy. (For more information, refer to the section "Modifying a Table.")

8. **A, C, D.** Entity integrity ensures that entities can be distinguished from one another, domain integrity ensures that values for a column fall into an acceptable range, and referential integrity ensures that entities relate to each other accurately. (For more information, refer to the section "Using Constraints.")

9. **A.** Using the ALTER TABLE statement allows you to add columns with any nullablility to a table. It would be possible to drop and re-create the entire table to accomplish this task, and this was in fact the only way to accomplish the goal in previous versions, but it would be exceedingly wasteful. There is no sp_changenull system stored procedure in SQL Server. (For more information, refer to the section "Modifying a Table.")

10. **C, D.** Using procedural validation is more error prone due to its complexity and flexibility and it requires more overhead to run the coded checks. The flexibility, however, is what makes procedural validation worthwhile in some cases. (For more information, refer to the section "Using Constraints.")

11. **A, C, D.** Primary keys enforce uniqueness, and do not allow NULLs, both of which apply to entity integrity. It is true that PRIMARY KEY constraints are enforced by indexes, and default to clustered indexes. (For more information, refer to the section "PRIMARY KEY Constraint.")

12. **A, D.** A FOREIGN KEY constraint must reference either a PRIMARY KEY or a UNIQUE key in the referenced table. (For more information, refer to the section "FOREIGN KEY Constraint.")

13. **B.** However a constraint is defined, it runs the same in the end. The WITH NOCHECK option is never required to add a constraint, and many constraints can be added to a column at a time. (For more information, refer to the section "Using Constraints.")

14. **A.** Using the IDENTITY_INSERT option allows explicit values to be entered into the identity column of a table. (For more information, refer to the section "Using an IDENTITY Column.")

15. **A.** The scripts presented not only implement the needed changes, but also set up referential integrity by placing a FOREIGN KEY constraint on both columns of the new table. Note that it also correctly drops the existing FOREIGN KEY constraint on the SupplierID column in the Products database before it attempts to drop the column itself. (For more information, refer to the section "Modifying a Table" and "Managing Table Constraints.")

APPLY YOUR KNOWLEDGE

Suggested Readings and Resources

We recommend the following resources for further study in the area of planning:

1. SQL Server Books Online

   - data types

2. Transact-SQL Help File

   - CREATE TABLE

   - ALTER TABLE

   - sp_addtype

   - sp_droptype

This chapter helps you to prepare for the Microsoft exam by covering the following objectives:

Create and maintain indexes.

- **Choose an indexing strategy that will optimize performance.**

- **Given a situation, choose the appropriate type of index to create.**

- **Choose the column or columns to index.**

- **Choose the appropriate index characteristics, specifically FILLFACTOR, DROP_EXISTING, and PAD INDEX.**

▶ The type of database system you have will affect your indexing strategy. For example, if your database is used for online analytical processing (OLAP), you will want to make extensive use of indexes to speed data retrieval. If instead your database is used more for online transaction processing (OLTP), you will want to choose fewer indexes so there is less overhead slowing your high insert and update traffic.

▶ You should understand when to use a clustered rather than a non-clustered index in particular. It is also important to choose unique indexes where appropriate.

▶ Certainly the most important factor to an index is the data that is being indexed. You should be able to choose which columns of your table to index to get the performance you expect.

CHAPTER 4

Indexing

▶ The CREATE INDEX statement has a number of optional settings that let you fine tune the indexes behavior. In order to fully understand how to create and manage indexes, you need to understand all aspects of the CREATE INDEX statement.

Implement full-text search.

▶ You'll need to be able to configure a database, table, and columns for full-text searches, and be able to write queries that perform full-text searches.

▶ First, be sure you fully understand how indexes work, and how SQL Server uses them. You'll need to understand when you can expect SQL Server to use a particular index and when you can't. Remember that a table that is too small won't benefit from an index, and that an index on two columns won't be used to search the second item alone.

Next, learn the syntax of the CREATE INDEX statement. It's more important to fully learn the syntax of the Transact-SQL statement than it is to be able to use Enterprise Manager for the test. After you know the statement syntax, the options in Enterprise Manager will be intuitive and easy to use.

Finally, learn all about full-text searches. Remember that full-text searches are done through the Microsoft Search service. Although this service is well integrated with SQL Server, it is not a part of SQL Server itself.

Be sure to learn the purpose of the full-text stored procedures. There are five of them to correspond to the five levels of configuration behind full-text searching: Server, Database, Catalog, Table, and Column. Learn the uses of the CONTAINS and FREETEXT predicates, but don't get too caught up in every detail of the syntax.

INTRODUCTION

Indexes are an important part of any database implementation. Properly indexed tables allow SQL Server to quickly and efficiently access the data in a database. On the other hand, improperly indexed tables, although they might not slow SQL Server, can consume unnecessary space in the database. Understanding and applying the indexing options available to you is therefore vital not only for passing the test, but also for having a well-functioning database.

Full-text searches do not use standard database indexes, but rather implement a proprietary indexing scheme that is actually stored outside the database. Nonetheless, these indexes that support full-text searches require the same kind of planning to be properly applied. After full-text searching is completely set up, there are special commands implemented in Transact-SQL to implement full-text searches. Learning these commands allows you to perform extremely complex text searches against your data.

This chapter covers the information you need to know for the test and for effectively implementing indexing in a database. It starts with several sections that introduce you to SQL Server indexes and how they work, then progresses to discussions on implementing these indexes. The chapter concludes with a full discussion on implementing and running full-text searches. The topics include the following:

◆ Introduction to indexes

◆ Types of indexes

◆ Guidelines for indexing

◆ Managing indexes with Transact-SQL

◆ Managing indexes with Enterprise Manager

◆ Implement full-text search

INTRODUCTION TO INDEXES

Indexes are extremely beneficial if they are used properly in a database. Following are some of the advantages of using indexes:

◆ Indexes give SQL Server a much quicker path to any particular row in a table. Without an index, SQL Server must perform a search through all of the rows in a table.

◆ Indexes can enforce entity integrity (see Chapter 1, "Database Design") by guaranteeing that rows are not duplicated in a table.

◆ Indexes can improve the performance of queries that use joins to retrieve data from two or more tables. (See Chapter 6, "Retrieving Data," for more information about joins.)

◆ Indexes are always created in ascending order, based on the sort order of the database. (The sort order is determined when the SQL Server is installed. See New Riders' *MCSE Training Guide: SQL Server 7.0 Administration* for more information.) Because the rows are indexed in ascending order, they can be used to physically sort the rows in a table and greatly improve the performance of queries that use the ORDER BY clause.

Because indexes are so helpful, you might wonder why it is not advisable to index every column in every table. Well, the primary reason is that indexes can actually slow down the performance of queries that update data. SQL Server dynamically updates the index(es) on a table whenever the data in that table is changed. Indexes also consume space in the database, and take time to create. Maintaining many indexes on a large table can be impractical.

So, what exactly is an *index*? Indexes serve much the same purpose as a library's card catalog. A card catalog provides multiple ways to look up a book in a library. Books are listed alphabetically by title or author on index cards for easy searching, then the card provides a Dewey decimal number that enables you to quickly find the book in the library's stacks. Indexes in SQL Server are implemented in much the same way; SQL Server maintains an ordered list of the rows in a table so it may look them up quickly. The arrangement of the index information is based on the index's *key*—this is the column or columns in the table that SQL Server uses to perform the lookup. A card catalog also has a key; books can be indexed by title or author name, for instance.

SQL Server indexes differ from a card catalog in structure if not in function. Information in an index is arranged in a tree-like structure to increase the speed of searches performed with the index. At the top of the index tree is the *root* of the index. Starting at the root, SQL Server follows a path down through the levels of the index (the *non-leaf* pages) to get to the *leaf* pages, which then reference the actual data rows. A library card catalog can be thought of as an index with two levels. The first level is the labeling on the drawers of the catalog, which enables you to pick the correct drawer, perhaps for author names beginning with the letter B. You then refine your search by browsing through the index cards in the drawer. The card you are looking for points you to the correct book.

TYPES OF INDEXES

▶ Create and Maintain Indexes.

- Choose an indexing strategy that will optimize performance.

- Given a situation, choose the appropriate type of index to create.

- Choose the column or columns to index.

- Choose the appropriate index characteristics, specifically FILLFACTOR, DROP_EXISTING, and PAD INDEX.

SQL Server has two major types of indexes—clustered and non-clustered—that differ slightly in the way they are implemented. Indexes also can be created to permit only unique key values or can be created on more than one column.

Clustered Indexes

In a *clustered index*, the data pages of the table and the leaf pages of the index are one and the same. This reduces the number of jumps that SQL Server must make from the leaf page of the index to the appropriate data page in the table and has the added effect of physically sorting the rows by the index's key. Figure 4.1 shows a graphical representation of a clustered index.

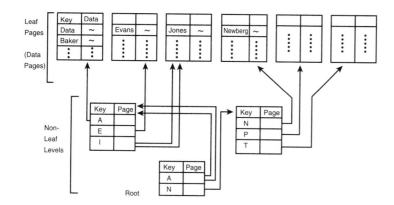

FIGURE 4.1
The structure of a clustered index.

Figure 4.1 shows how a table of authors might be indexed by authors' last names. At the top of the diagram are the table's data pages, which show several rows of data, keyed by authors' last names. Remember that because this is a clustered index, these pages also are the leaf pages of the index. On the next few levels of the index, the index pages contain key values and pointers to the next level of the index. Note how the index tapers off to the root index page.

To find the author *Jones*, for example, SQL Server would follow these steps:

1. *Jones* begins with a J, so SQL Server follows the left branch of the index. (The index is created in ascending order, and J comes before N).

2. The next page contains three values: A, E, and I. J comes after I, so SQL Server follows the rightmost branch from that page.

3. This path takes it to the data page, where SQL Server looks through the rows until it finds Jones.

Note that (unless the table is small) SQL Server looks at fewer pages when using an index than when scanning through every row in the table.

When you are creating a clustered index, keep the following in mind:

◆ Only one clustered index can be created per table.

◆ The leaf pages are the table's data pages, and the rows are physically stored in order according to the index key.

◆ Clustered indexes are smaller than non-clustered indexes. However, you need enough room in the database (about 1.2 times the original table's size) to initially create a clustered index.

For more information about when a clustered index should be chosen over a non-clustered index, see the later section "Guidelines for Indexing."

Non-Clustered Indexes

A *non-clustered index* works with a tree structure very much like a clustered index. The real difference comes when you get to the leaf pages. The leaf pages of a non-clustered index work very differently depending on whether there is a clustered index on the table. If there is no clustered index, the leaf pages of a non-clustered index point directly to the page and offset where the actual data can be found. However, if there is a clustered index on the table, the leaf pages of a non-clustered index contain the clustered key value of the row being sought. Thus, to find a row by reading a non-clustered index, SQL Server will also have to search through the clustered index on the table, if one exists. While this sounds like an odd way to do things, it has actually been found to be very efficient.

When the leaf pages of a non-clustered index point directly to a data page and offset, the index will need to be partially rebuilt every time a data page splits, or in some way changes. This results in quite a bit of overhead for the server. Clustered indexes do not suffer this penalty because they are part of the data pages. As the data pages change, the clustered index automatically represents the changes. Therefore, if non-clustered indexes can use clustered index references, they will not need to be reorganized when data pages change, because they use non-changing clustered index references. This reduction of overhead on the server has a beneficial impact on overall query performance.

When you are creating a non-clustered index, keep the following in mind:

◆ Up to 249 non-clustered indexes can exist on a table. Remember that some constraints create indexes, and these count against that total.

◆ The logical order of the rows as defined by the index's key is different than the physical order of the data.

◆ Because non-clustered indexes use clustered key references when they exist, create a clustered index before creating any non-clustered indexes. Otherwise, all non-clustered indexes will need to be rebuilt so that the leaf pages contain the new clustered key references.

◆ Non-clustered indexes are larger than clustered indexes because of the extra set of leaf pages. However, building a non-clustered index requires significantly less space than building a clustered index because the table does not need to be copied and sorted.

For more information about deciding which index should be clustered and which should be non-clustered, see the later section "Guidelines for Indexing."

Composite Indexes

A *composite index* is simply an index that has more than one column in its key. Composite indexes are helpful when you plan to write queries that search for rows based on all of the values in multiple columns, such as an author's last name and first name. Keep the following in mind when building and using composite indexes:

◆ Up to 16 columns can be used in an index. The combined size of the columns cannot exceed 900 bytes.

◆ The order in which the columns are used in the index is very important. An index of authors' last names and first names is not the same as an index of authors' first names and last names.

◆ SQL Server doesn't use the composite index unless the first column in the key is specified. So, specifying only an author's first name as criteria on a table with a last/first name index will not use the index. For this example, the index is used if you specify a last name as criteria, or both the last name and first name as criteria.

◆ When building a composite index, use the column with the widest range of values (the most unique) as the first column. This helps SQL Server narrow a search more quickly.

A composite index can be created as either a clustered or non-clustered index, subject to the requirements previously described for each. As a rule, however, keep in mind that a side benefit of indexes is that they tend to contain information on fewer columns than the base table. A small index row size allows more rows to fit on a page, which can reduce the number of pages that SQL Server has to scan to find the data it is looking for. Although a composite index spanning every column in a table is legal, and can improve searches run on the table, this use of composite indexes will eliminate the benefit of reduced row size and so should be used carefully.

Unique Indexes

A *unique index* has an additional requirement placed on its key values—namely, that the values must be unique within a table. Unique indexes are how SQL Server enforces PRIMARY KEY and UNIQUE constraints for entity integrity (Chapter 1 and Chapter 3, "Implementing a Physical Design," discuss entity integrity in more detail).

When you insert into a table with a unique index or update a table with a unique index, SQL Server checks the new key value against all other key values in the table. If the new key value duplicates an existing value, SQL Server disallows the insert or update.

When creating a unique index on a column that permits NULL values, no single column or multiple columns (as in a composite index) can contain NULLs in more than one row. SQL Server treats NULL values as distinctly unique value when used in an indexed column.

R E V I E W   B R E A K

Index Types

In this last section you have seen different types of indexes that SQL Server supports. The most important distinction to an index is whether it is clustered or non-clustered. The clustering type affects the very structure of the index, whereas the composite and unique types simply describe details of the index. Remember that clustered indexes physically order the data of the table itself, which is why there can only be one per table. Non-clustered indexes merely point to the actual rows either through direct pointers, or by storing the clustered key value if one exists. Composite indexes are indexes which are made on more than one column, and unique indexes provide automatic checking that the indexed column or columns values are unique.

Now that you understand the types of indexes that you can create, you are ready to explore some theory on how to decide which indexes to use in different situations. Then you will be ready to look at how to actually implement indexes in your database.

GUIDELINES FOR INDEXING

▶ Create and maintain indexes.

- Choose an indexing strategy that will optimize performance.

- Given a situation, choose the appropriate type of index to create.

- Choose the column or columns to index.

- Choose the appropriate index characteristics, specifically FILLFACTOR, DROP_EXISTING, and PAD INDEX.

There are no hard and fast rules for when you should or should not create an index, but there are some pretty good rules of thumb that you can follow. First, you should create indexes only for those columns that are used in queries. The lname column in the employee table might be a good candidate for an index, but if it is never used (or very infrequently used) in queries it should not be indexed.

Second, indexes should be chosen that are *selective*. SQL Server works best with indexes that narrow its search quickly. For example, if you were to index a table containing a listing of Kansas City's residents, indexing on last name would probably be a good idea. Even for a common name like Jones, the number of rows returned (perhaps 25,000) would be small in comparison to the total number of rows in the table (perhaps 1.3 million). The selectivity in this example is around 2 percent—finding all people with the surname Jones returns only about 2 percent of the table.

On the other hand, indexing on a column that is not very unique (such as gender) is useless to SQL Server. If we assume that Kansas City's distribution of women and men is roughly equal, then about half of the table will be returned if SQL Server tries to narrow its search with the index on gender.

Choosing Which Columns to Index

Here are some guidelines for choosing which columns to include in an index:

◆ Primary keys and foreign keys should nearly always be indexed. This provides SQL Server with the most number of methods to perform the join.

◆ Create indexes on columns that you often search on—in other words, columns often used in the WHERE clause of a query.

◆ Create indexes that cover the query. This is an index in which all the data usually retrieved from a query is held within the composite index.

◆ Create indexes on columns that are often searched for a range of values, like datetime fields.

◆ Create indexes on columns that are often used to sort the results of a query (those columns often included in an ORDER BY clause).

Knowing which columns to index is important. Equally important is knowing what type of index to create.

Choosing an Index Type

Keep the following in mind when you are choosing the type of index you will be creating:

◆ Create unique indexes on a primary key or alternate key. This allows SQL Server to enforce entity integrity.

(If you create PRIMARY KEY or UNIQUE constraints on a table as described in Chapter 3, SQL Server creates a unique index for you.)

◆ If you often retrieve data in sorted order by a particular column, consider putting a clustered index on that column. Because a clustered index physically sorts the rows in a table, SQL Server can retrieve rows very efficiently. The clustered index is most efficient for range queries and least useful when applied to simple IDENTITY columns.

◆ If two or more columns are often searched as a unit, consider placing a composite index on both columns.

◆ Consider using a non-clustered index on the primary key of a table if the table uses an IDENTITY column as its primary key. Placing a clustered index on an IDENTITY column causes all new rows to be inserted at the end of the table, which may cause concurrency problems if many users are inserting data into the table. Even with row-level locking, excessive insert activity on one data page will cause problems.

Indexes can be created or removed without affecting the data in a table, so feel free to experiment with different types of indexes if you need to.

MANAGING INDEXES WITH TRANSACT-SQL

▶ Create and maintain indexes.

- · Choose an indexing strategy that will optimize performance.

- · Given a situation, choose the appropriate type of index to create.

- · Choose the column or columns to index.

- · Choose the appropriate index characteristics, specifically FILLFACTOR, DROP_EXISTING, and PAD INDEX.

Part of the database designer's role in database implementation is managing the indexes on the database. One of the nicer features of SQL Server is that indexes may be created and dropped independently of their tables, so indexes may be changed without affecting the data in the database. Typically, these changes are accomplished through the use of the Transact-SQL statements covered in this section.

EXAM TIP

Exam Focuses on TSQL The Enterprise Manager application also may be used to manage indexes, as discussed later in the chapter. However, the exam focuses mainly on the Transact-SQL statements used to manage indexes.

Creating Indexes

To create an index on a table, you use the CREATE INDEX statement. There are a few restrictions you should be aware of before using this statement:

◆ Only tables can be indexed; you cannot create an index on a view.

◆ Columns of *bit*, *image*, or *text* data types cannot be used as an index's key.

◆ If the table is to have a clustered index, create it first before creating any non-clustered indexes. Otherwise, the non-clustered indexes will be rebuilt. Refer to the earlier section "Clustered Indexes."

The simplified syntax of the CREATE INDEX statement is as follows:

```
CREATE [UNIQUE] [CLUSTERED ¦ NONCLUSTERED]
        INDEX index_name ON table (column [,…n])
[WITH
                [PAD_INDEX]
                [[,] FILLFACTOR = fillfactor]
                [[,] IGNORE_DUP_KEY]
                [[,] DROP_EXISTING]
                [[,] STATISTICS_NORECOMPUTE]
]
[ON filegroup]
```

The following list takes a closer look at the parts of this syntax:

◆ The UNIQUE keyword specifies that the new index will disallow duplicate key values. If this keyword is omitted, then the index will be non-unique.

◆ The CLUSTERED and NONCLUSTERED keywords specify that the new index will be clustered or non-clustered. By default, a non-clustered index is created.

◆ index_name is the name of the new index. This name follows the naming conventions for tables and other objects in the database, and can be up to 128 characters in length.

◆ The ON keyword specifies the table and columns on which to create the index. You can create an index on a table in another database.

◆ The WITH keyword is used to specify various options for the new index. These options are discussed later in this section.

Following are some examples of using the CREATE INDEX statement in the Pubs sample database:

◆ This example creates a non-unique, non-clustered index on the job_desc column in the jobs table:

```
CREATE INDEX idx_job_desc ON jobs (job_desc)
```

◆ The following examples create a unique index on the title column in the titles table:

- To create a clustered index, use the following statement:

```
CREATE UNIQUE CLUSTERED INDEX uqcidx_title ON titles
(title)
```

- To create a non-clustered index, you can use one of the following statements (remember that by default, an index is non-clustered):

```
CREATE UNIQUE NONCLUSTERED INDEX uqncidx_title ON
titles (title)
```

```
CREATE UNIQUE INDEX uqncidx_title ON titles (title)
```

◆ This example creates a composite index on the au_lname and au_fname columns in the authors table:

```
CREATE INDEX idx_author_name ON authors (au_lname,
au_fname)
```

The index characteristics that can be set through the options following the WITH keyword deserve a lengthy discussion. The next two sections will describe these characteristics in depth.

Using the FILLFACTOR and PAD_INDEX Options

When you create an index, it is possible to fine-tune its performance by using several options shown already in the CREATE INDEX syntax.

When you create an index without specifying a fill factor, the fill factor value is 0. When SQL Server creates the index, it fills each leaf page full of index entries, and leaves room for two additional entries on the non-leaf pages. As data is inserted into the table, SQL Server must split the leaf pages (and possibly the non-leaf pages) to make room for the new index entries. This page splitting can cause the performance of data modification queries to suffer. To minimize page splitting, you can use the FILLFACTOR option.

A FILLFACTOR of 1 to 99 fills the leaf pages to the specified percentage of fullness. For example, a fill factor of 50 would leave the leaf pages half-full. The non-leaf pages still leave some empty space for additional entries.

A FILLFACTOR of 100 fills the leaf pages 100 percent full (as does a FILLFACTOR of 0), but the non-leaf pages are also filled to capacity. This results in the smallest possible index, but any inserted data is guaranteed to cause a page split in the index. A 100 percent fill factor is useful for read-only tables.

SQL Server's FILLFACTOR defaults to 0, but you can change this setting by using sp_configure.

The PAD_INDEX option is used in conjunction with the FILLFACTOR option. If PAD_INDEX is used, then the non-leaf pages are filled to the percentage specified by the fill factor. Again, a fill factor of 100 percent fills both leaf and non-leaf pages completely full.

This example creates an index on the titles table in which the leaf and non-leaf pages are 25 percent full:

```
CREATE INDEX idx_titles
ON titles (title)
WITH PAD_INDEX, FILLFACTOR = 25
```

Other Options for Index Creation

It has been stated earlier in this chapter that when a clustered index is dropped, all non-clustered indexes must be rebuilt. This is because non-clustered indexes use clustered index key values in their leaf pages. Therefore, if you wanted to completely rebuild a clustered index you could drop the index, and then create a new index with the same properties. This process would cause all non-clustered indexes on the table to be rebuilt twice, which can be quite time consuming. Fortunately, the DROP_EXISTING option of the CREATE INDEX statement can alleviate this burden. By using the DROP_EXISTING option on a clustered index, the index is dropped and re-created in one step, causing any non-clustered indexes to be rebuilt only once. The DROP_EXISTING option can also be used for non-clustered indexes simply to eliminate the need to drop the existing index in a separate step. The following statement shows an example of using the DROP EXISTING option.

```
CREATE UNIQUE CLUSTERED INDEX idx_titles
ON titles (title)
WITH DROP EXISTING
```

The IGNORE_DUP_KEY option in the CREATE INDEX statement controls
SQL Server's behavior when multiple rows are inserted from a single
statement. Setting this option causes SQL Server to ignore duplicate
key values being inserted into a table with a unique index from the
same statement. Instead of producing an error and allowing no
inserts, one of the rows is inserted, and the others are ignored. Note
that this option is only relevant for unique indexes. An example
utilizing this option follows:

```
CREATE UNIQUE CLUSTERED INDEX idx_titles
ON titles (title)
WITH IGNORE DUP KEY, DROP EXISTING
```

The last option is STATISTICS_NORECOMPUTE. By specifying this option
when building an index, you will prevent SQL Server from automatically maintaining index statistics. SQL Server uses these statistics to
determine which indexes are useful in different situations. If the statistics are out of date SQL Server may ignore a useful index. SQL
Server's use of statistics and a discussion of how to manually maintain them can be found in Chapter 11, "Maintaining a Database."
The following example shows the use of STATISTICS NORECOMPUTE.

```
CREATE UNIQUE CLUSTERED INDEX idx_titles
ON titles (title)
WITH IGNORE DUP KEY, DROP EXISTING, STATISTICS NORECOMPUTE
```

Dropping Indexes

The DROP INDEX statement is used to remove an index from a table.
Only the table owner or DBO can use this command. When an
index is dropped from a table, only the space used by the index is
reclaimed in the database; the table's data remains intact.

This statement can only be used to drop indexes created with the
CREATE INDEX statement. Indexes created by PRIMARY KEY or UNIQUE
constraints must be dropped by removing the constraint. For information about creating or dropping constraints, refer to Chapter 3.

The syntax of the DROP INDEX statement is as follows:

```
DROP INDEX [owner.]table_name.index_name [,
[owner.]table_name.index_name...]
```

Note that multiple indexes can be dropped in a single statement.
Also, there is no database specifier on the table name, so you must
execute the DROP INDEX statement from the database containing the
index you want to drop.

NOTE **Finding the Index Name** To determine the name of an index on a table,
use the sp_helpindex system stored
procedure.

Following are two examples of the DROP INDEX syntax:

◆ The following statement drops the index created in the first example of the CREATE INDEX examples. The USE statement causes the query to be executed from the specified database, in this case Pubs:

```
USE pubs
DROP INDEX jobs.idx_job_desc
```

◆ Following is an example of dropping multiple indexes in a single statement. This example drops the indexes created in the second and third examples of the CREATE INDEX examples:

```
USE pubs
DROP INDEX titles.uqcidx_title, authors.idx_author_name
```

Rebuilding an Index

As stated previously in the chapter, an index's fill factor is not maintained after the index is built. As data in the table is added or updated, the index pages are split to accommodate the new index rows on each index page. This means that over time, an index's pages may become only partially full. This can cause data modification queries to take longer to execute. Table pages also become fragmented over time as data in the table is modified. Rebuilding the table's clustered index physically reorganizes the table's rows and reduces fragmentation. This rebuilding takes place by using the DBCC DBREINDEX command.

It is possible for the table owner or DBO to drop and re-create each index manually by using DROP INDEX and CREATE INDEX statements. However, the DBCC DBREINDEX command has several advantages over the manual method:

◆ All indexes on the table can be rebuilt at once, including indexes created by PRIMARY KEY and UNIQUE constraints. This allows a table's indexes to be refreshed without knowing any index names or having to drop and re-create constraints.

◆ An index may be rebuilt with a new fill factor.

◆ All changes are automatically atomic; the re-indexing is automatically wrapped in a transaction so that all changes may be rolled back in the event of a problem.

As with the other index commands, only the table owner or DBO can issue the DBCC DBREINDEX command. The syntax of the command is as follows:

```
DBCC DBREINDEX
       (        [ 'database.owner.table_name' [, index_name
[, fillfactor ] ] ]
       ) [WITH NO_INFOMSGS]
```

The WITH NO_INFOMSGS keyword indicates that all errors with a severity of zero through ten are suppressed. These errors are simply warning messages that require no user action anyway, so they are safe to ignore.

Following are some examples of the DBCC DBREINDEX command:

◆ To rebuild all indexes on a table, simply specify a table name. The following example rebuilds all indexes on the titles table in the Pubs database:

```
DBCC DBREINDEX ('pubs..titles')
```

◆ To rebuild a particular index, specify both the table and index name:

```
DBCC DBREINDEX ('pubs..titles','titleind')
```

◆ A particular index can be rebuilt with an explicit fill factor:

```
DBCC DBREINDEX ('pubs..titles','titleind',80)
```

◆ Or all of a table's indexes can be rebuilt with an explicit fill factor:

```
DBCC DBREINDEX ('pubs..titles','',80)
```

Indexes and TSQL

R E V I E W   B R E A K

As was mentioned in the preceding section, the primary focus of the test will be on the Transact-SQL statements to create indexes. At this point you should now have a solid understanding of the CREATE INDEX command. Remember that you will need to understand all of the options for the CREATE INDEX statement to be prepared for the test. The following section rounds out the discussion of indexes by describing how to use SQL Server Enterprise Manager to create indexes.

MANAGING INDEXES WITH ENTERPRISE MANAGER

▶ Create and Maintain Indexes.

- Choose an indexing strategy that will optimize performance.

- Given a situation, choose the appropriate type of index to create.

- Choose the column or columns to index.

- Choose the appropriate index characteristics, specifically FILLFACTOR, DROP_EXISTING, and PAD INDEX.

The Enterprise Manager application provides an alternate way to manage the indexes in a database. All the indexes on each table in the database may be managed through Enterprise Manager's Design Table window.

To get to the Design Table window, perform the tasks outlined in Step by Step 4.1.

STEP BY STEP

4.1 Manipulating Indexes Using SQL Server Enterprise Manager

1. Load the SQL Server Enterprise Manager application if it is not already loaded.

2. From the left pane, select a server on which you want to manage indexes. You may have to expand server groups to get to the server you want. Expand the tree view by clicking the plus sign (+) to the left of the server.

3. Expand the Databases folder by clicking the plus sign next to the folder icon.

4. Expand the database of your choice by clicking the plus sign to the left of the database icon.

5. Click the tables icon to show a list of tables in the right pane of the Enterprise Manager. Right-click the table you want to work with to reveal the context menu.

6. Choose the Design Table option from the menu. The Design Table window will appear, as shown in Figure 4.2.

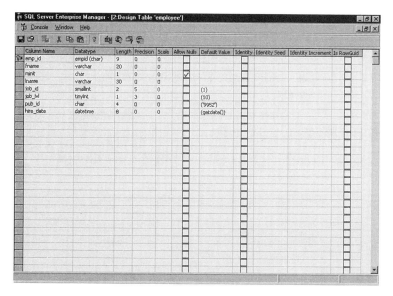

7. Click the second icon from the left in the toolbar at the top of the screen labeled Table and Index Properties. This will display a window that details properties of the table.

8. View the window's third tab, Indexes/Keys, to view information about the indexes on the table. The screen will look similar to Figure 4.3.

This window allows you to create, modify, and delete indexes on your table. Near the top of the window, a drop-down box displays the name of the index you are currently examining. Just below this drop-down box there are buttons allowing you to add a new index or drop the current index. A list box in the middle of the screen lists all of the columns involved in the index. A text box just below the column list displays the name of the index and allows you to enter the name of the index after clicking the New button. The rest of the options should be familiar to you if you are comfortable with the CREATE INDEX syntax described earlier in this chapter. You can mark

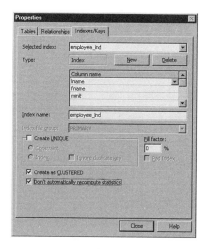

FIGURE 4.3▲
Indexes/Keys tab of Table and Index Properties.

the index as unique and clustered, and there is an option `Don't Automatically Recompute Statistics` that corresponds to the `WITH STATISTICS_NORECOMPUTE` option allowed by the `CREATE INDEX` command.

To actually create a new index using the Index tab of the Table and Index Properties dialog box, follow Step by Step 4.1 to open the dialog box, then continue with Step by Step 4.2.

STEP BY STEP

4.2 Create an Index Using SQL Server Enterprise Manager

1. Follow the steps outlined in Step by Step 4.1, "Manipulating Indexes with SQL Enterprise Manager," to display the Index tab of the Table and Index Properties dialog box.

2. Click the New button to prepare a new index.

3. Select the column or columns to be indexed in the Column Name list box. You will be allowed to select the columns from a drop down list on each row of the list box.

4. Enter the name of the index in the Index Name text box. The name must follow the standard rules for identifiers.

5. If you want to create the index in a particular file group, you can choose the file group from the Index File Group drop-down box. This corresponds with the file group following the optional `ON` keyword in the `CREATE INDEX` TSQL statement.

6. If you are creating a UNIQUE index, check the Create UNIQUE check box. You can also decide to create this UNIQUE index as a UNIQUE constraint by checking the Constraint option. By default, the index will not be created as a constraint.

7. If there is not already a clustered index on this table you can choose make this index clustered. To do so click in the Create as CLUSTERED check box.

8. If you do not want SQL Server to automatically keep the index's statistics up-to-date, check the Don't Automatically Recompute Statistics check box.

9. Click the Close button to finish describing the new index. The new index will not actually be created until you close the Design Table dialog box and save the changes to the table.

It has been stated earlier in this chapter that UNIQUE constraints, including PRIMARY KEY constraints, are actually enforced by UNIQUE indexes. This graphical interface allows you to create a constraint in this manner instead of just a UNIQUE index. The end result is still an index being created on the columns you choose, but by allowing you to create it as a constraint, Enterprise Manager provides the maximum flexibility to you.

IMPLEMENTING FULL-TEXT SEARCH

▶ Implement full-text search.

SQL Server 7.0 includes a new, powerful text-searching engine to allow complex keyword and keyphrase searches of your data. This is not a simple character-by-character comparison of a column; rather, a full-text search uses specially prepared indexes to be able to find words and phrases quickly. The full-text search capabilities include the ability to match singular or plural forms of the words you enter and multiple verb forms of the words you enter. Clearly this capability goes beyond the simple character pattern matching of the LIKE keyword. For more information about the LIKE keyword, see Chapter 6.

There are many levels of detail involved in the full-text search capability of SQL Server. You must configure the full-text search properties of each level before you can perform a full-text search. The Microsoft Search service must be installed and running on your SQL Server. Next, your database must be configured to allow full-text searching. A full-text catalog must then be created on your server. Finally, individual tables, and then columns in those tables must have full-text indexes defined on them. Do not confuse a full-text index with a common table index such as those discussed earlier in this chapter, they are two entirely different structures.

After full-text searching is enabled on your server and full-text indexes are populated for your tables, you will be ready to take advantage of the searching capability of SQL Server. This capability is accessed through the CONTAINS and FREETEXT predicates and the related CONTAINSTABLE and FREETEXTTABLE functions of the TSQL language. The predicates can be used as search criteria in standard query statements, and the equivalent functions perform the same operations but return the results in table format.

In the following sections you will first learn the details of how to configure full-text searching on your server, and then how to run full-text queries.

Enable Full-Text Searches

There are many details that must be set up to enable full-text searches on your data. There are configuration details on the server, database, table and column levels that must be addressed. Fortunately, this complexity can be largely bypassed through the use of the Full-Text Indexing Wizard that is included in Enterprise Manager (see Figure 4.4). This wizard simply asks you what database, table, and column you want to perform full-text searches on, and then presents default values that you can change or accept to fully enable full-text searching on your data. Because of the intuitiveness of this wizard, it does not require much attention here. This section will instead focus on the manual configuration of full-text searches. After you have an understanding of the manual configuration tasks, the operation of wizard will be transparent.

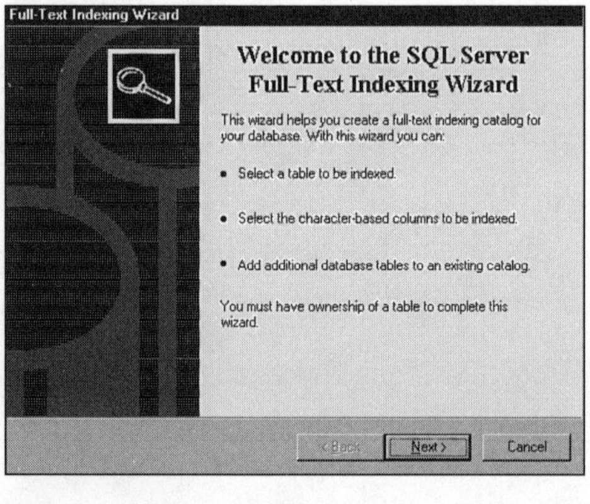

FIGURE 4.4
The Full-Text Indexing Wizard.

Preparing the Full-Text Service

SQL Server uses a separate service to actually perform full-text operations. This service is the Microsoft Search service, which is optionally installed with SQL Server. The Microsoft Search service can be started or stopped through the Windows NT Control Panel like any other service, or through the SQL Server Service Manager. This service must be running for full-text searches to work. It is important to note that the Microsoft Search service cannot be installed on the Windows 95 or Windows 98 platforms.

The Microsoft Search service has few configuration options. These can be accessed through the Properties dialog box of the Full-Text Search icon found under the Support Services folder under the server in Enterprise Manager, or by using the `sp_fulltext_service` stored procedure. Figure 4.5 shows the General tab of the Full-Text Search Service Properties dialog box.

Through the General tab you can change the account under which the Microsoft Search service runs. This is rarely necessary and is outside the scope of this book. At the bottom of the tab, however, you can see the default locations where full-text indexing files are stored. These locations can only be changed here through the use of Enterprise Manager.

The Performance tab of the Full-Text Search Service Properties dialog box has two properties, both of which can also be set through the `sp_fulltext_service` stored procedure mentioned earlier. Figure 4.6 illustrates this tab.

FIGURE 4.5▲
The General tab of the Full-Text Search Service Properties.

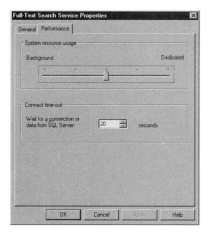

◄FIGURE 4.6
The Performance tab of the Full-Text Search Service Properties.

The System resource usage allows you to set the priority of the Microsoft Search service. A higher priority will cause the Microsoft Search service to demand more resources from Windows NT and will slow the performance of all other services on the server, including SQL Server. A low priority will sacrifice full-text search speed in order to ensure minimal impact on other server functions.

The default priority of three (out of five) is recommended. To affect this setting through the `sp_fulltext_service` stored procedure, use the following command:

```
Exec sp_fulltext_service 'resource_usage', 3
```

This command sets the resource usage to its default and recommended value of three.

The other setting on the Performance tab is the connection timeout. This is a setting of the number of seconds SQL Server will wait for results from full-text search. To affect this setting through the `sp_fulltext_service` stored procedure, use the following command:

```
Exec sp_fulltext_service 'Connect_timeout', 5
```

When using the stored procedure, the number you enter is multiplied internally by four to arrive at the number of seconds to wait.

There is one further option that the stored procedure offers. This is the `Clean_up` option and it takes no numerical value. When this option is set, the full-text service will search for full-text catalogs that are no longer in use, and remove them. This functionality can also be found in Enterprise Manager by right-clicking on the Full-Text Search icon under the server. This action displays a context menu that offers the `Cleanup Catalogs` option. To accomplish the same with the stored procedure, issue the following command:

```
Exec sp_fulltext_service 'clean_up', NULL
```

Configuring a Database for Full-Text Search

You have just seen how to configure the full-text search service through the Enterprise Manager and with stored procedures. Configuring the database level is even more basic. The only full-text setting at the database level is to enable or disable full-text searches within the database. Use the `sp_fulltext_database` stored procedure to enable full-text searches of the current database with the following syntax:

```
Exec sp_fulltext_database 'enable'
```

Replacing the parameter value of `enable` with `disable` will disable full-text searches within the current database. The only equivalent operation from within Enterprise Manager is in the Full-Text Indexing Wizard. The wizard is sensitive to the level at which it is started. If a database is currently selected, the wizard assumes you want that database enabled for full-text searches. Only if no database is selected in Enterprise Manager will the wizard prompt you to choose the database to work with.

Managing Full-Text Catalogs

Full-text searches are performed using special full-text indexes. These indexes are entirely different than standard database indexes. The Microsoft Search service maintains its own indexing information in full-text catalogs stored separate from any database files in the file system. Full-text catalogs are created and maintained within a database. A single database can contain several full-text catalogs, but a single catalog can reside in only one database. Multiple full-text indexes can reside in a single catalog. Full-text catalogs are managed through the sp_fulltext_catalog stored procedure, the syntax for which is shown here:

```
sp_fulltext_catalog  [@ftcat =] 'fulltext_catalog_name',
      [@action =] 'action'
      [, [@path =] 'root_directory']
```

The fulltext_catalog_name parameter is replaced with the name of the catalog you are managing. There are six different actions that can be specified in the second parameter, only one of which allows the use of the third, path, parameter. These six actions are detailed below.

◆ **CREATE**. Use this action to create an empty full-text catalog and register it within the current database. This is the only action that allows the use of the path parameter. The path parameter specifies a directory only, not a file name. If the path is not specified the default directory is used.

◆ **DROP**. Use this action to drop the specified full-text catalog. If the catalog is still in use by a full-text index, the command will fail.

◆ **START_INCREMENTAL**. Use this action to perform an incremental update of all the full-text indexes within the catalog. If the full-text enabled tables have timestamp columns, SQL Server can determine which rows have changed and can add only those rows to the index. Without a timestamp column, SQL Server assumes that all rows must be added.

◆ **START_FULL**. Use this action to completely repopulate all the full-text indexes in the catalog.

◆ **STOP.** Use this action to halt a currently running full-text catalogs population.

◆ **REBUILD.** Use this action to completely delete and rebuild the files related with the catalog. After it is rebuilt, the catalog will have no data and will need to be repopulated.

These actions can be performed through the Enterprise Manager as well. By expanding the Databases folder in the left pane of Enterprise Manager, and then expanding the database for which full-text indexing is enabled, you will see a Full-Text Catalogs folder. By right-clicking this folder to show a context menu, you will be presented with the same options. At this level, the choices will affect all catalogs in the database. In the left pane where all existing catalogs are shown, you can right-click to show a context menu that has options to affect just that catalog.

Managing Full-Text Indexing on Tables

Full-text indexing requires that involved tables have a unique index on a single, NOT NULL column. The data that is stored in the full-text index uses this single column value as a key to identify the row where the data came from. For this reason, a table must be registered with this key column before a full-text index can be fully defined. Furthermore, the previous section states that full-text indexes are populated for an entire catalog at a time. In order to provide you with more control over which tables are affected by repopulating, it is possible to activate and deactivate a registered table. When a table is deactivated, it is skipped from further full-text index populating.

These actions of registering individual tables and then activating and deactivating them for full-text index populating are performed through the sp_fulltext_table stored procedure. This procedure has the following syntax:

```
sp_fulltext_table [@tabname =] 'qualified_table_name',
      [@action =] 'action'
      [,[@ftcat =] 'fulltext_catalog_name',
      [@keyname =] 'unique_index_name'
```

The qualified_table_name parameter is replaced with a table name within the current database. There are then four distinct actions that can be supplied—only one of which allows the use of the last two parameters:

◆ **CREATE**. Use this action to register the table for full-text indexing in a given full-text catalog. The third parameter specifies the catalog, and the fourth parameter specifies a unique index on the table. This index must be on a single column that does not allow NULLs, as was specified above.

◆ **DROP**. Use this action to unregister the table for full-text indexing. It is not necessary to disable any columns that are currently being indexed for full-text searches before taking this action.

◆ **ACTIVATE**. Use this action to allow full-text indexes on the table to be populated with the rest of the catalog. At least one column must be defined for full-text indexing before the table can be activated. Defining columns for full-text indexing is discussed in the next section.

◆ **DEACTIVATE**. Use this action to disallow further populating of full-text indexes defined on this table. The next time the catalog is populated, this table will be ignored.

These tasks can be duplicated through Enterprise Manager by right-clicking on the table to bring up the context menu. The menu includes an option `Full-Text Index Table` that leads to a pop-up menu to define, edit, or remove full-text indexing.

Managing Full-Text Indexing on Columns

After a table has been registered for full-text indexing, you can define columns from the table to be indexed. Columns can only be defined for full-text indexing if the table is currently deactivated, as described above. To add a column to full-text indexing, you can use the `sp_fulltext_column` stored procedure. The syntax for this procedure follows:

```
sp_fulltext_column [@tabname =] 'qualified_table_name',
      [@colname =] 'column_name',
      [@action =] 'action'
```

The `qualified_table_name` is the table that has already been added to full-text indexing. The `column_name` is the name of the column to add to full-text indexing. The final parameter has two values—ADD and DROP—to add or drop the column to full-text indexing.

Run Full-Text Searches

As was mentioned before, full text searches are implemented in TSQL through the use of two predicates: CONTAINS and FREETEXT. Both of these predicates have equivalent functions: CONTAINSTABLE and FREETEXTTABLE. The difference is that the predicates are used as search criteria in a standard TSQL statement, whereas the functions scan a full-text index for matches and return the results in the form of a table that that is joined to in the statement. The simpler predicates will be discussed first, followed by discussions about the special uses of the functions.

Using CONTAINS

The CONTAINS predicate is used as a search criteria to filter rows in a result set. The filtering that this predicate provides is a very powerful full-text search. The syntax for the CONTAINS predicate is quite simple on the surface and is as follows:

```
CONTAINS ({column ¦ *}, '<contains_search_condition>')
```

The complexity of the CONTAINS predicate lies in the <contains_search_condition>. There are five kinds of search conditions that can be applied and which can be conjoined together with AND and OR conjunctions. The syntax and an explanation of each search condition will follow, but first a word on the search column.

The CONTAINS keyword is followed by a set of parenthesis that enclose all details of the command. The first argument in the parenthetical list is the column to search on. It is also permissible to use an asterisk (*) to specify all columns in the table that have full-text indexes defined should be used for the search. Whether a column is explicitly given or the asterisk is used, a table must be specified when there is any ambiguity.

The <contains_search_condition> parameter has the following syntax:

```
<contains_search_condition> ::=
        {
                <simple_term>
        ¦ <prefix_term>
        ¦ <proximity_term>
        ¦ <generation_term>
        ¦ <weighted_term>
        ¦ (<contains_search_condition>)
        }
```

```
        [       {
                        {AND ¦ AND NOT ¦ OR}
<contains_search_condition>
                }
        ] [...n]
```

This syntax may seem a bit confusing, but what it comes down to is that there are five distinct types of search conditions that can be used, any number of them can be grouped by parenthesis, and they can be conjoined by an AND, OR, or AND NOT conjunction. Parenthetical groups are evaluated first, the NOT operator is applied next, then the AND conjunctions are evaluated before OR conjunctions. It is important to note that the NOT operator cannot be used with an OR conjunction, and that it cannot precede the first search condition; it can follow only an AND conjunction.

It has been stated a few times now that there are five types of search conditions that can be used. Each of these types has its own syntax, which has been encapsulated in the preceding syntax diagram by a simple label. Each of these labels will now be explored, and described in detail. First examine the simple term search condition:

```
<simple_term> ::=
        word ¦ " phrase "
```

A *simple* term condition is simply a single word, or a collection of one or more words (a phrase) grouped by double quotes. A match is made when all words in the simple term are found in the order specified. Although the matches are not case sensitive, the spelling must be exact; alternate verb forms and plurals will not be matched. Punctuation should not be included in the word or phrase, and any punctuation in the columns searched will be ignored.

The Microsoft Search service has a list of *noise words* that it automatically ignores. These words include "a," "and," "the," "is," "this," and similar words. Noise words are not included in the full-text index, and therefore cannot be searched upon. You should not include noise words in your simple term if they can be avoided. If a simple term search contains only noise words, an error will be returned.

The following example demonstrates the use of a simple term in a query:

```
SELECT *
FROM Titles
WHERE CONTAINS(Title, 'Computer')
```

The next search condition is the *prefix* term. This condition is quite similar to the simple term, except that each individual word in the total phrase is fuzzily matched to words in the full-text index. The exact syntax and full explanation follows:

```
<prefix term> ::=
        { "word * " ¦ "phrase * " }
```

As indicated previously, the syntax is quite similar to the simple term condition described earlier. The differences are that even a single word must be enclosed in double quotes, and that an asterisk is added just before the closing quote. The asterisk (*)indicates that each of the words in the preceding phrase should be matched exactly in the full-text index, except that zero, one, or more characters can be appended to find a match. Thus, the word "Tom" would match "Tomas" and "tomboy" (remember that none of the matches are case-sensitive). Remember also that each of the words in the phrase are wild card-matched this way. For example, if your prefix term were "plant garden", rows containing the following phrases within them would match; "The plantation's gardening staff" and "to plant gardens is a joy". Both examples are used in the following queries, which demonstrate the use of a prefix term in a simple query:

```
SELECT *
FROM Titles
WHERE CONTAINS(Title, '"Tom *"')

SELECT *
FROM Titles
WHERE CONTAINS(Title, '"plant garden *"')
```

The third condition is a *proximity* term. This term specifies that two or more phrases should be found, but they can be separated by other words. The syntax follows:

```
<proximity_term> ::=
        {<simple_term> ¦ <prefix_term>}
        {        {NEAR() ¦ ~} {<simple_term> ¦ <prefix_term>}
} [...n]
```

The syntax shows that a proximity term consists of two or more simple or prefix terms joined by the keyword NEAR(). Note that the tilde (~) is an equivalent short-hand for the keyword NEAR(). The NEAR() keyword operates similarly to an AND operator in that it requires both terms on either side of it to exist; however, the NEAR()

keyword assigns a ranking value to the match according to how far apart the two terms are. This ranking value is more important to the CONTAINSTABLE function that will be described later, but for the CONTAINS predicate, if the conditions are composed solely of proximity terms and the ranking is sufficiently low (zero), the row will not be returned. The concept of ranking will be discussed in more detail later in the section addressing the CONTAINSTABLE function. An example of using a proximity term will also be withheld until the discussion of the CONTAINSTABLE function.

The CONTAINS predicate also supports a as a condition. A *generation term* contains a simple term where the words in the simple term are matched to singular or plural forms of themselves, and verbs are matched to any verb form. The syntax follows:

```
<generation_term> :: =
        FORMSOF (INFLECTIONAL, <simple_term> [,...n] )
```

The *generation* term begins with the keyword FORMSOF followed by a parenthetical list, indicating that the simple terms that follow are matched to various forms of themselves. The first item in the parenthetical is the keyword INFLECTIONAL, then any number of comma-separated simple terms follow. The following is an example of a simple query using a generation term:

```
SELECT *
FROM Titles
WHERE CONTAINS(Title, 'FORMSOF (INFLECTIONAL, "Run")')
```

Finally, the last search condition is the *weighted* term. A weighted term consists of a parenthetical list of terms where each is given a weighting between zero and one. A row will be returned if any one of the weighted terms is satisfied; however, a satisfied term with a higher weighting will receive a higher rank. Again, the concept of rank will be discussed in more detail in relation to the CONTAINSTABLE function, later in this chapter. The syntax for a weighted term follows:

```
<weighted_term> :: =
        ISABOUT
                (       {       {
                                        <generation_term>
                                        ¦ <prefix_term>
                                        ¦ <proximity_term>
                                        ¦ <simple_term>
                                }
                                [WEIGHT (weight_value)]
                } [, ...n]
                )
```

The ISABOUT keyword indicates that a weighted term follows. A weighted term consists of a parenthetical, comma-separated list of terms. The terms can be of any other type, not including weighted terms. Each term can optionally be followed by the keyword WEIGHT, which introduces the weighting to be assigned to that term. The following example shows the use of a weighted term:

```
SELECT *
FROM Titles
WHERE CONTAINS(Title, 'ISABOUT ( "Cooking" WEIGHT (.1),
➥"Stress" WEIGHT (.9))')
```

Using FREETEXT

Having examined the CONTAINS predicate, you can see that there are many keywords to use, and precise syntaxes to remember. The FREETEXT predicate is the deliberate antithesis of CONTAINS, in that its term consists of a string of text that obeys no rules of syntax at all. The manner in which the full-text search works with this string of text follows this view of the syntax:

```
FREETEXT({column ¦ * }, 'freetext_string')
```

The column parameter works identically to the CONTAINS predicate. The freetext_string that follows can be any list of words and punctuation without regard to any syntax or keywords. The full-text search engine will parse the string to find "important" words that it uses to compile a list of search terms. The engine then internally assigns weights to each search term and finds matches similarly to the way the CONTAINS predicate operates on a weighted term. Because the parsing of important words and the assigning of weights is done behind the scenes by the full-text search engine, you have much less control over the matches found than you do with the CONTAINS predicate; FREETEXT, however, is much easier to use.

Using Full-Text Functions

The full-text functions are CONTAINSTABLE and FREETEXTTABLE. These functions perform searches on criteria in an identical manner as their full-text predicate counterparts, CONTAINS and FREETEXT, described earlier. The functions, however, return the matches in the form of a result table that can be used in a join statement. Examine the basic syntax of the following two functions before continuing:

```
CONTAINSTABLE (table, {, column ¦ *},
'<contains_search_condition>')

FREETEXTTABLE (table, {column ¦ *}, 'freetext_string')
```

You should note that the basic syntax of the functions is identical to its predicate counterpart, except for the addition of the `table` parameter. This parameter indicates the table to be searched. The result table of either function has two columns: `KEY` and `RANK`. The `KEY` column contains values from the table searched that uniquely identify rows that were matched. Remember that in order to activate full-text capabilities on a table, a single, not `NULL` column with a unique index must be specified. It is this unique column which the full-text functions use to return the `KEY` column values. The `RANK` column contains an integer between 0 and 1000 which represents how "good" a match is. The higher the rank value is, the better the match is.

As was stated earlier, the full-text functions are used in the `FROM` clause of a query to represent a table. Most commonly, this result table is joined back to the original table to retrieve the matched rows. In addition, the `RANK` values provided by the full-text function can be used to order the matched values, or to eliminate poor matches. An example using the `CONTAINSTABLE` function follows:

```
SELECT title_id, rank, notes
FROM titles
JOIN CONTAINSTABLE(titles, notes, '"stress" near
"Computer"') ct
  ON titles.title_id = ct.[key]
```

CASE STUDY: BUILDING A KNOWLEDGE BASE

ESSENCE OF THE CASE

Here are the essential elements in this case:

▶ Consultants in the field often need technical advice.

▶ Senior consultants, who are most qualified to offer advice, are also the most likely to be too busy to help.

▶ A method is needed to store and distribute technical articles to all consultants.

SCENARIO

You work for a consulting company that contracts mainly with small to mid-size businesses in your city. One of your company's strengths is that even the most inexperienced consultants can call back to the main office and get advice from an expert in any area they need help with. Unfortunately, there are times during which all the experts are busy, and this system breaks down. You are put in charge of the internal

continues

CASE STUDY: BUILDING A KNOWLEDGE BASE

continued

project to build a knowledge base that can supplement this direct help desk system. As the consultants come across any particularly bothersome problem on their projects, they will be encouraged to write a brief article describing the problem and the solution they came up with. The idea is to collect these articles and make them available to everyone in the company. This knowledge base can eventually become a first line of contact when someone on a job runs into a problem. This system could even be used to store common code routines if the routines could be cataloged well enough.

ANALYSIS

The full-text search capabilities of SQL Server offer an ideal solution. SQL Server is a natural choice for storing data, but simple pattern matches would not likely be powerful enough to search through hundreds or thousands of lengthy technical articles. With full-text searching however, even the kinds of "fuzzy" searches required would be child's play. You could easily build a Web-based front-end application to take the search patterns and return the list of articles found. In fact, Microsoft has long used a similar (perhaps the very same?) technology for its popular Tech-Net product, and its Books Online publications. Now with the inclusion and integration of the Microsoft Search service with SQL Server, you can take advantage of this powerful technology to produce similar knowledge bases of your own.

CHAPTER SUMMARY

KEY TERMS

Before you take the exam, make sure you are comfortable with the definitions and concepts for each of the following key terms:

- clustered index
- non-clustered index
- unique index
- Microsoft Search service
- full-text catalog

In this chapter you learned how to use indexes to make for speedier, more efficient access to your databases. You should understand how SQL Server uses its indexing structure to find data quickly, and realize that full-text searches are implemented through an external search engine powered by the Microsoft Search service. You also learned that improperly indexed tables, although they may not slow SQL Server, can consume unnecessary space in the database. Understanding the indexing options available in SQL Server is important to being able to provide an optimally functioning database.

APPLY YOUR KNOWLEDGE

Exercises

4.1   Creating Indexes

In this exercise, you create several indexes on the tables in the Pubs sample database.

Estimated Time: 5 minutes

1. Open the SQL Query Analyzer application if it is not already running. Log in to your server.

2. Expand the DB drop-down box at the top of the screen and select the Pubs database.

3. First, you will create an index on the authors table on the au_lname column. Type the following into the query window:

   ```
   CREATE INDEX idx_au_lname on authors
   (au_lname)
   ```

4. Execute the query by typing **Alt + X** or by clicking the Execute Query button on the toolbar. The index will be created. The index will be named idx_au_lname, and is a non-clustered, non-unique index.

5. Next, execute the following query to create a unique non-clustered index on the au_id column in the authors table:

   ```
   CREATE UNIQUE INDEX idxuq_au_id on authors
   (au_id)
   ```

6. Create a composite index on the au_lname and au_fname columns by executing this query:

   ```
   CREATE UNIQUE INDEX idxcomp_au_name on
   authors (au_lname,au_fname)
   ```

7. Finally, create a clustered index on the roysched table. First, look at the rows in the table by executing this query:

   ```
   SELECT * FROM roysched
   ```

8. Look at the results of the previous query. Note that the results are returned in no particular order. Now, create a clustered index on the royalty column by executing this query:

   ```
   CREATE CLUSTERED INDEX idxcl_royalty ON
   roysched (royalty)
   ```

9. Notice the message that you were returned when you built the clustered index. You should have received a message indicating that an index was being rebuilt. By creating a clustered index, all non-clustered indexes had to be rebuilt. Re-examine the rows in the roysched table by executing this query:

   ```
   SELECT * FROM roysched
   ```

   Note that the results are now sorted according to the values in the royalty column.

4.2   Dropping an Index

This exercise walks you through the steps required to drop one of the indexes you created in Exercise 4.1.

Estimated Time: 1 minute

1. Open the SQL Query Analyzer application if it is not already running. Log in to your server.

2. Expand the DB drop-down box at the top of the screen and select the Pubs database.

3. Drop the unique index you placed on the au_id column in Exercise 4.1 by executing this query:

   ```
   DROP INDEX authors.idxuq_au_id
   ```

4.3   Setting Up a Full-Text Search on a Column

This exercise walks you through the steps required to create a full-text index on a column.

Estimated Time: 10 minutes

APPLY YOUR KNOWLEDGE

1. Open the SQL Query Analyzer application if it is not already running. Log in to your server.

2. Expand the DB drop-down box at the top of the screen and select the Pubs database.

3. First, you need to enable the database for full-text indexing. Type the following command:

```
Sp_fulltext_database 'enable'
```

4. After the database is enabled, you can create a full-text catalog in this database. Type the following command and note that the location of the full-text catalog is being left to the default directory:

```
sp_fulltext_catalog 'ft_pubs_cat', 'create'
```

5. After creating a catalog, you can begin to work with tables. For this example you should use the titles table. Note that there should be an existing unique index on the `Title_id` field named `UPKCL_titleidind`.

```
sp_fulltext_table 'titles', 'create',
'ft_pubs_cat', 'UPKCL_titleidind'
```

6. When the table is first created for full-text indexing, it is disabled by default. That works fine because you can only add columns when the table is disabled. You will add two columns to full-text indexes for this example by following these commands:

```
exec sp_fulltext_column 'titles', 'title',
➥'add'

exec sp_fulltext_column 'titles', 'notes',
➥'add'
```

7. Now you can finally enable the table, and then populate the catalog. After the catalog is populated you'll be able to run full-text searches on the titles table. Run the following commands, and keep in mind that it may take a short time for the catalog to fully populate.

```
exec sp_fulltext_table 'titles', 'activate'

exec sp_fulltext_catalog 'ft_pubs_cat',
'start_full'
```

Exercise 4.4   Running a Full-text search

In this exercise you will use the full-text search capabilities you set up on the titles table.

Estimated Time: 5 minutes

1. Open the SQL Query Analyzer application if it is not already running. Log in to your server.

2. Expand the DB drop-down box at the top of the screen and select the Pubs database.

3. First, you can prove the existence of full-text searching to yourself with a simple FREETEXT command. Use the following command to find all the titles with a form of the word "study" in them.

```
select title_id, title
from titles
where freetext(title, 'study')
```

Notice that the command returned a title that contained "studies". You can see that this is a more powerful search than simply using the LIKE operator with a wildcard. The full-text service recognized that "studies" and "study" had the same root.

4. The CONTAINSTABLE command can perform more specific searches for you. Use the following command to find books that most importantly have the word "stress" in the notes, but also should have the word "computer." Note that the Rank column from the CONTAINSTABLE function is also displayed to show you how well each book matched the criteria.

```
SELECT title_id, rank, notes
FROM titles
JOIN CONTAINSTABLE(titles, notes, 'ISABOUT
```

APPLY YOUR KNOWLEDGE

```
("stress" WEIGHT(.9), "computer"
WEIGHT(.1))') ct
  ON titles.title_id = ct.[key]
```

The book with the `title_id` PS7777 was the best match because it had both the required words. The other two only had the word "computer," which wasn't weighted highly.

Review Questions

1. What is the *primary* difference between a clustered and non-clustered index?

2. What are the advantages and disadvantages of using indexes?

3. What is a unique index?

4. What is a composite index?

5. What are the two main Transact-SQL commands used for managing indexes?

6. What are the five levels of full-text configurations?

7. After using the `create` action on a table, what is left before you can perform a full-text search?

8. What characteristic of a table is necessary for full text indexing?

9. What is the purpose of the table-based full-text search functions?

Exam Questions

1. What are some of the reasons indexes are used in a database? Select all that apply.

    A. Indexes improve the performance of data retrieval.

    B. Indexes can enforce entity integrity.

    C. Indexes can improve the performance of sorting and grouping queries.

    D. Indexes can reduce the space requirements for a table.

    E. Indexes can improve the performance of joins.

2. Choose the statement that best describes a clustered index.

    A. The leaf pages of the index contain pointers to the data pages of the table.

    B. The leaf pages of the index are the data pages of the table.

    C. The leaf pages of the index contain pointers to the data rows of the table.

    D. The non-leaf pages of the index contain pointers to the data rows of the table.

3. Choose the statement that best describes a non-clustered index on a table with no other indexes.

    A. The leaf pages of the index contain pointers to the data pages of the table.

    B. The leaf pages of the index are the data pages of the table.

    C. The leaf pages of the index contain pointers to the data rows of the table.

    D. The non-leaf pages of the index contain pointers to the data rows of the table.

4. Which of the following statements about clustered indexes are *not* true?

    A. Clustered indexes are smaller than non-clustered indexes.

B. Clustered indexes physically sort the data rows in a table by the index key.

C. Clustered indexes require less space to create than non-clustered indexes.

D. Clustered indexes are best used on IDENTITY columns.

E. The data pages of the table are the leaf pages of the clustered index.

5. How many clustered indexes can be created on a table?

   A. One

   B. Up to 256

   C. Up to 249

   D. Unlimited, provided there are enough server resources

6. How many non-clustered indexes can be created on a table?

   A. One

   B. Up to 256

   C. Up to 249

   D. Unlimited, provided there are enough server resources

7. Choose the statement that best describes a composite index.

   A. It physically sorts the rows in a table.

   B. It contains multiple keys.

   C. It logically sorts the rows in a table in both ascending and descending order.

   D. It contains multiple columns in its key.

8. Which columns are good candidates for indexing? Select all that apply.

   A. Primary keys and foreign keys

   B. Columns used to order the results of a query

   C. Columns that have few distinct values throughout the rows in a table

   D. Columns with high selectivity

9. What is the correct syntax for creating a unique, non-clustered index on the au_id column in the authors table?

   A. `CREATE NONCLUSTERED INDEX idxau_id ON authors (au_id)`

   B. `CREATE UNIQUE INDEX idxau_id ON authors (au_id)`

   C. `CREATE UNIQUE CLUSTERED INDEX idxau_id ON authors (au_id)`

10. Roger wants to create an index on a read-only table. What is the best option he should use when creating the index?

    A. `FILLFACTOR = 100`

    B. `FILLFACTOR = 0`

    C. `PAD_INDEX, FILLFACTOR = 100`

    D. `PAD_INDEX, FILLFACTOR = 0`

11. Mary would like to minimize page splitting for an index on a table that will have many rows inserted. What option should she use when creating the index?

    A. `FILLFACTOR = 100`

    B. `FILLFACTOR = 0`

APPLY YOUR KNOWLEDGE

C. PAD_INDEX, FILLFACTOR = 50

D. PAD_INDEX, FILLFACTOR = 1

12. Brian wants to create an index on a table that will have a moderate amount of new data inserted into it. He wants to reduce page splitting, but also wants the index to be of reasonable size. Which setting should he use for FILLFACTOR?

 A. FILLFACTOR = 0

 B. FILLFACTOR = 50

 C. FILLFACTOR = 100

13. Josh is attempting to drop an index on the titles table in the Pubs database with the DROP INDEX statement. However, he is receiving the error message "Cannot drop the index 'titles.titleind' because it doesn't exist in the system catalogs." What are some possible causes of this error?

 A. The index is unique, and he should use DROP UNIQUE INDEX.

 B. The titleind index does not exist on the titles table.

 C. The titles table does not exist in the database.

 D. He is not executing the query from the Pubs database.

14. Bill wants to set up full-text searching on the Comments column of his OrderDetail table in the BillCo database. The OrderDetail table has a composite key made up of the OrderID and the ProductID field. He ensures that full-text searching in enabled on his server, and then issues the following commands.

```
exec Sp_fulltext_database 'enable'
exec sp_fulltext_catalog 'ft_BillCo_cat',
➡'create'
```

```
exec sp_fulltext_table 'OrderDetail',
➡'create', 'ft_BillCo_cat',
➡'UPKCL_OrderProdind'
➡exec sp_fulltext_column 'OrderDetail',
➡'Comments', 'add'
exec sp_fulltext_table 'OrderDetail',
➡'activate'
exec sp_fulltext_catalog 'ft_BillCo_cat',
➡'start_full'
```

Is this a good solution to Bill's problem?

 A. This is an outstanding solution to the problem. It correctly prepares full-text searches on the column and populates the index immediately.

 B. This is a fair solution to the problem. It correctly prepares full-text searches on the column, but does not complete the job.

 C. This is a poor solution to the problem. It enables full-text searches on the database and table, but does not prepare or populate an index on the column.

 D. This is not a solution to the problem. It will not prepare either the table or column for full-text searches.

15. To use full-text searching to find all rows containing forms of the verb "swim" you should use which CONTAINS predicate?

 A. CONTAINS (columnname, FORMSOF(INFLECTIONAL, "Swim"))

 B. CONTAINS (columnname, "Swim", "Swims")

 C. CONTAINS (columnname, FINDALL("Swims"))

 D. CONTAINS (columnname, "Swim *")

APPLY YOUR KNOWLEDGE

Answers to Review Questions

1. In a clustered index, the data pages of the table are the leaf pages of the index. The rows in a table with a clustered index are physically ordered by the index key. A non-clustered index has leaf pages that point to the table's data pages or to the clustered key if one exists. The rows in a table without a clustered index are not physically ordered by the index key. (For more information, refer to the section "Introduction to Indexes.")

2. Indexes allow quick retrieval of table rows, and can be used to enforce entity integrity. However, indexes consume space in a database, and can slow data modifications. (For more information, refer to the section "Guidelines for Indexing.")

3. A unique index enforces entity integrity by guaranteeing that the index key will be unique in the table. (For more information, refer to the section "Unique Indexes.")

4. A composite index is an index whose key is composed of two or more columns. (For more information, refer to the section "Composite Indexes.")

5. CREATE INDEX and DROP INDEX. (For more information, refer to the section "Managing Indexes with Transact-SQL.")

6. The five levels of full-text configurations are Server, Database, Catalog, Table, and Column. (For more information, refer to the section "Enable Full-Text Searches.")

7. After you have enabled a table for full-text searches by performing the create action of the sp_fulltext_table procedure, you still have to enable columns in the table, activate the table, and then begin population of the catalog the table is associated with. (For more information, refer to the section "Enable Full-Text Searches.")

8. Any table that will be involved in full-text searches must have a unique index defined on a single column. For more information, refer to the section "Managing Full-Text Indexing on Tables".)

9. The functions CONTAINSTABLE and FREETEXTTABLE allow you to issue the same free-text queries as CONTAINS and FREETEXT, but instead of a simple Boolean response for matches, the table-based functions return information about how good or poor a match was. (For more information, refer to the section "Using Full-Text Functions.")

Answers to Exam Questions

1. **A, B, C, E.** Although indexes can provide many advantages to database performance, saving space is not one of them. Indexes always require additional storage space to the space the table requires. (For more information, refer to the section "Introduction to Indexes".)

2. **B.** Answer D is not correct because the non-leaf pages of the clustered index contain pointers to the data *pages* of the table. (For more information, refer to the section "Clustered Indexes".)

3. **C.** The leaf pages of a non-clustered index on a table with no other indexes point directly to the row on a page where the data can be found. If the table also had a clustered index, then the leaf pages of a non-clustered index would contain the key values of the clustered index columns. (For more information, refer to the section "Non-Clustered Indexes".)

APPLY YOUR KNOWLEDGE

4. **C, D.** Placing a clustered index on an IDENTITY column can cause a *hotspot*, or concurrence problem, if many users are inserting rows into a table. Because clustered indexes physically reorder the data in a table, they require more space to build, but they actually use less space than a non-clustered index after they are built. (For more information, refer to the section "Clustered Indexes".)

5. **A.** Because a clustered index physically orders the data in a table, there can be only one clustered index on a table. (For more information, refer to the section "Clustered Indexes".)

6. **C.** SQL Server allows 249 non-clustered indexes on a single table. Remember that primary key and unique constraints are enforced with indexes, and these count against that total. (For more information, see section "Non-Clustered Indexes".)

7. **D.** An index only has one key, which may be composed of more than one column. (For more information, refer to the section "Composite Indexes".)

8. **A, B, D.** Because primary keys and foreign keys are often used to join tables, they are good potential candidates for indexing. Any index should be built on columns with many distinct values, compared to the number of rows. These columns are said to have a high selectivity. (For more information, refer to the section "Choosing Which Columns to Index.")

9. **B.** Non-clustered indexes are created by default, so it is not necessary to specify NONCLUSTERED. Unique indexes are not created by default so UNIQUE must be specified in the CREATE INDEX statement. (For more information, refer to the section "Managing Indexes with Transact-SQL".)

10. **C.** Because the table is read only and will not be changed, the index should be built with no extra room allowed for changes. This will keep the index as small as possible. (For more information, refer to the section "Using the FILLFACTOR and PAD_INDEX Options.")

11. **D.** The options in answer C will reduce page splitting because the leaf and non-leaf pages will only be partially filled, but answer D will result in the least page splitting. (For more information, refer to the section "Using the FILLFACTOR and PAD_INDEX Options.")

12. **B.** A FILLFACTOR value of 50 represents the best balance between tightly filling the index to conserve space, and leaving space for new insertions out of the choices given. (For more information, refer to the section "Using the FILLFACTOR and PAD_INDEX Options.")

13. **B, C, D.** SQL Server cannot find either the table or index in the database. This could mean that the command is misspelled, or it could mean that the command is being issued in the wrong database. (For more information, refer to the section "Dropping Indexes".)

14. **D.** The code proposed would not implement full-text searching on the table or column. It is not possible to implement full-text searching on a table that does not have a unique key on a single field. Because the OrderDetail table has a composite key the first sp_fulltext_table command would have failed. (For more information, refer to the section "Enable Full-Text Searches.")

15. **A.** The generation-term that is introduced by the FORMSOF keyword attempts to match simple terms to all verb forms in the columns being searched. The prefix-term which is indicated by the asterisk

APPLY YOUR KNOWLEDGE

following a simple term as in choice D will perform a "fuzzy match" to the word "swim," which provides almost the same results. The fuzzy match will find "swim," "swims," and "swimming," but not "swam." The generation-term should be able to find that past-tense form. (For more information, refer to the section "Run Full-Text Searches.")

Suggested Readings and Resources

We recommend the following resources for further study in the area of planning:

1. SQL Server Books Online

   - Implementation of Full-text Search

   - Indexes

   - Using Clustered Indexes

2. Transact-SQL Help file

   - CONTAINS

   - FREETEXT

   - CONTAINSTABLE

   - FREETEXTTABLE

   - CREATE INDEX

   - DROP INDEX

   - sp_freetext_table

   - sp_freetext_column

This chapter helps you prepare for the Microsoft exam by covering the following objective:

Populate the database with data from an external data source. Methods include bulk copy program and Data Transformation Services (DTS).

▶ Loading a set of data into SQL Server is a common task. You need to be able to demonstrate an understanding of the data import tools that SQL Server provides you. Specifically mentioned are bulk copy program (BCP) and DTS, but you should understand the BULK INSERT statement, as well.

CHAPTER 5

Populating a Database

STUDY STRATEGIES

▶ You will want to read through the command-line switches available for the BCP.EXE utility several times before the test. Although you won't need to know the letter used for each option, you should be able to recognize valid switches if they are used in a question.

If you know the BCP.EXE utility, the BULK INSERT statement will be no problem. The BULK INSERT statement has the advantage of using more meaningful names for the options, making it easier to learn.

Spend more time with the DTS Package Designer than the DTS Wizard. As is pointed out in the chapter, the Wizard offers no functionality that can't also be found in the Package Designer anyway, and it's the functionality you want to be familiar with.

INTRODUCTION

Databases are rarely put into production empty. In most cases, before a database is ready to be used, it must be populated with existing data from an external source. This data can take any number of forms. It may be imported from another Relational Database Management System (RDBMS) or from a simple text file. The data can be well-known and clean, or it can have numerous inconsistencies. In any case, populating a database is a common challenge that most every SQL Server developer will have to deal with eventually. It is important, therefore, to understand the tools at your disposal for manipulating data. This chapter explores these tools in the following sections:

◆ Using bulk copy to import and export data

◆ Using the BCP command-line utility

◆ Using the BULK INSERT statement

◆ Using Data Transformation Services (DTS) to import and export data

USING BULK COPY TO IMPORT AND EXPORT DATA

▶ Populate the database with data from an external data source. Methods include bulk copy program and Data Transformation Services (DTS).

Bulk copy is an Application Programming Interface (API) built into SQL Server that allows data to be imported or exported in the most efficient manner possible. This interface is built directly into SQL Server's architecture. Bulk copy (BCP) is designed to deal with large amounts of data at once. Whereas an INSERT statement issued by an external client can insert a single row into a table, BCP is optimized to import (or export) thousands, or even hundreds of thousands, of rows into (or out of) a SQL Server database in a single session. BCP is the fundamental method of transferring data into or out of SQL Server.

As was stated previously, BCP is an API defined by SQL Server. Currently, this interface is exposed only through ODBC and DB-LIB data access libraries. The DB-LIB interface remains unchanged since version SQL Server version 6.0, but the ODBC interface continues to evolve and support new features and improvements. The fact that BCP has a well-defined public API means that you can write your own utilities to import or export data from SQL Server. These utilities you write will be able to harness the full power and speed of BCP. SQL Server provides a utility (BCP.EXE) that most users think of as being "BCP." However, this tool is simply a user interface placed in front of the standard API. Your programs can provide identical functionality and power.

Now that you have an understanding of what BCP is and the functionality it provides, you are ready to look at ways of implementing BCP. The two primary methods are the BCP command-line utility, and the BULK INSERT Transact-SQL statement.

Using the BCP Command-Line Utility

▶ Populate the database with data from an external data source. Methods include bulk copy program and Data Transformation Services (DTS).

The BCP command-line utility is a simple interface to SQL Server's bulk copy functionality. It is called a "simple" interface because it performs little work on its own. The BCP.EXE simply collects information and passes it to the BCP API defined in ODBC. The BCP utility offers a dizzying array of options that can be set to control the program's behavior. For the most part, each option that can be set on the command line represents exactly an option that can be set through the BCP API. The BCP utility does very little for you; rather, its purpose is to expose the full power, and sometimes the unfortunate complexity, of the API to you.

In talking to SQL Server veterans you will probably find that a love-hate relationship exists with the BCP utility. No one will dispute that it provided an extremely fast method of importing from and exporting data to SQL Server; however, you will likely find a few who feel that more time is lost setting up BCP than is gained by its transfer speed. This doesn't have to be the case. If you carefully learn the options the BCP utility provides and are especially careful with your format file, everything should run smoothly. You will see a discussion of a format file later in this chapter, but first some common terminology and the BCP options will be discussed.

BCP Terminology

Before you begin using BCP, you should learn about the jargon surrounding the use of this utility. Following are some of the more common terms you will encounter when using BCP:

♦ **Data file**. This is the operating system file that contains the data to be imported into SQL Server, or the file that contains exported data. You will often see this called a *source* file when the data is to be imported. The data can be in either native or character format.

♦ **Character format**. BCP can import from or export to a *character* (or *text*) file. These files use the standard ASCII character set to store information and are often used when transferring data between heterogeneous sources (such as a SQL Server and a mainframe). Columns in a character file are divided by delimiters (such as a comma or a tab character) or defined to be of a certain size (a fixed-width file). You can use a text editor such as Notepad to view the contents of a character file.

♦ **Native format**. BCP also can import from or export to a native file. *Native* files are binary files that contain the data in the same format that SQL Server uses to internally store data. Native files are generally used to transfer data between SQL Servers.

♦ **Format file**. When transferring data into or out of a character data file, you may use a *format* file to specify the column and row delimiters used in the data file. Format files also are useful for importing only parts of the data file into a table. The format file is covered later in this section.

♦ **Batch size**. By default, BCP loads all rows from the data file into SQL Sever in a single transaction. By specifying a batch size, you can tell BCP to load the data in smaller chunks. See the section "Command-Line Syntax" later in this chapter for more information.

◆ **Source table/destination table**. These terms are often used to describe the table from which data will be exported or the table to which data will be imported, respectively.

Permissions Required to Use BCP

To use the BCP utility, you must have a valid logon ID on the SQL Server and a valid user ID in the database involved in the data transfer. In addition, you must have the following permissions:

◆ If the data file resides on an NTFS partition, you must have permissions to read from the file (for imports) and create or modify the file (for exports).

◆ When importing data, you must have INSERT permission on the destination table. If you own the table, you will automatically have INSERT permission; otherwise, the table owner must grant this to your database user ID.

◆ When exporting data, you must have SELECT permission on the source table or view. The table owner has this permission to select data and may grant this permission to other database users. In addition, you must have SELECT permission on three tables in the database's catalog: sysobjecs, *syscolumns,* and sysindexes.

BCP Data Transfer Behavior

Knowing about how BCP transfers data into and out of SQL Server can save you hours of frustration. The first thing to remember is that when importing data into a table, rows are appended to the end of the table—existing rows are left intact. Alternately, when exporting to a file, the file is overwritten if it already exists.

When BCP is importing data into a table, other users in the database can be using that table. The rows inserted by BCP become visible after a batch has been completed. Keep in mind that, by default, the entire contents of the data file are loaded in a single batch. When

BCP is exporting data from a table, other users may be using the table as well. However, BCP exports a "snapshot" of the table as it existed when the BCP was started. Data modifications made by users after the BCP has started are not reflected in the data file. For this reason, it is often a good idea to prevent users from accessing the database (or at least the table) while data is being exported.

When BCP is importing data into a table, two different methods may be used: logged or non-logged BCP. Keep in mind that BCP, whether it be logged or non-logged, is many times faster than any other SQL Server data transfer method. Regardless of the transfer method, column data types and NULL options are always enforced. Attempting to import data of the incorrect type, or attempting to import a NULL value into a column that forbids NULLs will cause the BCP batch to fail. Fortunately, any default constraints are honored during a BCP import by default.

Non-Logged BCP

Non-logged BCP is the preferred method for transferring very large amounts of data because it is extremely fast—several thousand rows can be inserted per second. In a non-logged BCP, SQL Server only logs the page allocations used to increase the size of the destination table.

For a non-logged BCP to take place, a number of conditions must be met:

◆ The Select Into/Bulkcopy option for the database must be turned on. This allows non-logged operations to occur, such as BCP. (The log writes due to page allocations are built into the normal operations of SQL Server; thus, this mode of BCP is considered non-logged.)

◆ The TABLOCK option must be used. This option locks the table during an import process, and is described in full later in this chapter.

◆ The destination table cannot be marked for replication.

◆ The destination table can have indexes only if the table is empty. If the table has indexes defined and contains data rows, a logged BCP will be used.

If these conditions are not met, a logged BCP takes place.

WARNING

Non-Logged Operations Trade Safety for Speed Permitting non-logged operations in a database means that you lose the ability to perform up-to-the-minute recovery with the transaction log; only the full database can be backed up and restored. (SQL Server still performs automatic recovery in the event of a system failure.)

For this reason, you should perform a full backup of a database (if it has data) before importing large amounts of data. After the data load is complete, perform another full backup, and turn off the Select Into/Bulkcopy option.

NOTE

Standard Features of Command-Line Options   Command-line options are case sensitive, so -f and -F, for example, are different options. In addition, you can use either a slash (/) or a dash (-) to prefix the option.

Logged BCP

During a logged BCP, the inserted data is logged in the transaction log just as if an INSERT statement had been executed. Any constraints on the table are enforced, as are unique indexes. Because the amount of logging increases with a logged BCP, it is often much slower than a non-logged BCP, often by a factor of ten.

A logged BCP is a fully logged operation, so up-to-the-minute recovery is possible with a current transaction log dump. However, the transaction log may fill up if a large amount of data is imported.

Command-Line Syntax

The syntax of the BCP command-line utility follows. The executable file, BCP.EXE, can be found in the BINN subdirectory under the SQL Server installation directory.

```
bcp {[[database_name.][owner].]table_name ¦ "query"}
{in ¦ out ¦ queryout ¦ format} data_file
[-m max_errors] [-f format_file] [-e err_file]
[-F first_row] [-L last_row] [-b batch_size]
[-n] [-c] [-w] [-N] [-6] [-q] [-C code_page]
[-t field_term] [-r row_term]
[-i input_file] [-o output_file] [-a packet_size]
[-S server_name] [-U login_id] [-P password]
[-T] [-v] [-k] [-E] [-h "hint [,…n]"]
```

This BCP command-line syntax is explored more closely in the following list:

{in ¦ out ¦ queryout ¦ format} specifies whether data will be imported or exported from the table or whether you want BCP to create a format file for you. The queryout option is a special case of exporting that allows the data to be taken from a query instead of a table. The queryout option can only be used if a double-quote delimited query was given, rather than a table name.

datafile specifies the name of the data file.

/m is used to specify the maximum number of errors that may occur before the transfer is canceled. If this option is omitted, BCP fails after ten errors.

/f specifies the name of the format file, if used.

/e specifies the file to which error messages will be logged. By default, error messages are reported onscreen as they are generated.

/F specifies the number of the first row to copy. If omitted, BCP starts transferring with the first row of the data file or source table.

/L specifies the number of the last row to copy. If this option is omitted, BCP ends the transfer with the last row of the data file or source table.

/b enables you to specify the batch size (in number of rows) for the data transfer. If this option is omitted, BCP transfers all rows in a single batch. This option is useful if the entire BCP batch fills the transaction log due to page allocations. Specifying a smaller batch size and turning on the database trunc. log on chkpt. option can prevent the transaction log from filling up. In addition, reducing the batch size can prevent SQL Server from running out of locks during the import of data.

/n specifies that the data file is a native format file or that the data file created from an export should be in native format.

/c specifies that a character-format data file will be used for the transfer. The default column delimiter is a tab, and the default row delimiter is a newline character.

/w specifies that a unicode character format data file will be used for the transfer. Just as with the /c option, a tab is used for a column delimiter and a newline character for row delimiters. The w stands for "wide" character—hence unicode.

/N specifies that the data file uses SQL Server native format for numerical data and unicode for character-based data types.

/6 specifies that the data file uses SQL Server version 6.5 data types. This option is used to modify the /n and /c options.

/q specifies that the three-part table name identifier contains non-ANSI standard characters. The identifier should be enclosed by quotation characters.

/C *code_page* specifies a particular code page that the data file uses. Characters with ASCII values of less than 32 or greater than 127 are represented differently in different code pages, so this option lets you specify the code page to use. The possible values for *code_page* are as follows:

> ACP specifies the ANSI standard code page.
>
> OEM specifies the default code page for the client.
>
> RAW specifies that no code page conversion should be used.
>
> *<value>* specifies a specific code page to use by number.

/t specifies the column (or field) terminator for a character format data file.

/r specifies the row terminator for a character format data file.

/i specifies a file that contains input to redirect to BCP.

/o specifies an output file for all BCP messages (other than errors).

/a specifies the network packet size used when BCP loads data into a SQL Server over the network.

/S specifies the name of the SQL Server that is participating in the data transfer. This option can be omitted if you are executing BCP on the local SQL Server machine. If possible, perform data transfers on the machine that hosts SQL Server—this reduces the overhead generated by sending data across the network.

/U is used when BCP is to log in to the SQL Server in mixed or standard security modes. It specifies the name of the database user ID to use for the transfer.

/P is used when BCP is to log in to the SQL Server in mixed or standard security modes. It specifies the password of the database user ID given with the /U parameter.

/T specifies that BCP should log in to the SQL Server with a trusted security connection.

/v prints the DB-Library version information.

/k specifies that NULL values should be inserted for empty columns. This option overrides the default by disabling default constraints on the table.

/E specifies that the BCP transfer will be importing data into a table with an identity column, and that the values for the identity column will be explicitly provided in the data file. This option has no effect if data is being exported.

/h this option allows several "hints" to be specified for use during an import operation. The hints that can be supplied are as follows:

> ORDER (*column* [ASC ¦ DESC] [,...*n*]) specifies to SQL Server that the data being imported is already ordered. This allows SQL Server to optimize the insertions to the table if the order given matches that of a clustered index on the table. If the order given does not match that of a clustered index, the hint is ignored.

ROWS_PER_BATCH specifies the number of rows that should be inserted in each batch when the entire file is imported within a transaction. This hint is not valid if the /b option was also used.

KILOBYTES_PER_BATCH specifies the approximate number of kilobytes in a batch. This provides an alternative to specifying a batch size in "number of rows" units with the /b option.

TABLOCK specifies that the table being imported into should be locked during the import process. When this option is used, multiple BCP processes can load data in parallel while the table is protected from other forms of modification.

CHECK_CONSTRAINTS specifies that check constraints defined on the table are enabled. By default check constraints are disabled.

The following are some examples of using BCP to transfer data into and out of the sample database Pubs, which comes with SQL Server:

1. This example exports data from the authors table into a character file called C:\authors.txt. The file's columns are tab-delimited, with a new row on each line. A trusted connection is used to connect to the local server.

```
BCP pubs..authors out C:\authors.txt /c /T
```

The results of this command will look something like this:

```
Starting copy...

23 rows copied.
Network packet size (bytes): 4096
Clock Time (ms.): total =     20 Avg =      0 (1150.00
rows per sec.)
```

2. This example imports the data file from Example 1 back into the authors table in the Pubs database:

```
BCP pubs..authors in C:\authors.txt /c /T
```

Because data already exists in the authors table, this import attempts to insert duplicate data. BCP returns the following error message:

```
Starting copy...
Msg 2627, Level 14, State 1:
Line 1:
Violation of PRIMARY KEY constraint 'UPKCL_auidind':
➥Attempt to insert
duplicate key in object 'authors'.
```

3. This example exports the contents of the authors table into a native format file called C:\authors.dat:

```
BCP pubs..authors out C:\authors.dat /n /T
```

Using Format Files

BCP format files enable you to fine-tune the way data files are imported into a table or how a table's data is exported into the data file. You can specify different column or row terminators, adjust the length of the data transferred, or rearrange the order in which table columns are transferred. You will most often create a format file when importing a mainframe text file into SQL Server. Each part of the format file is marked so you may distinguish between the different parts used.

The purposes of each part of the format file are detailed in the following list:

◆ **Version**. This is the version number of the BCP program. This is "7.0" for SQL Server version 7.0.

◆ **Number of columns.** This is the number of columns in the data file.

Although you can use the BCP utility to create format files, if you have a data file with extra columns or unusual delimiters, you may need to modify the format file by hand. It is very easy to overlook the Number of Columns field when adding or removing rows to the format file. If your format file just isn't working, check this field for accuracy, it is a common source of error.

◆ **Host file field order**. This is the order in which the columns appear in the data file. These are usually just listed in sequential order.

◆ **Host file Data Type**. Specifies the data type of the column in the data file. For text files, always use SQLCHAR. For native format files, use the name of the table column's data type, such as SQLSMALLINT, for a smallint column.

Remember that the Host File Data Type refers to the type of data in the file you are importing. In a text file, all fields are always character fields, even if they are numbers. Use other data types only if you are importing a binary file. Thinking that you are importing numbers and therefore using SQLINT for a text file is another common source of error.

◆ **Prefix length**. This value is used with native format files to specify a storage area in the file used to hold the length of the data in the column. For text files, always use 0.

◆ **Host file Data Length**. This value specifies the actual length of the data in the data file for a particular column. For text files, this is the maximum length of a column. For instance, when a tinyint column is represented as characters, the number may range from 0 to 255. This field allows for a maximum of three characters.

◆ **Terminator**. The terminator column is used to specify column terminators for all but the last column and a row terminator for the last column. Typically, tabs (\t) or commas (,) are used to delimit columns, and a CRLF (\r\n) is used to delimit rows.

◆ **Server column order**. This specifies the column that SQL Server should insert into or retrieve from in the destination or source table.

◆ **Server column name**. The name of the column in the source or destination table. SQL Server does not actually use this to determine which column data will be inserted to or retrieved from, so you may enter any value here. However, you cannot leave this column blank.

See the SQL Server Books Online for more in-depth information about how format files may be used in a data transfer.

BCP.EXE

The BCP utility (BCP.EXE) is a program that exposes the full functionality of SQL Server's bulk copy interface. It can run in either logged or non-logged mode depending on conditions in the database and on your tables. Although it supports a vast array of options, each one is reasonably simple, and well-documented. You have seen a brief description of each option in this section, and more detailed information can be found in the SQL Server Books Online. Finally, you were introduced to the use of format files to supplement the command-line format options. A format file allows greater flexibility in the assignment and format of data to particular fields in the table.

In the next section you will be introduced to a Transact-SQL command that is closely related to the BCP utility. The BULK INSERT statement provides all the same functionality of BCP.EXE, but can be run from a query window.

USING THE BULK INSERT STATEMENT

▶ Populate the database with data from an external data source. Methods include bulk copy program and Data Transformation Services (DTS).

It is now possible to access the functionality of the bulk copy program (BCP) directly from inside a query tool by using the BULK INSERT Transact-SQL statement. As the name implies, the BULK INSERT statement is only used for importing data into SQL Server; it cannot be used to export data.

The best introduction to the BULK INSERT statement is to simply examine the syntax. Keep in mind that this statement is just an alternate front-end to the standard BCP functionality. All the rules governing permissions needed and conditions for a logged or non-logged BCP apply to the BULK INSERT statement just as they do for any other BCP function. You'll notice that the options here will be quite similar to the options available in the BCP utility described above:

```
BULK INSERT [['database_name'.]['owner'.]{'table_name'
➥FROM data_file}
        [WITH
                (
                        [ BATCHSIZE [= batch_size]]
                        [[,] CHECK_CONSTRAINTS]
                        [[,] CODEPAGE [= 'ACP' ¦ 'OEM' ¦
➥'RAW' ¦ 'code_page']]
                        [[,] DATAFILETYPE [=
                                {'char' ¦ 'native'¦
➥'widechar' ¦ 'widenative'}]]
                        [[,] FIELDTERMINATOR [=
➥'field_terminator']]
                        [[,] FIRSTROW [= first_row]]
                        [[,] FORMATFILE [=
➥'format_file_path']]
                        [[,] KEEPIDENTITY]
                        [[,] KEEPNULLS]
                        [[,] KILOBYTES_PER_BATCH [=
➥kilobytes_per_batch]]
                        [[,] LASTROW [= last_row]]
                        [[,] MAXERRORS [= max_errors]]
                        [[,] ORDER ({column [ASC ¦ DESC]}
➥[,...n])]
                        [[,] ROWS_PER_BATCH [=
➥rows_per_batch]]
                        [[,] ROWTERMINATOR [=
➥'row_terminator']]
                        [[,] TABLOCK]
                )
        ]
```

Noticeably lacking from the list of available options are the switches to specify the server, username, and password, or to force a trusted connection. In order to run a BULK INSERT statement, you must already have an open connection to SQL Server, making these parameters unnecessary. Note that all the options shown above are optional. If no options are specified, the operation will default to using a character data file with tab field delimiters and newline (\n) row delimiters, with the OEM codepage translation.

> **NOTE**
>
> **An Easy Way to Export Data from a Query Tool** Although the BULK INSERT statement is used only to import data from an external source, a simple SELECT statement can effectively export data from a query tool. Using the SQL Server Query Analyzer, for example, you can issue a query, and then save the results to a file by choosing File, Save from the menu bar.

Using Data Transformation Services to Import and Export Data

▶ Populate the database with data from an external data source. Methods include bulk copy program and Data Transformation Services (DTS).

The Data Transformation Services, usually referred to simply as DTS, use OLE-DB technology to transfer data from one application to another, optionally manipulating the data in the process. It is important to note that neither of these data sources is required to be SQL Server. In fact, DTS is not a part of SQL Server, but a standalone product in itself that is simply packaged as a tool to use with SQL Server. Microsoft's OLE-DB technology provides a method for accessing data in virtually any format, and DTS provides the bridge-work. DTS is commonly described as a "data pump". It reads data in from one source and pumps it out to another. As DTS reads in the data in preparation to write it back out, you are allowed to script code that will execute on the individual records being transferred. This data manipulation is the essence of the "transformation" in DTS.

With its functionality to access data in virtually any source and write that data into SQL Server, DTS is an important tool for populating SQL Server databases. The BCP functionality described earlier can use only limited formats, ASCII text files and SQL Server native binary files, when it is used to import data. In addition to DTS's excellent flexibility in working with data sources, its ability to perform transformations on data makes it a particularly useful tool.

The data manipulations supported by DTS are entered through the use of the scripting language of your choice. DTS is extensible to support new languages, but is shipped with the ability to use VB Script, Perl Script, or Jscript. The scripts you write can reference any of the data in a single record as that record is transferred. The most basic script is simply a series of assignments from the source fields to the destination fields, though any functions supported by the scripting language could be used before or during the assignments. A common use of these manipulations would be to properly format phone numbers, social security numbers, and so on, during a data transfer.

As was stated earlier, DTS is a tool that is separate from SQL Server. The DTS tool is implemented as an application that follows scripted commands that are contained in a proprietary data format called a "package". A DTS *package* is a collection of commands that tell DTS what data to collect, and how to write it out to a destination. In addition, a package can contain other commands called *tasks* that are basically action statements. These tasks can take a variety of forms such as DOS style commands, TSQL scripts, or even a command to send email.

In the following sections you will learn how to use DTS in two forms. First, you will be introduced to the DTS Package Designer. The Package Designer allows you to create packages with the full complexity that DTS allows. You will learn to use the DTS Wizard to create simple packages quickly. Both the DTS Package Designer and the DTS Wizard are tools that are run through the SQL Enterprise Manager to create packages and then call DTS to execute them.

Using the DTS Package Designer

The DTS Package Designer is a tool found in SQL Server Enterprise Manager that allows you to define DTS packages. It has been stated that DTS packages are collections of commands that tell DTS what to do. The DTS Package Designer defines these commands as one of two types: transforms and tasks. Tasks have been defined within the context of a DTS package as action commands; *transforms* define the movement of data between two data sources.

The term *data source* is used in the same sense as an OLE-DB data source. In other words, it is any collection of data that can be referenced through OLE-DB. Realize that a data source can have data written to it. Therefore, don't be confused when a data source is described as a destination for data.

The Package Designer is a graphical tool that represents data sources and tasks as icons, which can be placed in the Designer window. Transforms are represented by arrows, which connect two data sources, pointing from the source to the destination. Tasks are executed by being placed at the head or tail of a precedence constraint. A precedence constraint connects tasks together or indicates a transform should occur before or after a task is completed. By placing a precedence constraint from a task to a data source you indicate the transform associated with the data source should occur after the task, reversing the arrow's direction indicates the task follows the transform. There are three different precedence constraints to operate: On Completion, On Success, and On Failure. These concepts are better explained by viewing a sample package design, such as the one shown in Figure 5.2.

FIGURE 5.2
A sample DTS package design.

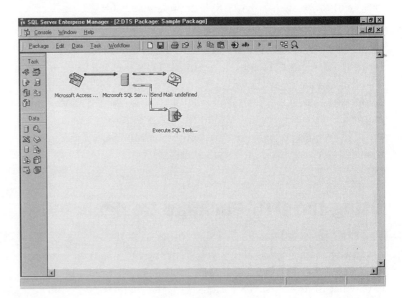

In the figure, a Microsoft Access database is used as a source for data to be transferred to SQL Server. The black arrow that connects the Access data source to the SQL Server represents the transformation. You will also notice two tasks defined in the figure. The Send Mail task is connected to the SQL Server data source with a red arrow, and the Execute SQL task is connected to the SQL Server data source with a green arrow. The fact that both the arrows lead from the destination data source indicates that the tasks should take place after the data transformation to the SQL Server. The red arrow is an On Failure precedence constraint, indicating that the Send Mail task should take place if the data transformation fails; the green arrow is an On Success precedence constraint, indicating that the Execute SQL task takes place only if the transformation succeeds. An On Completion precedence constraint is shown as a blue arrow, and would cause a task to run regardless of success or failure. This is a good example of a simple transformation because it uses the Send Mail task to report errors and it demonstrates the ability to take some predetermined action, such as creating an index on the newly transferred table, upon completion.

With this idea of a DTS package in mind, the following sections will detail how to create data sources, transforms, and tasks. In each section you will be escorted through a series of steps to create examples of each package object which will build on each other. At the end you will have a fully formed, albeit simple, DTS package.

Data Source Properties

Each data source defined in the Package Designer will expose properties that are unique for the source. The list of data sources corresponds to the OLE-DB drivers that you have installed on your system. Because every driver is somewhat different, and even the list of drivers changes from system to system, it is not possible to detail the use of every data source here. The important thing to realize is that every source will need to be given enough information to establish a connection to the actual data source. This usually involves a user name and password, but it can also include other information such as the filename of an Access database. Step by Steps 5.1 and 5.2 will show you how to create both a SQL Server Data Source and an Access Data Source, respectively.

STEP BY STEP

5.1 Creating a SQL Server Data Source

1. Open SQL Server Enterprise Manager and choose your server from the tree. You may have to open a Server Group to find your server.

2. Click the plus sign (+) to the left of your server to reveal the list of server components. Right-click the Data Transformation Services icon and choose New Package from the context menu. The DTS Package window is revealed as shown in Figure 5.3.

continues

continued

FIGURE 5.3
The DTS Package window.

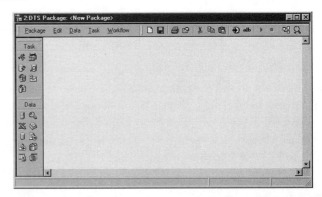

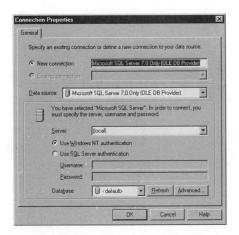

FIGURE 5.4
The Connection Properties dialog box for a SQL Server 7.0 data source.

3. Under the Data heading in the tool collection to the left of the window, examine the available tools to find the Microsoft SQL Server 7.0 Only data source. Drag and drop this icon onto an open space in the window. The Connection Properties dialog box will be displayed, as shown in Figure 5.4.

4. Keep the setting of New Connection, but change the name of the connection to My SQL Server.

5. Leave the data source as Microsoft SQL Server 7.0 Only (OLE-DB Provider).

6. Set the server to your SQL Server.

7. Set the authentication mode as appropriate to log in to your server. Enter the user name and password for SQL Server authentication if needed.

8. Choose a sample database that you have permissions to create tables in and click OK to complete configuring the data source.

In Step by Step 5.2, you will see how to set up an Access data source. If you do not have an Access database at your disposal, you can simply repeat Step by Step 5.1 and create another SQL Server data source. If you will be using two SQL Server data sources, you may want to name the second source the My Access Source, anyway, so that you can follow the remaining examples.

STEP BY STEP

5.2 Creating a Microsoft Access Data Source

1. Open a DTS Package Design window as described in steps 1 and 2 of Step by Step 5.1.

2. Under the Data heading in the tool collection to the left of the window, examine the available tools to find the Microsoft SQL Server 7.0 Only data source. Drag and drop this icon onto an open space in the window. The Connection Properties dialog box will be displayed, as shown in Figure 5.5.

3. Keep the setting of New Connection, but change the name of the connection to My Access Source.

4. Do not change the Data Source setting.

5. Enter the filename and, if necessary, the username and password for your Access database.

6. Click OK to create the data source. If you do not have an access database at your disposal, click Cancel.

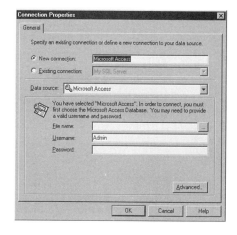

FIGURE 5.5▲

The Connection Properties dialog box for a Microsoft Access data source.

Transform Properties

It was noted earlier that transforms are represented by black arrows. By right-clicking the transform you can edit the properties of the transform. There are four tabs on the Properties dialog box detailing the source and destination of the transformation, a column-by-column detail of the transformation itself, and an Advanced tab that lets you set general properties. Figure 5.6 shows the Source tab from the example described earlier.

On the Source tab of the Data Transformation Properties dialog box, you need to determine the table that will be transferred. You can choose a literal table from the data source, or you can transfer a derived table which is the result set of a SQL query. By entering a query, you can transfer selected rows from a table, or you can even perform a join of several tables when transferring to a different data model. If you choose to export the results of a query, there are command buttons below the query box that allow you to build the

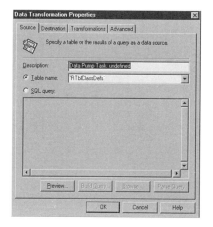

FIGURE 5.6▲

The Source tab of a Data Transformation Properties dialog box.

query using a graphical interface, check the syntax of your query, and preview the result set from the query.

Step by Step 5.3 shows an example of populating the Source tab of a Data Transformation Properties dialog box. This Step by Step assumes you have an open DTS package window and two data sources, named My SQL Server and My Access Source. These prerequisites can be met by following Step by Steps 5.1 and 5.2.

STEP BY STEP

5.3 Populating the Source Tab of the Data Transformation Properties Dialog Box

1. Select the data source My Access Source. This defines the source data source. Hold the Ctrl key and then select the My SQL Server data source. This defines My SQL Server as a destination.

2. In the Workflow menu item, choose Add Transform. This defines a transform from the source to the destination data sources.

3. Right-click the black transform arrow, and choose Properties. You will be presented with the Data Transformation Properties dialog box similar to the one shown in Figure 5.6.

4. Change the name of the transform to Sample Transform.

5. Keep the Table Name option selected, and keep the default table listed. Alternatively, you can choose a different table or even experiment by entering a SQL query with no detrimental impact on this example. This is all the information needed for the Source tab of the dialog box.

On the Destination tab of the Data Transformation Properties dialog box (see Figure 5.7) you must select a table that will receive the data. You can choose from tables that are already defined in the drop-down box, or you can choose to create a new table. You should realize that by choosing to create a table, the table you define will be created immediately, not when the transformation is run. Naturally, you must have appropriate rights and permissions on the database to create a new table.

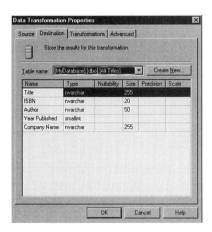

◄FIGURE 5.7
The Destination tab of a Data Transformation Properties dialog box.

Step by Step 5.4 demonstrates creating a new table to act as the destination to a transform. This Step by Step assumes that you have run Step by Steps 5.1 through 5.3, and that a Data Transformation Properties dialog box is open.

STEP BY STEP

5.4 Populating the Destination Tab of the Data Transformation Properties Dialog Box

1. Click the Destination tab of the Data Transformation Properties dialog box. ·

2. Ignore the table selected by default. Click the Create New button. The Create Destination Table dialog box will appear similar to the one shown in Figure 5.8.

3. The dialog box should automatically populate with a CREATE TABLE statement that is compatible with the table format of the source table. Accept the default and choose OK.

4. This is all the information needed to populate the Destination tab.

FIGURE 5.8▲
The Create Destination Table dialog box.

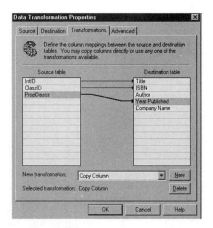

FIGURE 5.9▶
The Transformations tab of a Data Transformation Properties dialog box.

The Transformations tab (see Figure 5.9) allows you to perform column mappings from the source to the destination. If you simply want to transfer the contents of the table without changes, a graphical tool is presented that shows how the contents of the source are sent to the individual columns in the destination. If some columns are not supposed to be transferred, or the mapping is non-intuitive to SQL Server, the arrows can be deleted or moved. Figure 5.9 shows a default data transfer.

If you need to perform any transformations on a table's contents as the transfer is performed, you can change the selection in the New Transformation drop-down box near the bottom of the window. For example, you could choose to execute an ActiveX script to manipulate the data, as shown in Figure 5.10. This is a relatively uninteresting script that simply serves to convert the author's name to uppercase letters during the transformation. Figure 5.10 uses Visual Basic as the scripting language, but others are available and even more scripting languages can be added in the future. The important thing to note about scripting transformations is that although you can reference data from other columns, you cannot reference data from other rows. There is, however, an advanced feature of DTS that allows data to be examined from different tables. This feature is called a *lookup*, and is described later in this chapter.

FIGURE 5.10▶
Scripting a transformation.

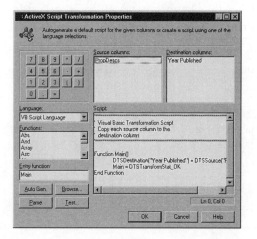

Step by Step 5.5 takes you through the process of populating the Transformations tab. This example assumes you have completed Step by Steps 5.1 through 5.4, and that the Data Transformation Properties dialog box is open.

STEP BY STEP

5.5 Populating the Transformations Tab of the Transform Properties Dialog Box

1. Click the Transformations tab of the Data Transformations Properties dialog box.

2. For this example you will modify one of the default transforms with a scripted transformation. Choose a character field in the Source and Destination tables. Click the black arrow that connects the two tables to select that transformation. Change the New Transformation drop-down box to ActiveX Script, then click New. The ActiveX Script Transformation Properties dialog box will appear.

3. In the Script text field, change the default field assignment to execute the UCase function. The assignment will end up looking something like the following:

```
DTSDestination("FieldName") =
➥Ucase(DTSSource("FieldName"))
```

4. Click OK to complete the script. This completes the actions needed to transform the data.

5. It will not be necessary to modify any settings of the Advanced tab. Click OK to complete your configuration of the Data Transformation Properties dialog box.

The last tab covers advanced features of the transformation properties. These properties are divided into three sections: error handling, data movement, and SQL Server—specific properties (see Figure 5.11).

Under the error handling section, you can specify an allowable number of errors before the transformation will be halted. Any transformed rows that cause errors can be written to an exception file defined here as well. You can specify the row and column delimiters used in the exception file through the last two controls in the error handling section.

The data movement section allows you to control properties that affect what data SQL Server transfers and how. The Insert Commit Size control adjusts the number of rows that are submitted before an

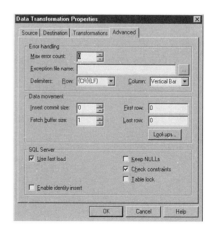

FIGURE 5.11
Advanced tab of Data Transformation Properties dialog box.

explicit commit is issued to the receiving data source. The Fetch Buffer Size control adjusts the number of rows that are transferred in a single batch. Neither of these controls should be adjusted unless you are explicitly familiar with specific capabilities of the receiving data source. The defaults will work for all data sources, and adjusted values can severely hurt performance on many data sources. The First Row and Last Row controls allow you some control over what rows get transferred. These controls are commonly used to skip header rows before transferring data. The last control in this section allows you to define lookups. Lookups are a complicated feature that demands individual coverage. You will return to a full discussion of lookups at the end of this section.

The final section, SQL Server properties, allows you to adjust settings specific to SQL Server. These properties are meaningful only when SQL Server is the receiving data source. All these properties should be familiar to you as properties relating to BCP, described earlier in this chapter. When DTS imports to SQL Server, it is able to take advantage of the BCP interface and this section allows you some control over the BCP properties it will use.

Data Transform Lookups

Lookups are a feature of DTS that allow you to define a parameterized query that retrieves a single row and a single column from a data source not participating in the transformation. Then, during an ActiveX script transformation, the lookup is referenced by name and passed the parameter values that it requires from the current row's column values. The lookup then executes the query and returns the resulting value. Lookups are commonly used to translate a code value to a meaningful description or vise versa.

Clicking the Lookups button on the Advanced tab of a Data Transform Properties dialog box will expose the Data Transformation Lookups dialog box, as shown in Figure 5.12. This dialog box simply allows you to give a name to a lookup and specify the connection that the lookup will execute on. Remember that the connection used by a lookup cannot be a connection that is in use by either the source or destination of a transformation. However, it is permissible to use a connection not involved in the transformation that points to the same data source as one involved in the transformation. You also can set a number relating to how many transformed rows should be cached in memory. If you are performing lookups on a relatively

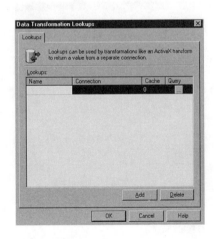

FIGURE 5.12
Data Transformation Lookups dialog box.

small table, you could set this cache to the number of rows in the lookup table so that each row is looked up only once, saving time on subsequent lookups. The final setting is the most important—defining the lookup query. Click the ellipsis button in the Query column to reveal the Data Transformation Services Query Designer dialog box, as shown in Figure 5.13.

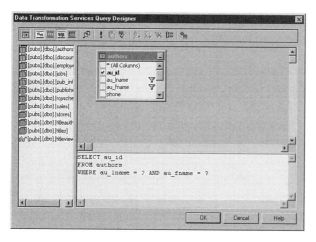

FIGURE 5.13
Data Transformation Services Query Designer.

The query you enter should use question marks as placeholders indicating that an exact value will be supplied at run time. The following is an example of a parameterized query that returns the author's ID (au_id) when passed the first and last names (au_fname and au_lname):

```
SELECT au_id
FROM authors
WHERE au_lname = ? AND au_fname = ?
```

This lookup is then used by an ActiveX script. The script code references the lookup by name and supplies all needed arguments; the lookup then returns the single column value that was looked up. The following routine could be used in a VB script to access the lookup defined above:

```
Function Main()
        DTSDestination("au_id") =
DTSLookups("lkAuthorID").Execute(DTSSource("au_lname")
➥.Value, DTSSource("au_fname").Value )
        Main = DTSTransformStat_OK
End Function
```

Through the use of lookups, you can reference values from other tables during your transformations. These values allow you to make more sophisticated and useful transformations and can particularly aid in a detailed normalization process.

Task Properties

There are many tasks that come predefined with SQL Server. These include a Bulk Insert task, Send Mail task, Execute SQL task, and Execute Process task. Each of these tasks performs a very different action, as you might guess from their names. Because each task is so different, there is no representative property sheet that can be easily described. As a rule, you should simply realize that you will be prompted to enter the command that you want executed. Each task is quite straightforward and self-explanatory to use.

The following lists the tasks that are predefined with SQL Server, and includes a short description of the properties needed for each.

◆ **Active Script task.** The Active Script task allows you to choose the language of the script, and to enter the code to be scripted. When the task is executed, your script will be run. You can interact with global variables during this task. A common use for an Active Script task would be to set up global variables or to perform error checking scans on the source or destination data sources to ensure prerequisites are met.

◆ **Execute Process task.** The Execute Process task allows you to execute a DOS based process. You can enter a description for the task, and the name of the process. If the process accepts parameters, those can be entered as well. A successful return code can also be entered so that the task can determine if the process succeeded or not. The process defined will be run asynchronously to DTS. To prevent DTS from waiting indefinitely for a process that has encountered an error and will not complete, you can enter a timeout value to indicate the number of seconds you are willing to wait for the process to complete. A value of zero (default) indicates that you will wait indefinitely. If you enter a non-zero value you can also indicate whether you want to terminate a process that has taken too long to complete, or if you wish to let it continue. A common use for the Execute Process task is to run an external process to create a data source before it can be transformed.

◆ **Execute SQL task.** The Execute SQL task allows you to execute a single SQL statement. A data source must first exist to use this task. You can enter a description for this task, and then you must choose an existing data source in the DTS

Package Designer. You can either enter a SQL statement your-self, or you can use the Query Designer tool to help you create a query. This task is similar to the Execute Process task in that it runs asynchronously to DTS. Therefore, you can enter a timeout value to indicate how long you are willing to wait for the query to complete. Again, a value of zero indicates that DTS should wait indefinitely. Unlike the Execute Process task, however, this task will always be terminated after the timeout.

◆ **Data Driven Query task.** The Data Driven Query task is rather different from the others discussed so far. This task actually performs a standard transformation and then runs a query based on the data inserted into the destination. This task takes a source and a destination data source as inputs, which must exist when the task is created. It then behaves exactly as a standard transform and has the same Source, Destination, and Transformation tabs as a standard transformation. In addition, however, it contains a Queries tab on which you can enter a parameterized query. Also on this tab is a list of fields in the destination data source that are used as the parameters to the query. The task as a whole, then, runs a standard transformation from the source to destination, then as each transformed row is entered into the destination, a query is run using the destination fields as input. This query can either insert, update, or delete the destination table or (more likely) any other table in the data source based on this new data. A common use for the Data Driven Query task would be to see if a value in the destination table already exists in a code table and then insert a new row to that code table.

◆ **Transfer Objects task.** The Transfer Objects task works to transfer objects between two SQL Server 7.0 data sources. It requires two SQL Server 7.0 data sources, and then requests information about what objects to transfer. Although this task can transfer data along with any tables that are transferred, its true purpose is to transfer objects of any type—not just tables. You may choose to transfer as many or as few objects as you wish.

◆ **Send Mail task.** The Send Mail task simply requires a mail profile that has already been configured on the DTS machine, addressing information, and a message. This task will then send mail to the addressees, from the mail account defined by the profile. The profile must be supplied with a password. Remember that the profile must be configured on the machine from which DTS is being run, which is usually the local machine. You can include attachments in this mail task. A common use might be to mail an error file as an attachment when a transfer fails.

◆ **Bulk Insert task.** The Bulk Insert task will automate BCP (as defined earlier in this chapter) to give you maximum optimization of a bulk data transfer from an ASCII text file into SQL Server. During a standard transformation to a SQL Server 7.0 data source, bulk copy functionality may be used if conditions permit. This task, however, allows you to fully configure and guarantee a bulk copy of the data into SQL Server.

Using the DTS Wizard

The DTS Wizard provides an alternative interface to creating and running packages via the DTS Package Designer described earlier. Although the DTS Package Designer is built into the SQL Enterprise Manager Tool itself, the DTS Wizard is a separate entity that can be found in the BINN directory of your SQL Server install directory (usually MSSQL7). The executable name is DTSWIZ.EXE, and it can be run independently of SQL Enterprise Manager. Nonetheless, Enterprise Manager contains links to run the DTS Wizard, and this is how it is most commonly run.

The DTS Wizard is designed to help you quickly transfer data from one data source to another. It asks simple questions about the data sources you will use and allows you to select the tables whose data you wish to transform. You are given the ability to use ActiveX scripts to perform transformations on the data, to simply define a column to column mapping between tables. All parts of the wizard will look familiar to you if you have already studied the Package Designer. It is more important to understand what can be done with the DTS Wizard than to understand every control you can adjust during the process. A description of each screen in the DTS Wizard follows, and the section will complete with a Step by Step description of the actual use of the DTS Wizard.

The DTS Wizard takes you through a step-by-step process to define a complete, though simple, DTS package. The DTS Wizard offers you a subset of the properties described above in each element of the DTS Package Designer. First, you are required to define two data sources for the source and destination of the data transfer. This is done by presenting to you, from inside the wizard, the data source property sheets for the sources you choose. You are then given the choice of transferring tables (this meaning the contents of the tables), or transferring the result set of a query. If you are transferring between two SQL Server 7.0 data sources, you are also given the option of transferring objects as well as data.

Whether you have chosen to transfer a query-based result set of data or multiple tables, you will be shown a list of the table objects that can be transferred, similar to the one shown in Figure 5.14.

Individual tables from this list can be chosen or disregarded by checking or clearing the checkboxes on the left. Also on this list is the ability to detail the column by column transformations by checking the ellipsis buttons at the far right of every table. This option will allow you to control the structure of the table that is the target of the transfer, as shown in Figure 5.15. If you are importing into an existing table, you will not want to adjust any of the table settings, so that your existing data is preserved. Otherwise, you can choose to create the table that will receive the data either by accepting the table properties that are given or modifying the table creation script by clicking the Edit SQL button. The grid shown at the bottom of this dialog box lets you define mappings between the source and destination columns.

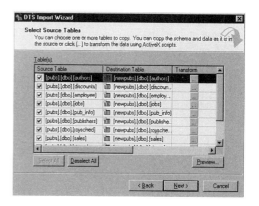

FIGURE 5.14▲
Select Source Tables dialog box with all tables selected.

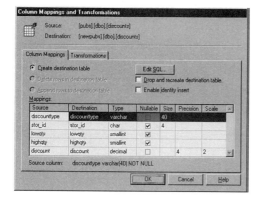

◀FIGURE 5.15
Column Mappings and Transformations dialog box.

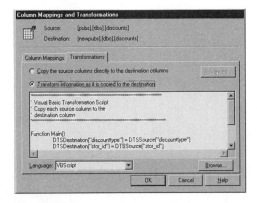

FIGURE 5.16
Transformations tab of the Column Mappings and Transformations dialog box.

To perform more detailed transformations on your data, you can choose the Transformation tab, shown by Figure 5.16. Here, you can choose a scripting language, and script your transformations. Unfortunately, you should note that you cannot use lookups, as defined earlier in this chapter, from the DTS Wizard. Even if you choose not to script any transformations, the Advanced button will allow you to control some aspects of the data type transformations.

There are three options on the Advanced Transformation Properties dialog box. These options allow all possible data type conversions (this is the default), to require exact data type matches, or to specify custom transformation flags. If you choose Custom, your further options are to allow 16-bit data types to be promoted to 32-bit data types, to allow the opposite demotions, and whether to allow a NOT NULL field to be converted to a field that allows NULLs.

After you have selected the table to transfer and enabled all necessary transformations, you have only to decide how and when to run your package. The package can be run immediately or scheduled for later. You also can decide to save the package, possibly run it again later, or let it be thrown away after it is used one time. After making these choices, you have only to review a last screen where the wizard briefly describes the actions it will take. At this point you have completed the DTS Wizard.

Now that you've seen how the DTS Wizard works, you can run through one example of using the DTS Wizard. Step by Step 5.6 takes you through the process of using the DTS Wizard to copy several tables from the Pubs database to another database where you have permissions to create tables. If you do not have a database readily available to you, the Step by Step will also describe how to create a new database to act as a destination through the DTS Wizard.

STEP BY STEP

5.6 Running the DTS Wizard to Transfer Multiple Tables

1. From SQL Server Enterprise Manager, choose Tools from the menu, then Wizards. You should be shown the Select Wizard dialog box, seen in Figure 5.17.

2. Click the plus sign (+) next to Data Transformation Services to expose the DTS Export Wizard and DTS Import Wizard choices. Both provide identical functionality but differ slightly in their defaults. Choose the DTS Import Wizard.

3. Click Next to move past the introduction screen.

4. Choose a Microsoft SQL Server 7.0 data source. Change the server name to the name of your server.

5. Select either Windows NT authentication or SQL Server authentication as appropriate for your server.

6. Select the Pubs database.

7. Click Next to complete your configuration of the source.

8. Again, choose a Microsoft SQL Server 7.0 data source. Change the server name to the name of your server. This may be the same server as the source.

9. Select the authentication mode as appropriate for your server.

10. In the Database drop-down box, either select a database where you have permissions to create tables or choose New. If you choose to create a new database, the Create Database dialog box will appear (see Figure 5.18). All you need to enter is the name of the database and the size of the data and log. The database will be created with auto-sizing of both the data and log files, so choosing the exact size is not critical. Enter the name of your new database and let the sizes default to 1MB for both the data and log, then click OK.

11. Click Next to complete your configuration of the destination.

12. Keep the default to copy tables from the source database and click Next. Notice that because you are using two SQL Server 7.0 data sources, the option to transfer objects is available to you. Don't use this option here, but note that it is available because you are using two SQL Server 7.0 data sources.

FIGURE 5.17▲
The Select Wizard dialog box from SQL Enterprise Manager.

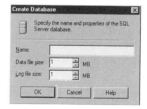

FIGURE 5.18▲
The Create Database dialog box from DTS Wizard.

13. You should now have the opportunity to choose tables to transfer. Select the Jobs table and the Sales table.

14. As you selected each table, you should have seen that destination tables were also set to defaults. The defaults can be changed by clicking in the Destination Table column. You can also choose to enable additional transformations on the individual columns being transferred by clicking the ellipsis (…) button in the Transform column. The screen should look similar to Figure 5.19. Click Next to continue.

FIGURE 5.19▶
The Select Source Tables window of the DTS Wizard.

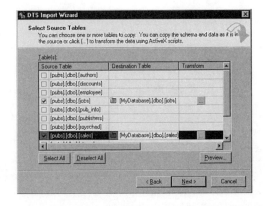

15. The wizard now has all the information it needs to perform the transformation. You can now choose to run the package immediately or schedule it for later. You can also choose to save the package regardless of the run mode. Figure 5.20 details the different options. Leave the default of Run Immediately and choose Next.

16. The wizard is now complete. The final screen shows a summary of the actions you directed it to take. Click Finish to run the package.

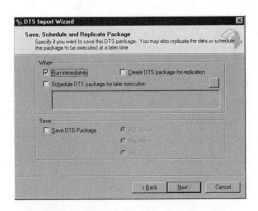

FIGURE 5.20▲
The Save, Schedule, and Replicate Package window of the DTS Wizard.

DTS

In the preceding sections, you learned about using the Data Transformation Services. You should fully understand that a DTS package is a collection of commands that tells DTS what to do. A package contains not only data transfer commands, but also tasks that can perform a variety of actions. You should be able to use either the Package Designer or the DTS Wizard to create and run packages.

CASE STUDY: IMPORTING DATA TO A NORMALIZED DESIGN

ESSENCE OF THE CASE

Here are the essential elements in this case:

▶ Import text files into SQL Server.

▶ Change data format to a more normalized form during import.

▶ Data scrubbing should not be an important factor.

▶ The Import process will run several times, but not on a regular basis.

SCENARIO

You have been given an assignment to take a series of data files that were dumped from a mainframe database application and import them into a more normalized SQL Server database. After examining the data, you have derived a data model utilizing fourteen tables derived from the five data files output by the mainframe application. The files you have been given are complete, but they are meant only for testing because they went out of date minutes after being dumped out for your use. Therefore, you will certainly need to run this transfer process again, when the system switchover is ready, but there will not be an ongoing data synchronization between the mainframe and SQL Server.

You have a concern about the need to "clean" the data during import to avoid bad data types and codes that aren't standard, so you take some time to interview the mainframe operator. She assures you that they run checks on the data once a week to ensure that all codes are valid, and that there are no mistyped records such as a last name consisting of nothing but numbers, and quantity fields containing an entry

continues

CASE STUDY: ADD TITLE HERE

continued

of "one." Of course, the proof of these assertions will be found only by actually importing the data and tracking any errors generated.

ANALYSIS

You have two basic options at your disposal to use for any import task: BCP and DTS. Whether you run it from the command-line utility or through the BULK INSERT statement, BCP will be the fastest method for getting the data into SQL Server. The problem would be that you cannot use this method for changing the data to a new model. You could instead transfer the data as-is into a temporary area, perhaps a separate import database, and then use Transact-SQL statements to manipulate the data into the normalized model. This solution would grant you a great deal of power to manipulate the data; however, these manipulations are subject to the logging overhead of SQL Server. You would also have to import most all your data into nullable character fields if you had any concerns about bad data types in the import files. BCP cannot fix data types on the fly, and would fail if a character were inserted into a numeric field. In addition, the speed of the actual import is not very important to this limited use application anyway.

Your next option is DTS. With DTS, you could pull different distinct subsets of columns out of the tables in many passes to break the wide files into a more normalized structure. You would also probably want to convert code fields such as SubscriberType into an integer code that points to a table listing all possible codes with a meaningful description. This code conversion can be done using a DTS lookup. If you use the DTS Wizard to create your package, you cannot make transformations from a single table to multiple tables. Furthermore, the DTS Wizard will not allow you to use lookups for converting code fields. Therefore, your best bet would be to use the DTS Package Designer in Enterprise Manager. This tool will allow you to make as many transformations of a single table as is necessary to complete the task. The process to query the source for distinct records may be a little slow, but speed is not the greatest concern on this task anyway. Because you are importing into SQL Server, DTS will even take advantage of the BCP interface to give you what speed it can. You can help the process by setting the Select into/Bulk Copy database option to ON and ensuring that the destination tables are empty to gain a non-logged BCP. Although data scrubbing is not supposed to be an issue, DTS will be capable of checking data types and range limitations before any bad data ever makes it to SQL Server.

CHAPTER SUMMARY

Data transfers are a common part of any Database Administrator's job. Fortunately, data transfers were a major part of Microsoft's strategy for SQL Server version 7.0. The existing bulk copy mechanism has been improved to work even better with SQL Server, and still offers the fastest performance for importing data into a SQL Server database. In addition, Microsoft has released the Data Transformation Services to tackle jobs more complex than a simple data load from a text file. DTS allows data to be taken from a wide variety of sources and imports that data into just as many. Remember that DTS does not even require the use of SQL Server at either end of the transfer. Knowing how to use these tools effectively will undoubtedly be an important part of your work with SQL Server.

KEY TERMS

Before you take the exam, make sure you are comfortable with the definitions and concepts for each of the following key terms:

- BCP
- non-logged versus logged BCP
- format file
- codepage
- native format
- DTS
- DTS package

APPLY YOUR KNOWLEDGE

Exercises

5.1   Exporting the Contents of the Employee Table

In this exercise, you export the rows in the employee table to a text file and a native file.

Estimated Time: 10 minutes

1. Open a DOS window and change to the directory in which you wish to create the data files.

2. At the command prompt, type the following command to export the employee table to a text file. This example assumes that you can access SQL Server through a trusted connection. If you cannot, specify a user name and password by using the /U and /P command-line parameters.

    ```
    BCP pubs..employee out empl.txt /T /c
    ```

    BCP should give a message similar to the following:

    ```
    Starting copy...

    43 rows copied.
    Network packet size (bytes): 4096
    Clock Time (ms.): total =     30 Avg =       0
    (1433.33 rows per sec.)
    ```

3. Examine the contents of the empl.txt file by issuing the following command:

    ```
    type empl.txt
    ```

4. Export the employee table again, this time in native format:

    ```
    BCP pubs..employee out empl.dat /T /n
    ```

5. Examine the contents of the empl.dat file by issuing this command at the DOS prompt:

    ```
    type empl.dat
    ```

Note that the file is difficult, if not impossible, to read as straight text. This is because the file is stored in a more efficient binary format. If you compare the size of the two files, the native file will be smaller.

5.2   Importing the Contents of the Employee Table

In this exercise, you delete the contents of the employee table and load the contents of one of the data files you created in Exercise 5.1.

Estimated Time: 5 minutes

1. Start the SQL Query Analyzer application and log on to your server.

2. Select the Pubs database from the DB combo box.

3. Type the following query:

    ```
    DELETE employee
    ```

4. Execute the query by typing **Alt + X** or by clicking the Execute Query button on the Query window toolbar. The contents of the employee table are deleted.

5. Now, import one of the data files into the employee table. If you want to import the text file, use empl.txt as the data file name and use the DATAFILETYPE = 'Char' option. If you want to import the native file, use empl.dat as the data file name and use the DATAFILETYPE = 'Native' option. The following command imports the character-based file:

    ```
    BULK INSERT employee
    FROM 'c:\empl.txt'
    WITH (DATAFILETYPE = 'char')
    ```

APPLY YOUR KNOWLEDGE

6. Verify that the contents of the data file have been imported into the table:

```
SELECT * FROM employee
```

5.3 Transferring the Pubs Database

In this exercise, you will transfer the contents of several tables in the sample Pubs database to a new database by using the DTS Package Designer.

Estimated Time: 15 minutes

1. Start the SQL Server Enterprise Manager and select the server containing the Pubs database that you want to transfer.

2. Expand the folders under the server to show the Data Transformation Services folder. Right-click this folder to reveal the context menu, and choose New Package.

3. The Package Designer window should now be displayed on the screen. On the left side of the screen there will be a list of data sources. By hovering the mouse over each source, you should see a label describing the source. You are looking for the Microsoft SQL Server 7.0 Only data source. When you have located it, drag and drop the icon to an open space in the window to your right.

4. You should immediately be presented with the Connection Properties dialog box. Rename the connection in the topmost text box as Pubs Source.

5. Leave the Data Source property as Microsoft SQL Server 7.0 Only.

6. In the Server drop-down box, choose the server that has the Pubs database you wish to transfer. If the server is not listed you may type the name of the server yourself.

7. Choose the authentication mode appropriate to your login with the server. Enter your login name and password if using SQL Server authentication.

8. Now choose the Pubs database from the drop-down list. This list is populated dynamically from the server you chose earlier, so if you do not see the Pubs database, it could mean that it does not exist on that server, or that you do not have access rights to the database. Click OK to complete the connection.

9. Repeat the process in steps 3 through 8 to create a Pubs Destination data source. If you have only one SQL Server at your disposal, this exercise works identically even if you choose the same server again. Also note that because you are transferring to a SQL Server 7.0 data source, you have the option of choosing New as a database. This option will prompt you for a name a starting size for the database and will then create it for you. You should use a database named PubsNew with a starting size of at least 1MB for data and 1MB for the log.

10. Having created the two data sources, you should be back to the Package Design window. First select the Pubs Source icon by clicking it. Next, hold the Shift or Ctrl key while clicking the Pubs Destination icon. Now, with both data sources selected in the correct order, you can choose Workflow|Add Transform from the menu. Alternatively, there is a toolbar button with a black arrow over a yellow gear that will also add a transform to two selected data sources.

11. Right-click the transform (the black arrow) and choose Properties. Note that the correct menu choice is Properties—not Workflow Properties.

APPLY YOUR KNOWLEDGE

12. You should now be looking at the Source tab of the Data Transformation Properties dialog box. In the Description text box, enter the name Authors Transform. Choose the Table Name option button, and from the drop-down box choose the Authors table.

13. Now switch to the Destination tab. When you do so, if you are using a new database that has no table objects, you will be immediately presented with a Create Destination Table modal dialog box. This simple box consists only of a text box that presents a CREATE TABLE statement. By default, this statement takes the form to create a duplicate of the Authors table that you are transferring. Accept the defaults and click OK.

14. The Authors table in PubsNew was immediately created, as selected as the destination table. Move on to the Transformations tab.

15. The Transformations tab will default to a column mapping that is just what you want. Note that by changing the New Transformation drop-down box to ActiveX script and selecting one or more columns, then pressing the New button, you could perform a scripted transform on the selected columns.

16. You will not need to adjust any Advanced properties—therefore, simply click OK at the bottom of the Data Transformation Properties dialog box to complete the transform of the Authors table.

17. You can now repeat the procedure in steps 10 through 16 to transfer other tables.

18. When you are ready, you can save your package by selecting Package, Save As from the menu. You can execute the package from the Package menu as well.

Review Questions

1. What is the purpose of the bulk copy program (BCP)?

2. What is the difference between a logged BCP and a non-logged BCP?

3. What are the differences between using the BCP command utility, and the BULK INSERT TSQL statement?

4. What does DTS stand for?

5. Describe the relationship between DTS and SQL Server.

6. What is a DTS package?

7. What is a DTS task?

8. What is a DTS transform?

Exam Questions

1. When using BCP to copy data into a table, which of the following statements apply?

   A. Database users will not be able to access the table because BCP will lock it.

   B. Database users will see the rows inserted by BCP after each batch is complete.

   C. You must have Insert permission on the table.

   D. Existing rows in the table are replaced by BCP.

   E. A non-logged BCP can occur even if the table has triggers or rules defined.

2. When using BCP to transfer data out of a table, which of the following statements apply?

APPLY YOUR KNOWLEDGE

A. Database users will not be able to access the table because BCP will lock it.

B. You must have Select permission on the table.

C. Data changes made by other users during the BCP will not be reflected in the data file.

D. The contents of the data file are replaced if the data file already exists.

3. For a non-logged BCP to occur, which conditions must be met?

A. The destination database must have its Select into/Bulk Copy option turned on.

B. The table cannot have constraints or indexes defined.

C. The data file must be in native format.

D. The destination table cannot be marked for replication.

E. The destination table cannot have triggers defined.

4. Why would you use the /E command-line switch during a BCP? Select the best answer.

A. Because the destination table has an identity column defined

B. To enable the enhanced features of BCP

C. Because the destination table has an identity column defined, and the source file explicitly provides values for that column

D. Because the source table has an identity column, so it will not be exported

5. What are the primary reasons for using a format file? Select all that apply.

A. To provide alternative row and column terminators

B. To provide column names for a new table created during an import

C. To rearrange the order in which columns are imported into a table

D. To parse a text file in a non-standard format

6. What does DTS calls its saved jobs?

A. DTS files

B. Packages

C. Format files

D. DTS scripts

7. How many table sources can be transferred through a single transform?

A. 1.

B. 16.

C. 255.

D. A single transform is capable of transferring all the tables in a database.

8. DTS Package Designer tasks can be set to run in what ways?

A. On completion

B. On failure

C. On error

D. On success

APPLY YOUR KNOWLEDGE

9. Jennifer needs to generate a report to list data that is collected and formatted through a view called JenRept. She decides to use BCP to output the data from the view, but she doesn't want to use the awkward command-line utility. Instead she decides to use the BULK INSERT command to create the report.

   Evaluate Jennifer's solution.

   A. This is an optimal solution to the problem. BULK INSERT is a good choice to avoid running the command-line BCP tool.

   B. This is a good solution to the problem. The command-line tool would actually give better performance, but BULK INSERT will still give equivalent functionality.

   C. This is a poor solution to the problem. Jennifer's solution will work, but it would be easier and faster to select the data from the view and save it in a file.

   D. This is not a solution to the problem.

10. Steve has two different databases in SQL Server 7.0 that model incoming orders, suppliers and inventory, and sales and shipping information. Both databases contain a number of views and stored procedures to help his programs work. He decides that he wants to combine these databases into one unified model. He decides to use DTS to transfer all the objects from one of his databases to the other. He will then alter the tables to set up referential integrity between the two models.

    Evaluate Steve's solution.

    A. This is an optimal solution to the problem. DTS can transfer all of his objects quickly and easily.

    B. This is a good solution to the problem. Although Steve can transfer all his objects this way, he will have to move the data separately.

    C. This is a poor solution to the problem. Views cannot be transferred through DTS, but everything else will work.

    D. This is not a solution to the problem. DTS can only transfer data and tables. It cannot be used to transfer an entire database structure.

Answers to Review Questions

1. BCP is used to transfer large amounts of data into SQL Server from a file, or transfer large amounts of data out of SQL Server into a file. (For more information, refer to the section "Using Bulk Copy to Import and Export Data.")

2. A non-logged BCP is not logged (except for page allocations), whereas a logged BCP logs all data inserted into a table. A logged BCP is used if the table has indexes and is not empty, if the table is marked for replication, or if non-logged operations are not permitted in the table's database. A non-logged BCP is many times faster than a logged BCP. (For more information, refer to the section "BCP Data Transfer Behavior.")

3. The BCP command-line utility uses the identical API to perform its work as does the BULK INSERT statement. The most notable difference is that BCP.EXE can export data, whereas BULK INSERT cannot. The other primary difference is the fact that BULK INSERT runs as a TSQL statement, and BCP.EXE must be run from a DOS command-line. (For more information, refer to the sections "Using the BCP Command-Line Utility" and "Using the BULK INSERT Statement.")

APPLY YOUR KNOWLEDGE

4. DTS stands for Data Transformation Services. (For more information, refer to the section "Using Data Transformation Services to Import and Export Data.")

5. DTS is a set of services that can be used with any OLE-DB–compliant data source. SQL Server is an OLE-DB–compliant data source, and works extremely well with DTS. The SQL Server Enterprise Mangager hosts applications to create DTS packages, but these applications are simple plug-ins that could conceivably be offered with other applications by Microsoft. Unlike BCP, which is a SQL Server–specific API hosted by SQL Server itself, DTS is a standalone application. (For more information, refer to the section "Using Data Transformation Services to Import and Export Data.")

6. A DTS package is a collection of commands that tell DTS what data to transform and how. A package can contain both transformations and tasks to perform. (For more information, refer to the section "Using Data Transformation Services to Import and Export Data.")

7. A DTS task is an action to perform. For example, it can be a TSQL command to run, a DOS program to execute, or even a data driven query that will transform data and then run a parameterized query on the data. (For more information, refer to the section "Using Data Transformation Services to Import and Export Data.")

8. A DTS transform is a command to transfer data from a source to a destination. A transform can also contain code to manipulate the data as it is transferred. (For more information, refer to the section "Using Data Transformation Services to import and Export Data.")

Answers to Exam Questions

1. **B, C, E.** By default, BCP will not lock a table during its import process. Therefore, users will see records being added as each batch completes. BCP never destroys existing data in a table. The existence of triggers or rules will not necessarily prevent a non-logged BCP. (For more information, refer to the section "Using the BCP Command-Line Utility".)

2. **B, C, D.** BCP will not lock a table during an export process. It will, however, capture a "snapshot" of the data so that changes that take place during the export will not be reflected in the export. Although BCP never destroys existing data in a SQL Server table, it will overwrite an existing data file during an export. (For more information, refer to the section "Using BULK COPY to Import and Export Data.")

3. **A, D.** Triggers will not prevent a non-logged BCP. Indexes will not necessarily prevent a non-logged BCP, but the table must be empty of data rows if indexes exist to gain a non-logged BCP. Not mentioned is the fact that the TABLOCK option must be used to gain a non-logged BCP. (For more information, refer to the section "Non-Logged BCP.")

4. **C.** The /E switch has no effect during exports. If a table has an identity column that is ignored during an import, normal identity assignments will occur automatically. If a table has an identity column, but the data imported needs to preserve its values for that column, the /E switch will allow an identity insert. (For more information, refer to the section "Command-Line Syntax.")

APPLY YOUR KNOWLEDGE

5. **A, C, D.** A table cannot be created through the use of BCP. A format file does provide for many different types of data parsing by rearranging columns, and providing non-standard row or column terminators. (For more information, refer to the section "Using Format Files.")

6. **B.** Although when DTS saves packages to a file, it uses a .DTS extension by default, these files are still referred to as packages. A format file is used to provide detailed column definitions to BCP and is not used by DTS. (For more information, refer to the section "Using the DTS Package Designer.")

7. **A.** Although a single transform can actually transfer a query result set that may have joined many tables, the query is still considered a single table source. (For more information, refer to the section "Transform Properties.")

8. **A, B, D.** Although it sounds legitimate, On Error is not a valid precedence constraint. (For more information, refer to the section "Using the DTS Package Designer.")

9. **D.** This is not a solution. Data cannot be exported with the BULK INSERT statement. The BCP command-line utility could be used to perform this task, but the best solution would probably be to write a SELECT statement to retrieve the results and then save those results to disk. (For more information, refer to the section "Using the BULK INSERT Statement.")

10. **A.** This is an optimal solution. As long as you are using two SQL Server 7.0 data sources, either the DTS Wizard or the Package Designer can be used to transfer any or all objects, with or without data. (For more information, refer to the section "Using Data Transformation Services to Import and Export Data.")

Suggested Readings and Resources

We recommend the following resources for further study in the area of planning:

1. SQL Server Books Online

   - Indexes (Level 1)
   - Data Import/Export Architecture

   - Logged and Nonlogged Bulk Copies
   - BCP Utility
   - Using the BCP Format file

2. Transact-SQL Help File

   - BULK INSERT

This chapter helps you to prepare for the Microsoft exam by covering the following objectives:

Write INSERT, DELETE, UPDATE, and SELECT statements that retrieve and modify data.

▶ INSERT, DELETE, UPDATE, and SELECT SELECT statements are the four most fundamental statements in the SQL language. Even casual users of SQL Server need to be able to use these statements to query and modify data. This chapter actually discusses only the SELECT statement. Chapter 7, "Modifying Data," discusses the other three statements.

Write Transact-SQL statements that use joins or sub-queries to combine data from multiple tables.

▶ All four of the basic SQL statements (INSERT, DELETE, UPDATE, and SELECT) are capable of using joins and sub-queries to combine data from multiple tables. This chapter explains these concepts using the SELECT statement. The identical syntax can then be applied to the INSERT, DELETE, and UPDATE statements in Chapter 7.

Create result sets that provide summary data. Query types include TOP _n_ PERCENT, and GROUP BY, specifically HAVING, CUBE, and ROLLUP.

▶ Summary data includes the use of aggregate functions in combination with the GROUP BY phrase. These functions allow you to report the summations, averages, and minimum or maximum values from a collection of rows. The CUBE and ROLLUP phrases modify a SELECT statement to return additional summations automatically. The TOP _n_ PERCENT phrase instructs a SELECT statement to show the first or last several rows that match a set of criteria.

CHAPTER 6

Retrieving Data

▶ Be sure you are thoroughly familiar with writing SELECT statements. You should be able to return specific columns and give them custom column headings.

You will need to be able to write join statements with inner, outer, and cross joins. Realize that outer joins come in three varieties: left, right, and full. In any join statement, the join criteria should be kept in the FROM clause rather than the WHERE clause.

Learn to provide summary data by using the GROUP BY clause in combination with aggregate functions. This lets you return summaries of distinct groups in your result set. You should also review the CUBE and ROLLUP options of the GROUP BY clause. These options cause additional summary information to be included in the results.

Finally, be sure you can use sub-queries. These can be simple SELECT statements that return a single row and column that can be used anywhere in a query (including INSERT, DELETE, and UPDATE statements) that would otherwise accept a literal value, or they can return single column lists of values to compare to. You should be familiar with correlated sub-queries that can reference table values from the outer query. You can also use sub-queries to return a derived table that can be used in a join statement.

INTRODUCTION

Retrieving data may be the most important function of a database. All the data in the world is worthless if it cannot be accessed. The basis for retrieving data in the SQL language is the SELECT statement. This chapter introduces you to the SELECT statement and describes how to retrieve formatted output from a single table.

The SELECT statement has a very modular syntax. It is made up of many different optional clauses. Therefore, you will first learn the basic structure of a SELECT statement, and then be introduced to new clauses in turn, adding additional power and complexity to the SELECT statements you can write. By the end of the chapter, you will be able to understand and write queries of high complexity. Specifically, the following topics will be covered:

◆ Writing SELECT statements: an overview

◆ Choosing columns

◆ Using DISTINCT and ALL keywords

◆ Choosing rows

◆ Sorting result rows

◆ Generating summary data

◆ Using joins

◆ Using sub-queries

WRITING SELECT STATEMENTS: AN OVERVIEW

▶ Write INSERT, DELETE, UPDATE, and SELECT statements that retrieve and modify data.

Again, the basis for retrieving data in the SQL language is the SELECT statement. SELECT statements tell SQL Server what data you are interested in. In the statement, you must describe to SQL Server what information you want and where to go to get it. The rigid

syntax of a SELECT statement is simply the way that you and SQL
Server agree to communicate. If you properly form a SELECT command, the syntax forces you to put key information exactly where
SQL Server expects to find it. Some of the information you must
provide consists of the following:

◆ The tables where the data can be found

◆ The columns of interest in those tables

◆ The criteria that the data must meet to qualify for being
  returned

◆ The order and format in which you want the data to be
  returned

You will see that you must know how to get the information you
want before you can tell SQL Server how to get it. This is why a
clear, appropriately normalized data model is so important. SQL
Server will never have a problem finding the tables where the information you need is kept because you will always have to provide a
clear plan to access the data yourself.

You are the one who must understand the data model and know
how to use it. SQL Server does determine the optimal method of
following your plan. SQL Server doesn't use any tables you don't tell
it to or follow any criteria you don't provide. However, it tries to
determine for itself how best to read the tables and what indexes, if
any, it should use. If you consider your data model a roadmap, you
must tell SQL Server where to go, but it decides what path to take
to get there.

Here is the basic syntax for the SQL SELECT statement:

```
SELECT [ALL ¦ DISTINCT] select_list
[INTO [new_table_name]]
[FROM {table_name ¦ view_name}[(optimizer_hints)]
[WHERE {search_conditions}]
[ORDER BY {column_name}]
```

Because the square brackets denote optional parameters, you can see
that very little is actually required for a proper SELECT statement. A
legitimate statement can consist of nothing more than the SELECT
keyword and a select_list.

There are four clauses that are used most often in SELECT statements. They are:

◆ **SELECT.** Specifies the columns to be returned

◆ **FROM.** Specifies the table

◆ **WHERE.** Specifies the rows to be returned

◆ **ORDER BY.** Specifies a sorting order

These four clauses together can allow data to be retrieved from tables and formatted to your needs. There are other keywords that can be used to build more powerful queries, and they are described in a later section: "Generating Summary Data."

Here is an example of a simple SELECT statement executed in the sample database, Pubs, that comes with SQL Server.

```
SELECT *
FROM authors
WHERE au_lname >= 'Smith'
ORDER BY au_lname
```

This statement returns all the rows from the Authors table where the author's last name is greater than or equal to Smith in alphabetical order.

With this introduction in mind, the next section will begin to offer you details about how to actually use the SELECT statement to return information from a table. You will then have a solid understanding of the way the select list works in a SELECT statement so that you can move on to more complicated topics.

CHOOSING COLUMNS

▶ Write INSERT, DELETE, UPDATE, and SELECT statements that retrieve and modify data.

A SELECT * command is perhaps the simplest possible statement for retrieving data. It simply returns all the columns from the table specified in the order in which the table was originally created. This allows a statement to be written very quickly, with minimal knowledge about the structure of the table you are querying.

The ease of this command is offset, however, by its inflexibility. Most often you will want to specify exactly what columns to retrieve and what order they should be in. Specifying columns also enables you to add formatting commands to each column to perform arithmetic operations, capitalize strings, and many other operations to improve the appearance of your data.

Specifying Columns and Column Order

In the preceding section, the following query was offered as an example of a simple SELECT statement:

```
SELECT *
FROM authors
WHERE au_lname >= 'Smith'
ORDER BY au_lname
```

It is the asterisk, *, following the keyword SELECT that commands SQL Server to return all columns. To return specific columns, you include a list of all the columns you want to see, in the order that you want to see them. To do this, simply replace the asterisk with the names of the specific columns you want to return, separated by commas.

If you only wanted to see the names of the authors, you could rewrite the example like this:

```
SELECT au_fname, au_lname
FROM Authors
WHERE au_lname >= 'Smith'
ORDER BY au_lname
```

Notice that in this example, not only is the output limited to just the name fields, the order in which the columns are returned is changed by specifying au_fname first.

Specifying Column Headings

When you specify the columns you want to see, you also have the opportunity to change the headings that SQL Server returns. By default, the heading of each column is the name of the column itself in the table. Unfortunately, column names are not always very meaningful to an end user. For example, a column containing a person's first name may be called Fname. By specifying your own

NOTE

How to Generate a SELECT List Explicitly entering every column from a table in the SELECT list can be tedious and more likely to lead to spelling and typing errors. To quickly obtain a list of all columns, start by running a SELECT * statement in your query tool. The result set you get back has all the column names of the table in the first line of the heading. This line can be copied right over the asterisk (*) in your SELECT statement, giving you an automatic list of all the column names. You still need to put commas between the column names, and you will almost certainly want to eliminate the extra spaces you end up with, but for a table containing ten or more columns, this can be a real timesaver.

NOTE

Limit the Data Retrieved to Improve Performance Specifying the columns in your queries serves a greater purpose than just formatting. It also enables you to limit the amount of data that needs to be returned to you from the server. The transfer of data over a network to a local machine can often be the slowest portion of issuing a query. For the best response, you should always try to limit your results to only the columns needed.

column heading you can make this something more meaningful such as First Name. The heading can be changed in either one of two ways.

The first is by including the keyword AS after the column name, followed by your own label. Or you can include the label before the column name with an equal sign between the two.

The syntax for each is as follows (respectively):

```
SELECT column_name [AS] column_heading [, column_name…]
FROM table_name

SELECT column_heading = column_name [, column_name…]
FROM table_name
```

Note that the keyword AS in the first form of the syntax is optional and can be omitted. Your column headings may include spaces if you desire, but to do so the entire heading must then be surrounded by quotes. The syntax is shown below, followed by two examples:

```
Column_heading = 'string literal' ¦ string_literal

SELECT au_fname 'first name', au_lname 'last name'
FROM Authors

SELECT 'first name' = au_fname, 'last name' = au_lname
FROM Authors
```

This process of supplying column headings is often referred to as *column aliasing.*

Using Literals as Columns

It is also possible to specify literals in the returned columns. A *literal* is a value that is wholly supplied to SQL Server, and requires no lookup of data from a database. In particular, a string literal is a string that is given for SQL Server to simply use as is. These can be in the form of *literal strings* (essentially labels inserted into the result set) or constant arithmetic expressions. Both expressions are inserted into the column list as though they were columns themselves. Literal strings are surrounded by quotes to distinguish them from column names, but arithmetic expressions are automatically recognized without special delimiters.

The syntax is as follows:

```
SELECT column_name ¦ 'string literal' ¦
arithmetic_expression [, column_name…]
FROM table_name
```

Using string literals in columns can enable you to embed labels into your result sets. The value of using numeric literals can be as simple as using SQL Server as an overpriced calculator. See the following examples:

```
SELECT 'The book ', title, ' costs $', price
FROM Titles

SELECT 2+2
```

Formatting Column Output

SQL Server has many functions built in to allow you to manipulate data before it is output. Some of these functions have been hinted at by the previous example, which showed how to use SQL Server as a simple calculator. In fact, all the simple arithmetic operators you'd expect—add, subtract, multiply, and divide—are included along with many advanced mathematical functions, such as square-root, logarithms, and various trigonometric functions. In addition, there are functions to manipulate character strings. These functions allow you to break strings into fixed-length pieces, find particular character patterns, and concatenate multiple character strings into one.

These functions let you perform operations on the data returned by a SELECT statement before it is presented to you. The use of such functions can greatly improve the readability of your data. For example, first and last name fields can be concatenated together to show a simple name, and items sold can be multiplied by a price column to display earned revenue. Although Microsoft does not explicitly promise to test you on the use of common functions, no discussion of writing SELECT statements would be complete without some reference to them.

The Transact-SQL Help file lists all the functions with excellent descriptions of each. Nothing can be added in these pages that would improve on the coverage in the Help file, either in organization, or detail. Although there are a large number of functions listed, you should at least read through the String Functions, Date and Time Functions, and Mathematical Functions. These topics can be found in the Contents of the Transact-SQL Help file, under Transact-SQL Help, Functions.

NOTE **Literal Columns Will Not Have Headings** Note that string literals and arithmetic expressions don't automatically receive column headings in the result set returned by SQL Server. This is because there is no column name for the heading to default to. If a heading is needed, it can be supplied in the same fashion as explained in previous section.

USING DISTINCT AND ALL KEYWORDS

▶ Write INSERT, DELETE, UPDATE, and SELECT statements that retrieve and modify data.

There are two optional keywords that can be used in the SELECT clause of a SELECT statement. DISTINCT and ALL specify whether to include duplicate rows in the result set.

ALL is the default assumed if neither option is specified. ALL indicates that all rows meeting the SELECT criteria should be returned to the user regardless of duplicate information.

DISTINCT indicates that of all rows in the result set which are exact duplicates, only one should be returned. This does not mean that the rows filtered out by the DISTINCT keyword are duplicates in the table from which they were retrieved—only that the data included in the columns returned formed duplicates. If a column with a unique index is part of the result set of a query on a single table, the DISTINCT keyword will not alter the output.

The following example illustrates the use of the ALL keyword in the SELECT statement and its effect on the resulting output (see Figure 6.1):

```
SELECT ALL State
FROM Authors
```

FIGURE 6.1
Result of the ALL keyword example.

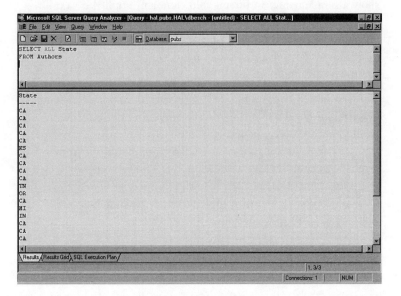

The following example illustrates the use of the DISTINCT keyword in the SELECT statement and its effect on the resulting output (see Figure 6.2):

```
SELECT DISTINCT State
FROM Authors
```

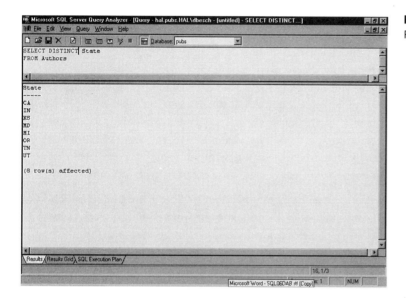

FIGURE 6.2
Result of the DISTINCT keyword example.

CHOOSING ROWS

▶ Write INSERT, DELETE, UPDATE, and SELECT statements that retrieve and modify data.

As noted previously, it is rare that you would ever need to return all the information that is in a table. Most often there is a particular piece or a specific set of entities for which information is needed. Limiting the number of columns isn't the only option. Instead of returning the entire contents of a table and looking for the rows you need, the WHERE clause enables you to tell SQL Server exactly what rows you are looking for in the table. For example, the following statement will return from an Authors table all authors who live in the state of California.

```
SELECT *
FROM Authors
WHERE State = 'CA'
```

> **NOTE**
>
> **The DISTINCT Keyword Affects All Columns** Note that the DISTINCT keyword refers to the entire row of data being returned. It is not possible to use DISTINCT to eliminate duplicates in just one column. The GROUP BY clause explained a little later in this chapter *can* be used to group multiple rows together based on specific columns.

N O T E

Note: Use `sp_helpsort` to Determine the Server's Sort Order To determine the sort order that your server is using, issue the command `sp_helpsort`. This stored procedure is provided by SQL Server to briefly describe the sort order and to show all the allowable characters in order. Note that some characters are considered equal to each other even though they are different characters. This is especially true for orders in which lowercase and uppercase characters are not differentiated. The results of the command are seen in Figure 6.3.

The following sections will explain how this example works, and will then go on to describe how even more complex statements can be built.

Introducing the WHERE Clause

The WHERE clause of a SELECT statement enables you to filter out certain rows from a table. The most common operations to perform for making row selections are simple comparisons. These operations enable you to specify rows that are equal to, greater than, or less than values you supply. All of these operations rely heavily on the sort order that your server is using to determine what values are "greater than" others. The idea of greater and lesser values is very straightforward when dealing with numbers. The very nature of a number system makes comparisons of this type very simple.

With character data things are not so clear. For example, which value is greater than the other when comparing 'A' and 'a'? SQL Server uses the sort order defined at installation to make the judgement as to which characters have precedence in comparisons.

The sort order defines a ranking of all the possible characters to make comparisons easy. This ranking lets you know what to expect when making comparisons with character data.

FIGURE 6.3
Result of stored procedure sp_helpsort.

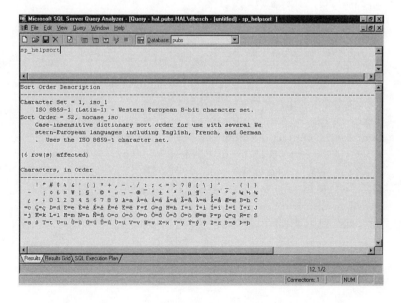

Defining Comparison Operators

The set of simple comparison operators follows:

- ◆ = Equal to
- ◆ > Greater than
- ◆ < Less than
- ◆ >= Greater than or equal to
- ◆ <= Less than or equal to

- ◆ <> Not equal to
- ◆ != Not equal to
- ◆ !> Not greater than
- ◆ !< Not less than

Using AND and OR Statements

You also can select specific rows based on multiple criteria. This is done by using the keyword AND or OR between each of the selection expressions. The conjunction AND specifies that all selection criteria must be met for a row to be returned, whereas OR specifies that either of the joined expressions is enough to make a selection.

Using the AND and OR keywords allows you to narrow down your row selections to the most exact criteria you can come up with. Not only will this make the query results shorter, and therefore easier to read, but it will reduce the load on your network.

Parentheses should be used to group AND and OR conjunctions together to avoid ambiguity over which expressions should be evaluated first and subsequently performed in the query. If parentheses are not used, SQL Server evaluates AND clauses first.

The following is an example of the syntax used for AND and OR statements:

```
SELECT rtrim(au_fname) + ' ' + rtrim(au_lname) 'Author
Name', state, city
FROM Authors
WHERE (state = 'CA' AND City != 'Oakland')
OR     (City = 'Salt Lake City')
```

Figure 6.4 provides the data you would expect from the example.

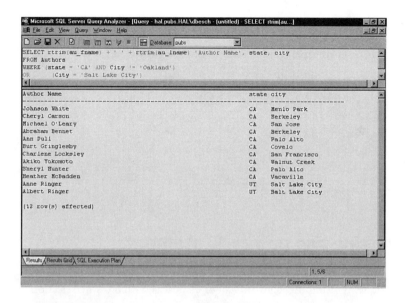

Using the BETWEEN and NOT BETWEEN Keywords

SQL Server provides a useful tool for specifying data within a set range of values by supporting the BETWEEN keyword. BETWEEN specifies an inclusive range of values in a shorthand notation.

The following examples are exactly equivalent statements:

```
SELECT *
FROM Titles
WHERE Price BETWEEN 5.00 AND 20.00

SELECT *
FROM Titles
WHERE Price >= 5.00
AND Price <= 20.00
```

Note that the BETWEEN keyword does not provide any unique functionality; it only allows for shortened notation of statements that could be built without the use of BETWEEN.

It is possible to find all values that do *not* fall in the range specified by including the NOT keyword before BETWEEN.

Using IS NULL and IS NOT NULL Keywords

There are a few special considerations to keep in mind when choosing rows with NULL values. SQL Server provides the special value of NULL to represent unknown values. NULL does not so much indicate any value as much as it indicates no value.

For example, if you didn't know the price of a certain book, you could set a price of $0.00, but that isn't very clear because $0.00 isn't a legal value for a price. It is better that you specify the price as NULL, indicating not that the book is free, but that you don't know the value.

Because NULL indicates the lack of any value, it behaves differently in comparison statements. In a comparison, a NULL value is neither greater nor less than any other value. Comparing any value to be greater or less than NULL always returns false.

Equal and not equal comparisons can be expressed against the keyword NULL with expected results, but these comparisons between columns do not return NULL records. Returning all the rows from a table in which the Price column equals itself, for example, does not return any rows with a price of NULL. Returning all the rows from a table in which the price does not equal itself does not return any rows whatsoever. In either case, the NULL values were excluded from the results. This behavior of the keyword NULL, acting as it does in one manner, but acting differently with column values of NULL, can be very confusing.

For this reason, SQL Server provides the IS keyword. Using IS NULL is the preferred method of specifying that you want to return NULL values. The NOT keyword can be used in conjunction with the IS keyword to specify that you want to return rows where a field IS NOT NULL. By always using the IS keyword to compare a value to the keyword NULL, this confusing behavior of NULL comparisons can be avoided. Unless you use the IS keyword, you can expect NULL values to be excluded from equal comparisons.

The following statement does not return any records in which the price is NULL:

```
SELECT Title, Price
FROM Titles
WHERE Price = Price
```

The following is an example of the syntax used for the IS NULL statement to return all the books that have not yet had a price set:

```
SELECT Title, Price
FROM Titles
WHERE Price IS NULL
```

Figure 6.5 depicts the results of the query.

FIGURE 6.5
Result of the IS NULL keyword example.

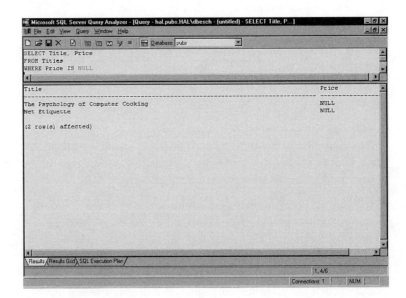

The following is an example of the syntax used for the IS NOT NULL statement. Here, you are trying to assemble a list of only those titles that have a price set:

```
SELECT Title, Price
FROM Titles
WHERE Price IS NOT NULL
```

Figure 6.6 depicts the results of the query.

NULL values always sort first regardless of the server's sort order.

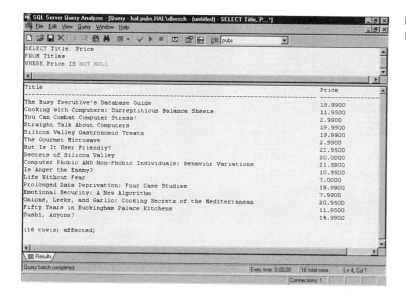

FIGURE 6.6
Result of the IS NOT NULL example.

Using IN and NOT IN Statements

SQL Server provides a method to choose rows that match any one of multiple criteria in a shorthand notation. Rather than comparing columns to individual values, you can instead find where a column value is equal to any single member of a list. This enables a much more compact syntax than multiple "equal to" expressions chained together by OR clauses. By performing comparisons to lists, SQL Server also is able to optimize its search, giving better performance than evaluating multiple OR clauses. Comparing to lists is accomplished with the IN keyword, by evaluating where the values of a column are IN a parenthetical list of values separated by commas.

The syntax follows:

```
SELECT select_list
FROM table_list
WHERE [NOT] expression [NOT] IN (value_list)
```

Using LIKE Statements

It also is possible to choose rows by performing wildcard matching on strings. The keyword LIKE is used in place of the equal sign to indicate a wildcard matching expression.

> **NOTE**
>
> **Use the NOT Keyword Effectively**
> Note that the syntax allows two possible locations for the NOT keyword, either before or after the expression. Although the statement can be negated by including the NOT keyword in either location, using NOT in both locations results in the two canceling each other's effect.

SQL Server provides four different wildcards for pattern matching expressions, as shown in Table 6.1.

TABLE 6.1

WILDCARD EXPRESSIONS

Wildcard	Meaning
%	Any string of zero or more characters
_ (underscore)	Any single character
[ ]	Any single character within the specified range ([a-f]) or set ([abcdef])
[^]	Any single character not within the specified range ([^a-f]) or set ([^abcdef])

When constructing a pattern string, remember that every character in that string is significant, including spaces. Although trailing spaces are usually ignored in comparisons, if they are explicitly stated in the pattern string, then they must exist in the data string found.

The following is an example of the syntax for the LIKE keyword (with the results shown in Figure 6.7):

```
SELECT rtrim(au_fname) + ' ' + rtrim(au_lname) 'Author
Name', state, city
FROM Authors
WHERE au_lname LIKE '%ger'
```

FIGURE 6.7
Result of the LIKE keyword example.

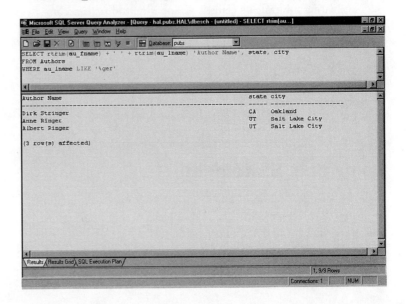

The LIKE operator is extremely useful when comparing a specific time or date. The datetime data type holds many different parts, including month, day, year, hour, minute, and more. Very often, only a specific date is needed and the time is considered irrelevant. Using the LIKE operator, a pattern can be easily constructed that specifies the date, but will accept any time. This method is usually easier than specifying a range of dates and times to search on.

The datetime data type can be searched as if it were a literal with the following format:

Mon dd yyyy hh:mmAM

For example, entering the following command will select only those books with the publish date that is Aug 10, regardless of the year or time parts:

```
SELECT Title,Pubdate
FROM Titles
WHERE Pubdate LIKE 'Aug 10%'
```

Choosing Rows

You have just completed the information on choosing rows. The WHERE clause that is used to choose specific rows in your queries is the most complex of any of the SELECT statement clauses, but it is also vital that you understand it completely. Later in this chapter, you will see that most all of the information you learned here will be used to join data from multiple tables together as well, which makes it doubly important that you are comfortable with the ideas presented here.

The WHERE clause allows you to specify criteria to use in choosing rows in a number of different formats. Simple comparison operators stating data should be equal, greater, or less than some criteria are probably the most commonly used expressions. More complex comparisons are accomplished through the use of the LIKE, IN, and IS NULL operations. Any comparison expression you build with these operators can be used in combination with other expressions by using the AND and OR keywords. In this way you can build complex logical expressions that will return exactly the data you want.

SORTING RESULT ROWS

▶ Write INSERT, DELETE, UPDATE, and SELECT statements that retrieve and modify data.

In addition to choosing the rows to return in a result set, you may want to exercise control over the order in which those rows appear in the set. SQL Server provides a straightforward means for sorting result rows.

The Importance of Sorting

The ORDER BY clause enables you to specify that SQL Server should return the data in a specific order. Order can be crucial to efficient and accurate interpretation of large result sets. By default, the data you request is returned in what is called *database order*. This is simply the order in which the data happens to reside in the table. In effect, however, you have no guarantees that the data will be in any order whatsoever if no ORDER BY clause is specified.

Very often, when a database is created, the data is first loaded into it in large loads. This data that is loaded may be sorted by some value, resulting in the data residing in sorted order in the tables. When this data is queried it may therefore appear in the order desired coincidentally. As records are modified, however, this order gradually disappears. When the data is queried in the future, it may seem to be in the order desired but with several records scattered randomly throughout or even miscellaneous records gathered together at the end of the list. Thus, key information being sought may be missed.

Using the ORDER BY Statement

The ORDER BY statement has the following syntax:

```
SELECT select_list
FROM table_list
WHERE search_conditions
ORDER BY column_name ¦ select_list_number ¦ expression [ASC
➡¦ DESC] [,column_name ¦ select_list_number ¦ expression
➡[ASC ¦ DESC] ..]
```

The items in the ORDER BY clause determine the ordering of the results in decreasing importance. The listed items are normally columns in the SELECT list. In this case the first column listed is sorted throughout the result set, the second column is sorted within duplicates of the first, and so on.

The items in the sort list should be referenced by column heading if one is given. If a function is used on a table column, SQL Server supplies no name for that result column unless a column heading is given. If a column heading is not supplied, the entire result column description, function name and all, can be used in the ORDER BY. Alternately, the columns in the SELECT list can be referenced by their ordinal position. Although it is less clear to anyone reading your query later, it can be much faster to simply list the number of the column to sort by instead of entering a long formula as a column identifier. Finally, SQL Server enables you to sort by a table column that is not even returned by the query.

The following examples are equivalent (and would all produce the results found in Figure 6.8):

```
SELECT rtrim(au_fname) + ' ' + rtrim(au_lname) 'Author
➥Name', state, city
FROM Authors
ORDER BY state, rtrim(au_fname) + ' ' + rtrim(au_lname)

SELECT rtrim(au_fname) + ' ' + rtrim(au_lname) 'Author
➥Name', state, city
FROM Authors
ORDER BY 2, 1

SELECT rtrim(au_fname) + ' ' + rtrim(au_lname) 'Author
➥Name', state, city
FROM Authors
ORDER BY state, 'Author Name'
```

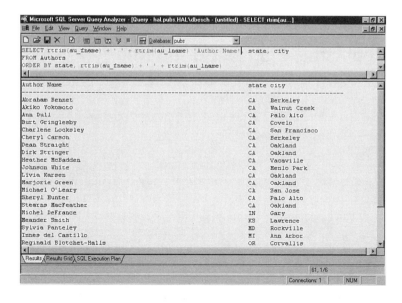

FIGURE 6.8
Result of the ORDER BY clause examples.

GENERATING SUMMARY DATA

▶ Create result sets that provide summary data. Query types include TOP *n* PERCENT, and GROUP BY, specifically HAVING, CUBE, and ROLLUP.

The golden rule in query design is always to return the least amount of information you need. This will make the results easier to understand, due to brevity, and will place less of a load on your network since less data is transferred. So far in this chapter you have seen how to return just the columns that you need, and just the rows that have the information you care about. This section will go one step further by describing different methods of collapsing multiple result rows into single row summaries of the information.

The basis for summarizing data in SQL Server is the aggregate functions. An *aggregation* is a collection of data expressed as a single piece of information. The *aggregate functions* can let you find information such as the number of rows in a set, or the sum or average of multiple values. After you understand the aggregate functions, you will learn different ways of breaking a result set into multiple groups to be aggregated using the GROUP BY and HAVING clauses of the SELECT statement. Then you will examine the use of the CUBE and ROLLUP operators, which modify the behavior of the GROUP BY clause. Finally, in a break from the discussion of aggregates, you will examine the TOP option, which does not so much summarize data as it returns a sampling of data.

Reporting Aggregate Information

SQL Server supports many functions that report *aggregate* information about a column. That is, information is derived from all the rows in a column. Aggregate functions all share a similar syntax, as shown in the following example:

```
aggregate_function ([ALL ¦ DISTINCT] expression)
```

In this syntax, the expression is almost always a column name. The function then operates on all the rows in that column to return the information requested. A listing of all the aggregate functions with a description of each is contained in Table 6.2.

TABLE 6.2

AGGREGATE FUNCTIONS

Aggregate Function	Description
Avg	Returns the average of all the values, or only the DISTINCT values, in the expression. Avg can be used with numeric columns only. NULL values are ignored.
Count	Returns the number of non-NULL values in the expression. When DISTINCT is specified, Count finds the number of unique non-NULL values. Count can be used with both numeric and character columns. NULL values are ignored.
Count(*)	Returns the number of rows. Count(*) takes no parameters and cannot be used with DISTINCT. All rows are counted, even those with NULL values.
Max	Returns the maximum value in the expression. Max can be used with numeric, character, and datetime columns, but not with bit columns. With character columns, Max finds the highest value in the collating sequence. Max ignores any NULL values. DISTINCT is available for ANSI compatibility, but it is not meaningful with Max.
Min	Returns the minimum value in the expression. Min can be used with numeric, character, and datetime columns, but not with bit columns. With character columns, Min finds the value that is lowest in the sort sequence. Min ignores any NULL values. DISTINCT is available for ANSI compatibility, but it is not meaningful with Min.
Sum	Returns the sum of all the values, or only the DISTINCT values, in the expression. Sum can be used with numeric columns only. NULL values are ignored.

Normally, an aggregate function returns a single value based on all the rows dictated by the WHERE clause (or the entire table if the WHERE clause is omitted). In these circumstances, an aggregate function cannot be combined in a SELECT list with simple column names because the single value returned by the aggregate function cannot be combined with the multiple values that would be returned from the column named in the table. The following is an example of such an invalid statement:

```
SELECT title, sum(price)
FROM title
```

Aggregate functions also cannot be used in a WHERE clause. The aggregation is performed on all the rows in a result set, whereas the

WHERE clause is used to compile that result set. Therefore, because the aggregate function is computed after the WHERE clause is applied, its value does not exist to be used in the WHERE clause.

Used by themselves, aggregate functions are most useful when a quick answer is needed about a table. Just by replacing the SELECT list of a query, the Count(*) function can be used to get a feel for how much data may be returned by a query before actually executing the full statement. Before inserting a new row into a table, the highest current ID can be determined with the Max function so the new row can use the next highest value. Application developers therefore use queries with such simple aggregations most often when they experiment with the data, rather than being used in reporting tools.

These limitations on the use of aggregate functions make them seem to be of only limited use. However, you will see that aggregate functions are central to the concept of grouping together similar rows using the GROUP BY clause. In this way, aggregate functions take on tremendous power and versatility.

Using the GROUP BY Clause

The GROUP BY clause enables you to group together similar rows from a result set. That is, by specifying columns in the GROUP BY clause, SQL Server takes all the rows in the result set where the values in those columns, taken as a whole, are identical and combines them into a single row. In its simplest case, the GROUP BY does nothing more than the DISTINCT keyword. The following statement returns all the values of the Pub_ID and Type columns of the Title table in the Pubs database, with identical values of Pub_ID and Type grouped together:

```
SELECT pub_id, type
FROM titles
GROUP BY pub_id, type
```

The results of the query are shown in Figure 6.9.

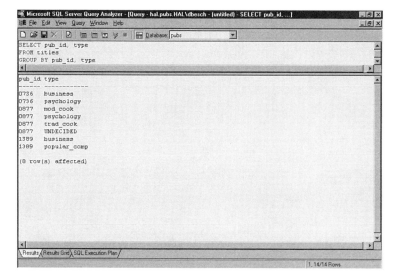

FIGURE 6.9
An example of a SELECT statement with a GROUP BY clause.

The example results exemplify the simplest case mentioned previously; the query returns results no different than what can be done through the DISTINCT keyword. Note that when used this way, all the columns named in the SELECT list must also be included in the GROUP BY clause. This is because there is no way to return the distinct values of one column, while multiple distinct values exist in another column. To illustrate this point, consider adding titles to the SELECT list of the above example without including it in the GROUP BY clause. If all the titles were shown for a given Pub_id/Type pair, there would be no grouping of Pub_id and Type at all; except, perhaps, an ordering that would more properly be done by an ORDER BY clause.

Although all the items in the SELECT list must exist in the GROUP BY clause, the reverse is not true. It would be perfectly acceptable to not show Pub_id in the SELECT list of the example above. It may be that not having the information listed would result in your result set being less clear and more difficult to understand, but it is legitimate to do so.

The GROUP BY clause shows its true value when it is combined with the use of aggregate functions in the SELECT list. When used in a statement containing a GROUP BY clause, an aggregate function operates on all the rows that were grouped to form a single result row.

NOTE

SELECT Statements Must Follow Specified Order It is important to always remember the order in which SQL Server expects to see each clause in a statement. Note that any of these clauses can be omitted (except the SELECT clause itself), as long as the rest maintain the same relative order:

```
SELECT select_list
FROM table_name
WHERE clause
GROUP BY clause
HAVING clause
ORDER BY clause
COMPUTE clause
```

When used this way, summary results can be returned for groups of rows in a result set. The following code based on the titles table of the Pubs database returns the total year-to-date sales for all the titles of similar subject matter released by each publisher:

```
SELECT pub_id, type, sum(ytd_sales)
FROM titles
GROUP BY pub_id, type
```

Those results are presented in Figure 6.10.

FIGURE 6.10
An example of returning summary data with a GROUP BY clause.

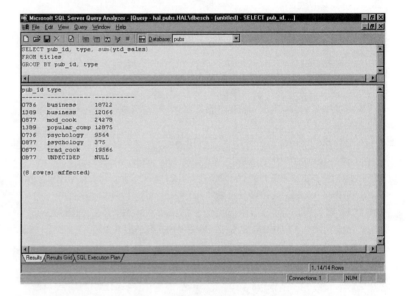

Using the HAVING Clause

As stated earlier in this section, aggregate functions cannot be used in the WHERE clause of a SELECT statement because the aggregate values are not created until after the where clause is evaluated. Instead, along with the GROUP BY clause, SQL Server supports the HAVING clause. The HAVING clause works just like the WHERE clause, except that it operates after aggregate functions have been calculated. Therefore, if you wanted to return only those rows in the above example where the year-to-date sales where greater than $10,000, you could use the following statement:

```
SELECT pub_id, type, sum(ytd_sales)
FROM titles
GROUP BY pub_id, type
HAVING sum(ytd_sales) > 10000.00
```

Although the HAVING clause specifically is needed to support filtering rows based on the values of aggregate functions, it also can be used for more mundane selections. In the preceding example, you could also state in the HAVING clause not to include any books about business. These kinds of standard conditions can be included in either the HAVING or the WHERE clause with no effect on the query results. It is better, however, to use the WHERE clause wherever possible. By operating on the results first, the WHERE clause can eliminate unnecessary data from the result set before SQL Server has to perform aggregate functions on those results. Any work that you can spare SQL Server from doing naturally improves its—and your—performance.

Putting conditions on the WHERE clause wherever possible is not only more efficient, it also is more versatile. The conditions that can be put in a WHERE clause are nearly limitless, in that they can reference any column of any table involved in the query. The HAVING clause, because it operates on the results determined by the rest of the query, can only contain conditions relating to aggregate functions, or columns named in the GROUP BY clause. Note that this is not the same as saying that the HAVING clause can reference only those columns that are contained in the SELECT list. The difference is that any aggregate function can be used in the HAVING clause, not just those that are in the SELECT list. The aggregate functions used in a HAVING clause may even reference columns that are not referred to in any way by the SELECT list.

For example, a correlated sub-query in the HAVING clause of an outer query. Consider this example using the Titles table in the Pubs database:

```
SELECT t1.Type
FROM Titles t1
GROUP by t1.Type
HAVING MAX(t1.Advance) >= ALL
       (SELECT 2 * AVG(t2.Advance)
        FROM Titles t2
        Where t1.Type = t2.Type)
```

This query returns the type of books in which the maximum advance is greater than twice the average within a given group.

Although the HAVING and the WHERE clauses have many similarities, each fills a specific role, and care should be taken to use each properly. The WHERE clause, as you have seen, is to be used to create a result set. The WHERE clause should therefore be designed to return the smallest result set possible to minimize the work that SQL Server must do. The HAVING clause is used to make selections on the result set after it has been grouped according to the GROUP BY list. Therefore, the HAVING clause should always contain conditions that can only be accomplished after the initial result set is compiled. Because non-aggregate functions on columns in the GROUP BY clause also can be operated on by the WHERE clause, they should be used in the HAVING clause only in conjunction with conditions on an aggregate function.

Using CUBE and ROLLUP

When using the GROUP BY clause, you can specify either of two additional options: WITH CUBE or WITH ROLLUP. Both of these options insert super-aggregations into your result set. A *super-aggregation* is the aggregation on one or more result rows. The GROUP BY clause causes all rows having the same values in the specified columns to be grouped together in a single row. Any specified aggregations are then applied to all the rows in each group. The CUBE command, for example, then takes every possible grouping of the groups and provides the requested aggregations on each of the super-groups. This concept is best expressed with examples. The following queries and the results they return all come from the Pubs sample database that ships with SQL Server.

Consider this example from the Titles table in the Pubs database:

```
SELECT Type, Pub_ID, sum(Royalty) Royalties
FROM Titles
GROUP BY Type, Pub_ID
WITH CUBE
```

The result set that follows is from the previous query. Note that where there are NULL values in the GROUP BY columns, that row is showing the aggregation of all the rows in the specified GROUP BY column, without regard to the NULL column. When all GROUP BY columns are NULL, that row represents the aggregations of all rows in the result set:

```
type        pub_id Royalties
— — — — —   — — —  — — — — — .
business    0736   24
business    1389   30
business    (null) 54
mod_cook    0877   36
```

```
mod_cook       (null) 36
popular_comp 1389   26
popular_comp (null) 26
psychology     0736   42
psychology     0877   10
psychology     (null) 52
trad_cook      0877   34
trad_cook      (null) 34
UNDECIDED      0877   (null)
UNDECIDED      (null) (null)
(null)         (null) 202
(null)         0736   66
(null)         0877   80
(null)         1389   56
```

The ROLLUP option works similarly to the CUBE option. Whereas the CUBE option calculates all possible groupings, the ROLLUP performs super-aggregations on a subset of the possible groupings. Thus, all the data returned by ROLLUP is also returned by CUBE. Remember that where NULLs are inserted into the GROUP BY columns of the result set, aggregations are applied to the group of data matching the values in the remaining GROUP BY columns. The ROLLUP option inserts NULLs in the last GROUP BY column first, then to the last two columns, and so on. With the ROLLUP option, if any column is held to NULL, all following columns will be held to NULL as well. Again, this is best explained through an example:

```
SELECT Type, Pub_ID, sum(Royalty) Royalties
FROM Titles
GROUP BY Type, Pub_ID
WITH ROLLUP

Type         Pub_ID Royalties
------       ---    ------.
business     0736   24
business     1389   30
business     (null) 54
mod_cook     0877   36
mod_cook     (null) 36
popular_comp 1389   26
popular_comp (null) 26
psychology   0736   42
psychology   0877   10
psychology   (null) 52
trad_cook    0877   34
trad_cook    (null) 34
UNDECIDED    0877   (null)
UNDECIDED    (null) (null)
(null)       (null) 202
```

Notice that the difference between the CUBE and ROLLUP examples is that the last several result rows of the CUBE statement are left off the ROLLUP statement's results.

Using the TOP Option

The TOP option of the SELECT statement is new to SQL Server 7.0, and it was sorely missed in the previous versions. It does not exactly summarize data, but rather returns a sampling of data. It could be said, however, that such a sampling may be representative of the entire table, and as such, the TOP option can be used to summarize a table's contents.

This option effectively returns only the first specified number of rows in the result set, yielding a truncated set of rows. Although the TOP option does not require that the ORDER BY clause be used, it has limited use without it. If the ORDER BY clause is not used, then the requested number of rows is returned, but there is no guarantee of which rows those will be. The ORDER BY clause will yield a predictable set of data every time.

The TOP option normally works by specifying the keyword TOP followed by a numeric value before the SELECT list in a SELECT statement, in which the numeric value (which must be an integer) denotes the number of result rows to return. An example of this basic syntax follows:

```
SELECT TOP 5 *
FROM TitleAuthor
```

The TOP option can be modified by adding the keyword PERCENT after the numeric value. When the PERCENT keyword is used, a numeric value N will cause the first N% of all result rows to be returned. When using the PERCENT keyword you may use a real number rather than just integers. The following query shows an example of using the TOP option with PERCENT:

```
SELECT TOP 20 PERCENT *
FROM TitleAuthor
```

There is one further modifier to the TOP option that can be used: The WITH TIES keyword can be used with or without the PERCENT modifier, but it does require that an ORDER BY clause be used. The WITH TIES modifier indicates that if the last row returned has any duplicate values in the result set, those duplicates should be returned as well, even though this would return more rows than were specifically requested. For example, read the following query:

```
SELECT TOP 2 WITH TIES *
FROM TITLEAUTHOR
ORDER BY Au_ID
```

The query calls for only two rows to be returned; however, the second value for Au_ID has a duplicate in the TitleAuthor table. Therefore, three rows are actually returned, as shown here:

```
au_id        title_id au_ord royaltyper
------------ -------- ------ ----------
172-32-1176  PS3333   1      100
213-46-8915  BU1032   2      40
213-46-8915  BU2075   1      100
(3 row(s) affected)
```

USING JOINS

▶ Write Transact-SQL statements that use joins or sub-queries to combine data from multiple tables.

Perhaps the most fundamental ability of a Relational Database Management System such as SQL Server is its ability to store data in multiple logical units (in other words, tables), and then relate those tables to each other through joins. A *join* is a single query that accesses data from multiple tables. It is this ability to correlate data from many different tables into a single result set that makes the Relational Database Model so powerful.

The SQL language supports three distinct kinds of joins:

◆ Inner joins

◆ Outer joins

◆ Cross joins

These three join types are discussed in depth in the following sections.

Using Inner Joins

An *inner join*, also known as an *equi-join*, is the most common type of join. In an inner join, the rows from two tables are combined wherever data in specified columns from each table are equal. In other words, an inner join returns results that contain the instances that the two tables have in common. It is possible in an inner join for a single row from one table to be matched to multiple rows in

N O T E

> **SQL Server Limits the Tables that Can Be Joined**   Although there is no limit inherent in the syntax, SQL Server imposes a limit of 32 tables that can be joined in one query.

another table. In an inner join, if none of the rows from one table match any rows in the other table, no rows are returned. The only rows that are returned in an inner join are those that have an exact match, according to the specified criteria, in the other table. It is worth noting that in a true inner join, at least one criterion must be specified to relate the two tables.

In the FROM clause, both tables are specified with the keywords INNER JOIN between them, and the keyword ON follows. The conditions of the join follow the keyword ON and may contain any number of individual criteria chained together with the standard conjunctions AND and OR. The following is an example of a simple ANSI-style INNER JOIN that returns all the author IDs for every title in the Titles table:

```
SELECT Au_ID, Title
FROM TitleAuthor
INNER JOIN Titles
ON Titles.Title_ID = TitleAuthor.Title_ID
```

Theoretically, any number of tables could be joined together in one query. To join more than two tables, the first join structure, including all conditions following the keyword ON, is simply followed by the keywords INNER JOIN again, then the third table name and the ON expression. In each ON expression, any column from any preceding table may be referenced. Optionally, each join phrase of two tables and an ON expression can be surrounded by parentheses to indicate that each such join can be considered a single combined table that each successive table then joins to.

With inner joins, this grouping is not significant because inner joins are commutative. That is, they can be performed in any order equivalently. SQL Server obeys the parenthetical order where such order would affect the outcome of the query. Where such grouping is irrelevant (such as with inner joins), SQL Server optimizes the query as it sees fit, regardless of the parentheses. Explicitly grouping joins becomes important when outer joins are discussed in the next section.

The syntax diagram for the SELECT statement, including the INNER JOIN syntax, follows:

```
SELECT select_list
FROM table_name [INNER] JOIN table_name ON
search_conditions
[[INNER] JOIN table_name ON search_conditions]
```

Notice that the keyword INNER is optional in the syntax. Inner joins are always assumed when no other qualifier is present.

It also is significant that the search_conditions that follow the keyword ON are equivalent to the search_conditions that can be contained in the WHERE clause. Any condition that can be written in the WHERE clause can be included in the conditions in an ON expression in the FROM clause. Likewise, it is permissible to put JOIN conditions in the WHERE clause, although some expression for the search_conditions must be present in the ON phrase to fulfill the syntax requirements.

This may seem to imply that the WHERE clause is irrelevant and can be ignored. Although it is true that any kind of a condition can be included in the FROM clause, it is extremely poor practice to do so. The FROM clause should be used to state all the tables that are to participate in the join, and specifically how those tables relate to each other. Then any filtering of data to specify exactly what rows in each table may participate in the query should be contained in the WHERE clause. Adhering to this style vastly improves the readability of a query.

When multiple tables are joined together, all the columns from each of the tables can be referenced throughout the query. If any tables happen to have columns with the same name (such as two tables that each have a "Change_Date" column, for example), it would be unclear which table was being referred to wherever that column name is used. To avoid this ambiguity, the column name can be preceded by the table name with a dot notation. Thus the "Change_Date" column for a table named "Sales" could be referenced as "Sales.Change_Date". This kind of notation can be used even where no ambiguity exists—making the query easier to read and maintain.

SQL Server provides a method of renaming tables for the purpose of a query. This feature, known as *aliasing*, enables long or obscure table names to be aliased to short, clear names within a query. This feature does not in any way affect the actual naming of the table, it only has meaning within a single query where such aliasing is used.

To alias a table, simply follow the table name in the FROM clause with the keyword AS and the alias name desired. The keyword AS, used in aliasing, is in fact optional and can be omitted. When a table name is replaced with an alias, that replacement spans the entire query.

NOTE SQL Server Support for Obsolete Join Syntax There is an alternate join syntax that is left over from before the SQL-92 standard was formalized and finally adopted into SQL Server. In this variant, all the tables that would be used in the query were included in a comma-separated list following the keyword FROM. All search conditions, including the relations between tables, are contained in the WHERE clause.

This old-style join syntax is much more difficult to read and maintain. No distinction is made between join criteria and row restrictions, often resulting in a seemingly random ordering of conditions. With no guidance offered though the syntax to order the join conditions and separate out row restricting criteria, complicated queries joining multiple tables can be very difficult to decipher. It is for this reason that the newer ANSI standard joins are preferred.

Table Aliases Affect the Entire Query It is worth pointing out that when a table name is aliased in a query, the replacement extends even to the SELECT list, which precedes the FROM clause. If a column name needs to be clarified by a table name in the SELECT list, any alias that exists for that table must be used. SQL Server parses the query in such a way that it can identify aliases in the SELECT list even though the FROM clause defines those aliases after the fact.

An alias must be used everywhere in the query that the table name would otherwise go:

```
SELECT TA.Au_ID, T.Title
FROM TitleAuthor AS TA
JOIN Title AS T
ON T.Title_ID = TA.Title.ID
```

Using Outer Joins

Outer joins differ from inner joins in that rows that do not have matches in a joined table can be returned. In an outer join, the conditions are specified in a manner similar to those for the inner join. The only difference is that the keyword JOIN is preceded by one of the outer qualifiers. The qualifier used with the keyword JOIN specifies which table retains all of its rows, and which table must have matches. Therefore the outer join syntax comes in three varieties: *left*, *right*, and *full* outer joins. In a left outer join, all rows are shown from the table to the left of the JOIN keyword, whereas in a right outer join all rows are retained from the right. In a full outer join, all rows are retained from both tables.

In an outer join, when a row from the specified table has no matching row from the other table, NULL values are returned for the missing column values.

The following code listing demonstrates a left outer join query:

```
SELECT Au_Fname + ' ' + Au_Lname, Title_ID
FROM Authors LEFT JOIN TitleAuthor
ON TitleAuthor.Au_ID = Authors.Au_ID
```

Figure 6.11 displays the results (although not in their entirety—some of them have scrolled below the bottom of the window).

In a full outer join, all the rows from both tables are returned. Where a row in either table has no match in the other table, that row is returned with NULL values filling the fields from the table with no matches. This full outer join has no equivalent in the old syntax.

The OUTER Keyword Is Optional The keywords LEFT, RIGHT, and FULL are not required to be accompanied by the keyword OUTER. OUTER is assumed when any of these qualifiers are present.

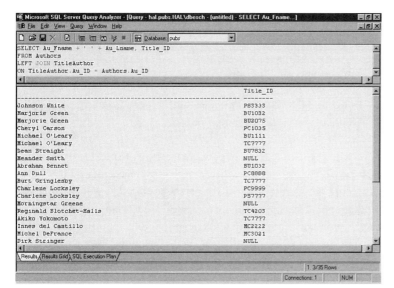

FIGURE 6.11
An example of ANSI standard left outer joins.

Using Cross Joins

The third distinct join form is the *cross join*. In a cross join, all rows in the left table are matched with all rows in the right table. The result of a cross join is known as a *Cartesian Product* of the two tables. A cross join can be thought of as an inner join where there are no restrictions defined.

To perform a cross join, the first table name is followed by the key-words CROSS JOIN, which are followed by the second table name. The keyword ON is not included in the syntax, and there are no conditions specified in the FROM clause, as shown by the following example:

```
SELECT Au_id, Au_lname, Title_ID, Title
FROM Authors
CROSS JOIN Titles
```

NOTE

Old-Style Join Syntax Poses Limitations with Outer Joins   The old-style outer join syntax is quite different from the ANSI-standard style. In the old style, the expressions that relate the two tables are joined with a *= for a left outer join and =* for a right outer join. This kind of syntax is inferior to the new style. With the old style, there could be ambiguities about whether limiting criteria should be applied before or after the join operation because all criteria are contained in the WHERE clause. The SQL-92 syntax separates search criteria and join criteria so that there is no such ambiguity. In an outer join this ambiguity would otherwise cause serious limitations.

N O T E

Cross Joins Can Cause Data Overload Cross joins tend to return an extreme amount of data. Where there are *X* number of rows in the first table and *Y* rows in the second, a cross join returns $X*Y$ rows. On tables of any significant size at all, this can quickly overload a system. Extreme care should be used with cross joins.

USING SUB-QUERIES

▶ Write INSERT, DELETE, UPDATE, and SELECT statements that retrieve and modify data.

▶ Write Transact-SQL statements that use joins or sub-queries to combine data from multiple tables.

Sub-queries are an extremely powerful feature of the SQL language. *Sub-queries* enable you to embed a query inside another query. This allows queries to retrieve data with a single step that would otherwise require several steps. Rather than execute a query and store the results, only to immediately reference the results in another query, the first query can be embedded directly inside the second. Thus, sub-queries save you the step of saving intermediate results.

The syntax for a sub-query is identical to a regular SELECT statement (with some limitations, discussed later) except that the sub-query is enclosed by parenthesis. The limitations imposed on the query have much to do with how the query is being used. The following sections will describe the use of sub-queries as a simple expression that returns a single value, and as fully formed SELECT statements whose results are treated as a table to be joined in the query. In addition, you will see how sub-queries can be either independent statements that could be run on their own or directly tied to the outer-query so that they return data that correlates with the data from the outer query.

Sub-Queries Used in Expressions

The simplest use of a sub-query is to return a single value that is used in an expression. This kind of a sub-query returns a single row, and a single column. The sub-query is evaluated early in the total execution plan, and the resulting value is simply plugged in as a literal from that point on. A simple example of this type of sub-query would be to return all the titles of books that have a price that is less than the average book price:

```
SELECT title
FROM Titles
WHERE price < (
       SELECT avg(price)
       FROM Titles
)
```

This kind of single-valued sub-query can be used anywhere in a query in place of a single literal value. It can even be used in INSERT, UPDATE, and DELETE statements (these statements are discussed in Chapter 7).

Using Correlated Sub-Queries

A *correlated* sub-query is one that uses values from the outer query in the sub-query. Any column from any table in the outer query can be referenced in the WHERE clause of the sub-query. In this situation, the sub-query is evaluated for every value of the column in the outer query. Thus the sub-query is executed repeatedly with different values in the WHERE clause each time. Correlated sub-queries can be used either in conjunction with list operators in expressions, or as derived tables in join operations. The list operators that are particularly useful with correlated sub-queries are discussed in the next few sections, and derived tables are discussed subsequently.

Using List Operations with Correlated Sub-queries

There are several operators in the SQL language that work against lists of data. These lists can be provided by enclosing a comma-separated list of literal values in parenthesis, or by using a sub-query that returns a single column, but any number of rows. These list operators include the IN operator that was discussed earlier in this chapter. Two other operators—EXISTS and the ANY, ALL, and SOME comparison modifiers—are primarily useful with correlated sub-queries, and are detailed here. You should note that no list operations actually require correlated sub-queries, and that any can be used with them. The operators discussed here are especially useful with correlated sub-queries, however, and are best described in that context.

Using the EXISTS Operator

The EXISTS keyword is a singleton operator. This means that it operates on a list without any other values needed. The EXISTS operator simply examines a list to determine if it is empty or not. The following is an example of using a correlated sub-query to show a

Publisher's name where at least one of their books has a price greater than $10.00:

```
SELECT Pub_Name
FROM Publishers
WHERE EXISTS (
      SELECT *
      FROM Titles
      WHERE Pub_id = Publishers.Pub_id
      AND Price > 10.00
)
```

The EXISTS operator is unique in that it operates on the list as a whole rather than on the values in the list. For this reason, the sub-queries used in conjunction with the EXISTS operator are allowed, and even encouraged, to use the asterisk (*) as the select-list. It would be misleading to imply that the EXISTS operator was examining any particular column values; therefore the asterisk select-list is preferred. The EXISTS operator can also be used with the NOT operator to check whether a list is empty rather than full.

Using the ANY, ALL, and SOME Operators

The value of a column can be compared to all the values of a list returned by a sub-query. This is accomplished with a standard comparison operator modified by one of the keywords ANY, ALL, or SOME. In this kind of expression, the value of the column is compared to each of the values in the list to find if the comparison is true for any, all, or some of the individual expressions. The ANY and SOME keywords are equivalent, and cause the expression to return true if the comparison is true in at least one case. The ALL keyword specifies that the comparison must be true for all values in the list. It is also possible to test if the values of a column equal any value in a list with the IN keyword. Using the IN keyword is equivalent to using the equal comparison with the ANY or SOME modifying keywords.

The following is an example of using a correlated sub-query to show the names of all Publishers whose books all have a price greater than $10.00:

```
SELECT Pub_Name
FROM Publishers
WHERE 10.00 < ALL (
      SELECT Price
      FROM Titles
      WHERE Pub_id = Publishers.Pub_ID
      AND Price IS NOT NULL
)
```

Sub-Queries Used in Joins as Tables

There is a special use for sub-queries that is introduced by the SQL-92 standard syntax. In the FROM clause, the results from a sub-query can be joined into the rest of the query as though that result set were a table itself. Such a sub-query is called a *derived table*. It is always necessary to alias this derived table because it has no inherent name of its own. This is the only time it is acceptable for a sub-query to return multiple columns. All of the columns returned in a derived table must have column headings that can serve as column names for the table. Such a query and its results are illustrated in the following statements and Figure 6.12:

```
SELECT Au_fname, State, Title
FROM Authors
LEFT JOIN (
        SELECT Au_id, Title
        FROM TitleAuthor
        JOIN Titles
        ON Titles.Title_ID = TitleAuthor.Title_ID
) AS AuthorTitles
ON Authors.au_id = AuthorTitles.au_id
```

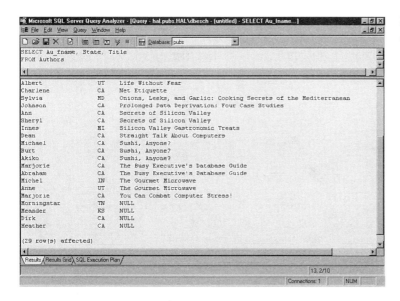

FIGURE 6.12

An example of a derived table in a join.

Review Break: Sub-Queries

Sub-queries allow you to combine multiple statements, which pass results to one another, into a single, multi-part query. This has the advantage of reducing the number of individual queries that are sent to SQL Server, which can result in better performance. Sub-queries can generally be categorized as ones that return a single value to an expression, a list of values to a comparison operator, or a result set to be used as a virtual table.

CASE STUDY: USING THE SELECT STATEMENT TO COLLECT DATA FOR REPORTS

ESSENCE OF THE CASE

Here are the essential elements of the case:

▶ The company is migrating from Mainframe system to SQL Server.

▶ The IT manager needs to show that SQL Server is already tracking company data accurately.

▶ Standard reports from SQL Server are still under development.

SCENARIOS

You return from lunch one day to find an urgent request from your supervisor waiting for you. He has a meeting this afternoon and needs to get some sales data out of the database. Your company has only recently set up this SQL Server database as an upgrade to your previous mainframe system, and not all the reports have been migrated yet. As one of the resident SQL Server experts, you get calls like this all the time, supporting special requests while the standard reporting tools are under development. Being in the IT department, your supervisor is probably looking for a comparison of data between the old system and the new to show that the migration is on track and SQL Server is handling the same data as the old mainframe.

ANALYSIS

Sure enough, when you call for details, you find that is exactly what is needed, a concise comparison of sales data from the old system versus the new. A detailed listing of sales from every department in every branch office is going to be too much data to compare by hand anyway, let

CASE STUDY: USING THE SELECT STATEMENT TO COLLECT DATA FOR REPORTS

alone in time for a meeting in about an hour. Your suggestion should be printing up a report of the sales, earned revenue, and expenses of every department in each branch, so that if the totals match, you have a fair comfort level that all the data is fine underneath. This is a one-query solution using the CUBE or ROLLUP feature of SQL Server. All you have to do is write a SELECT statement that groups by branch and department and performs a Sum aggregation on the Sales, Earned Revenue, and Expense columns. By

applying the CUBE or ROLLUP at the end, summaries of the summarized financial columns will be inserted into the result set for all the departments in each branch. The only question you face is whether the full detail of the CUBE function rather than the ROLLUP is needed in this case. Because the original reports from the mainframe weren't quite that detailed, and you are only grouping by two columns, you figure the ROLLUP will do fine.

CHAPTER SUMMARY

This chapter covered several objectives that assist in retrieving information from a database. These objectives included writing a SELECT statement and selecting specific columns and specific rows based on many different criteria. You can format and sort the query results, and provide summary information.

In addition, you can now retrieve data from any number of tables through joins. You can use joins to get only matching data through inner joins, data with or without matches through outer joins, or you can even do full matches between two tables without any regard to matches by using cross joins.

Finally, sub-queries were discussed. With sub-queries you can embed single results anywhere in a query, or perform comparisons against the results of another query. You also can use correlated sub-queries to return comparison results unique to each row in the outer query.

KEY TERMS

Before you take the exam, make sure you are comfortable with the definitions and concepts for each of the following key terms:

- query
- SELECT list
- aggregation
- inner join
- outer join
- cross join
- join criteria
- search criteria
- sub-query
- correlated sub-query
- derived table

APPLY YOUR KNOWLEDGE

Exercises

Pubs, the sample database that comes with SQL Server, is used throughout these exercises.

6.1 Executing a Simple Query

The purpose of this exercise is to use the Query tool in Enterprise Manager to execute a simple query.

Estimated Time: 5 minutes

1. Load the Query Analyzer from the Microsoft SQL Server 7.0 program group.

2. From the Database drop-down box, choose Pubs.

3. Type in the following SELECT statement to retrieve all columns and all rows from the Titles table:

```
SELECT *
FROM Titles
```

4. Run the query by hitting the Execute Query button, or by pressing Ctrl + E.

   The Results tab in the bottom half of the screen quickly fills with the results of your query.

6.2 Returning Selected Rows from a Table

The purpose of this exercise is to return only selected rows from the Titles table.

Estimated Time: 5 minutes

1. Write a query to return all the titles (title column) from the Titles table in which the price is greater than $15.00.

2. Use the BETWEEN keyword to modify your query to return all the titles where the price is greater than or equal to $15.00 and less than or equal to $22.00.

3. Modify your query to further restrict the rows returned to those with Year-to-Date sales (ytd_sales column) greater than 1,000.

   The final query should look similar to the following:

```
SELECT Title
FROM Titles
WHERE Price BETWEEN 15.00 AND 22.00
AND ytd_sales > 1000
```

6.3 Using the LIKE Statement

This exercise gives you practice using the LIKE statement.

Estimated Time: 5 minutes

1. Write a query to return all the titles (title column) that begin with the word "The" from the Titles table, using the LIKE statement with the % wildcard.

2. Write a similar query to return all the titles that have the word "Computer" anywhere in them.

3. Finally, use the square brackets along with the % wildcard to find all the titles that have either a comma or a semicolon anywhere in them.

   The three queries should look similar to the following:

```
SELECT Title
FROM Titles
WHERE Title LIKE 'The %'

SELECT Title
FROM Titles
WHERE Title LIKE '%Computer%'

SELECT Title
FROM Titles
WHERE Title LIKE '%[,;]%'
```

APPLY YOUR KNOWLEDGE

6.4 Use of Aggregate Functions to Return Simple Summary Data

The purpose of this exercise is to use the various aggregate functions to return simple summary data.

Estimated Time: 5 minutes

1. Load Enterprise Manager and open a Query Window by choosing SQL Query Tool from the Tools menu.

2. Write a single statement to return the number of rows in the Titles table.

3. Write another statement to return both the minimum and maximum prices from the Titles table.

4. Write a statement to find the sum total of all advances paid for every book in the Titles table.

5. Write a statement to return the number of books that have a price defined using the DISTINCT keyword with the Count function.

   Your queries should look similar to the following:

   ```
   SELECT count(*)
   FROM Titles

   SELECT min(Price), max(Price)
   FROM Titles

   SELECT sum(Advance)
   FROM Titles

   SELECT count(DISTINCT Price)
   FROM Titles
   ```

6.5 Generate Summary Data with the GROUP BY Clause

The purpose of this exercise is to demonstrate the use of the GROUP BY clause for generating summary data.

Estimated Time: 5 minutes

1. First write a query to return the publisher ID and the type from the Titles table.

2. Now you can eliminate the duplicates by adding the GROUP BY clause to your statement. You must group by both of the columns in your result set.

3. To find the average price of all the books by a publisher in each category, simply add the Avg aggregate function to your SELECT list.

   Your final query should look similar to the following:

   ```
   SELECT Pub_ID, Type, Avg(Price)
   FROM Titles
   GROUP BY Pub_ID, Type
   ```

6.6 Generating Summary Data Using the HAVING Clause

In this exercise you use the HAVING clause to restrict the data brought back by a SELECT statement containing a GROUP BY clause.

Estimated Time: 5 Minutes

1. Duplicate the solution to Exercise 5.2 to produce a statement to show the average price of the books by each publisher in every category.

2. Add a HAVING clause to the statement to restrict the results to show only the publishers and categories whose the average price is NOT NULL.

   Your resulting query should be similar to the following:

   ```
   SELECT Pub_ID, Type, Avg(Price)
   FROM Titles
   GROUP BY Pub_ID, Type
   HAVING Avg(Price) IS NOT NULL
   ```

APPLY YOUR KNOWLEDGE

6.7 Correlate Data Using an Inner Join

This exercise is a simple introduction to writing joins.

Estimated Time: 5 minutes

1. Before attempting the join, write a query to return just the publisher ID and the title (Pub_ID, Title) of every book in the Titles table.

2. Now you can use a join to the Publisher table to include the name of the publisher (Pub_name) to your results. To do this, you need to pull all the rows in which the Titles table's publisher ID equals the Publishers table's publisher ID. Remember to specify the table name before the Publisher ID field name to avoid ambiguity.

   Here is an example of the final query:

   ```
   SELECT Publishers.Pub_ID, Pub_Name, Title
   FROM Titles
   JOIN Publishers
   ON Titles.Pub_ID = Publishers.Pub_ID
   ```

6.8 Correlate Data Using Outer Join

This exercise gives you practice writing an outer join.

Estimated Time: 5 minutes

1. This exercise borrows from Exercise 5.6 to demonstrate using an outer join to return all the publishers and any matching titles. Copy the query from Exercise 5.6 to receive a statement that returns all the books from the Titles table and the name of the publisher for each.

2. In the old style, you would modify the equal comparison between the publisher IDs to use the *= or =* outer join comparison. Remember that the * is on the side on which you want to keep all the rows.

If you're using the new-style joins, modify the JOIN keyword to perform a left outer or right outer join. Remember that the LEFT or RIGHT keyword specifies which side should retain all the rows.

What follows is an example of the join to solve the exercise:

```
SELECT Publishers.Pub_ID, Pub_Name, Title
FROM Titles
RIGHT JOIN Publishers
ON Titles.Pub_ID = Publishers.Pub_ID
```

Review Questions

1. What is the syntax for a simple SELECT statement?

2. You want to return all the names and addresses of everyone in the Authors table. What statement would you use to accomplish this task?

3. You want to return every column from the Authors table, except one, without having to name every column. What statement would be the best way to accomplish this task?

4. You want to return all the names from the Authors table in a single column with a heading of Names. What statement would you use to accomplish this task?

5. Write a SELECT statement to return from the Titles table all the titles and what the prices would be if discounted 10%.

6. Write a SELECT statement to return from the Titles table all the titles and the price, where the price is less than $15.

7. Write a SELECT statement to return all the names from the Authors table, where the last name ends in "ger."

APPLY YOUR KNOWLEDGE

8. Write a SELECT statement to return all the titles of books that have no price from the Titles table.

9. Write a SELECT statement to return all the names and states, ordered by the state and last name from the Authors table.

10. Write a SELECT statement to return the number of records in the TitleAuthor table from the Pubs database.

11. John wants to know the highest price of any book in the Titles table. What statement would return this value?

12. Sandy wants to know the total amount of advances paid out by each publisher for the books in the Titles table. Write a statement that would return this information.

13. Carol would like to find the average price of the books from each category (of each type) in the Titles table. Write a statement to find this information.

14. Bill needs to find out how many authors who are under contract live in each state. What statement could he write involving the Authors table to find this information?

15. Sandy would like to be able to see a listing of all titles and the name of the publisher for each title. Write a statement that could return this list from the Titles and Publishers tables.

16. Peter needs a list of names of all the authors in the Authors table and the IDs of the books they have written, if any. He knows that the TitleAuthor table contains a listing of every author ID (Au_ID) with the ID of the book they wrote (Title_ID). What statement could return the list he needs?

17. Laura needs to be able to see the author and title of every book in the Titles table. Write a statement that will return every title along with its author(s).

Exam Questions

1. Which of the following are parts of a SELECT statement?

    A. FROM

    B. SORT BY

    C. WHERE

    D. SELECT

2. Choose all the SELECT clauses that will return the au_fname columns as "Name."

    A. SELECT au_fname as 'Name'

    B. SELECT 'Name' = au_fname

    C. SELECT Name

    D. SELECT au_fname 'Name'

3. What statement would you use in the WHERE clause to select all the names beginning with "B" from a table?

    A. WHERE name = 'B%'

    B. WHERE name = 'B*'

    C. WHERE name LIKE 'B%'

    D. WHERE name LIKE 'B*'

4. What statement could you use in the WHERE clause to select all the rows in a table where no price is defined?

A. `WHERE price IS NOT NULL`

B. `WHERE price IS < 0`

C. `WHERE price != 0`

D. `WHERE price IS NULL`

5. Choose all the statements that you could use in the `WHERE` clause to find only the rows where the first name is "Bobby" or "Bobbi."

   A. `WHERE name = "Bobby" or name = "Bobbi"`

   B. `WHERE name LIKE "Bobb_"`

   C. `WHERE name LIKE "Bobb%"`

   D. `WHERE name LIKE "Bobb[iy]"`

6. Which queries will return all the names in the Authors table sorted by first name, then last?

   A. `SELECT au_fname, au_lname`
      `FROM Authors`
      `SORT BY 1, 2`

   B. `SELECT au_fname, au_lname`
      `FROM Authors`
      `ORDER BY au_fname, au_lname`

   C. `SELECT au_fname, au_lname`
      `FROM Authors`
      `SORT BY au_fname, au_lname`

   D. `SELECT au_fname, au_lname`
      `FROM Authors`
      `ORDER BY 1, 2`

7. Which of the following are aggregate functions?

   A. `Sum`

   B. `ABS`

C. `Max`

D. `Count`

8. What is a valid `GROUP BY` clause for the following `SELECT` list?

   `SELECT Pub_ID, Type, Max(Price)`

   A. `GROUP BY Pub_ID, Type, Max(Price)`

   B. `GROUP BY Pub_ID, Type, Price`

   C. `GROUP BY Pub_ID, Type`

   D. `GROUP BY Max(Price)`

9. Which of the following statements are true of the `HAVING` clause?

   A. The `HAVING` clause can be used in any statement instead of the `WHERE` clause.

   B. The `HAVING` clause can restrict rows based on the values of aggregate functions.

   C. The `HAVING` clause must be accompanied by the `GROUP BY` clause.

   D. The `HAVING` clause can refer to fields not in the `GROUP BY` clause.

10. Mary wants to create a summary of the advances paid out by publishers for all the different types of books they publish. She would also like a summary of the total advances paid out by the publishers regardless of the book types. She decides to use the `CUBE` operator in her query to return the additional summary information about the publisher as a whole, without having to write a separate query. The statement she uses is as follows:

    ```
    SELECT Pub_ID, Type, Sum(Advance)
    FROM Titles
    GROUP BY Pub_ID, Type
    WITH CUBE
    ```

APPLY YOUR KNOWLEDGE

Which of the following best describes her solution?

A. This is an optimal solution that yields exactly the results she wanted.

B. This is a good solution that yields all the data she wanted, in addition to some data she doesn't need.

C. This is a poor solution that yields most of the data she wanted.

D. This is not a solution because the query will not work.

11. Which one of the following statements will return *all* the author IDs from the Authors table along with any title IDs on matching rows from the TitleAuthor table?

A. SELECT Authors.Au_ID,
   TitleAuthor.Title_ID
   FROM Authors JOIN TitleAuthor
   ON Authors.Au_ID = TitleAuthor.Au_ID

B. SELECT Authors.Au_ID,
   TitleAuthor.Title_ID
   FROM Authors RIGHT JOIN TitleAuthor
   ON Authors.Au_ID = TitleAuthor.Au_ID

C. SELECT Authors.Au_ID,
   TitleAuthor.Title_ID
   FROM TitleAuthor LEFT JOIN Author
   ON Authors.Au_ID = TitleAuthor.Au_ID

D. SELECT Authors.Au_ID,
   TitleAuthor.Title_ID
   FROM TitleAuthor RIGHT JOIN Author
   WHERE Authors.Au_ID = TitleAuthor.Au_ID

12. Which of the following statements are true of sub-queries?

A. A sub-query must be enclosed in parentheses.

B. A sub-query always returns multiple columns.

C. A sub-query in the WHERE clause can refer to fields from the outer query.

D. A sub-query can always be run as an independent statement.

13. Which of the following statements is true of correlated sub-queries?

A. A correlated sub-query is any sub-query that includes a join operation.

B. A correlated sub-query can be used to make a derived table in the SQL-92 join syntax.

C. A correlated sub-query always includes a join.

D. A correlated sub-query can only be executed once.

14. Which of the following SQL features is used to generate summary data?

A. Outer joins

B. Sub-queries

C. Derived tables

D. Aggregate functions

15. What do joins enable you to do? Select all that apply.

A. Correlate data from multiple tables.

B. Generate summary information on a table.

C. Return result columns that are derived from multiple columns in a table.

D. Identify unmatched rows between two tables.

Answers to Review Questions

1. ```
   SELECT select_list
   FROM table_name
   WHERE search_conditions
   ORDER BY sort_list
   ```

   (Refer to the section "Writing SELECT Statements: An Overview" for more information.)

2. ```
   SELECT au_fname,au_lname,address,city,state
   FROM Authors
   ```

   (Refer to the section "Writing SELECT Statements: An Overview" for more information.)

3. You would have to explicitly name every column that you intend to return. There is no method to exclude a single column from a SELECT * statement. (Refer to the section "Choosing Columns" for more information.)

4. ```
   SELECT au_fname + ' ' + au_lname Names
   FROM Authors
   ```

   (Refer to the section "Specifying Column Headings" for more information.)

5. ```
   SELECT title, price * .90
   FROM Titles
   ```

   (Refer to the section "Using Literals as Columns" for more information.)

6. ```
   SELECT title, price
   FROM Titles
   WHERE price < 15.00
   ```

(Refer to the section "Defining Comparison Operators" for more information.)

7. ```
   SELECT au_fname, au_lname
   FROM Authors
   WHERE au_lname LIKE '%ger'
   ```

   (Refer to the section "Using LIKE Statements" for more information.)

8. ```
   SELECT title, price
   FROM Titles
   WHERE price IS NULL
   ```

   (Refer to the section "Using IS NULL and IS NOT NULL Keywords" for more information.)

9. ```
   SELECT au_fname, au_lname, state
   FROM Authors
   ORDER BY state, au_lname
   ```

   (Refer to the section "Using the ORDER BY Statement" for more information.)

10. ```
    SELECT count(*)
    FROM TitleAuthor
    ```

    (Refer to the section "Generating Summary Data" for more information.)

11. ```
    SELECT max(Price)
    FROM Titles
    ```

    (Refer to the section "Generating Summary Data" for more information.)

12. ```
    SELECT Pub_id, sum(Advance)
    FROM Titles
    GROUP BY Pub_id
    ```

    (Refer to the section "Using the GROUP BY Clause" for more information.)
    ```

APPLY YOUR KNOWLEDGE

13. ```
SELECT Type, avg(Price)
FROM Titles
GROUP BY Type
```

    (Refer to the section "Using the GROUP BY Clause" for more information.)

14. ```
SELECT State, count(State)
FROM Authors
WHERE Contract = 1
GROUP BY State
```

    (Refer to the section "Using the GROUP BY Clause" for more information.)

15. ```
SELECT Publishers.Pub_Name, Titles.Title,
Price
FROM Publishers
JOIN Titles
ON Titles.Pub_ID = Publishers.Pub_ID
```

    (Refer to the section "Using Inner Joins" for more information.)

16. ```
SELECT au_fname + ' ' + au_lname, title_id
FROM TitleAuthor
RIGHT JOIN Authors
ON Authors.Au_ID = TitleAuthor.Au_ID
```

    (Refer to the section "Using Outer Joins" for more information.)

17. ```
SELECT au_fname + ' ' + au_lname, title
FROM (TitleAuthor
JOIN Titles
ON Titles.Title_ID = TitleAuthor.Title_ID)
JOIN Authors
ON Authors.Au_ID = TitleAuthor.Au_ID
```

    (Refer to the section "Using Inner Joins" for more information.)

# Answers to Exam Questions

1. **A, C, D.** To return a sorted result set use the ORDER BY clause. SORT BY is not a part of the SQL language. (For more information, refer to the section "Using the ORDER BY Clause.")

2. **A, B, D.** There are three different ways to rename a column heading, all of which were used as answers here. (For more information, refer to the section "Specifying Column Headings.")

3. **C.** To perform any pattern matching you must use the LIKE operator. The percent sign (%) is the wildcard that matches any number of characters. (For more information, refer to the section "Using LIKE Statements.")

4. **D.** SQL Server provides the value of NULL to represent undefined values. (For more information, refer to the section "Using IS NULL and IS NOT NULL Keywords.")

5. **A, D.** Answers B and C are incorrect because they would match any character in the last position, not just the "I" or "y" that would be correct. (For more information, refer to the section "Using LIKE Statements.")

6. **B, D.** There is no such operator as SORT BY. The ORDER BY clause can accept column names to operate on, or it can accept numeric positions of columns in the select-list. (For more information, refer to the section "Sorting Result Rows.")

7. **A, C, D.** The valid aggregate functions are Sum, Min, Max, Count, and Avg. (For more information, refer to the section "Generating Summary Data.")

8. **C.** When a GROUP BY clause is used when an aggregate function appears in the SELECT list, all
```

APPLY YOUR KNOWLEDGE

values in the SELECT list not involved with aggregate functions must appear in the GROUP BY clause. (For more information, refer to the section "Using the GROUP BY Clause.")

9. **B, C, D.** Although a HAVING clause can contain all the same search conditions that a WHERE clause can, the HAVING clause *must* be accompanied with the GROUP BY clause. (For more information, refer to the section "Using the HAVING Clause.")

10. **B.** The ROLLUP operator would have yielded exactly the data that Mary wanted. The CUBE operator calculates all super-aggregates, whereas the ROLLUP operator returns only a subset of all super aggregates. (For more information, refer to the section "Using CUBE and ROLLUP.")

11. **D.** To return all the values from a particular table, and only those that match from a second table, use an outer join. A right outer join will return all values from the table to the right of the RIGHT JOIN keywords, regardless of the order of the search conditions following the ON keyword. Notice that answers B and C are equivalent

statements. (For more information, refer to the section "Using Outer Joins.")

12. **A, C.** It is true that all sub-queries are always enclosed in parenthesis, and that a sub-query anywhere, including in the WHERE clause, can refer to fields from the outer query. Sub-queries can only return multiple columns when they are used as derived tables. Correlated sub-queries cannot be run independent of the outer query, because they reference the outer query. (For more information, refer to the section "Using Sub-Queries.")

13. **B.** Correlated sub-queries can be used as derived tables. (For more information, refer to the section "Using Correlated Sub-Queries.")

14. **D.** Aggregate functions specifically exist to generate summary data. (For more information, refer to the section "Generating Summary Data.")

15. **A, D.** Joins allow you to compare data from multiple tables. These comparisons allow a great deal of flexibility to make any determinations about the data in the tables. (For more information, refer to the section "Using Joins.")

Suggested Readings and Resources

We recommend the following resources for further study in the area of planning:

1. Transact-SQL Help
   - SELECT: overview
   - WHERE clause: described

2. SQL Server Books Online
   - Sub-query fundamentals
   - Correlated Sub-Queries with Comparison Operators
   - Using Aggregate Functions in the SELECT List
   - Choosing Rows with the HAVING Clause

This chapter helps you to prepare for the Microsoft exam by covering the following objective:

Write INSERT, DELETE, UPDATE, and SELECT statements that retrieve and modify data.

▶ INSERT, DELETE, UPDATE, and SELECT statements are the four most fundamental statements in the SQL language. Even casual users of SQL Server need to be able to use these statements to query and modify data. This chapter will not discuss the SELECT statement. Chapter 6, "Retrieving Data," discussed the SELECT statement, while this chapter discusses the remaining three.

CHAPTER 7

Modifying Data

▶ Practice writing queries with these three statements (INSERT, DELETE, and UPDATE). Syntax diagrams are no replacement for the solid
experience of seeing the statements in action.

Keep in mind that only one table at a time can
be modified with the INSERT, UPDATE, and DELETE
statements, even if you are modifying a view
that has many base tables.

Learn the rules of how the DEFAULT keyword
works for columns you don't know the values for.

INTRODUCTION

This chapter introduces you to the Structured Query Language (SQL) commands used to modify data in a database: INSERT, UPDATE, and DELETE. These three commands are known collectively as the *Data Manipulation Language (DML)* statements. A number of examples are shown for each SQL command to explain the syntax. If you have access to a SQL Server, these commands work on the Pubs database. By the end of this chapter, you will be able to insert, modify, and delete rows in a table by using these commands.

THE INSERT STATEMENT

▶ Write INSERT, DELETE, UPDATE, and SELECT statements that retrieve and modify data.

The INSERT statement is used to add a single row or multiple rows of data to a table or a view. (For more information on views, see Chapter 9, "Miscellaneous Programming Techniques.") By default, only the table owner can insert rows into a table, although this permission can be transferred to other users. When using the INSERT statement, keep the following in mind:

◆ Attempting to insert data of the incorrect data type into a column causes an error, and the INSERT statement will be rolled back. Likewise, explicitly inserting a NULL value into a column that does not accept NULLs causes an error.

◆ When inserting data into a view based on more than one table, data may only be inserted into one base table at a time. For more information on the restrictions placed on views, see Chapter 9 and the SQL Server Books Online.

◆ If the inserted data violates a rule or constraint, then the INSERT fails and returns an error message.

◆ When inserting characters into a column of type varchar or into a char column that accepts NULLs, whether trailing spaces are removed from the string is determined by setting the ANSI_PADDING server option when the column was created.

◆ When inserting data into a char column that does not accept NULLs, all strings (even empty strings) are right-padded to the defined length of the column.

N O T E

Use the Pubs Database to Follow Examples Throughout this chapter, the Pubs database will be used to demonstrate the use of the DML statements. Don't worry about damaging your database by following the examples, because SQL Server gives you scripts to repopulate the sample databases, including Pubs. Look in the INSTALL directory under your default SQL Server directory, which in most cases is MSSQL7. You will find the INSTPUBS.SQL file, which when run through SQL Server Query Analyzer will completely rebuild the Pubs database. The complete path for a standard installation would be as follows:

C:\MSSQL7\INSTALL\INSTPUBS.SQL

To get the most out of this chapter, it is highly recommended that you run the examples given.

Typically, INSERT statements are executed from the Query Analyzer Tool; however, INSERT statements can also be executed from other front-end applications written in Visual Basic or Visual C++.

Basic Syntax

The syntax of the INSERT statement is as follows:

```
INSERT [INTO] {table_name ¦ view_name}
   [(column_list)]
   {DEFAULT VALUES ¦ VALUES (values_list) ¦
➥select_statement ¦ stored_procedure}
```

The INSERT command consists of three basic parts. The first is the INSERT keyword itself, followed by the name of the table or view to which data is being added. Note that the INTO keyword is always optional. Next, the columns that data will be inserted into are listed. If this column list is omitted, SQL Server assumes that you will be inserting a value in every column. The last part of the INSERT statement defines where the column values will come from for the data row(s).

The table name or view name may be fully qualified in the form [database.[owner].]tablename or [database.[owner].]viewname. This enables you to insert records into a table or view that resides in another database or that is owned by another user.

Note that when you omit the column list, you must provide a value for every column in the table. When you use a column list, you need only provide values for the columns that you list. The columns in the column list can appear in any order. Some rules apply to the column(s) omitted from the column list:

- ◆ If the omitted column(s) does not allow NULLs, and does not have a default or default constraint, the INSERT statement will fail. Note that an Identity or Timestamp column is considered to have a default in this context.

- ◆ If the omitted column(s) does not allow NULLs, but has a default bound to it (or a default constraint defined), then the default value will be used for the column.

- ◆ If the column permits NULL values, then a NULL will be inserted (unless a default exists for that column).

Column values can come from four different sources. The DEFAULT VALUES and VALUES keywords are used to specify column values when inserting a single row. A SELECT statement or stored procedure may be used to provide column values for one or more rows. Take a look at some examples of inserting a single row (the multiple row inserts using SELECT statements are covered a bit later in this section):

1. This statement attempts to insert a row into the authors table in the Pubs database by using all default values:

```
INSERT authors DEFAULT VALUES
```

However, the DEFAULT VALUES keyword only works if all columns that disallow NULLs have a default defined. In this case, the au_id, au_lname, au_fname, and contract columns disallow NULLs and have no defaults. This query results in an error message because of the not null columns.

2. A single row may be inserted by specifying column values with the VALUES keyword. The list of values must be enclosed in parentheses; character strings and date/time values must be enclosed in single quotes ('). This example inserts a new row and provides a value in every column:

```
INSERT authors
    (au_id, au_lname, au_fname, phone, address, city,
➥state, zip, contract)
    VALUES ('111-22-3333','Davies','Joshua','302 444-
➥1515','14 N. Bluff','Atlanta','GA','55111',1)
```

Note that the preceding example explicitly lists all the columns in the table. If a value is to be inserted in every column, a shorthand way of writing the INSERT is to omit the column list, as shown here:

```
INSERT authors
    VALUES ('111-22-3333','Davies','Joshua','302 444-
➥1515','14 N. Bluff','Atlanta','GA','55111',1)
```

3. The first example showed that only four columns in the authors table prohibit NULLs and have no default. All other columns either allow NULLs or have a default defined. Thus, you can insert a record for this table by specifying values only for those four columns:

```
INSERT authors
    (au_id, au_lname, au_fname, contract)
    VALUES ('111-22-4444','Cook','Fergus',1)
```

278 Part I EXAM PREPARATION

The address columns all allow NULLs, so they will contain NULL values. The phone number column defaults to UNKNOWN. Note that because the columns in the column list may appear in any order, this statement is equivalent to the previous one:

```
INSERT authors
    (contract, au_id, au_fname, au_lname)
    VALUES (1,'111-22-4444','Fergus','Cook')
```

4. A special keyword, DEFAULT, can be used in the values list to indicate that you want the default value (if one exists) to be used for that column:

```
INSERT authors
    (au_id, au_lname, au_fname, phone, address, contract)
    VALUES ('111-33-4444','Cook','Angus', DEFAULT,
➥DEFAULT, 1)
```

The column for which you use the DEFAULT keyword must have a default if it prohibits NULLs. Otherwise, SQL Server provides a NULL value for a column that does not allow NULLs, and an error will occur. In this example, the phone column contains the value UNKNOWN because that is the default for the column, and the address column contains a NULL, because it has no default.

Using INSERT on a Table with an IDENTITY Column

There are some special considerations you need to keep in mind when inserting rows into a table that contains an identity column. The following examples use the jobs table in the Pubs database:

1. When omitting the column list, do not specify a value for the IDENTITY column in the VALUES list, like so:

```
INSERT jobs
    VALUES ('Mailroom Clerk',20,30)
```

2. When using a column list, do not include the IDENTITY column in the column list or the VALUES list:

```
INSERT jobs
    (job_desc, min_lvl, max_lvl)
    VALUES ('Mailroom Clerk',20,30)
```

Including the IDENTITY column in the list will cause an error, because an IDENTITY column normally cannot have a value explicitly defined for it. Consider the following statement:

```
INSERT jobs
    (job_id, job_desc, min_lvl, max_lvl) VALUES
    ➥(42, 'Mailroom Clerk',20,30)
```

It causes this error:

```
Msg 544, Level 16, State 1
Attempting to insert explicit value for identity column
in table 'jobs' when IDENTITY_INSERT is set to OFF
```

3. If an explicit value must be supplied for an IDENTITY column, a special option (IDENTITY_INSERT) must be turned on for the table, and a column list must be used.

For example, if the Editor job (with a job_id of 12) was deleted accidentally, the following SQL batch would reinsert the row:

```
SET IDENTITY_INSERT jobs ON

INSERT jobs
    (job_id, job_desc, min_lvl, max_lvl)
    VALUES (12, 'Editor',25,100)

SET IDENTITY_INSERT jobs OFF
```

Using a Nested SELECT Statement with INSERT

It is possible to use a SELECT statement to provide column values for the INSERT statement. The columns returned by the SELECT statement must match the columns in the inserted table or in the column list of the INSERT statement. In addition, the data types of the columns returned by the SELECT must match the data types for the inserted column(s). Using a nested SELECT also allows multiple rows to be inserted in a single statement. For more information about the SELECT statement, refer to Chapter 6.

If you want to experiment with the examples presented in this section, first execute the following SQL statement in the Pubs database to create the authors_examples table:

```
CREATE TABLE authors_examples (
    au_id     smallint     NOT NULL,
    au_lname  varchar (40)  NOT NULL ,
```

N O T E **Example Has No Primary Key** The primary key for the authors_examples table is intentionally omitted so that rows from the authors table can be inserted multiple times. This omission is used only for demonstrating the various forms of the INSERT SELECT syntax. Generally, every table should have a primary key.

N O T E **Query Analyzer Allows You to Run Selected Portions of a Query** To check the rows returned by the SELECT statement, you can use a trick in the Query Analyzer that enables you to execute a small portion of the query. Use the Shift + arrow keys or the mouse to highlight only the portion of the query you want to execute (in this case, the SELECT statement without the INSERT). Then, type **Alt** + **X** or click the Execute Query button. Only the highlighted portion of the query will be executed.

```
    au_fname   varchar (20)    NOT NULL ,
    phone      char (12)       NOT NULL DEFAULT ('UNKNOWN'),
    address    varchar (40)    NULL ,
    city       varchar (20)    NULL ,
    state      char (2)        NULL ,
    zip        char (5)        NULL ,
    contract   bit             NOT NULL
)
```

The following list contains examples of INSERT statements of varying complexity. If you have created the authors_examples table suggested above, you can enter each of the following examples yourself to gain practice with the INSERT statement:

1. This example shows the most basic form of the INSERT SELECT syntax. It copies all columns and all rows from the authors table to the authors_examples table:

```
INSERT authors_examples
    SELECT * FROM authors
```

2. To copy only a subset of the rows from one table to another, a WHERE clause can be used with the SELECT statement. This example inserts only the authors from California into the authors_examples table:

```
INSERT authors_examples
    SELECT *
    FROM authors
    WHERE state LIKE 'CA'
```

3. The SELECT statement can also use a join to filter rows based on values in a related table, or pull column values from a related table. In this example, only those authors having a royalty percentage of 100% are added to the authors_examples table:

```
INSERT authors_examples
    SELECT authors.*
    FROM authors INNER JOIN titleauthor
        ON authors.au_id = titleauthor.au_id
    WHERE titleauthor.royaltyper = 100
```

4. The columns receiving inserted data can be restricted by using a column list in the INSERT statement. The selected columns must match the columns inserted. In this example, only the author ID, first name, last name, and contract are copied into the authors_examples table. The phone column for every inserted author will default to UNKNOWN; all other columns will be NULL:

```
INSERT authors_examples
    (au_id, au_fname, au_lname, contract)
        SELECT au_id, au_fname, au_lname, contract
          FROM authors
```

5. Constant values can be used in the SELECT portion of the statement to give all inserted rows the same value in a particular column. This example is similar to example 4, except that every author's phone number is set to 800 555-1212:

```
INSERT authors_examples
    (au_id, au_fname, au_lname, contract, phone)
        SELECT au_id, au_fname, au_lname, contract, '800
➥555-1212'
          FROM authors
```

Using a Stored Procedure with INSERT

It is also possible to write INSERT statements that insert rows into a table based on the results of a stored procedure. This syntax has basically the same restrictions and advantages as using a nested SELECT statement: The columns returned by the stored procedure must match the inserted columns, and the stored procedure can return multiple rows to be inserted. All types of stored procedures (user, system, and extended) can be used to supply values to the INSERT statement.

For example, this SQL batch creates a new table called dboptions as it inserts the results of the stored procedure sp_dboption into the table:

```
CREATE TABLE dboptions (option_name varchar(255) NOT NULL)
GO

INSERT dboptions
    EXECUTE  sp_dboption pubs
```

The main advantage of using a stored procedure rather than a SELECT statement is that the stored procedure gives you the ability to fetch information from a remote server. For example, this statement pulls information from another server to populate a table in the local database:

```
INSERT employees
    EXECUTE
remoteserver.employeesdb.dbo.sp_getemployeeinfo
```

For more information about using stored procedures in the INSERT statement, see the SQL Server Books Online.

Using the INSERT Statement

The INSERT statement has several forms to allow you to insert data. You can use a simple VALUES clause to insert a single row of data or combine the INSERT with a SELECT statement to return multiple rows. In its third form, you can combine the INSERT statement with a stored procedure. You have seen examples of all these forms and should be comfortable using the INSERT statement.

THE UPDATE STATEMENT

▶ Write INSERT, DELETE, UPDATE, and SELECT statements that retrieve and modify data.

The UPDATE statement is used to modify one or more rows of data in a single table or view. The table owner is granted the permission to update rows and can grant this permission to other database users. The UPDATE statement has some restrictions that are very similar to those of the INSERT statement:

◆ If a column is updated in such a way that its new value violates the data type, NULL option, rule, or CHECK constraint on that column, the UPDATE fails and the changes are rolled back.

◆ When updating a view based on more than one table, only the data from a single table may be updated at a time. For more information about the restrictions placed on views, see Chapter 9 and the SQL Server Books Online.

◆ char and varchar columns behave as described in the "The INSERT Statement" section in this chapter with regard to empty strings and padding.

As with all DML statements, UPDATE can be executed from the Query Analyzer tool or other front-end applications written in Visual Basic or Visual C++.

Basic Syntax

The syntax for a standard UPDATE statement follows. In later sections you will be shown extensions that Microsoft has added to the UPDATE statement in Transact-SQL that make it easier to use:

```
UPDATE {table_name ¦ view_name}
SET
  { column_name = {NULL ¦ DEFAULT ¦ expression} }
  [,{ column_name = {NULL ¦ DEFAULT ¦ expression}...]
[WHERE {search_conditions ¦ CURRENT OF cursor_name}]
```

The SET keyword defines which columns to update in the table or view. The column name is specified, along with the new value for the column. Using the NULL keyword explicitly updates the column to a NULL value. Using the DEFAULT keyword updates the column to its default value, or NULL if no default exists. Otherwise, the column can be updated to a constant value, the results of a function, or the results of a sub-query.

The WHERE clause can be omitted entirely, in which case all rows in the table or view are updated. If a WHERE clause is used, then rows can be updated based on standard search criteria or a single row may be updated in a cursor. For more information about using WHERE clauses, see Chapter 6; for more information about cursors, see Chapter 8, "Programmability."

The following are some examples of using simple UPDATE statements:

1. This example updates the authors table and sets each author's phone number back to the default value:

```
UPDATE authors
  SET phone = DEFAULT
```

Because this example has no WHERE clause, it affects all rows in the table. The phone column could also have been set to a constant value, as shown in this example:

```
UPDATE authors
  SET phone = 'NO PHONE'
```

2. A column may also be updated based on an arithmetic expression. This example updates the titles table to give each author a well-deserved 10 percent increase on their book advances:

```
UPDATE titles
  SET advance = advance * 1.1
```

3. To update only certain rows in a table, use a WHERE clause. This example gives all authors of computer books an additional 10 percent increase on their book advances:

```
UPDATE titles
    SET advance = advance * 1.1
    WHERE title LIKE '%computer%'
```

4. To update the current row of a cursor, use the WHERE CURRENT OF keywords, as shown here:

```
UPDATE jobs
    SET min_lvl = 20
    WHERE CURRENT OF jobs_cursor_to_update
```

The preceding examples 2 and 3 show how it is possible to update a column based on an arithmetic expression that involves columns from the same table. It is also possible to use a sub-query to provide a value for a column. The WHERE clauses in the prior examples use criteria from the table being updated. In the ANSI standard form, it is possible to update rows in a table based on information stored in another table only by using a sub-query. Microsoft, however, has extended its definition of the UPDATE statement to include a FROM clause that makes referencing other tables even easier and more efficient. First, you will be shown the standard method before being introduced to the Transact-SQL extensions to the UPDATE statement.

Using Sub-Queries with the UPDATE Statement

Recall from Chapter 6 that sub-queries are queries that are embedded in another query. Sub-queries can be used with the UPDATE statement in two different ways:

◆ A sub-query can be used to provide a value for a column in the SET statement. The sub-query must return a value of zero or one. This example shows how a sub-query is used to raise the salary level of all employees hired on or before June 30, 1990, to the maximum salary for their job:

```
UPDATE employee
    SET job_lvl =
        (SELECT max_lvl FROM JOBS WHERE employee.job_id =
➥jobs.job_id)
    WHERE hire_date <= '6/30/1990'
```

Note that because the sub-query is correlated (the sub-query references the outer query—see Chapter 6 for more information), and every employee has a matching job in the jobs table, this sub-query always returns one value.

◆ A sub-query can be used in the WHERE clause of the UPDATE statement to update records based on records in other tables. A criteria value in the WHERE clause can be matched exactly to a sub-query that returns one value or the criteria value can be matched to a sub-query returning multiple values by the use of the IN or EXISTS keyword. As an example, consider the following query, which adds $10,000 to the salary of every employee who works for a publisher that publishes computer books:

```
UPDATE employee
    SET job_lvl = job_lvl + 10
    WHERE pub_id IN
        (SELECT publishers.pub_id FROM publishers INNER
➥JOIN titles
         ON publishers.pub_id = titles.pub_id
        WHERE type LIKE 'popular_comp'
        )
```

As was mentioned earlier, sub-queries are the ANSI standard way to reference other tables in an UPDATE statement. However, Microsoft has extended the syntax of the UPDATE statement to make referencing other tables easier, as shown in the next section.

Transact-SQL Extensions to the UPDATE Statement

The Transact-SQL UPDATE statement features a FROM clause that allows other tables to be referenced and joined without using a sub-query. The extended syntax is as follows:

```
UPDATE {table_name ¦ view_name}
SET
  { column_name = {NULL ¦ DEFAULT ¦ expression} }
  [,{ column_name = {NULL ¦ DEFAULT ¦ expression}...]
[FROM {table_list}]
[WHERE {search_conditions ¦ CURRENT OF cursor_name}]
```

The new FROM clause is used just like the FROM clause on a SELECT statement. Joins can be created between tables by using the old TSQL syntax or the new ANSI-standard syntax. (Chapter 6 discusses joins in more detail.)

N O T E

SQL Server-Specific Syntax This syntax is specific to SQL Server and may not work with other relational database systems. The sub-query syntax presented previously works with all databases that comply with the ANSI SQL syntax.

The following examples show how the queries presented in the previous section can be rewritten to use the Transact-SQL syntax:

1. This query updates the employee table to give employees hired on or before June 30, 1990 the maximum salary for their job:

```
UPDATE employee
    SET job_lvl = jobs.max_lvl
    FROM employee INNER JOIN jobs ON employee.job_id =
jobs.job_id
    WHERE employee.hire_date <= '6/30/1990'
```

2. This query updates the employee table to give the employees of publishers of computer books a $10,000 raise:

```
UPDATE employee
    SET job_lvl = job_lvl + 10
    FROM employee INNER JOIN
        (publishers INNER JOIN titles
            ON publishers.pub_id = titles.pub_id)
        ON employee.pub_id = publishers.pub_id
    WHERE titles.type LIKE 'popular_comp'
```

Note how the query syntax is more consistent when the TSQL extension is used. Many people find that queries with joins are easier to read and write than queries with sub-queries. Use whichever you are most comfortable with, with the understanding that the Transact-SQL syntax is specific to SQL Server.

THE DELETE STATEMENT

▶ Write INSERT, DELETE, UPDATE, and SELECT statements that retrieve and modify data.

The DELETE statement is used to delete one or more data rows from a table or view. By default, only the table owner can delete rows from a table, although this permission may be granted to other database users. The DELETE statement affects only a single table at a time, so it cannot be used with views that are based on more than one table. DELETE reclaims the database space used by the deleted data rows and any corresponding index rows.

As with all DML statements, DELETEs can be executed from the Query Analyzer tool or other front-end applications written in Visual Basic or Visual C++.

Basic Syntax

The syntax of the DELETE statement is as follows:

```
DELETE [FROM] [[database.][owner].]{table_name ¦ view_name}
    [WHERE {search_conditions ¦ CURRENT OF cursor_name}]
```

The FROM keyword is always optional and is usually just included for readability. The WHERE clause may be omitted entirely, in which case all rows are deleted from the table or view. If a WHERE clause is used, then rows may be deleted based on standard search criteria or a single row may be deleted from a cursor. For more information about using WHERE clauses, see Chapter 6; for more information about cursors, see Chapter 8.

Following are some examples of simple DELETE statements at work:

1. These examples delete all rows in the discounts table:

   ```
   DELETE discounts

   DELETE FROM discounts
   ```

2. This example deletes the sales records prior to January 1, 1994:

   ```
   DELETE Sales
       WHERE ord_date < '01/01/1994'
   ```

3. This example deletes the current row of the cursor named employee_service:

   ```
   DELETE Sales
       WHERE CURRENT OF employee_service
   ```

Note that in the preceding examples, rows are deleted based on criteria from the table containing the deleted rows. It is possible to delete rows from a table based on information stored in another table, as shown in the next two sections.

Using a Sub-Query in the WHERE Clause

Sub-queries can be used in the WHERE clause of a DELETE statement in much the same way that they are used in a SELECT statement. In the WHERE clause, a criteria value may be matched against a set (by using the IN or EXISTS keyword), or a criteria can be matched to a sub-query that returns a single value. Sub-queries can be *correlated*, which means that they reference a value in the main, or "outer" query. For a more thorough discussion of sub-queries, refer to Chapter 6.

> **NOTE**
>
> **How to Fix the Pubs Sample Database** If you execute the examples in this section, data is deleted from the Pubs database. To restore this database, you can execute the script found in the file \MSSQL7\INSTALL\INSTPUBS.SQL. Execute this script while in the master database, and Pubs is restored to its original state.

The following are examples of how sub-queries may be used to delete records from a table based on the records present in another table or tables:

1. To delete the employees that have a salary range of $25,000 to $100,000, a sub-query is used to first select the job_id for every job that matches this description. The DELETE statement then deletes those employees whose job_id falls within the set of job_ids returned by the sub-query:

```
DELETE employee
    WHERE job_id IN
        (SELECT job_id FROM jobs WHERE
        min_lvl = 25 AND max_lvl = 100)
```

This is an example of matching a criteria value to a set of values returned by a sub-query. The sub-query can return zero or more values.

2. This query deletes the royalty schedule records for book titles that feature information about traditional cooking:

```
DELETE roysched
    WHERE title_id =
        (SELECT title_id FROM titles
        WHERE title_id = roysched.title_id
          AND type LIKE 'trad_cook')
```

This is an example of a criteria value being matched to a sub-query that returns a single value. The sub-query must return zero or one value. The example also shows the use of a correlated sub-query; the sub-query selects information from the titles table based on the title_id in the roysched table.

Sub-queries are the ANSI standard way to reference other tables in a DELETE statement. However, another syntax exists, as discussed in the next section.

Transact-SQL Extension to the DELETE Statement

Microsoft has extended the syntax of the DELETE statement to make delete queries based on multiple tables easier to read and write. An additional FROM clause is added to the DELETE statement so that multiple tables can be referenced and joined:

```
DELETE [FROM] [[database.][owner].]{table_name ¦ view_name}
    [FROM {table_list}]
    [WHERE {search_conditions ¦ CURRENT OF }]
```

The new FROM clause is used just like the FROM clause on a SELECT statement. Joins can be created between tables by using the old TSQL syntax or the new ANSI-standard syntax. (Chapter 6 discusses joins in more detail.)

The two examples presented previously are rewritten here using the Transact-SQL syntax:

1. This query deletes those employees with a salary range of $25,000 to $100,000:

```
DELETE employee
    FROM employee INNER JOIN jobs
        ON jobs.job_id = employee.job_id
    WHERE jobs.min_lvl = 25 AND jobs.max_lvl = 100
```

2. This query deletes the royalty schedules for books on traditional cooking:

```
DELETE roysched
    FROM roysched INNER JOIN titles
        ON roysched.title_id = titles.title_id
    WHERE titles.type LIKE 'trad_cook'
```

Using the TRUNCATE TABLE Statement

The TRUNCATE TABLE statement is very similar to an unrestricted DELETE in that it removes all rows from a table, but is usually much faster. When a DELETE statement is executed, every row deletion is logged in the transaction log. When a TRUNCATE TABLE statement is executed, whole data pages are deallocated, and only the page deallocations are logged. While the TRUNCATE TABLE and unrestricted DELETE are basically the same, there are some subtle differences you need to be aware of:

◆ Because TRUNCATE TABLE does not log each individual row deletion, it cannot be rolled back if executed from within a transaction.

◆ TRUNCATE TABLE does not activate the DELETE trigger on a table.

◆ TRUNCATE TABLE cannot be used on a table that is referenced by a FOREIGN KEY constraint.

NOTE **SQL Server-Specific Syntax** Again, this syntax is specific to SQL Server and may not work with other relational database systems. The sub-query syntax presented previously works with all databases that comply with the ANSI SQL syntax.

NOTE **Test Your DELETEs before Running Them!** If you want to see which rows will be deleted by these queries, you can comment out the DELETE <tablename> portion of the query and replace it with SELECT * FROM <tablename>. This turns the DELETE statement into a SELECT statement so you can verify that the correct rows will be deleted.

◆ The TRUNCATE TABLE command will remove index statistics along with the all index information.

◆ If an IDENTITY column exists on the truncated table, it will be reset to its original seed value.

The syntax of the TRUNCATE TABLE statement is as follows:

```
TRUNCATE TABLE [[database.[owner].]table_name
```

For example, this statement removes all rows from the authors_examples table used in the INSERT section:

```
TRUNCATE TABLE pubs..authors_examples
```

R E V I E W   B R E A K

Using the DELETE Statement

The DELETE statement works similarly to an UPDATE statement in that they both must make use of sub-queries or special Transact-SQL extensions to reference other tables. You have now seen, and should have used yourself, both methods of writing DELETE statements. In addition you were introduced to the TRUNCATE TABLE statement. The TRUNCATE TABLE statement works similarly to an unrestricted DELETE statement, but it is more dangerous because it is not logged. Remember that you are trading safety for performance when using the TRUNCATE TABLE statement.

CASE STUDY: RECOVERING DATA FROM REDUNDANT COPIES

ESSENCE OF THE CASE

Here are the essential elements of the case:

▶ The data in a production table was damaged through a user's carelessness.

▶ It is believed that a good copy of the data exists in another database on the same server.

SCENARIO

Jim, a developer in your company, is working on an application that will allow a table containing a list of your companies clients to be maintained in a simple, graphical environment. After a demonstration that he was giving to some of the eventual users of the system, Jim realized that he had been running the application against the live data in production database. While demonstrating some of the features of the application,

CASE STUDY: RECOVERING DATA FROM REDUNDANT COPIES

Jim deleted four client records and set the city, state, and ZIP code fields of every client to NULL.

Fortunately, earlier that morning, Jim had asked you to create a fresh copy of the client table in his development database so that he could have good, up-to-date data to test with. 'He's already determined that no changes should have been made to the client table since you gave him his copy of it, so 'he's hoping that you can put that copy back into production for him before anyone notices.

ANALYSIS

You could try to fix the situation by restoring the table from last night's backup, but as long as you've got a good copy of the data sitting right there on the server you might as well use it. Besides, getting the data restored from backup would mean going through the Network Support department, which would really get your friend Jim in trouble.

Jim's request that you just take all the data from the development database and put it back into production, however, would require you to delete the existing data in the table, which would be a problem with several tables referencing the

ClientID as a foreign key. All those REFERENCES constraints would first have to be disabled to perform the delete, which seems like it would be a lot of work. Jim still remembers exactly which records he deleted, so you decide to insert those back one at a time. SQL Server allows tables from different databases to be referenced in the same statement simply by preceding the table name with the database name and the owner name. So you can write an INSERT statement that uses a SELECT statement to select the records you want from the development database. After those four records have been replaced, you need to fix the address information of all the clients. This is made easy by SQL Server's extensions to the UPDATE statement that allow joins. All you have to do is join the two client tables together on their primary key, and set the production table's address fields equal to the development table's address fields.

Jim is still going to have to explain the situation to his supervisor. He'll have to be certain that no important reports were run with the bad address data and that no side effects of the bad data hurt anyone else's work. Because you were able to fix the data so quickly, however, he should get off with just a stern warning to be more careful in the future.

CHAPTER SUMMARY

KEY TERMS

Before you take the exam, make sure you are comfortable with the definitions and concepts for each of the following key terms:

- INSERT
- UPDATE
- DELETE
- IDENTITY column
- DEFAULT keyword

This chapter introduced you to the INSERT, UPDATE, and DELETE commands, the SQL keywords used to modify data in a database. These commands allowed you to insert, modify, and delete rows in a table. With this information, combined with the details about the SELECT statement from the previous chapter, you have the fundamentals of the SQL Language. This is a powerful understanding that will serve you well in any SQL environment, not just SQL Server.

APPLY YOUR KNOWLEDGE

Exercises

6.1 Inserting a Record into the authors Table

This exercise walks you through the steps required to insert a record into the authors table in the Pubs database. You can insert a record that makes you an author.

Estimated Time: 5 minutes

1. Start the SQL Enterprise Manager application. In the Server Manager window, select a SQL Server that contains the Pubs database.

2. From the application's main menu, select Tools, SQL Query Tool. The Query window appears.

3. Select the Pubs database from the DB combo box.

4. Type the following query:

```
INSERT INTO authors (au_id, au_lname,
➡au_fname, phone, address, city, state, zip,
➡contract)
VALUES ('<your ssn>','<your last
➡name>','<your first name>','<your phone
➡number>',
        '<your address>','<your
➡city>','<your state>','<your zip code>',1)
```

Your query should look similar to the following:

```
INSERT INTO authors (au_id, au_lname,
➡au_fname, phone, address, city, state, zip,
➡contract)
VALUES ('111-22-9999','Author','Joe','816
➡555-1212',
        '123 anystreet','Kansas
➡City','MO','64114',1)
```

5. Type **Alt + X** or click the Execute Query button on the query window toolbar to execute the query. The following message should appear:

```
(1 row(s) affected)
```

6.2 Modifying Records in the titles Table

In this exercise, you update all the computer titles in the titles table to increase the advance amount by 10%.

Estimated Time: 5 minutes

1. Start the SQL Enterprise Manager application. In the Server Manager window, select a SQL Server that contains the Pubs database.

2. From the application's main menu, select Tools, SQL Query Tool. The Query window appears.

3. Select the Pubs database from the DB combo box.

4. Type the following query:

```
UPDATE titles
    SET advance = advance * 1.1
    WHERE type LIKE 'popular_comp'
```

5. Type **Alt + X** or click the Execute Query button on the query window toolbar to execute the query. A message similar to the following should appear:

```
(3 row(s) affected)
```

6.3 Deleting a Record from the authors Table

In this exercise, you delete the record you inserted in Exercise 6.1 from the authors table in the Pubs database.

Estimated Time: 5 minutes

1. Start the SQL Enterprise Manager application. In the Server Manager window, select a SQL Server that contains the Pubs database.

2. From the application's main menu, select Tools, SQL Query Tool. The Query window appears.

3. Select the Pubs database from the DB combo box.

APPLY YOUR KNOWLEDGE

4. Type the following query:

```
DELETE authors
    WHERE au_id = '111-22-9999'
```

If you used your own social security number when inserting the record, use that in the preceding query. If you used the example INSERT statement in Exercise 6.1, this query deletes the sample record:

```
DELETE authors
    WHERE au_id = '<your ssn>'
```

5. Type **Alt + X** or click the Execute Query button on the query window toolbar to execute the query. The following message should appear:

```
(1 row(s) affected)
```

Review Questions

1. What are the purposes of the INSERT, UPDATE, and DELETE statements?

2. How many rows can be modified by using the INSERT, UPDATE, and DELETE statements?

3. How many tables can be modified by using the INSERT, UPDATE, and DELETE statements?

4. What do the Transact-SQL extensions for UPDATE and DELETE statements allow?

5. What benefit, besides ease of use, do the Transact-SQL extensions for UPDATE and DELETE offer?

6. What are the three different methods of using the INSERT statement?

7. Contrast the benefits of using TRUNCATE TABLE against using an unrestricted DELETE.

8. What happens when you run TRUNCATE TABLE on a table with foreign key constraints?

Exam Questions

1. When using an INSERT statement, data to be inserted may come from which of the following? Select all that apply.

   A. The VALUES clause

   B. A stored procedure

   C. Another database

   D. A SELECT statement

2. What is the purpose of the column list in the INSERT statement?

   A. It provides values to be inserted into each column.

   B. It lists which columns will have data inserted into them.

   C. It lists which columns will be excluded from having data inserted in them.

   D. SQL Server does not use the column list; it is used only as a means for the developer to document the columns used in the INSERT statement.

3. You want to insert data into the jobs table of the Pubs database, which has an IDENTITY column. Which statements enable you to insert a row into this table?

   A. INSERT jobs (job_id, job_desc, min_lvl, max_lvl) VALUES (42,'Temp Employee',10,10)

   B. INSERT jobs (job_desc, min_lvl, max_lvl) VALUES ('Temp Employee',10,10)

APPLY YOUR KNOWLEDGE

C. INSERT jobs VALUES (42,'Temp Employee',10,10)

D. SET IDENTITY_INSERT jobs ON
   INSERT jobs (job_id, job_desc, min_lvl,
   ➡max_lvl) VALUES
   (42,'Temp Employee',10,10)
   SET IDENTITY_INSERT jobs OFF

4. If the column list is omitted from the INSERT statement, which columns must be provided in the VALUES clause? (Assume that IDENTITY_INSERT is turned off.)

   A. All columns

   B. Only those columns that do not allow NULLs

   C. Only the columns without defaults defined

   D. All columns except the identity column

5. What is the purpose of the DEFAULT keyword when used in the VALUES clause of the INSERT statement?

   A. To define a default value for a column

   B. To explicitly use the default value of a column

   C. To specify a default value for that column if the SELECT statement provides a NULL value

   D. To explicitly use the column's default value if the column allows NULLs

6. If the DEFAULT keyword is used in the INSERT or UPDATE statement, and no default exists for that column, what are the results? Select all that apply.

   A. A NULL value will be provided for the column.

   B. The query will fail.

   C. The query may fail if the column does not allow NULLs.

   D. A value of 'UNKNOWN' is placed in the column.

7. In the SET portion of an UPDATE statement, where may the new value for a column come from? Select all that apply.

   A. Another table by way of a single-result sub-query or table join in the FROM clause.

   B. An arithmetic expression or constant value.

   C. Values for multiple rows in the update may come from a sub-query that returns more than one value.

   D. Another column within the table itself.

   E. An explicit NULL value may be specified.

8. An UPDATE statement may modify how many tables?

   A. One or more tables, provided the UPDATE statement is not operating on a view

   B. Only one, except when updating a view based on multiple tables

   C. One

   D. Up to sixteen

9. Omitting the WHERE clause of an UPDATE or DELETE statement has what effect?

   A. All rows in the specified table are affected.

   B. The query returns an error because the WHERE clause is required.

   C. Only the current row of the specified cursor is affected.

APPLY YOUR KNOWLEDGE

10. A sub-query that returns multiple values may be used in what parts of an UPDATE statement?

    A. The SET clause only

    B. The SET and WHERE clauses

    C. The WHERE clause only

11. What are the purposes of the additional FROM clause in the extended Transact-SQL syntax for the UPDATE and DELETE statements?

    A. Allows data modifications to more than one table

    B. Allows data modifications based on data in other tables

    C. Allows column values in the UPDATE statement to come from columns in other tables

    D. Provides an alternative way to perform sub-queries

12. How does a TRUNCATE TABLE statement differ from an unrestricted DELETE? Select all that apply.

    A. A TRUNCATE TABLE cannot be rolled back, even if it occurs within a transaction.

    B. An unrestricted DELETE resets an IDENTITY column to its original seed, whereas the TRUNCATE TABLE does not.

    C. If the table is referenced by a FOREIGN KEY constraint, only the DELETE may be used.

    D. The TRUNCATE TABLE causes a DELETE trigger to be fired, whereas the DELETE does not.

    E. A TRUNCATE TABLE is often much faster than an unrestricted DELETE.

13. Rick is an application developer who is writing a database-aware program that he hopes to market for any ODBC database. Because he has carefully chosen an open standard for database access, he knows his program will work with any database that he can get ODBC drivers for. Therefore, he decides to use the TSQL extensions for UPDATE and DELETE statements to maximize his query performance.

    Rate Rick's solution as one of the following:

    A. This is an optimal solution. He is adhering to a well-defined and widely accepted standard, which will allow him access to a wide market.

    B. This is a fair solution. His program will work with ODBC, but he should use OLE-DB to reach the widest market segment.

    C. This is a poor solution. Non-Microsoft ODBC drivers do not always implement the Transact SQL extensions efficiently.

    D. This is not a solution. His program will not work with many databases.

Answers to Review Questions

1. The INSERT statement adds row(s) to a table. The UPDATE statement modifies existing row(s) in a table. The DELETE statement removes row(s) from a table. (Refer to the sections "The INSERT statement," "The UPDATE Statement," and "The DELETE Statement," respectively, for more information.)

2. Zero or more rows may be affected by the three data modification statements. (Refer to the sections "The INSERT Statement," "The UPDATE Statement," and "The DELETE Statement" for more information.)

APPLY YOUR KNOWLEDGE

3. Only one table may be affected at a time by using the data modification commands. (Refer to the sections "The INSERT Statement," "The UPDATE Statement," and "The DELETE Statement" for more information.)

4. The TSQL extensions for the UPDATE and DELETE statements allow you to use a FROM clause to join to multiple tables. (Refer to the sections "The UPDATE statement" and "The DELETE Statement" for more information.)

5. The ANSI standard UPDATE and DELETE statements do not allow multiple tables to be referenced directly. Instead, it is necessary to use sub-queries to reference other tables during these statements. (Refer to the sections "The UPDATE statement" and "The DELETE Statement" for more information.)

6. SQL Server can process joins enabled by the FROM clause due to the TSQL extensions for the UPDATE and DELETE statements more efficiently than it can process sub-queries. (Refer to the sections "The UPDATE statement" and "The DELETE Statement" for more information.)

7. Using a TRUNCATE TABLE statement is a non-logged operation and cannot be recovered. Because it is non-logged it is extremely fast, but using the DELETE statement maintains transactional consistency in your database. You should always back up your database after any non-logged operation, such as TRUNCATE TABLE. (Refer to the section "The DELETE Statement" for more information.)

8. A TRUNCATE TABLE statement is unaffected by the fact that a table may have FOREIGN KEY constraints. The TRUNCATE TABLE statement cannot be run on a table that is referenced by foreign key constraints however. (Refer to the section "The DELETE Statement" for more information.)

Answers to Exam Questions

1. **A, B, C, D.** All the choices are correct. Data may come from another database by means of a remote stored procedure. (For more information, refer to the section "The INSERT Statement.")

2. **B.** In a way, the columns list also implies which columns will not have data inserted into them; they are noted by their absence, but the list does not actually list them. (For more information, refer to the section "The INSERT Statement.")

3. **B, D.** In choices A and C, an explicit value is being set to the identity column, which is not allowed unless the IDENTITY_INSERT option is turned on. (For more information, refer to the section "The INSERT Statement.")

4. **D.** If the column list is omitted, you normally must supply some value to every column. SQL Server makes an exception to this rule for the identity column, but no others. (For more information, refer to the section "The INSERT Statement.")

5. **B.** By using the DEFAULT keyword in the values list, you can explicitly state that you do not have a specific value to place in the column and will be satisfied with any default value SQL Server can provide. If the column has a default value defined, that value is used. If the column has no default value but allows NULLs, a NULL value is assigned. If the column has no default value, and does not allow NULLs; an error occurs just as if you had tried to assign a NULL to the column. (For more information, refer to the section "The INSERT Statement.")

6. **A, C.** By choosing to allow a default assignment to a column that has no explicit default value assigned, a NULL value is assigned to the column. If the column does not allow NULLs, then an error will occur. (For more information, refer to the section "The INSERT Statement.")

APPLY YOUR KNOWLEDGE

7. **A, B, D, E.** Only option C is not allowed. A sub-query returning multiple rows cannot be used to make a different assignment to multiple rows in the UPDATE statement. Such a sub-query could probably be rewritten as a join in the UPDATE statement to assign a specific joined value to each row affected by the UPDATE. (For more information, refer to the section "The UPDATE Statement.")

8. **C.** Under no circumstances can an UPDATE statement affect more than one table. (For more information, refer to the section "The UPDATE Statement.")

9. **A.** By omitting the WHERE clause of an UPDATE or DELETE statement, all rows in the table are affected. (For more information, refer to the sections "The UPDATE Statement" and "The DELETE Statement.")

10. **C.** A sub-query returning multiple values is useful in the WHERE clause as a means of comparing rows in the UPDATED table to a list of values to determine which rows should be updated. Such a sub-query cannot be used in the SET clause to assign different values to different rows being updated. (For more information, refer to the section "The UPDATE Statement.")

11. **B, C, D.** The Transact-SQL extensions that allow the FROM clause allow an alternative to using sub-queries to compare values from other tables. These values that are joined in can also be used to make assignments in the UPDATE query. (For more information, refer to the section "The UPDATE Statement.")

12. **A, C, E.** A TRUNCATE TABLE operation removes data pages directly from the table structure. This has the same end result as a DELETE operation, but the TRUNCATE TABLE statement is faster. Because the TRUNCATE TABLE statement operates on the datapages and not the data itself, triggers and constraints cannot be checked. For this reason, the TRUNCATE TABLE is simply disallowed if REFERENCE constraints exist on the table, although triggers are simply ignored. (For more information, refer to the section "The DELETE Statement.")

13. **D.** Rick's use of ODBC as a widely accepted standard has nothing to do with the fact that he is using non-standard syntax. Because he is using SQL Server-specific syntax, he will not be able to work with all ODBC compliant databases. (For more information, refer to the section "The UPDATE Statement" and section "The DELETE Statement.")

Suggested Readings and Resources

We recommend the following resources for further study in the area of planning:

1. SQL Server Books Online

   • New Features of Microsoft Transact-SQL: Note the discussion of how TSQL handles empty strings.

   • Using Character Data: Note the discussion of when characters are padded with spaces.

2. Transact-SQL help file

   • INSERT: Described

   • UPDATE: Described

   • DELETE: Described

This chapter helps you to prepare for the Microsoft exam by covering the following objectives:

Create scripts using Transact-SQL. Programming elements include control-of-flow methods, local and global variables, functions, and error handling methods.

▶ The idea behind this objective is to make sure you are comfortable programming with the Transact-SQL (TSQL) language. This chapter explains each of the control-of-flow methods, such as IF statements and WHILE loops, and describes the use of variables and system functions. The importance and use of error handling methods also is discussed.

Create and manage explicit, implicit, and distributed transactions to ensure data consistency and recoverability.

• **Define the transaction isolation level.**

• **Design transactions of appropriate length.**

• **Avoid or handle deadlocks.**

• **Use optimistic locking appropriately.**

• **Implement error handling by using @@TRANCOUNT.**

▶ The transaction isolation level is set through the TSQL SET TRANSACTION ISOLATION LEVEL command. Using this command allows you to control SQL Server's locking behavior inside transactions.

▶ Transactions have the potential to lock large amounts of data, which can prevent other users from working. A certified SQL Server developer should always be careful to keep transactions as short as possible.

CHAPTER 8

Programmability

▶ Deadlocks present a subtle problem that arises from editing data inside of transactions. It is important to know what causes deadlocks and how to avoid them whenever possible.

▶ Optimistic locking is a strategy that involves minimal locking of the database while still allowing consistent updates. It requires some work on the part of developers to implement this strategy effectively, however, so it is an important concept to understand.

▶ This objective is really talking about the proper use of nested transactions. Transactions can nest implicitly when using stored procedures and triggers, so you'll need to understand the unique problems that can occur when nested transactions encounter errors.

Manipulate data by using Transact-SQL cursors.

- **Choose the appropriate type of cursor.**

- **Define the appropriate level of sensitivity to change.**

- **Choose the appropriate navigation.**

- **Choose the scope of the cursor, specifically global or local.**

▶ These four specifics about cursors all relate to the options that can be chosen in the DECLARE CURSOR statement. Each of the four classes of options has two or three values, which results in hundreds of distinct types of cursors that can be declared. You'll need to know how each of the options affect the cursor operation so you can get the kind of performance you need.

OUTLINE	STUDY STRATEGIES

▶ Be familiar with the terms batch and block and how they each group individual statements differently.

▶ Even if you don't know all the intimate details of every control-of-flow statement, at least familiarize yourself with the different keywords. Don't be tripped up on the exam by choosing to use a FOR loop (which doesn't exist in TSQL) instead of a WHILE loop!

▶ Be aware that the @@ERROR function returns only the error code returned by the last statement, and that even checking the value will cause it to change.

▶ Understand all the locking issues involved with transactions.

▶ Understand what data you should expect from a cursor. Be aware of which kinds of cursors will show changes made to the underlying tables and which will not.

INTRODUCTION

Microsoft SQL Server supports the Transact SQL language, or TSQL, for interactive queries and scripting. Since version 6.5, TSQL complies with ANSI standards for SQL as well as certain enhancements beyond the ANSI requirements. Version 7.0 adds to these enhancements making programming tasks even easier.

TSQL is a powerful programming language that can be used to create scripts that can be interpreted at execution time; commands also can be collected into stored procedures that SQL Server precompiles to improve performance. Using the TSQL language to the fullest, you can create batch jobs that evaluate the outcome of individual statements and can adjust the program logic based on the results.

This chapter covers SQL Server 7.0 general programmability through the following main sections:

◆ Control-of-flow statements

◆ Managing errors

◆ Using transactions

◆ Implementing cursors

CONTROL-OF-FLOW STATEMENTS

▶ Create scripts using Transact-SQL. Programming elements include control-of-flow methods, local and global variables, functions, and error handling methods.

The key to getting started using TSQL is understanding the *control-of-flow* structures that are available to you. These commands enable you to test conditions and take action based on the results. Examples of control-of-flow statements are IF statements for conditional execution, WHILE statements for looping, and GOTO statements for branching. Proper use of these and other control-of-flow statements gives you tremendous control over SQL Server's execution of your code.

Understanding Scripts and Batches

When submitting a large group of commands to be executed by SQL Server, it is important to understand how the individual commands are grouped for execution. The group of all commands submitted to SQL Server at one time is called a *script*. Within a script, commands can be further grouped into logical units known as *batches*. By properly grouping statements into scripts and batches, you can control the logical flow of execution through your commands, as described next.

A batch is the set of TSQL statements that are executed together. A batch of statements is compiled once as a whole and then executed. If any statement within the batch has a syntax error that prevents it from compiling, the entire batch fails to compile and is not run. Any following batches can still compile and run, however. Multiple explicit transactions can exist within a single batch, and a single script submitted to SQL Server for execution can be broken into multiple batches. The keyword GO signifies the end of a batch to SQL Server.

Using Variables

Variables are supported by TSQL to hold single values. In TSQL scripts, variables play less of a role than they do in other languages, such as Visual C++ and Visual Basic. This is because TSQL is a set-based language rather than an iterative one. Common TSQL data manipulation commands such as SELECT, INSERT, UPDATE, and DELETE normally operate on large sets of data at a time, whereas in many other languages, all operations act upon one piece of information at a time. Therefore, in TSQL, most data is stored in tables rather than in individual variables. Still, variables are needed to allow iterative programming and to store return codes and other single pieces of information. In particular, variables are useful to branching statements such as IF, WHILE, and CASE (all these are described in following sections) to control the logical execution of your scripts.

TSQL allows users to define and use local variables. Local variables are recognized by preceding the name by a single "at" sign (@). These user-defined variables continue to exist until the end of the current batch.

NOTE **Global Variables Are Now Called System Functions**   Previous versions of SQL Server supported system defined *global variables*, which were always available. SQL Server 7, however, has redefined global variables as *system functions*. Despite this change in terminology, these functions behave in identical fashion to the global variables of previous versions. These system functions are preceded by two "at" signs (@@) just as they were in previous versions. System functions return values from system tables, and are the preferred method of retrieving this data since Microsoft reserves the right to change system tables in future versions of the product. Although these system functions look and behave like variables, users should not attempt to change their assignments.

Local, user-defined variables are created through the DECLARE statement. Any number of variables can be created together in the same statement—even ones of different data types. The syntax for the DECLARE statement is as follows:

```
DECLARE @variable_name datatype
[, @variable_name datatype...]
```

After declaring local variables, you generally need to assign them. Assignment of local variables is done in either of two ways: with the SET statement or with the SELECT statement.

To assign a value using the SET statement, simply follow the keyword SET with the variable name followed by an equal sign (=) and the value to assign. The value assigned can be any TSQL expression, including constants, system functions, or even a value returned by a sub-query. Multiple variables can be set in a single statement by separating the individual assignments with commas.

To assign a variable to a value from a table, the SELECT statement is most often used. In the SELECT list of the statement, local variables can be listed followed by an equal sign and the value to assign.

In the following example, the SELECT statement returns the maximum Employee ID from the Pubs database.

```
USE PUBS
GO
DECLARE @EmpIDVariable INT

SELECT @EmpIDVariable = MAX(Emp_Id)
FROM EMPLOYEE
GO
```

In this way, variables can be assigned to constants, function results (such as those from Aggregate or System functions), or even table columns. Variables are generally assigned to a single value, but if a variable is assigned to a column returning multiple values, only the last value in the column is retained in the variable.

Using BEGIN and END Keywords

The BEGIN and END keywords are used to define a block of statements. A block causes all the statements contained within it to be treated by SQL Server as a single statement. Because all the statements in a block are grouped together, a block must be completely contained within a batch, as defined earlier. In other words, a batch terminator, the GO statement, cannot be used inside a block. The primary purpose of statement blocks is to define the group of statements that are affected by other control-of-flow statements such as IF, WHILE, and CASE. Each of these control-of-flow statements operates with only a single statement, or a statement block.

Using the IF Keyword

The IF statement enables you to control whether statements are executed based on the results of a Boolean expression. The statement following the IF statement is executed only if the Boolean expression returns True. If the Boolean expression returns False, the statement following is skipped. The syntax for the IF statement follows:

```
IF Boolean_expression
{sql_statement | statement_block}
 [ELSE [Boolean_expression]
{sql_statement | statement_block}]
```

In the preceding syntax listing, you can see that either a single statement or a block of multiple statements, delimited by the BEGIN and END keywords (explained earlier), can follow the Boolean expression.

The Boolean expression generally consists of some form of a comparison operation. All that is required is that the expression return a single value of TRUE or False. A SELECT statement can be used in a Boolean expression, but it must be contained within parentheses.

The following example demonstrates IF statements followed by single statements and blocks. In this example, the first statement following the IF will not execute because the condition is false; the second statement will execute, however, because it is outside the range of the IF statement.

```
IF 1=0
SELECT 'This statement will not execute'
SELECT 'This statement will execute'
```

By using the BEGIN and END keywords described earlier, the IF statement can affect multiple statements, as seen in this example:

```
IF 1=0
BEGIN
SELECT 'This statement is controlled by the IF statement'
SELECT 'And so is this one!'
END
SELECT 'This statement is unaffected by the IF statement'
```

There is an optional keyword: ELSE. If the initial Boolean expression returns False, the statement or block following the ELSE statement executes. If the initial expression returns True, however, the ELSE block does not execute. If the ELSE is followed by another Boolean expression, the statement following executes only if the initial expression is false but the ELSE expression returns True. The following example demonstrates this:

```
IF 1=0
SELECT 'Execute when IF boolean_expression is TRUE'
ELSE 1=1
BEGIN
SELECT 'Execute when IF boolean_expression is FALSE...'
SELECT '...And the ELSE boolean_expression is TRUE.'
END
```

The statement blocks following the IF or ELSE expression can contain almost any kind of statement, including other IF statements. SQL Server does not impose any limits on the number of IF statements that can be nested together. Note that because any statement block must be wholly contained in a batch, the GO command cannot be contained in an IF block.

Using the WHILE Statement

A WHILE statement allows for looping in a TSQL script or procedure. A WHILE statement is followed by both a boolean expression, which controls the looping, and a SQL statement, which performs the desired actions. The statement following is repeatedly executed until the expression that follows the WHILE keyword returns False. A description of the WHILE syntax follows:

```
WHILE Boolean_expression
{sql_statement | statement_block}
[BREAK]
{sql_statement | statement_block}
[CONTINUE]
```

The Boolean expression must follow the same rules as expressions in an IF statement. New to the WHILE statement are the two keywords BREAK and CONTINUE. These commands must be contained in a statement block following a WHILE. When either of these commands is encountered in a block, the execution of that block is interrupted. The difference between BREAK and CONTINUE is where execution resumes. The BREAK command causes execution to resume after the

WHILE statement block; the CONTINUE command causes the WHILE expression to be re-evaluated immediately and execution to resume according the result of that expression.

The following batch demonstrates controlling a WHILE loop with a variable. Note that as the scripts become more complicated, they are more difficult to read, as in this example. In all subsequent examples, spaces will be placed before statements in a statement block to clearly denote the statement blocks:

```
DECLARE @CountVar int
SET @CountVar = 1
WHILE @CountVar < 10
BEGIN
SELECT 'This statement will execute 9 times'
SET @CountVar = @CountVar + 1
END
```

Here is an example of an equivalent batch that relies on the BREAK statement to halt the WHILE loop. In addition, notice how using spaces to indent the commands in each statement block improves the readability of the code:

```
DECLARE @CountVar int
SET @CountVar = 1
WHILE 1=1
BEGIN
        SELECT 'This statement will execute 9 times'
        SET @CountVar = @CountVar + 1
        IF @CountVar >= 10
        BEGIN
                BREAK
        END
END
```

Using the CASE Expression

The CASE expression is a very powerful feature of TSQL. Although in many ways it simply provides the same functionality as nested if...else structures, the CASE expression can actually be used within the body of a SELECT statement. Note, however, that CASE is an expression—not a statement, like IF. As an expression, CASE cannot be executed by itself; it must be used as a part of another command that can be executed independently.

As stated previously, the CASE expression provides functionality similar to that of an IF statement. A CASE expression is specified along with any number of additional expressions. When the CASE expression equals one of the additional expressions, an expression associated with the matched expression is returned. The following syntax helps explain this better:

```
CASE expression
WHEN expression1a THEN expression1b
[[WHEN expression2a THEN expression2b] [...]]
[ELSE expressionNb]
END
```

In the preceding syntax, when the expression that follows CASE is equal to expression1a, expression1b is returned as the value of the CASE expression. This comparison is done on all of the WHEN expressions until a match is found. If no WHEN expression equals the CASE expression, the ELSE expression is returned (if one is provided). If no match is found and no ELSE expression is provided, the CASE expression returns NULL.

Here is an example of using a CASE expression in a SELECT statement:

```
DECLARE @IntVar INT
SET @IntVar = 1
SELECT CASE @IntVar
       WHEN 0 THEN 'This won't show'
       WHEN 1 THEN 'This will show'
       ELSE 'This won't show'
       END
```

There also is an alternate form of the CASE syntax. In this syntax no initial expression is provided for comparison. Rather, each WHEN expression must return a Boolean value. Each WHEN expression is evaluated until one returns TRUE; the related THEN expression is returned. If no WHEN Boolean expression returns TRUE, the ELSE expression is returned. This form of the syntax is called a *searched CASE*. The following syntax illustrates this:

```
CASE
WHEN Boolean_expression1 THEN expression1
[[WHEN Boolean_expression2 THEN expression2] [...]]
[ELSE expressionN]
END
```

The following example uses a searched CASE to form a more complicated example of using a CASE expression:

```
USE Pubs
GO
DECLARE @IntVar INT
SET @IntVar = 1
```

```
SELECT authors.au_lname, authors.state
FROM authors
WHERE CASE
        WHEN @IntVar = 0 THEN 'KS'
        WHEN @IntVar = 1 THEN 'CA'
        ELSE 'NY'
        END = authors.State
```

In the preceding example, by changing the value of @IntVar, you can cause authors to be returned from different states.

Using the GOTO Command

The GOTO command causes the execution of a batch to immediately resume at a label. A *label* is simply an identifier that is followed by a colon to identify it as an independent entity. A label can be placed anywhere in your script as a commenting feature, regardless of whether a GOTO refers to it.

The GOTO command itself is followed by the name of the identifier without the colon. When the GOTO is executed, the batch continues execution from the label onward. The label referred to by the GOTO can appear either before or after the GOTO itself, but it must be within the same batch. It is permissible to use a GOTO within an IF or WHILE command.

The following is an example of a GOTO command at work:

```
SELECT 'This command will execute'
GOTO SkipToHere
SELECT 'This command will not execute'
SkipToHere:
SELECT 'This command will execute'
GO
```

Using the RETURN Command

The RETURN command enables you to immediately stop execution of a batch. When the RETURN command is executed, the script execution resumes at the beginning of the next batch in the script. When used in a script, the RETURN command takes no parameters. It is executed as an independent statement.

The following example shows the RETURN command in action:

```
SELECT 'This command will execute'
RETURN
SELECT 'This command will not execute'
SELECT 'Nor will this'
GO
SELECT 'This command will execute'
GO
```

The RETURN command also can be used to terminate execution of a stored procedure, which is discussed later in this chapter. When RETURN is used in a stored procedure, it can accept an optional parameter enclosed in parentheses as the value that it returns. If the procedure was called from an EXEC statement, the RETURN value from the procedure can be assigned to a variable and examined for the cause of the procedure's termination. The following syntax shows this use of the RETURN command:

```
RETURN [(integer_expression)]
```

REVIEW   BREAK

Control-of-Flow Statements

You have now been introduced to control-of-flow commands in Transact-SQL. These commands form the basis of programming with this language. You have learned to group code into scripts, batches, and blocks. You can also define and use your own variables to store values to be used in later statements. You can control the execution of your scripts using IF, GOTO, RETURN, and WHILE, and you can use the CASE statement to perform complex branching in a TSQL statement.

The next section in this chapter deals with managing errors that could arise in your scripts.

MANAGING ERRORS

▶ Create scripts using Transact-SQL. Programming elements include control-of-flow methods, local and global variables, functions, and error handling methods.

When writing large TSQL scripts and procedures, you will quickly find situations in which errors can occur. You cannot always guarantee that users will enter the kind of data you expect, and this can cause duplicate key violations or other forms of constraint violations. It is often impractical to pre-examine entered data for every possible violation that could occur, and even then, it is wise to protect your code against changes to the database structure that could cause errors for which you could not have planned. SQL Server provides the ability to check for and respond to unexpected errors and to respond to bad data by raising errors of your own.

By controlling errors in your code, you can take automated responses to predefined conditions, or you can simply ensure that the error message is displayed to the user so that he can take any necessary response. SQL provides two different ways of generating such messages to the user: RAISERROR and PRINT. These statements are discussed in the following sections.

Responding to Errors

After the execution of any TSQL statement, the global variable @@ERROR is always set to indicate success or failure. A value of zero indicates success, and any other value means that some error occurred. Good code should always check the value of @@ERROR after any statement. Very often scripts or procedures do their work inside transactions to ensure consistency. In these cases, it is especially important to check for errors so that a partially completed transaction is not committed.

As previously stated, any TSQL statement causes @@ERROR to be reset to indicate success or failure of that statement. This means that the very act of checking @@ERROR for a non-zero status causes it to be reset. Therefore, even though you will learn the results of your comparison, you can no longer use @@ERROR to report the error value that occurred. If you need to know the exact error value that was returned by a statement, you must immediately assign @@ERROR to a user-defined variable, and then perform your validation on that variable.

Because it is so important to maintain the value of @@ERROR after a statement, it is common to see similar code following every statement in a script. This code would resemble the following:

```
SET @ErrVal = @@ERROR
IF @ErrVal > 0
BEGIN
        --Respond to Error here
END
```

The preceding block of code assumes that the variable @ErrVal has been defined earlier. You will also notice that the key portion of the code that actually acts on the error is missing. This section of code should use the value of @ErrVal to perform some meaningful action. The following section will help you fill in the blanks by introducing the RAISERROR statement.

Using the RAISERROR Statement

If you detect any condition within your code about which you need to warn the user, you can raise your own custom-defined errors to return. This is done with the RAISERROR statement. With the RAISERROR statement you can either raise errors that you have defined and registered in the database, or create an ad-hoc error message to return. The syntax for RAISERROR follows:

```
RAISERROR ({msg_id | msg_str}, severity, state
[, argument1 [, argument2]] )
[WITH option]
```

The severity and state parameters are used by RAISERROR to report additional information to the client application. The severity should be an integer between 1 and 25. Errors with a severity of 1 to 10 are considered informational only—the user might want to note the occurrence, but should feel safe to ignore it. Errors with a severity of 11 through 16 are those that are generated by the user and can be corrected by the user. Examples of these would be constraint violations caused by bad data being sent by the user. Errors with severity 17 through 19 are hardware or software errors. These errors indicate that the user can continue working, although a serious problem exists that may affect the server's performance. Errors returned with a severity of 20 through 25 indicate a fatal problem. Returning these errors causes the client connection to be disconnected.

Only the system administrator can raise an error with a severity of 19 or greater, and then the WITH LOG option must be specified (refer to Table 8.1). The error state should indicate the source of the error, if the error can be raised from more than one place. An error state of -1 should be used to indicate no particular state.

The WITH option allows one of three optional behaviors to occur. The three options are described in Table 8.1.

TABLE 8.1

OPTION PARAMETERS FOR THE RAISERROR STATEMENT

Option	Meaning
LOG	The error will be written to SQL Server's error log. All errors with a severity of 19 or greater must use the WITH LOG option.
NOWAIT	The error will be sent immediately to the client.
SETERROR	The @@ERROR function value will be set to *msg_id* or 50000.

Either a predefined error or an ad-hoc message can be returned by RAISERROR. A predefined error is one that has been registered in the sysmessages system table. You can register and remove errors of your own using the sp_addmessage and the sp_dropmessage stored procedures. The messages RAISERROR uses, whether supplied explicitly or pulled from sysmessages, are subject to parameter replacement so that specific values can be inserted into the string to make the message more relevant. Special format strings are included in the error string to mark the point at which the RAISERROR parameters argument1, argument2, and so on, should be inserted. The arguments can be of any data type as long as they match the type required by the format string. The syntax for the format string follows:

```
% [[flag] [width[.precision]] [{h | l}]] type
```

The flag parameter allows the values shown in Table 8.2.

TABLE 8.2

flag PARAMETERS FOR THE RAISERROR STATEMENT

Value	Formatting	Description
– (minus)	Left-justified	The result will be left-justified within the specified field width.
+ (plus) – (minus)	+ (plus) or – (minus)	The output value will be preceded with a + or –.
0 (zero)	Zero padding	The result will be padded with zeros on the left. This flag will be overridden by the – (minus) flag if both are used together.
# (number)	0x prefix for hexadecimal type of x or X	When used with the o, x, or X format, the # flag will preface any nonzero value with 0, 0x, or 0X, respectively. This value will be ignored with all other formats.

continues

TABLE 8.2		*continued*

flag PARAMETERS FOR THE RAISERROR STATEMENT

Value	Formatting	Description
(blank)	Space padding	The result will be padded with spaces on the left. This flag will be ignored if included with the + flag.

The width parameter defines the minimum width the replacement argument takes up in the resulting message. Values are normally right-justified within the width specified, although this can be changed by some of the preceding specified values. This parameter can optionally be modified by following it with a decimal point (.) and a precision parameter. The precision specifies a width within the total width that printed characters show. For an integer value, this precision specifies the minimum number of digits to print. For a string, the precision specifies the maximum characters to print.

The type parameter indicates the data type that will be embedded into the message string. Note that only integer and character data types are allowed. When this parameter indicates an integer type it can be followed by either the h or l option to indicate a short or long integer type, respectively. Table 8.3 describes the values for this parameter.

TABLE 8.3

DATA TYPES FOR FORMAT STRINGS IN THE RAISERROR STATEMENT

Type Code	Data Type
d or i	Signed integer
o	Unsigned octal
p	Pointer
s	String
u	Unsigned integer
x or X	Unsigned hexadecimal

The previous section, "Responding to Errors," showed a section of common error handling code, and stated that it would be elaborated on here. Now that you are familiar with the RAISERROR statement, you can use it to respond to an error with a descriptive message to the user. Examine the changes in the following code:

```
SET @ErrVal = @@ERROR
IF @ErrVal > 0
BEGIN
        RAISERROR("Error number %d was detected. The
➥current batch will be halted.", 16, 1, @ErrVal)
        RETURN
END
```

This works well for a simple error catcher that will halt a batch at the first sign of trouble. The RAISERROR statement allows you to return the error number to the user along with a simple message.

Using the PRINT Statement

The PRINT statement is used to return a message to the client application. The message can be any kind of text up to 1024 characters in length. String literals, character variables, and functions returning character data can be used in a PRINT statement. Multiple expressions can be concatenated together to form a complete string to be printed.

The messages that the PRINT statement returns are well suited for error messages and debugging messages in batches. The RAISERROR statement defined earlier will also return descriptive messages, but it also causes an error to occur that can interrupt normal processing. Use the PRINT statement to return messages to the user without affecting the normal process flow. Here is the example used to demonstrate a WHILE loop earlier in the chapter, improved with the use of the PRINT statement:

```
DECLARE @CountVar int
SET @CountVar = 1
WHILE @CountVar < 10
BEGIN
        PRINT 'The loop has executed ' +
convert(varchar(5), @CountVar) + ' times.'
        SET @CountVar = @CountVar + 1
END
```

Managing Errors

If you never run more than a single TSQL statement at a time, error handling will not be very important to you. If a statement fails, you will immediately evaluate and deal with the error yourself before writing the next statement. In order to do any programming in the TSQL language, however, you will quickly realize the need for error handling. Because a batch does not automatically stop when errors are encountered, it is important that you monitor the state of the @@ERROR function after every statement so that you can respond to errors correctly. You can then use the RAISERROR and PRINT statements to return messages to the user as a result of an error. The PRINT statement is also particularly useful in returning messages about the current state of variables or other conditions in your scripts so that you can track down where problems are arising.

USING TRANSACTIONS

▶ Create and manage explicit, implicit, and distributed transactions to ensure data consistency and recoverability.

- Define the transaction isolation level.
- Design transactions of appropriate length.
- Avoid or handle deadlocks.
- Use optimistic locking appropriately.
- Implement error handling by using @@TRANCOUNT.

Transactions are groups of statements that are all dependent on the execution of the whole. In any transaction, either all statements are committed together, or all results are cancelled together. A transaction is begun with the BEGIN TRANSACTION statement, and is ended with either a COMMIT TRANSACTION statement or a ROLLBACK TRANSACTION statement. A COMMIT TRANSACTION will commit the results of all statements in the transaction and a ROLLBACK TRASACTION statement will undo all the results of the transaction.

Transactions are an important feature whenever you need to perform multiple related actions. Transactions allow you to combine your

TSQL statements into "all or nothing" groups. Consider the Pubs database that is installed with SQL Server. If you were to add a new book into the database, you would want to make sure that the book was inserted into both the Titles table and the TitleAuthor table in the same transaction. In this way you could be certain that if any errors occurred, you would not end up with a title that had no author referenced to it. By encompassing the statements in a transaction, either both the inserts would happen together, or not at all.

Although transactions are a necessary feature of any relational database, they can cause certain problems. As a normal part of its operations, SQL Server cannot allow two people to change the same data at the same time. However, by opening a transaction you are declaring that your changes cannot be completed until you close the transaction. Therefore, while your transaction is open, you may be preventing others from working. The following sections will discuss the ramifications of transactions on multi-user data access.

Define the Transaction Isolation Level

One of the primary functions of any database management system, such as SQL Server, is to allow many users to read and update data at the same time. After all, a database wouldn't be nearly as useful if only one person could see the data at a time. The ability of a server to allow multiple people to work together is described by its concurrency. There are, however, times when a single user needs to take control of a particular portion of data for a limited time. Using transactions exerts this control. By performing work within a transaction, a user can guarantee that multiple actions take place together, or not at all. This ability of one person to control a portion of the data is described as the user's isolation. The question of where to draw the line between concurrency and isolation is solved by the transaction isolation level.

There are four distinct settings for the transaction isolation level; each of them represent a different trade off between concurrency and isolation. The following illustrates the syntax to set the transaction isolation level:

```
SET TRANSACTION ISOLATION LEVEL
{READ COMMITTED |
READ UNCOMMITTED |
REPEATABLE READ |
SERIALIZABLE}
```

READ COMMITTED is the SQL Server default. At this level, SQL Server will hold locks on data that is modified inside a transaction, but will not lock data that is selected inside a transaction. Because data being modified is locked until the changes are committed, other users are protected from reading changes to data that could be rolled back later. Reading data that is later rolled back, and therefore considered never to have actually existed, is commonly called a dirty read. With the READ COMMITTED isolation level it is possible, however, for a user to read data inside a transaction, and then have someone else change that data. If the first user were to reread the data after the changes, she would not see the same data again. When previously read data is changed, it is known as a non-repeatable read, when new data appears in a previously read dataset, it is known as *phantom data*. The READ COMMITTED isolation level prevents dirty reads, but not non-repeatable reads or phantom data.

The lowest isolation level is READ UNCOMMITTED . At this level no shared locks are issued, and no exclusive locks are honored. With this level selected, dirty reads are possible and rows can appear and disappear from the data before the transaction is complete.

The REPEATABLE READ isolation level places locks on all data used in a query, preventing other transactions from updating it, guaranteeing repeatable reads, but it will not prevent phantom data.

SERIALIZABLE is the highest isolation level where transactions are guaranteed to be able to read and re-read the same data at any time during the transaction. Locks in the database are managed to completely isolate one transaction from another to make it appear as if the transactions are run in some serial order. This isolation level will prevent dirty reads, non-repeatable reads, and phantom data.

Design Transactions of Appropriate Length

When editing data within a transaction, it is important to realize that your actions can have a serious impact on other users. Even on the lowest isolation level, two users cannot edit the same data at the same time; and on high isolation levels, even reads will prevent others from accessing that data. When you open a transaction you must be aware that you may be preventing others from working.

Therefore, it is important to keep transactions as short as possible. A good rule of thumb is to never keep a transaction open while waiting on user input. Otherwise, you'll eventually have someone take an extended lunch, and shut down your database for the afternoon.

Avoid or Handle Deadlocks

Deadlocks occur when each of two users holds locks on tables to which the other needs reference. In this situation, both users will wait for the other to release their locks before they will complete their transaction and release their own locks. This can be a difficult situation to resolve when it happens. Fortunately, SQL Server has methods to recognize such deadlocks, and it will automatically roll back one of the deadlocked transactions. What this means to you as a database developer is that you should be prepared to handle the error that will occur if your transaction is ever rolled back for this reason. Whenever you are making modifications to data, you can never be certain that your statements will succeed. Deadlocks are just a good illustration of the point that statement failures can happen for perfectly valid reasons—not just as a result of poor programming or a server problem. Therefore, it is always important to check for error conditions after your data modification statements, and either resubmit, or cancel your actions.

Even though SQL Server can automatically handle a deadlock situation, it is a complicated process. The detection process itself is wasteful of the server's resources, and then the rollback and eventual re-submittal of the transaction is wasted work. For this reason it is always better to avoid a deadlock situation in the first place.

There are several strategies that can be employed to avoid deadlocks. The first is to always access objects in the same order. If two different processes must update the same tables, they can only deadlock with each other if each has a lock on data that the other wants. That can't happen if both processes access the tables in the same order, because one of the two processes would get a lock on the table first, preventing the other from even getting started. A deadlock occurs when each process locks different tables and then waits forever to get a lock on the table that the other process already has. Moving database access into stored procedures on the server can make it easier to enforce this rule by centralizing code. You should also attempt to keep transactions as short as possible. Deadlocks always occur because of bad timing. If transactions are kept short there is less time for conflicts to occur. Submitting entire transactions in a single batch can help speed by reducing round trips to the server. You can also shorten the time that locks are held, by not leaving transactions open while waiting on user input. Finally, it is a good idea to keep the transaction isolation level as low as possible. This will reduce the number of locks generated by a transaction.

Use Optimistic Locking Appropriately

When writing On Line Transaction Processing (OLTP) applications, a common need is to examine and update existing records in the database. A common problem in solving this need is how to prevent changes to the data being examined without holding locks in the database that could prevent work by other users. It has already been mentioned that it is best not to hold locks on data while waiting on user interaction. This scheme is implemented by the default transaction isolation level (READ COMMITTED). The scheme is also known as *optimistic locking*. With optimistic locking you leave the data unlocked until it is time to actually write your changes in the optimistic hope that no one will change it behind your back.

In some situations you may not care if the data was changed, and you will simply want to make your own changes regardless. More commonly, however, you will want to discover how or why the data was changed while you were examining it. In this approach, you should attempt to detect such changes, and then handle them accordingly. The detection can be done by performing a second read of the data just before your update; this time your read *should* lock the data because your following actions will take place in rapid succession. After the second read, compare the values found to your original values. If they are the same, no one has changed the data and you can safely update the data; otherwise, you should take some action to determine if your changes should still take place. Note that if this action involves user input, you should first free the locks you have taken. Timestamp columns and update triggers can aid this change detection by guaranteeing that any update to a row will cause some identifiable change to a particular field. In this case, only that one field would have to be examined for changes, which simplifies things considerably.

The kind of change detection scheme advocated here is handled automatically by some data access models. In the next major section of this chapter, "Implementing Cursors," you will see that SQL Server cursors have two different methods for implementing optimistic locking with change detection.

Implement Transactional Error Handling

When working inside a transaction, it is important to check for errors so that the transaction can be rolled back if any part cannot succeed. This seems simple enough, but things can get slightly more complicated when nesting transactions inside stored procedures or triggers.

Suppose you want to update some data by calling several predefined stored procedures that your company developed for just this purpose. You decide that you want the stored procedure calls inside a transaction so that either they all succeed or no data will be changed. It is entirely possible that the procedures themselves will have transactions inside them as well. In addition, perhaps there are triggers on the tables that the stored procedures update, with transactions in the triggers. In this way, the transactions can nest quickly, and sometimes in subtle ways. Although SQL Server allows nested transactions, they don't behave the way you might expect; therefore, it is important to pay special attention to error handling in transactions.

SQL Server provides a system function, @@TRANCOUNT, to allow you to keep track of nesting transactions. Every time a BEGIN TRANSACTION is encountered, SQL Server increments the value of @@TRANCOUNT. This allows you to easily track the level of nesting of your transactions.

It is important to note that SQL Server does not truly nest transactions with each one operating independent of the surrounding transactions. In reality, only the outermost transaction is valid. When a COMMIT TRANSACTION is encountered, if the @@TRANCOUNT is equal to 1, the transaction is committed and resources held by the transaction are freed. If the @@TRANCOUNT is greater than 1, then the @@TRANCOUNT is simply decremented by 1; no other actions take place. A ROLLBACK TRANSACTION statement works very differently, however. Because nested transactions are not independent of the outer transaction, a ROLLBACK TRANSACTION is taken much more seriously than a nested COMMIT TRANSACTION. A nested ROLLBACK TRANSACTION will actually roll the transaction back to the outermost level, and cause @@TRANCOUNT to be set to 0.

Note that in the scenario in which a transaction is nested inside a stored procedure, a ROLLBACK TRANSACTION statement will still roll the transaction back to the outermost transaction, even if that is outside the stored procedure. In this case, when the procedure ends, the informational error number 266 will be raised to indicate that the transaction was rolled back inside the stored procedure. Triggers will work similarly, in that a ROLLBACK TRANSACTION will reset the outermost transaction, but the informational error 266 will *not* be raised because well-designed triggers will tend to return their own errors via the RAISERROR statement discussed earlier in this chapter. If a ROLLBACK TRANSACTION occurs in either a stored procedure or trigger, execution of the current batch ends at the point at which the procedure or trigger was called and resumes with the next batch. Therefore, any error handling must be done at the beginning of the next batch.

Because ROLLBACK TRANSACTION commands can cause a more extensive rollback condition than might be anticipated, it is a good idea to check the @@TRANCOUNT system function to see how many levels of transactions will be reset. The reverse is also true—after running stored procedures or any statements that could cause a trigger to fire, you should check @@TRANCOUNT to see whether any explicit transactions you started are still in effect.

R E V I E W   B R E A K

Transactions

Although transactions can be an important tool for maintaining data consistency by grouping changes together, they can also cause problems if not handled correctly. In the previous sections, you were introduced to the problems that can arise from transactions: lowered concurrency and deadlocking. You were also shown how to limit these problems through careful setting of the transaction isolation level, optimistic locking, and keeping transaction lengths to a minimum. Finally, you learned how to handle errors in transactions so that your ROLLBACK commands don't cause even more errors.

IMPLEMENTING CURSORS

▶ Manipulate data by using Transact-SQL cursors.

 · Choose the appropriate type of cursor.

 · Define the appropriate level of sensitivity to change.

 · Choose the appropriate navigation.

 · Choose the scope of the cursor, specifically global or local.

Cursors provide you with the ability to work with data in SQL Server iteratively (one row at a time), rather than in sets. SQL is inherently a set-based language. All its most fundamental data manipulation statements (SELECT, UPDATE, INSERT, and DELETE) normally work with entire sets of data at a time. Cursors enable you to define a set of data and work with that data one row at a time. To work with data in this way, you generally need to use some form of a loop to iterate through the set, which is why using cursors is called an *iterative* approach.

As a rule, SQL Server can work with data as a set faster than it can respond to an iterative series of commands. Because most iterative solutions can be expressed as set operations with a little work, cursors should generally be avoided. Thinking in terms of whole sets of data rather than individual rows is what makes the SQL language so different from other traditional programming languages. Looking for set-oriented solutions to problems is, however, an important transition to make.

When cursors are found to be necessary, they can be implemented quickly and efficiently in SQL Server. SQL Server supports server-based cursors, in which the server maintains the entire set of data that makes up the cursor and keeps track of the current position in the set of the cursor. Before SQL Server 6.0, these operations had to be handled through client libraries, which was much less efficient. By handling all the data itself, SQL Server can process any commands necessary without having to transport data to another application that could possibly be running over a slow network connection.

The following sections will detail exactly how cursors are implemented in SQL Server. The entire life span of a cursor will be examined, from the time it is first declared, while it is opened and iterated, until it is closed and deallocated. There is a TSQL command for each phase of a cursor's existence, and each will be examined.

Declaring Cursors

To use cursors in TSQL, you must first define the type of cursor and the data set it operates on. There are two distinct syntaxes allowed for defining cursors: the SQL-92 standard for cursor definition, and the TSQL extended syntax. Predictably, the SQL-92 standard is somewhat more limiting than the TSQL enhancements. There are many keywords that can be used in the declaration of a cursor to specify various options for the cursor's behavior, and the data set to operate on is specified by embedding a SELECT statement in the declaration. The SQL-92 standard cursor declaration and the TSQL extensions will be described in the following subsections.

Declaring SQL-92 Standard Cursors

The following details the syntax for a SQL-92 standard cursor declaration:

```
DECLARE cursor_name [INSENSITIVE] [SCROLL] CURSOR
FOR select_statement
 [FOR {READ ONLY | UPDATE [OF column_list]}]
```

The keyword INSENSITIVE specifies that the result set of the cursor be held in the temporary database, tempdb, so that changes to the underlying tables while the cursor is open will not affect the results of the cursor. These cursors cannot be updated because the only data that is maintained is in tempdb. There is no tie maintained with the underlying table.

The keyword SCROLL specifies that the cursor can be positioned forward or backward and by specified amounts. The different options for scrolling are described by the FETCH command later in this section.

By specifying that the cursor is scrollable, SQL Server needs to maintain a collection of key information about all the rows in the cursor so that it can uniquely identify its position as it moves around. If all the tables involved have unique indexes, then this condition is easily satisfied. If any table does not have a unique index, then the data from that table must be manipulated in the temporary database, tempdb, where each row can be assigned a unique identifier. By storing this information in tempdb, however, SQL Server cannot maintain a connection to the real table because there is no way to identify any specific row without a unique index. This is why scrollable cursors cannot be updated if any table does not have a unique index. SQL Server creates the cursor as INSENSITIVE, which is non-updateable.

The select_statement specified in the DECLARE command is a standard SELECT statement with a few limitations. The keywords COMPUTE, COMPUTE BY, FOR BROWSE, and INTO cannot be used in the declaration of a cursor. If the keywords DISTINCT, UNION, GROUP BY, or HAVING are used in the select_statement, then the cursor is not updateable and declaring it so results in an error. This is because using these options requires SQL Server to store the data in tempdb so that the results can be ordered and otherwise manipulated. Again, because the data is in tempdb, the cursor is created as INSENSITIVE, which is non-updateable.

The cursor is also INSENSITIVE if the select_statement includes a derived column. This is any column that does not come directly from a single column from some table. The cursor also is INSENSITIVE if one of the tables in the query does not have a unique index and the SCROLL option is used, as was discussed earlier in this section.

The READ_ONLY keyword ensures that the cursor allows no modifications. Because non-insensitive cursors are updateable by default, this option is needed to prevent unintentional updates or deletes.

The UPDATE keyword ensures that the cursor will allow modifications. Because the nature of the tables and the type of SELECT statement that is used can implicitly disallow updates, it is a good idea to explicitly use the UPDATE keyword to ensure that the cursor actually allows data modifications to occur. If the UPDATE demand cannot be honored because of the nature of the rest of the declaration, an error is returned, and the cursor is not declared.

If the UPDATE keyword is used, all columns in the cursor are updateable. Using the OF modifier to UPDATE enables you to explicitly list the columns you intend to modify. Note that the UPDATE keyword does not simply mean that updates are allowed to the rows in the result set—it also indicates that deletions are allowed.

The following are examples of an updateable and an insensitive cursor:

```
DECLARE cur_Update SCROLL CURSOR FOR
SELECT *
FROM Authors
FOR UPDATE of au_fname, au_lname

DECLARE cur_Insensitive INSENSITIVE CURSOR FOR
SELECT *
FROM Authors
FOR READ_ONLY
```

> **NOTE**
>
> **Using the SCROLL Option Affects Cursor Performance** If the SCROLL option is not used, the cursor only positions itself one row at a time in the forward direction. This is known as a *forward-only* cursor. Because positioning in this situation is so predictable, no keysets need to be created and stored in tempdb, allowing the cursor to be opened more quickly and positioning speed is much faster. The predictability of scrolling through a forward-only cursor is also why such a cursor can be updateable even if no unique indexes are available.

Declaring Cursors with TSQL Extensions

The syntax for a cursor with the TSQL extensions is as follows:

```
DECLARE cursor_name CURSOR
[LOCAL ¦ GLOBAL]
[FORWARD_ONLY ¦ SCROLL]
[STATIC ¦ KEYSET ¦ DYNAMIC]
[READ_ONLY ¦ SCROLL_LOCKS ¦ OPTIMISTIC]
FOR select_statement
[FOR UPDATE [OF column_list]]
```

The keywords LOCAL and GLOBAL define the scope of a cursor. LOCAL is the default. A LOCAL cursor's declaration is valid only within the batch, stored procedure, or trigger in which it is defined. A GLOBAL cursor can be used for the duration of the connection in which it was defined. If you do not open the cursor within the batch where it is declared, or you reopen the cursor in a later batch, you will need to declare a global cursor.

The keywords FORWARD_ONLY and SCROLL behave exactly as does the SCROLL option in the SQL-92 standard syntax. FORWARD_ONLY cursors will respond only to the FETCH NEXT command (described later in this chapter), whereas SCROLL cursors can be repositioned in any direction or distance.

There are three distinct types of cursors allowed in the TSQL extended syntax: static cursors, keyset driven cursors, and dynamic cursors. Each of these types can be specified by the STATIC, KEYSET, and DYNAMIC keywords in the extended DECLARE CURSOR syntax.

A *static* cursor is the same as an insensitive cursor in the SQL-92 standard. It is non-editable, and all values are stored in tempdb when the cursor is opened.

A *keyset-driven* cursor has its membership and the order of its values set when the cursor is opened. A keyset-driven cursor also uses tempdb; however, only unique row identifiers are stored in tempdb. In a keyset-driven cursor, inserts to the base table will not be seen because the keyset cannot grow. Updates made to non-key values on the base tables will be seen through the cursor when that row is scrolled to. Scrolling to a row that has been deleted will be noted by the system function @@fetch_status being set to a value of -2 (a full description of the @@fetch_status system function can be found later in the section "Using the FETCH Command").

A *dynamic* cursor is one in which the base tables for the cursor are examined directly. In a dynamic cursor, the full population of the cursor is never fully known. Scrolling can take place by only a single row at a time, and the row scrolled to is not known until you get there. Therefore, new rows can be added and existing rows deleted from the base tables throughout the lifetime of the cursor, and they will be seen as the cursor is repositioned.

There are three different levels of locking that can be chosen for the cursor. The lowest level is READ_ONLY, which will implement no locking whatsoever on the base tables of the cursor. A READ_ONLY cursor cannot be updated. Using the SCROLL_LOCK option implements the highest level of locking. When the SCROLL_LOCK option is used, records are locked as they are read in. The SCROLL_LOCK option guarantees that the records scrolled to can be updated or deleted, because the cursor has exclusive control over the records. The next level of locking is implemented by specifying the OPTIMISTIC option. With optimistic locking, the table is locked only for the time an actual UPDATE requires. SQL Server will either use a timestamp value on the row in the cursor or will calculate a checksum when the row is read by the cursor. This value is used to determine if the row to be changed has been changed since the time it was read—if it has, the positioned update or delete will fail.

The select_statement after the keyword FOR is treated identically as the equivalent section in the SQL-92 standard definition. This is the select statement that actually retrieves the rows that the cursor operates on. Similarly, the FOR UPDATE phrase is equivalent to that of the SQL-92 standard. The FOR UPDATE indicates that the cursor will be allowed to modify some or all of the columns in the data retrieved.

After you have declared the cursor, it is ready to be used. The following sections will describe how to open, use, and eventually close the cursor.

Using the OPEN Command

The DECLARE command does all the work of defining a cursor, but it does not actually create a cursor as an object that can be used. The cursor isn't created until it is opened through the OPEN command.

The OPEN command requires only the name of the cursor. If the cursor was declared as a GLOBAL using the extended TSQL DECLARE statement, then the keyword GLOBAL should preface the name of the cursor in the OPEN command as well. All the complicated options were taken care of in the DECLARE command, so the OPEN syntax is simple, as shown here:

```
OPEN { { [GLOBAL] cursor_name } ¦ cursor_variable_name}
```

When the cursor is opened, the SELECT statement in the DECLARE command is executed and any results needed for the cursor are collected. If the cursor is INSENSITIVE, this means all the rows are collected and stored in tempdb. If the cursor is forward-only, almost no information is collected. Rather, each successive fetch gathers one more row and information from the previous row is discarded. The OPEN command does not implicitly perform an initial FETCH on the data.

Using the FETCH Command

The FETCH command retrieves requested rows from the cursor's result set. The data from these rows can be stored in variables specified in the FETCH command. The syntax for the FETCH command is as follows:

```
FETCH [[NEXT | PRIOR | FIRST | LAST
| ABSOLUTE {n | @nvar} | RELATIVE {n | @nvar}]
FROM] { { [GLOBAL] cursor_name } ¦ cursor_variable_name}
  [INTO @variable_name1, @variable_name2, ...]
```

The @variable_name parameters each correspond to the columns from the SELECT statement used in the declaration of the cursor. Note that no variables need be provided, and fewer variables may be provided than columns in the SELECT. It is not possible, however, to specify which variable receives data from which column, except by position. Therefore, any columns not stored into given variables start from the rightmost in the SELECT list of the declaration. Any variables used in the FETCH command must be declared first.

When positioning the cursor with the FETCH command, you must pay careful attention to the global variable @@FETCH_STATUS. After each FETCH, this variable indicates success or failure. A value of 0 indicates a successful FETCH. A value of -1 indicates that the position requested was before the beginning or beyond the end of the cursor. A value of -2 indicates that although the position requested existed when the cursor was opened, it has since been deleted. Note that this does not occur in a forward-only, dynamic, static, or insensitive cursor, because these cursors keep no record of membership, and so can't say whether any given row used to exist or not, or they maintain their own data set which cannot be modified.

The NEXT position specifier is the default if no other is provided. This causes the very next row in the result set to be fetched. This is also the only specifier allowed for forward-only cursors.

The PRIOR position specifier fetches the results from the row just before the current row. This does not mean that the row fetched is the one previously fetched, however, because other positioning commands may jump over several rows.

The FIRST and LAST specifiers fetch the results from the very first or the last rows in the result set, respectively. This can be useful to reset the cursor's position to a known point.

The ABSOLUTE and RELATIVE specifiers set the position to a point that could be any distance from the current point. Both of these options require that a distance be specified, either by an integer literal, or by a variable. ABSOLUTE positions the cursor at N number of rows from the FIRST position, where N is the specified distance. RELATIVE positions the cursor N rows away from the current position. A dynamic cursor cannot use the ABSOLUTE or RELATIVE specifier because no membership information exists for that cursor, so SQL Server cannot easily deduce where to go except one step at a time.

Using the CLOSE and DEALLOCATE Commands

The CLOSE and DEALLOCATE commands take the cursor name as their only parameter. The CLOSE command releases any data being held by the cursor since it was opened. This may be significant in the case of an insensitive cursor or relatively minor in the case of a forward-only cursor. No further positioning or editing can be done on a closed cursor.

The DEALLOCATE command removes the definition of the cursor from the server's memory. After a DEALLOCATE command, the cursor cannot be re-opened.

Using the CURRENT OF Keyword

Updateable cursors enable both updates to the individual columns of a cursor and deletions of rows. This is done through UPDATE and DELETE commands, with the CURRENT OF keyword as the only phrase in the WHERE clause. The syntax for each is shown here:

```
UPDATE table_name
SET column_name1 =
{expression1 | NULL | (select_statement)}
[, column_name2 =
{expression2 | NULL | (select_statement)}...]
WHERE CURRENT OF cursor_name

DELETE FROM table_name
WHERE CURRENT OF cursor_name
```

With these features, positioned updates and deletions through cursors use the same sort of syntax with which developers are already familiar. This makes data modifications through cursors simple and familiar. You will notice that insertions are not supported through cursors, however. Insertions should be made directly to the table where the data belongs, through a normal INSERT statement.

REVIEW BREAK

Cursors

Cursors are an important part of the SQL language because they provide the only way to work with data iteratively. Remember that cursors will not generally perform as well as an equivalent set statement, but when the only way to accomplish a task is with an iterative approach, cursors are the way to go. The best way to review the commands needed to implement a cursor is to see it in action. Step by Step 8.1 will walk you through the process of declaring and running a cursor.

STEP BY STEP

8.1 Running a Cursor

1. Load the SQL Server Query Analyzer and connect to your server.

2. Use the DB drop-down box to set the database to the Pubs sample database that is installed with SQL Server.

3. First, you will need to declare your cursor. Write a DECLARE statement to define a global, forward-only, static, read-only cursor that will retrieve all the names in the authors table. Enter and execute the following statement to accomplish this:

```
DECLARE myCursor CURSOR
GLOBAL FORWARD_ONLY STATIC READ_ONLY
FOR SELECT au_lname, au_fname
```

4. You will need two variables to hold the values for the first name and last name fields. Because variable declarations last only within the batch in which they are declared, the following commands should not be run until you are instructed to do so. Enter the following DECLARE statement to create the variables:

```
DECLARE @au_lname char(40), @au_fname char(20)
```

5. Open the cursor and fetch the first values with the following command:

```
OPEN myCursor
FETCH NEXT FROM GLOBAL myCursor INTO @au_lname,
@au_fname
```

6. Enter the following command to implement a WHILE loop to iterate through the cursor:

```
WHILE @@FETCH_STATUS = 0
BEGIN
PRINT 'The name is ' + @au_fname + ' ' + @au_lname
FETCH NEXT FROM GLOBAL myCursor INTO @au_lname,
@au_fname
END
```

7. Close and deallocate the cursor as shown here:

```
CLOSE myCursor
DEALLOCATE myCursor
```

8. Run the preceding commands from step 4 through step 7 to see the cursor in action.

CASE STUDY: NIGHTLY JOB NEEDS HIGHER ISOLATION

ESSENCE OF THE CASE

Here are the essential elements of the case:

▶ The summarization process to be run nightly.

▶ Other users may be working.

▶ The summarization must have perfect transactional consistency.

▶ The summarization has top priority.

SCENARIO

One of the database developers you work with, Jane, asks for advice about a script she is writing. The script is supposed to run every night and collect summary information on a few specific tables. This summary information must then be written to a summary table, overwriting any information that is already there. She must be able to guarantee that this process is getting the correct information to summarize. She must be sure that when this process runs, no other changes will occur in those tables that would affect the final totals. Her process will end up scanning the tables several times for different summaries, but all must be accomplished on the same data with no additions, changes, or deletions. The client for whom the software is being developed has dial-up connectivity for many of its employees to work from home. The client can't guarantee that no one will be working in the database overnight when this process runs, but has made it clear that this summarization process is the number-one priority when it is running. No one and nothing should be allowed to interfere with the summarization.

ANALYSIS

The solution to this problem is quite straightforward. Jane needs to run her script inside a transaction to guarantee that all the updates with the summarized data take place together or not at all. In addition, the reads that she performs on the data should be contained within the same transaction to guarantee that the data will be unchanged from the first read to the final update. To prevent non-repeatable reads and phantom

CASE STUDY: NIGHTLY JOB NEEDS HIGHER ISOLATION

data from affecting her process, before beginning her transaction she should set the transaction isolation level to SERIALIZABLE. This is the highest isolation level and will cause the tables she reads to be locked until the end of the transaction.

Using this high isolation level will prevent other users from accessing the data that is involved in

Jane's summary process. This is why the job is scheduled to run in the wee-hours of the morning, when database traffic will be at a minimum. Eventually, there are bound to be some people whose work will be interrupted by this process. Because of the strict requirements the company has made on transactional consistency, however, this is just the price they must pay.

CHAPTER SUMMARY

The language of SQL Server, Transact SQL, contains a rich set of commands to enable you to program SQL Server. By utilizing the features of TSQL, you can write complicated scripts that can take action based on conditions found in data and respond to unexpected errors. When writing scripts, you will often need to ensure that a set of actions take place together or not at all, where a partial change would leave the database in an inconsistent state. SQL Server provides transactions for this purpose. Transactions group statements so that all the commands take place together or none do. The statements that you write in TSQL are generally set based in nature, that is, they work on many rows at a time. If you find a situation in which something needs to be done iteratively (one row at a time), however, you can use a cursor. Cursors are specially designed to access and manipulate data one row at a time.

KEY TERMS

Before you take the exam, make sure you are comfortable with the definitions and concepts for each of the following key terms:

- batch
- variable
- IF
- control of flow
- WHILE
- CASE
- GOTO
- RETURN
- @@ERROR
- @@TRANCOUNT
- transaction
- cursor
- deadlock
- optimistic locking

APPLY YOUR KNOWLEDGE

Exercises

These exercises should all be performed in the Pubs database.

8.1 Syntax Errors in Batches

This exercise is the first of two that will examine how errors are handled in batches. In this exercise, you will enter a deliberately flawed statement to see how a syntax error is handled. Syntax errors usually occur because of typing errors, and therefore happen when a script is first being tested. During this testing phase, you will need to be familiar with the effects of syntax errors so that you can recognize them and take appropriate action.

Estimated Time: 15 minutes

1. Load SQL Query Analyzer. Accumulate the commands that follow into a single script and wait to execute the script until the exercise instructs you to do so. The exercise also indicates where batch separators should go.

2. First, you need to create a temporary table to work with in this exercise. Because you may want to run this exercise repeatedly, you also need to be able to drop this table if it already exists. For simplicity, the code to drop and then re-create the table, #MyTable with the single field, myint, is given here. Copy this code into your query window:

```
IF EXISTS (SELECT * FROM tempdb..sysobjects
WHERE Name LIKE '#MyTable%')
DROP TABLE #MyTable
GO

CREATE TABLE #MyTable (
myint int NOT NULL
)
GO
```

3. To see how batch processing reacts to syntax errors, you can deliberately write a flawed statement followed by a legitimate statement in the same batch. Write an INSERT statement to insert the number 1 into #MyTable, but misspell the word INSERT.

4. Now write a statement to select all of the data from #MyTable. Put a column header (such as Flawed Batch) in the statement to indicate that the SELECT statement is in the flawed batch. Follow this SELECT with the batch separator GO.

5. In the new batch that follows the error, duplicate the same SELECT statement as in step 5, but change the header to indicate that it is executing in the new batch.

6. Now execute the script and examine the results. The table creation should produce no results at all, but the INSERT statement produces an error message indicating a syntax error near the keyword INTO. Following the error message you should see the results from your second query that was in the new batch. The query in the flawed batch never executed at all, demonstrating that all statements in a batch are compiled together and that if any command in the batch fails to compile, the batch is skipped.

7. To further demonstrate the same point, add another SELECT statement before the INSERT and rerun the script. Although the error follows the first SELECT, the valid SELECT statement does not run because the error occurred at compile time, before any statement in the batch could run.

The following code listing is an example of what your final script should look like:

```
IF EXISTS (SELECT * FROM tempdb..sysobjects
WHERE Name LIKE '#MyTable%')
```

APPLY YOUR KNOWLEDGE

```
DROP TABLE #MyTable
GO

CREATE TABLE #MyTable (
myint int NOT NULL
)
GO

SELECT 'First Batch Results' = myint
FROM #MyTable

INSRET INTO #MyTable (myint)
VALUES ('A')

SELECT 'Flawed Batch Results' = myint
FROM #MyTable
GO

SELECT 'New Batch Results' = myint
FROM #MyTable
```

8.2 Run-Time Errors in Batches

In Exercise 8.1, you saw how a compile-time error caused a batch not to run. This exercise modifies the results from Exercise 8.1 to show the effect of a run-time error. Run-time errors can happen at any time a script is run. You will generate a run-time error deliberately by using "bad" data, but general locking or deadlocking problems can also cause an unpredictable run-time error.

Estimated Time: 5 minutes

1. Load Enterprise Manager and put the script you created from Exercise 8.1 into a Query window.

2. Correct the spelling mistake in the INSERT statement, and then change the value inserted to NULL. This conflicts with the NOT NULL constraint placed on the column in the table, but the constraint will not be checked until run time.

3. Execute the script. You should see that although the INSERT statement again generates an error, the three SELECT statements successfully execute.

8.3 Control-of-Flow Statements

In this exercise, you practice the use of control-of-flow statements. These statements allow you to write conditional code. Your script need not be linear, but may instead respond to conditions such as the data it reads or errors that occur. Based on the changing conditions, your script can take different actions to make up a fully robust system.

Estimated Time: 15 minutes

1. Type the following code into a Query window and try to predict what output you should expect to see when you execute the code:

```
IF 0 = 1
Print 'First Print Statement'
Print 'Second Print Statement'
```

The IF statement causes only one statement following it to run or not to run, depending on the Boolean expression. Therefore, only the second print statement is executed.

2. Now use a WHILE loop to execute a PRINT statement exactly 10 times. Use a variable @Count as an integer to keep track of the number of iterations. Also declare a variable of type char(30) named @CharCount. In each iteration of the loop, assign the message Loop N, where N is the value of @Count, to @CharCount, and print its value. Your script should look something like the following:

```
DECLARE @Count int,
@CharCount char(30)
SELECT @Count = 1

WHILE @Count <= 10
BEGIN
SELECT @CharCount = 'Loop ' + Convert(char,
➥@Count)

PRINT @CharCount

SELECT @Count = @Count + 1
END
```

APPLY YOUR KNOWLEDGE

3. To examine the uses of the CASE expression, you can write a SELECT statement to calculate the profitability of the books in the Titles table and display the results in three easy-to-read categories. Your SELECT statement should show all rows from the Titles table. Use the following formula to calculate the profitability of the books: (Price × Ytd_Sales) / (Advance + (Royalty × Ytd_Sales)). Use a CASE expression to evaluate the profitability of each book and print Very Profitable if the result is greater than 1.5, Profitable if the result is equal to or greater than 1.0, or Lost Money if the result is less than 1. Include the title of the book in the results. Your final statement should be similar to this:

```
SELECT      Title,
'Profitability' = CASE
WHEN (Price * Ytd_Sales) / (Advance +
(Royalty * Ytd_Sales)) > 1.5
THEN 'Very Profitable'
WHEN (Price * Ytd_Sales) / (Advance +
(Royalty * Ytd_Sales)) >= 1.0
THEN 'Profitable'
WHEN (Price * Ytd_Sales) / (Advance +
(Royalty * Ytd_Sales)) < 1.0
THEN 'Lost Money'
End
FROM Titles
```

8.4 Using a Cursor to Repeatedly Execute a Stored Procedure

In this exercise you will use a cursor to execute the sp_help stored procedure on every user table in the Pubs database. Because many stored procedures can only operate on a single piece of data at a time, it is not uncommon to run a stored procedure through a cursor so that an entire set of data can be acted upon by the procedure.

Estimated Time: 10 minutes

1. First, declare a character type variable named @Tablename to hold the names of the tables.

2. Second, declare a LOCAL, FORWARD_ONLY, STATIC, READ_ONLY cursor curTable that will select the Name field of the sysobjects table, where the type field is U.

3. Open the cursor and select the first name into the @Tablename variable.

4. Set up a WHILE loop to execute until the @@FETCH_STATUS function is not zero, indicating there are no more records. You need to use the BEGIN and END keywords to enclose the body of the loop in a statement block.

5. Immediately inside the loop, use the EXEC statement to execute the string SP_HELP concatenated with the @Tablename variable to execute the stored procedure.

6. Also inside the loop, fetch the next table name from the cursor.

7. After the loop, close and deallocate the cursor.

   Your results should look much like the following:

```
DECLARE @Tablename char(30)
DECLARE curTable CURSOR LOCAL FORWARD_ONLY
STATIC READ_ONLY FOR
SELECT Name
FROM sysObjects
WHERE Type = 'U'

OPEN curTable

FETCH NEXT FROM curTable INTO @Tablename

WHILE @@FETCH_STATUS = 0

BEGIN
EXEC ('SP_HELP ' + @Tablename)

FETCH NEXT FROM curTable INTO @Tablename
END

CLOSE curTable
DEALLOCATE curTable
```

APPLY YOUR KNOWLEDGE

8.5 Using a Cursor to Perform Positioned Updates Against a Table

In this exercise, you create a table to hold all the Author IDs from the Authors table, then assign each of the rows in the table a unique monotonically increasing value starting at 1. Positioned updates of this kind are often used to write values from stored procedures as described in the previous exercise.

Estimated Time: 10 minutes

1. First create a temporary table called #HoldAuthors to hold the IDs from the Authors table. Include two fields in the table, called Ident and Au_Id. These should be integer and char(11) types, respectively. Note that the Ident field must allow NULLs. Because you may want to re-run the script several times, you should first include code to drop the table if it already exists.

2. Insert the values from the Au_Id field of the Authors table into the Au_Id field from the #HoldAuthors table.

3. Declare a LOCAL, FORWARD_ONLY, DYNAMIC, OPTIMISTIC cursor that retrieves the Ident column from the #HoldAuthors table.

4. Declare an integer variable @Count and initialize the value to 0.

5. Open the cursor, and then fetch the first record. You do not need to store the value from the FETCH statement.

6. Set up a WHILE loop to execute while the @@FETCH_STATUS global variable remains 0, indicating no problems during the FETCH. You also need to begin a statement block to contain the body of the loop.

7. In the WHILE loop, update the #HoldAuthors table to set the Ident field to the value of @Count, using the CURRENT OF syntax for the UPDATE statement.

8. Next, increment the value of the @Count variable by 1. Then fetch the next record, and end the statement block of the loop.

9. Finally, select all the values from the #HoldAuthors table to see the results. Your final script should look something like the following:

```
IF EXISTS (SELECT * FROM tempdb..sysobjects
WHERE Name LIKE '#HoldAuthors%')
DROP TABLE #HoldAuthors
GO

CREATE TABLE #HoldAuthors (
Ident int NULL,
Au_ID char(11) Not NULL
)

INSERT INTO #HoldAuthors (
Au_ID
)
SELECT Au_ID
FROM Authors

DECLARE cur_Author CURSOR FOR
SELECT Ident
FROM #HoldAuthors
FOR UPDATE OF Ident

DECLARE @Count int
SET @Count = 0

OPEN cur_Author

FETCH NEXT FROM cur_Author

WHILE @@FETCH_STATUS = 0
BEGIN
UPDATE #HoldAuthors
SET Ident = @Count
WHERE CURRENT OF cur_Author

SET @Count = @Count + 1
```

APPLY YOUR KNOWLEDGE

```
FETCH NEXT FROM cur_Author
END
GO

SELECT *
FROM #HoldAuthors
```

8.6   Using Transactional Error Handling to Rollback Changes as a Result of an Error

In this exercise, you will write several data modification statements and error handling code to roll back your changes as the result of an error. The script itself will be written to complete normally, but should an unforeseen error occur, the script will respond by rolling back the changes in the transaction.

Estimated Time: 10 minutes

1. Use the BEGIN TRANSACTION statement to begin the transaction, and declare an integer variable to hold the value of @@ERROR for use in error handling.

2. Write an INSERT statement to insert a single author into the Authors table. Invent the values you need for the author's characteristics. The solution at the end of this exercise has sample data you can copy.

3. Include the following error handling code to trap the value of @@ERROR and roll back the transaction if the value is not 0. Also use RAISERROR to send a message and stop execution of the batch. This example assumes that the variable declared in step 1 is named @ErrVal.

```
SET @ErrVal = @@ERROR
IF @ErrVal <> 0
BEGIN
    ROLLBACK
    RAISERROR("Error number %d was detected.
The current batch will be halted.", 16, 1,
➡@ErrVal)
    RETURN
END
```

4. Write a statement to insert a single book into the Titles table, and follow it with error handling code. Again, an example can be found at the end of the exercise.

5. Finally, insert a record relating the Title and the Author in the TitleAuthor table, and follow it with error handling code.

6. To complete the exercise, issue the COMMIT command and terminate the batch.

The following script demonstrates a successful solution to the exercise:

```
BEGIN TRANSACTION
DECLARE @ErrVal INT

INSERT INTO Authors
(au_id, au_lname, au_fname, phone, address,
➡city, state, zip, contract)
VALUES ('123-45-6789', 'Doe', 'John', '212
➡555-1212', '1313 Mockingbird Lane', 'New
➡York', 'NY', '10101', 1)


SET @ErrVal = @@ERROR
IF @ErrVal <> 0
BEGIN
    ROLLBACK
    RAISERROR("Error number %d was detected.
➡The current batch will be halted.", 16, 1,
➡@ErrVal)
    RETURN
END

INSERT INTO Titles
(title_id, title, type, pub_id, price,
➡advance, royalty, ytd_sales, notes)
VALUES ('BU1234', 'Make Money', 'Business',
➡'0736', 22.75, 5000.00, 10, 2500, 'The
➡bottom line in business')


SET @ErrVal = @@ERROR
IF @ErrVal <> 0
BEGIN
    ROLLBACK
    RAISERROR("Error number %d was detected.
➡The current batch will be halted.", 16, 1,
➡@ErrVal)
```

APPLY YOUR KNOWLEDGE

```
        RETURN
END

INSERT INTO TitleAuthor
(au_id, title_id, au_ord, royaltyper)
VALUES ('123-45-6789', 'BU1234', 1, 100)


SET @ErrVal = @@ERROR
IF @ErrVal <> 0
BEGIN
    ROLLBACK
    RAISERROR("Error number %d was detected.
➡The current batch will be halted.", 16, 1,
➡@ErrVal)
    RETURN
END

COMMIT
GO
```

Review Questions

1. If one of the statements inside a batch causes an error, what happens to the execution of that batch?

2. What happens if a statement in a batch has a syntax error?

3. What is the scope of a local variable?

4. What is a Boolean expression?

5. How many statements can follow an IF statement that returns TRUE?

6. What two statements enable you to interrupt execution of a WHILE loop?

7. Where can the CASE structure be used?

8. What command must be issued before a cursor can be opened?

9. What phrase is used to perform positioned updates and deletes with cursors?

10. How can you cause user-defined errors to be written to the SQL Server error log?

11. Can transactions be nested?

12. What is a deadlock?

13. What is the transaction isolation level?

Exam Questions

1. What is the lifetime of a user-defined variable?

   A. Duration of the script

   B. Duration of the statement block

   C. Duration of the batch

   D. Duration of the current SQL Server connection

2. What is the significance of the GO statement? Select all that apply.

   A. It ends the current transaction.

   B. It causes all commands since the last GO to be compiled and executed.

   C. It ends the current batch.

   D. It causes all commands since the last GO to be compiled and executed, and ends the script.

3. Which of the following commands can be used to interrupt processing of a loop? Select all that apply.

   A. BREAK

   B. HALT

   C. EXIT

   D. CONTINUE

APPLY YOUR KNOWLEDGE

4. A GOTO command can cause execution of a batch to resume where?

   A. At a label

   B. At an absolute line number

   C. At a relative line number

   D. Anywhere in the next batch

5. Insensitive cursors provide what functionality?

   A. They enable users to see data inserted since the time the cursor was opened.

   B. They allow faster updates because the data for the cursor is stored in tempdb.

   C. They cannot be scrolled backward because the data is discarded from the temporary storage after it is fetched.

   D. They ensure an unchanging view of the data as it was when the cursor was opened.

6. User-defined errors can be written to the SQL Server error log through what mechanism?

   A. Using the RAISERROR command with a severity of greater than or equal to 19

   B. Using the PRINT command with the WITH LOG option

   C. Using the RAISERROR command with the WITH LOG option

   D. Using the LOGERROR command

7. Which of the following are valid options for a FETCH command?

   A. FORWARD

   B. BACK

C. ABSOLUTE

D. RELATIVE

8. Susan is writing a script that will make modifications to several related tables in a high-usage database. This is a short, very fast script that will be run several times a day by the shipping department whenever a new shipment is ready. Because it is absolutely critical that incomplete information is never found in this system, she decides to enclose the script within a transaction so that all her changes are made together. Because it is such a high-use database, however, she sets the transaction isolation level to READ COMMITTED so that this process will disrupt other users as little as possible.

How would you rate Susan's solution?

   A. This is an optimal solution. The transaction encompasses the changes, and the isolation level is kept low so as not to disturb other users.

   B. This is a fair solution. Her script will work, but by eliminating the transaction she would disturb no one.

   C. This is a poor solution. Her script will work, but due to the low isolation level she will expose inconsistent data to other users.

   D. This is not a solution. Her transaction cannot work at this isolation level.

9. Which of the following will help reduce deadlocks in your database? Select the best answer.

   A. Keeping the transaction isolation level as high as possible with out hurting user concurrency.

B. Always accessing tables in the same order in all programs.

C. Never completing transactions until a user can confirm that the changes are correct.

D. Always checking the state of @@TRANCOUNT before issuing a ROLLBACK command

10. Which of the following is a problem associated with a transaction isolation level of SERIALIZABLE?

A. Dirty reads

B. Non-repeatable reads

C. Phantom data

D. Excessive locking

Answers to Review Questions

1. Execution resumes after the error, and the system function @@ERROR is set to reflect the error code. (Refer to the section "Using Scripts and Batches" for more information.)

2. The entire batch fails to compile and execution resumes with the next batch. (Refer to the section "Using Scripts and Batches" for more information.)

3. A local variable has scope only within the batch in which it is declared. (Refer to the section "Using Variables" for more information.)

4. A Boolean expression is an expression that returns TRUE or FALSE. (Refer to the section "Using the IF Keyword" for more information.)

5. Only one statement or statement block (defined by a BEGIN/END keyword pair) is executed

following an IF statement. (Refer to the section "Using the IF Keyword" for more information.)

6. The BREAK and CONTINUE statements can be used to interrupt normal execution of a WHILE loop. The BREAK statement exits the WHILE loop and causes execution to resume at the statement following the body of the loop. The CONTINUE statement halts execution of the current loop and causes the Boolean expression to be reevaluated, possibly resuming the WHILE loop. (Refer to the section "Using the WHILE Statement" for more information.)

7. The CASE structure is used in an expression. CASE does not form a statement that can be executed by itself. (Refer to the section "Using the CASE Expression" for more information.)

8. A cursor must be declared with the DECLARE CURSOR statement before it can be opened. (Refer to the section "Declaring Cursors" for more information.)

9. Positioned updates and deletes are performed through otherwise standard UPDATE and DELETE statements using the CURRENT OF phrase in the WHERE clause. (Refer to the "Using the CURRENT OF Keyword" for more information.)

10. Errors can be written to the error log using the RAISERROR command along with the WITH LOG option specified. (Refer to the section "Using the RAISERROR statement" for more information.)

11. Transaction can be nested. SQL Server will actually maintain a single transaction corresponding to the outermost transaction definition, but it is acceptable to define transactions within the scope of that outermost one. When a nested transaction

is begun, SQL Server increments the value of the @@TRANCOUNT function, and when the transaction is committed, @@TRANCOUNT is decremented. If a ROLLBACK is seen anywhere within a transaction, however, the entire outermost transaction is rolled back. (Refer to the section "Using Transactions" for more information.)

12. A deadlock is a situation in which neither of two processes can continue until one completes. SQL Server can detect this problem and automatically terminate one of the competing processes. Deadlocks are normally caused because scripts running in transactions cannot release their locks until the transaction completes. These long-held locks can block other processes and lead to a deadlock. (Refer to the section "Avoid or Handle Deadlocks" for more information.)

13. The transaction isolation level is a setting that affects the level of protection you want for processes against reading uncommitted changes in transactions. While a transaction is in progress, any changes made prevent the original data from being read, but the changes themselves are not permanent until the transaction is completed. The transaction isolation level will affect what kinds of uncommitted changes other processes can see. (Refer to the section "Define the Transaction Isolation Level" for more information.)

Answers to Exam Questions

1. **C.** The lifetime of a user-defined variable is equal to the batch in which it is declared. (For more information, refer to the section "Using Variables.")

2. **B, C.** SQL Server compiles and executes statements in a batch together, and the GO statement indicates the end of a batch. Transactions can span multiple batches; therefore, a GO statement has little effect on any open transaction. (For more information, refer to the section "Using Scripts and Batches.")

3. **A, D.** Both the BREAK and CONTINUE statements will interrupt the normal execution of a WHILE loop. The BREAK statement will immediately cause the execution of the batch to skip to the end of the WHILE loop. The CONTINUE statement will cause the Boolean expression controlling the loop to be immediately reevaluated, and continued execution of the loop, or termination, is conditioned on the results. (For more information, refer to the section "Using the WHILE Statement.")

4. **A.** The GOTO statement can be used only to set execution of the batch to a label that is explicitly declared elsewhere in the batch. Because SQL Server compiles and executes only one batch at a time, a GOTO cannot be used to send execution outside of the batch being processed. (For more information, refer to the section "Using the GOTO Command.")

5. **D.** Insensitive cursors collect all of the data reference by a cursor and copy it to a temporary location. Because insensitive cursors reference only a copy of the actual data, edits are not allowed. Navigation in an insensitive cursor is controlled by the SCROLL option, just as with any other cursor. (For more information, refer to the section "Implementing Cursors.")

6. **C.** Using the RAISERROR command with the WITH LOG option will cause the message of the error to be written to the error log. Any RAISERROR with a

APPLY YOUR KNOWLEDGE

severity of 19 or greater must use the WITH LOG option, but it is still that option that causes the error to be written to the error log, not the severity. The PRINT statement has no mechanism to write to the error log, and there is no such command as LOGERROR. (For more information, refer to the section "Managing Errors.")

7. **C, D.** The valid options for a FETCH command are FIRST, LAST, NEXT, PREVIOUS, ABSOLUTE, and RELATIVE. To move forward, use the NEXT option; to move back use the PREVIOUS option. (For more information, refer to the section "Using the FETCH Command.")

8. **C.** This is a poor solution to the problem given. The key point of the question was that users must never be shown inconsistent data. Although it was a busy database, no restriction was made that users must not be interrupted. Therefore, it is better to keep the transaction isolation level high and potentially interrupt users

than to show inconsistent data. The fact that the script runs very fast will help minimize the user interruptions as well. (For more information, refer to the section "Using Transactions.")

9. **B**. The transaction isolation level should be kept low, tables should be accessed in the same order, and transactions should never wait on user interaction to avoid deadlocks. Checking the @@TRANCOUNT function before issuing a ROLLBACK is always a good idea, but it will not affect deadlocking. (For more information, refer to the section "Avoid or Handle Deadlocks.")

10. **D**. Although the transaction isolation level of SERIALIZABLE is the highest level and therefore avoids all problems of inconsistent data, it comes at the price of lower user concurrency. The price of consistency is high numbers of locks on your tables, which can prevent other users from working. (For more information, refer to the section "Define the Transaction Isolation Level.")

Suggested Readings and Resources

We recommend the following resources for further study in the area of planning:

1. SQL Server Books Online
   - Set Transaction Isolation Level
   - Isolation Levels
   - Avoiding Deadlocks
   - Coding Efficient Transactions
   - Four Concurrency Problems

   - Rollbacks in Stored Procedures and Triggers
   - Nesting Transactions

2. Transact-SQL Help file
   - Control-of-Flow Language
   - RAISERROR: described
   - PRINT: described
   - DECLARE CURSOR

This chapter helps you to prepare for the Microsoft exam by covering the following objectives:

Create and execute stored procedures to enforce business rules, to modify data in multiple tables, to perform calculations, and to use input and output parameters.

- **Implement error handling by using return codes and the RAISERROR statement.**

- **Choose appropriate recompile options.**

▶ Stored procedures are a big part of SQL Server's programmability. Stored procedures are the preferred method of combining multiple Transact-SQL statements into a single easy-to-run unit. Stored procedures can utilize all the programming features of the Transact-SQL language to perform complex tasks with a simplified interface. To become certified in SQL Server design and implementation, you should understand how to use standard features of stored procedures such as the return code, both input and output parameters, and the recompile option.

Design, create, use, and alter views.

- **Modify data through a view.**

- **Query data through a view.**

▶ Views are an important feature for abstracting the physical design of your database. You need to know both the practical matters of how to create and use views and the philosophy behind the use of views.

Miscellaneous Programming Techniques

Create triggers that implement rules, that enforce data integrity, and that perform cascading updates and deletes.

- **Implement transactional error handling.**

▶ Triggers give you nearly unlimited power to review and act upon the actions of inserting, updating, and deleting data from tables. Triggers have much the same power as stored procedures, but they are called automatically in response to data modifications. Here again, the philosophy dictating when to use triggers effectively is as important as knowing the actual syntactical rules.

Access data from static or dynamic sources by using remote stored procedures, linked servers, and openrowset.

- **Evaluate where processing occurs when using OPENQUERY.**

▶ The use of distributed queries that can access data from any OLE/DB data source is a powerful new feature of SQL Server 7.0. This feature provides an open framework for SQL Server to work with data not only with other SQL Servers, an important feature in its own right, but with other data sources as well. This particular point focuses primarily on different SQL Servers working with each other's data, but you'll need to be familiar with how the same features allow operation with other database servers and even non-database data sources.

STUDY STRATEGIES

▶ Anyone certified in SQL Server Design needs to have strong understanding of stored procedures. Stored procedures allow you to encapsulate complex code into a procedure that can simply be called by name. This allows a SQL Server developer to produce optimized procedures that can be called by applications developers that need not know the details of the executing code.

The objectives have a very mechanical focus on views. You'll want to have an understanding of how views can be used in your database design, but the emphasis is on the actual syntax for creating views and the limitations of views.

There isn't a lot of syntax to learn for the CREATE TRIGGER statement. You'll want to focus on how triggers behave in SQL Server. Be sure you understand how the inserted and deleted tables are used, and learn the rules for nesting triggers.

While you are studying triggers, be sure you are still familiar with the concepts of transactions in SQL Server, which were discussed in Chapter 8. Triggers always run inside a transaction to allow the trigger to roll back the data modification statement that initiated the trigger. The discussion about transactions in this chapter assumes you are comfortable with the concepts from the previous chapter.

Finally, learn which commands are used to write distributed queries that work with data on other servers. Although some of these commands have a complicated syntax in order to establish connections to remote data sources, don't spend time memorizing every parameter. Every data source you connect to requires different connection parameters, so you'll never learn them all. It is more important to understand the options that are available to you when you need to get data from outside your local SQL Server.

INTRODUCTION

This chapter expands on the programmability of the TSQL language. You will be introduced to programming objects in your SQL Server database that enforce business rules, and the features of SQL Server that allow the use of distributed data sources throughout the enterprise. Stored procedures, views, and triggers are all objects to which you attach code in order to perform tasks on a repetitive basis. Linked servers are statically defined remote data sources that allow your SQL Server to access data in another SQL Server, database provider, or even non-relational database sources. The OpenRowset function provides a method for linking to a server in an one time, ad-hoc method in the same way as accessing remote data through a static link. Finally, the OpenQuery function will be looked at as a way to perform remote processing on a linked server.

STORED PROCEDURES

▶ Create and execute stored procedures to enforce business rules, to modify data in multiple tables, to perform calculations, and to use input and output parameters.

- Implement error handling by using return codes and the RAISERROR statement.

- Choose appropriate recompile options.

The use of stored procedures is an important part of any database scheme. *Stored procedures* can be thought of as precompiled scripts. Stored procedures can contain any commands that can be put in a script, including control-of-flow structures, any kind of data modification or data retrieval statements, cursors, and, of course, error handling. Stored procedures offer many benefits to developers and users alike.

Stored procedures are excellent tools for encapsulating complex programming logic. With stored procedures you can write code once and let other users run them any number of times without needing to understand the logic behind them.

A normalized data model will often have many table chained together through FOREIGN KEY relationships. However, programs may find it easier to present the data in these tables to a user as a denormalized whole. The user then makes changes and expects to save all his modifications in a single command. A stored procedure can be written to take all of the values for the multiple tables, and handle the logic of updating the multiple tables together. By encapsulating this logic into a single stored procedure you have easier, more reliable code.

Stored procedures are also great for encapsulating business rules and complex computations for the same reasons as above. The complex logic involved in these tasks can be written once and then reused. The upcoming sections describe these benefits and show you how to put stored procedures to work.

Query Plans are Re-entrant A major improvement in the way SQL Server handles stored procedures in version 7.0 is that query plans are now *re-entrant*. This means that the same query plan can be used by multiple users at the same time. In previous versions, SQL Server had to load and store multiple versions of the same plan so different users could run the same procedure. Because of this change, SQL's handling of stored procedures will likely be tested to make sure you are aware of all the benefits of the new version.

Precompiled Code

One of the major benefits of using stored procedures is that they are precompiled and therefore can run with less overhead than would be experienced by submitting the logic in a script. When a procedure is created, it is converted to a form that SQL Server can execute quickly. This process is called *normalization* and is SQL Server's internal representation of the logic behind a stored procedure. The normalization process that is done when the stored procedure is created saves any subsequent calls to the procedure from having to go through this step. Then, when a procedure is run for the first time, it is compiled into a query plan that is saved into the procedure cache. This *query plan* is the optimized set of instructions that tells SQL Server exactly what to do. Because this query plan is then stored into the procedure cache, subsequent calls to the procedure may not have to do even the work of finding an optimized plan.

Sharing Application Logic

Another distinct benefit you get from using stored procedures is that common tasks can be shared between any number of different applications. By writing your stored procedures in small, logical units, the individual pieces can be put together in other stored procedures to accomplish a specific task. Then, some of those same individual units can be reassembled along with other pieces to form a procedure to accomplish a different task. In this way, code can be shared among different applications.

Reliability

The approach of using many procedures to accomplish one specific task also enables you to evaluate the effectiveness of each individual piece of a complicated process so that it can be debugged more effectively. This should result in a much more stable final process. In addition, return codes can be returned from each piece to ensure that if any piece fails for any reason, appropriate actions can be taken. This provides even further reliability.

Security

Stored procedures also can be used as an integral part of your security system on SQL Server. Stored procedures always run in the security context of their owner. Therefore, anyone granted execute privileges to a stored procedure does not also need to be granted permissions to query or edit every table that stored procedure references. This allows permissions to be set very tightly to allow users only the access they truly need. Then, carefully designed stored procedures can be created to allow users to query or edit tables in a controlled manner.

Creating Stored Procedures

Stored procedures are created with the CREATE PROCEDURE statement. Parameters are defined and certain options set during the initial definition, then a series of TSQL commands may follow. When a user executes your stored procedure, he can supply values to the parameters you defined to affect the operation of the stored procedure.

There are two options that can be specified with the CREATE PROCEDURE statement. These are RECOMPILE and ENCRYPTION, and they can be specified either together or separately. The RECOMPILE option causes the stored procedure to not cache its query plan in memory at execution. Use this option when the procedure will be passed parameters that could require significantly different query plans on different runs. The ENCRYPTION option causes the text of the stored procedure to be stored in an encrypted fashion. This option can allow you to distribute a stored procedure without giving away the source code.

Stored procedure parameters can be defined with the OUTPUT option, which allows the variables to be passed back to the user who called the procedure. Output parameters also receive values that can be used in the stored procedure just like any other parameter, and these values may be used and even modified throughout the procedure. Whereas the final value of other parameters is lost when the procedure ends, the final value of output parameters can be passed back to the calling statement.

Special attention should be paid to creating stored procedures that support cursors as output parameters. A stored procedure can define and open a cursor, and then pass the cursor back to the calling statement for further manipulation of the cursor's result set. When a cursor is defined as a parameter in a stored procedure, the VARYING and OUTPUT keywords must also be used. The VARYING option applies only to cursor parameters.

The actual syntax to create a stored procedure is very straightforward once you understand all the options that can be applied. All the options shown should look familiar in the context that they were just described:

```
CREATE PROC[EDURE] procedure_name [;number]
        [
                {@parameter data_type} [VARYING] [=
➥default] [OUTPUT]
        ]
        [,…n]
[WITH
        {
                RECOMPILE
                ¦ ENCRYPTION
                ¦ RECOMPILE, ENCRYPTION
        }
]
[FOR REPLICATION]
AS
        sql_statement [...n]
```

In the syntax diagram above, you can see that parameters are optional, and that multiple parameters can be defined. SQL Server does impose a limit of 1,024 parameters, however. The WITH keyword introduces the recompile and encryption options that were described earlier.

The FOR REPLICATION keywords are used to indicate that stored procedure is to be used by the replication process to operate on local data, rather than replicating all the results of the stored procedure. When these keywords are specified, the stored procedure is dedicated to the use of the replication process and cannot be used by the subscriber.

Following the keyword AS are the TSQL commands that make up the body of the procedure. The body contains all the logic needed to perform the task that will define your procedure. It is even possible to call other stored procedures from the body of a stored procedure which allows you to break a task in to multiple procedures which can call one another. By defining procedures to perform small generic tasks you can encourage code resuse. SQL Server imposes a limitation on the size of the body at 128MB.

There is one piece of the syntax that was not yet described. After the procedure name, you can specify a number preceded by a semicolon. If specified, this number can be used to differentiate multiple stored procedures with the same name that can be dropped as a group. This feature is commonly used so that all procedures that support a certain application can be grouped under a common name. Then if the application is uninstalled, all the supporting procedures can be dropped as a unit.

Returning Information from a Stored Procedure

Output parameters have been described as a method of passing information from the stored procedure to the calling statement. It has also been noted that cursor variables pointing to result sets created inside stored procedures can be passed as output parameters as well. Another, more limited way to pass values back to the calling statement from inside a stored procedure is with the use of return codes. The keyword RETURN can be used in a stored procedure to stop the execution of the procedure. An integer expression that may follow the RETURN statement will be passed back to the calling statement. The final method for returning information from inside a stored procedure is using the RAISERROR statement that was discussed previously in Chapter 8, "Programmability."

The use of output parameters and return codes requires the use of the EXECUTE statement to work in TSQL. The EXECUTE statement is used to call stored procedures with the following syntax:

```
[[EXEC[UTE]]
        {
                   [@return_status =]
                            {procedure_name [;number] ¦
➥@procedure_name_var
        }
        [[@parameter =] {value ¦ @variable [OUTPUT] ¦
➥[DEFAULT]]
                   [,…n]
[WITH RECOMPILE]
```

If a return status is expected from a stored procedure any integer variable can be specified for the @return_status parameter to receive that return code. The procedure itself can be specified either literally as the procedure_name parameter, or the name of the procedure can be stored in a variable as shown by the @procedure_name_var parameter. A comma-separated list of parameters can then be passed to the stored procedure. The @parameter in the syntax indicates that the name of the stored procedure's parameter may be specified so that the parameters can be passed in any order. If named parameters are not used, the parameters passed to the procedure must be in the same order as they were defined. Either a literal value or a variable of the appropriate type may be used to pass values. Null values can be passed to parameters. It is also possible to simply specify the keyword DEFAULT to indicate that the default value of a parameter should be used. If a parameter is being passed into an output parameter in a stored procedure, and you want to receive the value, you must use a variable and specify the OUTPUT keyword.

The RAISERROR statement is valuable in stored procedures because it passes an unmistakable message back to the caller that something notable happened in the stored procedure. Usually the RAISERROR statement should only be used to denote that an error occurred in the procedure that forced the abnormal termination of the procedure, but it could also be used to return simple warning messages by lowering the severity parameter. The following error handling code was recommended by Chapter 8, which introduced the RAISERROR statement:

```
SET @ErrVal = @@ERROR
IF @ErrVal > 0
```

```
BEGIN
        RAISERROR("Error number %d was detected. The
➥current batch will be halted.", 16, 1, @ErrVal)
        RETURN
END
```

This same code is useful in stored procedures to check for and
handle errors, with a slight modification. The RETURN command is
used to stop processing of a batch in the preceding example; in a
stored procedure a simple integer value should be added to the
RETURN command as was noted above. This integer value can then be
received by the calling statement to gain additional information
about the condition of the procedure when it finished.

Altering Stored Procedures

After a stored procedure is created, it is sometimes necessary to
modify the logic to adapt to changing requirements. In such cases, it
can be time consuming and even error prone to ensure that no user
permissions or dependant objects are disturbed as when the procedure is dropped and then recreated. For this reason, SQL Server 7.0
introduces the ALTER PROCEDURE statement. This statement has an
identical syntax to the CREATE PROCEDURE statement discussed earlier
and so will not be detailed here. When the ALTER PROCEDURE statement is run, the procedure with the given name is overwritten with
the parameters, options, and code specified. The procedure retains
the same internal identifier when it is altered, and therefore the user
permissions and all dependencies are unaffected.

R E V I E W   B R E A K

Stored Procedures

Stored procedures provide you with a method of encapsulating code
into easily referenced objects. Stored procedures are precompiled, so
the can run faster that the equivalent set statements. In addition,
they allow you to share application logic to increase reliability and
security.

Both in the way that stored procedures are precompiled for efficiency
and in the wide range of programming benefits that are made available to you by encapsulating your code, SQL Server promotes the use
of stored procedures. You should take advantage of all the benefits
that stored procedures offer by implementing your business rules and
data manipulation routines into stored procedures whenever possible.

VIEWS

▶ Design, create, use, and alter views.

· Modify data through a view.

· Query data through a view.

A view is a structure provided by SQL Server that enables you to represent a standard query in the form of a table. This section covers the concept of views, starting with the benefits of using them. Discussion then moves to creating views, then to altering them, and finally, a look at their limitations.

Recognizing the Benefits of Using Views

A *view*, in most ways, can be treated exactly like an actual table. However, it is actually a subset or superset of data from one or more tables. This can allow you to address security issues by restricting user access only to views that show data that is considered appropriate for that user. It also can provide a method of abstracting your data to an unchanging interface. Third-party applications can connect to this interface so that your underlying data model can continue to evolve.

A view is a method of turning the data returned by a single unchanging query into a pseudo-table. That is, a view presents the data returned by a SELECT statement to a user as though that data were contained in a single table.

A view can be used to provide a simplified interface to users. The actual data model may provide for all kinds of information that is not relevant to a particular user. A system of views can be created for that user that provides only the information of interest. Views also can simplify the data access of a user. If a user consistently has to use a complex join to retrieve the information he wants, these joins can be written into a view so that only the qualifying information needs to be supplied each time.

In addition to simplifying the interface to the user, views also can be used to hide or leave out sensitive information that is not necessary to the user. For example, a view can provide access to credit information but filter out actual account numbers and credit card numbers that are considered too sensitive for that user. Then permissions can be granted to the user to access the view rather than the table itself.

Over time, a data model may need to be modified to meet a company's changing needs. New tables may be added or existing ones changed to allow for more informative data to be stored. These changes, however, can often cause existing applications to fail. Views can be used to present an unchanging interface to applications so that this problem is avoided. Applications can be written to access only the views, not tables themselves. Then when the data model changes, the views can be changed to retrieve the same information they always have. The application is therefore protected from changes to the underlying data model.

Creating Views

The following is the syntax for creating views:

```
CREATE VIEW view_name [(column [,…n])]
[WITH ENCRYPTION]
AS
select_statement
[WITH CHECK OPTION]
```

The heart of a view is the `select_statement` that follows the keyword AS. The view shows the data returned by the `select_statement` to the user, without the user needing to know about the complexity such a statement might entail.

The list of column names in the syntax is optional and can be omitted. This list overlays the column headings that the SELECT statement can contain. If it is omitted, the normal column headings from the SELECT statement become the columns of the view. Whether or not this column list is included, the view must have standard, legal identifiers for all the columns or an error will occur.

The WITH ENCRYPTION option encrypts the copy of the CREATE VIEW syntax for your view that SQL Server stores in the *syscomments* table. This prevents anyone from seeing the exact syntax used to create the view. The WITH CHECK OPTION from the syntax causes SQL Server to perform additional checks on data modified through the view. Both of these options are described in greater detail later in the chapter.

The following are several examples of common kinds of views:

```
CREATE VIEW v_ProjectionView
AS
SELECT Au_fname, Au_lname, City, State, Zip
FROM Authors

CREATE VIEW v_JoinExample
AS
SELECT Pub_Name, Title, Price
FROM Publishers
JOIN Titles
ON Titles.Pub_ID = Publishers.Pub_ID

CREATE VIEW v_ComputedColumn
(Title, Discount, Disc_Price)
AS
SELECT Title, '10%', Price * 0.90
FROM Titles

CREATE VIEW v_AggregateExample
(Category, Avg_Price)
AS
SELECT Type, Avg(Price)
FROM Titles
GROUP BY Type
HAVING Avg(Price) IS NOT NULL

CREATE VIEW v_ViewOfView
AS
SELECT *
FROM v_ComputedColumn
WHERE Disc_Price > 15.00
```

The preceding examples illustrate the CREATE VIEW syntax. You can
see that views are very flexible. Almost any SELECT statement can be
used as the basis of a view. The restrictions on the kinds of views
that can be created are discussed later in this chapter.

Altering Views

After you have created a view, you can modify the structure of the
view by using the ALTER VIEW command. With this command you
can change or totally rewrite the select statement in a view, or
change the ENCRYPTION or WITH CHECK OPTION. The syntax for the
ALTER VIEW statement follows:

```
ALTER VIEW view_name [(column [,…n])]
[WITH ENCRYPTION]
AS
select_statement
[WITH CHECK OPTION]
```

This syntax is identical to that of the CREATE VIEW statement discussed earlier, so the particular phrases will not be repeated here. As was stated earlier, any option can be changed from the original CREATE VIEW command. It is possible to alter a view to the point that it is unrecognizable from the original. The only thing that cannot be changed with this statement is the name of the view.

The only benefit to altering a view as opposed to dropping and recreating a new view with the same name is that the ALTER VIEW syntax allows changes with a single command.

Recognizing the Limitations of Views

There are certain limitations to the kinds of SELECT statements that can be used in creating a view. For example, a view cannot reference temporary tables. Temporary tables are considered too short-lived to make them useful to reference through views. Furthermore, the ORDER BY, COMPUTE, and COMPUTE BY operators cannot be used in the creation of a view, and of course the creator of a view must have sufficient rights to access the data that the view will return.

There are two stored procedures that provide useful information on views. The stored procedure sp_helptext outputs the actual SELECT statement used to create the view if the WITH ENCRYPTION option was not used. What sp_helptext does is display the information SQL Server stores in *syscomments* at the time the view is created. The WITH ENCRYPTION option is used for the sole purpose of encrypting that information so it cannot be displayed. To find out what objects the view depends on and what other objects depend on the view, use the system stored procedure sp_depends.

If the view is created with the WITH CHECK OPTION statement included, INSERTs and UPDATEs behave differently on that view than they would otherwise. This option causes additional checks to be performed on INSERT and UPDATE statements to ensure that the data affected will be a part of the view and will not be inserted into the underlying table invisible to the view.

Remember that views do not contain any data themselves; the data is stored in the underlying tables. If a view is showing only rows from a table that meet a certain criteria, then it would be possible to write an UPDATE against that view that would cause one or more rows to no longer meet the view's criteria. These rows would still exist in the table. However, they would seem to have disappeared from the view. Similarly, a row could be inserted into the view that would not meet the view's criteria, but would still be allowed into the underlying table. The WITH CHECK OPTION statement causes an error to occur if data updated in or inserted to a view would not appear as part of the view. Table 9.1 runs down the various view options for the WITH CHECK OPTION statement.

TABLE 9.1

WITH CHECK OPTION VIEW OPTIONS

View Definition WHERE Clause Reference Data IN/OUT of Range	WITH CHECK OPTION Not Specified	WITH CHECK OPTION Specified
IN Range (INSERT, UPDATE, and DELETE)	Successful	Successful
OUT of Range (INSERT)	Successful	Error Message (INSERT fails)
OUT of Range (UPDATE changes Value out of Range)	Successful	Error Message (UPDATE fails)
OUT of Range (UPDATE)	0 rows affected	0 rows affected
OUT of Range (DELETE)	0 rows affected	0 rows affected

It is permissible to write UPDATE and INSERT statements that include views. However, there are limitations. The data modified by UPDATE or INSERT must not affect more than one table. So if a view is presenting data obtained from many tables, an UPDATE written against that view could only affect those columns that happen to contain data from a single table. Similarly, an INSERT statement can only cause data to be inserted into one of the tables.

Modifications to data through views are also limited by the fact that views may contain certain columns that cannot be updated or used in an INSERT statement. Any column presented by a view that is a computed value or is the result of a built-in function (such as Trim or Format) cannot be modified. This is simply because such columns do not correspond directly to a column in a table where such modifications must be stored.

INSERT statements have an additional limitation. A view may present only certain columns from its underlying table. If an INSERT statement is written for this view, only columns displayed by that view can be specified. Any additional columns in the table receive default information if any are defined for the column or are left as NULL. If columns exist in the table that do not allow NULL and no default is specified, then no INSERT into a view that does not contain that column can be successful.

Although it is possible to alter data through views, it is generally not advisable to do so. Just as a view is treated like a real table in a SELECT statement, INSERTs, UPDATEs, and DELETEs can be written to affect views the same as they would real tables. However, the limitations that apply to such modification make it bad practice to rely on changing data through views.

It already has been shown that it is good practice for applications to reference views rather than user tables directly. This practice allows the underlying data model to evolve to meet changing needs while still providing a static interface to the applications that access the database. However, such changes may cause a view that once pulled data from one table to now require a JOIN to collect all the data it needs. Because UPDATEs, INSERTs, and DELETEs can only be written against views such that they cause changes to only one table underlying the view, if a view that once referenced one table now must join two or more, any UPDATEs written against that view will now likely fail. Instead, data modifications should always be done through stored procedures, and views should be used strictly for retrieving data.

Even seemingly simple views can cause problems to UPDATEs and INSERTs. A simple view with no joins and no computed columns can still cause errors when updated if it was built on other views that *do* contain computed columns and joins. In this way, views can hide complexity that would otherwise warn the user of such problems.

It is important to keep in mind that views are not tables, despite all their similarities. Views have no user data associated with them at all. In SQL Server, all user data is stored with tables; views merely allow an alternate method of accessing that data. Therefore, views cannot be indexed. Indexes provide information to SQL Server about the physical storage of data to allow quick access to that data. Views have no data, therefore they cannot be indexed. If queries using views are found to be too slow, the actual data stored in tables should be indexed and the views written to take advantage of such indexes. Similarly, triggers cannot be created on views. Triggers can only be written to activate when data is modified in a table. Whether the modification is as a result of a statement written using a view or the table itself is irrelevant.

It is important to know how views are dependent on the tables they reference. Even when a table is dropped and re-created, any view dependent upon it will still reference it correctly, provided the fields referenced by the view still exist. The order in which the table's columns are defined, and even the data types, may be changed. The columns a view references are stored explicitly when the view is created; therefore, as long as the view can find those columns when it is executed, the view continues to work. What this also means is that even if a view is created with a SELECT * statement, new columns added to the table aren't automatically added to the view. You can, however, use the ALTER VIEW command to modify the view to begin using the new columns.

Earlier in this chapter it was stated that even if a table is re-created with a different data type for a column referenced by a view, the view can still reference that column. It is important to note, however, that if the view contains any statement that would fail against the new data type (such as an addition on a character field, for example), the next statement executed against that view will fail. This is not because the view was unable to reference that column; it is because SQL Server was unsuccessful at performing the requested operation on the column it found.

> **NOTE**
>
> **Use Special Naming Convention with Views** Because views present themselves to users just like tables, they can often be mistaken for tables until an UPDATE fails because it would modify more than one underlying table, or an index fails to be built against it. Therefore, it is a good idea to use a special naming convention with views to set them apart from user tables. A common approach is to preface a descriptive name with v.

> **NOTE**
>
> **Use a View to Export Multiple Tables** Exporting data out of SQL Server is commonly done with the Bulk Copy program (BCP). Limitations of BCP include that it only exports data from one table, and that it cannot be limited to only certain rows of that table. Views can be used to present a "single" table to BCP even when the data is joined from many tables. By the same token, views can present only rows from a table that meet a certain criteria to BCP.

Views

Views are an important part of a robust data model. They allow a layer of abstraction between users and the actual data that help provide a level of independence to applications that use your database. They also can provide security benefits for much the same reason. Users aren't seeing the data directly. Finally, they can simplify data access for less experienced users.

TRIGGERS

▶ Create triggers that implement rules, that enforce data integrity, and that perform cascading updates and deletes.

· Implement transactional error handling.

Triggers are a powerful part of the SQL Server programming model. A *trigger* can be thought of as a stored procedure that is registered to be run whenever a data modification event (INSERT, UPDATE, or DELETE) happens to a defined table. A trigger can contain many Transact-SQL statements that are run as a batch when the trigger is executed, similar to a stored procedure. Multiple triggers can be created for a single operation on a single table.

The primary use for triggers is to enforce business rules on the data in a table. Although constraints can perform a wide variety of data validation and can enforce data integrity rules very efficiently, a trigger puts all the power of the TSQL language at your disposal for complex tasks. The power of triggers, however, is also their weakness. Every time any data modification statement is run against a table with an appropriate trigger, all the complex logic of that trigger must be executed. Think about a database with very high transaction rates of many rows of data being modified every second, and you will realize what a daunting task trigger execution can be. As a rule, if a business rule can be implemented through the use of a constraint, the constraint is the best way to go.

If triggers should be used only when constraints cannot be, then you need to be aware of situations in which triggers are necessary. Triggers can ensure referential integrity to data in different databases. Just as a TSQL statement can use a three-part identifier to specify the database, owner, and object to be referenced, these complex identifiers can be used in the statements that make up a trigger. A reference constraint, on the other hand, cannot reference a table outside the database it exists in. Another common use for triggers is to perform cascading updates and deletes. In related tables, if a parent record is updated it may be desirable to propagate some of these changes to the dependent entities. Triggers can examine the changed data and perform further updates to the dependent tables. Similarly, if a parent record is deleted, a trigger could delete all dependent records as well. Care should be taken in these scenarios because even seemingly simple changes to a table's data can cause significant changes throughout the database (and even other databases).

When a trigger makes modifications to other tables, or even its own table, it is possible for triggers on those tables to be invoked. This is known as the *nested execution of triggers* and could conceivably get out of hand. If triggers are written to modify their own table, the same trigger could be fired again recursively. Similarly, a trigger on one table could modify a second table, which could then fire a trigger to modify the first table resulting in the first trigger firing again. These situations could lead to infinite loops, which could overload a server. For this reason, SQL Server tracks and limits the nesting level of triggers. The limit is set through the "nested triggers" option of sp_configure. The limit can be set from 0, prohibiting the nested firing of triggers, up to a maximum of 32. The special case of recursive firing of triggers can be specifically prohibited through the "recursive triggers" option of sp_dboption. This second option is simply set to TRUE or FALSE. The full syntax and use of the sp_configure and sp_dboption stored procedures can be found in the TSQL help file.

> **NOTE**
>
> **Determine What Tables Have Triggers Defined** You can determine which tables already have triggers assigned to them by using the system stored procedure sp_depends.

Creating Triggers

The basic syntax for creating a trigger looks like the following:

```
CREATE TRIGGER [owner.]triggername
ON [owner.]tablename
FOR {INSERT, UPDATE, DELETE}
 [WITH ENCRYPTION]
AS
/*Trigger text follows */
```

The CREATE TRIGGER portion of the statement is used to assign a name to the trigger and establish ownership. Ownership is defaulted to the user executing the statement unless otherwise specified. The table for which you are creating the trigger is specified following the ON keyword. The owner of the table can be specified if necessary. Each trigger is created for a single table only. The keyword FOR specifies the type of trigger that is to be created: INSERT, UPDATE, or DELETE. Any combination can be specified. In other words, a single trigger can be created to handle INSERT, UPDATE, and DELETE or any combination of those actions. The WITH ENCRYPTION option is used to hide the contents of a trigger. The text is encrypted similarly to

> **WARNING**
>
> **Limitations of Statements in Triggers** Certain commands cannot be executed from a trigger. You cannot use any CREATE, ALTER, or DROP statements. You cannot GRANT or REVOKE from a trigger. LOAD, RESTORE, and TRUNCATE commands are prohibited as well. A specific list of all prohibited commands can be found in the TSQL Help file.

an encrypted stored procedure. Finally, the AS keyword is used to lead into the body of the trigger. At this point, the set of SQL statements to be executed should be incorporated.

Implementing Transactional Error Handling in Triggers

While the code of a trigger is executing, an explicit transaction is always in place. Although the transaction is opened automatically without user intervention, it is called an explicit transaction here because it can be explicitly committed or rolled back through code. Remember that SQL Server does not truly nest transactions independently; rather, any ROLLBACK command completes all outstanding transactions, and COMMIT commands only reduce the @@Trancount value by one. Therefore, if a transaction is open when a trigger fires, a ROLLBACK command issued by the trigger will roll back all previous changes contained in the outer-most transaction, whereas a COMMIT command does not guarantee the changes validated by a trigger will not eventually be rolled back. If a trigger completes normally without an explicit transaction command, the transaction is committed.

Good error handling in a trigger requires that if an error occurs, or the trigger successfully detects bad data, a ROLLBACK command should executed. This will prevent the data modification statement that caused the trigger to fire to be undone. You will find a sample trigger to enforce referential integrity in the next section. This sample trigger includes statements to issue a ROLLBACK if bad data is found.

Using the Inserted and Deleted Tables

If the base table is examined while a trigger is executing, the table will appear to already have been changed by the statement that caused the trigger to fire. There are two special tables that SQL Server makes available to the code of a trigger that hold the original values of all the changed rows. These tables are called Inserted and Deleted. The Inserted table holds copies of all the rows that were inserted into the base table. The Deleted table holds the rows that were deleted from the base table. An update can be thought of as a delete followed by an insert to understand the data that will be found in the Inserted and Deleted tables. The code inside a trigger can reference these tables to determine the changes that were made as part of data validation.

For example, you could use the Inserted and Deleted tables in an update trigger to enforce referential integrity. For simplicity this example will refer to tables within the Pubs database, but declarative referential integrity can do this job better than a trigger. The true usefulness of triggers to enforce referential integrity is the fact that they can reference tables in other databases. Because constraints cannot enforce referential integrity across databases, a trigger is your best tool for that job.

The following trigger will fire whenever the Titles table is updated, and it will ensure that all referential integrity is enforced in the Titles table:

```
CREATE TRIGGER tu_titles
ON Titles
FOR UPDATE
AS
DECLARE @HoldCnt int
-- Count number of titleids referenced in
-- Sales that have been deleted in Titles.
-- Note that any titleid that is in Deleted
-- but not in Inserted was deleted.
SELECT @HoldCnt = Count(*)
FROM (Deleted d
LEFT JOIN Inserted i
  ON i.title_id = d.title_id)
JOIN Sales s
  ON s.title_id = d.title_id
WHERE i.title_id IS NULL

IF @HoldCnt > 0
Begin
        RAISERROR('Cannot delete Title in use by Sales.',
➥16, 1)
        ROLLBACK TRANSACTION
        RETURN
End

-- Count number of titleids referenced in
-- RoySched that have been deleted in Titles.
SELECT @HoldCnt = Count(*)
FROM (Deleted d
LEFT JOIN Inserted i
  ON i.title_id = d.title_id)
JOIN RoySched r
  ON r.title_id = d.title_id
WHERE i.title_id IS NULL
```

```
IF @HoldCnt > 0
Begin
        RAISERROR('Cannot delete Title in use by
➥RoySched.', 16, 1)
        ROLLBACK TRANSACTION
        RETURN
End

-- Count number of titleids referenced in
-- TitleAuthor that have been deleted in Titles.
SELECT @HoldCnt = Count(*)
FROM (Deleted d
LEFT JOIN Inserted i
  ON i.title_id = d.title_id)
JOIN TitleAuthor ta
  ON ta.title_id = d.title_id
WHERE i.title_id IS NULL

IF @HoldCnt > 0
Begin
        RAISERROR('Cannot delete Title in use by
➥TitleAuthor.', 16, 1)
        ROLLBACK TRANSACTION
        RETURN
End

-- Count number of pubids that don't exist
-- in Publishers table
SELECT @HoldCnt = Count(*)
FROM Inserted i
LEFT JOIN Publishers p
  ON p.Pub_ID = i.Pub_ID
WHERE p.Pub_ID IS NULL

IF @HoldCnt > 0
Begin
        RAISERROR('Cannot Update with Pub_ID that does not
➥exist.', 16, 1)
        ROLLBACK TRANSACTION
        RETURN
End
GO
```

REVIEW BREAK

Triggers

Triggers can be thought of as stored procedures that are called automatically in response to data modifications on a table. Triggers are objects that are attached to a specific table and are registered to execute in response to an INSERT, UPDATE, or DELETE on that table. A single trigger can be set to respond to any or all data modifications. In addition, multiple triggers can be created to respond to each data modification.

Triggers always execute within a transaction. If an error condition is detected by a trigger, the transaction can be cancelled through the standard ROLLBACK command. To aid in error checking, there are two special tables that can be referenced by a trigger. The Inserted and Deleted tables exist only during the execution of a trigger, and they can be referenced only by the trigger for which they were created. The Inserted table contains copies of all the new records being added to a table during an Insert or Update (an Update in this context is thought of as a DELETE followed by an INSERT).

DISTRIBUTED QUERIES

▶ Access data from static or dynamic sources by using remote stored procedures, linked servers, and OpenRowset.

  • Evaluate where processing occurs when using OpenQuery.

The term *distributed queries* encompasses a wide range of features. In brief, it covers the interaction between a SQL Server and any other data source. SQL Server uses the OLE-DB technology developed by Microsoft to communicate with heterogeneous data sources. A *heterogeneous data source* is any data source that is not SQL Server. A *data source* is simply any source of data. Data sources include both relational and non-relational database management systems, as well as mail systems, text documents, and spreadsheet data. OLE-DB drivers exist to allow you to interact with any of these sources and more.

Distributed queries can be used in any of the programming constructs that have been discussed in this book. For example, stored procedures and triggers can be written to use distributed queries to collect or reference data from external data sources as part of their work. Views can even be written to present data from an external data source as though it were a local table.

Distributed queries can use either statically defined or dynamically defined data sources. Statically defined data sources, or linked servers, are fully discussed in the following section. You can dynamically connect to remote data source using the OpenRowset function, which is also defined in a later section.

EXAM TIP

Watch for Marketing Questions
Microsoft is very proud of SQL Server's ability to use the new OLE-DB technology to access heterogeneous data sources. Because they are so proud of this feature, they will certainly want you to be aware of it on the test. For example, you may be presented with a list of data sources and asked which ones SQL Server can access. When in doubt, choose them all.

As a rule, if you are unsure of a question on the test that compares SQL Server to other products or that discusses limitations of SQL Server, go ahead and choose the answer that puts SQL Server in the best light. As a SQL Server certified professional, Microsoft will want you to spread the praises of SQL Server at every opportunity, and is not above phrasing questions to put you in the right mindset.

Defining and Using Linked Servers

One implementation of the distributed query technology is the concept of the linked server. A *linked server* is a statically defined data source that is stored on the SQL Server so that scripts and procedures executing on the server can easily reference these external data sources by a simple name. All information that SQL Server needs to communicate with this data source is pre-defined, so that a single name is sufficient to allow access. A linked server is defined on a SQL Server through the use of the `sp_addlinkedserver` stored procedure. This stored procedure accepts differing arguments to connect to different data sources; therefore, a complete description of the stored procedure is outside the scope of this book. Refer to the Transact-SQL Help File for a complete description of `sp_addlinkedserver`. Using `sp_addlinkedserver` to connect to a SQL Server is quite simple, and the simplified syntax is described below:

```
Sp_addlinkedserver @server, 'SQL Server'
```

In the syntax above, the `@server` parameter is the name of the SQL Server you want to explicitly link to. After you have linked to this server, you can access objects in any of the databases to which you have permissions. To access objects in the linked SQL Server database, the following four-part object name is used:

```
[[[server.][database].][owner].]object
```

Note that in the syntax shown, only the object is required. To access an object on a linked server, naturally the server name would be required. If the server name is omitted, the current server you are connected to is used. If a server is specified, the database name is still optional. If the server is specified but no database name is given, the default database for your login is used. If the owner name is not specified, then dbo is assumed. If the object cannot be found as owned by dbo, then the ownership defaults to your user name. If the object cannot be found under your user name, then the reference fails, and an error is reported. To omit the database or owner name, simply enter the period separator with no data, not even spaces. For example, to run the `sp_who` stored procedure on a linked server named LinkedServer without specifying the database or owner name, you would use the following statement:

```
Exec LinkedServer...sp_who
```

NOTE

Remote Servers Are Obsolete If you've been using SQL Server before version 7.0, you may be familiar with the concept of a remote server. *Remote servers* are statically defined just like linked servers, and distributed queries can be referenced through a four-part object reference identical to the reference used for a linked server. Remote servers, however, were designed using proprietary SQL Server technology that has now been made obsolete by SQL Server 7.0's use of OLE-DB, which is an open solution. Remote servers are included in SQL Server 7.0 for backward compatibility only. Linked Servers are now the preferred method of performing distributed queries.

For the remainder of this chapter, the term *remote server* will be used to refer to any data source other than the local SQL Server.

This style of four-part object reference can be used anywhere an object reference is allowed. Wherever you are accustomed to using a table name in a query, for example, you can use the full four-part name to perform a distributed query.

Accessing Data Using Remote Stored Procedures

Remote stored procedures are simply stored procedures that exist on servers other that the one you are currently connected to, such as a linked server. Stored procedures can simplify activity on a linked server by encompassing queries so that you need not understand the data model of the linked server to access data. The other well-known benefits of simplified interface and precompiled execution plans also apply.

To execute a remote stored procedure, simply use the four-part object reference to specify the stored procedure name. The stored procedure from the remote server will be executed and return data from the remote server. Note that the local server will actually execute the remote stored procedure, although it will do so in the context of the remote database in which the stored procedure resides. In other words, the local server will perform the queries, but it will retrieve the data from the remote database.

> **NOTE**
>
> **Security Concerns with Linked Servers** To access another SQL Server through distributed queries, you must have the appropriate rights on that machine. In addition, the linked server must be able to recognize your login. The simplest situation is between two SQL Servers running on operating systems that support security account delegation. In this case, NT authentication can be used to gain rights between the servers. Unfortunately, neither Windows NT 4.0 nor Windows 9x supports this delegation. However, the stored procedure sp_addlinkedsrvlogin allows a local login to be mapped to a remote SQL Server login. A full discussion of SQL Server logins and NT Authentication is needed for the Administering SQL Server 7.0 test and is outside the scope of this book. Look for the sp_addlinkedsrvlogin stored procedure documentation in the Transact-SQL Help File for more information.

Accessing Data Using the OpenQuery Function

The OpenQuery function allows passthrough queries to be executed on the linked server. Normally the local server queries the linked server for the data needed, but joins and other data processing are done on the local server. The OpenQuery function takes a fully formed query and causes it to be executed on the remote data source. This removes the burden of processing from the local machine. It also allows joins on remote data to be performed locally on the remote data source, which will often be more efficient. Even where the complexity of joins is not needed, data from a single remote table can be limited using search criteria on the remote data source before sending it to the local server to be used. This can significantly reduce network traffic. The syntax for the OpenQuery function is as follows:

```
OPENQUERY(linked_server, 'query')
```

In the preceding syntax, the *linked_server* parameter is simply the name of the predefined linked server. The *query* parameter is a fully formed TSQL statement that will run in the context of the linked server. Object names in the query should be formed to refer to the objects locally on the linked server.

The OpenQuery function can be used in TSQL statements wherever a table name is normally used. The result set returned by the OpenQuery function treated the same way as a derived table from a sub-query.

Accessing Data Using OpenRowset

The OpenRowset function can be used to return data from a remote data source. The OpenRowset function provides an alternative to using a predefined linked server. Whereas a linked server is statically defined on a SQL Server, the OpenRowset function provides all the information needed to make a connection to the remote data source and issue a one-time query to be executed by that remote data source. The query is executed on the remote data source in the same way that the OpenRowset function works. The following details the OpenRowset syntax:

```
OPENROWSET('provider_name'
        {
                'datasource';'user_id';'password'
                ¦ 'provider_string'
        },
        {
                [catalog.][schema.]object
                ¦ 'query'
        }
```

The *provider_name* parameter specifies the OLE-DB driver that will be used. For example, there are OLE-DB drivers for SQL Server, ODBC, ORACLE, and others. The OLE-DB driver for ODBC can be used to access any ODBC data source. The second parameter provides information for connecting to the specific data source. This connection information can be presented in two forms. The 'datasource';'user_id';'password' string can be passed, which provides the three parameters as interpreted by the OLE-DB driver.

The other form is a '*provider_string*' that is specifically requested by the OLE-DB driver. The third argument specifies the object that should be returned as a result set or is in the form of a query which is executed by the OLE-DB data source. A full discussion of OLE-DB is outside the scope of this book, but the following example will illustrate how to connect to a remote SQL Server:

```
SELECT *
FROM OPENROWSET('MSDASQL',
'DRIVER={SQL
➥Server};SERVER=RemoteServer;UID=user1;PWD=thispass',
        'SELECT * FROM pubs.dbo.Titles WHERE Pub_ID =
➥''0736''')
```

The previous example uses the OLE-DB provider for ODBC, which is the provider name parameter of 'MSDASQL'. It then uses the SQL Server ODBC driver to connect to a remote SQL Server named 'RemoteServer', and log in as 'user1' with the password 'thispass'. Finally, the query, which selects all columns from the Titles table for a particular publisher ID, is executed on the remote SQL Server. You'll notice that the query that is sent uses a three-part object reference to the Titles table where the server is not specified. This is because the entire query is being executed on the remote server so that by not specifying a server in the object reference, the local server is the SQL Server named RemoteServer.

Distributed Queries

REVIEW BREAK

Distributed queries allow you to reference data from sources outside the SQL Server to which you are connected. There are two primary forms of distributed queries: those which utilize a statically linked data source, and those that dynamically link to a data source at the time the query is made. A data source can be statically linked to your SQL Server through the linked server mechanism. After a data source is defined as a linked server, users connected to the SQL Server can access information on the linked server by its name. This is the simplest method for your users to use, but it requires you to set up all needed data sources before hand. A dynamic distributed query requires no setup before hand, but it requires the end user to be able to perform all the configuration necessary to attach to the data source. A dynamic distributed query is accomplished through the OpenRowset function.

CASE STUDY: ABSTRACTING A DATA MODEL

ESSENCE OF THE CASE

Here are the essential elements of the case:

▶ You want to run existing applications against new SQL Server database for performance reasons.

▶ Performance can be further improved by normalizing the data model.

▶ Cascading deletes need to be implemented on SQL Server.

SCENARIO

Your company is upgrading a database and all related applications to SQL Server from Microsoft Access. During the initial stages of this process, you decide that the current data model has some room for improvement, but you know that the existing applications must remain in production until the new development effort is completed. You are expecting a performance gain in the short term simply by upgrading to a more powerful SQL Server even with the existing applications. Fortunately, these existing applications were written using ODBC so that they do not specifically require an Access database—just a valid ODBC data source. In addition, Microsoft Access has an option to allow for cascading deletes that you'll need to preserve.

ANALYSIS

You certainly have your work cut out for you on this one. You can make some significant changes to the data model and still use views to present the data in the style of the old tables to your users; however, if the views involve joins, data modification statements against them will likely fail. A single data modification statement can affect only a single table at a time, even through a view. Therefore, a data modification made against a view that is composed of multiple tables will fail unless the statement affects columns from only one of the tables. This makes it unlikely that the existing applications could be tricked into working against views abstracting an enhanced data model. It would be possible to create old style "shadow" tables in your data

CASE STUDY: ABSTRACTING A DATA MODEL

model and use triggers to keep the old and new tables synchronized, but that would really defeat the purpose of implementing the new data model.

You'll likely still get a performance boost by running your existing applications against the original data model implemented on SQL Server simply due to the power of a dedicated server,

which may make the immediate upgrade to SQL Server worthwhile. You can go ahead with your plans to implement a new data model for future development efforts in a separate database, and use triggers to offer similar cascading deletes that your developers expect. Of course, triggers would have to be implemented on your existing data model to allow provide for cascading deletes in any case.

CHAPTER SUMMARY

With the concepts presented in this chapter, you will be able to exercise greater control over your database, and you will be in a position to respond more flexibly to your users' requests for data. Successful administration includes rapid and positive responses to changes as well as stable reliability. To successfully implement a manageable database, you need to understand all options at your disposal, and stored procedures, views and triggers are particularly valuable ones. In addition, the use of distributed queries allows you to integrate your data more tightly, to keep you and your users better informed.

KEY TERMS

Before you take the exam, make sure you are comfortable with the definitions and concepts for each of the following key terms:

- views
- triggers
- stored procedures
- linked server
- OpenQuery
- OpenRowset
- inserted table
- deleted table
- distributed query

APPLY YOUR KNOWLEDGE

Exercises

9.1 Using a Query Tool to Create a View

In this exercise, you create a view that joins the Authors, TitleAuthor, and Titles tables.

Estimated Time: 5 minutes

1. Load SQL Query Analyzer and log on to your server.

2. Choose the Pubs database from the Database dropdown box.

3. Enter the CREATE VIEW statement to create a view with the name v_AuthorTitles.

    For this example, do not set any special options, and do not specify a column list outside the select statement.

4. Enter a select statement to return the first and last name of every author along with the titles of all their books and the advance they were paid.

5. Execute the statement to create the view. Your final statement should look similar to the following:

    ```
    CREATE VIEW v_AuthorTitles AS
    SELECT Au_fName, Au_lName, Title, Advance
    FROM Authors, TitleAuthor, Titles
    WHERE Authors.Au_ID = TitleAuthor.Au_ID
    AND TitleAuthor.Title_ID = Titles.Title_ID
    ```

9.2 Modifying an Existing View

Now, you will use the ALTER VIEW statement to modify the view you just created.

Estimated Time: 5 minutes

1. Make sure you have the Query Analyzer loaded and connected to your server and that the Pubs database is chosen in the Databases dropdown box.

2. Begin your ALTER VIEW statement to alter the v_AuthorTitles view.

3. Enter a column list for the view that will display four columns labeled FirstName, LastName, Title, and AdvancePaid. Also add the encryption option this time.

4. Use the same select statement as you did in Exercise 9.1 to complete the view.

5. Execute the statement to re-create the altered view. The statement you end up with should resemble the following:

    ```
    ALTER VIEW v_AuthorTitles
    (FirstName, LastName, Title, AdvancePaid)
    WITH ENCRYPTION
    AS
    SELECT Au_fName, Au_lName, Title, Advance
    FROM Authors, TitleAuthor, Titles
    WHERE Authors.Au_ID = TitleAuthor.Au_ID
    AND TitleAuthor.Title_ID = Titles.Title_ID
    ```

9.3 Creating an Update Trigger

In this exercise you create an update trigger that stops the user from changing the column hired_dt in the table employee. The requirements are as follows:

- The trigger is an update trigger.

- The trigger will be on the Authors table.

- The trigger will need to determine if the column au_lname has been changed.

- If the user attempts to change au_lname, then an error needs to be presented to the user.

APPLY YOUR KNOWLEDGE

Estimated Time: 15 minutes

1. Begin the script with the CREATE statement:

```
CREATE TRIGGER Authors_tu
ON Authors
FOR UPDATE
AS
```

2. Add the check for au_lname to the script.

```
IF update(au_lname)
begin
--Error code goes here
end
```

3. Between begin and end, the error code needs to be added.

```
RAISERROR ('The authors last name cannot be
➥changed.', 10, 1)
ROLLBACK TRANSACTION
```

4. Altogether, the script should look like the following:

```
CREATE TRIGGER Authors_tu
ON Authors
FOR UPDATE
AS
IF update(au_lname)
begin
RAISERROR ('The authors last name cannot be
➥changed.', 10, 1)
ROLLBACK TRANSACTION
end
```

9.4   Creating a Delete Trigger

In this exercise you create a delete trigger that prevents the user from deleting rows from the titles table if the book is referenced in the titleauthor table. The requirements are as follows:

- The trigger is a delete trigger.

- The trigger is on the titles table.

- The trigger needs to check the titleauthor table for references to the book being deleted.

- If references exist, stop the transaction from being processed.

Estimated Time: 15 minutes

1. Begin the script with the CREATE statement:

```
CREATE TRIGGER titles_td
ON titles
FOR DELETE
AS
```

2. Now check the titleauthor table for references to the deleted book.

```
IF (SELECT count(*)
FROM titleauthor ta JOIN deleted d
  ON ta.title_id = d.title_id) > 0
begin
--Error code goes here
end
```

3. Between begin and end, the error code needs to be added.

```
RAISERROR ('The book is referenced by an
➥author and cannot be deleted.', 10, 1)
ROLLBACK TRANSACTION
```

4. Altogether, the script should look like the following:

```
CREATE TRIGGER titles_td
ON titles
FOR DELETE
AS
IF (SELECT count(*)
FROM titleauthor ta JOIN deleted d
  ON ta.title_id = d.title_id) > 0
begin
RAISERROR ('The is referenced by an author
➥and cannot be deleted.', 10, 1)
ROLLBACK TRANSACTION
end
```

9.5   Creating a Stored Procedure

In this exercise you will create a simple stored procedure to insert a new book into the titles table and attach an existing author to that book. As you follow

APPLY YOUR KNOWLEDGE

this exercise, you will be asked to create the procedure one step at a time. Enter all your commands into a continuous script, and do not execute any commands until the entire stored procedure is assembled.

Estimated Time: 10 minutes

1. First enter the CREATE PROCEDURE statement. The name of the procedure will be usp_AddTitle. The procedure will accept one parameter for each field in the Titles table, plus one extra to hold the author ID. The command should resemble the following:

```
CREATE PROCEDURE usp_AddTitle
     @title_id char(6),
     @au_id char(11),
     @title varchar(80),
     @type char(12),
     @pubdate datetime,
     @pub_id char(4) = NULL,
     @price money = NULL,
     @advance money = NULL,
     @royalty int = NULL,
     @ytd_sales int = NULL,
     @notes varchar(200) = NULL
AS
```

Note that in the example all required arguments are arranged as the first arguments listed. Because the Titles table has many nullable fields, the arguments relating to these fields can be set up as optional arguments that default to NULL.

2. Write an insert statement that will insert a title into the Titles table.

```
INSERT INTO Titles
(title_id, title, type, pub_id, price,
advance, royalty, ytd_sales, notes, pubdate)
VALUES
(@title_id, @title, @type, @pub_id, @price,
➥@advance, @royalty, @ytd_sales, @notes,
➥@pubdate)
```

3. Write an insert statement that will insert a record into the TitleAuthor table. Only the title_id and au_id fields need to be inserted; all other fields can be left to default to null.

```
INSERT INTO TitleAuthor
(au_id, title_id)
VALUES
(@au_id, @title_id)
```

4. Run all the previous commands you have entered in this exercise together as a batch to create the procedure.

9.6   Running a Distributed Query

In this exercise you will run a distributed query against a dynamically defined remote data source. You will need a SQL Server to act as your remote source. If you have only one SQL Server at your disposal, the exercise can still be performed using your server's name as the remote server. You will need to have a login defined for SQL Authentication that has permissions to the Pubs database.

Estimated Time: 10 minutes

1. First you must identify the information you will need to dynamically link to the remote server. Fill in the following list:

   - RemoteServer:
   - UserID:
   - Password:

2. Set up a query that will simply relate tables within a single server and a single database. The next statement will replace one of the tables with a distributed query to return the same information from a remote data source. Write a query that joins the Titles table to the TitleAuthor table, and returns the author ID, title ID, and the title of all books.

```
SELECT ta.Au_ID, t.Title_ID, t.Title
FROM Titles t
JOIN TitleAuthor ta
  ON ta.Title_ID = t.Title_ID
```

APPLY YOUR KNOWLEDGE

3. Now you will simply replace the Titles table with a dynamically linked distributed query. This is done with the OpenRowset function. Replace the RemoteServer, UserID, and Password arguments with the information you supplied in step 1.

```
SELECT ta.Au_ID, t.Title_ID, t.Title
FROM OPENROWSET('MSDASQL', 'DRIVER={SQL
➥Server};SERVER=RemoteServer;UID=UserID;PWD=
➥Password',
'SELECT * FROM pubs.dbo.Titles') t
JOIN TitleAuthor ta
  ON ta.Title_ID = t.Title_ID
```

Review Questions

1. What is a view?

2. Why can't you index a view?

3. Can you view present data from more than one table at a time? Why or why not?

4. Paul has accidentally dropped a table from his database, but was able to re-create it and recover all his data. What should he plan to do to ensure that the views he is using to reference the table will still work?

5. Courtney uses a view to present data from the Persons table along with the persons' address information stored in the Addresses table to simplify printing mailing labels. Dan is developing an application that will enable a user to update all of this address information. Is it a good idea for Dan to utilize this view to perform his updates? Why or why not?

6. What is a trigger?

7. How can you view the script of a trigger already created in the database?

8. Why might you nest triggers?

9. What are the inserted and deleted tables?

10. What is the proper syntax for creating an insert trigger for the authors table?

11. In general, how could you prevent data in one table, table_1, from being deleted if there is related data in another table, table_2?

12. What are the advantages triggers have over other methods of enforcing data integrity?

13. What is a linked server?

14. With what kinds of data sources can SQL Server communicate?

15. How does a stored procedure improve query performance?

16. How does a stored procedure improve code reliability?

Exam Questions

1. What does the WITH ENCRYPTION option do when creating a view? Select the best answer.

   A. For security reasons, queries accessing this view are encrypted before being sent to the SQL Server.

   B. SQL Server encrypts the entries in the syscomments table so that no one but the view owner can see how the view was created.

   C. SQL Server encrypts the entries in the syscomments table so that no one, not even the view owner, can see how the view was created.

APPLY YOUR KNOWLEDGE

D. SQL Server deletes the entries about this view in the syscomments table so that no one can see how the view was created.

2. Which of the following statements about views are true?

   A. Modifications can affect only one table in a single statement.

   B. Views can reference temporary tables.

   C. Creating an index on a view can improve performance.

   D. Views can include computed columns.

3. What of the following statements cannot be used to create a view? Select all that apply.

   A. GROUP BY

   B. HAVING

   C. COMPUTE

   D. ORDER BY

4. What are the space requirements of views? Select the best answer.

   A. Views require as much space as all the tables they are created from.

   B. Views require as much space as would a table that presented the same data.

   C. Views do not store data and therefore use no space.

   D. Views require the space used to store a few records in various system tables.

5. How do you find out what triggers have already been created?

   A. Run sp_configure.

   B. Run sp_helptriggers.

   C. Run sp_depends.

6. Why is the option WITH ENCRYPTION useful for triggers? Select the best answer.

   A. It causes the triggers text to be encrypted when placed in syscomments so that any user selecting off syscomments or using sp_helptext cannot view the triggers script.

   B. It requires a password to use the trigger.

   C. It gives the user the option of using encryption on the table data via the trigger.

7. Which of the following are valid options in the FOR clause of the CREATE TRIGGER statement? Select all that apply.

   A. UPDATE

   B. INSERT, UPDATE

   C. SELECT

   D. SELECT, DELETE

8. Which of following are valid SQL commands in a trigger? Select all that apply.

   A. EXEC

   B. SELECT INTO

   C. GRANT

   D. UPDATE

APPLY YOUR KNOWLEDGE

9. An update trigger typically accesses which of the following? Select the best answer.

   A. The updated table

   B. The inserted table only

   C. The inserted and deleted tables

   D. The deleted table only

10. Which of the following statements best describes referential integrity?

    A. It maintains consistency between related data in the same table.

    B. It has the ability to reference data in another table.

    C. It maintains the references established between two entities.

11. What are two advantage of triggers over rules and constraints?

    A. The ability to define the boundaries within which the data must reside

    B. The ability to use looping structures

    C. The ability to reference data in other databases

    D. The ability to check the data before it is logged

12. If table_a has an insert trigger that performs an update on table_b, in which case will the update trigger on table_b be fired?

    A. If 'nested triggers' has a value of 1 or greater

    B. If 'nested triggers' has a value of TRUE

    C. If 'nesting' is set to 0

    D. If 'nesting' is set to 1

13. Which of the following statements are true of stored procedures?

    A. They can be fired by data modifications on tables.

    B. They are precompiled.

    C. They can return only integers and result sets.

    D. They can be executed by only one person at a time.

14. Which of the following are benefits of stored procedures?

    A. They can be tested for improved reliability.

    B. They are precompiled.

    C. They run with a higher priority than ad-hoc queries.

    D. They enable you to share business rule logic.

15. Diane needs to enforce referential integrity on one of her tables. The data in one of the columns should contain key values from a table residing in a database on the corporate server, as opposed to her departmental server where her database resides. She decides to write triggers that will use distributed queries to reference the other server to enforce integrity.

    How would you rate this solution?

    A. This is an optimal solution. Using triggers and distributed queries is the best way to accomplish this task.

    B. This is a fair solution. Although her idea will work, she should simply use distributed queries to verify referential integrity before modifying the table, thereby eliminating the need for triggers.

    C. This is a poor solution. FOREIGN KEY constraints are far more efficient at enforcing referential integrity than triggers.

D. This is not a solution. Distributed queries cannot be used inside a trigger.

16. Which of the following are legitimate data sources for distributed queries?

    A. Relational databases

    B. Non-relational databases

    C. Spreadsheets

    D. Text files

Answers to Review Questions

1. A view is an object created in SQL Server to present data derived from one or more tables in the database. A view is referenced just like a table, but it stores no data itself. A view is created with a specific SELECT statement, and the data it shows are the results of that SELECT statement. (For more information, refer to the section "Views.")

2. Views do not store data themselves; they only reference the data from actual tables. Because views do not own data directly, there is nothing to index. (For more information, refer to the section "Recognizing the Limitations of Views.")

3. Yes. The SELECT statement used to create the view can join data from any number of tables. (Note that SQL Server actually imposes a limit of 256 tables on any SELECT statement.) (For more information, refer to the section "Creating Views.")

4. Nothing needs to be done. The table can be dropped and re-created, and the view will continue to reference it correctly. (For more information, refer to the section "Recognizing the Limitations of Views.")

5. No. Data modifications made to a view can affect only one underlying table or an error occurs. (For more information, refer to the section "Recognizing the Limitations of Views.")

6. A trigger is a set of SQL statements that is executed when an INSERT, UPDATE, or DELETE occurs on a table. (For more information, refer to the section "Creating Triggers.")

7. The system stored procedure sp_helptext can be used to display the script for a trigger unless the trigger was created with the WITH ENCRYPTION option. (For more information, refer to the section "Triggers.")

8. Nesting triggers is useful for performing cascading updates and deletes. (For more information, refer to the section "Triggers.")

9. The inserted and deleted tables are used to hold the data changes that have taken place in a table, but have yet to be committed. (For more information, refer to the section "Using the Inserted and Deleted Tables.")

10. The syntax used to create an insert trigger for the authors table would resemble the following:

    ```
    CREATE TRIGGER authors_ti
    ON authors
    FOR INSERT
    AS
    ```

    (For more information, refer to the section "Creating Triggers.")

11. A FOREIGN KEY constraint on table_2 or a delete trigger on table_1 could be used to prevent the data in table_1 from being deleted while it is still being referenced by table_2. (For more information, refer to the section "Triggers.")

12. The advantages triggers have over other methods of enforcing data integrity include the ability to

include error checking, looping structures, and access to values in other columns. (For more information, refer to the section "Triggers.")

13. A linked server is a remote data source that has been registered with your local SQL Server with enough information so that a connection can be established. After a linked server has been registered, the data from that linked server can be referenced by name. (For more information, refer to the section "Defining and Using Linked Servers.")

14. SQL Server can access data from any OLE-DB data source. These data sources can be either statically or dynamically defined. (For more information, refer to the section "Using Distributed Queries.")

15. When a stored procedure is first run, the execution plan is stored in the procedure cache to be reused by future calls to the stored procedure. Reusing a stored execution plan will save resources and time. (For more information, refer to the section "Precompiled Code.")

16. By encapsulating your business rules and all data modifications through stored procedures, you can exhaustively test those few stored procedures and eliminate them as a possible cause for error. (For more information, refer to the section "Reliability.")

Answers to Exam Questions

1. **C.** The text of the statement used to create the view are encrypted in such a way that no one can read it. Exceptions are not made for the owner, and the text is still stored in the syscomments table. The encryption option for a view does not enhance security for queries written to reference the view. (For more information, refer to the section "Creating Views.")

2. **A, D.** INSERTs, UPDATEs, and DELETEs can be executed against views and will affect the underlying data, but only one table can be affected in a single statement. Views can display the results from most any Select statement, including computed columns. Views cannot reference temporary tables, and they cannot be indexed. (For more information, refer to the sections "Views" and "Recognizing the Limitations of Views.")

3. **C, D.** A COMPUTE statement causes additional result sets to be returned from a SELECT statement and so cannot be included in a view. ORDER BY statements also are not allowed. (For more information, refer to the section "Recognizing the Limitations of Views.")

4. **D.** Although both C and D are based on the correct premise that views store no data, answer D is *more* correct because it addresses the fact that the defining information for the view must be stored in system tables. (For more information, refer to the section "Views.")

5. **C.** The sp_depends stored procedure lists all the objects that are dependent on the given object. This includes all the triggers that are defined against it. (For more information, refer to the section "Triggers.")

6. **A.** The WITH ENCRYPTION option in the CREATE TRIGGER statement encrypts just the text of the create statement. It does not increase the security of your queries or table data. (For more information, refer to the section "Creating Triggers.")

APPLY YOUR KNOWLEDGE

7. **A, B.** Triggers cannot be created to operate when SELECT statements are used. A single trigger can be defined to operate for multiple data modification statements. (For more information, refer to the section "Creating Triggers.")

8. **A, D.** Both GRANT and SELECT INTO statements are disallowed in triggers. (For more information, refer to the section "Creating Triggers.")

9. **C.** Although any type of trigger can access either the iInserted or deleted table, both tables are populated only during the execution of an UPDATE trigger. (For more information, refer to the section "Using the Inserted and Deleted Tables.")

10. **C.** Referential integrity is all about maintaining references between two entities, even if those entities belong to the same table or tables in a different database. (For more information, refer to the section "Triggers.")

11. **B, C.** Triggers can contain much more complex logic than rules and constraints, which typically allow only simple Boolean expressions. Triggers can also reference other databases, just as any TSQL statement can. (For more information, refer to the section "Triggers.")

12. **A.** The setting 'nested triggers' defines the number of triggers that can be executing at the same time in response to a single data modification statement. (For more information, refer to the section "Triggers.")

13. **B, D.** Stored procedures contain a batch of Transact-SQL statements just as triggers do; triggers, however, are registered to execute in response to a data modification statement. The code of a stored procedure is precompiled to speed total execution time. Stored procedures can return a single integer return code and multiple

result sets, and can return data through output parameters. Although only a single connection can execute a single query plan in memory at a time, multiple query plans may be in use at the same time. (For more information, refer to the section "The Benefits of Using Stored Procedures.")

14. **A, B, D.** Stored procedures are precompiled after the first execution. Stored procedures also allow you to encapsulate common application logic to be reused by multiple applications. This encapsulation allows you to fully test the code in one place, which improves reliability. Although stored procedures can improve performance because they don't always need to be compiled, they do not run with a higher priority than any other query. (For more information, refer to the sections "Precompiled Code," "Reliability," and "Sharing Application Logic.")

15. **A.** Writing triggers to use distributed queries is the best solution to this problem. Although it would be possible to write applications that always verified referential integrity for themselves before making data modifications, this approach is less reliable than using triggers or FOREIGN KEY constraints. FOREIGN KEY constraints cannot reference other databases or other servers so they would not help in this situation. (For more information, refer to the sections "Triggers" and "Distributed Queries.")

16. **A, B, C, D.** SQL Server can reference data in any OLE-DB data source. OLE-DB drivers have been written for all of these types of systems. (For more information, refer to the section "Distributed Queries.")

APPLY YOUR KNOWLEDGE

Suggested Readings and Resources

We recommend the following resources for further study in the area of planning:

1. SQL Server Books Online

   - Programming Stored Procedures

   - Managing Security with Linked Servers

   - Adding a Linked Server Login

2. Transact-SQL Help file

   - Create Procedure

   - Create Trigger

   - Create View

   - `sp_addlinkedserver`

   - `OpenQuery`

   - `OpenRowset`

This chapter helps you to prepare for the Microsoft exam by covering the following objectives:

Access data by using the dynamic SQL model.

▶ Applications that access SQL Server have the ability to submit queries for SQL Server to process immediately. In these cases, SQL Server usually has to completely compile the statements before executing the compiled plan. This kind of scenario is called the dynamic SQL model because SQL Server cannot predict or plan for the queries beings sent. Instead it must dynamically build and execute the commands.

Access data by using the Stored Procedure model.

▶ Applications also have the option of submitting queries to SQL Server to be precompiled and then sending final arguments later at execution time. These prepared statements are treated in the same way as stored procedures in that their execution plan is stored in the procedure cache so that SQL Server can quickly execute the plan upon request.

Configure session-level options.

▶ There are many options that you can set to modify SQL Server's behavior in a session. These are accessed through the TSQL SET command. The SET command will be discussed and its relation to ODBC and OLE-DB.

CHAPTER 10

Client Accessibility

▶ The first two objectives shouldn't give you too much trouble on the test. The idea of using the Stored Procedure model versus the dynamic SQL model is very theoretical and doesn't have much in the way of solid facts to memorize. Keep in mind that Microsoft is a little vague on these objectives themselves so keep an open mind when you see the terms Stored Procedure model or dynamic SQL model on the test; your version of the test may have a slightly different take on these topics. Read through the sections here, and just focus on the theory.

Configuring session-level options requires using the SET command. There are many options to try to memorize, but they have been broken into sections to help make it a little easier. In addition, each section highlights a few that are particularly useful in each section. Read through them all, and if any look particularly useful or confusing to you, pull them up in the Transact-SQL help file for a more detailed description.

INTRODUCTION

So far, the material in this book has dealt primarily with learning to work with SQL Server from its own tools and its own language. You have learned how to accomplish the task of creating and populating a database, and then manipulating the data therein through the use of the SQL Server Enterprise Manager and with Transact-SQL statements issued directly to SQL Server from the SQL Server Query Analyzer. The majority of the users of SQL Server will not be trained on these tools, however, and they will not have any need for them. Rather, the majority of users will be using custom-built applications that handle the access of SQL Server invisibly to the user. As a professional database developer certified in the use of SQL Server, you will need to understand how these applications access SQL Server, and what abilities they have to control SQL Server's behavior.

In this chapter, you will first learn about how SQL Server processes dynamic queries, and how it uses the procedure cache to speed execution of similar queries. By understanding SQL Server's optimization strategies, you can deliberately tailor your applications to allow SQL Server to maximize its performance. Second, you learn what configurable settings SQL Server supports that allow your applications to control SQL Server's default behavior.

DYNAMIC MODEL VERSUS STORED PROCEDURE MODEL

▶ Access data by using the dynamic SQL model.

▶ Access data by using the Stored Procedure model.

As you have followed the examples and exercises throughout this book you have primarily been using the dynamic model of data access. You have written statements to accomplish various tasks and then submitted them to be executed by SQL Server. When you issue the execute command from the SQL Server Query Analyzer, you have expected SQL Server to immediately process your queries and return the results to you as fast as the server was capable. Each time you submitted your scripts, SQL Server had no prior knowledge of what commands you would be sending it. Therefore, in every case

SQL Server has to interpret the text of your commands dynamically, and parse them into an execution plan that it then must immediately carry out. This is the least efficient method of data access and is called the *dynamic model*, but because of the unpredictability of the queries that you would be sending, it was unavoidable.

Fortunately, most of the applications you will be writing will not be nearly so unpredictable. Rather, in most cases there will be a discrete number of actions that can be taken at any point of your application. For example, in a data access application used by employees of a call center to take order information, your application will primarily retrieve and enter client information, and then retrieve and enter order information. Certainly, a real-world application has quite a bit more complexity than this simplification, but in a nutshell the program has six queries to select, insert, and update both client and order information. Therefore, you have a good idea of the queries that will be needed for this application—you just don't know exactly which client, and which orders you will be working with.

Because you know you will be performing the same six queries repeatedly, it seems like a waste of resources for SQL Server to have to completely re-evaluate each query every time you send it. SQL Server's strategy to alleviate this situation is the *Stored Procedure model.* Your applications can use features of SQL Server to explicitly prepare statements and request that SQL Server hold the plans in memory for repeated use later. Whereas the dynamic SQL model involves sending ad-hoc statements for SQL Server to parse, compile and execute, the Stored Procedure model involves preparing common statements once, and then calling the prepared plan to get results. These two models are described in more depth in the following sections.

Stored Procedure Model

The Stored Procedure model is based on SQL Server's ability to store an execution plan for reuse. Even a *parameterized* query, which is an incomplete query containing placeholders indicating where values will be supplied later, can be cached. Therefore, a query to retrieve order information can be cached and reused even when later calls to the query supply different part numbers to search on.

There are two methods of accessing the benefits of the Stored Procedure model. One is by encapsulating your queries, and even some associated business rules, into stored procedures, which are stored in SQL Server and are accessed by applications later. The other method allows applications to send queries to SQL Server with the request that the execution plan be held in the same procedure cache as stored procedures. This is known as preparing a query for execution, or creating a prepared statement. For both stored procedures and prepared statements, later calls can access the execution plan directly, saving execution time.

A stored procedure is an object in SQL Server, and like all objects it has an object identifier that is automatically assigned at creation time. SQL Server can use this object identifier to exactly locate an execution plan stored in the procedure cache so the plan can be reused. There is, however, an exception to this rule. SQL Server does not create an execution plan for the stored procedure at the time the object is created. Rather, it waits until the first execution of the procedure to create the plan. Remember from Chapter 9, "Miscellaneous Programming Techniques," that stored procedures take advantage of deferred name resolution. This means that stored procedures can refer to objects that may not exist until run time. Since the objects may not exist when the procedure is created, the first execution plan cannot be created until run time.

When a prepared statement is created on SQL Server, an identifier is created by which the execution plan can be referenced later. Although SQL Server supports prepared statements natively, this functionality is accessed only through an API that is referenced from an external source. Native SQL Server scripts instead use stored procedures to gain comparable functionality. The database applications that you write can use the API to prepare specific, often-used statements. Your applications, however, will undoubtedly use some data access method that exists between your application and SQL Server to handle all database calls. By far the most common of these are ODBC, and the newer (and now preferred by SQL Server 7.0) OLE-DB. By way of example, ODBC uses the SQLPrepare function, and OLE-DB uses the ICommandPrepare interface to access prepared statement functionality. You should refer to the documentation of the data access method you are using to learn the exact implementation of prepared statements.

Dynamic SQL Model

Through the dynamic SQL model, fully formed statements are sent to SQL Server for immediate execution. No warnings are given to SQL Server to prepare for the statement, and no logic is predefined on the server, as is the case with stored procedures. It was stated earlier that this is a less efficient method of querying SQL Server than the Stored Procedure model. The dynamic model is less efficient because you must assume that your query will have to be completely processed from scratch.

There are two things to keep in mind, however, that overcome the inefficiencies in the dynamic model. The first is the simple fact that for any query, an execution plan must always be built at some point. Therefore, if a query will only be run infrequently, or even just once, taking extra steps to prepare the statement for execution is actually more wasteful than just letting the query run independently. The second point is that even dynamic queries will be cached.

Any query that is sent to SQL Server will result in a plan being used from the procedure cache or a plan being built in the procedure cache. Thus, even a dynamic query might get lucky and be matched to a cached plan, with all the benefits that implies. Of course, if the plan is not found the search is wasted, but Microsoft is quick to point out that the resources used by this search are far fewer than what would be required to build the plan from scratch, and so the search is well worth the price.

You should note that there is something you can do to help the process of dynamic plan reuse. In order for the algorithm to work efficiently, you should always fully qualify object names used in your query. SQL Server is far more likely to identify a fully qualified name than one that is not. Therefore, it is worth your effort to specify the database name and object owner in your queries.

Stored Procedure versus Dynamic

When writing database-enabled applications, you have many choices about how to query the database. Using stored procedures improves query performance through execution plan reuse, and it can encapsulate some program logic so that intermediate results do not need to be sent back to the application. Otherwise your applications can use prepared statements to get the same benefits of execution plan reuse. Your final option is to simply execute your queries dynamically. This saves a small amount of complexity in your application, but may increase the overhead on SQL Server because execution plan reuse is not guaranteed.

CONFIGURING SESSION-LEVEL OPTIONS

▶ Configure session-level options.

As your applications work with SQL Server, they always do their work in the context of a session. This session corresponds to a single connection made to the server. When queries are interpreted and results are returned to your application, there are many defaults that are in place to control SQL Server's actions. Your applications can issue commands to SQL Server to modify these defaults when necessary.

The default settings are controlled through the SET command. SQL Server defines seven different categories of statements (explored in next several subsections) to group the almost 40 different settings that you can control with the SET command. The following sections will *not* give you a detailed description of every form of the SET statement—rather, they will focus on giving you an overview of what the different statements can do. You should consult the Transact-SQL help file for a complete reference on the implementation of each command.

Remember also that all of these commands affect only the current connection from which they are issued. Many of these commands have equivalent options at the server or database level. Session-level options will always override server or database defaults for the connection in which they are issued.

Date and Time Statements

The date and time category of session options deals with the way that date and time information is interpreted by default. There are many conflicting standards dictating the format that a date or a time is presented in. You can use these standards to control the way SQL Server will assume dates and times should look. The following list describes the commands Date and Time session-level options:

SET DATEFIRST. Changes SQL Server's understanding of the first day of the week.

SET DATEFORMAT. Changes the way SQL Server interprets character strings during implicit conversion to `datetime` format.

Locking Statements

The session-level options that deal with locking will allow you to specify how you want your queries to react when faced with blocking locks. You can set your queries to be more likely to terminate in the event of a deadlock, and you can control how long you are willing to wait for blocking locks to be released. The following list details the session-level options to control locking behavior:

SET DEADLOCK_PRIORITY. Can be used to make queries issued from this connection to be more or less likely to be chosen as deadlock victims.

SET LOCK_TIMEOUT. Sets the time in milliseconds to wait for a blocking lock to be released before returning the query with an error.

If you believe that deadlocks will be common for your application, you might want to set the deadlock priority based on the user, so that the CEO or senior accountant is less likely to be the victim when SQL Server detects a deadlock. Alternatively, you may be aware that deadlocks often occur during specific user activities. One of those activities may be more important than the others, so you may want to set the deadlock priority differently based on the actions of the user. The following example shows how to make the current session less likely to be chosen as a deadlock victim:

```
SET DEADLOCK_PRIORITY LOW
```

You can use the LOCK TIMEOUT session-level option to cause your queries to timeout and fail due to blocking locks rather than waiting forever. You must supply a value representing the number of milliseconds to wait before the timeout occurs. A value of −1 will cause the session to wait indefinitely, and a value of zero will timeout immediately upon encountering any blocking lock. The following example will set a timeout value for the session of 10 seconds:

```
SET LOCK_TIMEOUT 1000
```

Miscellaneous Statements

The miscellaneous session-level statements are difficult to categorize. Within this category there are many statements that affect SQL Server's compliance with certain standards, and some that are obsolete or are used only with the obsolete DB-Library data access library. The options of particular usefulness are detailed after the following list:

SET CONCAT_NULL_YIELDS_NULL. Controls whether a NULL value concatenated to a string will result in the whole string being null, or whether the NULL is treated as an empty string.

SET_CURSOR_CLOSE_ON_COMMIT. Affects SQL Server's compliance with SQL-92 standards. If this option is set to ON, any cursors that are open within the scope of a transaction will be closed when the transaction is committed in accordance with the SQL-92 standards.

SET DISABLE_DEF_CNST_CHK. Is an obsolete option and is included for backward compatibility only.

SET FIPS_FLAGGER. Controls compliance-level warnings. This setting accepts values relating to four levels of compliance to the FIPS 127-2 standard, which is based on the SQL-92 standard. Warning messages will be generated when SQL Server receives commands that do not meet the specified compatibility level.

SET IDENTITY_INSERT. Allows you to insert explicit values into an Identity column. After the insert, the base of the Identity column is adjusted to a value greater than the new highest base.

SET LANGUAGE. Affects default datetime formats and system messages for a particular session. This option must be set to a value from the syslanguages table.

SET OFFSETS. Is used only in DB-Library applications. It accepts of comma-separated list of Transact-SQL keywords, and returns the position, relative to the start of a statement, of those keywords to the DB-Library application.

SET PROCID. Is used only in DB-Library applications. It will cause the identification number of a stored procedure to be returned to the calling DB-Library application before the procedure's result set.

SET QUOTED_IDENTIFIER. Causes SQL Server to interpret all strings in double quotes to be treated as identifiers rather than literal strings. When this option is set, identifiers that are delimited by double quotes do not need to conform to the normal rules for identifiers. Therefore, this option can be used to allow you to use TSQL reserved words as identifiers, and you can use identifiers that incorporate otherwise forbidden characters such as spaces.

The IDENTITY INSERT option was mentioned briefly in Chapter 3, "Implementing a Physical Design." It is common to create a table with an identity column, but have a set of data that needs to be immediately inserted before the database is opened up to public use. You can use the IDENTITY INSERT option to allow explicit values to be entered into the identity column, then the option is turned off and the column will start generating values upon insert again, starting a new minimum value greater than the maximum value you entered. The following example demonstrates this scenario:

```
SET IDENTITY_INSERT MyIdentityTable ON
INSERT INTO MyIdentityTable
(IdentityColumn, CharDataColumn)
VALUES (101, 'Sample Data')
SET IDENTITY_INSERT MyIdentityTable OFF
```

The QUOTED IDENTIFIER option is important when using a database with a nonstandard naming scheme. Although you can use this option to create table names that would not otherwise be allowed, this makes your database more difficult to use. Therefore, although it is important to be familiar with this option in case you need to reference a nonstandard object name, you should not count on this option to allow you to break the default rules except in controlled situations. The following example will allow you to create a table named with the reserved word "group" by utilizing the session-level option:

```
SET QUOTED_IDENTIFIER ON
CREATE TABLE "GROUP" (
        GroupCode char(3) NOT NULL PRIMARY KEY,
        GroupName char(30) NOT NULL
)
```

Query Execution Statements

There are many important session level options that affect query execution. The following statements allow you to control the way SQL Server executes your statements. You can control how arithmetic errors are handled during query execution, and you can cause your queries to run only partially, or not at all, for testing or performance reasons. You should pay particular attention to this list because these options are used very often:

SET ARITHABORT. Causes SQL Server to terminate a query when an overflow or divide-by-zero error occurs. When this option is not set, SQL Server will continue to process the remainder of a query after one of these errors is encountered.

SET ARITHIGNORE. Controls whether SQL Server will return a warning message after a statement that encounters an overflow or divide-by-zero error. This option is subordinate to SET ANSI_WARNINGS; that is, if SET ANSI_WARNINGS is set to ON, then these arithmetic warning messages are always returned regardless of the setting of SET ARITHIGNORE.

SET FMTONLY. Is used to cause SQL Server to return only the column heading information from a query. This setting causes no rows to be processed and no data to be returned.

SET NOCOUNT. Is used to prevent SQL Server from returning informational messages stating the number of rows affected by the query.

SET NOEXEC. Is used to prevent SQL Server from actually executing a query. Rather, when this option is turned on, SQL Server will compile a query and return any errors found as a result of the compilation, but the query will not be executed.

SET NUMERIC_ROUNDABORT. Causes SQL Server to generate a warning or error when rounding in an expression causes a loss of precision to some value in the expression. If SET ARITHABORT is set ON along with this option, an error occurs when rounding causes a loss of precision; otherwise, only a warning is issued, and the expression evaluates to NULL.

SET PARSEONLY. Checks for syntax errors in a TSQL statement. Whereas the SET NOEXEC option causes compilation of a statement, which can find errors in variables, this option causes statements only to be parsed, which is a more cursory examination.

SET QUERY_GOVERNOR_COST_LIMIT. Sets a value, in seconds, that all queries must complete within. Any query that runs longer than this limit is terminated by SQL Server.

SET ROWCOUNT. Limits the number of rows processed by a query. All queries issued for this connection will stop processing when this number of rows is reached.

SET TEXTSIZE. Controls the amount of data, in bytes, that will be returned from a text or ntext field.

If you are calculating values from data in a table, you may sometimes come across arithmetic errors. By using the ARITHABORT options you can simply tell SQL Server to ignore any errors for a query you know will cause them. On the other hand, you may be attempting to calculate very precise values and need to be sure that you are getting exactly the data you expect. Setting the NUMERIC_ROUNDABORT option will cause SQL Server to warn you when data is being lost due to automatic rounding. Both of these options are set with a simple ON or OFF value, as shown in the following example:

```
SET ARITHABORT ON
SET NUMERIC_ROUNDABORT ON
```

The NOEXEC option allows you to cause an exceptionally long-running query to compile but not run. When this option is combined with the SHOWPLAN options defined later, you can return the execution plan for a query without actually taking the time to run the query. In this way, the query can be optimized much faster. This option also takes a simple ON or OFF value, as shown in the following example:

```
SET NOEXEC ON
```

When you are writing applications that return search results to the user, you will often want to limit the amount of data returned in case the search is too vague, and returns too much data. The SET ROWCOUNT option will allow you to set a maximum number of rows that will be returned in these situations. The following example shows how to limit the rows returned to three, run a sample query, then set the ROWCOUNT option back to unlimited:

```
SET ROWCOUNT 3
SELECT * FROM Authors
SET ROWCOUNT 0
```

The NOCOUNT option is useful when you are writing a reporting script that will return a series of result sets to a user. In these cases you may not want system supplied messages about the rows affected to interrupt your output. This is another option that is set with simple ON and OFF values, as shown by the following example:

```
SET NOCOUNT ON
```

SQL-92 Settings Statements

The options in the following list all control SQL Server's compatibility with the ANSI SQL-92 standards. Although SQL Server can run in complete compliance to the SQL-92 standard, some of the requirements are unnecessarily restrictive. You can use these options to increase or decrease SQL Server's compliance as you need:

SET ANSI_DEFAULTS. Causes the settings of all SQL-92 compliance settings to be turned on. This option is simply shorthand for setting all SQL-92 compliance settings at once.

SET ANSI_NULL_DFLT_OFF. Causes columns in CREATE TABLE statements that do not explicitly state their nullability to default to NOT NULL.

SET ANSI_NULL_DFLT_ON. Causes columns in CREATE TABLE statements that do not explicitly state their nullability to default to NULL.

SET ANSI_NULLS. Controls whether a NULL value can be logically compared to itself with the equals (=) or not-equals (<>) operator. If this option is true, then a NULL value compared to itself will yield NULL as a result instead of TRUE or FALSE.

SET ANSI_PADDING. Controls whether strings are padded with extra spaces to fill a fixed width column. When strings are inserted into a variable-length column, this option controls whether trailing spaces are trimmed.

SET ANSI_WARNINGS. Causes warnings to be generated when certain ANSI-defined error conditions occur.

It is important to know the setting of ANSI padding, because this value will change the way strings are stored in your tables. By default, if you are using Microsoft's ODBC or OLE-DB providers, this option is turned on. Microsoft recommends that this option always be left on through the equivalent server level option. The following example shows how to override the server level option at the session level:

```
SET ANSI_PADDING ON
```

The ANSI NULLS option controls whether NULL can be compared to itself as any normal value can. When working with a set of values that contains NULLs, it can be more convenient to treat NULLs as though they were real values; sometimes, however, it is more important to have NULL values treated specially because they represent a lack of datarather than any real value themselves. The following command demonstrates setting this option:

```
SET ANSI_NULLS ON
```

Statistics Statements

All the following statistics statements relate to generating information about the way your queries run. By turning on these options, SQL Server will return information about how your query was optimized or how well it ran. This information can be useful in determining whether additional indexes are needed, or whether a join clause is not working as you expect:

SET FORCEPLAN. Forces SQL Server to perform join operations in the order in which the tables appear in the FROM clause of SELECT statements. This option limits the ability of the query optimizer to find the best query plan.

SET SHOWPLAN_ALL. Causes a detailed execution plan in the form of a hierarchical tree to be returned along with query results.

SET SHOWPLAN_TEXT. Produces an execution plan similar to SET SHOWPLAN_ALL but with less detail.

SET STATISTICS_IO. Causes SQL Server to return information relating to the amount of disk activity a statement generates.

SET STATISTICS_PROFILE. Causes SQL Server to return the additional result sets of SET SHOWPLAN_ALL along with additional columns relating to the number of rows processed by each operator.

SET STATISTICS_TIME. Causes SQL Server to return the amount of time, in milliseconds, that it took to parse, compile, and execute statements.

The SHOWPLAN options will be explained in detail in Chapter 11, "Maintaining a Database." These options are especially useful to find out why a query is performing poorly. Both SET SHOWPLAN_ALL and SET SHOWPLAN_TEXT are set with simple ON and OFF values.

The STATISTICS_TIME option will show you how long it took a query to run, which can be useful to determine if modifications to a query are helping or hurting performance. This option also takes a simple ON and OFF value as shown in the following command:

```
SET STATISTICS TIME ON
```

Transactions Statements

The following options affect the way transactions are handled by SQL Server. It is possible to cause SQL Server to automatically begin transactions when certain events take place, which can improve the recoverability of your database. You can also control the severity of locking during transactions, which can improve consistency, but hurt concurrency:

SET IMPLICIT_TRANSACTIONS. Implicitly begins a transaction when certain statements are issued. Implicitly generated transactions must be explicitly closed or they are rolled back when the connection is closed.

SET REMOTE_PROC_TRANSACTIONS. Causes SQL Server to begin a distributed transaction when a remote procedure is executed within an existing transaction.

SET TRANSACTION_ISOLATION_LEVEL. Controls SQL Server's locking behavior inside of transactions.

SET XACT_ABORT. Controls whether SQL Server automatically rolls back transactions when a run-time error is encountered.

The transaction isolation level affects the amount of locking that is performed by queries while running in a transaction. This option was discussed in detail in Chapter 8, "Programmability."

By setting the XACT_ABORT option, you can guarantee that a transaction is rolled back if any error is encountered in a batch. When this option is set, you can be sure that you don't commit a partial transaction because you overlooked an error. The option takes a simple ON or OFF value as shown here:

```
SET XACT_ABORT ON
```

CASE STUDY: DEVELOPING A DATABASE-AWARE WEB SITE

ESSENCE OF THE CASE

Here are the essential elements in this case:

▶ VB scripting on active server pages is a necessity.

▶ The developers intend to use OLE-DB for data access.

▶ High traffic is expected.

▶ There are a limited number of predetermined queries.

▶ The query model must be determined.

SCENARIOS

You are on a team working to develop a database-aware Web site. The Web developers have decided to use active server pages to allow them to use VB scripts, which will in turn use the OLE-DB provider for SQL Server to access the database. You expect usage for the site to be over ten thousand page hits per day. When users come to the Web site, they will be allowed to enter information about the products and services about which they are interested, and then virtually every page hit after this first one will require data to be pulled from the database.

The developers with whom you are working are experienced with both Visual Basic and in writing active server pages. They have written applications in Visual Basic that use SQL Server, but have only limited experience in database-aware active server pages. They will be relying on you to decide on standards for database access.

ANALYSIS

Because this is a Web-based application, you could potentially have thousands of users requesting that queries be run all the time. In a traditional desktop environment, it is generally easier to predict a program's usage because the program can be run only on as many machines as it is installed on. With the Web-based Internet access that this application uses, you need to be very concerned with the efficiency of your queries because of the potential for high activity. With this in mind, you will certainly want to take advantage of the Stored Procedure model.

Using stored procedures would allow you to control queries to your database from SQL Server, which gives you centralized administration. More importantly, after the procedures are called, their

CASE STUDY: DEVELOPING A DATABASE-AWARE WEB SITE

execution plans will be stored in SQL Server's procedure cache for easy reuse. When the plans are stored in this manner, any reference to the database that requests this query will benefit from the cached plan.

You could instead choose to use prepared statements over stored procedures. The application is using OLE-DB for data access, which you know supports the capability to prepare a statement for reuse. After you have prepared the statement, you can reissue the query on your connection and reap the benefits of precompiled execution plans. In addition, the queries would be stored in the active server pages which are all executed from the Internet Information Server, which can also be centrally administered.

The tiebreaker is the caveat mentioned briefly in the discussion of prepared statements. After the query is prepared for execution, it can quickly be run on that connection. Web-based applications, however, do not maintain open connections against the database. Rather, when each user requests data by clicking a button on her browser, the Web server interprets this as an entirely new request for information. This is why Web applications are often called "stateless"— because there is no lasting information to determine the current state of the applications. Thus, if a prepared statement were used, every new user would prepare yet another version of the same procedure and run that. SQL Server would actually be able to interpret that the same query was being requested and would store the query only once, but the active server page would be wasting time and energy making needless requests. Because of this, you would almost certainly be best off placing all your queries in stored procedures and letting the Web requests call those.

CHAPTER SUMMARY

This chapter dealt with some of the issues involved with accessing SQL Server from client applications. You were introduced to the procedure cache, which saves optimized query execution plans for later reuse. You learned that you can use data access libraries such as ODBC and OLE-DB to prepare individual statements to guarantee plan reuse through the Stored Procedure model, and you learned that queries that are run infrequently through the Dynamic SQL model will not necessarily benefit from reuse.

You also have learned a little about the kinds of options you can set to control how your queries run on a particular connection. It is most important that you are aware what kinds of options are available to you than it is to memorize the nearly 40 commands that exist.

KEY TERMS

Before you take the exam, make sure you are comfortable with the definitions and concepts for each of the following key terms:

- Stored Procedure model
- dynamic SQL model
- prepared statement
- execution plan
- SET statement
- session
- session-level option

APPLY YOUR KNOWLEDGE

Exercises

10.1 Using Session-Level Options to Monitor Execution Plan Reuse

In this exercise you will use the SET STATISTICS TIME command to monitor the parse and compile time of a query. By issuing the same query twice, you will see the time required to parse and compile the query on the first run. Then, because of plan reuse, the second query will require very little time to parse and compile because the compilation will be skipped in favor of the cached plan.

Estimated Time: 10 minutes

1. Load the SQL Server Query Analyzer and log on to your server. From the DB drop-down box, choose the Northwind database.

2. Enter the following statement into the query window.

   ```
   SET STATISTICS TIME ON
   ```

3. All subsequent statements issued on your current connection, (from this query window), will return information listing the length of time it took to parse, compile, and execute each query.

   You should note that the SQL Server Query Analyzer sends additional information to SQL Server just before running your queries. Because of this, you will actually see multiple timing information being returned before the information about your query. Usually, this will consist of a parse and compile message followed by three execution time messages. The messages that relate to your query are the parse and compile message just before, and the execution time message just after, the query results.

Now that you have some idea of what to expect, enter the following query:

```
SELECT e.FirstName, e.LastName, od.ProductID,
➥s.CompanyName
FROM northwind.dbo.Employees e
JOIN northwind.dbo.Orders o
  ON o.EmployeeID = e.EmployeeID
JOIN northwind.dbo.[Order Details] od
  ON od.OrderID = o.OrderID
JOIN northwind.dbo.Products p
  ON p.ProductID = od.ProductID
JOIN northwind.dbo.Suppliers s
  ON s.SupplierID = p.SupplierID
```

4. Execute the query you have just entered. Remember that if you wish to execute only this query from a window containing many statements, you can highlight the query and the Query Analyzer will send only the highlighted text to SQL Server for execution. The results you see should resemble the following, though your numbers will certainly differ.

```
SQL Server parse and compile time:
   CPU time = 0 ms, elapsed time = 117 ms.

SQL Server Execution Times:
   CPU time = 0 ms,  elapsed time = 8 ms.

SQL Server Execution Times:
   CPU time = 0 ms,  elapsed time = 4 ms.

SQL Server Execution Times:
   CPU time = 0 ms,  elapsed time = 12 ms.
SQL Server parse and compile time:
   CPU time = 60 ms, elapsed time = 85137 ms.
FirstName LastName  ProductID  CompanyName
--------- --------  ---------  --------------------
Nancy     Davolio   2          Exotic Liquids
Nancy     Davolio   5          New Orleans Cajun
                               Delights
Nancy     Davolio   32         Formaggi Fortini s.r.
```

Only the first three lines of the results set are included here in the interest of brevity. Remember that the first four messages do not concern us; rather, you should examine the SQL Server parse and compile time: message just before the result set. In this case, the CPU time is 60 ms.

APPLY YOUR KNOWLEDGE

5. Scroll to the bottom of the result set and examine the output. You should see results similar to the following:

```
Anne    Dodsworth  21   Specialty Biscuits, Ltd.
Anne    Dodsworth  60   Gai pâturage
Anne    Dodsworth  61   Forêts d'érables

(2155 row(s) affected)

SQL Server Execution Times:
   CPU time = 410 ms,  elapsed time = 440020 ms.
```

Note that the execution time for the query is 410 ms.

6. Run the same query again so that you can compare results. The following is condensed version of the output you should expect for this second query.

```
SQL Server parse and compile time:
   CPU time = 0 ms, elapsed time = 25 ms.
FirstName LastName ProductID CompanyName
--------- -------- --------- ------------
Nancy     Davolio  2         Exotic Liquids
Nancy     Davolio  5         New Orleans
                             ➥Cajun Delights
Nancy     Davolio  32        Formaggi Fortini
                             ➥s.r.l.
```

Note that this time the CPU time is 0 ms. During the second execution, SQL Server was able to parse and compile the plan so quickly, that it could not accurately measure the time. Of course, this is because the query was matched to one already in the procedure cache so that no compilation was necessary.

7. Scroll to the bottom of the result set and examine the output. You should see results similar to the following:

```
Anne    Dodsworth  21   Specialty Biscuits, Ltd.
Anne    Dodsworth  60   Gai pâturage
Anne    Dodsworth  61   Forêts d'érables

(2155 row(s) affected)

SQL Server Execution Times:
   CPU time = 440 ms,  elapsed time = 445086 ms.
```

You should notice that although the query took less time to parse and compile, it still took approximately the same time to execute. This is logical because the query used the same plan to execute the query.

10.2 Examining How Stored Procedures Are Cached

This exercise will be similar to the preceding exercise in that you will use the SET STATISTICS TIME command to examine how a stored procedure is cached *after* it is run the first time.

10 minutes

1. Load the SQL Server Query Analyzer and log on to your server. From the DB drop-down box, choose the Northwind database.

2. First you need to create the stored procedure. The idea is just to create a stored procedure that will take a noticeable time to run, so the same query from the previous example will work well. Enter the following statement into the query window, and run it:

```
CREATE PROCEDURE TestProc
AS
SELECT e.FirstName, e.LastName, od.ProductID,
➥s.CompanyName
FROM northwind.dbo.Employees e
JOIN northwind.dbo.Orders o
  ON o.EmployeeID = e.EmployeeID
JOIN northwind.dbo.[Order Details] od
  ON od.OrderID = o.OrderID
JOIN northwind.dbo.Products p
  ON p.ProductID = od.ProductID
JOIN northwind.dbo.Suppliers s
  ON s.SupplierID = p.SupplierID
GO
```

3. After creating the procedure, you are ready to turn on the statistics. Enter the following statement and execute it.

```
SET STATISTICS TIME ON
```

APPLY YOUR KNOWLEDGE

4. Now you just need to run the procedure with the timing statistics on, and pay attention to the "parse and compile" number just before the result set. Execute the following statement to run the procedure:

```
EXECUTE TestProc
```

5. You should see a parse and compile time comparable to the one you received by running the non-cached query in the previous exercise. Here is an example of some of the results you might expect (again some leading results have been left off for the sake of brevity):

```
SQL Server parse and compile time:
   CPU time = 80 ms, elapsed time = 18810 ms.
FirstName LastName ProductID CompanyName
--------- -------- --------- -----------
Nancy     Davolio  2         Exotic Liquids
Nancy     Davolio  5         New Orleans
                             Cajun Delights
Nancy     Davolio  32        Formaggi Fortini
                             s.r.l.
```

6. When you execute the procedure again, you should see the CPU time number is reduced, possibly down to zero, as in this example:

```
SQL Server parse and compile time:
   CPU time = 0 ms, elapsed time = 21 ms.
FirstName LastName ProductID CompanyName
--------- -------- --------- -----------
Nancy     Davolio  2         Exotic Liquids
Nancy     Davolio  5         New Orleans
                             Cajun Delights
Nancy     Davolio  32        Formaggi Fortini
                             s.r.l.
```

Review Questions

1. What is the Dynamic SQL model?

2. What is the Stored Procedure model?

3. What is another term for a session?

4. What is the basic command for configuring session-level options?

5. What does SET STATISTICS TIME do?

6. What can you do to improve the odds of SQL Server matching your query to an existing execution plan?

7. What is a prepared statement?

8. What are two things that happen every time a query is compiled?

Exam Questions

1. When is an execution plan for a stored procedure cached? Select the best answer.

   A. When the procedure is created

   B. Whenever the procedure is run

   C. The first time the procedure is run

   D. The first time the procedure is run from a connection

2. Which of the following statements are true about the Stored Procedure model?

   A. SQL Server doesn't always need to compile execution plans.

   B. SQL Server doesn't always need to parse the queries.

   C. SQL Server creates temporary stored procedures to speed ad-hoc query processing.

   D. Users submit queries in a way to maximize execution plan reuse.

APPLY YOUR KNOWLEDGE

3. Joan is working on a client-server database application that uses OLE-DB to access SQL Server. In one area of the application she allows the user to search for a product by any of six different criteria. For three of the possible criteria, the query will have to join to other tables to gather the detail information it needs to match the user's input. This aspect of the program will probably be used only a few times a day for each user.

   She decides to write a stored procedure to which the six different criteria will be passed. In the stored procedure, she uses a series of IF statements to assemble a string that has all the needed clauses to form the query she needs. She then uses the EXECUTE statement to dynamically execute the ad-hoc query string.

   Which of the following best describes Joan's solution?

   A. This is an optimal solution. It uses the Stored Procedure model to execute the query, in order to maximize performance.

   B. This is a good solution. Although it is not able to make use of the Stored Procedure model, it does place the query-building code on the server for ease of maintenance.

   C. This is a poor solution. Although it will work, it deliberately overlooks ways to use the Stored Procedure model.

   D. This is not a solution. The query cannot be properly assembled and executed in this manner.

4. In what situations might the dynamic SQL model be advantageous?

   A. When ad-hoc queries must be assembled based on user input

   B. When a query will be run infrequently or perhaps once in an application

   C. When a query contains more than three join statements

   D. When a query must accept variable input to a parameter, such as a client ID

5. Which of the following statements is true about session-level options?

   A. Once set, the options remain in effect until the server is rebooted.

   B. The options can be used to control the settings of all users in a database.

   C. Once set, the options affect all queries sent on that connection.

   D. Once set, many options can be overridden by changing the equivalent database setting.

6. A consulting company considers all billing done on a weekend to count towards the previous week's total. When running reports, the employees use the Datepart function to return which week of the year to which any particular billing entry belongs. In order to force the days to fall into the correct billing period (the correct week of the year), they use the SET DATEFIRST session-level option to make Monday the first day of the week.

   A. This is an optimal solution. The data will be returned exactly as expected.

   B. This is a good solution. Although the correct information is returned, the output format for dates cannot be changed.

APPLY YOUR KNOWLEDGE

C. This is a bad solution. Although no errors are produced, the reports will return erroneous information.

D. This is not a solution. Date functions such as Datepart cannot be used when the DATEFIRST option is being used.

7. Sarah needs to return the square root of all the values in particular column of a table. This can be done by raising each value to the one-half power using the POWER function in SQL Server. She knows that it is possible that some of the values may be negative, however, and that it is mathematically impossible to take the square root of a negative number. She would like to be able to avoid this error, but she would also like to receive some warning that she does indeed have a bad data set.

Sarah decides to use the ARITHIGNORE option set to OFF so that she will receive warning messages when errors occur, and to use the absolute value function on the values before using the POWER function to prevent query from being halted by bad data.

A. This is an optimal solution to the problem. Errors will be avoided, and the ARITHIGNORE setting will generate warnings if any data is negative.

B. This is a good solution to the problem. Errors will be avoided, but no warnings will be generated.

C. This is a poor solution to the problem. Erroneous values could be introduced into the result set, and no errors will produced.

D. This is not a solution to the problem. No correct values will be produced.

8. Which of the following problems can be addressed by configuring a session-level option? Select all that apply.

A. Change the default input format of dates and time values.

B. Change all character-based output to uppercase.

C. Change the way NULL values are compared.

D. Change the color of the output displayed on the screen.

9. Which of the following problems can be addressed by configuring session-level options? Select all that apply.

A. Cause timing information to be returned for queries.

B. Insert ANSI compliance messages before your result set.

C. Reduce the amount of data returned from a field of text data type.

D. Associate a program to run that will interpret binary data.

10. In what situations might you favor the dynamic SQL model?

A. When executing infrequently run queries

B. When executing queries with known parameter lists

C. When executing ad-hoc queries that perform joins based on user-input

D. When executing queries with long WHERE clauses

Answers to Review Questions

1. The dynamic SQL model defines a situation in which queries are sent to SQL Server with no regard to whether an execution plan for the query exists in the procedure cache. (For more information, refer to the section "Dynamic SQL Model.")

2. The Stored Procedure model defines a situation in which queries are sent to SQL Server with the expectation that the execution plan exists in the procedure cache and it can be reused. (For more information, refer to the section "Stored Procedure Model.")

3. Sessions are defined by the scope of a single connection to SQL Server. (For more information, refer to the section "Configuring Session-Level Options.")

4. Session-level options are set through the use of the SET command. (For more information, refer to the section "Configuring Session-Level Options.")

5. The SET STATISTICS TIME command causes SQL Server to return information about the length of time necessary to process queries. Information is returned about both the parse and compile time and the time to execute the query. (For more information, refer to the section "Statistics Statements.")

6. SQL Server prefers to receive queries built with objects specified with fully qualified names. SQL Server is more likely to match a query to its execution plan if it sees object names built in the fully qualified name format of database, owner, then object name. (For more information, refer to the section "Dynamic SQL Model.")

7. A prepared statement is a query that has been sent to SQL Server with instructions to compile and store the execution plan for the statement. The execution plan can then be invoked repeatedly to execute the query without compiling it first. (For more information, refer to the section "Stored Procedure Model.")

8. Every time a query is sent to SQL Server, either the query is matched to an existing execution plan, or the query is compiled to create a new execution plan and that plan is stored for future reference. (For more information, refer to the section "Dynamic SQL Model.")

Answers to Exam Questions

1. **C.** A stored procedure's execution plan is created the first time the procedure is run. The execution plan is not recompiled every time the procedure is run; after a plan is created, it can be reused by any other user through any other connection. (For more information, refer to the section "Dynamic Model versus Stored Procedure Model.")

2. **A, D.** In the Stored Procedure model, queries are sent to SQL Server in such a way that the query can be matched to an execution plan, if one exists, without fail. Because of this, a query may not need to be compiled. (For more information, refer to the section "Stored Procedure Model.")

APPLY YOUR KNOWLEDGE

3. **B.** The solution proposed does not truly use the Stored Procedure model because the data gathering query is executed dynamically from inside the procedure. The procedure cannot maintain an execution plan for a query that is assembled and run at execution time. However, the solution does not take this approach at the expense of an obviously better solution because the query is dynamic by nature and cannot be predetermined. (For more information, refer to the section "Dynamic Model versus Stored Procedure Model.")

4. **A, B.** Ad-hoc or infrequently run queries often benefit by being run without special preparations because the overhead of preparations is often high enough to offset the benefits of plan reuse when the query is run few times. The complexity, including the number of its joins, of a query should not be considered a barrier to the Stored Procedure model. Prepared statements and stored procedures alike can use parameters to supply simple variable input. (For more information, refer to the section "Dynamic Model versus Stored Procedure Model.")

5. **C.** Session-level options affect only the connection from which they were issued. Session-level options do not affect the entire server or other users of a database. Both server and database options can be overridden with session-level options. (For more information, refer to the section "Configuring Session-Level Options.")

6. **A.** This is an optimal solution. By changing SQL Server's understanding of the first day of the week, queries can be built to return billing information grouped by the same week using the DatePart function. The DATEFIRST session-level option has no affect on the formatting of dates. (For more information, refer to the section "Date and Time Statements.")

7. **C.** This is a poor solution to the problem. By changing all values to the absolute value, all arithmetic errors from taking the square root of a negative number will be avoided because there will be no negative number. This not only hides warning messages that Sarah would like to see, but it also results in square root values being returned for made-up values. All negative values will be changed, and then the square root function will be applied to the bogus values without informing the user which values are erroneous. A better solution to this problem would be to set ARITHABORT to OFF during the query so that the bad values would not halt the query, but the ARITHIGNORE setting would still generate a helpful warning message. (For more information, refer to the section "Query Execution Statements.")

8. **A, C.** The DATEFORMAT session-level option will change the default input format for date and time values, and the ANSI_NULLS option affects the way null comparisons are made. There are no options to automatically cause all character output to be returned in upper case or to affect the colors of output in your query tool. (For more information, refer to the section "Session-Level Options.")

9. **A, B, C.** The STATISTICS TIME option will return timing information about a query. The ANSI_WARNINGS option will return warnings if statements violate ANSI standards compliance. The TEXTSIZE option controls the maximum size of text data that will be returned from queries. (For more information, refer to the section "Configuring Session-Level Options.")

10. **A, C.** Dynamic queries are best used for infrequent queries or those that must involve different tables at run time. A lengthy WHERE clause need not have any adverse affect on using the Stored

APPLY YOUR KNOWLEDGE

Procedure model as long as it is static. Both stored procedures and prepared statements can take parameter lists as long as the list is well

defined and does not change the number of elements on an ad-hoc basis. (For more information, refer to the section "Dynamic SQL Model.")

Suggested Readings and Resources

We recommend the following resources for further study in the area of planning:

1. SQL Server Books Online

    • Server Enchancements—section "Stored Procedures"

• Execution Plan Caching and Reuse
• Transact-SQL Reference—see the "SET" statement

This chapter helps you prepare for the Microsoft exam by covering the following objectives:

Evaluate and optimize the performance of an execution plan by using DBCC SHOWCONTIG, SHOWPLAN_TEXT, SHOWPLAN_ALL, and UPDATE STATISTICS.

▶ This objective lists specific tools you should be familiar with before taking the test. Learn how to use these commands and how to interpret their results.

Evaluate and optimize the performance of query execution plans.

▶ You should be familiar with query execution plans and how to interpret them. In particular, you will need to be able to create and examine a graphical query plan and identify operations within the plan that could be improved.

Diagnose and resolve locking problems.

▶ It is possible for applications to lock portions of your database and hold them for extended periods of time. As a certified professional, you should be able to identify these situations and be able to fix them.

Identify SQL Server events and performance problems by using SQL Server Profiler.

▶ The SQL Server Profiler is a new tool in SQL Server, so it is important to know what it can do for you. It monitors predefined events that occur in SQL Server, and reports information about those events to you.

CHAPTER 11

Maintaining a Database

▶ The most important information to gain from this chapter is an understanding of the way that the SQL Server Query Optimizer works through the study of execution plans. You will want to be very familiar with the ideas of physical and logical operators and how they can be used to construct a flow chart that describes the processing of your query.

Because the test objectives explicitly mention the DBCC SHOWCONTIG and the UPDATE STATISTICS commands, you'll certainly want to be familiar with them before attempting to take the test.

Understand the use of the SQL Server Profiler for monitoring activity on SQL Server. Learn all of the event categories that the Profiler can monitor and be at least casually familiar with the events in each category.

INTRODUCTION

Handling the design and implementation of a database in SQL Server is only part of a database developer's role. Because applications are built to use the database, you will need to be able to support the database-related issues of software design. If the application developers feel that their queries are running too slowly, or that your database server is dropping their connections "for no good reason," you should be able to negotiate on SQL Server's behalf. As a certified professional you will need to be able to find out from SQL Server how the queries are being handled and why connections are being dropped. You can then add needed indexes, suggest query changes, and point to long-running transactions in the application that cause other connections to time out. You should be able to work with the developers to effect changes in both the database and the application to allow both to work well together.

In this chapter you will learn to examine the execution plans that SQL Server builds for the queries you issue, how to identify locking problems, and how to monitor SQL Server's activities. By examining the execution plans that SQL Server builds, you can learn to optimize the queries being sent so that SQL Server will appear to run faster and more efficiently. Identifying locking problems will allow you to explain to users and developers alike why their connections appear to freeze up or are dropped altogether. Finally, by monitoring activity on the server itself, you can hope to spot problems that are occurring so that you can better identify other reasons why the server seems to run slowly or connections are being dropped.

CREATING, EXAMINING, AND OPTIMIZING EXECUTION PLANS

▶ Evaluate and optimize the performance of an execution plan by using DBCC SHOWCONTIG, SHOWPLAN_TEXT, SHOWPLAN_ALL, and UPDATE STATISTICS.

▶ Evaluate and optimize the performance of query execution plans.

A common activity of an advanced SQL Server developer is optimizing queries. For the most part, you must trust that the Database Administrator for your server is keeping the server's performance optimized. If you find queries that are performing poorly, you must first assume that the fault is in your table design or the queries themselves, before assuming that your server is running poorly. To this end, SQL Server provides the ability to produce the execution plan for a given query, so that you can see what steps SQL Server is taking to process your requests. You should be able to use the SQL Server tools to generate these execution plans and interpret them. You should also be able to recognize situations in which a query plan can be improved and those in which the query is executing optimally.

As was just stated, SQL Server provides the ability to output a query's execution plan. The *execution plan* describes the steps that SQL Server takes in order to process a query. These steps describe every join in a query and how individual rows are found in tables. There are more than sixty different operations that SQL Server can perform during the course of a query. These operations include every join strategy, row lookup, and more. There are too many operations to effectively list them all here, so the common ones will be presented.

After examining the plans, you will be introduced to some things you can do to optimize your queries. You will learn what to look for in a table or index that could be causing SQL Server to work inefficiently. Using these procedures will allow you to correct problems in both your queries and your database itself.

Create a Graphical Execution Plan

A graphical execution plan is normally displayed using the SQL Query Analyzer. You already have used the Query Analyzer for many examples throughout this book to issue queries and examine the results. You can also use the Query Analyzer to request that SQL Server return execution plan information. The Query Analyzer is capable of interpreting the execution plan information and displaying it in a graphical form, which is easy to read and interpret. Every operation that SQL Server performs is represented as an icon in this graphical plan, and arrows are drawn to denote the logical processing flow.

This concept is best understood by generating a graphical execution plan for yourself. Step by Step 11.1 guides you through the process of generating a graphical execution plan on a simple three-table join.

STEP BY STEP

11.1 Generating a Graphical Execution Plan

1. Load the SQL Server Query Analyzer and log on to your server. From the DB drop-down box choose the Pubs database.

2. Enter the following query into the query window:

```
select top 10 a.au_id, t.title_id
from authors a
join titleauthor ta
  on ta.au_id = a.au_id
left join titles t
  on t.title_id = ta.title_id
```

3. The Query Analyzer can either estimate an execution plan or can be set to actually run the query and return the actual execution plan. First, estimate an execution plan.

To the right of the database drop-down box is a button with a short flowchart pictured on it. The tool-tip for this button reads Display Estimated Execution Plan. Either click this button or press Ctrl + L to display the estimated execution plan.

4. Instead of the normal Results tab at the bottom of the query window, you will be presented with the Estimated Execution Plan tab, where you will see the graphical execution plan, which should be similar to the one in Figure 11.1.

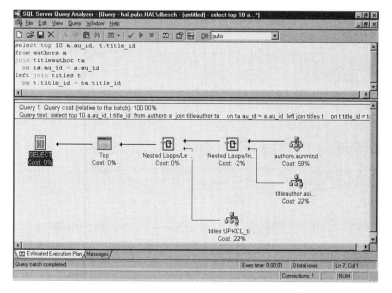

FIGURE 11.1
A graphical execution plan on a three-table join query.

continues

continued

---

5. To actually run the query, you must set the query mode. Hover your mouse over the toolbar buttons until you find the one with a tool-tip that reads Query Mode. Click the small down arrow to the right of the button, and choose Show Execution Plan. Then either click the Execute Query button, or press Ctrl + E to execute the query and show the execution plan.

---

6. This time, you will be presented with both a Results tab and an Execution Plan tab.

Create a Textual Execution Plan

Any query tool can request a textual execution plan. Although special logic must be included to interpret an execution plan and display a graphical representation of it, SQL Server will return a text-based execution plan to any query tool. If you find yourself in a situation in which SQL Server Query Analyzer is not available, the text-based plans are a viable alternative to the graphical plans. The execution plan that SQL Server returns is in a tabular format. There is a single row in the result table for every operation SQL Server must perform to execute the query. There are two levels of detail that you can request an execution plan for. The simplest level of detail returns only a description column detailing the steps taken by the query. If you request the higher level of detail, additional detail columns will be returned. These levels of detail are called upon through the SET SHOWPLAN_TEXT and the SET SHOWPLAN_ALL commands for low and high detail, respectively.

Using SHOWPLAN_TEXT

The SET SHOWPLAN_TEXT statement has two settings: ON and OFF. This statement must be run in its own batch; therefore, it must be followed by the batch terminator (the GO command). Step by Step 11.2 illustrates an execution plan using SET SHOWPLAN_TEXT.

STEP BY STEP

11.2 Generating a Textual Execution Plan Using SET SHOWPLAN_TEXT

1. Load the SQL Server Query Analyzer and log on to your server. From the DB drop-down box choose the Pubs database.

2. Enter the following query into the query window:

```
SET SHOWPlAN_TEXT ON
GO
SELECT TOP 10 a.au_id, t.title_id
FROM Authors a
JOIN TitleAuthor ta
  ON ta.au_id = a.au_id
LEFT JOIN Titles t
  ON t.title_id = ta.title_id
GO
SET SHOWPLAN_TEXT OFF
GO
```

3. The result set from the query will be displayed in the Results tab as shown in Figure 1 1.2.

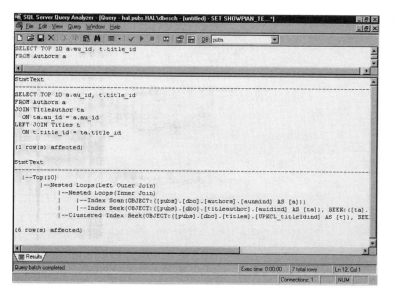

FIGURE 11.2

A text-based execution plan for a simple query.

Using SHOWPLAN_ALL

Using SET SHOWPLAN ALL causes SQL Server to return more detailed information on the execution plan it uses to run your queries than it does for SET SHOWPLAN TEXT. Similarly to SET SHOWPLAN_TEXT, the SET SHOWPLAN_ALL statement has two settings: ON and OFF. This statement must also be run in its own batch; therefore, it must be followed by the batch terminator (the GO command). Step by Step 11.3 illustrates an execution plan using SET SHOWPLAN_ALL.

STEP BY STEP

11.3 Generating a Textual Execution Plan Using SET SHOWPLAN_ALL

1. Load the SQL Server Query Analyzer and log on to your server. From the DB drop-down box choose the Pubs database.

2. Enter the following query into the query window:

```
SET SHOWPLAN_ALL ON
GO
SELECT TOP 10 a.au_id, t.title_id
FROM Authors a
JOIN TitleAuthor ta
  ON ta.au_id = a.au_id
LEFT JOIN Titles t
  ON t.title_id = ta.title_id
GO
SET SHOWPLAN_ALL OFF
GO
```

3. The result set from the query will be displayed in the Results tab.

   The SHOWPLAN_ALL statement causes more detail to be displayed than the previous SHOWPLAN_TEXT statement in Step by Step 11.2. This detail is shown in Figure 11.3. Notice that the Results tab is scrolled to the right to display the addition fields.

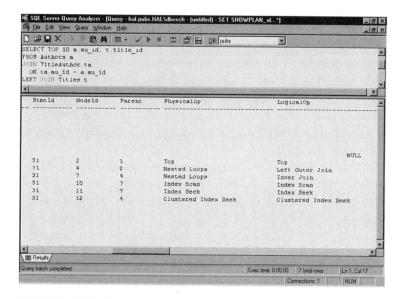

FIGURE 11.3
The detail columns of a text-based execution plan for a simple query.

Examine an Execution Plan

Now that you have seen how to generate a query execution plan, you will want to learn more about how to interpret the data it gives you. As was stated earlier, there are over 60 operations that SQL Server may need to perform to accomplish your query. This is too many to examine in detail here. Instead, you will receive an overview of the types of operations that SQL Server routinely performs, so that you can quickly recognize when your query is bound by an expensive operation. Refer to the SQL Server Books Online for a complete listing of all physical and logical operators.

Physical and Logical Operators

When examining an execution plan, you will encounter both logical and physical operators. *Physical operators* describe the actual operation that takes place, and *logical operators* represent different methods of accomplishing the physical operation. In many cases the physical operator is also a logical operator. Physical operators tell you generally what SQL Server is doing, and logical operators can specify more precisely how SQL Server accomplishes the task.

Scans, Seeks, and Spools

There are several physical *scan* operators, including table scans, index scans, and clustered index scans. Each scan is both a physical and logical operator. In each case, a scan indicates that SQL Server will read from the beginning of the object straight through to the end. Scanning indexes can yield two benefits for SQL Server. Because indexes generally cover fewer columns than are in the table, more index rows can often fit on a single page than table data rows. Therefore, if the data being sought is included in columns found in an index, SQL Server can scan the smaller data set of the index rather than searching through the larger data set of the entire table. In addition, when SQL Server scans an index, it can choose to follow the index tree in order, which can result in ordered output. This saves the effort of a separate sort operation in a query with an ORDER BY clause.

A *seek* operation takes place only on an index. A seek utilizes the index to quickly find specific rows. A seek operation can take place in response to a WHERE clause that requires specific rows, or to find matching rows in response to a join operation.

Similar to a scan is the *spool* operation. A spool reads all rows from the object; however, as it reads them the first time, they are stored in a hidden location in tempdb database. This worktable in tempdb is discarded immediately after the query, and cannot be referenced by any other process. After the first pass, SQL Server will refer to this spooled data instead of reading directly from the object.

There are three physical spool operators:

◆ Table spool

◆ Index spool

◆ Row count spool

Both *table spools* and *index spools* return columns from the object, but a *row count spool* returns only the number of rows that match its conditions. As a table is spooled, SQL Server stores in tempdb only the columns that will be needed, which reduces the amount of data that will need to be scanned. An index spool will also create an index on the spooled rows to aid in later scans.

Each of these physical operators can use either of two logical operators: eager spool and lazy spool. An *eager spool* will consume the entire table immediately, whereas a *lazy spool* reads only one row from the table when requested, in the hopes that the next row will be the one needed, and the entire input will not need to be consumed.

Join Operators

There are three physical join operators:

- ◆ Nested loops
- ◆ Merge join
- ◆ Hash match

The *nested loops* operator is the simplest one to understand. In a nested loops operation, the first (outer) object is scanned one row at a time. Then the second (inner) object is searched repeatedly for matching rows.

In a *merge join*, both inputs are required to be sorted on the merge column (as defined by the equality clauses in the join). A merge join operation can exploit the sorted nature of the inputs to search both inputs at the same time, knowing that wherever non-matching rows are found, the lower value can be safely discarded because no match for that row can exist in the other input. Note that a merge join does not guarantee a single pass through each input because in a Many-to-Many or inequality relationship, one of the inputs will have to be rewound to the start of the duplicates after finding all matches for one row.

A *hash match* has two inputs: a *build input* (the smaller table) and a *probe input* (the larger table). Like merge joins, hash joins can be used only if there are one or more columns equated between the two tables. However, because most joins are used to reconstruct relationships, this is often the case. The entire build input is scanned and the join columns assembled into a hash key using a deterministic algorithm. The hash key values are then grouped together with like values into hash buckets. The hash buckets are kept in memory or in temporary tables if the build input is very large. In the second phase of the join, the probe input is scanned and each join column(s) assembled into a hash key. The hash bucket for this key is scanned, and matches are produced.

There are three types of hash joins used. The first is an *in-memory hash*, in which the hash buckets from the build input all fit in memory. The second is a *grace hash join*, in which the build input is divided into partitions that each fit into memory and are joined in separate operations. The third is a *recursive hash join*, in which the build input is so large that sub-partitions must be made to fit into memory. This can lead to an error known as a *hash bail*, in which the recursive limit is reached and SQL Server must find an alternate way to process the remaining data. This usually results from skewed input data.

Optimize an Execution Plan

After you have evaluated an execution plan, you will want to optimize it. Optimization is more of an art than a science, but there are still several rules of thumb you can follow. First, scans and spools are generally inferior to seek operations. Keep in mind, however, that some join operations require at least one scan or spool. For instance, a nested loops operation must scan the outer object, unless there is a predicate in the WHERE clause that restricts the outer rows enough to warrant an indexed seek. Therefore, you should carefully consider scans and spools, but do not automatically disregard them.

Be especially careful when a physical index spool is being used. This indicates that SQL Server is so convinced that an index would be useful to the join that it would rather build an index and throw it away afterwards rather than try to join without one. If the query causing this will be run repeatedly, an index may very likely be justified.

If a table involved in a scan or spool operation has an index on the columns being scanned, there may be a problem with that index. A common issue here is that the table is simply too small for an index to be useful. If a table has less than one page of data, it will almost always be more efficient to read all the data than it would be to trace through an index. If this is not the case, however, there are other causes you can investigate. As data is updated in a table, the changes are rarely applied evenly across all pages. There will often tend to be places in which more data was deleted than was inserted and vice versa. When this happens, your data will become somewhat fragmented, making it more difficult for SQL Server to read. SQL Server also maintains detailed statistics on indexes that tend to lose relevance over time. If the statistics are out of date, SQL Server can use, or not use, that index inappropriately. Fortunately, there are commands that you can use to investigate such problems so that they may be corrected. These commands are discussed in the following sections.

Using DBCC SHOWCONTIG

The DBCC command is the *DataBase Consistency Checker*. This command has many options to detect problems in your databases. An important one is DBCC SHOWCONTIG. This command will scan a table or index and report how densely packed the data is. If the data is very sparse, then SQL Server will have to read more pages to get all the data. The following details the syntax for this command:

```
DBCC SHOWCONTIG [(table_id [, index_id])]
```

As you can see, both the table and index arguments are optional. If no table is specified, all indexes on all tables will be reported. If a table is specified without an index, all indexes on that table will be reported. A table must be specified before an index may be used. If both table and index arguments are supplied, then only the one index on the table will be checked. Note that both table and index must be specified by their IDs, and that a table without a clustered index will have an index with an ID of zero (0), representing the data itself.

The DBCC SHOWCONTIG command outputs nine different pieces of information, but there are three that are of particular importance. The first of these three is *Scan Density*. This row displays a percentage representing the average density of the data, as well as two numbers representing the best possible number of extent changes, and the actual number of extent changes. An extent change occurs when SQL Server finished scanning one extent and must read in another. If the density is very low, or the difference between actual count and best count is very high, your data could be more tightly compacted to save space, and to give SQL Server less space to look through.

The other two key rows are *Logical Scan Fragmentation* and *Extent Scan Fragmentation*. These rows are only relevant when scanning indexes or a table with a clustered index. A high fragmentation indicates that the data is not held in contiguous locations on the physical media (disk drives). This fragmentation makes it more difficult to retrieve the next page needed as the data is searched.

NOTE

Use the OBJECT_ID Function to Get the ID of a Table The DBCC SHOWCONTIG command requires the objectid of a table. This ID is stored in the sysobjects system table found in every database. An easier way to obtain it, however, is simply to use the OBJECT_ID function SQL Server provides.

If you suspect that your data is too sparse or too highly fragmented, you can cause the data to be reorganized correctly by dropping and recreating the index in question. A shortcut to accomplish this is the DBCC DBREINDEX command, which can be given a table name and an index name to drop and rebuild in a single step.

Using UPDATE STATISTICS

SQL Server maintains information about how "selective" an index is. This tells SQL Server how much duplicate information is contained in the index, which lets SQL Server determine how quickly the index will help it narrow down its search. As data is changed in the table, this information can become obsolete and misleading. SQL Server will normally recalculate these statistics periodically and keep the information up to date, but this option can be disabled for performance reasons. Therefore, to force an immediate recalculation of the statistics, you can use the UPDATE STATISTICS command.

```
UPDATE STATISTICS table
        [
                index
        ]
        [       WITH
                [
                        [FULLSCAN]
                        ¦ SAMPLE number {PERCENT ¦ ROWS}]
                ]
                [[,] NORECOMPUTE]
        ]
```

You must specify a table in the current database for the UPDATE STATISTICS command. If you chose to specify an index name, only that index will be affected. You can omit an index name to recompute statistics for all indexes. After the WITH keyword you can request that either all the data be examined to guarantee accurate statistics or that only a random sampling be taken to increase performance, by specifying the FULLSCAN or SAMPLE keyword.

If you want to disable automatic statistics gathering on an index or table, you can also use the NORECOMPUTE keyword after the WITH keyword. This can improve performance when you know that a table is rarely, or never, updated.

Execution Plans

In the preceding sections you learned a great deal about execution plans. First, you learned how to create the execution plans. SQL Server can always be requested to output a execution plan in tabular format, but a special tool such as SQL Server Query Analyzer can be used to interpret the tabular execution plan and display it graphically for better readability. Second, you were introduced to the kinds of operators that SQL Server lists in its execution plans. You learned to differentiate between a scan, a seek, and a spool operation when SQL Server is reading a table, and you were introduced to join operations. Finally, you studied optimization strategies. You learned how to discover if a table or index has become fragmented and how to reorganize the table or index if it has. Now you can also keep index statistics up-to-date manually with the UPDATE STATISTICS command.

In the next section, you learn to deal with common locking problems in a database. The section discusses both how to recognize when such locking problems exist and what to do about them.

DIAGNOSING AND RESOLVING LOCKING PROBLEMS

▶ Diagnose and resolve locking problems.

Part of the day-to-day job of a SQL Server database operator is simply to be around and able to respond in case problems arise. One of the more common problems that can occur and will prevent users from working with the server results from improper locking of data. The most serious issue with this problem is that it cannot always be predicted. Any user with adequate permissions to update data can cause a locking problem at any time. The user must only begin a transaction, update the data, and then never complete the transaction. The locks held by this action can prevent other users from accessing the data. A detailed explanation of locking issues is found in Chapter 8, "Programmability."

The important thing to learn from this section is how to recognize the existence of a locking problem and how to fix it. You will probably first learn that a locking problem exists when a user informs you that he issued a query and his connection either timed out or froze up. The user was most likely prevented from accessing data by locks being held by another user. Locks are primarily placed by data modification queries and are held until the end of such a query. A query that takes an excessive time to run can hold these locks long enough to block others' access to the locked data. In addition, a query run inside a transaction cannot be fully committed until the end of the transaction. Therefore, if a user forgets to close the transaction or simply holds it open for an extended period of time, the locks can be held long enough to interfere with other users.

The first thing you will want to check is whether any processes are being blocked by the locks held by another process. You can determine if any process is being blocked by running the sp_who stored procedure. The sp_who stored procedure lists all connections on the server by their process identifiers. This *process identifier* is known as a *spid*. It also lists a column labeled blk, which will contain the spid of another process that is blocking the process in question. Normally the blk column will list only zeros, indicating that all processes are proceeding normally. When the blk column is non-zero, then there may be a serious locking problem. By examining the login name, host name, the name of the database that the blocking process is in, you must determine whether the process is acting appropriately or not. If it is acting inappropriately, you can ask the user controlling the connection to halt its operation and free the locks. If the user is unable to do so, you have another command that can force the process to terminate: KILL. Simply issue the command KILL followed by the spid of the offending process, and SQL Server will halt the process immediately.

Keep in mind that a "killed" process must roll back any changes that it could not complete. This rollback cannot be prevented, nor stopped prematurely. If a considerable amount of data was changed, the rollback can take several minutes to complete. No locks can be freed until the rollback is finished.

Using SQL Server Profiler

▶ Identify SQL Server events and performance problems by using SQL Server Profiler.

SQL Server Profiler is an important tool for monitoring activity on SQL Server. The Profiler allows you to specify the kinds of activity you would like to monitor, and then records all actions that take place on the server that meet your criteria. With SQL Server Profiler, you can monitor most or all activity during a stress test of your server, or monitor just the activity from one user, or one application during a program test. You can even define high standards to record any statement meeting certain criteria that is ever run on your server. These criteria should be held to a high enough standard, however, to avoid recording more data than can be easily examined.

SQL Server Profiler exposes events that represent certain types of activity on the server. You can define *traces* on these events that will record to command or commands that cause the events you choose. This section will discuss the events that can be monitored and the performance problems that the events may indicate.

The *Cursors* event category can be used to monitor cursors being used on your server. Specifically, you can monitor when cursors are opened, closed, defined, and undefined among others. If a user is having trouble with a cursor, you can use SQL Server Profiler to capture all the commands issued dealing with the cursor so that it can be determined what commands may be missing or malformed and causing problems.

The *Error and Warning* event category allows you to monitor possible error conditions so that you know right away when problems occur. You can monitor events such as errors being written to the SQL Server error log or the NT Application Log, warnings and exceptions that occur to users from SQL Server, and selected warnings that could indicate malformed queries. In particular, there are events that indicate hash joins that were too large for SQL Server to handle, unrestricted join statements, and missing column or index statistics. Although none of these events are necessarily bad, they indicate queries that could likely be improved with careful optimization.

The *Locks* event category is normally used either to monitor the locking behavior of a single process or to warn of more serious problems occurring anywhere on the server. The acquisition and release of individual locks is normally monitored only for a single process, or for all processes from a single application or user because these events fire so frequently. It can be useful to monitor any occurrence of a deadlock, however, because this is a situation in which SQL Server is forced to terminate a process to resolve the situation. Similarly, you can monitor any occurrence when a process times out waiting to access locked data. Deadlocks and similar locking issues are detailed in Chapter 8.

The *Misc.* event category contains many interesting, but usually not dangerous, events. There is an event that fires anytime SQL Server automatically generates statistics, and others that indicate that a login failed or that someone has requested an execution plan. There are even events that fire any time a SQL Query is prepared or unprepared. Events in this category are normally traced only when tracking down a particular problem with an application or a user.

The *Objects* event category is easily defined. A different event exists to track every time an object is opened, closed, created, or deleted. These events occur very often on even a moderately busy server, so tracing these events can lead to excessive overhead on the server and very large trace files.

The *Scans* event category contains events that fire whenever a table or index scan is begun or stopped. It was noted earlier in this chapter that scans often result from a poor query, or a lack of needed indexes. This event category therefore lets you identify that potentially slow queries are being executed. This is another category that can easily overwhelm a busy server.

The *Sessions* event category is used to track user connections on a server. Any time a connection is established or closed, the event can be monitored. There is also an event that will fire whenever there is activity on an existing connection.

The *SQL Operators* event category contains an event for SELECT, INSERT, UPDATE, and DELETE statements. Whenever one of these SQL operators is executed, the appropriate event is fired.

The *Stored Procedures* event category contains two different kinds of events relating to stored procedures. There are events that monitor procedure cache activity and events that monitor procedure execution. Those that monitor cache activity allow you to judge how often stored procedures are found in memory and how often they need to be recompiled to satisfy a user request. If many, or even most, stored procedures need to be re-cached every time they are run, you may need to increase the amount of memory assigned to SQL Server (therefore increasing the size of procedure cache).

The *Transactions* event category tracks transaction usage. One event is fired every time a transaction takes place that is controlled by the Distributed Transaction Coordinator. Another monitors all SQL transactions, and a third event fires every time a transaction of any kind is written to the transaction log.

The *TSQL* event category can track the beginning or end of remote procedure calls, TSQL statements, or batches. The events in this category can yield a great amount of detail on a particular connection. You should note that these events can track the exact SQL commands that SQL Server is receiving. The particular data access library that you are using to communicate with SQL Server will often include additional commands to configure your connection. By tracking the exact SQL commands that were sent, you may be able to spot an error that you didn't even realize was happening.

The *User-configurable* event category has five identical events that are fired through deliberate user actions. These events are activated when the xp_trace_generate_event extended stored procedure is run. This extended stored procedure specifies which of the five events should be fired, giving the programmer complete control over this category. These events can allow user applications to communicate directly to the SQL Server Profiler for specific debugging purposes.

Running a Simple Trace

Now that you have learned about what you can trace and how you can use that information, you should practice that knowledge by creating a simple trace. In Step by Step 11.4, you will be guided through the steps to create a generic trace. It will be up to you to decide what events you want to experiment with. This example will provide the framework so that you can use and learn many different events.

STEP BY STEP

11.4 Running a Generic Trace

1. Load the SQL Server Profiler tool. In the File menu choose New and then Trace. This will display the Trace Properties dialog box, which you can use to enter all the information you need to define a trace.

continues

continued

2. The Trace Properties dialog box will initially be set to the General tab. In the Trace Name text box, enter a name for the trace. To begin with, Sample Trace will do fine.

3. Choose the server that you want to trace from the SQL Server drop-down box. Note that you have to ability to record the information that the trace captures to a file or a table. You should not need to use either option for a test case such as this, however.

4. Change to the Events tab to choose the events that you want to trace. You will see all the available events grouped in the event categories described earlier in the section. Use the Add and Remove buttons to choose the events to trace.

5. You should not need to change any setting in the Data Columns tab; instead proceed directly to the Filters tab. Here you can limit the events to those that happen to a particular database, user, or even connection. Examine the list and enter values appropriate for the selection.

6. Click OK to complete the dialog and begin the trace.

CASE STUDY: PROFILING PERFORMANCE PROBLEMS

ESSENCE OF THE CASE

Here are the essential elements in this case:

▶ You are noticing slow performance on a Web site that uses stored procedures to pull data from a SQL Server 7.0 database.

▶ None of the stored procedures take longer than six seconds to run during your tests.

▶ The Web pages in question do not work of any significance other than run the stored procedures and display the results.

SCENARIO

Your company has just redesigned its intranet Web site that allows employees to find information about the company. This redesign has made the site extremely database driven. Rather than running static reports every month and simply displaying them, the site will actually pull live data and generate reports detailing the company's production and productivity information, and even let individual employees query their vacation balance.

Unfortunately the performance of the Web site isn't quite as good as you had hoped. You wrote most of the stored procedures that the application uses to get data from the database and you

CASE STUDY: PROFILING PERFORMANCE PROBLEMS

know that they ran pretty well. Your mandate is to get at a minimum ten-second response time on every report. The site developers tell you that they simply run the stored procedures and then output the data on the final report pages, and they know there is nothing they can do to speed that up.

Naturally, you go back and review your stored procedures. You run them interactively through the SQL Server Query Analyzer to test them, and quickly find that the procedures run in far less than 10 seconds. You even run execution plans for some of the slower queries and are able to improve them somewhat, but although some of your stored procedures take five to six seconds to run, none take longer than this. Nonetheless, when you run the Web pages, you are still receiving 11- to 12-second response times on the slower pages.

ANALYSIS

Certainly, there is something happening that you have not been told about. In all your testing of the stored procedures you know that they can't be behaving quite so poorly as the Web page performance indicates. What you realize is that you have tested the speed of the stored procedures independently, but you don't really know how long they take when run from the scripted code in the Web page. There is no reason to believe the time

to run the procedures would be any different, but the only way to vindicate your procedures would be to show exactly how long they take to run from the Web page.

To accomplish this, you can use SQL Server Profiler. The Profiler tool can monitor all TSQL batches that are executed from a particular application, in this case the active server page running on the internet information server that hosts the Web page. When you run this trace, you will obtain the information you were looking for. You will receive information detailing the length of time it took for your stored procedures to run.

It is also worth noting that this approach might yield results you did not expect. This author came across a similar problem and found that every time the Web page was displayed, the stored procedures were being run twice! With this information to guide them, the site developers were able to find that they were reading the entire result set to determine the number of rows returned and then attempting to reset the cursor to the first row. Unfortunately, they were using a forward-only, server-based result set (the principle is the same as using a forward-only cursor in TSQL as described in Chapter 8). The Data Access layer being used, ADO (Advanced Data Objects), responded to the move-first command on a forward-only result set by reissuing the query from scratch. Thus, Web pages were taking twice as long to process as they should have.

CHAPTER SUMMARY

KEY TERMS

Before you take the exam, make sure you are comfortable with the definitions and concepts for each of the following key terms:

- execution plan
- SET SHOWPLAN_ALL
- SET SHOWPLAN_TEXT
- UPDATE STATISTICS
- DBCC SHOWCONTIG
- graphical execution plan
- Logical Operators
- Physical Operators
- SQL Server Events

The information in this chapter should allow you to keep your database in an optimized condition on an ongoing basis. If problems arise after several months of use, you should be able to evaluate queries to determine if they are still using optimized execution plans, tables to determine if they have become heavily fragmented, and indexes to ensure that their statistics are up to date. You can also use the SQL Server Profiler to monitor the activity on your server periodically to alert you to long-running queries and warn you of repeated deadlocking or other problems.

APPLY YOUR KNOWLEDGE

Exercises

11.1 Generating an Execution Plan Using SET SHOWPLANALL

In this exercise you will generate an execution plan using the SET SHOWPLAN ALL command.

Estimated Time: 10 minutes

1. Load the SQL Server Query Analyzer and log on to your server. From the DB drop-down box choose the Northwind database.

2. Enter the following query into the query window:

```
SET SHOWPLAN_ALL ON
GO
SELECT e.FirstName, e.LastName,
➥od.ProductID, s.CompanyName
FROM Employees e
JOIN Orders o
  ON o.EmployeeID = e.EmployeeID
JOIN [Order Details] od
  ON od.OrderID = o.OrderID
JOIN Products p
  ON p.ProductID = od.ProductID
JOIN Suppliers s
  ON s.SupplierID = p.SupplierID
GO
SET SHOWPLAN_ALL OFF
GO
```

3. Notice that the GO command (batch separator) is inserted between each statement. The SET SHOWPLAN_ALL statement must be run in a separate batch.

4. Execute the script by pressing Ctrl + E or by clicking the Execute Query button. The execution plan will be displayed in the Results tab at the bottom of the window.

5. Examine the execution plan. You should notice that because the query requires simple joins on indexed columns, SQL Server uses the nested loops join method on all joins. In addition, SQL

Server was able to make use of existing indexes to perform its searches. You should see index seeks, or clustered index seeks, in all but one case. As is expected with a nested loops join, the outermost table requires a scan operation, but it is able to scan an index even here.

11.2 Generating a Graphical Execution Plan Using SQL Query Analyzer

In this exercise you will generate a graphical execution plan using the SQL Query Analyzer.

Estimated Time: 10 minutes

1. Load the SQL Server Query Analyzer and log on to your server. From the DB drop-down box choose the Northwind database.

2. You can use the same query as in Exercise 11.1, but remove the SET SHOWPLAN_ALL statements. The query is repeated here for your convenience.

```
SELECT e.FirstName, e.LastName, od.ProductID,
➥s.CompanyName
FROM Employees e
JOIN Orders o
  ON o.EmployeeID = e.EmployeeID
JOIN [Order Details] od
  ON od.OrderID = o.OrderID
JOIN Products p
  ON p.ProductID = od.ProductID
JOIN Suppliers s
  ON s.SupplierID = p.SupplierID
```

3. Execute the script by clicking the Display Estimated Execution Plan button. The execution plan will be displayed in the Estimated Execution Plan tab at the bottom of the window.

4. Examine the execution plan. You should notice all the same features you saw in Exercise 11.1; however, you will likely grasp this graphical representation much faster than you did the text output you received above.

APPLY YOUR KNOWLEDGE

5. Hover your mouse pointer any of the operation icons represented. A pop-up display should give you detailed information about the operation. This same information can be found through the SET SHOWPLAN_ALL command, but again, is much clearer here.

11.3 Diagnosing Locking Problems

In this exercise you will generate a locking situation and resolve it.

Estimated Time: 5 minutes

1. Load the SQL Server Query Analyzer and log on to your server. From the DB drop-down box choose the Pubs database.

2. Enter commands to begin, but not end, a transaction, and then delete records to generate locks on a table. You may use the following command as a guide. Note that the transaction will eventually be rolled back and the data restored.

```
BEGIN TRANSACTION
GO
DELETE TITLEAUTHOR
```

3. Execute the script by clicking the Execute Query button. In the Results window you will receive output stating the number of rows affected. Remember that the transaction is still open, however, so the deleted rows are being held in the transactions log where they can be recovered. In the mean time a lock is held on the table because the rows aren't really gone, but they certainly aren't available.

4. Open a new connection by pressing Ctrl + N or by selecting Query, New Query from the menu. In this window issue a query to select all rows from the table you deleted the records from. The lock held by your other connection will prevent this query from completing.

5. Open yet another connection to the server. Enter the sp_who command with no parameters and execute it. For this command in particular, you will find it easier to use the Execute into Grid feature of the Query Analyzer. Examine the blk column in the output. You should see one row that contains a non-zero spid. Use the KILL command to terminate that spid. No output is returned for the KILL command.

6. Using the Window menu item, return to the previous connection where you issued the SELECT query. You should see that the command has now completed because the blocking process was terminated. Note that the abnormal termination of the process caused it to be rolled back, rather than committing it; therefore, the SELECT query returned all the data you would expect to find in the table.

11.4 Monitoring Server Events with SQL Server Profiler

In this exercise you will practice monitoring the server with the SQL Server Profiler tool. You will use the Profiler tool to track deadlocks on the server and then deliberately cause a deadlock with the query tool so that you can monitor the results.

Estimated Time: 15 minutes

1. Load the SQL Server Query Analyzer and log on to your server. From the DB drop-down box choose a test database where you can create and destroy objects.

2. First, you can set up the objects that you can use to initiate the deadlock. This simply involves creating two simple tables, and entering some sample data. You may copy the following code, or use two existing tables, but be aware that you will be deleting the data in the tables you choose.

APPLY YOUR KNOWLEDGE

```
CREATE TABLE TestTable1 (
    Col1 int NOT NULL,
    Col2 char(10) NOT NULL
)
go

CREATE TABLE TestTable2 (
    Col1 int NOT NULL,
    Col2 char(10) NOT NULL
)
go

INSERT INTO TestTable1 (Col1, Col2)
VALUES (1, 'first')
INSERT INTO TestTable1 (Col1, Col2)
VALUES (2, 'second')
INSERT INTO TestTable2 (Col1, Col2)
VALUES (10, 'tenth')
INSERT INTO TestTable2 (Col1, Col2)
VALUES (11, 'eleventh')
```

3. Now you are ready to begin your trace on the server. Load the SQL Server Profiler, and in the Tools menu, choose Create Trace Wizard.

4. Choose Next to skip the introduction screen. You will then be prompted for the server to monitor and the problem you want to profile. Enter your server into the first box (note that only servers that are registered through Enterprise Manager will be available), and then choose Identify the Cause of a Deadlock from the Problem drop-down box. Choose Next when you are done.

5. The next screen asks you for the database that you want to trace. Enter the database you identified earlier in this exercise and click Next.

6. Finally, you can enter a customized name for the trace, or simply allow the default. Click Finish to begin the trace.

7. Switch tasks back to the Query Analyzer. To cause a deadlock to occur, you can open a transaction in each of two connections, and delete the two tables in a different order on each connection. In this way, each connection will have to wait for the other to finish before it can delete its second table. This results in a deadlock. In the first connection, begin the transaction and delete the first table you had chosen. The following command will work if you are using the test tables created by the example provided in step 2.

```
BEGIN TRANSACTION
DELETE TestTable1
go
```

8. Now you need to open a second connection to your server and the database you have been working in. Again, you will begin a transaction, but this time you can delete both tables. Again, the following example will work if you are using the test tables created by the example provided in step 2.

```
BEGIN TRANSACTION
DELETE TestTable2
go

DELETE TestTable1
go
```

Note that this second connection cannot complete until the locks held on the first table are released by the first connection.

9. You can now return to the first connection and delete the second table. Remember, however, that the first connection is holding locks on the second table, so this deletion will be blocked. Because the second connection cannot complete its transaction until this transaction completes, and this connection cannot complete until the second one does, you will be in a deadlock situation.

```
DELETE TestTable2
Go
```

Just after issuing the command, you should receive a message informing you that this process was chosen as a deadlock victim, and your transaction was rolled back.

APPLY YOUR KNOWLEDGE

10. Return to the SQL Server Profiler. You should see information that a deadlock occurred, and details about the processes that were affected. Figure 11.4 shows an example of the kinds of information you should expect. Note that if there were others working in your database at the same time, you might see slightly different results.

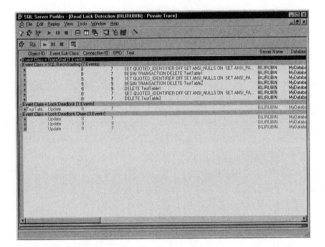

FIGURE 11.4
An image of the SQL Server Profiler after a deadlock has been detected.

Review Questions

1. What are the two commands to return a text-based query plan from SQL Server?

2. What is the difference between a logical and a physical operator?

3. How are logical operators represented in a graphical execution plan?

4. What command will terminate a process in SQL Server?

5. How can you produce a list of blocking processes currently running on the server?

6. Is there a way to track all the actions of a particular user?

7. How does the User-Configurable event category work?

8. Why might the commands from a TSQL event trace differ from the commands you thought you were tracing?

Exam Questions

1. What are the three join operations SQL Server supports?

   A. Nested loops

   B. Merge join

   C. Index spool

   D. Hash match

2. Of the following, which is likely to be the fastest operation?

   A. Index spool

   B. Table scan

   C. Table spool

   D. Index seek

3. With which of the following commands can you refresh the statistics on a table's indexes? Select the best answer.

   A. DBCC RECOMPILE_STATS

   B. UPDATE STATISTICS

APPLY YOUR KNOWLEDGE

C. GENERATE STATISICS

D. sp_createstats

4. With which of the following commands can you reorganize a table to eliminate excessive fragmentation? Select the best answer.

   A. DBCC REORGANIZE

   B. UPDATE STATISTICS

   C. DBCC REINDEX

   D. sp_tabledefrag

5. Which of the following commands can best diagnose locking problems?

   A. sp_lock

   B. sp_who

   C. DBCC SHOWLOCKS

   D. SET SHOWLOCKS

6. SQL Server Profiler can trace which of the following events? Select all that apply.

   A. New connections

   B. SQL operators

   C. Writes to the SQL Server error log

   D. TSQL batch completion

7. If you want to trace all of the exact commands that are being sent to SQL Server from a particular connection, in which event category would you look?

   A. Misc.

   B. Sessions

C. SQL Operators

D. TSQL

8. The graphical execution plan presented by SQL Server Query Analyzer uses different icons to represent which of the following? Select the best answer.

   A. Physical operators

   B. Logical operators

   C. TSQL commands

   D. Process flow

9. Anna is working with database issues of a team of developers writing an application that uses SQL Server. As the developers begin full-scale testing on their application, they notice that during certain complicated insert or delete routines, the process sometimes fails.

   To get to the answer, Anna asks to be notified immediately when the problem occurs again so that she can run sp_who to identify the cause.

   Rate the solution as one of the following:

   A. This is an optimal solution to the problem. Anna is using the best tool for the job.

   B. This is a good solution to the problem. Anna will find the answer if she can run the procedure quickly enough.

   C. This is a poor solution to the problem. Anna will find the answer, but she is not using the best tool at her disposal.

   D. This is not a solution. Anna should not expect to find the cause of the problem using the sp_who stored procedure.

APPLY YOUR KNOWLEDGE

10. Which of the following are expected results of using the KILL command on a connection? Select all that apply.

    A. The connection is halted and then dropped.

    B. Open transactions on the connection are halted and rolled back.

    C. Commands currently executing on the connection are allowed to complete and commit their changes before the process is stopped.

    D. Locks held by the connection are freed.

Answers to Review Questions

1. Both SET SHOWPLAN_TEXT and SET SHOWPLAN_ALL will cause SQL Server to output execution plans for the following commands. (For more information, refer to the section "Create a Textual Execution Plan.")

2. A physical operator describes the action the SQL Server will take. A logical operator specifies the particular strategy SQL Server will take to accomplish the physical operation. (For more information, refer to the section "Physical and Logical Operators.")

3. Logical operators are not directly shown in a graphical execution plan. Rather, physical operators are shown as icons and the logical operations are listed in the detail of the physical operation. (For more information, refer to the section "Examine an Execution Plan.")

4. The KILL command can be used to terminate a process. You must know the ID of the process, known as the *spid*, in order to use the KILL command. (For more information, refer to the section "Diagnosing and Resolving Locking Problems.")

5. The stored procedure sp_who can be used to quickly list all processes on the server. Part of the process information is whether the process is blocked by another process. (For more information, refer to the section "Diagnosing and Resolving Locking Problems.")

6. The SQL Server Profiler can track many kinds of events that occur on SQL Server. It is possible to filter these events for a single user, a single connection, or a single application. (For more information, refer to the section "Using SQL Server Profiler.")

7. The User-Configurable event category has events that can be triggered by the use of the xp_trace_generate_event extended stored procedure. By placing calls to this extended stored procedure from inside your code, you can trace your own code. (For more information, refer to the section "Using SQL Server Profiler.")

8. The data access library used to help your programs communicate with SQL Server will often send configuration commands along with your statements, which could sometimes lead to unexpected results. (For more information, refer to the section "Examine an Execution Plan.")

Answers Exam Questions

1. **A, B, D.** An index spool is an operator, but it does not represent a join. The hash match join actually has three forms. (For more information, refer to the section "Join Operators.")

2. **D.** A seek operation is generally expected to be faster than either a scan or a spool. (For more information, refer to the section "Scans, Seeks, and Spools.")

3. **B.** The UPDATE STATISTICS command can be used to recalculate statistics on an index. The other choices represent bogus commands. (For more information, refer to the section "Using UPDATE STATISTICS.")

4. **C.** The DBCC REINDEX command can be used to rebuild an index. By rebuilding a clustered index, a table's data will be reorganized to reduce fragmentation. (For more information, refer to the section "Using DBCC SHOWCONTIG.")

5. **B.** The sp_who stored procedure will list which process is being blocked by another process and give you the spid of the blocking process. (For more information, refer to the section "Diagnosing and Resolving Locking Problems.")

6. **A, B, C, D.** The SQL Server Profiler can trace all these events and more. (For more information, refer to the section "Using SQL Server Profiler.")

7. **D.** The TSQL event category has events that will allow you to trace all commands sent to SQL Server. Any trace can be limited to examine only events from a specific connection. The SQL Operators event category allows you to trace only specific SQL operations—not all TSQL commands. (For more information, refer to the section "Using SQL Server Profiler.")

8. **A**. Physical operators are represented as icons in a graphical execution plan. The logical operator is listed as a detail of the physical operator. The actual SQL command is listed as a physical operator, which is represented as an icon. (For more information, refer to the section "Using SQL Server Profiler.")

9. **D.** After the statements have failed and stopped running, they are no longer blocked. Because the sp_who stored procedure takes special note only of blocked processes, Anna will not be able to spot the cause of the problem. She should be tracing processes with SQL Server Profiler instead, probably starting by tracing deadlocks. (For more information, refer to the section "Using SQL Server Profiler.")

10. **A, B, D.** Open transactions are rolled back when the connection is killed. Currently executing commands are not only halted, but are also rolled back. Because locks are always held by a connection and the connection is dropped, locks are freed when the connection is killed. (For more information, refer to the section "Diagnosing and Resolving Locking Problems.")

Suggested Readings and Resources

We recommend the following resources for further study in the area of planning:

1. SQL Server Books Online

   - "Query Tuning" and all related subtopics

   - Monitoring with SQL Server Profiler

   - Events monitored by SQL Server Profiler

2. Transact-SQL help file

   - sp_who

   - KILL

FINAL REVIEW

Fast Facts

Study and Exam Prep Tips

Practice Exam

Now that you have thoroughly read through this book, worked through the exercises, and picked up as much hands-on exposure to SQL Server as possible, you're ready to take your exam. This chapter is designed to be a last-minute cram for you as you walk out the door on your way to the exam. You can't reread the whole book in an hour, but you will be able to read this chapter in that time. This chapter is organized by objective category and summarizes the basic facts you need to know regarding each objective. If you know what is in here, chances are the exam will be a snap.

DEVELOPING A LOGICAL DATA MODEL

▶ Group data into entities by applying normalization rules.

▶ Identify primary keys.

▶ Choose the foreign key that will enforce a relationship between entities and that will ensure referential integrity.

▶ Identify the business rules that relate to data integrity.

▶ Incorporate business rules and constraints into the data model.

▶ In a given situation, decide whether denormalization is appropriate.

First Normal Form: Eliminate repeating groups of attributes in an entity. If the entity can have multiple instances of an attribute, place that attribute into its own separate entity and define a One-to-Many relationship between the parent entity and the new child entity.

Fast Facts

SQL SERVER 7 DATABASE DESIGN

Second Normal Form: Eliminate partial key dependencies. If an attribute's value can be fully determined by the values of a collection of attributes belonging to the primary key, then there is no need to store that information with the entity. Instead, a new entity defined by the partial key should be defined with the dependent attribute.

Third Normal Form: Eliminate dependencies between non-key attributes. If any attribute's value can be fully determined by the values of a collection of one or more other non-key attributes, all those attributes should combine to define a new entity. After a primary key is defined for that new entity, only the primary key should be stored in the original entity.

A primary key must uniquely identify an entity—that is, a row in a table.

As a rule, a primary key should be the smallest (in terms of byte size) candidate key available. If the smallest candidate key is still "large" (for example, greater than the size of four integers, or 16 bytes), consider adding a surrogate key. A *surrogate* key is a candidate key composed of values deliberately added for the sole purpose of providing uniqueness. An auto-numbering field (called an IDENTITY field in SQL Server) is an excellent example of a surrogate key.

Foreign keys are always made up from a candidate key in the related table.

A NULL value is a special value that indicates "unknown". An attribute that allows NULL values is called *nullable*.

Nullability, uniqueness, and allowing changes are business rules that affect data integrity. Attributes in your entities should have these business rules applied to them where appropriate.

Denormalization is the process of breaking the rules of normalization to increase performance. Denormalization always reduces the flexibility of your data model; therefore, you should be sure you will get a large enough performance gain to warrant it.

If normalization will increase the storage requirements of your data, denormalization may be appropriate.

If normalization will require a join to take place every time an entity is retrieved (in other words, one entity is *never* retrieved without the other), denormalization may be appropriate.

DERIVING THE PHYSICAL DESIGN

▶ Assess the potential impact of the logical design on performance, maintainability, extensibility, scalability, availability, and security.

Normalization will tend to increase the maintainability, extensibility, and scalability of your database by breaking large, inflexible entities into smaller ones. Smaller entities tend to require more relationships, which gives you more flexibility to change the degree of the relationships.

Normalization tends to reduce data redundancy, which makes your database more consistent. This increases the availability and security of your database.

Denormalization tends to increase performance by reducing joins.

CREATING DATA SERVICES

▶ Access data by using the dynamic SQL model.

▶ Access data by using the Stored Procedure model.

▶ Manipulate data by using Transact-SQL cursors.

◆ Choose the appropriate type of cursor.

◆ Define the appropriate level of sensitivity to change.

◆ Choose the appropriate navigation.

◆ Choose the scope of the cursor, specifically global or local.

▶ Create and manage explicit, implicit, and distributed transactions to ensure data consistency and recoverability.

◆ Define the transaction isolation level.

◆ Design transactions of appropriate length.

◆ Avoid or handle deadlocks.

◆ Use optimistic locking appropriately.

◆ Implement error handling by using @@trancount.

▶ Write INSERT, DELETE, UPDATE, and SELECT statements that retrieve and modify data.

▶ Write Transact-SQL statements that use joins or sub-queries to combine data from multiple tables.

▶ Create scripts using Transact-SQL. Programming elements include control-of-flow methods, local and global variables, functions, and error handling methods.

▶ Design, create, use, and alter views.

◆ Modify data through a view.

◆ Query data through a view.

▶ Create and execute stored procedures to enforce business rules, to modify data in multiple tables, to perform calculations, and to use input and output parameters.

◆ Implement error handling by using return codes and the RAISERROR statement.

◆ Choose appropriate recompile options.

▶ Create triggers that implement rules, that enforce data integrity, and that perform cascading updates and deletes.

◆ Implement transactional error handling.

▶ Create result sets that provide summary data. Query types include TOP *n* PERCENT and GROUP BY, specifically HAVING, CUBE, and ROLLUP.

▶ Configure session-level options.

▶ Access data from static or dynamic sources by using remote stored procedures, linked servers, and openrowset.

◆ Evaluate where processing occurs when using OpenQuery.

The dynamic model is used when queries are sent to SQL Server with no preparation. That is, with no expectation of reusing an execution plan.

The stored procedure model is used when queries are sent to SQL Server in such a way to reuse an existing execution plan. ODBC and OLE-DB allow you to prepare statements by storing the execution plan for later reuse. SQL Server always stores the execution plan of a stored procedure for reuse.

SQL-92 cursor syntax:

```
DECLARE cursor_name [INSENSITIVE] [SCROLL]
CURSOR
FOR select_statement
 [FOR {READ ONLY | UPDATE [OF column_list]}]
```

Transact-SQL enhanced cursor syntax:

```
DECLARE cursor_name CURSOR
[LOCAL ¦ GLOBAL]
[FORWARD_ONLY ¦ SCROLL]
[STATIC ¦ KEYSET ¦ DYNAMIC]
[READ_ONLY ¦ SCROLL_LOCKS ¦ OPTIMISTIC]
FOR select_statement
[FOR UPDATE [OF column_list]]
```

An *insensitive* cursor in SQL-92 syntax equates to a *static* cursor in the enhanced TSQL syntax.

A global cursor can be referenced outside of the batch in which it was declared. Global cursors can be referenced as long as the connection remains valid.

Insensitive or static cursors work on a copy of the actual data so that changes cannot affect "live" data.

Scrollable cursors require extra overhead, and require more space than forward-only cursors. Forward-only cursors are therefore considerably faster, although less flexible.

Static cursors will not reflect changes made to the base tables because they operate on a static data set.

Keyset cursors collect a set of unique keys to identify the records on which the cursor will operate. Therefore, keyset cursors will reflect changes to the existing data in base tables. Inserts to the base tables will not be seen by the cursor, however, because the keyset is fixed at the time the cursor is opened.

Dynamic cursors will show all updates, inserts, or deletes against the base tables.

Transactions are begun with the `BEGIN TRANSACTION` statement and are completed by either the `COMMIT TRANSACTION` or `ROLLBACK TRANSACTION` statement.

If a transaction is rolled back, all actions that took place within the scope of the transaction are undone.

Transaction isolation levels:

◆ **Read Committed.** Prevents dirty reads, but allows phantom data and non-repeatable reads. Locks held by updates will prevent the modified data from being read.

◆ **Read Uncommitted.** Allows dirty reads in addition to phantom data and non-repeatable reads. Reads do not respect locks held by any data modifications in process.

◆ **Repeatable Reads.** Prevents dirty reads and non-repeatable reads, but allows phantom data. Locks held by updates will prevent the modified data from being read. Reads made within transactions will prevent updates to data, but not inserts.

◆ **Serializable.** Prevents dirty reads, non-repeatable reads, and phantom data. Locks held by updates will prevent the modified data from being read. Reads made within transactions will prevent updates and inserts to data.

Because of the extra locking that takes place within transactions to allow the changes to be rolled back, transactions should be kept as short as possible.

Tips for avoiding deadlocks:

◆ Always access objects in the same order.

◆ Keep transactions short.

◆ Never allow an open transaction to wait on user input.

◆ Run transactions in a single batch to reduce waiting on network traffic.

◆ Keep the isolation level as low as is practical for your situation.

Note that using stored procedures can help to ensure that objects are accessed in the same order between applications, and can be used to ensure transactions run in a single batch.

Optimistic locking means data is not locked during reads. This is implemented by the default transaction isolation level of Read Committed.

Applications using optimistic locking should check whether the records that were read earlier and are about to be updated have been changed in the mean time. Timestamp columns and update triggers can aid this process considerably.

Although transactions can be nested, only the outermost transaction is truly enforced. Each nested transaction increments the value of the @@TRANCOUNT system function, and COMMIT statements ending nested transactions decrement the value of @@TRANCOUNT. Any ROLLBACK statement, no matter how deeply nested, will roll back the entire outermost transaction, and set @@TRANCOUNT to zero.

Because a nested ROLLBACK statement will end the entire transaction at all levels, subsequent COMMIT or ROLLBACK statements issued on the assumption that the transaction is still open will cause errors. Therefore, it is important to check the value of @@TRANCOUNT when there is any possibility that a nested transaction may have already ended your transaction level.

Syntax for SELECT, INSERT, UPDATE, and DELETE statements:

```
SELECT [ALL ¦ DISTINCT] select_list
[INTO [new_table_name]]
[FROM {table_name ¦
view_name}[(optimizer_hints)]
[WHERE {search_conditions}]
[ORDER BY {column_name}]

INSERT [INTO] {table_name ¦ view_name}
   [(column_list)]
   {DEFAULT VALUES ¦ VALUES (values_list) ¦
select_statement ¦ stored_procedure}

UPDATE {table_name ¦ view_name}
SET
  { column_name = {NULL ¦ DEFAULT ¦ expression}
}
  [,{ column_name = {NULL ¦ DEFAULT ¦
expression}...]
[FROM {table_list}]
[WHERE {search_conditions ¦ CURRENT OF
cursor_name}]

DELETE [FROM] [[database.][owner].]{table_name
¦ view_name}
    [FROM {table_list}]
    [WHERE {search_conditions ¦ CURRENT OF
cursor_name}]
```

In the FROM clause of each of these statements, multiple tables can be listed with the JOIN keyword to provide multi-table joins.

INNER JOIN is the default. Rows are returned from the two tables where the ON criteria are met.

LEFT OUTER JOIN: All rows are returned from the table to the left of the JOIN keyword, and rows from the right are returned where the ON criteria can be satisfied. Where the ON criteria cannot be met, NULL values are returned for columns from the table on the right.

RIGHT OUTER JOIN: Same as LEFT OUTER JOIN, with the left and right tables reversed.

FULL OUTER JOIN: All rows are returned from both tables. Rows from both tables are returned together wherever the ON criteria can be met.

CROSS JOIN: Returns a Cartesian product between the two tables. Each row from the first table is matched with every row from the second table. No ON criteria are needed or allowed.

Transact-SQL allows multiple tables to be joined together in UPDATE and DELETE statements, but only the single table listed immediately after the keyword UPDATE or DELETE is modified. All other tables are there only to provide values, or to aid in filtering the rows to modify.

Sub-queries are fully formed SELECT statements that are enclosed in parentheses and return data dynamically to be used in the statement that called them.

Sub-queries that return a single row and column can be used wherever an expression is allowed.

Sub-queries that return a single column but multiple rows can be used in place of lists in query (for example, following the IN operator).

Sub-queries that return multiple rows and multiple columns can only be used as derived tables.

Derived tables are created by a sub-query that is used in place of a table name in a JOIN clause. In this way the results of the sub-query are treated as though they are an actual table.

Correlated sub-queries are sub-queries that refer to values from the outer query. Every distinct value in the outer query will require the correlated sub-query to re-run in order to take that value into account.

A *script* is a series of TSQL commands. A script may contain one or more batches.

A *batch* is a series of TSQL commands that are compiled and run as a unit. Any syntax error in a batch that prevents any command from compiling will prevent the entire batch from compiling.

Any run-time error that occurs in a batch will prevent the particular statement from completing but will not stop the batch.

Control-of-Flow statements in TSQL are conditional execution and looping statements, including IF, GOTO, WHILE, RETURN, and CASE.

User-definable variables are always local, which last only within the batch in which they were defined. Local variables must begin with the character @.

A *Boolean* expression is an expression that returns either True or False.

The IF statement provides conditional execution based on the result of a Boolean expression.

The GOTO statement provides a method of unconditional branching.

The WHILE loop will continuously repeat the execution of the statement block that follows until a Boolean expression returns False.

The WHILE loop can be immediately and unconditionally halted with the BREAK statement.

The WHILE loop can be immediately and unconditionally reset to the evaluation of the Boolean expression with the CONTINUE statement.

The RETURN statement will halt the execution of the current batch. The RETURN statement can also be used in stored procedures to halt the procedure and return an integer value.

The CASE command operates as part of a regular expression, and allows one of several values based on Boolean conditions.

The RAISERROR statement can be used to raise a predefined error number or an ad-hoc error message.

The syntax for the RAISERROR statement is as follows:

```
RAISERROR ({msg_id | msg_str}, severity, state
[, argument1 [, argument2]] )
[WITH option]
```

The WITH option in the RAISERROR statement allows the LOG keyword to direct the error raised to the error log where it is "permanently" recorded.

The PRINT statement does not raise an error condition but will return a message to the user.

Views are virtual tables created through a predefined SELECT statement. The data returned by the query is presented to the user as though the data existed in the table itself.

The syntax to create a view is as follows:

```
CREATE VIEW view_name [(column [,…n])]
[WITH ENCRYPTION]
AS
select_statement
[WITH CHECK OPTION]
```

Data modification statements can be written to change the data presented by a view. When a view presents information joined from multiple tables SQL Server must be able to unambiguously determine what table the data modified comes from or an error will occur.

The WITH CHECK OPTION in the CREATE VIEW syntax ensures that any data modifications made to data in a view will not cause the data to "disappear" from the view; that is, the data must still meet the criteria of the view after the modifications.

The WITH ENCRYPTION option encrypts the CREATE VIEW statement stored in the syscomments system table so that it cannot be read.

Stored procedures consist of a series of commands that are stored under a well-defined name. All the actions of the commands can be carried out simply by executing the stored procedure by name.

Stored procedures can accept parameters into variables, which can then affect the way the execution of the procedure.

Stored procedures are compiled the first time they are run, and then the execution plan is stored so that it can be reused. Reusing a stored execution plan saves time on future calls to the stored procedures.

Stored procedures can encapsulate all the logic of your business rules so that these rules can be shared consistently across all applications that use the database.

To avoid deadlocks, all data modifications involving multiple tables should access the tables in the same way every time. By encapsulating the logic to perform these data modifications within stored procedures, this condition can be assured.

Stored procedures can use output parameters to return changed values in variables. Stored procedures can also return a single integer value through the RETURN statement. An error condition can be returned from a stored procedure by using the RAISERROR statement.

Stored procedures are created with the following syntax:

```
CREATE PROC[EDURE] procedure_name [;number]
    [
                {@parameter data_type} [VARYING]
[= default] [OUTPUT]
    ]
    [ ,…n]
[WITH
    {
            RECOMPILE
        ¦ ENCRYPTION
        ¦ RECOMPILE, ENCRYPTION
    }
```

```
]
[FOR REPLICATION]
AS
        sql_statement [ ...n]
```

By specifying the WITH RECOMPILE option, the execution plan will not be reused by future calls to the stored procedure. Using this option will guarantee a new execution plan each time.

Triggers are basically stored procedures that can be registered to automatically fire upon data modifications to a table.

A trigger can only be registered to a single table (although any number of tables can referenced through the code of the trigger).

A trigger can be registered to fire on any or all of the INSERT, UPDATE, or DELETE statements made to a table.

Multiple triggers can be registered to fire on any data modification statements.

Triggers give you full programmability to respond to data modifications, which can allow a more detailed response than you can get from constraints.

When accomplishing the same goal, constraints will generally give superior performance to triggers.

Triggers always execute within a transaction covering the original data modification. A trigger can therefore cancel the data modification that caused the trigger to execute by issuing a ROLLBACK statement.

Triggers can be nested. Therefore, triggers should always check the value of @@TRANCOUNT before issuing a ROLLBACK statement to avoid rolling back a transaction that other triggers may have already ended.

Aggregate functions operate on multiple rows in a result set to calculate a singe summary value. Examples include COUNT, SUM, AVG (average), MIN, and MAX.

The TOP *n* PERCENT modifier can be used in a SELECT statement to cause only the first *n* rows or the first *n* percent rows to be returned from a query.

The GROUP BY clause in a SELECT statement is used to collapse multiple rows with the same values in the columns defined into a single summary row. The GROUP BY clause is normally used along with aggregate functions to summarize groups of data in a result set.

The HAVING clause is normally used along with the GROUP BY to stipulate conditions on the summary rows returned. Although it works very much like the WHERE clause by stating conditions that resulting rows must meet, only the HAVING clause can operate on aggregate values.

The CUBE and ROLLUP clauses operate along with the GROUP BY clause to introduce super-aggregates into the result set. When using the CUBE and ROLLUP clauses, super-groups are created by grouping groups that share values in a subset of the total columns defined by the GROUP BY.

The ROLLUP clause systematically masks columns in the GROUP BY clause starting with the last, then the last two, then the last three, and so on, to define its super-groups to aggregate on.

The CUBE clause operates exactly like the ROLLUP, but then continues to make all possible super-groupings that the ROLLUP missed.

Session-level options are configured using the SET command.

Session-level options override equivalent system and database options.

Linked servers are statically defined with a name, and all other information needed to create an OLE-DB connection.

After they are defined, queries can reference data on a linked server simply by using a four-part naming convention of *server.database.owner.object.*

Stored procedures can be run on linked servers by using the four-part naming convention to specify the stored procedure from the EXECUTE command.

The OpenRowset function can be used in place of a table name in any query to dynamically define a remote data source and issue a simple SELECT statement, which will return data from the remote source in the form of a table.

The OpenQuery function is used to send a query to a remote data source and retrieve the results in the form of a table. The OpenQuery function causes the remote server to execute the query locally. Processing occurs on the remote server when using the OpenQuery function.

CREATING A PHYSICAL DATABASE

▶ Create and manage files, file groups, and transaction logs that define a database.

▶ Create tables that enforce data integrity and referential integrity.

◆ Choose the appropriate data types.

◆ Create user-defined data types.

◆ Define columns as NULL or NOT NULL.

◆ Define columns to generate values by using the IDENTITY property, the uniqueidentifier data type, and the NEWID function.

◆ Implement constraints.

▶ Create and maintain indexes.

◆ Choose an indexing strategy that will optimize performance.

◆ Given a situation, choose the appropriate type of index to create.

◆ Choose the column or columns to index.

◆ Choose the appropriate index characteristics, specifically FILLFACTOR, DROP_EXISTING, and PAD INDEX.

▶ Populate the database with data from an external data source. Methods include bulk copy program (BCP) and Data Transformation Services (DTS).

▶ Implement full-text search.

All databases are composed of at least one data file and at least one log file.

Data files store the information contained in a database. This information includes all object definitions, including tables and indexes for example, and all data for those objects, such as the rows in a table, and the data that makes up an index.

Log files store information that describes all modifications that have been made to a database since the log was last reset. Because all changes to a database are stored in the log file, this information can be used to recover the state of a database in case of a failure.

The first data file in any database is the primary data file.

The primary data file should be given the extension .mdf according to Microsoft conventions.

Any additional data files defined are secondary data files and should be given the extension .ndf according to Microsoft conventions.

Log files should be given the extension .ldf according to Microsoft conventions.

File groups are groups of data files, to which objects may be created.

All data files belong to one and only one file group.

The primary data file always belongs to the predefined primary file group.

All data files not specifically assigned to a user-defined file group belong to the primary file group.

The primary file group is always the default file group when the database is created.

All objects are stored in one and only one file group.

All objects not specifically stated otherwise are created in the default file group.

Because the primary file group, which contains the primary data file, is always the default when the database is created, the system tables are always created in the primary file group.

The default file group may be changed after the database is created.

The data for an object is stored in all data files that make up the file group. The data is assigned proportionally to the amount of free space in each data file.

Log files do not belong to any file group.

Databases are created with the CREATE DATABASE statement. The syntax follows:

```
CREATE DATABASE database_name
[ ON [PRIMARY]
          [ <filespec> [,...n] ]
          [, <filegroup> [,...n] ]
]
[ LOG ON { <filespec> } ]
[ FOR LOAD ¦ FOR ATTACH ]

<filespec> ::=
   ( [ NAME = logical_file_name, ]
     FILENAME = 'os_file_name'
     [, SIZE = size]
     [, MAXSIZE = { max_size ¦ UNLIMITED } ]
     [, FILEGROWTH = growth_increment] ) [,...n]
<filegroup> ::=
FILEGROUP filegroup_name <filespec> [,...n]
```

Data files can be set to automatically grow when they become full by setting the MAXSIZE and FILEGROWTH optional parameters to the filespec.

The structure of a database can be changed using the ALTER DATABASE statement:

```
ALTER DATABASE database
{     ADD FILE <filespec> [,...n] [TO FILEGROUP
filegroup_name]
      ¦ ADD LOG FILE <filespec> [,...n]
      ¦ REMOVE FILE logical_file_name
      ¦ ADD FILEGROUP filegroup_name
      ¦ REMOVE FILEGROUP filegroup_name
      ¦ MODIFY FILE <filespec>
      ¦ MODIFY FILEGROUP filegroup_name
filegroup_property
}
```

Tables are created with the CREATE TABLE statement. They syntax is as follows:

```
CREATE TABLE [database.[owner].]table_name (
  { column_name data_type [null_option]
[col_constraint[, ...]]
   ¦table_constraint
  } [,...]
)
[ON {filegroup ¦ DEFAULT} ]
[TEXTIMAGE_ON {filegroup ¦ DEFAULT} ]
```

SQL Server supports the following data types:

◆ **Binary.** The binary, varbinary, and image types are used to store streams of binary information. The binary type is fixed length, whereas the varbinary and image types are variable length. Use the image type to store extremely large values greater than 8,000 bytes.

◆ **Character.** The char, varchar, and text types store alphanumeric characters. The char type is fixed length, whereas the varchar and text types are variable length. Use the char data type when you expect each value to be roughly the same size; use the varchar type if a character field can contain NULLs or will have data of widely varying lengths; use the *text* type to store extremely large strings longer than 8,000 characters.

◆ **Unicode Character.** The nchar, nvarchar, and ntext types store unicode characters. Because unicode characters are twice the size of standard characters, each of these types store only half as much data as their standard character counterparts. Use the ntext data type to store strings larger than 4,000 unicode charaters.

◆ **Date & Time.** The datetime and smalldatetime types both store date and time values. The difference between the two is the range of dates each can store and the accuracy of the time. smalldatetime is accurate to one second, whereas datetime is accurate to 3.33 milliseconds.

◆ **Exact Numeric.** The decimal, numeric, money, and smallmoney types can all store decimal numbers exactly. The numeric data type is actually just a synonym for the decimal type.

◆ **Floating Point (approximate numeric).** The float and real types both provide for the approximate storage of decimal numbers; the main difference between the two is the range of values each can store. The float type can be defined with a variable precision between 1 and 53. The real type is a synonym for float(24).

◆ **Integer.** The bit, int, smallint, and tinyint types all store integer data in varying ranges.

◆ **Special Numeric.** These are numerically based data types that have special properties beyond simply storing user-supplied data:

  • *cursor.* The cursor data type can be assigned the instance of a cursor that was defined with the DECLARE CURSOR syntax. The cursor type variable will then maintain a reference to the cursor and can be used to manipulate the cursor.

  • *uniqueidentifier.* The uniqueidentifier is a 16-byte number formatted as a globally unique identifier (guid) as defined by Microsoft. The NEWID function provided by SQL Server will generate numbers of this type that are guaranteed to be unique throughout the world.

  • *timestamp.* The timestamp data type provides a value unique to the database every time a column is inserted or updated. Note that this value is guaranteed to be unique to the database, but could conceivably be duplicated on other databases.

Unlike `uniqueidentifier` values, which must be set using some function, `timestamp` columns are updated by the system automatically when an insert or update occurs to the row.

A user-defined data type encapsulates many characteristics of a column in a simple definition. This encapsulation is useful for imposing consistent standards on related columns.

A user-defined data type encapsulates the following characteristics:

◆ **Base type.** This defines the main SQL Server data type for the user-defined type (UDT).

◆ **NULL option.** Specifies the default NULL option for columns that use this user-defined type. The UDT NULL option can be overridden when a table is created or changed.

◆ **Rule.** A UDT may have a rule bound to it that defines a range of values acceptable for the column.

◆ **Default.** A UDT may have a default bound to it that defines an initial value for the column. Default values are most often used with columns that do not allow NULLs.

A user-defined data type is created with the `sp_addtype` stored procedure. The syntax to create a user defined data type is as follows:

```
sp_addtype [@typename =] type,
       [@phystype =] system_data_type
       [, [@nulltype =] 'null_type']
```

The IDENTITY property of a table column will cause incrementing integer values to be automatically assigned to the column. This is useful for generating unique values for a primary key.

The following constraints can be defined for a column:

◆ **Unique.** Defines a set of columns whose values uniquely defined an entity. The uniqueness is enforced through a unique index.

◆ **Primary key.** Defines a set of columns whose values uniquely define an entity. This is a special case of a unique constraint, which defines the preferred method of identifying an entity for which more than one method exists. The uniqueness of a primary key constraint is enforced through a unique index.

◆ **Foreign key.** Defines a set of columns whose values must exist in the primary key, or unique key values of another table.

◆ **Check.** Defines a Boolean expression that must return True for the data to be allowed.

◆ **Default.** Defines a value that will be inserted into the column when no other value is supplied.

Indexes are objects created on tables that store data in an ordered fashion that can be searched quickly.

Indexes are created using the CREATE INDEX statement. The syntax follows:

```
CREATE [UNIQUE] [CLUSTERED ¦ NONCLUSTERED]
       INDEX index_name ON table (column [, n])
[WITH
              [PAD_INDEX]
              [[,] FILLFACTOR = fillfactor]
              [[,] IGNORE_DUP_KEY]
              [[,] DROP_EXISTING]
              [[,] STATISTICS_NORECOMPUTE]
]
[ON filegroup]
```

Clustered indexes store data from a table in a tree structure, which is extremely efficient for searching.

Clustered indexes impose a physical ordering on the data in the table. A table can have only one index.

Non-clustered indexes are stored outside of the table. A table can have multiple non-clustered indexes.

The leaf pages of a clustered index are the data pages of the table itself. This how the clustered index imposes a physical ordering of the tables data itself.

The leaf pages of a non-clustered index point to the data in the table. If the table has a clustered index, that clustered index key is stored, otherwise the actual data page and offset of the row in the page is stored.

As a rule, it is a good idea to index primary keys and foreign keys because these are commonly searched. Note that an explicitly defined primary key constraint automatically creates a unique index.

The FILLFACTOR characteristic of an index defines how much empty space should be left in an index to allow for growth. This empty space makes the index larger, and therefore more difficult to search, but it allows for new rows to be inserted into the table without having to make space, which speeds inserts.

If an index is created with the DROP_EXISTING option, the existing index of the same name will be automatically dropped at the same time the new one is created. This allows indexes to be rebuilt in a single command rather than first dropping and then creating the index in two steps.

When a clustered index is dropped or created, all non-clustered indexes must also be rebuilt because they depend on clustered index keys. To prevent the non-clustered indexes being rebuilt when a clustered index is dropped and re-created, use the DROP_EXISTING option.

The bulk copy program (BCP) of SQL Server defines a method for quickly importing and exporting data into and out of SQL Server.

BCP is supported as an application programming interface (API) in ODBC and DB-Lib data access libraries. You can bulk copy data into and out of SQL Server using these APIs.

BCP.EXE is a utility that uses the ODBC API to bulk copy data out of SQL Server into a file you name or into SQL Server from a file you name.

The Data Transformation Services (DTS) of SQL Server defines a set of services that transfer data between any OLE-DB data sources.

DTS executes a sequence of events defined in DTS packages.

DTS packages contain data source definitions, transforms, and tasks.

A DTS transform defines how to take the data from one data source and move it into another. The data can be manipulated through the use of a scripting language as it is transferred.

A DTS task is an instruction to do something. Examples include send email, or execute a WIN32 command.

The DTS Wizard is a program that takes you through the process of creating a package that moves data from a single table source to another table source. The full functionality of DTS packages cannot be accessed through the wizard.

The DTS Package Designer is a program that allows you to construct packages of arbitrary complexity.

Full-text searching is supported through the use of the Microsoft Search service.

Special full-text indexes must be created on columns in a table to allow a full-text search.

There are five levels of objects that must be configured to allow full-text searches. The levels and the stored procedures used to configure them are as follows:

◆ **Service.** sp_fulltext_service. This level configures the Microsoft Search service itself.

◆ **Database.** sp_fulltext_database. This level enables the database for full-text searches.

◆ **Catalog.** sp_fulltext_catalog. This level creates, enables, disables, and populates all full-text indexes in the catalog.

◆ **Table.** `sp_fulltext_table`. This level enables and disables the table for indexing.

◆ **Column.** `sp_fulltext_column`. This level defines the columns that will have full-text indexes created on them.

A *catalog* is an external file that is created for a particular database where the Microsoft Search service stores the data for the full-text indexes it creates.

A table must have a single non-nullable unique column to participate in full-text searching.

A full-text index is not updated to reflect changes to the column. Use the `sp_fulltext_catalog` stored procedure to refresh the full-text index periodically.

Full text searches are implemented through the CONTAINS and FREETEXT predicates in the WHERE clause of a statement. Full-text searches can also be implemented through the equivalent CONTAINSTABLE and FREETEXTTABLE functions, which return all rows that meet the specified criteria in the form of a table that can be joined to.

The full-text predicates simply return True or False depending on whether a row meets the criteria specified.

The full-text functions return result sets in the form of tables that can be joined to through the JOIN clause of a statement. The full-text functions return a rating defining how close a match is, and the unique key value of the table that was searched to be used in the join.

The FREETEXT predicate and FREETEXTTABLE functions take a simple phrase as their criteria which it uses to find any matches that are sufficiently "close". The ease of use of FREETEXT is offset by its impreciseness.

The CONTAINS predicate and CONTAINSTABLE function take a complex criteria as defined by the syntax below:

```
<contains_search_condition> ::=
        {
                <simple_term>
        ¦ <prefix_term>
        ¦ <proximity_term>
```

```
        ¦ <generation_term>
        ¦ <weighted_term>
        ¦ (<contains_search_condition>)
        }
    [       {
                        {AND ¦ AND NOT ¦ OR}
<contains_search_condition>
                }
    ] [...n]

<simple_term> ::=
        word ¦ " phrase "

<prefix term> ::=
        { "word * " ¦ "phrase * " }

<proximity_term> ::=
        {<simple_term> ¦ <prefix_term>}
        {   {NEAR() ¦ ~} {<simple_term> ¦
<prefix_term>} } [...n]

<generation_term> :: =
        FORMSOF (INFLECTIONAL, <simple_term>
[,...n] )

<weighted_term> :: =
        ISABOUT
                (       {       {
<generation_term>
<prefix_term>
<proximity_term>
<simple_term>
                                }
                                [WEIGHT
(weight_value)]
                } [, ...n]
                )
```

MAINTAINING A DATABASE

▶ Evaluate and optimize the performance of an execution plan by using DBCC SHOW CONTIG, SHOWPLAN_text, SHOWPLAN_ALL, and UPDATE STATISTICS.

▶ Evaluate and optimize the performance of query execution plans.

▶ Diagnose and resolve locking problems.

▶ Identify SQL Server events and performance problems by using SQL Server Profiler.

DBCC SHOW CONTIG can be used to determine whether your tables or indexes are fragmented, or split up among non-continuous data pages. Fragmented tables and indexes are more difficult to search and can slow queries. Re-creating a clustered index will defragment a table as well as the index itself. Re-creating a non-clustered index will defragment the index.

The SET SHOWPLAN_TEXT and SET SHOWPLAN_ALL commands instruct SQL Server to return information describing the execution plan of a query. The SHOWPLAN_ALL option returns more detailed information relating to the number of rows affected and times expected.

An execution plan consists of logical and physical operations. A *physical* operation describes the action being taken, and the *logical* operation describes the method SQL Server has chosen to implement the action.

SQL Server stored statistics on indexes to tell it how useful the index is. As data is modified in a table, the statistics can fall out of date. Running the UPDATE STATISTICS command on a table or a particular index will re-create the statistics to reflect the current data.

The sp_who stored procedure lists all processes on the server and will list which are blocked by locks held by another process.

The kill command can be used to kill a process on the server. For example, a process found to be holding locks that are preventing other users from working can be killed to free those locks.

The SQL Server profiler can be used to monitor the work being done by SQL Server. Actions can be monitored by user, connection, application, or database, or for the entire server. Specific events also can be monitored.

Study and Exam Prep Tips

This chapter provides you with some general guidelines for preparing for the exam. It is organized into three sections. The first section addresses your pre-exam preparation activities and covers general study tips. This is followed by an extended look at the Microsoft Certification exams including a number of specific tips that apply to the Microsoft exam formats. Finally, changes in Microsoft's testing policies and how they might affect you are discussed.

To better understand the nature of preparation for the test, it is important to understand learning as a process. You probably are aware of how you best learn new material. You may find that outlining works best for you, or you may need to "see" things as a visual learner. Whatever your learning style, test preparation takes place over time. Obviously, you can't start studying for these exams the night before you take them; it is very important to understand that learning is a developmental process. Understanding it as a process helps you focus on what you know and what you have yet to learn.

Thinking about how you learn should help you recognize that learning takes place when we are able to match new information to old. You have some previous experience with computers and networking, and now you are preparing for this certification exam. Using this book, software, and supplementary materials will not just add incrementally to what you know; as you study you actually change the organization of your knowledge as you integrate this new information into your existing knowledge base. This will lead you to a more comprehensive understanding of the tasks and concepts outlined in the objectives and of computing in general. Again, this happens as a repetitive process rather than a singular event. Keep this model of learning in mind as you prepare for the exam, and you will make better decisions concerning what to study and how much more studying you need to do.

STUDY AND EXAM PREP TIPS

STUDY TIPS

There are many ways to approach studying just as there are many different types of material to study. However, the tips that follow should work well for the type of material covered on the certification exams.

Study Strategies

Although individuals vary in the ways they learn information, some basic principles of learning apply to everyone. You should adopt some study strategies that take advantage of these principles. One of these principles is that learning can be broken into various depths. Recognition (of terms, for example) exemplifies a more surface level of learning in which you rely on a prompt of some sort to elicit recall. Comprehension or understanding (of the concepts behind the terms, for example) represents a deeper level of learning. The ability to analyze a concept and apply your understanding of it in a new way represents a further depth of learning.

Your learning strategy should enable you to know the material at a level or two deeper than mere recognition. This will help you do well on the exams. You will know the material so thoroughly that you can easily handle the recognition-level types of questions used in multiple-choice testing. You will also be able to apply your knowledge to solve new problems.

Macro and Micro Study Strategies

One strategy that can lead to this deeper learning includes preparing an outline that covers all the objectives and subobjectives for the particular exam you are working on. You should delve a bit further into the material and include a level or two of detail beyond the stated objectives and subobjectives for the exam. Then expand the outline by coming up with a statement of definition or a summary for each point in the outline.

An outline provides two approaches to studying. First, you can study the outline by focusing on the organization of the material. Work your way through the points and sub-points of your outline with the goal of learning how they relate to one another. For example, be sure you understand how each of the main objective areas is similar to and different from another. Then do the same thing with the subobjectives; be sure you know which subobjectives pertain to each objective area and how they relate to one another.

Next, you can work through the outline, focusing on learning the details. Memorize and understand terms and their definitions, facts, rules and strategies, advantages and disadvantages, and so on. In this pass through the outline, attempt to learn detail rather than the big picture (the organizational information that you worked on in the first pass through the outline).

Research has shown that attempting to assimilate both types of information at the same time seems to interfere with the overall learning process. Separate your studying into these two approaches and you will perform better on the exam.

Active Study Strategies

The process of writing down and defining objectives, subobjectives, terms, facts, and definitions promotes a more active learning strategy than merely reading the material. In human information-processing terms, writing forces you to engage in more active encoding of the information. Simply reading over it exemplifies more passive processing.

Next, determine whether you can apply the information you have learned by attempting to create examples and scenarios on your own. Think about how or where you could apply the concepts you are learning. Again, write down this information to process the facts and concepts in a more active fashion.

The hands-on nature of the Step by Step tutorials and the Exercises at the ends of the chapters provide further active learning opportunities that will reinforce concepts as well.

Common-Sense Strategies

Finally, you should also follow common-sense practices when studying. Study when you are alert, reduce or eliminate distractions, take breaks when you become fatigued, and so on.

Pre-Testing Yourself

Pre-testing enables you to assess how well you are learning. One of the most important aspects of learning is what has been called "meta-learning." Meta-learning has to do with realizing when you know something well or when you need to study some more. In other words, you recognize how well or how poorly you have learned the material you are studying.

For most people, this can be difficult to assess objectively on their own. Practice tests are useful in that they reveal more objectively what you have learned and what you have not learned. You should use this information to guide review and further studying. Developmental learning takes place as you cycle through studying, assessing how well you have learned, reviewing, and assessing again until you feel you are ready to take the exam.

You may have noticed the practice exams included in this book. Use it as part of the learning process. The TestPrep software on the CD-ROM also provides a variety of ways to test yourself before you take the actual exam. By using the Practice Exams, you can take an entire practice test. By using the Study Cards, you can take an entire practice exam, or you might choose to focus on a particular objective area, such as Planning, Troubleshooting, or Monitoring and Optimization. By using the Flash Cards, you can test your knowledge at a level beyond that of recognition; you must come up with the answers in your own words. The Flash Cards also enable you to test your knowledge of particular objective areas.

You should set a goal for your pre-testing. A reasonable goal would be to score consistently in the 90-percent range.

See Appendix C, "What's on the CD-ROM," for a more detailed explanation of the test engine.

Exam Prep Tips

Having mastered the subject matter, the final preparatory step is to understand how the exam will be presented. Make no mistake, a Microsoft Certified Professional (MCP) exam will challenge both your knowledge and test taking skills. This section starts with the basics of exam design, reviews a new type of exam format, and concludes with hints targeted to each of the exam formats.

The MCP Exam

Every MCP exam is released in one of two basic formats. What's being called exam format here is really little more than a combination of the overall exam structure and the presentation method for exam questions.

Each exam format uses the same types of questions. These types or styles of questions include multiple-rating (or scenario-based) questions, traditional multiple-choice questions, and simulation-based questions. It's important to understand the types of questions you will be asked and the actions required to properly answer them.

Understanding the exam formats is key to good preparation because the format determines the number of questions presented, the difficulty of those questions, and the amount of time allowed to complete the exam.

Exam Format

There are two basic formats for the MCP exams: the traditional fixed-form exam and the adaptive form. As its name implies, the fixed-form exam presents a fixed set of questions during the exam session. The adaptive form, however, uses only a subset of questions drawn from a larger pool during any given exam session.

Fixed-Form

A fixed-form computerized exam is based on a fixed set of exam questions. The individual questions are presented in random order during a test session. If you take the same exam more than once you won't necessarily see the exact same questions. This is because two or three final forms are typically assembled for every fixed-form exam Microsoft releases. These are usually labeled Forms A, B, and C.

The final forms of a fixed-form exam are identical in terms of content coverage, number of questions, and allotted time, but the questions are different. You may notice, however, that some of the same questions appear on, or rather are shared among, different final forms. When questions are shared among multiple final forms of an exam, the percentage of sharing is generally small. Many final forms share no questions, but some older exams may have a 10 percent to 15 percent duplication of exam questions on the final exam forms.

Fixed-form exams also have a fixed time limit in which you must complete the exam. The TestPrep software on the CD-ROM that accompanies this book carries fixed-form exams.

Finally, the score you achieve on a fixed-form exam, which is always reported for MCP exams on a scale of 0 to 1,000, is based on the number of questions you answer correctly. The exam's passing score is the same for all final forms of a given fixed-form exam.

The typical format for the fixed-form exam is as follows:

◆ 50–60 questions.

◆ 75–90 minute testing time.

◆ Question review is allowed, including the opportunity to change your answers.

Adaptive Form

An adaptive-form exam has the same appearance as a fixed-form exam, but its questions differ in quantity and process of selection. Although the statistics of adaptive testing are fairly complex, the process is concerned with determining your level of skill or ability with the exam subject matter. This ability assessment begins by presenting questions of varying levels of difficulty and ascertaining at what difficulty level you can reliably answer them. Finally, the ability assessment determines if that ability level is above or below the level required to pass that exam.

Examinees at different levels of ability will see quite different sets of questions. Examinees who demonstrate little expertise with the subject matter will continue to be presented with relatively easy questions. Examinees who demonstrate a high level of expertise will be presented progressively more difficult questions. Individuals of both levels of expertise may answer the same number of questions correctly, but because the higher-expertise examinee can correctly answer more difficult questions, he or she will receive a higher score and is more likely to pass the exam.

The typical design for the adaptive form exam is as follows:

◆ 20–25 questions.

◆ 90 minute testing time, although this is likely to be reduced to 45–60 minutes in the near future.

◆ Question review is not allowed, providing no opportunity to change your answers.

The Adaptive-Exam Process

Your first adaptive exam will be unlike any other testing experience you have had. In fact, many examinees have difficulty accepting the adaptive testing process because they feel that they were not provided the opportunity to adequately demonstrate their full expertise.

You can take consolation in the fact that adaptive exams are painstakingly put together after months of data gathering and analysis and are just as valid as a fixed-form exam. The rigor introduced through the adaptive testing methodology means that there is nothing arbitrary about what you'll see. It is also a more efficient means of testing, requiring less time to conduct and complete.

As you can see from Figure 1, there are a number of statistical measures that drive the adaptive examination process. The most immediately relevant to you is the ability estimate. Accompanying this test statistic are the standard error of measurement, the item characteristic curve, and the test information curve.

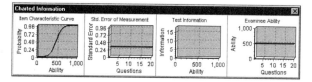

FIGURE 1▲
Microsoft's Adaptive Testing Demonstration Program.

The standard error, which is the key factor in determining when an adaptive exam will terminate, reflects the degree of error in the exam ability estimate. The item characteristic curve reflects the probability of a correct response relative to examinee ability. Finally, the test information statistic provides a measure of the information contained in the set of questions the examinee has answered, again relative to the ability level of the individual examinee.

When you begin an adaptive exam, the standard error has already been assigned a target value it must drop below for the exam to conclude. This target value reflects a particular level of statistical confidence in the process. The examinee ability is initially set to the mean possible exam score (500 for MCP exams).

As the adaptive exam progresses, questions of varying difficulty are presented. Based on your pattern of responses to these questions, the ability estimate is recalculated. Simultaneously, the standard error estimate is refined from its first estimated value of one toward the target value. When the standard error reaches its target value, the exam terminates. Thus, the more consistently you answer questions of the same degree of difficulty, the more quickly the standard error estimate drops, and the fewer questions you will end up seeing during the exam session. This situation is depicted in Figure 2.

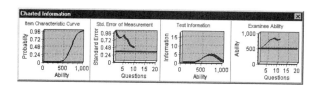

FIGURE 2▲
The changing statistics in an adaptive exam.

As you might suspect, one good piece of advice for taking an adaptive exam is to treat every exam question as if it is the most important. The adaptive scoring algorithm attempts to discover a pattern of responses that reflects some level of proficiency with the subject matter. Incorrect responses almost guarantee that additional questions must be answered (unless, of course, you get every question wrong). This is because the scoring algorithm must adjust to information that is not consistent with the emerging pattern.

New Question Types

A variety of question types can appear on MCP exams. Examples of multiple-choice questions and scenario-based questions appear throughout this book and the TestPrep software. Simulation-based questions are new to the MCP exam series.

Simulation Questions

Simulation-based questions reproduce the look and feel of key Microsoft product features for the purpose of testing. The simulation software used in MCP exams has been designed to look and act, as much as possible, just like the actual product. Consequently, answering simulation questions in a MCP exam entails completing one or more tasks just as if you were using the product itself.

The format of a typical Microsoft simulation question consists of a brief scenario or problem statement along with one or more tasks that must be completed to solve the problem. An example of a simulation question for MCP exams is shown in the following section.

A Typical Simulation Question

It sounds obvious, but your first step when you encounter a simulation is to carefully read the question (see Figure 3). Do not go straight to the simulation application! You must assess the problem being presented and identify the conditions that make up the problem scenario. Note the tasks that must be performed or outcomes that must be achieved to answer the question and review any instructions on how to proceed.

The next step is to launch the simulator by using the button provided. After clicking the Show Simulation button, you will see a feature of the product, as shown in the dialog box in Figure 4. The simulation application will partially cover the question text on many test center machines. Feel free to reposition the simulation or move between the question text screen and the simulation by using hotkeys, point-and-click navigation, or even clicking the simulation launch button again.

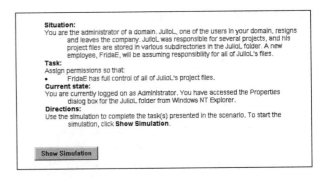

FIGURE 3▲
Typical MCP exam simulation question with directions.

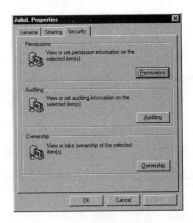

FIGURE 4▲
Launching the simulation application.

It is important to understand that your answer to the simulation question will not be recorded until you move on to the next exam question. This gives you the added capability to close and reopen the simulation application (using the launch button) on the same question without losing any partial answer you may have made.

The third step is to use the simulator as you would the actual product to solve the problem or perform the defined tasks. Again, the simulation software is designed to function, within reason, just as the product does. But don't expect the simulation to reproduce product behavior perfectly. Most importantly, do not allow yourself to become flustered if the simulation does not look or act exactly like the product.

Figure 5 shows the solution to the simulation example problem.

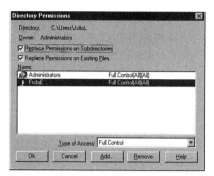

FIGURE 5
The solution to the simulation example.

There are two final points that will help you tackle simulation questions. First, respond only to what is being asked in the question; do not solve problems that you are not asked to solve. Second, accept what is being asked of you. You may not entirely agree with conditions in the problem statement, the quality of the desired solution, or the sufficiency of defined tasks to adequately solve the problem. Always remember that you are being tested on your ability to solve the problem as it is presented.

The solution to the simulation problem shown in Figure 5 perfectly illustrates both of those points. As you'll recall from the question scenario (refer to Figure 3), you were asked to assign appropriate permissions to a new user, Frida E. You were not instructed to make any other changes in permissions. Thus, if you had modified or removed the Administrator's permissions, this item would have been scored wrong on a MCP exam.

Putting It All Together

Given all these different pieces of information, the task now is to assemble a set of tips that will help you successfully tackle the different types of MCP exams.

More Pre-Exam Preparation Tips

Generic exam-preparation advice is always useful. Tips include the following:

◆ Become familiar with the product. Hands-on experience is one of the keys to success on any MCP exam. Review the exercises and the Step by Steps in the book.

◆ Review the current exam-preparation guide on the Microsoft MCP Web site. The documentation Microsoft makes available over the Web identifies the skills every exam is intended to test.

◆ Memorize foundational technical detail, but remember that MCP exams are generally heavy on problem solving and application of knowledge rather than just questions that require only rote memorization.

◆ Take any of the available practice tests. We recommend the one included in this book and the ones you can create using the TestPrep software on the CD-ROM. Although these are fixed-form exams, they provide preparation that is just as valuable for taking an adaptive exam. Because of the nature of adaptive testing, these practice exams cannot be done in the adaptive form. However, fixed-form exams use the same types of questions as adaptive exams and are the most effective way to prepare for either type. As a supplement to the material bound with this book, try the free practice tests available on the Microsoft MCP Web site.

◆ Look on the Microsoft MCP Web site for samples and demonstration items. These tend to be particularly valuable for one significant reason: They help you become familiar with any new testing technologies before you encounter them on a MCP exam.

During the Exam Session

The following generic exam-taking advice you've heard for years applies when taking a MCP exam:

◆ Take a deep breath and try to relax when you first sit down for your exam session. It is very important to control the pressure you may (naturally) feel when taking exams.

◆ You will be provided scratch paper. Take a moment to write down any factual information and technical detail that you committed to short-term memory.

◆ Carefully read all information and instruction screens. These displays have been put together to give you information relevant to the exam you are taking.

◆ Accept the Non-Disclosure Agreement and preliminary survey as part of the examination process. Complete them accurately and quickly move on.

◆ Read the exam questions carefully. Reread each question to identify all relevant detail.

◆ Tackle the questions in the order they are presented. Skipping around won't build your confidence; the clock is always counting down.

◆ Don't rush, but also don't linger on difficult questions. The questions vary in degree of difficulty. Don't let yourself be flustered by a particularly difficult or verbose question.

Fixed-Form Exams

Building from this basic preparation and test-taking advice, you also need to consider the challenges presented by the different exam designs. Because a fixed-form exam is composed of a fixed, finite set of questions, add these tips to your strategy for taking a fixed-form exam:

◆ Note the time allotted and the number of questions appearing on the exam you are taking. Make a rough calculation of how many minutes you can spend on each question and use this to pace yourself through the exam.

◆ Take advantage of the fact that you can return to and review skipped or previously answered questions. Record the questions you can't answer confidently, noting the relative difficulty of each question, on the scratch paper provided. Once you've made it to the end of the exam, return to the more difficult questions.

◆ If there is session time remaining once you have completed all questions (and if you aren't too fatigued!), review your answers. Pay particular attention to questions that seem to have a lot of detail or that require graphics.

◆ As for changing your answers, the general rule of thumb here is *don't*! If you read the question carefully and completely and you felt like you knew the right answer, you probably did. Don't second-guess yourself. If, as you check your answers, one clearly stands out as incorrectly marked, however, of course you should change it in that instance. If you are at all unsure, go with your first impression.

Adaptive Exams

If you are planning to take an adaptive exam, keep these additional tips in mind:

◆ Read and answer every question with great care. When reading a question, identify every relevant detail, requirement, or task that must be performed and double-check your answer to be sure you have addressed every one of them.

◆ If you cannot answer a question, use the process of elimination to reduce the set of potential answers, then take your best guess. Stupid mistakes invariably mean additional questions will be presented.

◆ Forget about reviewing questions and changing your answers. Once you leave a question, whether you've answered it or not, you cannot return to it. Do not skip any questions either; once you do, it's counted as incorrect.

Simulation Questions

You may encounter simulation questions on either the fixed-form or adaptive-form exam. If you do, keep these tips in mind:

◆ Avoid changing any simulation settings that don't pertain directly to the problem solution. Solve the problem you are being asked to solve and nothing more.

◆ Assume default settings when related information has not been provided. If something has not been mentioned or defined, it is a non-critical detail that does not factor into the correct solution.

◆ Be sure your entries are syntactically correct, paying particular attention to your spelling. Enter relevant information just as the product would require it.

◆ Close all simulation application windows after completing the simulation tasks. The testing system software is designed to trap errors that could result when using the simulation application, but trust yourself over the testing software.

◆ If simulations are part of a fixed-form exam, you can return to skipped or previously answered questions and change your answer. However, if you choose to change your answer to a simulation question or even attempt to review the settings you've made in the simulation application, your previous response to that simulation question will be deleted. If simulations are part of an adaptive exam, you cannot return to previous questions.

FINAL CONSIDERATIONS

Finally, there are a number of changes in the MCP program that will impact how frequently you can repeat an exam and what you will see when you do.

◆ Microsoft has instituted a new exam retake policy. This new rule is "two and two, then one and two." That is, you can attempt any exam twice with no restrictions on the time between attempts. But after the second attempt, you must wait two weeks before you can attempt that exam again. After that, you will be required to wait two weeks between subsequent attempts. Plan to pass the exam in two attempts or plan to increase your time horizon for receiving a MCP credential.

◆ New questions are being seeded into the MCP exams. After performance data is gathered on new questions, the examiners will replace older questions on all exam forms. This means that the questions appearing on exams will be regularly changing.

◆ Many of the current MCP exams will be republished in adaptive form in the coming months. Prepare yourself for this significant change in testing as it is entirely likely that this will become the preferred MCP exam format.

These changes mean that the brute-force strategies for passing MCP exams may soon completely lose their viability. So if you don't pass an exam on the first or second attempt, it is entirely possible that the exam's form will change significantly the next time you take it. It could be updated to adaptive form from fixed form or have a different set of questions or question types.

The intention of Microsoft is clearly not to make the exams more difficult by introducing unwanted change, but to create and maintain valid measures of the technical skills and knowledge associated with the different MCP credentials. Preparing for a MCP exam has always involved not only studying the subject matter, but also planning for the testing experience itself. With the recent changes, this is now truer than ever.

Practice Exam

This portion of the Final Review section consists of a practice examination. This practice exam is representative of what you should expect on the actual exam. The answers are at the end of the exam. It is strongly suggested that when you take this exam, you treat it just as you would the actual exam at the test center. Time yourself, read carefully, and answer all the questions as best you can.

Some of the questions are vague and require deduction on your part to come up with the best answer from the possibilities given. Many of them are verbose, requiring you to read a lot before you come to an actual question. These are skills you should acquire before attempting the actual exam.

1. Which of the following best normalizes a person's name and street address?

   A. Name
      Address
      CityStateZip

   B. Name
      Address
      City
      State
      Zip

   C. LastName
      FirstName
      Address
      City
      State
      Zip

   D. LastName
      FirstName
      Address
      City
      Zip

2. Some of your users are complaining about long response times when running a particular query. If query response time for other queries on other tables is acceptable, what is the most probable cause for the long response time?

   A. The server is overloaded and should be upgraded.

   B. There are locks preventing records from being read.

   C. The database is corrupt.

   D. The network is slow.

3. Which of the following is *not* an advantage of using stored procedures for data access?

   A. Server-based management of data access

   B. Stored execution plans

   C. Allows programs the most flexible access to SQL Server data

   D. Provides isolation between clients and the server, so the server side can change independently of the client

4. Sam needs to use a cursor to loop through a record set and perform an update to a data field in a table independent of the cursor. The cursor will contain, at most, a few thousand records. Which type of cursor should Sam use?

   A. Static cursor

   B. Dynamic cursor

   C. Forward-Only cursor

   D. Keyset-driven cursor.

Refer to the following table definitions for questions 5 through 9:

Users
```
UserID int IDENTITY
FirstName char(50)
LastName char(50)
```

UserDepartments
```
UserID int
DepartmentID int
```

Departments
```
DepartmentID int IDENTITY
DepartmentName char(30)
```

5. Jim needs to change the last name of a record in the **Users** table. The user Daisy Mae just got married and wants her last name changed to "Smith." Which of the following will most easily accomplish this task?

   A. `UPDATE Users SET LastName = 'Smith' Where LastName = 'Mae'`

   B. `UPDATE Users SET LastName = 'Smith' WHERE FirstName = 'Daisy' and LastName = 'Mae'`

C. UPDATE Users SET LastName = 'Mae' where
FirstName = 'Daisy'

D. Find Daisy's UserID by querying the UserID
table, and then update the correct record by
using the UserID in an UPDATE query.

6. Sandy needs to find out how many users are in
each department in her company. Which query
will produce the best report?

A. SELECT DepartmentName, Count(*) FROM
Departments

B. SELECT DepartmentID, count(*) FROM Users

C. SELECT DepartmentName, Count(*)
FROM UserDepartments UD
INNER JOIN Departments D
ON UD.DepartmentID = D.DepartmentID
GROUP BY DepartmentName

D. SELECT DepartmentID, Count(*)
FROM UserDepartments UD
GROUP BY DepartmentID

7. After producing the report in Question 6, Sandy
is told that the report had too much information—the executives want to know only the
departments with more than 10 people in them.
Which of the following, when added to a query
from Question 6, will produce that report? Select
the best answer.

A. HAVING DepartmentID > 10

B. HAVING Count(*) > 10

C. TOP 10 PERCENT

D. WITH CUBE

8. Rob wants to create a view that will show users'
full names and their departments' names. Which
of the following will produce the view Rob
wants? Select the best answer.

```
CREATE VIEW RobsView AS
    SELECT FirstName, LastName,
DepartmentID
    FROM Users
        INNER JOIN UserDepartments
            ON USERS.UserID =
Departments.DepartmentID
```

A. CREATE VIEW RobsView AS
    SELECT FirstName, LastName,
DepartmentID
    FROM Users
        INNER JOIN UserDepartments
            ON USERS.UserID =
Departments.DepartmentID

B. CREATE VIEW RobsView AS
    SELECT FirstName, LastName,
DepartmentName
    FROM Users U
        INNER JOIN UserDepartments UD
            ON U.UserID = UD.UserID
        INNER JOIN Departments D
            ON UD.DepartmentID =
D.DepartmentID

C. CREATE VIEW RobsView FOR
    SELECT FirstName, LastName,
DepartmentID
    FROM Users U
        INNER JOIN UserDepartments UD
            ON U.UserID = UD.UserID
        INNER JOIN Departments D
            ON UD.DepartmentID =
D.DepartmentID

D. CREATE VIEW RobsView AS
    SELECT FirstName, LastName,
DepartmentID
        FROM Departments

9. Now that the view from Question 8 is created,
Rob wants to query it. Which of the following
will query the view? Select the best answer.

A. `SELECT * FROM RobsView`

B. `SELECT * FROM VIEW RobsView`

C. `SELECTVIEW * FROM RobsView`

D. `sp_selectview RobsView`

10. Which of the following techniques is used to uniquely identify a database row?

   A. The `UNIQUEIDENTIFIER` data type

   B. The `TIMESTAMP` data type

   C. The `IDENTITY` qualifier on an integer field

   D. All of the above

11. Jane needs to add a unique identifier field to a table. Which of the following commands will correctly add the field called `ID` to the table Pictures? Select the best answer.

   A. `ALTER TABLE Pictures ADD ROWIDGUIDCOL ID`

   B. `ALTER TABLE Pictures ADD ID UNIQUEIDENTIFIER null`

   C. `ALTER TABLE Pictures ADD ID ROWIDGUIDCOL`

   D. `ALTER DATABASE Pictures ADD ID ROWIDGUIDCOL`

12. After adding the field to the table in Question 11, Jane wants to go back and populate all of the existing records with a GUID. Which of the following will perform this operation? Select the best answer.

   A. The operation was automatically performed when the column was created.

   B. `ALTER TABLE Pictures ALTER COLUMN ID ADD ROWIDGUIDCOL`

   C. `ALTER TABLE Pictures ALTER COLUMN ID ADD UNIQUEIDENTIFIER`

   D. `UPDATE Pictures SET ID = NEWID()`

13. Now that all the current data is updated from Question 12, Jane needs to set up the ID column so it automatically updates to a new GUID for each inserted row. Which of the following best describes the procedure for accomplishing this task?

   A. Nothing needs to be done; this was accomplished when the column was created.

   B. Nothing needs to be done; this was accomplished when the `ROWIDGUIDCOL` property was turned on for the ID column.

   C. `ALTER TABLE Pictures ADD CONSTRAINT IDDefault DEFAULT NewID() FOR ID`

   D. `ALTER TABLE Pictures ADD DEFAULT CONSTRAINT = NewID()`

14. Cliff needs to add to an existing table a field that will hold social security numbers. It will be updated in every record in the table with current data and shouldn't ever be `NULL`. Which of the following data types is the best choice?

   A. `int`

   B. `char(9)`

   C. `varchar(9)`

   D. `smallint`

The following table format is used for questions 15 through 17:

```
Table1
ID int not null IDENTITY
LastName char(50)
FirstName char(50)
ZipCode char(5)
```

15. Which of the following index definitions would work best for creating a list sorted by last name then first name?

A. `CREATE UNIQUE CLUSTERED INDEX foo`
   `ON Table1(LastName, FirstName, ID)`

B. `CREATE INDEX foo`
   `ON Table1(LastName, FirstName)`

C. `CREATE INDEX foo`
   `ON Table1(LastName, FirstName, ID)`

D. `CREATE UNIQUE INDEX foo`
   `ON Table1(LastName, FirstName)`

16. If Table1 was used in an inner join, with the ID field being the inner join key, which of the following indexes would provide the best performance?

A. `CREATE UNIQUE CLUSTERED INDEX foo`
   `ON Table1(LastName, FirstName, ID)`

B. `CREATE UNIQUE CLUSTERED INDEX foo`
   `ON Table1(ID, LastName, FirstName)`

C. `CREATE UNIQUE CLUSTERED INDEX foo`
   `ON Table1(ID)`

D. `CREATE UNIQUE INDEX FOO`
   `ON Table1(ID)`

17. If Table1 is going to be joined on 90% of the time on ID, and used to generate lists 10% of the time, which of the following combinations of indexes would provide the best performance to the most queries?

A. Clustered unique index on ID; non-clustered index on LastName, FirstName

B. Clustered index on LastName, FirstName; non-clustered unique index on ID

C. Clustered index on FirstName, LastName; non-clustered unique index on ID

D. Non-clustered, unique index on ID; non-clustered index on LastName

18. When creating an index, `FILLFACTOR` describes which of the following?

A. The number of columns in the index

B. The number of pages used by index

C. The amount of time it takes to build the index

D. The number of files on which the index is used

19. Which of the following describes a good composite primary key?

A. Social Security Number

B. Last Name, First Name

C. Last Name, First Name, Address, Age

D. Last Name

20. Consider the following query:
```
SELECT *
FROM OpenQuery(OracleSrvr, 'Select name, id
from authors')
ORDER BY name
```
On which server does the sorting occur?

A. On the server OracleSrvr

B. On the SQL Server executing the query

C. By the OLE-DB driver

D. By the SQL*Net driver

21. For which of the following actions can a trigger *not* be created? Select the best answer.

A. Select

B. Insert

C. Update

D. Delete

Questions 22 through 25 use the following table and trigger definitions:

Table1
UserID int IDENTITY
FirstName char(50)
LastName char(50)
DepartmentID int
BillingID int

```
CREATE TRIGGER Table1_InsertUpdate
ON Table1
FOR INSERT, UPDATE
AS
BEGIN
        IF UPDATE(DepartmentID)
                IF (Select count(*) from Table1
inner join Deleted on Table1.DepartmentID =
                    deleted.departmentid) = 0
                BEGIN
                    RAISERROR ('Cannot remove
the last member of a department.', 16, 1)
                    ROLLBACK
                END
END
```

22. Assuming this is the only trigger bound to the table, is it possible for the last member of a department to be deleted?

    A. No; the trigger prevents that from happening.

    B. Yes; the trigger has not been activated yet.

    C. Yes, if a new record is inserted on top of the existing one.

    D. Yes, by using a DELETE command.

23. How could this trigger be modified to set the BillingID to 1 if the department was successfully changed? (Assume the nested trigger's configuration setting is set to its default.)

    A. It cannot because a trigger can only act on one field at a time.

    B. By adding an ELSE clause to the IF (SELECT...) statement that makes the appropriate update.

C. It cannot because a table cannot be updated during a trigger.

D. It cannot because nested triggers are not allowed.

24. What does the ROLLBACK statement in the trigger do?

    A. It causes the transaction to roll back, aborting the insert or update that caused the trigger to run, but not aborting the transaction that the offending statement was part of.

    B. It causes the transaction containing the offending statement to roll back.

    C. Nothing; the keyword EXIT should have been used to cause the transaction to abort.

    D. It causes the transaction log to fill up.

25. The RAISERROR statement in the trigger performs what function?

    A. It provides the connection with an error message.

    B. It provides the connection and the SQL Server error log file with an error message.

    C. It provides the connection, the SQL Server error log file, and the Windows NT application event log with an error message.

    D. It causes a server-wide severity one message, stopping SQL Server.

26. When is it important to use the WITH RECOMPILE option when creating a stored procedure?

    A. Always use WITH RECOMPILE.

    B. On servers that aren't busy, the WITH RECOMPILE option should be used all the time.

    C. Only if the query plans used by the stored procedure change frequently.

D. When any tables that are going to be used by the stored procedure are routinely dropped and re-created.

27. Which one of the following statements will correctly execute the stored procedure sp_foo and receive an output parameter @Identifier into the variable @ID? Assume the variable @ID is correctly declared.

    A. SELECT @ID = sp_foo @Identifier

    B. EXEC (select @ID = sp_foo @Identifier)

    C. EXEC sp_foo @ID = @Identifier OUTPUT

    D. EXEC sp_foo @Identifer = @ID OUTPUT

28. The transaction log in the database Northwind has filled up. What is the safest way to empty it?

    A. Take SQL Server offline and delete the log files.

    B. Truncate the syslogs system table.

    C. Use the Transact-SQL command BACKUP LOG with either the NO_LOG or TRUNCATE_ONLY option.

    D. Use the Transact-SQL command BACKUP LOG with no options.

29. Which of the following are situations in which implementing file groups would provide performance benefits? Select all that apply.

    A. On a server without RAID 5 but with multiple disk drives, file groups can be used to split data onto separate physical disks.

    B. On a server with one large physical drive, file groups should be used to spread data out across the drive.

    C. On a server with RAID 5, file groups should be used to spread data out across several drives.

D. On servers that have slower tape drives, or for large databases that can't be backed up conveniently, file groups can be used to partition data for backups.

30. What is the most appropriate scenario for denormalizing a database model?

    A. A database that is read-only and used for reporting

    B. A database with volatile data

    C. A database that is used to track sales data

    D. A database that contains personnel records

31. Barney needs to run a report against a table that has a very high transaction volume. He's concerned that if he runs the report, he might lock users out of the table. Which transaction isolation level can Barney set to ensure that he won't be competing for locks with the rest of the users?

    A. Serializable

    B. Repeatable Read

    C. Read Committed

    D. Read Uncommitted

32. Janet is doing the monthly payroll report. It is after the deadline for time reporting, but she needs to make sure that no updates occur in the tables on which the report is being built until the report is done. What transaction isolation level can ensure that Janet will have the level of concurrency she wants?

    A. Serializable

    B. Repeatable Read

    C. Read Committed

    D. Read Uncommitted

33. Which of the following is not a good way to pre-vent deadlocks?

    A. Perform transactions in the same order every time.

    B. Allow user input during transactions.

    C. Keep transactions short.

    D. Avoid using high transaction isolation levels, reducing the number of locks held at a time.

34. Which of the following will enable a transaction to be chosen as a victim automatically if it is involved in a deadlock? Select the best answer.

    A. `SET TRANSACTION_ISOLATION_LEVEL 1`

    B. `SET DEADLOCK_PRIORITY LOW`

    C. There is no way to change a deadlock priority.

    D. Set the deadlock priority status of the user's account to low.

35. What types of queries justify using the dynamic SQL model of programming? Select the best answer.

    A. Queries that require different joins depending on which criteria are chosen.

    B. Queries that involve complex where clauses.

    C. Queries that use permanent tables that are created and destroyed routinely.

    D. All of the above.

Questions 36 through 40 use the following table structures:

Users
UserID int NOT NULL IDENTITY
UserName char(30)
FirstName char(50)
LastName char(50)

UserDepartments
UserID int NOT NULL
DepartmentID int NOT NULL

Departments
DepartmentID int NOT NULL IDENTITY
DepartmentName char(30)

36. What is the best choice for primary key for the UserDepartments table?

    A. The `UserID` field.

    B. The `DepartmentID` field.

    C. The `UserID` and `DepartmentID` fields form a composite key.

    D. There is no primary key relationship possible.

37. The relationship between the User and Department tables can be characterized as which of the following?

    A. One-to-Many.

    B. Many-to-One.

    C. Many-to-Many.

    D. There is no apparent relationship.

38. Which of the following constraints defined on the UserDepartments table best describes the relationship between the User and UserDepartments table?

    A. `FOREIGN KEY UserID REFERENCES Users (UserID)`

    B. `FOREIGN KEY DepartmentID REFERENCES Departments (DepartmentID)`

    C. `FOREIGN KEY UserID REFERENCES UserDepartments (UserID)`

    D. `FOREIGN KEY UserID REFERENCES Users (FirstName)`

39. XYZ Corporation has a company policy that all users must belong to at least one department. What is the best way to enforce this business rule?

   A. Business rules cannot be enforced in database structures.

   B. Use a default constraint.

   C. Use a foreign key constraint.

   D. Use a trigger.

40. XYZ Corporation has a company policy that all users must have a company-defined user name, which is a combination of their first and last names, and their UserID in case of duplication. What is the best mechanism to use to enforce this rule?

   A. Business rules cannot be enforced in database structures.

   B. Use a default constraint.

   C. Use a foreign key constraint.

   D. Use a trigger.

41. When using cursors, what restrictions are there on a cursor of type FAST_FORWARD? Select the best answer.

   A. SCROLLABLE and READ_ONLY

   B. FORWARD_ONLY and READ_WRITE

   C. FORWARD_ONLY and READ_ONLY

   D. SCROLLABLE and FOR_UPDATE

42. A global cursor can be used by which of the following? Select the best answer.

   A. Any connection on the server

   B. The connection that created the cursor

   C. The connection that created the cursor, but only within the current transaction

   D. The connection that created the cursor, but only within the current batch

43. How is a global variable in Transact-SQL made available?

   A. Only by the current connection.

   B. Only by the current connection in the current batch.

   C. Only by the current connection in the current transaction.

   D. There are no global variables in Transact-SQL.

44. How is a local variable in Transact-SQL made available?

   A. Only by the current connection.

   B. Only by the current connection in the current batch.

   C. Only by the current connection in the current transaction.

   D. There are no local variables in Transact-SQL.

45. What is the value of @foo after the following Transact-SQL statement is run?

```
declare @foo int
select @foo = 0

while @foo < 5
begin
    print @foo
    if @foo = 5
            continue
    select @foo = @foo + 1
end
```

   A. 5

   B. 4

   C. 3

   D. 2

46. A `ROLLBACK TRANSACTION` statement will cause which of the following events? Select the best answer.

    A. Abort the current transaction

    B. Abort all open transactions

    C. Abort the current transaction and close the current connection.

    D. Abort the current transaction and decrement the `@@TRANCOUNT` counter by 1.

47. For a bulk import to be non-logged, which of the following *cannot* be true? Select the best answer.

    A. The Select into/Bulk Copy option must be turned on.

    B. The table has some rows in it and has indexes.

    C. The table has some rows in it with no indexes.

    D. The BCP command uses a table lock.

48. For which one of the following cases would a format file need to be used with the bulk copy program (BCP)?

    A. The data file is comma delimited.

    B. The data file is delimited by a space.

    C. The Select into/Bulk Copy option is not turned on in the target database.

    D. The data file is column delimited (has fixed-width columns).

49. Suzy needs to load a lot of data from a Microsoft Access database into SQL Server. She's planning to use the Data Transformation Services to directly import the data from Microsoft Access.

    Evaluate Suzy's solution.

    A. This is an optimal, efficient solution to the problem.

    B. This is a good solution to the problem, but not the most efficient.

    C. This is a poor solution to the problem. It will not work reliably in all cases.

    D. This is not a solution to the problem.

50. Suzy needs to load a lot of data from a Microsoft Access database into SQL Server. She's planning to export the data from Microsoft Access.

    Evaluate Suzy's solution.

    A. This is an optimal, efficient solution to the problem.

    B. This is a good solution to the problem, but not the most efficient.

    C. This is a poor solution to the problem. It will not work reliably in all cases.

    D. This is not a solution to the problem.

51. Suzy needs to load a lot of data from a Microsoft Access database into SQL Server. She's planning to export the data from Microsoft Access into a delimited text file, and use non-logged BCP to import the data.

    Evaluate Suzy's solution.

    A. This is an optimal, efficient solution to the problem.

    B. This is a good solution to the problem, but not the most efficient.

    C. This is a poor solution to the problem. It will not work reliably in all cases.

    D. This is not a solution to the problem.

52. Jason is using SQL Server Query Analyzer to examine a query. He wants to see his query plan, so he uses `SET SHOWPLAN_ALL ON`.

    Evaluate Jason's solution.

A. This is an optimal, efficient solution to the problem.

B. This is a good solution to the problem, but not the most efficient.

C. This is a poor solution to the problem. It will not work reliably in all cases.

D. This is not a solution to the problem.

53. Jason is using SQL Server Query Analyzer to examine a query. He wants to see his query plan, so he uses SET SHOWPLAN_TEXT ON.

Evaluate Jason's solution.

A. This is an optimal, efficient solution to the problem.

B. This is a good solution to the problem, but not the most efficient.

C. This is a poor solution to the problem. It will not work reliably in all cases.

D. This is not a solution to the problem.

Questions 54 and 55 use the following table structures:

Users
UserID int IDENTITY
UserName char(30)
FirstName char(50)
LastName char(50)

54. Donna needs to copy 100 records in the user table into a new table called NewUsers so she can test some new update routines. The Select into/Bulk Copy option is turned on. She plans to run the following script:

```
SELECT * INTO NewUsers FROM Users
```

Evaluate Donna's solution.

A. This is an optimal, efficient solution to the problem.

B. This solution to the problem will work, but has undesirable side effects.

C. This is a poor solution to the problem. It will not work reliably in all cases.

D. This is not a solution to the problem.

55. Donna needs to copy 100 records in the user table into a new table called NewUsers so she can test some new update routines. The Select into/Bulk Copy option is turned on. She plans to run the following script:

```
SET ROWCOUNT 100
SELECT * INTO NewUsers FROM Users
SET ROWCOUNT 0
```

Evaluate Donna's solution.

A. This is an optimal, efficient solution to the problem.

B. This solution to the problem will work, but has undesirable side effects.

C. This is a poor solution to the problem. It will not work reliably in all cases.

D. This is not a solution to the problem.

56. Mark is building a large database that will house historical transactions for several years. The data storage required is currently 50GB, and is expected to grow at a rate of 5GB per year. Mark's solution is to put all of the data into one large table, which would be used for reporting and for transaction processing.

Evaluate Mark's solution.

A. This is an optimal, efficient solution to the problem.

B. This solution to the problem will work, but has undesirable side effects.

C. This is a poor solution to the problem. It will not work reliably in all cases.

D. This is not a solution to the problem.

57. Mark is building a large database that will house historical transactions for several years. The data storage required is currently 50GB and is expected to grow at a rate of 5GB per year. Mark's solution is to horizontally partition the data by year and move records to a new table every month to keep the OLTP table smaller.

    Evaluate Mark's solution.

    A. This is an optimal, efficient solution to the problem.

    B. This solution to the problem will work, but has undesirable side effects.

    C. This is a poor solution to the problem. It will not work reliably in all cases.

    D. This is not a solution to the problem.

58. Mark is building a large database that will house historical transactions for several years. The data storage required is currently 50GB, and is expected to grow at a rate of 5GB per year. Mark's solution is to horizontally partition the data by year and move records to a new table every month to keep the OLTP table smaller. The data that isn't current would be stored in a separate, read-only database to ease load on the backup system.

    Evaluate Mark's solution.

    A. This is an optimal, efficient solution to the problem.

    B. This solution to the problem will work, but has undesirable side effects.

    C. This is a poor solution to the problem. It will not work reliably in all cases.

    D. This is not a solution to the problem.

59. Sam is investigating a query plan and notices that all of his searches on different keys of a table are done as a clustered index scan.

    Evaluate Sam's query.

    A. His query is using a clustered index to search for the data; it is the most efficient search possible.

    B. His query is using a normal index to search for the data; it is the most efficient search possible.

    C. His query is reading through the whole table and is not very efficient.

    D. His query is reading through the whole table, which is very efficient.

60. Becky needs to query the table ClientList and find all the cities that are not mentioned in the table CityList so she can determine which clients are in new cities. Becky plans to use the following script:

    ```
    SELECT * FROM ClientList WHERE City NOT IN
    (SELECT City FROM CityList)
    ```

    Evaluate Becky's solution.

    A. This is an optimal, efficient solution to the problem.

    B. This a good solution to the problem, but not the most efficient.

    C. This is a poor solution to the problem. It will not work reliably in all cases.

    D. This is not a solution to the problem.

61. Becky needs to query the table ClientList and find of the cities that are not mentioned in the table CityList so she can determine which clients are in new cities. She plans to use the following script:

    ```
    SELECT ClientList.*
    FROM ClientList
        INNER JOIN CityList
            ON ClientList.City <> CityList.City
    ```

    Evaluate Becky's solution.

    A. This is an optimal, efficient solution to the problem.

B. This a good solution to the problem, but not the most efficient.

C. This is a poor solution to the problem. It will not work reliably in all cases.

D. This is not a solution to the problem.

62. Bart is trying to track down a problem with an Internet application that uses ADO. He suspects that the developer of the application has misspelled some table names. Bart is going to use the SQL Profiler to determine what is being sent to the server.

Evaluate Bart's solution.

A. This is an optimal, efficient solution to the problem.

B. This a good solution to the problem, but not the most efficient.

C. This is a poor solution to the problem. It will not work reliably in all cases.

D. This is not a solution to the problem.

63. Lisa is writing a stored procedure that will use a cursor to update 50,000 records on an OLTP system. Lisa plans to use the optimistic locking strategy when declaring the cursor.

Evaluate Lisa's solution.

A. This is an optimal, efficient solution to the problem.

B. This a good solution to the problem, but not the most efficient.

C. This is a poor solution to the problem. It will not work reliably in all cases.

D. This is not a solution to the problem.

64. Lisa is writing a stored procedure that will use a cursor to update 50,000 records on an OLTP system. Lisa plans to use a FAST_FORWARD cursor to perform the update.

Evaluate Lisa's solution.

A. This is an optimal, efficient solution to the problem.

B. This a good solution to the problem, but not the most efficient.

C. This is a poor solution to the problem. It will not work reliably in all cases.

D. This is not a solution to the problem.

65. Homer is building a full-text index for the following table:

HomerTable
HomerID int null
HomerTxt char(8000)

He's building it so he can search through the HomerTxt field quickly and easily. The primary key in the table is the HomerID, which is externally generated and may be NULL.

Evaluate Homer's solution.

A. This is an optimal, efficient solution to the problem.

B. This a good solution to the problem, but not the most efficient.

C. This is a poor solution to the problem. It will not work reliably in all cases.

D. This is not a solution to the problem.

ANSWERS AND EXPLANATIONS

1. **D.** Using State and Zip is redundant because a ZIP code implies a state. Its true that you would-n't normally leave off the state in an address record because it's faster to hold the data in the local table, but the question did ask for normal-ization, not optimization. This question applies to the objective "Group data into entities by applying normalization rules."

2. **B.** If everything else is running OK except for one particular query, that implies the query is broken, so the problem cannot lie in the network, a database corruption problem, or the network hardware. This question applies to the objective "Diagnose and resolve locking problems."

3. **C.** Using stored procedures obligates the calling program to use the provided interface, which is not as flexible as the full range of INSERT, DELETE, UPDATE, and SELECT statements that are possible via a dynamic model. This question applies to the objective "Access data by using the Stored Procedure model."

4. **A.** Because the cursor is relatively small, Sam should use a static cursor because of the low processor overhead and low TempDB overhead. This question applies to the objective "Manipulate Data by using Transact-SQL Cursors."

5. **D.** Answer D is the best answer because if there were two different Daisy Mae's working for the company, the other queries would inadvertently update them both. This question applies to the objective "Write INSERT, DELETE, UPDATE, and SELECT statements that retrieve and modify data."

6. **C.** Options C and D will both provide the same counts, but answer C is better because the result set provides department names rather than meaningless ID numbers. This question applies to the objective "Create result sets that provide summary data."

7. **B.** The HAVING clause is designed for just this operation. This question applies to the objective "Create result sets that provide summary data."

8. **B.** Options C and B are functionally equiva-lent, but B returns the required department name. This question applies to the objective "Design, create, use, and alter views."

9. **A.** Views are queried just like tables are. This question applies to the objective "Design, create, use, and alter views."

10. **D.** All of the techniques will provide a unique identifier if used properly. This question applies to the objective "Create tables that enforce data integrity and referential integrity."

11. **B.** Adding a column for a GUID is just like adding any other column: the data type is UNIQUEIDENTIFIER. This question applies to the objective "Create tables that enforce data integrity and referential integrity."

12. **D.** Option B will set the column properties so SQL Server will take advantage of the GUID, but won't go back and fix the NULL entries. The only way to retrofit the data is to use the UPDATE query. This question applies to the objective "Create tables that enforce data integrity and referential integrity."

13. **C.** By using a default, and using the niladic function NewID(), the column will be perpetually updated. This question applies to the objective "Create tables that enforce data integrity and ref-erential integrity."

14. **B.** The integer and small integer types won't hold all of the range of a Social Security number, and because the field will always be populated, a char field is more space efficient than a varchar. This question applies to the objective "Create tables that enforce data integrity and referential integrity."

15. **A.** The ID column must be included to make sure that people with the same name don't violate the primary key, and it's always a good idea to make a clustered index unique if possible. This question applies to the objective "Create and maintain indexes."

16. **C.** The smaller the index, the faster the access; the name data doesn't add anything to any search anyway. This question applies to the objective "Create and maintain indexes."

17. **A.** A clustered index on the ID will make joins very fast, and the non-clustered index would help sorting and searching for names. This question applies to the objective "Create and maintain indexes."

18. **B.** This is a sneaky question. FILLFACTOR describes how full index pages are, so it indirectly determines how many pages the index will have. It's the only answer that makes sense. This question applies to the objective "Create and maintain indexes."

19. **C.** Option A is incorrect for two reasons: First of all, it's not really legal to use a Social Security number as an identifier for a person because of privacy laws. Also, SSN would not be a composite key because it's only one field. To get the best match for a person, go with the combination of Last, First, Address, and Age. Age helps to reduce problems of people who have suffixes like "Junior" or "Senior". This question applies to the objective "Identify primary keys." Note that this is probably a good case to use a surrogate key (an identity column) because big indexes like that can cause long search times, and create problems on inserts as well.

20. **B.** The sorting has to be done by either the remote server or the local server, so options C and D are out. Because the only thing the OracleSrvr server will see is the SELECT statement 'Select name, id from

authors', it won't know that it has to sort anything. This question applies to the objective "Access data from static or dynamic sources by using remote stored procedures, linked servers, and OPENROWSET."

21. **A.** The whole notion of a SELECT trigger is a bit silly. Triggers are only used during data modification, which implies INSERT, UPDATE, or DELETE. This question applies to the objective "Create triggers that implement rules, enforce data integrity, and perform cascading updates and deletes."

22. **D.** The trigger will fire for INSERT and UPDATE statements only, and the trigger is designed to prevent the last member of a department from being reassigned. This question applies to the objective "Create triggers that implement rules, enforce data integrity, and perform cascading updates and deletes."

23. **B.** The default state for nested triggers is TRUE, so the trigger can run and update the same record again, which will fire the trigger again. Assuming the nested trigger doesn't roll back the change, the changes will take effect perfectly. This question applies to the objective "Create triggers that implement rules, enforce data integrity, and perform cascading updates and deletes."

24. **B.** A rollback in a trigger will stop the offending action and roll back all currently open transactions. This question applies to the objective "Create triggers that implement rules, enforce data integrity, and perform cascading updates and deletes."

25. **A.** The necessary options (WITH LOG) aren't present to cause notification to the SQL Server error log or the Windows NT event log. This question applies to the objective "Create and execute stored procedures to enforce business rules, to modify data in multiple tables, to perform calculations, and to use input and output parameters."

26. **C.**   A new "feature" in SQL Server 7 is that the WITH RECOMPILE option *doesn't* handle cases in which a table's object ID changes. This question applies to the objective "Create and execute stored procedures to enforce business rules, to modify data in multiple tables, to perform calculations, and to use input and output parameters."

27. **D.**   Option D is the only syntactically correct option. Another correct statement for the same effect is EXEC sp_foo @ID OUTPUT. This question applies to the objective "Create and execute stored procedures to enforce business rules, to modify data in multiple tables, to perform calculations, and to use input and output parameters."

28. **C.**   Option C is the only way to safely clear a transaction log. This question applies to the objective "Create and manage files, file groups, and transaction logs that define a database."

29. **A, D.**   Options B and C just cause more management overhead with no real benefit. This question applies to the objective "Create and manage files, file groups, and transaction logs that define a database."

30. **A.**   Options B, C, and D are places in which denormalization should probably be avoided because it may cause synchronization issues. This question applies to the objective "In a given situation, decide whether denormalization is appropriate."

31. **D.**   The READ UNCOMMITTED option causes no locks to be issued at all, at the expense of data integrity. The other options cause various levels of locking. This question applies to the objective "Create and manage explicit, implicit, and distributed transactions to ensure data consistency and recoverability."

32. **A.**   A SERIALIZABLE read causes locks on all records and tables that are accessed by the query. This question applies to the objective "Create and manage explicit, implicit, and distributed transactions to ensure data consistency and recoverability."

33. **B.**   The general idea for reducing deadlocks is simply to reduce the amount of time locks are held overall; by eliminating user prompts during transactions, the lock times are reduced significantly. This question applies to the objective "Create and manage explicit, implicit, and distributed transactions to ensure data consistency and recoverability."

34. **B.**   Option B can be used for reporting applications so that information being written to a database won't be lost. This question applies to the objective "Create and manage explicit, implicit, and distributed transactions to ensure data consistency and recoverability."

35. **D.**   Dynamic queries are very flexible, so all of the options apply. This question applies to the objective "Access data by using the dynamic SQL model."

36. **C.**   About 99% of the time, an Identity column is going to be a primary key if it is present in a table. Plus, it makes sense for the User table because there really isn't another unique entity or combination of entities. This question applies to the objective "Identify Primary Keys."

37. **C.**   Many-to-Many relationships are characterized by the use of an intersection table—in this case, UserDepartment. This question applies to the objective "Choose the foreign key that will enforce a relationship between entities and that will ensure referential integrity."

38. **A.**   This is the Create Table syntax for that particular foreign key. Note that the referenced fields must be part of either a unique constraint or a primary key constraint (which would make them unique and not NULL). This question applies to the objective "Choose the foreign key that will enforce a relationship between entities and that will ensure referential integrity."

39. **D.**   Usually, triggers are the best means for enforcing business rules of any kind. This question applies to the objective "Identify the business rules that relate to data integrity."

40. **D.**   A trigger is really the best way to perform this operation. This question applies to the objective "Incorporate business rules and constraints into the data model."

41. **C.**   Cursors defined as FAST_FORWARD are both FORWARD_ONLY and READ_ONLY; they also have other optimizations to make them really fast. This question applies to the objective "Manipulate Data by using Transact-SQL Cursors."

42. **B.**   The term "global" in this case is a bit misleading. It refers to the fact that the cursor is available throughout any stored procedures called by the connection. This question applies to the objective "Manipulate data by using Transact-SQL Cursors."

43. **D.**   There are no global variables; the @@VAR variables are now implemented as functions. There never have been any user-defined global variables. This question applies to the objective "Create scripts using Transact-SQL."

44. **B.**   Local variables are good only in the current connection, batch, and statement block. This question applies to the objective "Create scripts using Transact-SQL."

45. **B.**   The Continue statement never gets executed. This question applies to the objective "Create scripts using Transact-SQL."

46. **B.**   The ROLLBACK TRANSACTION statement rolls back everything that's pending back unless it is used with a named transaction. This question applies to the objective "Create and manage explicit, implicit, and distributed transaction to ensure data consistency and recoverability" and "Create scripts using Transact-SQL."

47. **B.**   The table can have data in it, or it can have indexes, but not both. This question applies to the objective "Populate the database with data from an external data source."

48. **D.**   Format files are usually only used for column-delimited data. This question applies to the objective "Populate the database with data from an external data source."

49. **A.**   This is the best solution; it uses batch inserts into SQL Server, which goes really fast. This question applies to the objective "Populate the database with data from an external data source."

50. **C.**   When data is exported from Access, the data is actually sent as a CREATE TABLE statement and then a whole bunch of one-row INSERT statements. This will usually fill the transaction log, run the database out of locks, run the server out of memory, or some combination of all three. This question applies to the objective "Populate the database with data from an external data source."

51. **B.**   This is still better than exporting from Access, and actually works fairly well even with large data sets. This process is less efficient than Data Transformation Services because it makes a full duplicate of the data and translates it to and from text format. DTS doesn't perform the multiple translations, and doesn't need to write an intermediate file to disk, so it is more space efficient and more time efficient. This question applies to the objective "Populate the database with data from an external data source."

52. **A.**   The SHOWPLAN_ALL option is designed for windowing environments that can handle column output well. This question applies to the objective "Evaluate and optimize the performance of an execution plan."

53. **B.**   SHOWPLAN_TEXT is used for command-line environments. It provides similar information to SHOWPLAN_ALL, but is formatted for OSQL or similar applications. This question applies to the objective "Evaluate and optimize the performance of an execution plan."

54. **B.**   This will copy the entire table, which could be a nasty side effect, but it does copy 100 rows, plus anything else that's in the table. This question applies to the objective "Write INSERT, UPDATE, DELETE and SELECT statements that retrieve and modify data."

55. **A.**   The SET ROWCOUNT statements will copy 100 rows, and then turn off the restriction for the rest of the queries. This question applies to the objectives "Write INSERT, DELETE, UPDATE, and SELECT statements that retrieve and modify data" and "Configure Session-Level Options."

56. **D.**   It is a very bad idea to put OLTP data and reporting data into the same table, or even in the same database for that matter, because the two types of data are accessed in very different ways, requiring different indexing schemes. This question applies to the objective "Assess the potential impact of the logical design on performance, maintainability, extensibility, scalability, availability, and security."

57. **B.**   This is a good solution, but there are better solutions that are pretty obvious, such as the solution to question 58. This question applies to the objective "Assess the potential impact of the logical design on performance, maintainability, extensibility, scalability, availability, and security."

58. **A.**   The lock manager ignores read-only databases, so the queries will perform well, and because the data is almost static, it can be backed up less frequently. This question applies to the objective "Assess the potential impact of the logical design on performance, maintainability, extensibility, scalability, availability, and security."

59. **C.**   A clustered index scan is a whole-table scan that occurs on a table that just happens to have a clustered index on it. This question applies to the objective "Evaluate and optimize the performance of query execution plans."

60. **B.**   This is the simplest case for this query, and it works well. This question applies to the objective "Write Transact-SQL statements that use joins or sub-queries to combine data from multiple tables."

61. **D.**   This is a loose join that will almost return a Cartesian product. This question applies to the objective "Write Transact-SQL statements that use joins or sub-queries to combine data from multiple tables."

62. **A.**   SQL Profiler is a fairly easy-to-use tool to perform tasks such as finding out exactly what a client is saying to a server. It is a tool that database administrators should be very familiar with and is also very helpful to developers. This question applies to the objective "Identify SQL Server events and performance problems by using SQL Server Profiler."

63. **C.**   Optimistic locking in an OLTP system that is under any kind of load is probably…well…*optimistic*. It probably won't work. A better solution is to run this query late at night, or on a weekend, or use a different locking strategy and make sure the lock hold time is minimized. This question applies to the objective "Manipulate data by using Transact-SQL cursors."

64. **D.** FAST_FORWARD cursors are read-only. This question applies to the objective "Manipulate data by using Transact-SQL Cursors."

65. **D.** For a full-text search to work, a not-nullable single field must be the primary key. This question applies to the objective "Implement full-text search."

PART

III

APPENDIXES

A   Glossary

B   Overview of the Certification Process

C   What's on the CD-ROM

D   Top Score User's Manual

Glossary

@@ERROR   A system function that returns the value of the last error code.

@@TRANCOUNT   A system function that returns the number of nested transactions that are currently active.

A

aggregation   A single value that summarizes a set of values.

ALTER DATABASE   A TSQL statement used to change the structure of an existing database in SQL Server.

attribute   An additional characteristic or information defined for an entity.

B

batch   A collection of TSQL statements that are compiled and run together as a unit.

BCP   Acronym for Bulk CoPy. A proprietary mechanism for importing and exporting large quantities of data into and out of SQL Server.

C

candidate key   A collection of one or more attributes whose values uniquely identify an entity.

CASE   A TSQL expression that returns one of several values depending on the value of a test expression.

clustered index   An index that defines a physical ordering of the data in a table. Because it affects the ordering of the table's data, there can be only one clustered index per table.

codepage   A description of the allowable characters that SQL Server recognizes. Also known as a character set.

constraint   A characteristic of an attribute that provides special rules about the data that can be stored. SQL Server includes the following constraints: Check, Default, Foreign Key, Primary Key, and Unique.

control-of-flow   A description of statements that control the execution of a batch. Includes conditional execution statements and loops.

correlated sub-query   A sub-query that relies on values from the outer query.

CREATE DATABASE   A TSQL statement which is used to create a new database in SQL Server.

cross join   A join of data from two tables in which every row of the first table is matched to every row of the second table. Also known as a Cartesian product.

cursor   Allows you to examine and manipulate a result set from a select query one row at a time.

D

data type   A characteristic of an attribute that defines the type of information that can be stored in that attribute.

DBCC SHOWCONTIG   A statement that instructs SQL Server to return information about the arrangement of a table's data on the physical pages of the database. A table whose data is stored on non-continuous pages can be slower to search on.

deadlock   A condition in which each of two processes has a lock on an object that the other process requires before it will release its own lock. In this situation each process will wait indefinitely unless one of the processes are terminated.

DEFAULT keyword   A constraint that automatically generates a value for the column during inserts when no value is specified.

DELETE   A SQL statement that deletes existing data in a table.

deleted table   A special table with the same structure as the base table of a trigger, which contains all of the rows from the base table as they were before any changes. The data in this table includes all rows that were deleted and all rows as they existed before an update. This table is available only to the trigger and can be seen by no other process. This table allows the trigger to examine the changes that will be committed in the base table if the trigger allows them.

denormalization   The process of changing your data model to meet the requirements of a lower normal form. A data model is usually denormalized in an effort to achieve a specific performance gain.

derived table   A result set from a sub-query that is treated as a table in a query.

distributed query   A query that uses data from any source other than the server to which it was submitted. Queries may reference either linked servers or use the OpenRowset function to attach to the remote data source.

domain integrity   The requirement that column values fall within an acceptable range of values. Domain Integrity encompasses the data type and nullability characteristics of an attribute.

DTS   Acronym for Data Transformation Services. DTS is a program that can transfer data from any OLE-DB–compliant data source to any other.

DTS Package   A proprietary data format for storing DTS commands.

E

entity   A basic building block of a relational database design. An entity defines any person, place, thing, or concept for which data will be collected.

entity integrity   The requirement that entities are distinguishable from one another. This requirement can be satisfied through a unique or, better yet, a primary key constraint.

Execution plan   The sequence of logical and physical operators that SQL Server uses to perform a query's operations. This plan can be stored for later reuse by other processes.

F

file group   A collection of data files that objects in the database can be assigned to. All data files are members of a single file group, and all objects are created in a single file group.

foreign key   A collection of one or more attributes whose values must match the values in a predefined primary key.

format file   A file used by the BCP process to describe the data format in the data file.

full-text catalog   A file stored external to SQL Server's database files that contains full-text indexes.

G, H

GOTO   A TSQL statement that causes execution of the batch to continue at different location.

Graphical Execution plan   The SQL Server Query Analyzer tool has the ability to read an execution plan and display the same data in an easy-to-read, graphical format.

I

identity   A characteristic of an attribute that causes increasing integer values to be automatically assigned to the attribute when an new entity is assigned. Identity columns are usually used to create surrogate keys.

Identity column   A column that will have a unique, increasing integer value generated by default when new data is inserted.

IF   A TSQL statement that evaluates a Boolean expression and executes the following statement only if the expression returns TRUE.

inner join   A join of data from two tables where only data that matches criteria in both tables is returned.

INSERT   A SQL statement that inserts data into a table.

inserted table   A special table with the same structure as the base table of a trigger, which contains all of the newly changed rows in the base table. The data in this table includes all rows that were inserted and all existing rows after they have been updated. This table is available only to the trigger and can be seen by no other process.

This table allows the trigger to examine the changes that will be committed in the base table if the trigger allows them.

J, K

join criteria   The criteria that are used to relate the data in the two tables involved in a join. The join criteria are specified after the ON keyword.

L

linked server   A remote server that has been statically defined on the local server along with all information necessary to establish an OLE-DB connection. With this information, SQL Server is able to retrieve information and run stored procedures on the remote server at a users request. Although the connection must be predefined, this is then the easiest method for users to use to work with a remote server.

log file   A database file that holds transaction log data.

Logical Operators   A specific method that SQL Server will use to carry out the physical operation. The logical operation is a more specific, detailed operation than the physical one.

M

Many-to-Many relationship   A relationship in which any number of entities in a table can relate to any number of entities in another table. An example might be the relationships between people and addresses, in which an arbitrary number of people can have the same address and one person can have an arbitrary number of addresses (work, home, and so on).

This type of relationship is actually implemented in SQL Server through a One-to-Many relationship on each table to a third table. The third table consists of two foreign keys—one to each of the other two.

Microsoft Search service   A service that runs external to SQL Server which supports full-text searching.

N

native format   A description of a BCP data file that SQL Server has written with no data translations. Binary data is written in SQL Server's native binary format. Because this is a proprietary SQL Server format, no format files are necessary when using native format.

non-clustered index   An index that stores information duplicated from a table in a tree structure external to the table.

non-logged versus logged BCP   Applies only to BCP import processes. Determines whether the data imported is written to the transaction log of the database. A logged BCP can be restored through a transaction log backup in the event of a database failure. A non-logged BCP can offer significant speed improvements.

normal forms   There are three commonly used normal forms. Each form describes a series of criteria that a data model should meet.

Normal Form, First   Eliminates repeating groups of attributes in an entity. For example, there should not be multiple class attributes in a student entity. Instead, create a new entity to hold student classes and apply a One-to-Many relationship to that entity.

Normal Form, Second   Eliminates partial key dependencies. In other words, a single attribute should depend on the entire primary key, not just some of the attributes. Instead, create a new entity from the partial key and its dependent attributes.

Normal Form, Third   Eliminates dependencies between non-key attributes. In other words, the value of an attribute should not be determined by the values of a collection of other non-key attributes. Instead, create a new entity from the non-key attributes and the dependent attributes.

normalization   The process of changing your data model to meet the requirements of a higher normal form. There are three normal forms important to database design. Each normal form requires that the conditions of the previous normal form are met in addition to its own rules.

O

One-to-Many relationship   A relationship in which one entity can relate to any number of other entities. A variation of this relationship is a One-to-*exactly-N* relationship, in which *N* is any whole number.

One-to-One relationship   A relationship in which one entity implies the existence of one other entity. A variation of this relationship is a One-to-*exactly-One* relationship, in which one entity requires another entity.

OpenQuery   A function that takes a fully formed SQL query and sends that query to be executed by a remote server. Only the results of the query are sent back. All processing of the query takes place on the remote machine.

OpenRowset   A function that takes all parameters necessary to establish an ad-hoc connection to a remote server. This function allows a connection to be made to a remote server that has not been predefined as a linked server. Although this function is more complex to use than simply using the name of a linked server, it gives users a great deal more flexibility to attach to any remote data source.

optimistic locking A strategy of examining a set of data without locking it until you are ready to apply modifications. The data is then locked to prevent modifications while your application determines whether changes have been made since you first retrieved the records. If changes were made, the locks are immediately released and an error is returned to the user; otherwise, the data modifications are immediately carried out. The alternative is to lock records while changes are contemplated, which is easier to do; however, this option severely limits concurrent use of the database.

outer join A join of data from two tables in which all data is returned from one table, but only the data that matches the join criteria is returned from the other.

P

physical operators A general operation that SQL Server must carry out. A physical operation may describe that a table is searched, but a logical operation will describe exactly how that table is to be searched.

primary data file The data file for a database in which the system tables are stored.

primary key A collection of one or more attributes that will uniquely identify an entity. Where multiple candidates exist for the primary key, only one can be designated as the primary key.

Q

query Any SQL command that returns or modifies data.

R

referential integrity Refers to the requirement that primary and foreign keys remain synchronized between parent and child tables.

relationship A logical linkage between two entities that describes how the entities are associated with each other. Think of relationships as the logical links in a database that turn simple data into useful information.

RETURN A TSQL statement that causes execution of the current batch or stored procedure to halt.

S

search criteria The criteria that are used to filter results to be returned by a query.

secondary data file Any data file defined for a database that does not contain the system tables.

Select-list The list of columns to be returned by a SELECT statement.

SET SHOWPLAN_ALL A statement that instructs SQL Server to begin returning all information about the execution plans that are compiled for queries from this connection.

SET SHOWPLAN_TEXT A statement that instructs SQL Server to begin returning partial information about the execution plans that are compiled for queries from this connection.

SQL Server events SQL Server returns information every time it takes certain predefined actions. This information is returned in the form of an event that can be read by tools such as the SQL Server Profiler. By monitoring the events of a server, the SQL Server Profiler can report what the server is doing at any given time.

stored procedures   Objects in SQL Server that contain a batch of commands that are encapsulated together to execute on command. SQL Server stores the execution plan of a stored procedure, which can improve the performance of a stored procedure over ad-hoc commands.

sub-query   A select statement that is run within another query.

surrogate key   A candidate key composed of attributes that were added to the table for the sole purpose of adding an arbitrary identifier. An IDENTITY attribute is a surrogate key.

T

transaction   A group of statements that are all dependent on the execution of the whole. In any transaction, either all statements are committed, or all results are cancelled.

trigger   An object in SQL Server that contains a batch of commands that are executed in response to a data modification to a table. A trigger is defined to work with a single table, and can be defined to execute in response to any or all INSERT, UPDATE, or DELETE statements. Triggers can contain complex logic to make data integrity and referential integrity checks.

U

unique index   An index that allows only one instance of any value. May allow NULLs, and can be either clustered or non-clustered.

UPDATE   A SQL statement that modifies existing data in a table.

UPDATE STATISTICS   A statement that instructs SQL Server to recompile statistics about an index. These statistics tell SQL Server about how useful the index is likely to be in different circumstances. If this information is out of date, SQL Server will not be able to develop an optimal execution plan when accessing this table.

user-defined data type   An object that encapsulates the data type, nullability, defaults, and rule characteristics of an attribute. An attribute that is assigned a user-defined data type has all of these characteristics assigned automatically.

V

variable   A location in which to store a single value.

view   An objects in SQL Server that appears as a virtual table to the user. Views are created with a SELECT statement, which is used to retrieve a result set that is presented to a user as if it were a table.

W, X, Y, Z

WHILE   A TSQL statement that repeatedly executes the following statement or statement block while a Boolean expression evaluates to TRUE.

Overview of the Certification Process

You must pass rigorous certification exams to become a Microsoft Certified Professional. These closed-book exams provide a valid and reliable measure of your technical proficiency and expertise. Developed in consultation with computer industry professionals who have experience with Microsoft products in the workplace, the exams are conducted by two independent organizations. Sylvan Prometric offers the exams at more than 1,400 Authorized Prometric Testing Centers around the world. Virtual University Enterprises (VUE) testing centers offer exams at over 250 locations.

To schedule an exam, call Sylvan Prometric Testing Centers at 800-755-EXAM (3926) or VUE at 888-837-8616 (or register online with VUE at `http://www.vue.com/student-services/`). Currently Microsoft offers seven types of certification, based on specific areas of expertise.

TYPES OF CERTIFICATION

❖ **Microsoft Certified Professional (MCP).** Qualified to provide installation, configuration, and support for users of at least one Microsoft desktop operating system, such as Windows NT Workstation. Candidates can take elective exams to develop areas of specialization. MCP is the base level of expertise.

❖ **Microsoft Certified Professional+Internet (MCP+Internet).** Qualified to plan security, install and configure server products, manage server resources, extend service to run CGI scripts or ISAPI scripts, monitor and analyze performance, and troubleshoot problems. Expertise is similar to that of an MCP but with a focus on the Internet.

❖ **Microsoft Certified Professional+Site Building (MCP+Site Building).** Qualified to plan, build, maintain, and manage Web sites using Microsoft technologies and products. The credential is appropriate for people who manage sophisticated, interactive Web sites that include database connectivity, multimedia, and searchable content.

❖ **Microsoft Certified Systems Engineer (MCSE).** Qualified to effectively plan, implement, maintain, and support information systems with Microsoft Windows NT and other Microsoft advanced systems and workgroup products, such as Microsoft Office and Microsoft BackOffice. MCSE is a second level of expertise.

◆ **Microsoft Certified Systems Engineer+Internet (MCSE+Internet).** Qualified in the core MCSE areas, and also qualified to enhance, deploy, and manage sophisticated intranet and Internet solutions that include a browser, proxy server, host servers, database, and messaging and commerce components. An MCSE+Internet-certified professional is able to manage and analyze Web sites.

◆ **Microsoft Certified Solution Developer (MCSD).** Qualified to design and develop custom business solutions by using Microsoft development tools, technologies, and platforms, including Microsoft Office and Microsoft BackOffice. MCSD is a second level of expertise with a focus on software development.

◆ **Microsoft Certified Trainer (MCT).** Instructionally and technically qualified by Microsoft to deliver Microsoft Education Courses at Microsoft-authorized sites. An MCT must be employed by a Microsoft Solution Provider Authorized Technical Education Center or a Microsoft Authorized Academic Training site.

NOTE
For up-to-date information about each type of certification, visit the Microsoft Training and Certification World Wide Web site at http://www.microsoft.com /train_cert. You must have an Internet account and a WWW browser to access this information. You also can contact the following sources:

- Microsoft Certified Professional Program: 800-636-7544

- **mcp@msource.com**

- Microsoft Online Institute (MOLI): 800-449-9333

CERTIFICATION REQUIREMENTS

An asterisk following an exam in any of the lists below means that it is slated for retirement.

How to Become a Microsoft Certified Professional

Passing any Microsoft exam (with the exception of Networking Essentials) is all you need to do to become certified as a MCP.

How to Become a Microsoft Certified Professional+Internet

You must pass the following exams to become a MCP specializing in Internet technology:

◆ Internetworking Microsoft TCP/IP on Microsoft Windows NT 4.0, #70-059

◆ Implementing and Supporting Microsoft Windows NT Server 4.0, #70-067

◆ Implementing and Supporting Microsoft Internet Information Server 3.0 and Microsoft Index Server 1.1, #70-077

OR Implementing and Supporting Microsoft Internet Information Server 4.0, #70-087

How to Become a Microsoft Certified Professional+Site Building

You need to pass two of the following exams in order to be certified as an MCP+Site Building

- ◆ Designing and Implementing Web Sites with Microsoft FrontPage 98, #70-055

- ◆ Designing and Implementing Commerce Solutions with Microsoft Site Server 3.0, Commerce Edition, #70-057

- ◆ Designing and Implementing Web Solutions with Microsoft Visual InterDev 6.0, #70-152

How to Become a Microsoft Certified Systems Engineer

You must pass four operating system exams and two elective exams to become a MCSE. The MCSE certification path is divided into two tracks: Windows NT 3.51 and Windows NT 4.0.

The following lists show the core requirements (four operating system exams) for both the Windows NT 3.51 and 4.0 tracks and the electives (two exams) you can take for either track.

Windows NT 3.51 Track

The Windows NT 3.51 Track will probably be retired with the release of Windows NT 5.0. The Windows NT 3.51 core exams are scheduled for retirement at that time.

Core Exams

The four Windows NT 3.51 Track Core Requirements for MCSE certification are as follows:

- ◆ Implementing and Supporting Microsoft Windows NT Server 3.51, #70-043*

- ◆ Implementing and Supporting Microsoft Windows NT Workstation 3.51, #70-042*

- ◆ Microsoft Windows 3.1, #70-030*

    OR Microsoft Windows for Workgroups 3.11, #70-048*

    OR Implementing and Supporting Microsoft Windows 95, #70-064

    OR Implementing and Supporting Microsoft Windows 98, #70-098

- ◆ Networking Essentials, #70-058

Windows NT 4.0 Track

The Windows NT 4.0 track is also organized around core and elective exams.

Core Exams

The four Windows NT 4.0 Track Core Requirements for MCSE certification are as follows:

- ◆ Implementing and Supporting Microsoft Windows NT Server 4.0, #70-067

- ◆ Implementing and Supporting Microsoft Windows NT Server 4.0 in the Enterprise, #70-068

- ◆ Microsoft Windows 3.1, #70-030*

    OR Microsoft Windows for Workgroups 3.11, #70-048*

OR Implementing and Supporting Microsoft Windows 95, #70-064

OR Implementing and Supporting Microsoft Windows NT Workstation 4.0, #70-073

OR Implementing and Supporting Microsoft Windows 98, #70-098

◆ Networking Essentials, #70-058

Elective Exams

For both the Windows NT 3.51 and the 4.0 track, you must pass two of the following elective exams for MCSE certification:

◆ Implementing and Supporting Microsoft SNA Server 3.0, #70-013

OR Implementing and Supporting Microsoft SNA Server 4.0, #70-085

◆ Implementing and Supporting Microsoft Systems Management Server 1.0, #70-014*

OR Implementing and Supporting Microsoft Systems Management Server 1.2, #70-018

OR Implementing and Supporting Microsoft Systems Management Server 2.0, #70-086

◆ Microsoft SQL Server 4.2 Database Implementation, #70-021

OR Implementing a Database Design on Microsoft SQL Server 6.5, #70-027

OR Implementing a Database Design on Microsoft SQL Server 7.0, #70-029

◆ Microsoft SQL Server 4.2 Database Administration for Microsoft Windows NT, #70-022

OR System Administration for Microsoft SQL Server 6.5 (or 6.0), #70-026

OR System Administration for Microsoft SQL Server 7.0, #70-028

◆ Microsoft Mail for PC Networks 3.2-Enterprise, #70-037

◆ Internetworking with Microsoft TCP/IP on Microsoft Windows NT (3.5-3.51), #70-053

OR Internetworking with Microsoft TCP/IP on Microsoft Windows NT 4.0, #70-059

◆ Implementing and Supporting Microsoft Exchange Server 4.0, #70-075*

OR Implementing and Supporting Microsoft Exchange Server 5.0, #70-076

OR Implementing and Supporting Microsoft Exchange Server 5.5, #70-081

◆ Implementing and Supporting Microsoft Internet Information Server 3.0 and Microsoft Index Server 1.1, #70-077

OR Implementing and Supporting Microsoft Internet Information Server 4.0, #70-087

◆ Implementing and Supporting Microsoft Proxy Server 1.0, #70-078

OR Implementing and Supporting Microsoft Proxy Server 2.0, #70-088

◆ Implementing and Supporting Microsoft Internet Explorer 4.0 by Using the Internet Explorer Resource Kit, #70-079

How to Become a Microsoft Certified Systems Engineer+Internet

You must pass seven operating system exams and two elective exams to become a MCSE specializing in Internet technology.

Core Exams

The seven MCSE+Internet core exams required for certification are as follows:

◆ Networking Essentials, #70-058

◆ Internetworking with Microsoft TCP/IP on Microsoft Windows NT 4.0, #70-059

◆ Implementing and Supporting Microsoft Windows 95, #70-064

  OR Implementing and Supporting Microsoft Windows NT Workstation 4.0, #70-073

  OR Implementing and Supporting Microsoft Windows 98, #70-098

◆ Implementing and Supporting Microsoft Windows NT Server 4.0, #70-067

◆ Implementing and Supporting Microsoft Windows NT Server 4.0 in the Enterprise, #70-068

◆ Implementing and Supporting Microsoft Internet Information Server 3.0 and Microsoft Index Server 1.1, #70-077

  OR Implementing and Supporting Microsoft Internet Information Server 4.0, #70-087

◆ Implementing and Supporting Microsoft Internet Explorer 4.0 by Using the Internet Explorer Resource Kit, #70-079

Elective Exams

You must also pass two of the following elective exams for MCSE+Internet certification:

◆ System Administration for Microsoft SQL Server 6.5, #70-026

◆ Implementing a Database Design on Microsoft SQL Server 6.5, #70-027

◆ Implementing and Supporting Web Sites Using Microsoft Site Server 3.0, # 70-056

◆ Implementing and Supporting Microsoft Exchange Server 5.0, #70-076

  OR Implementing and Supporting Microsoft Exchange Server 5.5, #70-081

◆ Implementing and Supporting Microsoft Proxy Server 1.0, #70-078

  OR Implementing and Supporting Microsoft Proxy Server 2.0, #70-088

◆ Implementing and Supporting Microsoft SNA Server 4.0, #70-085

How to Become a Microsoft Certified Solution Developer

The MCSD certification is undergoing substantial revision. Listed below are the requirements for the new track (available fourth quarter 1998) as well as the old.

New Track

For the new track, you must pass three core exams and one elective exam. The three core exam areas are listed below as well as the elective exams from which you can choose.

The core exams include the following:

Desktop Applications Development (one required)

♦ Designing and Implementing Desktop Applications with Microsoft Visual C++ 6.0, #70-016

OR Designing and Implementing Desktop Applications with Microsoft Visual Basic 6.0, #70-176

Distributed Applications Development (one required)

♦ Designing and Implementing Distributed Applications with Microsoft Visual C++ 6.0, #70-015

OR Designing and Implementing Distributed Applications with Microsoft Visual Basic 6.0, #70-175

Solution Architecture (required)

♦ Analyzing Requirements and Defining Solution Architectures, #70-100

You must pass one of the following elective exams:

♦ Designing and Implementing Distributed Applications with Microsoft Visual C++ 6.0, #70-015

OR Designing and Implementing Desktop Applications with Microsoft Visual C++ 6.0, #70-016

OR Microsoft SQL Server 4.2 Database Implementation, #70-021*

♦ Implementing a Database Design on Microsoft SQL Server 6.5, #70-027

OR Implementing a Database Design on Microsoft SQL Server 7.0, #70-029

♦ Developing Applications with C++ Using the Microsoft Foundation Class Library, #70-024

♦ Implementing OLE in Microsoft Foundation Class Applications, #70-025

♦ Designing and Implementing Web Sites with Microsoft FrontPage 98, #70-055

♦ Designing and Implementing Commerce Solutions with Microsoft Site Server 3.0, Commerce Edition, #70-057

♦ Programming with Microsoft Visual Basic 4.0, #70-065

OR Developing Applications with Microsoft Visual Basic 5.0, #70-165

OR Designing and Implementing Distributed Applications with Microsoft Visual Basic 6.0, #70-175

OR Designing and Implementing Desktop Applications with Microsoft Visual Basic 6.0, #70-176

♦ Microsoft Access for Windows 95 and the Microsoft Access Development Toolkit, #70-069

♦ Designing and Implementing Solutions with Microsoft Office (Code-named Office 9) and Microsoft Visual Basic for Applications, #70-091

♦ Designing and Implementing Web Solutions with Microsoft Visual InterDev 6.0, #70-152

Old Track

For the old track, you must pass two core technology exams and two elective exams for MCSD certification. The following lists show the required technology exams and elective exams needed to become an MCSD.

Core Technology Exams

You must pass the following two core technology exams to qualify for MCSD certification:

◆ Microsoft Windows Architecture I, #70-160*

◆ Microsoft Windows Architecture II, #70-161*

Elective Exams

You must also pass two of the following elective exams to become an MSCD:

◆ Designing and Implementing Distributed Applications with Microsoft Visual C++ 6.0, #70-015

◆ Designing and Implementing Desktop Applications with Microsoft Visual C++ 6.0, #70-016

◆ Microsoft SQL Server 4.2 Database Implementation, #70-021*

   OR Implementing a Database Design on Microsoft SQL Server 6.5, #70-027

   OR Implementing a Database Design on Microsoft SQL Server 7.0, #70-029

◆ Developing Applications with C++ Using the Microsoft Foundation Class Library, #70-024

◆ Implementing OLE in Microsoft Foundation Class Applications, #70-025

◆ Programming with Microsoft Visual Basic 4.0, #70-065

   OR Developing Applications with Microsoft Visual Basic 5.0, #70-165

   OR Designing and Implementing Distributed Applications with Microsoft Visual Basic 6.0, #70-175

   OR Designing and Implementing Desktop Applications with Microsoft Visual Basic 6.0, #70-176

◆ Microsoft Access 2.0 for Windows-Application Development, #70-051

   OR Microsoft Access for Windows 95 and the Microsoft Access Development Toolkit, #70-069

◆ Developing Applications with Microsoft Excel 5.0 Using Visual Basic for Applications, #70-052

◆ Programming in Microsoft Visual FoxPro 3.0 for Windows, #70-054

◆ Designing and Implementing Web Sites with Microsoft FrontPage 98, #70-055

◆ Designing and Implementing Commerce Solutions with Microsoft Site Server 3.0, Commerce Edition, #70-057

◆ Designing and Implementing Solutions with Microsoft Office (Code-named Office 9) and Microsoft Visual Basic for Applications, #70-091

◆ Designing and Implementing Web Solutions with Microsoft Visual InterDev 6.0, #70-152

Becoming a Microsoft Certified Trainer

To understand the requirements and process for becoming a MCT, you need to obtain the Microsoft Certified Trainer Guide document from the following WWW site:

    http://www.microsoft.com/train_cert/mct/

At this site you can read the document as Web pages or display and download it as a Word file. The MCT Guide explains the four-step process of becoming a MCT. The general steps for the MCT certification are as follows:

1. Complete and mail a Microsoft Certified Trainer application to Microsoft. You must include proof of your skills for presenting instructional material. The options for doing so are described in the MCT Guide.

2. Obtain and study the Microsoft Trainer Kit for the Microsoft Official Curricula (MOC) courses for which you want to be certified. Microsoft Trainer Kits can be ordered by calling 800-688-0496 in North America. Those of you in other regions should review the MCT Guide for information on how to order a Trainer Kit.

3. Take the Microsoft certification exam for the product about which you want to be certified to teach.

4. Attend the MOC course for the course for which you want to be certified. This is done so you can understand how the course is structured, how labs are completed, and how the course flows.

If you are interested in becoming a MCT, you can obtain more information by visiting the Microsoft Certified Training WWW site at `http://www.microsoft.com/train_cert/mct/` or by calling 800-688-0496.

> **WARNING**
>
> You should consider the preceding steps a general overview of the MCT certification process. The precise steps that you need to take are described in detail on the WWW site mentioned earlier. Do not misinterpret the preceding steps as the exact process you need to undergo.

What's On the CD-ROM

This appendix is a brief rundown of what you'll find on the CD-ROM that comes with this book. For a more detailed description of the newly developed Top Score test engine, exclusive to Macmillan Computer Publishing, please see Appendix D, "Top Score User's Manual."

TOP SCORE

Top Score is a test engine developed exclusively for Macmillan Computer Publishing. It is, we believe, the best test engine available because it closely emulates the format of the standard Microsoft exams. In addition to providing a means of evaluating your knowledge of the exam material, Top Score features several innovations that help you to improve your mastery of the subject matter.

For example, the practice tests allow you to check your score by exam area or category to determine which topics you need to study further. Other modes allow you to obtain immediate feedback on your responses, explanations of correct answers, and even hyperlinks to the chapter in an electronic version of the book where the topic is covered. The simulator mode actually emulates the SQL Server product and tests your hands-on product knowledge. Again, for a complete description of the benefits of Top Score, see Appendix D.

Before running the Top Score software, be sure that AutoRun is enabled. If you prefer not to use AutoRun, then you can run the application from the CD by double-clicking the START.EXE file from Explorer. This simulator will run on Windows 95, Windows 98, and Windows NT with a minimum of 64 MB of RAM.

EXCLUSIVE ELECTRONIC VERSION OF TEXT

As referred to above, the CD-ROM also contains the electronic version of this book in Portable Document Format (PDF). In addition to the links to the book that are built into Top Score, you can use this version to help search for terms you need to study or other book elements. The electronic version comes complete with all figures as they appear in the book.

COPYRIGHT INFORMATION AND DISCLAIMER

Macmillan Computer Publishing's Top Score test engine: Copyright 1998 New Riders Publishing. All rights reserved. Made in U.S.A.

Using the Top Score Software

GETTING STARTED

The installation procedure is very simple and typical of Windows 95 or Window NT 4 installations.

1. Put the CD into the CD-ROM drive. The autorun function starts, and after a moment, you see a CD-ROM Setup dialog box asking you if you are ready to proceed.

2. Click OK, and you are prompted for the location of the directory in which the program can install a small log file. Choose the default (C:\Program Files\), or type the name of another drive and directory, or select the drive and directory where you want it placed. Then click OK.

3. The next prompt asks you to select a start menu name. If you like the default name, click OK. If not, enter the name you would like to use. The Setup process runs its course.

When setup is complete, icons are displayed in the MCSE Top Score Software Explorer window that is open. For an overview of the CD's contents, double-click the CD-ROM Contents icon.

If you reach this point, you have successfully installed the exam(s). If you have another CD, repeat this process to install additional exams.

INSTRUCTIONS ON USING THE TOP SCORE SOFTWARE

Top Score software consists of the following three applications:

◆ Practice Exams

◆ Study Cards

◆ Flash Cards

The Practice Exams application provides exams that simulate the Microsoft certification exams. The Study Cards serve as a study aid organized around specific exam objectives. Both are in multiple-choice format. Flash Cards are another study aid that require responses to open-ended questions, which test your knowledge of the material at a level deeper than that of recognition memory.

To start the Study Cards, Practice Exams, or Flash Cards applications, follow these steps:

1. Begin from the overview of the CD contents (double-click the CD-ROM Contents icon). The left window provides you with options for obtaining further information on any of the Top Score applications as well as a way to launch them.

2. Click a "book" icon, and a listing of related topics appears below it in Explorer fashion.

3. Click an application name. This displays more detailed information for that application in the right window.

4. To start an application, click its book icon. Then click on the Starting the Program option. Do this for Practice Exams, for example. Information appears in the right window. Click on the button for the exam, and the opening screens of the application appear.

Further details on using each of the applications follow.

Using Top Score Practice Exams

The Practice Exams interface is simple and straightforward. Its design simulates the look and feel of the Microsoft certification exams. To begin a practice exam, click the button for the exam name. After a moment, you see an opening screen similar to the one shown in Figure D.1.

Click on the Next button to see a disclaimer and copyright screen. Read the information, and then click Top Score's Start button. A notice appears, indicating that the program is randomly selecting questions for the practice exam from the exam database (see Figure D.2). Each practice exam contains the same number of items as the official Microsoft exam. The items are selected from a larger set of 150–900 questions. The random selection of questions from the database takes some time to retrieve. Don't reboot; your machine is not hung!

> **NOTE**
>
> **Some Exams Follow a New Format** The number of questions will be the same for traditional exams. However, this will not be the case for exams that incorporate the new "adaptive testing" format. In that format, there is no set number of questions. See the chapter "Study and Exam Prep Tips" in the Final Review section of the book for more details on this new format.

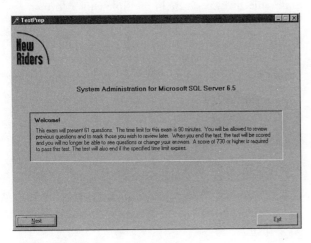

FIGURE D.1
Top Score Practice Exams opening screen.

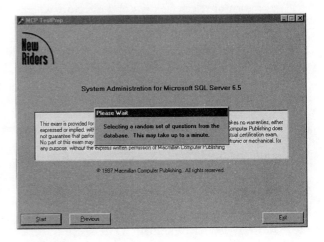

FIGURE D.2
Top Score's Please Wait notice.

After the questions have been selected, the first test item appears. See Figure D.3 for an example of a test item screen.

Notice several important features of this window. The question number and the total number of retrieved questions appears in the top-left corner of the window in the control bar. Immediately below that is a check box labeled Mark, which enables you to mark any exam item you would like to return to later. Across the screen from the Mark check box, you see the total time remaining for the exam.

The test question is located in a colored section (it's gray in the figure). Directly below the test question, in the white area, are response choices. Be sure to note that immediately below the responses are instructions about how to respond, including the number of responses required. You will notice that question items requiring a single response, such as that shown in Figure D.3, have radio buttons. Items requiring multiple responses have check boxes (see Figure D.4).

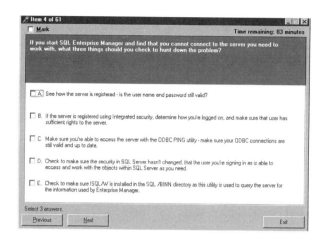

FIGURE D.4
A Top Score test item requiring multiple responses.

Some questions and some responses do not appear on the screen in their entirety. You will recognize such items because a scroll bar appears to the right of the question item or response. Use the scroll bar to reveal the rest of the question or response item.

The buttons at the bottom of the window enable you to move back to a previous test item, proceed to the next test item, or exit Top Score Practice Exams.

Some items require you to examine additional information referred to as *exhibits*. These screens typically include graphs, diagrams, or other types of visual information that you will need in order to respond to the test question. You can access Exhibits by clicking the Exhibit button, also located at the bottom of the window.

After you complete the practice test by moving through all the test questions for your exam, you arrive at a summary screen titled Item Review (see Figure D.5).

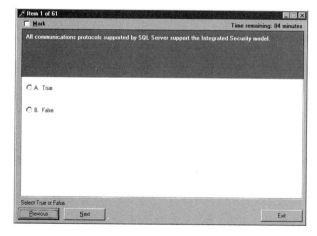

FIGURE D.3
A Top Score test item requiring a single response.

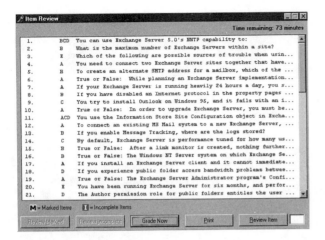

FIGURE D.5
The Top Score Item Review window.

This window enables you to see all the question numbers, your response(s) to each item, any questions you have marked, and any you've left incomplete. The buttons at the bottom of the screen enable you to review all the marked items and incomplete items in numeric order.

If you want to review a specific marked or incomplete item, simply type the desired item number in the box in the lower-right corner of the window and click the Review Item button. This takes you to that particular item. After you review the item, you can respond to the question. Notice that this window also offers the Next and Previous options. You can also select the Item Review button to return to the Item Review window.

> **NOTE**
>
> **Your Time Is Limited** If you exceed the time allotted for the test, you do not have the opportunity to review any marked or incomplete items. The program will move on to the next screen.

After you complete your review of the practice test questions, click the Grade Now button to find out how you did. An Examination Score Report is generated for your practice test (see Figure D.6). This report provides you with the required score for this particular certification exam, your score on the practice test, and a grade. The report also breaks down your performance on the practice test by the specific objectives for the exam. Click the Print button to print out the results of your performance.

You also have the option of reviewing those items that you answered incorrectly. Click the Show Me What I Missed button to view a summary of those items. You can print out that information if you need further practice or review; such printouts can be used to guide your use of Study Cards and Flash Cards.

Using Top Score Study Cards

To start the software, begin from the overview of the CD contents. Click the Study Cards icon to see a listing of topics. Clicking Study Cards brings up more detailed information for this application in the right window.

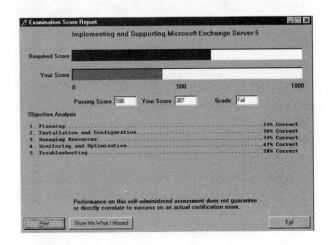

FIGURE D.6
The Top Score Examination Score Report window.

To launch Study Cards, click on Starting the Program. In the right window, click on the button for the exam in which you are interested. After a moment, an initial screen similar to that of the Practice Exams appears.

Click on the Next button to see the first Study Cards screen (see Figure D.7).

The interface for Study Cards is very similar to that of Practice Exams. However, several important options enable you to prepare for an exam. The Study Cards material is organized according to the specific objectives for each exam. You can opt to receive questions on all the objectives, or you can use the check boxes to request questions on a limited set of objectives. For example, if you have already completed a Practice Exam and your score report indicates that you need work on Planning, you can choose to cover only the Planning objectives for your Study Cards session.

You can also determine the number of questions presented by typing the number of questions you want into the option box at the right of the screen. You can control the amount of time you will be allowed for a review by typing the number of minutes into the Time Limit option box immediately below the one for the number of questions.

When you're ready, click the Start Test button, and Study Cards randomly selects the indicated number of questions from the question database. A dialog box appears, informing you that this process could take some time. After the questions are selected, the first item appears, in a format similar to that in Figure D.8.

Respond to the questions in the same manner you did for the Practice Exam questions. Radio buttons signify that a single answer is required, while check boxes indicate that multiple answers are expected.

Notice the menu options at the top of the window. You can pull down the File menu to exit from the program. The Edit menu contains commands for the copy function and even allows you to copy questions to the Windows clipboard.

Should you feel the urge to take some notes on a particular question, you can do so via the Options menu. When you pull it down, choose Open Notes, and Notepad opens. Type any notes you want to save for later reference. The Options menu also allows you to start over with another exam.

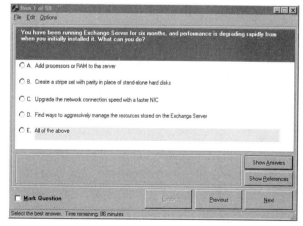

FIGURE D.8
A Study Cards item.

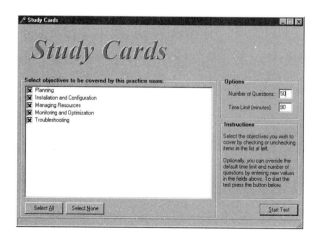

FIGURE D.7
The first Study Cards screen.

The Study Cards application provides you with immediate feedback of whether you answered the question correctly. Click the Show Answers button to see the correct answer, and it appears highlighted on the screen as shown in Figure D.9.

Study Cards also includes Item Review, Score Report, and Show Me What I Missed features that function the same as those in the Practice Exams application.

Using Top Score Flash Cards

Flash Cards offer a third way to use the exam question database. The Flash Cards items do not offer you multiple-choice answers to choose from; instead, they require you to respond in a short answer/essay format. Flash Cards are intended to help you learn the material well enough to respond with the correct answers in your own words, rather than just by recognizing the correct answer. If you have the depth of knowledge to answer questions without prompting, you will certainly be prepared to pass a multiple-choice exam.

You start the Flash Cards application in the same way you did Practice Exams and Study Cards. Click the Flash Cards icon, and then click Start the Program.

Click the button for the exam you are interested in, and the opening screen appears. It looks similar to the example shown in Figure D.10.

You can choose Flash Cards according to the various objectives, as you did Study Cards. Simply select the objectives you want to cover, enter the number of questions you want, and enter the amount of time you want to limit yourself to. Click the Start Test button to start the Flash Cards session, and you see a dialog box notifying you that questions are being selected.

The Flash Cards items appear in an interface similar to that of Practice Exams and Study Cards (see Figure D.11).

Notice, however, that although a question is presented, no possible answers appear. You type your answer in the white space below the question (see Figure D.12).

Compare your answer to the correct answer by clicking the Show Answers button (see Figure D.13).

You can also use the Show Reference button in the same manner as described earlier in the Study Cards sections.

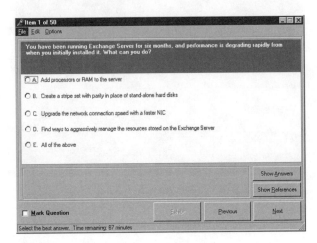

FIGURE D.9
The correct answer is highlighted.

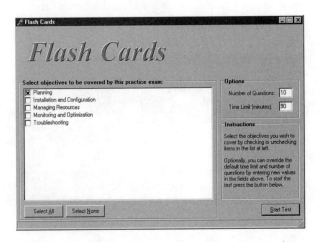

FIGURE D.10
The Flash Cards opening screen.

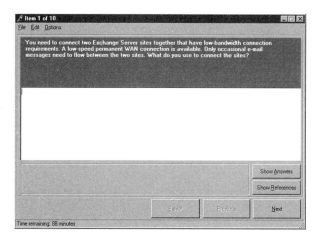

FIGURE D.11
A Flash Cards item.

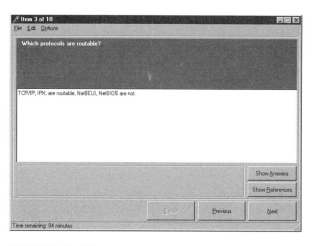

FIGURE D.12
A typed answer in Flash Cards.

The pull-down menus provide nearly the same functionality as those in Study Cards, with the exception of a Paste command on the Edit menu instead of the Copy Question command.

Flash Cards provide simple feedback; they do not include an Item Review or Score Report. They are intended to provide you with an alternative way of assessing your level of knowledge that will encourage you to learn the information more thoroughly than other methods do.

SUMMARY

The Top Score software's suite of applications provides you with several approaches to exam preparation. Use Practice Exams to do just that—practice taking exams, not only to assess your learning, but also to prepare yourself for the test-taking situation. Use Study Cards and Flash Cards as tools for more focused assessment and review and to reinforce the knowledge you are gaining. You will find that these three applications are the perfect way to finish off your exam preparation.

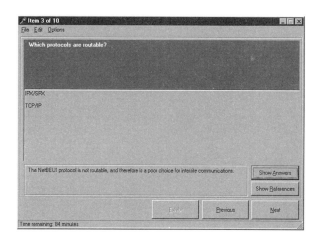

FIGURE D.13
The correct answer is shown.

Index

SYMBOLS

1NF, *see* first normal forms

2NF, *see* second normal form

3NF, *see* third normal form

@@ERROR, 311

@@TRANCOUNT, nesting transactions, 321

A

ABSOLUTE position specifier, FETCH command, 328

Access, creating data sources, 197-198

accessing

    data

        OpenQuery function, 369

        OpenRowset function, 369-370

        with remote stored procedures, 368

    remote stored procedures, 369

actions

    full-text catalogs, 160

    full-text indexing, 161-162

ACTIVATE, full-text indexing, 161

Active Script task, 204

adding constraints, 107

    Enterprise Manager, 109

    TSQL, 106-108

Advanced tab, Data Transformation Properties dialog box, 202-203

advantages of indexes, 138-139

aggregate functions, 243-245, 449

    HAVING clause, 247

    summary data, generating, 244-245

    super-aggregation, 249

    WHERE clause, 245

aliases, queries, 256

aliasing, 254

ALL keyword, 231-232

ALL operators, correlated sub-queries, 259

ALTER DATABASE statements, 75, 451

ALTER PROCEDURE statements, 354

ALTER TABLE statements, 102

    constraints, 108

ALTER VIEW command, 357

altering, *see* modifying

alternate keys, candidate keys, 26

AND keywords, choosing rows, 234-235

ANSI Null Default, 77

ANSI Nulls, 77

ANSI Warnings, 77

E

G

NEW RIDERS CERTIFICATION TITLES

TRAINING GUIDES
NEXT GENERATION TRAINING

 MCSE Training Guide: Networking Essentials, Second Edition

1-56205-919-X, $49.99, 9/98

 MCSE Training Guide: TCP/IP, Second Edition

1-56205-920-3, $49.99, 11/98

 A+ Certification Training Guide

1-56205-896-7, $49.99, 8/98

 MCSE Training Guide: Windows NT Server 4, Second Edition

1-56205-916-5, $49.99, 9/98

 MCSE Training Guide: SQL Server 7 Administration

0-7357-0003-6, $49.99, 5/99

TRAINING GUIDES
FIRST EDITIONS

MCSE Training Guide: Systems Management Server 1.2, 1-56205-748-0

MCSE Training Guide: SQL Server 6.5 Administration, 1-56205-726-X

MCSE Training Guide: SQL Server 6.5 Design and Implementation, 1-56205-830-4

MCSE Training Guide: Windows 95, 70-064 Exam, 1-56205-880-0

MCSE Training Guide: Exchange Server 5, 1-56205-824-X

MCSE Training Guide: Internet Explorer 4, 1-56205-889-4

MCSE Training Guide: Microsoft Exchange Server 5.5, 1-56205-899-1

MCSE Training Guide: IIS 4, 1-56205-823-1

MCSD Training Guide: Visual Basic 5, 1-56205-850-9

MCSD Training Guide: Microsoft Access, 1-56205-771-5

Microsoft Corporation is a registered trademark of Microsoft Corporation in the United States and other countries. New Riders Publishing is an independent entity from Microsoft Corporation, and not affiliated with Microsoft Corporation in any manner.

 MCSE Training Guide: Windows NT Server 4 Enterprise, Second Edition

1-56205-917-3, $49.99, 10/98

 MCSE Training Guide: SQL Server 7 Database Design

0-7357-0004-4, $49.99, 5/99

 MCSE Training Guide: Windows NT Workstation 4, Second Edition

1-56205-918-1, $49.99, 9/98

 MCSD Training Guide: Solution Architectures

0-7357-0026-5, $49.99, Q3/99

 MCSE Training Guide: Windows 98

1-56205-890-8, $49.99, 2/99

 MCSD Training Guide: Visual Basic 6 Exams

0-7357-0002-8, $69.99, 3/99

FAST TRACKS

The Accelerated Path to Certification Success

Fast Tracks provide an easy way to review the key elements of each certification technology without being bogged down with elementary-level information.

These guides are perfect for when you already have real-world, hands-on experience. They're the ideal enhancement to training courses, test simulators, and comprehensive training guides.

No fluff—simply what you really need to pass the exam!

MCSE Fast Track: Networking Essentials
1-56205-939-4,
$19.99, 9/98

MCSE Fast Track: Windows 98
0-7357-0016-8,
$19.99, 12/98

MCSE Fast Track: TCP/IP
1-56205-937-8,
$19.99, 9/98

MCSE Fast Track: Windows NT Server 4
1-56205-935-1,
$19.99, 9/98

MCSE Fast Track: Windows NT Server 4 Enterprise
1-56205-940-8,
$19.99, 9/98

MCSE Fast Track: Windows NT Workstation 4
1-56205-938-6,
$19.99, 9/98

A+ Fast Track
0-7357-0028-1,
$34.99, 3/99

MCSE Fast Track: Internet Information Server 4
1-56205-936-X,
$19.99, 9/98

MCSE Fast Track: SQL Server 7 Administration
0-7357-0041-9,
$29.99, Q2/99

MCSE/MCSD Fast Track: SQL Server 7 Database Design
0-7357-0040-0,
$29.99, Q3/99

MCSD Fast Track: Visual Basic 6, Exam 70-175
0-7357-0018-4,
$19.99, 12/98

MCSD Fast Track: Visual Basic 6, Exam 70-176
0-7357-0019-2,
$19.99, 12/98

MCSD Fast Track: Solution Architectures
0-7357-0029-X,
$29.99, Q3/99

NEW RIDERS CERTIFICATION TITLES

TESTPREPS

PRACTICE, CHECK, PASS!

Questions. Questions. And more questions. That's what you'll find in our New Riders *TestPreps*. They're great practice books when you reach the final stage of studying for the exam. We recommend them as supplements to our *Training Guides.*

What makes these study tools unique is that the questions are the primary focus of each book. All the text in these books support and explain the answers to the questions.

✓ **Scenario-based questions** challenge your experience.

✓ **Multiple-choice questions** prep you for the exam.

✓ **Fact-based questions** test your product knowledge.

✓ **Exam strategies** assist you in test preparation.

✓ **Complete yet concise explanations of answers** make for better retention.

✓ **Two practice exams** prepare you for the real thing.

✓ **Fast Facts** offer you everything you need to review in the testing center parking lot.

Practice, practice, practice—pass with New Riders TestPreps!

MCSE TestPrep: Networking Essentials, Second Edition

0-7357-0010-9, $19.99, 12/98

MCSE TestPrep: Windows 98

1-56205-922-X, $19.99, 11/98

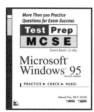
MCSE TestPrep: Windows 95, Second Edition

0-7357-0011-7, $29.99, 12/98

MCSE TestPrep: Windows NT Server 4, Second Edition

0-7357-0012-5, $19.99, 12/98

MCSE TestPrep: Windows NT Server 4 Enterprise, Second Edition

0-7357-0009-5, $19.99, 11/98

MCSE TestPrep: Windows NT Workstation 4, Second Edition

0-7357-0008-7, $19.99, 12/98

MCSE TestPrep: TCP/IP, Second Edition

0-7357-0025-7, $19.99, 12/98

A+ Certification TestPrep

1-56205-892-4, $19.99, 12/98

MCSD TestPrep: Visual Basic 6 Exams

0-7357-0032-X, $29.99, 1/99

TEST PREPS

FIRST EDITIONS

MCSE TestPrep: SQL Server 6.5 Administration, 0-7897-1597-X

MCSE TestPrep: SQL Server 6.5 Design and Implementation, 1-56205-915-7

MCSE TestPrep: Windows 95 70-64 Exam, 0-7897-1609-7

MCSE TestPrep: Internet Explorer 4, 0-7897-1654-2

MCSE TestPrep: Exchange Server 5.5, 0-7897-1611-9

MCSE TestPrep: IIS 4.0, 0-7897-1610-0

HOW TO CONTACT US

IF YOU NEED THE LATEST UPDATES ON A TITLE THAT YOU'VE PURCHASED:

1) Visit our Web site at www.newriders.com.

2) Click on the Product Support link, and enter your book's ISBN number, which is located on the back cover in the bottom right-hand corner.

3) There you'll find available updates for your title.

IF YOU ARE HAVING TECHNICAL PROBLEMS WITH THE BOOK OR THE CD THAT IS INCLUDED:

1) Check the book's information page on our Web site according to the instructions listed above, or

2) Email us at support@mcp.com, or

3) Fax us at (317) 817-7488 attn: Tech Support.

IF YOU HAVE COMMENTS ABOUT ANY OF OUR CERTIFICATION PRODUCTS THAT ARE NON-SUPPORT RELATED:

1) Email us at certification@mcp.com, or

2) Write to us at New Riders, 201 W. 103rd St., Indianapolis, IN 46290-1097, or

3) Fax us at (317) 581-4663.

IF YOU ARE OUTSIDE THE UNITED STATES AND NEED TO FIND A DISTRIBUTOR IN YOUR AREA:

Please contact our international department at international@mcp.com.

IF YOU WISH TO PREVIEW ANY OF OUR CERTIFICATION BOOKS FOR CLASSROOM USE:

Email us at pr@mcp.com. Your message should include your name, title, training company or school, department, address, phone number, office days/hours, text in use, and enrollment. Send these details along with your request for desk/examination copies and/or additional information.

WE WANT TO KNOW WHAT YOU THINK

To better serve you, we would like your opinion on the content and quality of this book. Please complete this card and mail it to us or fax it to 317-581-4663.

Name _____

Address _____

City _____ State _____ Zip _____

Phone _____ Email Address _____

Occupation _____

Which certification exams have you already passed? _____
_____
_____
_____

Which certification exams do you plan to take? _____
_____
_____
_____

What influenced your purchase of this book?
❑ Recommendation   ❑ Cover Design
❑ Table of Contents   ❑ Index
❑ Magazine Review   ❑ Advertisement
❑ Reputation of New Riders   ❑ Author Name

How would you rate the contents of this book?
❑ Excellent   ❑ Very Good
❑ Good   ❑ Fair
❑ Below Average   ❑ Poor

What other types of certification products will you buy/have you bought to help you prepare for the exam?
❑ Quick reference books   ❑ Testing software
❑ Study guides   ❑ Other

What do you like most about this book? Check all that apply.
❑ Content   ❑ Writing Style
❑ Accuracy   ❑ Examples
❑ Listings   ❑ Design
❑ Index   ❑ Page Count
❑ Price   ❑ Illustrations

What do you like least about this book? Check all that apply.
❑ Content   ❑ Writing Style
❑ Accuracy   ❑ Examples
❑ Listings   ❑ Design
❑ Index   ❑ Page Count
❑ Price   ❑ Illustrations

What would be a useful follow-up book to this one for you?_____

Where did you purchase this book? _____

Can you name a similar book that you like better than this one, or one that is as good? Why?_____
_____
_____

How many New Riders books do you own? _____

What are your favorite certification or general computer book titles? _____
_____

What other titles would you like to see us develop?_____
_____

Any comments for us? _____
_____
_____

MCSE TRAINING GUIDE: SQL SERVER 7 DATABASE DESIGN 0-7357-0004-4

Fold here and tape to mail

- -

New Riders
201 W. 103rd St.
Indianapolis, IN 46290

NEW RIDERS TOP SCORE TEST SIMULATION SOFTWARE SUITE

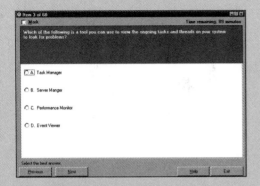

Practice Exams simulate the actual Microsoft exams. Option buttons and check boxes indicate whether there is one or more than one correct answer. All test questions are presented randomly to create a unique exam each time you practice—the ideal way to prepare.

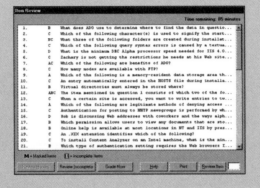

The Item Review shows you the answers you've already selected and the questions you need to revisit before grading the exam.

The Score Report displays your score for each objective category, helping you to define which objectives you need to study more. It also shows you what score you need to pass and your total score.

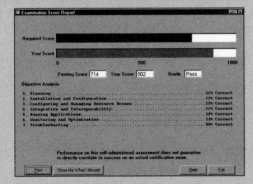

Study Cards allow you to test yourself and receive immediate feedback and an answer explanation. Link to the text for more in-depth explanations.